Context and Communication Behavior

CONTEXT AND COMMUNICATION BEHAVIOR

Edited by

James L. Owen
University of Nevada, Reno

CONTEXT PRESS
Reno, Nevada

Cover

The figure on the front cover was designed by Merle H. Owen as an illustration of Stephen C. Pepper's four "relatively adequate" world views: formism, mechanism, organicism, and contextualism. Each of these views has its own perspective on what counts as *events* and what counts as *context* (see Chapter 1).

In the upper left corner is a symbol of formism; next, moving clockwise, is a symbol for mechanism; then organicism. A symbol for contextualism dominates the center of the figure; Pepper approaches all world views from the perspective of a contextualist.

The initial work on this textbook-anthology was made possible by a sabbatical provided by the University of Nevada for the Spring semester of 1995.

Context and Communication Behavior / edited by James L. Owen. Managing editor, Merle H. Owen.

Hardback. 465 pp. Includes bibliographies.

ISBN# 1-878978-28-4

© 1997 CONTEXT PRESS
933 Gear Street, Reno, NV 89503-2729

All rights reserved.

No part of this book may be reproduced, stored in a retrieval system, or transmitted in any form or by any means, electronic, mechanical, photocopying, microfilming, recording, or otherwise, without written permission from the publisher.

Printed in the United States of America

To Merle

I remember when I was a boy going upon the beach and being charmed with the colors and forms of the shells. I picked up many and put them in my pocket. When I got home I could find nothing that I gathered—nothing but some dry ugly mussel and snail shells. Thence I learned that Composition was more important than the beauty of individual forms ... On the shore they lay wet and social by the sea and under the sky.

> Ralph Waldo Emerson (from his journal of May 16, 1834)

Table of Contents

Preface and Acknowledgments xiii

Part 1
Philosophical Perspectives:
Context and Communication Behavior

Chapter 1:
World Views as Context for Communication Studies 17
   James L. Owen, Ph.D.,
     University of Nevada, Reno

Chapter 2:
Objectivism as the Basic Context for Theory and
Research in Communication 41
   Nancy Grant Harrington, Ph.D.,
     University of Kentucky
   Robert N. Bostrom, Ph.D.,
     University of Kentucky

Chapter 3:
From Modernity to Postmodernity: Recontextualizing Communication Theory 59
   Alan D. DeSantis, Ph.D.,
     University of Kentucky

Part 2
Theoretical Perspectives: Context and
Communication Behavior

Chapter 4:
Pragmatism and Context: A Matter of Pattern 81
   Katherine L. Adams, Ph.D.,
     California State University, Fresno

Chapter 5:
The Meaning and Use of "Context" in the Theory of the Coordinated
Management of Meaning 97
    Jonathan G. Shailor, Ph.D.,
        University of Wisconsin-Parkside

Chapter 6:
Theories of Culture, Communication and Context 111
    Bradford 'J' Hall, Ph.D.,
        University of New Mexico

Chapter 7:
Social Contexts for Communication: Communicative Power as Past and
Present Social Consequences 133
    Bernard Guerin, Ph.D.,
        University of Waikato, New Zealand

Chapter 8:
Communication as History and Evolution: Comparing Contextualism
and Symbolic Interactionism 181
    Dennis C. Alexander, Ph.D.,
        University of Utah

Chapter 9:
Vygotsky's Contextualism: Cultural Historical Psychology 193
    Tom Whelan, Ph.D.,
        Boulder City, Nevada

Chapter 10:
Cognitive Representation of Rhetorical Situations 213
    Gary Cronkhite, Ph.D.,
        Indiana University

Chapter 11:
An Impersonal Basis for Shared Interpretations of Messages in Context 229
    Robert E. Sanders, Ph.D.,
        University at Albany, SUNY

Chapter 12:
Context's "Culture": Speech 251
    Frank E. X. Dance, Ph.D.,
        University of Denver

Chapter 13:
The Behavior-Context Interface in Interethnic Communication 261
  Young Yun Kim, Ph.D.,
    University of Oklahoma

Part 3
Context and the Applied Analysis of Communication Behavior

Section 1
Evolutionary Context and the Applied Analysis of Communication Behavior

Chapter 14:
Signs of the Apes, Songs of the Whales: Human Communication
in Evolutionary Context 295
  Jo Liska, Ph.D.,
    University of Colorado, Denver

Section 2
Social Context and the Applied Analysis of Communication Behavior

Chapter 15:
The Concept of Context in Social Communication Theory 319
  Wendy Leeds-Hurwitz, Ph.D.,
    University of Wisconsin-Parkside

Chapter 16:
The Researcher in Communication: The Primary Research Position 337
  Robyn Penman, Ph.D.,
    Communication Research Institute of Australia

Section 3
Conversational Context and the Applied Analysis of Communication Behavior

Chapter 17:
Context and Conversational Processes 355
  Robert E. Nofsinger, Ph.D.,
    Washington State University

Chapter 18:
Contingency Analysis Applied to the Pragmatics and Semantics
of Naturally Occurring Verbal Interactions 369
    Ullin T. Place, Ph.D.,
        University of Wales, Bangor

Section 4
Rhetorical Context and the Applied Analysis of Communication
Behavior

Chapter 19:
Rhetorical Contexts and Scholarly Inquiry 389
    Jeanine Czubaroff, Ph.D.,
        Ursinus College

Chapter 20:
Narrative and Context: Communication's Milieu 407
    Deborah S. Ballard-Reisch, Ph.D.,
        University of Nevada, Reno
    Barbara C. Thornton, Ph.D.,
        University of Nevada, Reno

Section 5
Cultural Context and the Applied Analysis of Communication Behavior

Chapter 21:
Culture as Communication Context: Finnish Cultural Characteristics
in Political Television Programs 425
    Maili Pörhölä, Ph.D.,
        University of Jyväskylä, Finland
    Aino Sallinen, Ph.D.,
        University of Jyväskylä, Finland
    Pekka Isotalus, Ph.D.,
        University of Jyväskylä, Finland

Chapter 22:
Between Challenge and Burden: Changing Contexts in
East Germany After Democratization 445
    Romy Fröhlich, Ph.D.,
        Institut für Journalistik und Kommunikationsforschung Hochschule für
        Musik und Theater, Hannover, Germany

Section 6
Technological Context and the Applied Analysis of Communication Behavior

Chapter 23:
Shifts in Identity: The Contextualizing Function of Communication Technologies 457
    Denice Yanni, Ph.D.,
        Fairfield University

Preface and Acknowledgments

Individuals who speak from different world views and different theoretical commitments would hardly disagree that *contexts* are important. Indeed, we are taught at a very young age that finding the meaning of a word often requires that we consider the context in which it is used. Also, most of us can justifiably argue that in one way or another our own particular view of things "takes into account" the topic of context. An experimentalist, for example, is likely to point to his or her interest in framing an experiment in a way that controls "extraneous" contextual influences. Or, he or she might point to the trend toward more detailed descriptions of the experimental settings within which independent variables are manipulated.

In any case, while most of us agree that context is important, few attempts have been made to open up the concept to see in detail what might be found. The central purpose of this book is to do just that. Many distinguished contributing authors have generously accepted an invitation to address the issue of context in the light of their particular theoretical orientation and disciplinary interests. Their articles not only address the general concept of context but also the very different roles it is conceived to have in relation to studies of human communication.

It is no accident that the topic of context should become a focal issue at this particular time. "Situated," "social," or "contextual" approaches to behavior in general and communication behavior in particular constitute one of the most remarkable contemporary movements within both the humanities *and* the social behavioral sciences.

Many deserve my sincere thanks for their considerable help in the creation and publication of this volume. Seminal thinkers including Willard Day, Steven Hayes, Linda Hayes, Sam Leigland, Jay Moore, and Bernard Guerin have been particularly influential with regard to my own thinking about the importance and nature of context in relation to communication behavior. Steve and Linda also made things happen by agreeing to publish this book with Context Press. Discussions with Bob Nofsinger, and his willingness to contribute the first article, were important motivating factors in the early stages. Numerous contacts with all contributing authors over the past two years were highly rewarding. They have been a constant source of stimulation and assistance; they have contributed excellent articles; to a person they have good naturedly helped resolved the numerous problems that inevitably occur during this type of project. My appreciation also goes to Scott Compton; because of his patience, sense of humor, and expertise in formatting the book, he was immensely helpful. Above all, I want to thank my wife Merle for designing the cover, for generously and competently serving as managing editor, and for working closely with me on every aspect of this book.

James L. Owen,
Reno, Nevada,
January 1997

Part 1
Philosophical Perspectives:
Context and Communication Behavior

Chapter 1

World Views as Context for Communication Studies

James L. Owen
University of Nevada, Reno

The last few years have seen a sharply increased amount of activity in the area of "contextual," "social," "ecological," or "situated" approaches to human behavior in general and human communication behavior in particular (for examples, see "Forum: Social Approaches," *Communication Theory* (Vols. 2 & 4, 1992).

In trying to sort out and explicate some of the major features and implications of a "contextual" approach, and the ways it differs from alternative ones, a number of scholars have found it useful to resurrect Stephen C. Pepper's *World Hypotheses: A Study in Evidence* (1942; see also Hayes, Hayes, & Reese, 1988; Hayes, Hayes, Reese, & Sarbin, 1993; Rosnow & Georgoudi, 1986; Hayes & Ghezzi, in press).

Pepper was a Mills Professor of Intellectual and Moral Philosophy and Civil Polity at the University of California, Berkeley. He is best known for his seminal work in *root metaphor theory* as captured in his most popular text, *World Hypotheses* (for Pepper, the terms "world hypotheses" and "world views" are interchangeable). Pepper presumes that most of us need some kind of helpful guide to get us through the world's very complex systems of ideas. Pepper's root metaphor theory provides his version of that guide.

In particular, Pepper's root metaphor theory helps us to see vividly the surprisingly small number of paradigmatic ways in which we typically characterize most things in our universe. With Pepper's help it becomes rather easy to see how most philosophies and theories actually collapse into a small number of paradigms. *World Hypotheses* identifies the assumptions, conceptual categories and "word games" of these alternative views; it also considers their implications for the ways we talk about the world, and their inherent limitations.

The purpose of the first part of this chapter is to briefly discuss the nature of Pepper's root metaphor theory, and the important distinctions he makes between "relatively adequate" and "relatively inadequate" world views. The second part will summarize some of the most salient features of what Pepper sees as the four "relatively adequate" world views: formism, mechanism, organicism, and contextualism. This summary includes a discussion of the ways in which each relatively adequate view explicitly or implicitly addresses the focal topic of this text, i.e., the nature of events and their *context*.

An analysis and discussion of Pepper's world views helps to locate our own interests relative to available paradigmatic alternatives. It also helps to identify one's conceptual allies. Typically, the effect of Pepper is not only to inform and sensitize us to the possibilities and limitations of our own preferred world view, but also to make us more respectful and tolerant of alternative ones. Underneath it all, however, Pepper is a contextualist, and that's what makes him particularly relevant to current interests in *contextual* approaches to the study of human communication behavior. Pepper's work is foundational to this chapter; at the same time, appeals are made to prominent contemporary writers who address similar issues. And, of course, my own interpretations of these sources are an inseparable part of the final product.

The Nature of Root Metaphors

Pepper's primary assumption is that we try to understand things by appealing to a familiar metaphor; we then proceed to interpret events in the "light" of this metaphor. The light of a particular metaphor carries with it the inherent assumptions and related categories that constitute a unique language game. Pepper argues (1) that root metaphors are located in everyday, common sense language and are supported by common sense evidence; (2) that the refinement of these basic metaphors leads to alternative world views; and (3) that a particular world view provides the basis for *categorizing* and *interpreting* the world in unique philosophical or theoretical ways.

Even with refinement, however, Pepper concludes that some metaphors lead to "relatively adequate" world views while others only lead to "relatively inadequate" ones. For Pepper, adequacy is based on his foundational criteria of precision and scope. *Precision* is the measure of a world view's ability to capture the details of a phenomenon. In the case of perfect precision only a small number of concepts and related interpretations are needed to capture the essence of a particular event. *Scope* is the measure of a view's capacity to embrace a broad spectrum of phenomena. In the case of perfect scope, only a small number of concepts are required to interpret the whole world. Briefly then, a perfect world view is one that provides a parsimonious way of capturing both perfect precision and perfect scope. Pepper argues that we do not have a perfect world view, but we do have four *relatively adequate* ones: *formism, mechanism, organicism,* and *contextualism*.

These world views are "relatively adequate" because they evidence *both* precision *and* scope. Nevertheless, two of these views, mechanism and organicism, are stronger on precision while weaker on scope; the other two, formism and contextualism, are stronger on scope while weaker on precision.

While the criteria of precision and scope provide the basis for Pepper's distinctions between relatively adequate and inadequate world views, he also differentiates among the relatively adequate views by appealing to two additional sets of bipolar terms: *analytic vs. synthetic;* and, *integrative vs. dispersive*.

The distinction between analytic theories (formism and mechanism) and synthetic theories (organicism and contextualism) does not imply "... that the analytical theories do not recognize and interpret synthesis, and the synthetic theories analysis..." (Pepper, 1942, p. 142). However, for analytical theories facts "... are mainly in the nature of elements or factors, so that synthesis becomes a derivative and not a basic fact..." (p. 142). For synthetic theories, "... basic facts ... are complexes or contexts, so that analysis becomes derivative" (p. 142).

Integrative views (mechanism and organicism) are based on the metaphysical assumption that the world exists in a singular ideal form. Accordingly, facts are related by assumption, order is categorical, and novelty is explained in terms of ignorance or error. It is assumed that knowledge moves progressively toward the discovery and integration of more and more facts. In contrast, from a *dispersive* view (formism and contextualism) facts are only related to the extent that they are found to be so. Contextualism is particularly clear about this pragmatic stance. It is self-consciously open to the possibility that the world may be constituted by both order and disorder and it recognizes the possibility of novel events. Contextualism's only fundamental commitment is to the concept of *change*.

As seen in the following Table, Pepper's three bipolar terms, i.e., (1) precision vs. scope, (2) analysis vs. synthesis, and (3) integration vs. dispersion, conveniently fit into a symmetrical 2 X 2 matrix. The matrix also notes that *integrative* world views (mechanism and organicism) are relatively strong on precision but weaker on scope, whereas *dispersive* world views (formism and contextualism) are stronger on scope but weaker on precision. Finally, the Table identifies, in brackets, each world view's root metaphor and truth criterion. These concepts are developed later in separate discussions of each world view.

Importantly, different root metaphors and the world views based on them are *orthogonally* related. That is, each is constituted by different assumptions, different

**Basic Features of Stephen Pepper's
Relatively Adequate World Views**

	INTEGRATIVE WITH PRECISION	DISPERSIVE WITH SCOPE
ANALYTIC	[A Machine] **MECHANISM** [Truth = Correspondnace] (1)	[Similarity] **FORMISM** [Truth = Correspondnace] (2)
SYNTHETIC	[Organic Development] **ORGANICISM** [Truth = Coherence]	[Act in Context] **CONTEXTUALISM** [Truth = Successful Working]

1. *Correspondence between a person's "physiological attitude" and his or her environment.*
2. *Correspondence between similar forms within a class.*

goals, different categories for interpreting the world, and different truth criteria. Accordingly, legitimate problems are to be found within a single world view, not between or among them. We do not advance the adequacy of our own world view or theory by challenging the adequacy of others; we can only do so by showing how our own conceptual commitments are successful relative to the criteria of precision and scope.

What follows then, is a brief discussion of Pepper's four "relatively adequate" world views and their implications for the ways we interpret and talk about our world. Much of the discussion will focus on the contextual world view; it is this view that is gaining in prominence but is probably the least understood.

Formism

The *root metaphor* for formism is *similarity in appearance or form*, e.g., sheets of paper, blades of grass (Pepper, 1942, p. 151). The *common sense evidence* for formism is that we often see things that look alike. This evidence supports the general perspective that the world is composed of different categories of similar things. The task of a formist is to name these things and to classify them. Among Pepper's four relatively adequate world views, formism is the simplest and the earliest to be systematized (Hayes, 1993, p. 12).

In the domain of human communication, a formist might focus on similarities in the topographical features of speakers, messages, channels, and listeners. For example, one might exlore the similarities (and differences) among a sample of speeches and then classify them as "informative," "persuasive," "ceremonial," "entertaining," etc.

Two Types of Formism

There are two types of formism: *immanent* (applied) and *transcendent* (ideal). The business of immanent formism is the classification of empirical events based on their *observed* topographical similarities (Pepper, 1942, pp. 151-152). In contrast, *transcendent* formism presumes abstract *ideal* forms. It focuses on similarities between these imagined forms and observed ones. For example, the transcendent formist would share Plato's interest in an "ideal" oak tree and the extent to which it corresponds to the oak tree we see before us; or, one might draw comparisons between an "ideal" speech and the one actually heard. Transcendent formism also embraces the concept of "normal" appearances.

Basic Categories

The basic categories for immanent formism are (1) characters, (2) particulars, and (3) participation (Pepper, 1942, p. 154). *Characters* pertain to the properties of an event; a *particular* is a single, individual event. Particulars which possess certain characters are said to *participate* in them.

The categories of transcendent formism are similar to those of immanent formism. The only important difference is that the transcendent formist starts with a *set* of characters that constitute a particular *form* (Pepper, 1942, p. 163). For example, a biologist might describe the *set* of characters that constitute a *good specimen* or *norm* for a species (p. 165). As noted by Pepper, "The biologist seems to have a pretty definite idea of the *normal* habits and the *normal* appearance of his species..." (p. 165). The same might be said of a speech instructor. That is, most seem to have a pretty definite idea about the normal habits of a good speaker, and the normal appearance of a good speech.

Both immanent and transcendent formisms embrace the idea of rudimentary relationships; for example, the side-by-sideness of sitting next to someone on a park bench, or the before-and-afterness of having a conversation with that person. But these "relationships" are also viewed as discrete particulars or *forms* identifiable by their own unique *characters*. More elaborate relationships referenced by terms such as "cause-effect," "fusion," "consolidation," and "emergence," etc., are not included within the purview of formism (they are included in alternative world views and provide a critical basis for distinguishing among them).

A formistic view is *analytic* in that it tries to make sense of something by studying its individual characters and by placing it in the appropriate category. Placing disparate but similar events into common categories brings order to our observations and to various reasoning processes. Formism is *dispersive* in that one's analysis moves outward in a horizontal fashion and encompasses more and more of the world's events. Knowledge is *incremental* but only in the sense that we can progressively categorize more things and can generate more elaborate categories. Knowledge is more refined to the extent that we can place events into increasingly fine-grained subcategories.

A formist in the field of human communication is likely to feel that one's work is finished when one's subject matter is properly "botonized." For example, when a person is able to exhaustively identify, name, and classify *types* of messages, speeches, audiences, etc. This botonization includes talk about process but only in the most rudimentary of terms. For example, one might speak of communication "process" in terms of a linear sequence of discrete events, i.e., "the speaker," "the message," "the channel," "the listeners," and "feedback." A formist stops short of talking about more complex processes.

Context, Narratives, and Truth

From the formistic view, *the context of an event is the category to which it belongs* based on the characters it possesses and shares with other members of the same class. An event's context also includes the location of its class within a larger taxonomic system. At the applied or "immanent" level, formistic narratives are stories about the similarities among empirical things, i.e., their common observable forms. For example, I might say, "These are all *informative* speeches because they take the *form* of explaining *how* to do something; unlike persuasive speeches they do not include specific arguments advocating *why* something *should* be done." At the ideal or "transcendent" level, narratives pertain to someone's concept of the "ideal" or "normal" in relation to the particulars actually observed.

The truth criterion for a formistic narrative is *correspondence*. In the case of immanent formism the correspondence at issue is the relation between observable things. In the case of transcendent formism, the correspondence at issue is the relation between an "ideal" or "norm" of something, and the particulars of an observable event that approximate that ideal or norm. Ordinarily the term correspondence "... is reserved for such objects as pictures, maps, diagrams, sentences, formulas, and mental images" (Pepper, 1942, p. 180). These objects may be viewed as "descriptions" which correspond, more or less, to "objects of reference" (p. 180). Accordingly, we can say that a picture is a "true" likeness of a person to the extent that it shares certain features with that person. Sentences do not capture the *form* of an object of reference in the manner of a picture or a map, but do so in the form of verbal *conventions* (pp. 180-181; see also Sanders, this volume); that is, words serve as convenient *symbolic substitutes* for the objects of reference. From this view, sentences, formulas, and other symbolic "descriptions" are *true* to the extent that they serve as conventional ways of capturing and representing some of the formal properties of the objects to which they refer.

Strengths and Weaknesses

At one point or another, scholars in all disciplines are formists in that they find it convenient to name and classify things. A few might even focus on this one task to the exclusion of others. Most, however, are also interested in more discriminating questions about the processes by which certain events "impact" or "influence" each other, or "merge" with other events. Nevertheless, these interests go beyond the agenda of a formist; to address them one must appeal to mechanistic, organicistic, or contextualistic views.

Transcendent formism can be particularly problematical. The presumption that any one of us can determine what is "ideal" or "normal" for a particular state of affairs raises questions about our qualifications for doing so. An alternative to a dogmatic stance on these issues can be found in processes involving mutual participation and the negotiation of meanings (see Shailor; Hall, this volume).

Formism has considerable scope in that our taxonomies can be modified and expanded on an ad hoc basis in order to provide a place for an infinite variety of events. Precision, however, is limited. The more we know about a "fact" the more difficult it becomes to place it in its proper category (Pepper, 1942, p. 144). This lack of precision makes formism appear to be "... the least adequate of the four favored ones..." (p. 144). Indeed, one might be tempted to abandon formism as a relatively adequate world view were it not for the strength of its root metaphor, i.e., the strength of our intuition about the *similarities* among things. As noted by Pepper, "No other root metaphor of a favored theory is blessed with nearly so strong a feeling of certainty..." (p. 144).

Mechanism

The *root metaphor* for the mechanistic world view is the *machine* (Pepper, 1942, p. 186). The mechanistic view assumes a real world constituted by events that interact and influence each other through the exercise of some type of *force*. It further assumes that we progressively "dis/cover" this world through careful observations and the construction of increasingly refined descriptions and related inferences or "speculations" (p. 224). The goal of the mechanist is to objectively "see" the world's parts and their lawful interactions.

Common sense evidence for a mechanistic view includes our observation that billiard balls, automobiles, football players, etc., bump into each other and exert *force through contact*. We can also see the influence of *force at a distance* as when the magnetic northpole turns the needle of a compass, or when the force of gravity pulls back to earth objects that are thrown into the air. The mechanistic view is further supported by an accumulation of refined evidence. For example, through observation and inference we have been able to construct a concept of the atom and its governing laws, one that has resulted in an impressive measure of predictability and control.

Two Types of Mechanisms

There are two types of mechanisms and each is based on its own unique root metaphor. The first is the *discrete* mechanism based on a push-and-pull type of machine which stresses action by contact (the lever serves as the root metaphor); the second is a *consolidated* mechanism based on action at a distance (an electromagnetic field serves as the root metaphor) (Pepper, 1942, pp. 186-187).

The *discrete* mechanism shares with formism the concept of a world of particulars (Pepper, 1942, p. 198). Additionally, however, it includes the concept of lawful relations among particulars described in terms of force. Even these laws, however, are seen as discrete entities, each being distinct from the other. The effect is a strange polarity between accident and necessity. For example, a discrete mechanist might reason that:

> ... since this atom [accidently] did *happen* to be at this place at this time and [necessarily] had been obeying the law of inertia, it was *inevitable* that the collision should have occurred (Pepper, 1942, p. 196).

With further refinements of the mechanistic view, particulars were eventually located in the context of time and space. Then came the amalgamation of time, space, and gravity; the move toward the concept of a *consolidated* mechanism was underway. Relativity theory became the crowning achievement because of its ability to deal with "the details of the spatiotemporal field" (Pepper, 1942, p. 213). In a consolidated mechanism, all "accidents" give way to necessity and inevitability. "A completely consolidated mechanism would be a completely mechanized and internally determined universe" (p. 207). In this world, events and laws are not separate particulars, rather they are consolidated into the structure or *context* of the field itself. Pepper argues that a "consolidated mechanism is not a dream, but is the most plausible theory of the nature of the world so far as physical evidence goes" (p. 214).

Essentially, discrete mechanism assumes that the functions of a machine can be understood primarily in terms of its internal dynamics, and with minimum regard for the greater field in which it happens to be located. In contrast, the concept of a consolidated mechanism makes an important distinction between the *internal* and *external* functions of a machine. As stated by Gregory (1981):

> A machine is generally conceived as a functional entity consisting of clearly defined parts, such that the internal functions can be understood from knowledge of the parts and how they interact. To understand its external functions—what it does—we must know about its "environment" (p. 73).

Gregory (1981) adds that when we wish to speak of a machine in its entirety we must consider it "... within a context within which it plays its part" (p. 83). From this view, a comprehensive mechanistic analysis goes well beyond the parts of a machine and their functional relations; it includes an analysis of the specific ways in which a machine *interfaces* and *interacts with* its *environment*.

In effect, a consolidated mechanism is more *context oriented*; it directs attention to a wider array of interacting variables and thus serves as a corrective to the more restrictive concept of a discrete machanism. Nevertheless, both discrete and consolidated mechanisms share the fundamental assumptions that the world is constituted by *discrete* events and that these events interact and influence each other through the exercise of some type of *force*. These fundamental assumptions serve to shape all mechanistic talk about the nature of events and their interactions within and with a context.

Basic Categories

The mechanistic view is constituted by two types of categories: *secondary categories* known directly through experience, and *primary categories* known indirectly through inference (Pepper, 1942, pp. 192-193). Both are necessary in order to provide the scope needed to qualify mechanism as a relatively adequate world view (p. 195). Further, secondary and primary categories "... need each other more directly still. It turns out that, ultimately, our cognitive evidence for the structure and detail of the cosmic machine described through the primary categories comes entirely from materials within the secondary categories" (p. 195).

In the sociobehavior sciences the distinction between secondary and primary categories has contributed significantly to the bifurcation of human behavior into a mind-body dualism (see Guerin, in press; Owen, 1989, 1990, 1993, 1994, in press). Specifically, observations of behavior (conceived as secondary categories) are frequently conducted for the purpose of drawing inferences about an imaginary "mind" (conceived as primary categories). The mind-body dualism has also led to the mechanistic concept of the mind as an information processing "computer" and has spawned several generations of cognitivists who envision their primary task as the mapping out of alleged mental processors (see Gardner, 1985).

A mechanistic view is *analytic*; it assumes that the "whole" is made up of discrete parts that are lawfully related. It is also *reductionistic*; presumably, that is, we get closer to the way things really are to the extent that we can reduce them down to their smallest parts, and the lawful relations among them.

In the sociobehavioral domain, students raised in the tradition of a mechanistic view were led to accept the notion that human behavior is "... the product of forces acting according to invariant universal laws" (Sarbin, 1993, p. 54). In some cases, events and their relations were conceptualized in terms of the now classic S-R model in which "S" represents an independent stimulus variable (such as a tap below the knee) and "R" a dependent response variable (such as a knee jerk). This model also provides the foundational paradigm for early conditioning studies. Nevertheless, other branches of behaviorism went on to develop additional formulations that differ categorically from the S-R paradigm (Owen, 1989, 1990, 1993, 1994). Importantly, some contemporary behaviorists, primarily in the area of *behavior analysis* (see Hayes et al., 1993) consider themselves to be *contextualists*, not mechanists. Nevertheless, popular mythologies die slowly—even professional ones—and many continue to associate all "behaviorisms" with the S-R model and a mechanistic approach.

A mechanistic view is *integrative*; the whole of something is seen as the sum of its organized parts. Knowledge is progressive; the mechanist presumes that an accumulation of discrete facts will eventually fit together and reveal the inherent structures and patterns of things, and thereby affirm one's faith in a unified world.

Context, Narratives, and Truth

From a mechanistic view the *context of an event is constituted by the force of action by contact, or action at a distance*. As stated by Sarbin (1993), the program of the mechanist is to make sense of things by answering the question: "What forces caused such and such an action?" (p. 52). From this view, we address the important aspects of context (and advance knowledge) by discovering (1) *objects* or *entities*, and (2) the ways in which they are necessarily, deterministically, and *lawfully* related.

The mechanistic view is consistent with the concept of "independent variables" acting on "dependent" ones. Experimentalism is the ultimate method of choice due to its alleged ability to isolate and manipulate specific variables and their forceful effects upon each other. Experimentalism is so closely associated with a mechanistic view that some who advocate a shift from mechanistic approaches (in studies of human behavior) also advocate a shift from experimental methods (Leeds-Hurwitz, 1992, p. 133). Nevertheless, a case can be made for the value of experimental methodologies at the *tactical level*, even within the purview of social-contextual approaches (see Hayes, 1993, pp. 24-25).

Mechanistic *narratives* are more sophisticated versions of formistic ones. Like formistic stories, they name and describe the properties of things, but they add a major new element: they also describe *necessary relationships* between individual parts. These relationships include the ways in which discrete parts interact with each other and fit together to form "wholes." Mechanistic narratives also include inferences about an "ideal" world described in terms of deterministic laws that govern "the grand machine."

Since discrete mechanism is little more than another version of formism, it follows that its *truth criterion* is also based on the idea of correspondence through similarities in form. For example, early mechanistic concepts of correspondence were based on naive *pictorial* and *symbolic* theories (see discussion under Formism). Eventually, however, mechanists realized that the correspondence at issue in these theories is one between a pair of perceptions (i.e., our perception of the picture and our perception of the thing; or, our perception of the symbolic representations and our perceptions of the objects or relationships represented). All perceptions are open to distortions, of course, and therefore the issue of how we make objective contact with the world remains unanswered. The upshot of all of this is that *predictive verifications* became the truth criterion for a mechanistic view. Specifically, symbolic representations of events—or relations among them—are regarded as true to the extent that they provide a basis for predicting future events (see Hayes, 1993, p. 12).

Eventually, consolidated mechanists attempted to bridge the gap between the external world and our representations of it through the "causal adjustment" theory of correspondence. Essentially, this theory argues that the real world makes *direct mechanical contact* with us by "bumping" into our nervous system and thereby motivating us to find verbal and nonverbal ways of adjusting to it. While this solution does provide a mechanistic way of bridging the gap between observations and symbolic representations, it is one that comes very close to the contextualist's criterion for truth, i.e., "successful working." As noted by Pepper (1942), "... discrete mechanism gravitates toward a correspondence or formistic theory of truth, while consolidated mechanism gravitates toward an operational or contextualistic theory of truth" (p. 225). Pepper's fundamental conclusion is that, "... the gap between the primary and the secondary categories still remains the center of inadequacy for mechanism" (p. 231).

Strengths and Weaknesses

The practice of analyzing things into their component parts, and reducing these to smaller and smaller ones has made the mechanist strong on precision, but relatively weak on scope. "Parts" appear to be almost infinitely divisible and a mechanistic narrative can easily get lost in a sea of details while losing sight of the bigger picture.

In the physical domain, the mechanistic view is supported by both common sense and a convincing amount of refined scientific evidence from the field of physics. Importantly, many of the objections to a mechanistic approach are based on the primitive concept of a discrete machine and deserve reconsideration when viewed in terms of a consolidated one. Perhaps the most impressive feature of a consolidated mechanism is that it can embrace numerous types of complex phenomena while at the same time retaining the basic mechanistic assumptions of discrete parts deterministically organized in terms of lawful forces.

Nevertheless, concepts of demonstrable value in the physical domain can be difficult to import consistently into the behavioral domain. For example, it is possible to see how people can exert "force" upon each other through direct contacts in the form of pushing and pulling, or even perhaps, through S-R conditioning operations; however, these concepts have not fared well when talking about more complex behaviors including numerous verbal phenomena. Also, "force at a distance" may serve as a metaphor for people being "attracted" or "repelled" by each other, but it is doubtful that these tendencies are literally under the control of a physical *force* resembling anything like magnetism. Nevertheless, a distinction can be made between an appeal to mechanistic predictions and mechanistic explanations. Mechanists in the field of human communication continue to provide useful predictions in a variety of practical areas. These findings have a useful life of their own apart from any appeal to explanatory devices.

Organicism

The *root metaphor* for the organicistic world view is *organic development* (Pepper, 1942, p. 280). "The organicist believes that every actual event in the world is a more or less concealed organic process" (p. 281).

The human life cycle provides strong *common sense evidence* for an organicistic view. We are born, we develop, and we die. We are surrounded by flora and fauna that do the same. Various minerals and crystals evolve through a predictable sequence of steps. The metaphor of organic development can also be extended to our interpersonal encounters: A relationship is initiated, it "develops" or "grows" and relationships end. From this view, events become meaningful when they can be seen in relation to the various steps or stages that constitute a particular organic process. At a cosmic level, the organicist assumes an ideal world in which all "individual processes" become integrated and reveal a singular, grand organic one.

Organicists seek answers to the question, "What steps or stages describe a particular process?" To answer this question, they construct step or stage models; and, they seek "... rules of change that are themselves unchanging" (Reese & Overton, 1970; cited in Hayes et al., 1988). Presumably the stability of these process rules can be attributed to the inherent dynamics of specific organic structures.

Organicists assume that facts which contradict each other, or do not immediately fit into process models, are testimony to our current ignorance. With more knowledge, it is presumed, these problems will be resolved (Pepper, 1942, pp. 283; 304). Organicists, like mechanists, assume that knowledge progressively reveals the ultimate nature of things.

Basic Categories

The organicistic perspective includes two sets of categories. The first pertains to *appearances;* i.e., how organic processes look to the observer. Appearances focus on "step" or "stage" models. Typical of an organicist's program is the construction of a process model that describes events in terms of their location in a series of *developmental* steps or stages.

Pepper (1942) identifies seven categories of organicistic appearances—but states that we could have more or less depending on how detailed we wish to be (p. 283). It will be noted that these categories constitute an analytical sequence that moves from lower to higher levels of *organic integration*. They include:

... (1) fragments of experience which appear with (2) *nexuses* or connections or implications, which spontaneously lead as a result of the aggravation of (3) *contradictions,* gaps, oppositions, or counteractions to resolution in (4) an *organic whole,* which is found to have been (5) *implicit* in the fragments, and to (6) *transcend* the previous contradictions by means of a coherent totality, which (7) *economizes,* saves, preserves all the original fragments of experience without any loss (p. 283).

Pepper (1942) illustrates this path of organic integration by reviewing critical stages in the development of knowledge about astronomy. Through this extended exemplar, he shows how each conceptual breakthrough from Anaximenes to Einstein resulted in a new and *more inclusive* "picture" of the universe; one that also fills previous gaps and resolves apparent contradictions among earlier fragmented observations. The overall effect of progress along this path is to embrace more facts (or fragments) and to incorporate them into a larger integrated whole. The organicistic program assumes that sooner or later all facts can be integrated into more inclusive process models that progressively exhibit the single grand organicistic process that constitutes the entire world.

The second set of organicistic categories pertain to this ultimate organic world fully known. This idealized world is described in terms of three categories: *inclusiveness, determinateness,* and *organicity* (Pepper, 1942, p. 310). Inclusiveness is achieved through historical integrations such as the one that occurred with astronomy and mechanics; determinateness is achieved through the fencing in of additional facts and greater penetration into the details and ramifications of these facts (p. 299). The concept of organicity presumes an ideal system in which "... every element ... implies every other ..." and "... the alteration or removal of any element would alter every other element or even destroy the whole system" (p. 300).

For the organicist, newly discovered levels of integration "... were really there all the time, working in nature" (Pepper, 1942, p. 242). For example, the earth was in the gravitational field of the sun long before we were able to see it that way. The organicist assumes that there is an "... inevitability of connections among fragments ..." and an "... implication of wholeness ..." (p. 242). At the same time, the progress of knowledge toward this wholeness might proceed through different routes. "There are many paths from error to truth" (p. 294).

In the sociobehavioral domain, the organicistic perspective is consistent with the efforts of "developmentalists" who construct step or stage models relative to alleged human, social, or cultural processes. For example, typical of the developmental approach is the effort to plot size of vocabulary against age, or to describe a sequence of stages that are alleged to constitute an inherent "life cycle." From this perspective one is led to expect a history of successive "breakthroughs" in knowledge that will progressively reveal inherent developmental processes that one can then appeal to in making general predictions about human behavior and in providing explanatory accounts.

Context, Narratives and Truth

Briefly then, at the applied level of "appearances," the program of the organicist is the development of sequential *process* models. And, from this view, the essential *context* for a given event is *its location relative to a series of steps or stages that constitute a particular process*. Practical narratives are stories about the various "steps" or "stages" that constitute a particular process and the location of particular events within them. At the idealized level narratives are about the inherent nature of the world; that is, a world that takes the form of a unified organic whole and can be described in terms of inclusiveness, determinateness, and organicity.

The *truth criterion* for an organicistic narrative is *coherence* (Pepper, 1942, p. 310). In this context, however, coherence is not to be confused with logical consistency (i.e., formal noncontradiction); it pertains to the ability of a theory to *encompass known facts*. "... consistency is mere formal noncontradiction whereas coherence is the positive organic relatedness of material facts ... It is not formal consistency but material coherence that the organicist sets up as truth" (p. 310).

Common sense tells us that a story can have formal consistency in the sense that nothing is said that contradicts itself. But from an organicistic view, a consistent story is only true to the extent that it embraces relevant facts. A story, of course, can be partially true if it embraces some of the facts. "There is more truth in Ptolemy than in Anaximenes, more in Kepler than in Ptolemy, more in Newton than in Kepler" (Pepper, 1942, p. 310). The ultimate test of material consistency takes the form of precise, verified predictions. Like the mechanistic view, precise predictions properly verified are seen as the strongest evidence of truth (p. 297).

Strengths and Weaknesses

Like mechanism, organicism is strong on precision while weaker on scope. However, while mechanism achieves precision by reducing things down to their component parts, i.e., through analysis, organicism does so through synthesis; that is, through the unification of factual "fragments," or partial facts, until they take their rightful place in organic process models.

In the human domain, for example, it has become commonplace to examine the "growth" of language fragments in infants and children and to organize this data into a sequence of developmental stages. Examples of this effort include the plotting of vocabulary size against age, or charting the progressive use of abstract terms.

Clearly, however, genetically "wired in" developmental processes cannot by themselves account for many aspects of human development (Lerner, 1993). For example, numerous studies have demonstrated that the rate at which language develops in children is also a function of manageable environmental influences. One of the most distinctive and defining *endowments* of a human being is one's capacity to be affected by, and adjust to, the diverse particularities that characterize one's environment, especially one's language environment. This uniquely human endowment (in degree if not kind) significantly complicates the efforts of organicists to find and describe reliable genetically based processes that are relatively free from sociocultural influences (see Liska, this volume). An organicist, of course, would argue that sociocultural influences might also be captured in the form of inherent organicistic process models.

Where humans are concerned, we must consider whether limited resources should be diverted to the discovery of organismically based stages and cycles, or whether most efforts should be directed at changeable and manageable environmental conditions that are already known to affect a person's innate potentials (see Guerin, 1994; Guerin, this volume; Owen, 1993). The organicist will no doubt argue that we need not choose between these two alternatives. And, that continued progress in knowledge about inherent organismic processes will increasingly inform the ways in which we might most profitably redesign and control influential aspects of our physical and sociocultural environments.

Contextualism

The *root metaphor* for contextualism is an *historic event* or *act* which is *alive* in the current setting (Pepper, 1942, pp. 232; 253). Contextualism is unique in its explanatory appeal to complex webs of historical events interpenetrating with current ones. Importantly, this web of historical events includes the unique history of each observer. For example, in the process of interpreting a text, many of one's previous experiences are functionally present and are part of what one has to say.

The Basic Category: Change

The fundamental category for contextualism is *change; novelty* is not assumed, but it can be accepted with no sense of embarrassment. Mechanism and organicism are required by their metaphysical commitments to view novelty as ignorance or error. In sharp contrast, contextualists remain open to the possible occurrence of novel events or acts. "... *change* and *novelty* accepted in the most radical sense will be regarded as the fundamental presuppositions of this theory" (Pepper, 1942, pp. 235-236). From a contextual point of view, order can come out of disorder and can return again to disorder (p. 234).

Contextualism assumes a real world, but one that is presented to us in complex, ever-changing ways; and, one that is experienced in novel ways by each individual (and by the same individual on different occasions). It follows then that the world is open to multiple interpretations. From a contextualist's view, one's verbal report is a point of convergence; it is a moment in time when one's personal and professional state of affairs converges and interpenetrates with the state of affairs one is looking at and talking about (see Penman, this volume; Owen, in press). For example, in describing the qualities of a table, Pepper (1942) states:

> ... the important point to note is that the qualities arise in the integration of the texture and belong neither to me alone nor to the table alone, but to the common texture. In seeing a table I am interacting with my environment and am so far out into it (p. 266).

Contextualism is uniquely a-ontological. That is, unlike mechanism and organicism (and to some extent formism), it does not presume a world organized in some ideal way. Its interests are more immediate and related to one's practical goals.

Two "Types" of Contextualism

A distinction can be made between *descriptive* (qualitative) and *instrumental* (functional) contextualisms (Pepper, 1942; Hayes, 1993).[1] The difference, however, is a matter of emphasis. And, importantly, "... it does not make much different in contextualism what traits are emphasized first; the others will all come in sooner or later" (Pepper, p. 260). Both descriptive and instrumental contextualists see the world through the same basic category of *change* and through related categories that serve to characterize the particulars of that basic category. The difference in emphasis between the two "types" of contextualism can be stated in terms of their focal purposes or goals.

The primary goal of a descriptive contextualist is *understanding:* For example, one might travel to a foreign country just to gain a better sense of what is going on there. This understanding is always more or less *personal* and *situational*. That is, an understanding can work for me but not you, and it can work for me at one time but not another. Also, one kind of understanding does not necessarily contribute to another. For example, an understanding of what it means to be growing older does not necessarily lead to an understanding of what it's like to give a public speech.

In effect, descriptive contextualists emphasize the very personal and idiosyncratic aspect of an analysis. They remind us, for example, that a speaker talking about the Civil War not only brings a particular perspective to the events in question but also unique interpretations in the light of unique personal and professional histories.

Instrumental contextualists recognize (1) the legitimate goal of personal understanding, and (2) the fact that the particulars of one's history contribute to how one functions as an analyst. However, instrumental contextualists are also interested in the goals of *prediction* and *influence* (Hayes, 1993). Influence includes not only the effects of informative and persuasive speaking but also the results of negotiations, including the negotiation of meanings (see Shailor; Hall, this volume).

Instrumental contextualists emphasize the value of any schemata such as plans, strategies, maps, guidelines, formulae, rules, etc., that increase one's ability to take successful action in settings that are both complex and changing. Importantly, a schema found useful during one's own era might remain pretty much "intact," while the circumstances to which it applies are subject to continual change (see Cronkhite, this volume). Quite often a scheme takes the form of an hypothesis about actions that lead to satisfaction in a particular setting; an hypothesis implies action, and if that action leads to satisfaction the hypothesis is said to be true

(Pepper, 1942, p. 269). From a contextual view, schemata need not reveal anything about the actual structures of the world as envisioned by the metaphysics of formism, mechanism, or organicism; they need only contribute to successful action.

In general, whether one's primary purpose is descriptive or instrumental, a contextual view is *synthetic* (as opposed to analytic); an observer's overall experience and description of the whole is primary. The central importance of the entirety of an event is particularly evident in one's experience of a painting, a dance, a speech, or some other work of art. Contextualism is also *dispersive* (as opposed to integrative); analysis moves outward from an event and provides a *description* of its interaction and interpenetration with other events.

The Categories of Quality and Texture

From a contextual view, change can "slow down" and "thicken up." Accordingly, we can differentiate among numerous events, and can provide qualitative descriptions and assessments of them including their apparent relationships (see Adams, this volume). The description of an event and its relationships is based on our experience of it; our intuitive sense of what it is and how it functions. For practical purposes we can distinguish between the quality of a whole event, and the qualities of its textures or details. In general, "... the quality of a given event is its intuited wholeness or total character; the texture is the details and relations that contribute to that character or quality" (Pepper, 1942, p. 238).

The categories of quality and texture are fundamental to a contextual analysis; nevertheless, some effort is required to appropriately distinguish between them. In the other three relatively adequate world views, major categories are easily divided into *subcategories.* Indeed, the notion of subcategories is so engrained in common sense that it is difficult to get beyond it—as one must—in grasping the uniqueness of the contextualist's categories.

For a contextualist, categories such as quality and texture do not distinguish between a *whole and its parts*; they distinguish between our shifts in *focus* from a *whole to its details.* The idea here is that the whole of something is experienced in its entirety and can be described in qualitative terms. But when we shift attention to the textures or details encompassed within a whole, each texture is itself experienced as a whole which can also be described in additional qualitative terms. For example, we might shift our attention from the qualities of a "whole" painting to the unique shades of green used by an artist in a particular detail of that painting. The distinction between a "whole" and its details depends upon our orientation at any given moment (Pepper, 1942, pp. 248; 257). In any case, both the whole of something and its details are presented to us with their own unique, distinctive, and *wholistic* qualities.

The Qualities of Textures: Strands and Their Contexts

If we wish to examine more closely some of the details of an event's texture we can do so by shifting our focus to its *strands* and their connections to different *contexts*. A strand is "... a contributing detail in a texture, but it also reaches out into a context and brings some of the quality of the context into the texture" (Pepper, 1942, p. 247). In examining a manuscript, for example, one might view a particular paragraph as one of its textures; in that case, individual sentences in that paragraph can be seen as strands that reach out to other sentences and to broader references. From this view, the complex ways in which a particular message is connected by its strands to a broader set of contexts contribute to its overall intuited "quality" or "meaning."

Categories of Change: Spread, Convergence, and Fusion

The contextualist's basic category of *change* can also be examined more closely in terms of our intuited sense of an event's *spread*, and its interpenetration with other events through processes of *convergence*, and on some occasions, *fusion*.

Spread pertains to the intuited quality of an event as we see it unfold out of the past and move into the future. Qualitative time (one's personal experience of spread) is distinguished from schematic time (a derived mathematical way of quantifying it). There is a transitive quality to one's intuited sense of an event's spread; a perception of before-and-afterness; a sense that an event has a history and is in transition toward a future.

The spread of an event can be further analyzed in terms of its participation in *processes* of *change*. The simplest process is a linear one in which an event moves forward in sequence from moment A to B to C. A *linear reference* is a description of an event in transition "... from an initiation to a satisfaction with a continuous intervening spread pointing both forward and backward" (Pepper, 1942. p. 253).

While the concept of a single linear reference captures the transitory nature of events, a contextual analysis typically involves a focus on *convergent* processes. "A *convergent* reference [or process] is a complex linear reference in which there are either several initiations [Events: A1, A2, A3...] converging upon one satisfaction [Event B] or several satisfactions [B1, B2, B3...] derived from one initiation" (Pepper, 1942, pp. 253-254). That is, multiple converging events can produce a single effect (such as a declaration of war); or, a single event (such as winning a lottery) can have multiple consequences. Contrary to some opinions then, contextualists do not object to linear thinking per se; they embrace it. What they do object to is the overly simplified linear analysis that fails to address the convergent processes that characterize most events. From a contextual view, a "single event" almost always turns out to be a complex web of textures and strands interpenetrating with their respective contexts and in transition from a past to a future.

Fusion is a special case of convergence where events not only interact with each other, but assimilate into new or "emergent" ones. The concept of "fusion" is captured in a now classic illustration by William James. He noted that in making lemonade we have three events: lemons, water, and sugar, each with its own perceived qualities. Yet, when we combine these events, we have a new one that *emerges* with its own distinctive qualities. That is, lemonade neither looks like, nor tastes like lemons, water, or sugar. On the contrary, it looks and tastes like something new, something we call "lemonade."

Problems Inherent in a Contextual Analysis

The person who chooses to do a contextual analysis is faced with at least two major problems. Firstly, there are no rules for where a contextual analysis should begin or end. Decisions about these matters must be made somewhat arbitrarily. Theoretically, a contextual analysis could start with any event that just happens to capture one's attention; it could then go on forever, or it could end when one's interests change or when one is exhausted.

Secondly, there are no rules for sorting out in advance just what it is that one should focus upon (see Leeds-Hurwitz, this volume). As noted by Pepper (1942), there is an inherent element of arbitrariness "... in selecting so much of one feature rather than another, or so much of one feature against so little of another" (p. 233). Theoretically, one could jump about endlessly among different events and their textures; and, one could follow forever a texture's numerous strands and the ways in which they reach out into different contexts.

The Central Importance of Purpose and Prior Experience

Contextualism has a strong affiliation with philosophical pragmatism, and it is one's *practical purposes* that keep a contextual analysis from spinning out of control (Hayes, 1993). A contextual analysis can be initiated in order to achieve a practical purpose; it can be terminated when that purpose is achieved, or perhaps, when it is apparent that one's goals are not achievable and one could move productively to new ones.

Importantly, a contextual analysis has *no significance in itself*. Its significance lies in the purpose we are pursuing (Pepper, 1942, pp. 250-251). In the case of a descriptive contextualist the focal purpose is practical action that leads to a satisfaciton in the form of understanding. In the case of an instrumental contextualist the focal purpose is practical action that leads to a satisfaction in the form of prediction, or to prediction and influence.

After determining one's practical purpose, decisions about where a contextual analysis should begin or end, or what it should focus upon, are best made in the light of one's previous experiences. Previous experience gives direction to a contextual analysis. This experience also leads to contextually oriented schemata which can facilitate future goal achievement (Pepper, 1942, p. 267). These schemata serve as "... a summary of past social experiences and a guide to future experiences ... they constitute what is called 'the science' of a period and change from period to period" (p. 267).

Context, Narrative, and Truth

From a contextual view, *events or acts and their contexts* "... cannot be fully distinguished because each contributes to the nature of the other" (Hayes et al.,

1988, p. 100). Specifically, an analysis of an *event or act* moves in the direction of contributing contexts. Concurrently, an analysis of a *context* moves in the direction of contributing events or acts. Take, for example, the speaker who prepares and delivers an informative speech to a particular audience. A contextual analysis of the speaker would consider the ways in which the interests of an audience reach out and affect the performance of a speaker. A contextual analysis of the audience would consider the ways in which the performance of a speaker reaches out and affects audience responses. From a contextual view then, *context is constituted by all events that are functionally related to the occurrence and qualities of a particular event.* And, *the description of a particular event is only meaningful to the extent that it includes the conditions that contribute to its occurrence and its qualities.*

Most contextualists are likely to conceptualize speakers "... as agents, as actors pursuing goals ... action in social contexts, conversations, dialogues and strategic interaction [are] the objects of study" (Sarbin, 1993, p. 56). A contextualist is likely to emphasize "... social and cultural forms, kinship and family, politics and economics, and recent and remote history" (p. 56). (For an unusually lucid and detailed discussion of this last point see Ratner, 1993.)

The synthetic and dispersive features of a contextual analysis are most easily captured within a *narrative* methodology (Sarbin, 1993). A *contextual narrative* is particularly well suited for describing the ways in which particular events "unfold" within their past and current settings, and participate in processes of change. Various forms of the narrative can be adapted to the more specific purposes of rhetorical analysis, conversation analysis, ethnography, ethology, historiography, biography, hermeneutics, semiotics, role-playing, theater, etc.

The *truth criterion* for contextualism is *workability* (i.e., the achievement of one's goals). A contextualist is a pragmatist who looks for workability or usefulness in one's era. However, in most societies successful action involves more than what is "good" for self. It also involves what we do that is good for others, and what we do that is good for our culture. It is through our support of deserving others and our contributions to the preservation and strengthening of useful social institutions and practices that we enhance successful working for now and generations to come.

Strengths and Weaknesses

A contextual view is strong on scope but relatively weak on precision. Scope is achieved by the fact that a contextual narrative is inherently capable of moving about in numerous directions while capturing the qualities and textures of events, along with their relationships and involvement in processes of change. However, this scope is achieved at a certain price in precision. As stated by Pepper (1942), "... there are many equally revealing ways of analyzing an event, depending simply on what strands you follow from the event into its context" (p. 250).

A particularly important contribution of contextualism is that it elevates the importance of practical everyday human activities (see DeSantis, this volume).

Things that people do and say become legitimate objects of study *on their own merits* (without the need to reduce them down to a more microscopic level of analysis, or to use them simply as a basis for inferring cognitive activity going on at some other level). Scientific generalizations or "rules" are still possible but they focus on contextual contingencies as opposed to neurological or mentalistic ones (see Guerin, 1994; Guerin, this volume; Owen, 1989, 1990, 1993, 1994, in press). From a contextual view, of course, it is not necessary for one's scientific efforts to evidence progress toward some presumed universal state of order or disorder. A descriptive contextualist might want to explore a particular territory simply for the purpose of making some kind of sense out of it. An instrumental contextualist might want to employ and refine certain strategems just because they have a history of helpling to solve practical problems.

At the same time, a major weakness of descriptive contextualism is the ease with which we can generate personal understandings that do not necessarily contribute to someone else's sense of understanding. While a particular understanding may work for one's self, others are free to vote with their feet. A major weakness of instrumental contextualism is that the schemata that contribute to prediction and influence in one setting may fail to do so in another, or they may fail to do so in the "same" setting at a different time. From a contextual view, much of our knowledge about these matters is situation specific and cumulative only in the relatively short term.

Ironically, as a contextualist is increasingly successful at generating reliable schemata, one is pulled in the direction of either a mechanistic or an organicistic view. That is, while contextualism accommodates regularity in the short term, "...it is constantly threatened with evidence of permanent structures in nature" (Pepper, 1942, p. 253). Accordingly, contextualism "...is constantly on the verge of falling back upon underlying mechanistic structures, or of resolving into the overarching implicit integrations of organicism" (p. 235).

To work consistently within the legitimate parameters of a contextual view, one must continually hurry back to the metaphor of historical events alive in the current, complex, and ever-changing present. One must be ready to accept order or disorder wherever they might be found. Where change speeds up and disorder appears to rule the day, "understanding" may be the most a contextualist can hope for (the same may be said of order that is so complex and changing that it can only be seen as disorder). Where change slows down and order appears to rule the day, the contextualist should be prepared to appreciate the instrumentalist's goals of prediction, or prediction and influence–at least for the short term. The trick for the contextualist is to remain committed only to the fundamental category of change, and to follow change through to whatever order or disorder it might reveal in one's own era. The essential interests of a contextualist must remain practical, not ontological.

Some Concluding Remarks

In sorting through the many things that Pepper has to say, it becomes increasingly clear that he speaks primarily from a contextual point of view. His seminal contribution is root metaphor theory, and this theory turned back on itself reveals its contextualistic origins.

Probably the most unique feature of Pepper's robust contextual view is its capacity to appreciate—while not categorically embracing—three alternative world views: formism, mechanism, and organicism. It is required to do so, of course, because of its truth criterion, *successful working*. Based on this criterion, relatively adequate language games need not light up the entire universe; like headlights on a car, they need only light up parts of it while in the service of more immediate practical purposes. Above all else, contextualism is a *pragmatic* point of view.

References

Adams, K. L. (1997). Pragmatism and context: A matter of pattern. In J. L. Owen (Ed.), *Context and communication behavior*. Reno, NV: Context Press.

Craig, R. T. (Ed.), & Leeds-Hurwitz, W. (Guest Co-Ed.). (1992). Forum: Social approaches. *Communication Theory, 2*(2), 131-172.

Craig, R. T. (Ed.), & Leeds-Hurwitz, W. (Guest Co-Ed.). (1992). Forum: Social approaches. *Communication Theory, 2*(2), 329-356.

Cronkhite, G. (1997). Cognitive representation of rhetorical situations. In J. L. Owen (Ed.), *Context and communication behavior*. Reno, NV: Context Press.

DeSantis, A. D. (1997). From modernity to postmodernity: Recontextualizing communication theory. In J. L. Owen (Ed.), *Context and communication behavior*. Reno, NV: Context Press.

Gardner, H. (1985). *The mind's new science*. New York: Basic Books, Inc.

Gregory, R. L. (1981). *Mind in science*. Cambridge, England: Cambridge University Press.

Guerin, B. (1994). *Analyzing social behavior: Behavior analysis and the social sciences*. Reno, NV: Context Press.

Guerin, B. (1997). Social contexts for communication: Communicative power as past and present social consequences. In J. L. Owen (Ed.), *Context and communication behavior*. Reno, NV: Context Press.

Guerin, B. (in press). How things get done: Socially, non-socially; with words, without words. In L. Hayes & P. Ghezzi (Eds.), *Investigations in behavioral epistemology*. Reno, NV: Context Press.

Hall, B. J. (1997). Theories of culture, communication and context. In J. L. Owen (Ed.), *Context and communication behavior*. Reno, NV: Context Press.

Hayes, L., & Ghezzi, P., (Eds.). (In press). *Investigations in behavioral epistemology*. Reno, NV: Context Press.

Hayes, S. (1993). Analytic goals and the varieties of scientific contextualism. In S. Hayes, L. Hayes, H. Reese, & T. Sarbin (Eds.), *Varieties of scientific contextualism* (pp. 11-27). Reno, NV: Context Press.

Hayes, S. C., Hayes, L. J., & Reese, H. W. (1988). Finding the philosophical core: A review of Stephen C. Pepper's WORLD HYPOTHESES: A STUDY IN EVIDENCE. *Journal of the Experimental Analysis of Behavior, 50,* 97-111.

Hayes, S. C., Hayes, L. J., Reese, H. W., & Sarbin, T. R. (Eds.). (1993). *Varieties of scientific contextualism.* Reno, NV: Context Press.

Leeds-Hurwitz, W. (1992). Forum introduction: Social approaches to interpersonal communication. *Communication Theory, 2,* 131-139.

Leeds-Hurwitz, W. (1997). The concept of context in social communication theory. In J. L. Owen (Ed.), *Context and communication behavior.* Reno, NV: Context Press.

Lerner, R. M. (1993). A developmental contextual view of human development. In S. Hayes, L. Hayes, H. Reese, & T. Sarbin (Eds.), *Varieties of scientific contextualism* (pp. 301-316). Reno, NV: Context Press.

Liska, J. (1997). Signs of the apes, songs of the whales: Human communication in evolutionary context. In J. L. Owen (Ed.), *Context and communication behavior.* Reno, NV: Context Press.

Owen, J. L. (1989). Interpersonal surrogates and communication theory: A behavioral view. *Communication Reports, 2,*(1), 48-50.

Owen, J. L. (1990). A closer look at the behaviorists' agenda. *Communication Reports, 3,*(2), 109-113.

Owen, J. L. (1993). On contextual interpretations of behavior. In S. Hayes, L. Hayes, H. Reese, & T. Sarbin (Eds.), *Varieties of scientific contextualism* (pp. 222-225). Reno, NV: Context Press.

Owen, J. L. (1994, February). *Behavior paradigms and communication theory.* Paper presented at the meeting of the Western States Communication Association, San Jose, CA.

Owen, J. L. (in press). A referent is not a thing: It's a process. In L. Hayes & P. Ghezzi (Eds.), *Investigations in behavioral epistemology.* Reno, NV: Context Press.

Penman, R. (1997). The researcher in communication: The primary research position. In J. L. Owen (Ed.), *Context and communication behavior.* Reno, NV: Context Press.

Pepper, S. (1942). *World hypotheses: A study in evidence.* Berkeley, CA: University of California press.

Ratner, C. (1993). A sociohistorical psychological approach to contextualism. In S. Hayes, L. Hayes, H. Reese, & T. Sarbin (Eds.), *Varieties of scientific contextualism* (pp. 169-186). Reno, NV: Context Press.

Rosnow, R. L., & Georgoudi, M. (Eds.). (1986). *Contextualism and understanding in behavior science: Implications for research and theory.* New York: Praeger.

Sanders, R. E. (1997). An impersonal basis for shared interpretations of messages in context. In J. L. Owen (Ed.), *Context and communication behavior.* Reno, NV: Context Press.

Sarbin, T. R. (1993). The narrative as the root metaphor for contextualism. In S. Hayes, L. Hayes, H. Reese, & T. Sarbin (Eds.), *Varieties of scientific contextualism* (pp. 51-65). Reno, NV: Context Press.

Shailor, J. G. (1997). The meaning and use of "context" in the theory of the coordinated management of meaning. In J. L. Owen (Ed.), *Context and communication behavior.* Reno, NV: Context Press.

Footnote

[1] Pepper (1942) does not use the term "descriptive" contextualist; he does use the term "instrumental" contextualism in reference to those contextualists who emphasize the goals of prediction and influence (p. 260). Hayes uses the terms "descriptive" and "functional" contextualists to distinguish between those primarily interested in personal understanding and those who also emphasize the value of prediction and influence (Hayes, 1993, pp. 21-25). The term "functional" is particularly appropriate for Hayes' target audience of behavior analysts. The term "instrumental" is more in keeping with the literature in communication studies.

Chapter 2

Objectivism as the Basic Context for Theory and Research in Communication

Nancy Grant Harrington
Robert N. Bostrom
University of Kentucky

There is no doubt that a substantial portion of our modern health problems stem from our behavior, not from sickness or accidents (Becker, 1992). The AIDS epidemic certainly has a physiological component, but probably never will be checked until appropriate behavioral components are addressed. Heart disease and cancer are both dramatic examples of specific illnesses that can be alleviated, if not eliminated altogether, by modifications in behavior. In the United States, although we claim to appreciate the power of prevention, apparently we prefer to expend more and more of our national resources on treating illnesses rather than preventing or avoiding them. Wouldn't it make sense to supplement "medical science" with "behavioral science"?

Many of us do indeed, remember "behavioral science." In the early 1960s, the prospect for the scientific study of human behavior seemed bright. Bernard Berelson (1963) described the new science this way:

> The scientific aim is to establish generalizations about human behavior that are supported by empirical evidence collected in an impersonal and objective way. The evidence must be capable of verification by other interested scholars and the procedures must be completely open to review and replication. The search for broad propositions about human behavior and the effort to build knowledge cumulatively require that general categories descriptive of behavior be set up and used more or less systematically. ...The ultimate end is to understand, explain, and predict human behavior in the same sense in which scientists understand, explain, and predict the behavior of physical forces or biological factors. (p. 3)

The statement and the agenda are clear, but after thirty years, reading Berelson's statement provokes only nostalgia and a longing for this kind of optimism. What happened to the study of behavior?

There are many possible explanations for the apparent decrease of interest in behavior. One is that the attempt to "objectify" behaviors led to the study of more specific and less interesting responses, such as eyelid blinks and finger taps. It is difficult to get excited about such things, much less to relate them to socially significant situations. Another possible explanation is that, in the attempt to operationalize variables of interest, researchers contrived elaborate representations of social situations that really weren't very meaningful to anyone. A third explanation is that behaviorism was marred by the Vietnam war – the associations with manipulation and control were hard to maintain in a climate of revolution and protest. These factors, coupled with the increasing emphasis among a number of communication researchers on originating, developing, and promoting theory, gave momentum to a movement that favored an entirely different focus for communication research – human *action*.

Action theory represents one of the earliest splits from the behaviorism of the sixties, and prides itself on being "subjective science." In this chapter, we first provide a brief introduction to action theory, noting its origin and elaborating its position against behavioral study and empiricism.[1] Next, we look at some of the arguments for action theory and show how most of them are flawed. Then, we discuss some of the serious negative implications for communication teaching, research and practice that would result if an action approach were followed literally. Finally, we contemplate the concept of human "action," and point out ways that this concept can be studied objectively.

A Brief Introduction to Action Theory

Historically, empirical (objectivist) approaches to communication theory have emphasized behavior and observation. The process of building theories based strictly on observations of behavior has a number of logical, practical, and ethical difficulties that are hard to reconcile, however. One logical problem involves the operational definition of theoretical terms. A strict, Bridgmanian (1938) definition would equate the theoretical term with the set of operations which defined it – so the question becomes why bother with the theory?[2] Even if we adopt a more reasonable approach to operationalization, creating a realistic <u>and</u> controlled environment in which to observe our operationalized terms is exceptionally demanding. And, because communication is a "human" science, we are severely limited in the way that we can ethically manipulate human behavior. We can't deliberately make people apprehensive, for example, and observe their behavior.[3] The best we can settle for is to ask people about their experience with apprehension. "Experience," however, is by nature private and inaccessible to observers.

A group of theorists who have taken the view that these limitations *demand* a degree of subjectivity in social science have come to be known as action theorists. Rather than solve some of the sticky problems in objective behavioral research, these theorists concluded that the limitations could be obviated with the introduction of a degree of subjectivity in social science. This subjectivity soon developed into a whole new kind of theory – action theory. In a recent essay, Hanna (1991) notes that critical, empirical and action theories have become institutionalized to the extent that they now are seen as "competing" models of communicative phenomena. And while most of us clearly understand and accept the differences between empirical and critical approaches, action theory – "subjective science" – is quite another question.

Action theorists treat individuals as active perceivers and interpreters of reality. They believe that the causes of human behavior reside in individuals' "inner environments" and therefore the inner environments, not just behavior, should be of utmost concern. Since scientists have no way of directly assessing what is in *someone else's* inner environment, however, we must rely on interpretation. To interpret, we depend on our own inner experiences and assume that others are experiencing events the same way we are. This interpretation takes the form of the question "If I performed that response in that fashion in that situation, what would I have been thinking?"

If the only difference between empirical theories and action theories was the assessment of interpretation, we would justifiably conclude that the differences were trivial and that basically the two kinds of theories were similar. But the leap to interpretive science is a more basic point of departure, having to do with some fundamental theoretical assumptions. At the center of the controversy lies the very nature of the data we observe, analyze and interpret. An empirical approach makes a clear distinction between data and theory, with interpretation taking place at the inferential/theoretical level, and not the observation/data level (Bostrom & Donohew, 1992). An action approach, on the other hand, argues that theory and data interact, with the nature of the theory *determining* the nature of the data.

Action explanations are at the heart of the constructivist and rules theory approaches to communication phenomena, and proponents of these theories think of themselves as action theorists. For example, Delia (1977) asserts that:

> In the constructivist perspective a person's understandings of others and their perspectives is understood as always in terms of construals, i.e., of images or impressions. The other's intentions, inner qualities or attitudes are never apprehended directly; rather in interpersonal perception, impressions of others and their perspectives are erected within cognitive structures (constructs) that perceiver brings with him [sic] to interpersonal situations. (p. 71)

Since what is studied is interpretive, say the adherents of action theory, does it not follow that the assessment process (and the theories on which they are based) is also interpretive? This view is expressed by Applegate and Sypher (1983), who state that theories should be "interpretive" in nature.

> [These theories] should embody a philosophical anthropology that treats people as active interpreters of their social environment: one that rejects determinism and recognizes the falsity of the nature/nurture dichotomy. Interpretive theories should focus upon the interpenetration of the developing symbolic capabilities of human organisms and the historical structures of culture within which the former emerge. (p. 64)

Interpretive theory is found in many aspects of communication study. For example, some organizational communication theorists (Eisenberg & Goodall, 1993) have taken the position that a "symbolic interactionist" perspective is the most productive way in which to study organizations, and draw on symbolic interactionism as a basic conceptual framework for organizational study. Morely (1993) depends on a basic interpretivism in explaining contemporary audience research – and so on.

Difficulties with Action Theory

Throughout the construction of this new "paradigm," action theorists have attacked empiricism and science in general. They assert that action theory is *demanded* because of what they see to be inherent difficulties in empiricism. In communication, the view that empiricism is a complete failure has been expressed by Delia, O'Keefe, & O'Keefe (1982) and Cushman, Valentinsen, & Dietrich (1982). Rather than articulate the deficiencies of empiricism in detail, they depend on Daniel O'Keefe's (1975) basic indictment of "positivism" as their principal argument for the inherent difficulties of empiricism in general.[4] In his indictment of positivism, O'Keefe faults empiricism for its reliance on operational definitions for mental predicates, asserting his belief in the reliability of *a priori* principles. Second, he asserts that empirical verification is impossible, and third, that all observations are theory-dependent, and therefore suspect. These deficiencies, and his preference for the subject matter of action theories make up the main thrust of his arguments.

Action theorists justify de-emphasis on behavior by contending that they study the unobservable mental events that mediate communicative effects, and they contend that to do so involves an interpretive act that can only be done by reference to introspective processes, with the goal of discovering intentionality. Further, they assert that scientific study of human behavior is interpretive since the process is interpretive. Theory just doesn't *explain* observations, it *creates* them. They go on to contend that empiricism is fatally flawed, and these flaws demand the adoption of social constructions in science. In short, they offer an elaborate justification for abandoning the study of behavior and substituting for it theories based on mental processes and their interpretation of them.

Unfortunately, the acceptance of this view means that replication is impossible, and further, that principles discovered by the scientific process are not generalizable. A truly depressing situation! Fortunately (at least from the point of view of us objectivists) these arguments are without merit. Let us look at some of them in a little more detail.

We will begin with the contentions that empiricism is fatally flawed because theoretical terms have a priori meaning and are infinitely extendable. To simply assert the existence of *a priori* meaning is to ignore the entire history of philosophy (Russell, 1945). The existence of universals is by no means agreed on, and never has been. Empiricism always has denied universals, and to assert that empiricism is wrong for this reason is highly circular.

Recently Bostrom and Donohew (1992) applied Russell's contentions about logic and metalogic to some of the ideas of confirmation advanced by the interpretivists, and showed that the contention that an observational system defines its subsequent analytical system is without merit. In addition, they demonstrated that the "theory-data" interaction which interpretivists place at the center of their argument against empiricism is allegedly supported by research that could not be believed if indeed there were a theory-data interaction. It seems clear that the interpretivists' contentions about "positivism" are worse than mistaken – they are inherently inconsistent.

But the most telling deficiency in the interpretivists' argument is Reichenbach's (1936) application of the Russell-Whitehead demonstration that a mathematical or logical system cannot contain within itself proofs of the system. Goedel demonstrated that *no* system could do so. Self-referential systems are inherently illogical, whether based in logic or mathematics. If Russell and Whitehead were wrong about this, then it would seem that the interpretivists ought to show exactly how and why. Mathematicians are careful to separate "meta-mathematical systems" from the systems they describe (Nagel & Newman, 1956). These philosophical and logical errors are glaring ones, and should convince us that an interpretive system is inherently deficient.

Theory and Practice

But rather than continue this discussion in an abstract vein, let us look at where interpretivism leads us. The practical implications of the application of interpretive science in our daily lives are unsettling, and we will demonstrate this with examples from academe. University professors typically are expected to engage in three principal activities – teaching, research, and service. In one of our courses, for example, we teach that patient compliance with medical directives is unacceptably low, and that the reason for this is not related to patient or physician characteristics in any consistent way, but rather has been found to be related to the nature of the physician-patient relationship. The communication between the physician and patient and the patient's satisfaction with the physician-patient relationship can impact a patient's compliance. In research studies, then, the question can be asked, "What types of message strategies might lead to patient satisfaction and compliance?" and physician-patient interactions can be studied to discover an answer to that question. Michael Burgoon and his colleagues (Burgoon, Birk, & Hall, 1991; Burgoon, Parrott, Burgoon, Birk et al., 1990; Burgoon, Parrott, Burgoon, Coker et al., 1990) have found, for example, that patients who receive less "verbally aggressive" compliance gaining messages from their physicians report greater satisfaction and greater compliance. This research adds to the store of knowledge about health communication and certainly is worthwhile. In translating this to community service, if we are asked to speak to medical students about the importance of communication with their patients and how to communicate in a more effective manner, we can talk about this and related research.

In all of these activities, the product that we are selling is, in fact, a *principle*. Communicable principles must be put in the form of statements, and the statement about verbal aggression and patient satisfaction and compliance goes like this:

Physicians who use verbally unaggressive compliance gaining messages will be more likely to achieve patient satisfaction and compliance than those who use moderately aggressive messages.

Since communication scholars are paid to distribute this principle, and even apply it, most theories of economics would hold that the principle has some intrinsic value – to students, to patients and physicians, and to our professional community. But the ultimate value of what we do depends on some very basic assumptions that all of us apparently are willing to make. Most of these assumptions are not just important – they are fundamental. For example, the most common assumption is that the future will resemble the past, or that human behavior next week will be very much like behavior last week. While the future is unknowable, and Humean views of verification tell us that we can only say that phenomena only exist in the past, it makes little sense to act as if pigs will begin to fly next week and that since you don't know whether your car will start this afternoon, you may as well walk home. Assumptions that pigs probably will stay in their pens, and that since the car started this morning, it probably will this afternoon, are what philosophers call "common sense" assumptions. And while philosophers look down their noses at "common sense," we have noticed that most of them *act* pretty much the way the rest of us do.

Additional assumptions that have been made in research on compliance gaining strategies, verbal aggression, and patient satisfaction and compliance include:

1. Physicians' compliance gaining messages differ in levels of verbal aggression;
2. Researchers can identify this message characteristic accurately (reliably);
3. This message characteristic produces different outcomes.

To verify each of these assumptions (and, of course, the many other assumptions not listed) alone is truly impossible. No individual has the time, ability, or energy to carry out all the research necessary to do this. So what we researchers do is depend on the efforts of other researchers (e.g., Professor Dominic Infante, who has investigated verbal aggression in great detail). Through conference papers and published work, we come to understand the phenomenon in question. Then, when we design our own experiments using previously applied protocols with different subjects, we can get the same results. The process, of course, is called *replication*. Without it, we have no product to sell, no credibility, and certainly no justification for our jobs.

Replication is a fundamental characteristic of any trade in knowledge. But the very possibility of replicating research from one place to another, from one time to another, and even from one person to another is called into question by the interpretivists. Rorty (1994), for example, advances the philosophical argument that

"...objectivity is not a matter of corresponding to objects but of getting together with other subjects – that there is nothing to objectivity except intersubjectivity" (p. 56). We would argue that there is much more to objectivity than this statement implies. There are degrees of intersubjectivity, and it can be either highly objective or highly subjective, in spite of its unfortunate name. The concept could easily have been named "interobjectivity."

Replicability seems like such a common sense idea – a "concept" or a principle has utility only if someone else can perform the same process and produce a similar result. The statement "verbal aggression produces poor problem solving" implies future problem solving as well as past problem solving, and is therefore "nonverifiable" in the Humean view of logic. Hübner (1983) notes that this logical limitation applies to even very well-known concepts, such as the gravitational constant, and that the existence of physical "laws" must depend on something other than strict inferential logic. But we know that the gravitational constant is a powerful descriptor of falling bodies and that the descriptions of communication satellites as well as firmly struck baseballs can only be accomplished by use of this constant. These logical difficulties are dealt with in a number of ways, and different thinkers in the philosophy of science have proposed rules that they hope will enable workers to justify the use of scientific concepts (Reichenbach, 1936).

Yet the assumption that the "hard sciences" deal with "laws" (highly general statements), and the social sciences deal with less exact ones is fairly widespread, and is frequently used to call into question the application of empirical principles to social science. Cushman and Pearce (1977) present the typical view, when they state "the number of staunch advocates of this approach [objectivist thinking] has been steadily declining. Social scientists have simply been unable to discover *laws* [italics added] which have generality and necessity comparable to those in the natural sciences" (Cushman & Pearce, 1977, p. 346). The scientific process of replication, however, is exactly the same in the "hard" and "social" sciences. Let's look at another example.

We all believe that individuals have "personalities" – yet this idea only makes sense if these personalities can be said to have some consistency over time and situations. Burger (1990), for example, defines personality as "consistent behavior patterns originating within the individual" (p. 3). He goes on to show that it makes little sense to term someone as being "aggressive" if they don't *consistently* exhibit behaviors that we can generally agree fit into a category of "aggressive." This consistency over time invokes the concept of replicability.

Replicability, of course, is a central concept in *operationism*, a view that holds that scientific statements need to be grounded in specific actions in order to be meaningful. Operationism is closely related to logical empiricism. Generally, logical empiricism has treated objective actions as a characteristic of statements, while operationism has treated the actions as a characteristic of concepts (Hempel, 1965, p. 123). Both claim that language has meaning if and only if the terms embodied in it can be referred to some direct procedure, and that other terms, which cannot, are essentially meaningless and empty. P. W. Bridgman, who is generally associated with originating the strongest arguments in favor of operationism, used the term *instrumental* operations to refer to gauges, devices, and measurements by which scientists typically use to "operationalize" concepts (Bridgman, 1938).

These instrumental operations, roughly speaking, are those which occur when, under a specific set of conditions, a particular response occurs. In other words, to specify that one gram is the weight of a cubic centimeter of water, it is necessary to elaborate all the specific circumstances that are necessary to achieve a consistent result – terms like "centimeter," but also "pure" as applied to water, certain temperatures, sea level, latitude, and so forth. Once all these conditions are satisfied, then a degree of agreement can be reached concerning the term in question.[5]

But rather than emphasize operation, the concern for theory in social science has led to the dramatic inflation of theoretical terms which represent the concepts around which raw data can be organized. Common sense tells us that "information" should not mean one thing in Miami and another thing in Minneapolis; "involvement" should mean at least the same thing approximately in 1992 as it did in 1962. But current practice in social sciences is somewhat at variance with this ideal position. Not too many years ago, "dissonance," "congruity," and "imbalance" were all applied to similar phenomena, with the adherents of each "school" using their chosen term without regard or mention of the other "schools."[6] Conversely, the term "attitude" has been applied to orientations toward sensory qualities, concrete objects, abstract concepts, verbal statements, systems of thought, actions, and "attitudes" themselves (Greenwald, Pratkanis, Leippe, & Baumgardner, 1986).

Characterization of phenomena in elevated terms also is commonplace. Being interested in the outcome of a message becomes "involvement" (Petty & Cacioppo, 1984); remembering details in a message is labeled "comprehension" (Bostrom, 1990); being aware of your own communicative behavior becomes "self-monitoring" (Snyder, 1974); using lots of adjectives in a writing sample becomes "construct complexity" (Delia et al., 1982); and being left-brain oriented becomes "asymmetrically lateralized" (Springer & Deutsch, 1989). The hope is, of course, that the specialized vocabulary will take us away from folk psychology (generally taken to mean that our behavior is influenced by our thoughts and ideas) and lead us to new discoveries. This can happen only, however, if the new term is rigidly applied and meticulously defined. And this has not been the case.

Let us recapitulate. The very definition of the terms "teaching" and "research" and "service" imply *replicable* principles, principles which we must hold to be useful and meaningful to our communities. One strategy in avoiding replicability has been the redefinition of conceptual terms, often to the point of absurdity. At the heart of the process seems to be an inordinate interest in theory, theorizing, and a disinterest in phenomena or events. Taylor (1991) has noted that the underlying structures implicit in scientific discourse historically have been characterized by the rhetorical forms of universalism, communism, disinterestedness, and skepticism, and that these characteristics (among others) constitute the demarcation of science from non-science. He also notes that the "boundary work" of scientific discourse is affected by the publicness of the audience for which it is intended. To abandon these rhetorical forms is to abandon their rhetorical force. In other words, not only are the arguments for action theory flawed, they lead to the denial of replicability, and in so doing, deprive statements of their applicability and usefulness.

Should we just abandon action theory? Should we get out our notes from the 1960s and return to a purer behaviorism? What is it that has made many of us interested in the idea of human "action"? We believe that the subject matter of action theories is really quite interesting and important, and that we might want to think again about the contention that studying interpretations is inherently interpretive. It certainly ought to be possible to study "actions" objectively. Let us look into this possibility in a little more detail.

An Objectivist Approach to Action Theory

The study of human action is interesting and important, both in communication and in behavior in general. Because it allows that an individual is an active perceiver and interpreter of his or her environment, with individual intentions and goals, it offers explanations that may have greater power than simple associations among communicative and behavioral events necessary when one attempts to avoid inferred dispositional or motivational states, and treats the individual simply as reactive. We propose that communication researchers accept the action view of the individual, but approach the study of that individual and his or her communication and behavior from an objectivist orientation. This proposition is not entirely radical. In fact, we would argue that much interpretivist research is really quite objectivist. Once the meta-theoretical trappings are discarded, the methodologies are in keeping with empiricism.

Let's look at some specific instances of how action theory within an objectivist framework might be applied to the study of communication and attitude or behavior change – what many of us call "persuasion."

Communication often aims at "change" and by this we mean that a message creates a difference in the things that we think or do. But how does that message create a difference? Instances of behavioral change can be said to be "mediated" by attitudes, in that attitudes clearly are implicated in these decisions. Behaviorists often invoke "behavioral intentions," but even with this more specific approach to potential acts, they are far from providing an adequate explanation for these changes. Even though attitudes and intentions are logically antecedent to these behaviors, as explanations, they are somehow unsatisfying. We are interested in specifying the underlying mechanism of this change.

Consider the following two cases in which behavioral change occurs:

CASE ONE: Audrey has been smoking cigarettes since she was fifteen years old. Now 40, she has recently begun to entertain the idea of quitting. She has been growing tired of feeling like a "second class citizen" at work and in businesses and restaurants. She also is aware of the health benefits associated with quitting smoking. Finally one day, she decides to join the ranks of non-smokers and signs up for a smoking cessation program she saw advertised at a local hospital. Through the program, she is able to quit smoking.

CASE TWO: David is a homosexual who has had many different sexual partners, and rarely used condoms in any of the encounters. He is very aware of the prevalence of AIDS and the risk of contracting HIV through unsafe sex practices. After a recent blood test revealed he was HIV-negative and his physician again lectured him on the importance of using condoms, he decides he'd better stop taking chances and start practicing safer sex, and he does.

Each of these instances of behavioral change can be said to be influenced by messages from individuals, the community, or the media, and also to be "mediated" by attitudes or behavioral intentions held by Audrey and David. Yet we all know of cases just like these in which the individual refuses to or "chooses" not to change. What accounts for the differences?

We suggest that a useful direction in which to point this investigation is toward schema theory. Bartlett (1932) generally is credited as being the first to develop a schema theory, suggesting that learning requires "effort after meaning" and remembering requires an active "process of construction." During learning, one must "assimilate the new material to existing schemas; during recall, an existing schema is used to construct details that are consistent with it" (Mayer, 1983, p. 212). From Bartlett's (1932) groundwork, a considerable literature on schemas has developed.

A schema generally may be defined as "an abstract or generic knowledge structure, stored in memory, that specifies the defining features and relevant attributes of some stimulus domain, and the interrelations among those attributes" (Crocker, Fiske, & Taylor, 1984, p. 197). In persuasion research, schemas have been defined as "hierarchically interrelated sets of expectancies or hypotheses, each of which relates either: 1) a self or other object to its presumed attribute, or 2) some specified action to its anticipated consequences" (Smith, 1982b, p. 336). Schemas function actively at all phases of information processing – they determine what we attend to, how we interpret, how we store and ultimately recall information (Fiske & Taylor, 1984; Smith, 1982a).

In distinguishing "action" research from "behavioral" research, Morris (1981) proposed that we distinguish between responses that *require* some introspection and those that do not. When the stimulus domain cannot be assessed without introspection (i.e., without consciously activating and accessing schemas), then evaluation of it is an "action" event. Morris (1981) used the following example to explain his types of responses. If he is asked to "provide a word that begins with 'C,'" and he says "cat," he may not be able to explain why. If he puts water in the coffee maker, and you ask "why?" he will be able to explain his motives, i.e., to make coffee. You certainly will recognize the distinctions between "mindless" and "mindful" phenomena (Kellerman, 1992; Motley, 1992). In other words, Morris contends that we should not ask persons about their mindless behavior, but that their answers to mindful behavior may well be very useful.

While both mindless and mindful behavior are guided by schemas, we would suggest that when persuasion or behavior change is mediated by messages from the environment (e.g., from other individuals, from the media), this is a change that is mindful and open to introspection, and therefore counts as an "action." But what is happening, in an objectivist sense, to the individual whose behavior changes? What has changed within the person to explain the external behavior change? What is the mechanism of change?

Underlying the variables studied in much of persuasion research, but not always examined explicitly by researchers in persuasion and attitude change, are cognitive processes. According to Cacioppo, Harkins, and Petty (1981), "Cognitive processes refer to such information-processing and -structuring activities as perceiving, abstracting, judging, elaborating, rehearsing and recalling from memory" (p. 37). A focus on cognitive processes seeks to illuminate how the very encoding, storage, and retrieval of information impinges upon persuasion and attitude change. Several recent studies have attempted to explicate the different ways in which people process and evaluate arguments in persuasive messages (Chaiken, 1980; Petty & Cacioppo, 1984; Wood, Kallgren, & Priesler, 1985).

Research on thought-induced attitude polarization (Chaiken & Yates, 1985; Judd & Lusk, 1984; Millar & Tesser, 1986; Tesser & Leone, 1977) has explicitly sought to examine the impact of schematic information processing on attitude change. Tesser's (1978) model of thought-induced attitude polarization maintains that schema-guided thought will lead to attitude polarization only when the schemas are well-developed. Possessing a well-developed schema is required for polarization to occur because it provides necessary organizational guidelines for thinking about the attitude object. Tesser argues that thought-induced attitude polarization is the result of persons generating consistent cognitions and suppressing or reinterpreting inconsistent ones. Millar and Tesser (1986) hypothesized that not only does schema content change in the direction of consistency, but that schema structure changes to reflect that consistency. Results from their research supported this hypothesis, with thought being associated with higher intercorrelations among schema dimensions, indicating increased consistency or unity (Zajonc, 1960) within the schema.

While the work in thought-induced attitude polarization is suggestive, there is a lack of understanding of schema change as a possible basis of persuasion through communication. Hamilton (1981) observes that "schema theories are ambiguous regarding how schema-inconsistent information is processed" (p. 140). On the one hand, some claim that inconsistent information is inefficiently processed and often forgotten or ignored because 1) it cannot be assimilated into the existing schema, and 2) accommodation of the schema to discrepant information is uncommon. On the other hand, some assume that the very difficulty of processing inconsistent information makes it especially salient and memorable. It is less likely to simply be absorbed into an existing schema and thus will produce lasting consequences (Fiske & Taylor, 1984).

It is possible to move toward a solution to the apparent problem of schema-inconsistent information by considering certain variable features of schemas and incoming information. Crocker et al. (1984) present three characteristics of schemas – development, accessibility, and disconfirmability – which may have a bearing on schema change. Schemas which are highly developed, inaccessible, or difficult to disconfirm tend to resist change. Schemas which are not well developed, which have been accessed by the incoming information, or for which disconfirming evidence is available are easier to change. Crocker et al. (1984) suggest that four characteristics vary for incoming information – discrepancy, ambiguity, organization, and memorability. They hypothesize that schemas will be more affected by information which has a high degree of discrepancy with existing schemas, is clear and unambiguous, is dispersed across a wide number of cases, and is highly memorable.

Rothbart (1981) has suggested two models for how schemas change. The "bookkeeping" model suggests that change takes place as each new bit of relevant, inconsistent information is processed. As new information is taken in, modifications to the schema occur in a deliberate, methodical, and predictable manner. The "conversion" model proposes that sudden and dramatic change occurs when the schema is confronted with some dramatic disconfirming instance. Change in this model is basically an all or none proposition, and it occurs in an erratic, impulsive, and unpredictable manner.

Weber and Crocker (1983) attempted to test the models which Rothbart had proposed as well as a third one, which they call the "subtyping" model. This model visualizes schemas as hierarchical structures with many subcategories or subtypes attached to each general schema. When new information is encountered, it is either placed in one of the existing categories, or if inconsistent, gathered together with other information to create a new category. In other words, inconsistent information leads to more schematic differentiation. Weber and Crocker (1983) wanted to find out which of the three models best predicts change under varying conditions of amount and distribution of evidence. They also included conditions of extremity of disconfirming evidence, representativeness and size of the disconfirming subgroup, and memory load conditions. Their results supported the bookkeeping and subtyping models, but Weber and Crocker (1983) also suggest that the conversion model might be valid under conditions which were not available in their experiments.

None of the preceding models adequately consider the nature of schemas as highly organized and structured when attempting to predict change. Wyer and Carlston (1979) propose such a network model in which memory structures consist of many interconnected nodes. They provide an extensive discussion of linkage within schemas when they discuss their model of person memory.

> Very briefly, we will propose a model in which concepts are connected by pathways of different widths, and in which the activation of one concept may lead to activation of a second as a result of "excitation" that travels through these pathways. The greater the width of a given pathway

connecting two concepts the more excitation can be transmitted along it, and therefore the more quickly one concept will activate a second. (Wyer & Carlston, 1979, p. 70)

The twelve postulates of this model provide a detailed description of the structure and function of schemas. Implied in this model is the notion that new links may be formed between concepts from different domains:

> In some instances the relations have been experienced in both directions; for example, the judge may often encounter the notion that Republicans are businessmen as well as the notion that businessmen are Republicans. In such cases, two paths may exist between the concepts, one in each direction. (Wyer & Carlston, 1979, p. 72)

Clearly, the concepts of "businessmen" and "Republicans" are thought to exist as independent concepts (or schemas) prior to their linking in this hypothetical example. Through incoming information (in the form of messages) these two become linked.

This suggests a fourth model of schema change which we will call the "linkage" model. In this model, incoming information may be initially perceived as inconsistent with a schema because it connects, or links, that schema with a discrepant schema which had previously been domain independent. If the information is accepted, the resulting connection provides a new pathway for information processing. Thus not only must the basic structures of both previous schemas change to accommodate the linkage, but inconsistent elements including attitudes must be modified in order to produce consistency (McGuire, 1981; Millar & Tesser, 1986). The basic idea of establishing connections between schemas, and the associated concept of attitude polarization provides a foundation for hypotheses concerning attitude change. This model can be extended and applied to people like Audrey and David to test hypotheses explaining behavior change, as well.

It seems clear to us that research into schemas has provided a good deal of basic knowledge about cognitive structures and the mechanism of persuasion. It also seems to us that those who call themselves action theorists should now examine the empirical framework of these discoveries, and go on to emphasize the study of actions within that framework. Doing so from an objectivist perspective, emphasizing observation and replication, will result in the accumulation of data, and the practice of empirical, scientific investigation.

References

Applegate, J. L., & Sypher H. E. (1983). A constructivist outline for cultural communication studies. In W. Gudykunst (Ed.), *Intercultural communication theory: Current perspectives* (pp. 63-78). Beverly Hills, CA: Sage.

Bartlett, F. C. (1932). *Remembering: A study in experimental and social psychology.* London: Cambridge University Press.

Becker, S. (1992, April). *An information campaign to reduce smoking*. Paper presented at the Second Annual Conference on Health Communication (University of Kentucky), Lexington, KY.

Berelson, B. (1963). *The behavioral sciences today*. New York: Harper and Row.

Bostrom, R. N. (1990). *Listening behavior: Measurement and application*. New York: Guilford.

Bostrom, R. N., & Donohew, R. L. (1992). The case for empiricism: Clarifying issues in communication research. *Communication Monographs, 59*, 109-129.

Bridgman, P. W. (1938). *The intelligent individual and society*. New York: The Macmillan Company.

Burger, J. M. (1990). *Personality*. Belmont, CA: Wadsworth.

Burgoon, M., Birk, T. S., Hall, J. R. (1991). Compliance and satisfaction with physician-patient communication: An expectancy theory interpretation of gender differences. *Human Communication Research, 18*(2), 177-208.

Burgoon, M., Parrott, R., Burgoon, J., Birk, T., Pfau, M., & Coker, R. (1990). Primary care physicians' selection of verbal compliance-gaining strategies. *Health Communication, 2*, 13-28.

Burgoon, M., Parrott, R., Burgoon, J., Coker, R., Pfau, M., & Birk, T. (1990). Patients' severity of illness, noncompliance, and locus of control and physicians' compliance-gaining messages. *Health Communication, 2*, 29-46.

Cacioppo, J. T., Harkins, S. G., & Petty, R. E. (1981). The nature of attitudes and cognitive responses and their relationships to behavior. In R. E. Petty, T. M. Ostrom, & T. C. Brock (Eds.), *Cognitive responses in persuasion* (pp. 31-54). Hillsdale, NJ: Lawrence Erlbaum Associates.

Chaiken, S. (1980). Heuristic versus systematic information processing and the use of source versus message cues in persuasion. *Journal of Personality and Social Psychology, 39*, 752-766.

Chaiken, S., & Yates, S. (1985). Affective-cognitive consistency and thought-induced attitude polarization. *Journal of Personality and Social Psychology, 49*, 1470-1481.

Crocker, J., Fiske, S. T., & Taylor, S. E. (1984). Schematic bases of belief change. In J. R. Eiser (Ed.), *Attitudinal judgment* (pp. 197-226). New York: Springer-Verlag.

Cushman, D. P., & Pearce, W. B. (1977). Generality and necessity in three types of communication theory. *Human Communication Research, 3*, 344-353.

Cushman, D. P., Valentinsen, B., & Dietrich, D. (1982). A rules theory of interpersonal relationships. In F. E. X. Dance (Ed.), *Human communication theory: Comparative essays* (pp. 90-119). New York: Harper and Row.

Delia, J. (1977). Constructivism and the study of human communication. *Quarterly Journal of Speech, 63*, 66-83.

Delia, J. G., O'Keefe, B. J., & O'Keefe, D. J. (1982). The constructivist approach to communication. In F. E. X. Dance (Ed.), *Human communication theory: Comparative essays* (pp. 147-191). New York: Harper & Row.

Eisenberg, E. W. (1992). Metaphor in the language of science. *Scientific American, 266*(5), 144.

Eisenberg, E. W., & Goodall, H. L., Jr. (1993). *Organizational communication: Balancing creativity and constraint.* New York: St. Martin's Press.

Fiske, S. T., & Taylor, S. E. (1984). *Social cognition.* New York: Random House.

Greenwald, A., Pratkanis, A. Leippe, M., & Baumgardner, M. (1986). Under what conditions does theory obstruct research progress? *Psychological Review, 93,* 216-229.

Hamilton, D. L. (1981). Illusory correlation as a basis for stereotyping. In D. L. Hamilton (Ed.), *Cognitive processes in stereotyping and intergroup behavior* (pp. 115-144). Hillsdale, NJ: Lawrence Erlbaum Associates.

Hanna, J. F. (1991). Critical theory and the politicalization of science. *Communication Monographs, 58,* 202-212.

Hempel, C. G. (1958). The theoretician's dilemma: A study in the logic of theory construction. In H. Feigl, M. Scriven, & G. Maxwell (Eds.), *Minnesota studies in the philosophy of science,* Vol II (pp. 37-98). Minneapolis: University of Minnesota Press.

Hempel, C. G. (1965). *Aspects of scientific explanation.* New York: The Free Press.

Hübner, K. (1983). *Critique of scientific reason* (P. Dixon & H. Dixon, Trans.). Chicago: University of Chicago Press. (Original work published 1982)

Judd, C. M., & Lusk, C. M. (1984). Knowledge structures and evaluative judgments: Effects of structural variables on judgmental extremity. *Journal of Personality and Social Psychology, 46,* 1193-1207.

Kellerman, K. (1992). Communication: Inherently strategic and primarily automatic. *Communication Monographs, 59,* 288-297.

Mayer, R. E. (1983). *Thinking, problem solving, and cognition.* San Francisco: W. H. Freeman and Company.

McGuire, W. J. (1981). The probabilogical model of cognitive structure and attitude change. In R. E. Petty, T. M. Ostrom, & T. C. Brock (Eds.), *Cognitive responses in persuasion* (pp. 291-307). Hillsdale, NJ: Lawrence Erlbaum Associates.

Millar, M. G., & Tesser, A. (1986). Thought-induced attitude change: The effects of schema structure and commitment. *Journal of Personality and Social Psychology, 51,* 259-269.

Morely, D. (1993, Autumn). Active audience theory: Pendulums and pitfalls. *Journal of Communication, 43,* 13-19.

Morris, P. (1981). The cognitive psychology of self-reports. In C. Antaki (Ed.), *The psychology of ordinary explanations of social behaviour.* New York: Academic Press.

Motley, M. (1992). Mindfulness in solving communicator's dilemmas. *Communication Monographs, 59,* 306-314.

Nagel, E., & Newman, J. R. (1956). Goedel's proof. In J. R. Newman (Ed.), *The world of mathematics* (Vol. 3, pp. 1668-1695). New York: Simon & Schuster.

O'Keefe, D. J. (1975). Logical empiricism and the study of human communication. *Speech Monographs, 42,* 169-183.

Petty, R. E., & Cacioppo, J. T. (1981). *Communication and persuasion*. New York: Springer-Verlag.

Petty, R. E., & Cacioppo, J. T. (1984). The effects of issue involvement on responses to argument quantity and quality: Central and peripheral routes to persuasion. *Journal of Personality and Social Psychology, 46*, 69-81.

Reichenbach, H. (1936). *Experience and prediction*. Chicago: University of Chicago Press.

Rorty, R. (1994). Does academic freedom have philosophical presuppositions? *Academe, 80*, 52-63.

Rothbart, M. (1981). Memory processes and social beliefs. In D. L. Hamilton (Ed.), *Cognitive processes in stereotyping and intergroup behavior* (pp. 145-181). Hillsdale, NJ: Lawrence Erlbaum Associates.

Russell, B. (1945). *A history of western philosophy*. New York: Simon & Schuster.

Smith, M. J. (1982a). Cognitive schemata and persuasive communication: Toward a contingency rules theory. In M. Burgoon & N. E. Doran (Eds.), *Communication Yearbook 6* (pp. 330-362). Beverly Hills: Sage.

Smith, M. J. (1982b). *Persuasion and human action: A review and critique of social influence theories*. Belmont, CA: Wadsworth Publishing Company.

Snyder, M. (1974). Self-monitoring and expressive behavior. *Journal of Personality and Social Psychology, 30*, 526-537.

Springer, S. P., & Deutsch, G. (1989). *Left brain, right brain*. New York: W. H. Freeman and Company.

Taylor, C. A. (1991). Defining the scientific community: A rhetorical perspective on demarcation. *Communication Monographs, 58*, 402-420.

Tesser, A. (1978). Self-generated attitude change. In L. Berkowitz (Ed.), *Advances in experimental social psychology, 11* (pp. 289-338). New York: Academic Press.

Tesser, A., & Leone, C. (1977). Cognitive schemas and thought as determinants of attitude change. *Journal of Experimental Social Psychology, 13*, 340-356.

Weber, R., & Crocker, J. (1983). Cognitive processes in the revision of stereotypic beliefs. *Journal of Personality and Social Psychology, 45*, 961-977.

Wood, W., Kallgren, C., & Priesler, R. (1985). Access to attitude relevant information in memory as a determinant of persuasion: The role of message attributes. *Journal of Experimental Social Psychology, 21*, 73-85.

Wyer, R. S., & Carlston, D. E. (1979). *Social cognition, inference, and attribution*. Hillsdale, NJ: Lawrence Erlbaum Associates.

Zajonc, R. B. (1960). The process of cognitive tuning in communication. *Journal of Abnormal and Social Psychology, 61*, 159-167.

Footnotes

[1] Action theory can refer to a) the view that the study of human action involves the acceptance of a methodological position that includes a commitment to philosophical interpretivism; or b) the study of plan-making and action-guiding schemas, usually done from an empirical framework. In this chapter, we devote most of our discussion to the first definition.

²This extreme view has long been considered unreasonable. See Hempel (1958) for an enlightening discussion on the resolution of this dilemma.

³It may be possible ethically to make someone apprehensive if his or her "informed consent" were obtained prior to the experiment. But prior knowledge of impending apprehension invites problems in terms of the validity of construct operationalization and renders the manipulation worthless.

⁴The use of the term "positivist" is a problematic one. There are few persons that subscribe to the positivist view, which is quite narrow. "Empiricism" is a much more descriptive term for a good deal of what is currently practiced in the social sciences (Bostrom & Donohew, 1992). Our own preference is for "objectivism."

⁵Exactly how good this agreement must be is usually not specified in the philosophy of science. Typical writers only mention it in passing, as does Hempel (1965, p. 127).

⁶It apparently was not possible for Leon Festinger to say to his colleagues, "Charles Osgood used the term *incongruous* for this phenomenon; I shall adopt his usage." The creation of the dissonance metaphor in and of itself was apparently persuasive. Eisenberg (1992) sees value in the use of metaphor in the description of scientific phenomena, but only when ordinary language fails to capture the essence.

Chapter 3

From Modernity to Postmodernity: Recontextualizing Communication Theory

Alan D. DeSantis
University of Kentucky

During the last two decades, the debate between traditional Modernism and Postmodernism increasingly has become a point of contention in artistic and academic communities around the world. Andreas Huyssen (1984) believes that the reason for such contention is "precisely because there is so much more at stake than the existence or non-existence of a new artistic style, so much more also than just the 'correct' theoretical line" (p. 12). At stake is how "reality" and "truth" are to be defined and actualized.

While the battle wages over whether Postmodernity is going to be our salvation or lead us to social damnation, fervent discussion continues over the term's meanings and merits. The nation hears from political conservatives, for example, that the deterioration of traditional family values can be blamed on the destructive Postmodern values of the Left. Modern architectural critics berate Postmodern buildings for their blatant irreverence of universal truths and the natural laws of design. In our thinktanks, international economists debate the benefits of Fordist Modernity versus Flexible Postmodernity in technocratic societies, while in New York City galleries, contemporary feminist artists, like Barbara Kruger and Hillary Leone, ride the wave of popularity with their condemnation of Modern society and their inclusion of alternative epistemologies. Even within our colleges and universities, myriad disciplines, from communication to physics, either are hailing the "Postmodern turn" as a liberating presence for marginalized voices or criticizing its anarchistic and deconstructive tendencies.

With such fervent debates surrounding Postmodernity, it is not surprising that many are confused as to this movement's definition, worth, and impact on the discipline of communication. Therefore, it is the purpose of this chapter to help clarify this ambiguity by supplying readers with a lucid summary and analysis of Postmodernity. This is accomplished by 1) reviewing Modernism's basic tenants, 2) analyzing the major characteristics of Postmodernism, and 3) critiquing Postmodernism's worth and impact on communication studies.

Modernism

Just as Postmodernism can be viewed as a reactionary movement away from Modernism, Modernism can be viewed as a reactionary movement away from the late Medieval and early Renaissance epochs–200-1600 A. D. (Harvey, 1989, p. 7). The Modernist project of the late 17th and 18th centuries, referred to by contemporary scholars as the Scientific Revolution and/or the Enlightenment, emerged from a climate universally hostile towards independent, skeptical thinking. According to historians Will and Ariel Durant, Europeans of the 1600s viewed "All natural objects, all planets . . . constellations and galaxies, as helpless islands in a supernatural sea" (Durant & Durant, 1963, p. 481). European intellectuals, including Joseph Glanvill in *Philosophical Considerations Touching Witches and Witchcraft* (1666) and Ralph Cudworth in *True Intellectual System of the Universe* (1678), denounced all who would deny the reality of witches. Glanvill found it a shocking wonder that "men otherwise witty and ingenious are fallen into the conceit that there is no such thing as a witch or apparition" (Lecky, 1910, p. 45).

European Churches augmented this Medieval superstition and insular thinking with censorship and intolerance. In Catholic Cologne, the Archbishop Elector censored all speech on religion while in Protestant Brandenburg, the Great Elector ordered a thorough censorship of all documents, sacred and secular. Even in England, where the western conception of liberty was born, the government, despite the *Act of Toleration* (1689), continued to imprison blasphemous authors and burn heretical books (Putman, 1906, pp. 264-65).

Slowly, however, tolerance and rational inquiry began to diffuse. Motivated primarily by commerce, countries and merchants from Holland to Venice, who once castigated alien ideas and religions, began to welcome differing perspectives. In 1670, Benedict (or Baruch) De Spinoza published his *Tractatus Theologico-Politicus* calling for full tolerance of heretical ideas, while the Englishman, John Locke, issued his *Letters on Toleration* (1689) viewing tolerance a virtue, rather than a vice. "Decade after decade the demand for intellectual freedom rose," asserts Durant, "and by the end of the 17th century no church would have dared to do what had been done to Bruno in 1600, or to Galileo in 1633" (Durant & Durant, 1963, p. 484).

Spinoza and Locke's treatises served as harbingers to the Enlightenment and helped propel Europe into the "Age of Reason." This new age was an effort on the part of European intellectuals to develop an objective and universal standard from which to view the world. Only through such a project, Enlightened thinkers believed, could eternal and immutable truths be discovered (Harvey, 1989, p. 12). By the turn of the 18th century, the church of science and Modern rationality was born and with it came a force of true believers: Bacon called men to labor for the advancement of knowledge through inductive, scientific experiments; Descartes married algebra to geometry to create a system of inquiry that supplied certainty; Guericke's air pump explored the possibility of the vacuum; Gregory and Newton made better telescopes; Hook improved the compound microscope to examine the cell; Amontons refined the accuracy of the thermometer; Boyal and Leibniz viewed nature as applied mathematics; Pierre de Fermat fathered the Modern theory of numbers; Riccioli discovered the first double star; Hevelius catalogued 1,564 stars, discovered 4 comets, and observed the movement of Mercury; and the rhetorical theories of Locke, Bacon, Hobbes and Descartes advocated mathematical plainness in scientific pursuit for order and precision (Durant & Durant, 1963, pp. 480-490; Conley, 1990, pp. 151-187).

More important than the individual ideas developed and discoveries made during the Enlightenment, however, was the Modernist foundation laid by these intellectuals. Even now these thinkers of the 18th and 19th centuries continue to shape the way western industrialized countries of the 20th century view reality. The ghosts of Descartes, Kant, and Bacon are evident in our schools, factories, cities, governments, prisons, and hospitals. Because of the Enlightenment, Steven Toulmin (1990) argues, our contemporary society has shifted from the particular to the universal, from the local to the general, and from the timely to the timeless (p. 75). Seen in this light, the 17th and 18th century's quest for certainty, and the 20th century's adaptation of their epistemology, can be viewed as "an attempt to decontextualize philosophy and science" (Gill, 1994, p. 199).

Specifically, the ideals of the Scientific Revolution and the Enlightenment have influenced the way the 20th century conceives of 1) truth and certainty, 2) linear progress, 3) alternative epistemologies and perspectives, and 4) the function and scope of rhetoric. A review of these major characteristics will follow.

Characteristics of Modernity

The dominant characteristic of what John Searl (1992) calls the "Western Rationalistic Tradition" is the belief in absolute, universal Truths, the capitalization of which implies transcendence (pp. 55-84). The search for universal Truths became the essential goal for the Modernist society, whether seeking the indisputable laws of metaphysics, music, or medicine. The rationalist doctrine that encourages this pursuit, argues Barry Barnes (1990), emphasizes the ultimate "power of the reasoning capabilities which all individuals possess" (p. 85). While such an idea may seem obvious to 20th century readers, within its 17th century context, the belief that any sound, logical human could discover indisputable Truths was quite revolutionary. This new conception of knowledge sounded especially treasonous to the clergy and monarchs who previously enjoyed the elitist privilege of determining Truth claims through divine epiphanies.

This view of rationality is paramount to the Eurocentric quest for Truth. The Modernist account of science, for example, views its "growth as the product of individual acts of reasoning" (Barnes, 1990, p. 85). Through the use of the scientific method, researchers believe they tap into the natural codes of life and construct formulas and theories that define, explain, and predict *a priori* Truths. Similarly, Modernist philosophers, sociologists, political scientists, and social theorists have regarded morality, goodness, and beauty as "eternal objects which are located and revealed through rationality." According to Richard Rorty (1991), such thinkers believe that there is a common moral consciousness that "contains certain intuitions concerning equality, fairness, human dignity, and the like, which need to be made explicit through the formulation of principles" ("Essay on Derrida," p. 90). Such principles, if constructed using the proper rules of Modernist reasoning, will provide an absolute and perfect insight into universal morals and ethics.

Implicit in the Modernist's faith in discoverable Truths is the belief that these Truths transcend context. As Carole Blair and associates (Blair, Marsha, Jeppeson, & Pucci, 1991) have stated, Modernists view their epistemology as "beyond cultural relativity in that their ideas and theories mirror natural laws" (p. 353). Indeed, cultural conventions only impede the search for absolute meaning and certainty. Unwanted variables, such as social pressure, political passion, context, economic interests, and personal feelings only bias the judgment of the intellect. Over time, Barnes (1990) writes, "these biases may transform thought into political ideology or religious dogma; they must be eliminated or neutralized if the understanding of nature is to be advanced or a contribution to science [and morality] made" (p. 86).

A second key aspect in the Modern worldview is teleology, or a belief in linear, systematic progress towards Truth. This theme induces the Western World to think that the study of morality, ethics, science, technology, politics, and medicine is moving with purpose and direction towards perfection. Milton in *Areopaegetica* imagined truth as a complete and finished entity that had been scattered around the earth. "Humankind gradually collected parts to truth as time went by, thereby getting closer and closer to the whole truth" (Railsback, 1983, p. 356). This concept manifests itself in the field of science, Thomas Kuhn argues, in the belief that knowledge is cumulative, "gradually increasing towards a correspondence with the reality it describes" (Barnes, 1990, pp. 85-86). The mission of the contemporary scientist, therefore, is the search for clearer and more accurate explanations, ultimately arriving at the absolute truth at the end of this process.

This teleological perspective also has invaded the way we design our communities and cities. Mary McLeod (1985) describes the principle of Modern architecture, for instance, as a "messianic faith in the new" (p. 19). Fisher (Fisher, Gleiniger-Neumann, Klotz, Schwartz, 1985) agrees, suggesting that Modernist architecture views the past not as a source, but an enemy of the new. "Modernity in the twentieth century" he claims, "has no intention of compounding the supposed error made in the past" (p. 8). Not surprisingly then, Modern architects see their designs as "something beyond style, the definitive fulfillment of a program" started by previous generations. In fact, much of the work of Modern architects is purposely void of any "traditional artistic style," reflecting their belief that their designs have teleologically evolved past aesthetic, national, and historical boundaries (Blair, et al., 1991, p. 265). Using the "box" as their prototype, blocked skyscrapers, functional factories, and uniformed housing projects proliferated throughout the industrialized west as testament to this Modernist faith in the new. Unfortunately, argue critics, this aggressive expansion too often has been at the expense of community, the extended family, and historical identity.

Even the study of morality and ethics is not exempt from the Modernist faith in progress. Teleological social theorists view their research regarding our societies, governments, cities, and values as moving towards perfection and truth. As Rorty (1991) has observed, Modernist philosophers believe that they are formulating "better and better principles, principles corresponding ever more closely to the moral law itself" ("Essay on Derrida," p. 91). Ultimately, once these absolute laws emerge, Modern philosophers, architects, government officials, scientists, and legislators believe they can design and order a social utopia that is 1) independent of cultural traditions, beliefs, religions, and values, 2) free from subjectivism and relativism, and 3) universally applicable.

A third characteristic of Modernist philosophy is an unequivocal certainty in rational/scientific Truths and a resulting intolerance towards alternative knowledge, i. e., nonrationalistic and nonscientific knowledge. For the Modernist there are iron-clad laws of rationality that must be obeyed if absolute Truths are to be discovered. Epistemologies and perspectives that break these rules by adopting a different set of assumptions, therefore, are inherently flawed. To grant legitimacy and equal status to such peripheral perspectives would be seen as subjective, relativistic, and situational. "As a matter of fact," Robert L. Scott (1967) argues, "if one can be certain, tolerating deviations from the demands of certainty may itself be deemed evil" (p. 16). Subsequently, alternative ways of knowing, religions, and cultures that fall outside the purview of western normality often are devalued and marginalized. An inventory of the hierarchical structure of American culture illustrates this Modernist bias: The physicist prized over the poet, the scientist over the mother, the western surgeon over the Native American shaman, the rationally thinking man over the emotionally feeling women, and the industrialized first-world over the tribalized third-world. American culture has become controlled by technocrats, scientists, and experts while elevating rationality and western logic to a position of preeminence. As Rorty (1991) argues, the European tradition "takes scientific truth as the center of philosophical concern and scorns the notion of incommensurable world-pictures" ("Essay on Derrida," p. 92). As a result, Modernism, ironically, has become totalitarian in its goal to liberate the world of oppression, a maneuver aptly termed by T. W. Adorno (1972) as the "Dialectic of Enlightenment."

The fourth characteristic of the Modern worldview is the insignificant and devalued role given to human communication. Rhetoric's function becomes one of communicating Truths that have been discovered by "legitimate disciplines that search for objectivity," i.e., natural science, metaphysical philosophy and, to a lesser extent, the social sciences. Since rhetoric, according to Modernism, deals only with the subjective, the relative, and the probable, it must be controlled by, and subservient to, mind-independent Truths, Truths that do not rely on the subjective mind of the knower but that exist independently of humans and language. Rhetoric should not, therefore, create reality, construct social morality, shape worldviews, or negotiate competing cultural tensions for Modernists. Robert L. Scott (1967) elaborates on the consequence of this Modernist perspective:

> Accepting the [Modernists] notion that truth exists, may be known, and communicated leads logically to the position that there should be only two modes of discourse: a neutral presenting of data among equals and a persuasive leading of inferiors by the capable. (p. 16)

The Modernist epistemology, therefore, greatly diminishes the scope and function of rhetoric and communication. Either rhetoric is a tool used by other disciplines to disseminate their research findings or it becomes a manipulative device, used by unethical lawyers and unscrupulous used-car dealers, distorting absolute Truths and destabilizing society. The ethical rhetorician, in the Modernist paradigm, is one who expresses scientific and social Truths as plainly and succinctly as possible, purging language of its ornamentational, poetic, literary, and metaphoric qualities.

The Modernist Project: Success or Failure?

The Modernist search for absolute Truths was not motivated solely by the drive to accumulate knowledge for knowledge's sake. A noble political and social agenda undergirds the work of the western rationalistic tradition. In the 19th century, "science and rationality were already being hailed as the key to unlocking the Utopia and saving mankind" (Durant & Durant, 1963, p. 530). According to the Modernist project, if knowledge could be standardized and absolute Truths discovered, then the world could be controlled and the perfect social order created. By the 20th century, faith in Modernism intensified and "Technological progress promised to constitute the aesthetic and provide the solution to social ills" (Blair et al., 1991, p. 535). Harvey (1989) expands:

> The development of a rational form of social organizations and rational modes of thought promised liberation from the irrationalities of myth, religion, superstition, and release from the arbitrary use of power as well as the dark side of our own human natures. (p. 12)

This overwhelming sense of optimism, however, was shattered under the pressure and harsh realities of the 20th century. Instead of a Utopia, the West created "death camps and death squads, militarism and two world wars, the threat of nuclear annihilation and the experience of Hiroshima and Nagasaki" (Harvey, 1989, p. 13). Instead of liberating individuals from want and the arbitrary use of power, Herbert Marcuse (1978) critically viewed modernization as fostering increased capitalistic exploitation, monologic rationality, bureaucracy, environmental devastation and pollution, the loss of community and the extended family, and individual alienation and isolation.

Additionally, critics claim the Modernist philosophy has become as totalitarian and oppressive as the Medieval church it reacted against. Just as Catholicism dogmatically insisted that Truth can come only from the authority of the church, Modernism preached the exclusivity of rationality in the search for mind-independent reality. The church of God was replaced by what author Robert Pirsig (1974) called the "church of reason" (p. 153)—both, however, monopolized epistemology while excluding and disempowering alternative voices. Such an ironic twist of history supports what Hegel, Marx, and Dewey maintained: Ideas and movements that were created as instruments of emancipation (Greek metaphysics, Christianity, the rise of the bourgeoisie, science) "typically, over the course of time, turn into instruments of repression" (Rorty, "Philosophical Presuppositions," 1994, p. 59). Confronted with mounting condemnation, critics began reconsidering the basic tenants of Modernity and its claims of Absolutism. While a myriad of alternative epistemologies emerged during the Post World War II epoch, one of the most significant threats to the Modernist world-view emerged out of France in the form of Postmodernity. In the section that follows, an explanation of the philosophy's history, characteristics, and shortcomings will be supplied.

Postmodernism

The term "Postmodernism" first was used in the 1930s by the literary critic, Federico de Onis, who used the term *postmodernismo* to describe a "kind of exhausted and mildly conservative *modernismo*." A comparable use of the term occurs in the late 1950s in America to "lament the exhaustion of the modern movement." However, it was not until the mid-1970s that the term began to be widely used and clearly defined (Smart, 1993, pp. 18-19).

The harbinger to the present Postmodern movement originated during the turbulent 1960s. America's youth, forced to confront issues of race, environmental pollution, industrialization, worker exploitation, and the Vietnam war, began to question the "Truths" of their Modernist society. Ideas and practices that generally were unquestioned and blindly obeyed became rallying cries for revolution. The traditional values that once "stabilized" previous generations were disdained while Modernist "taboos" were embraced in acts of defiance. This counter-culture "explored the realms of individualized self-realization through a distinctive 'new left' politics, through the embrace of anti-authoritarian, iconoclastic habits (in music, dress, language, and life-style) and the critique of everyday life" (Harvey, 1989, p. 38).

Initially centered in universities and supported by the leftist intelligentsia, the movement gained momentum and impacted on all aspects of mainstream society: Psychedelic rock and roll, vanguard jazz, sexual promiscuity, experimental drug use, back-to-nature movements, and Marxist communes attempted to undermine western Modernity and liberate the repressed human spirit. The culmination of this movement crested in a "vast wave of rebelliousness in Chicago, Paris, Prague, Mexico City, Madrid, Tokyo, and Berlin in the global turbulence of 1968" (Harvey, 1989, p. 38).

While the counter-cultural movement of the 1960s fell short of the political and economic revolution envisioned, the rebellion, nonetheless, can be viewed as a portent to the Postmodern turn. "Somewhere between 1968-1972, Postmodernism emerged as a full-blown, though still an incoherent, movement out of the chrysalis of the anti-Modern movement of the 1960s" (Harvey, 1989, p. 39). This embryonic movement soon became a philosophical passion for many critical theorists and social critics around the world. With the publication of such works as Thomas

Kuhn's *The Structure of Scientific Revolutions* in 1962, the translated forms of Michel Foucault's *Folie et deraison* (*Madness and Civilization*, 1965) and *Les mots et les choses* (*The Order of Things*, 1970); Jean-Francois Lyotard's *La Condition postmoderne* (*The Postmodern Condition*, 1979); and Jacques Derrida's *De La Grammatologie* (*Of Grammatology*, 1976), the philosophy's leading spokespeople and its general premises became widely disseminated and acknowledged.

Chief among Postmodern's characteristics are 1) a general distrust of all grand systems claiming transcendent, *a priori* Truths, 2) a belief that rhetoric constructs realities, 3) a view that truth emerges through intersubjective agreement, and 4) a political agenda that advocates change, pluralism, and empowerment . These characteristics are explored in the following section.

Distrust of all Grand Systems of Thought

The dominant theme that runs through all Postmodern discourse is the view that there are NO absolute, *a priori* Truths waiting to be discovered by the objective, unbiased mind. Postmodernists assert that the Modernist belief that pure knowledge can be discerned independent of language is essentially flawed, for individuals cannot free themselves from the linguistic and social constraints imposed on reality. Indeed, Postmodernists claim, language and society create human reality and our understanding of existence. "Elements of what we call language or mind penetrate so deeply into what we call 'reality,'" argues Hilary Putnam (1990), "that the very project of representing ourselves as being 'mappers' of something 'language independent' is fatally compromised from the start" (p. 28).

Essential to Modernist thinkers who claim to have mapped absolute Truth, is the belief that their epistemology is equally absolute and untainted by context. An epistemology is a grand system of thought that defines how absolute knowledge is derived and supplies universal standards of judgment. Plato's epistemology, for example, viewed True knowledge as derived from ideas of reason intrinsic to the mind and confined to the suprasensible world of forms and ideas. In opposition, British Empiricists, like John Locke and David Hume, argued that sense experience is the primary source of our ideas, and hence of knowledge. While Platonism, Empiricism, and 20th Century Modernism emerged out of different epochs, they are all united in that they claim 1) to produce the "Absolute Truth," and 2) their epistemology to be "ahistoric and natural."[1]

From the Postmodern perspective, however, this belief in the purity of epistemologies is problematic and dangerous. Such systems of knowledge (also referred to as a metanarrative or a discursive formation) are not transcendent procedures for unlocking the mysteries of the universe, but rhetorically constructed language games for finding what may be best viewed as contextually based knowledge. Far from being untainted by human contact, such systems supply their own particular presuppositions, methods, and criteria which must be followed if the status of Truth is to be granted.

The most disturbing aspect of these grand systems of thought for Postmodernists, however, is that society is trained to believe that the dominant epistemology is ahistoric and absolute. Once individuals lose sight of the contextual nature of truth, assertions that work within an epistemology's framework can ascend to the rarefied rank of "Truth," blindly accepted and unquestioned. If, however, as Postmodernists advocate, we deconstruct our epistemologies and realize that our metanarratives are products of human interaction and language, not external products of nature, then every idea becomes open for debate and consideration.

Two of Postmodernity's leading contributors that have explicitly attacked any notion that there might be a transcendent epistemology, metanarrative, or discursive formation through which all things can be connected or represented are Jean-Francois Lyotard and Michel Foucault. A review of their major claims will further clarify Postmodern's distrust of grand-systems, specifically the Modernist system.

Jean-Francois Lyotard

In 1979, the French Philosopher, Jean-Francois Lyotard published his seminal work, *The Postmodern Condition*, defining Postmodernism as, "incredulity towards metanarratives," or skepticism of "any science [grand system] that legitimates itself with reference to a discourse [epistemology]" (1984, p. xxiii). For Lyotard, all forms of knowledge, including Modern science, are constructed by language and society. Lyotard calls these knowledge forms narratives or discourse and sees science not as "the path to truth but merely one type of discourse." Knowledge has "no permanent, fixed, or privileged status. It is shifting, fragmented and indeterminate" (Gill, 1994, p. 201). What motivates Lyotard's writings, therefore, is Modern science's ability to masquerade as stable, whole, and absolute. When this is accomplished, as it has been in the 20th century, Modernity becomes an unchallenged power for the status quo.

This ability of metanarratives to create an illusion of permanence, explains Lyotard, is essentially the ability of metanarratives to self-legitimate—that is, these metanarratives supply society with the criteria for evaluating their own competence. For example, a scientific statement, such as "the world is round," is "verified through argumentation and proof, but what counts as proof and what qualifies as a good argument are determined by standards outside science." Those standards are part of a metanarrative that is accepted as true. But for Lyotard, as Gill (1994) eloquently states, "science cannot operate without this metanarrative, which is truly ironic, as the metanarrative is, by definition, unscientific; it is unavailable for testing and not subject to proof" (p. 200). Lyotard (1984) explains:

> Scientific knowledge cannot know and make known that it is the true knowledge without resorting to the other, narrative, kind of knowledge, which from its point of view is no knowledge at all. With such recourses it would be in the position of presupposing its own validity and would be stooping to what it condemns: begging the question, proceeding on

prejudice. But does it not fall into the same trap by using narrative as its authority? (p. 29)

For Lyotard then, Modern science is no different than any other form of knowledge (myths, religion, poetry, history). This conclusion, essential to most Postmodern thought, is further elaborated by the French philosopher and historian, Michel Foucault.

Michel Foucault

Perhaps the most influential force in the Postmodern movement is Michel Foucault. Throughout his prolific research career, his primary objective was to provide a critique of the way Modern societies, through claims of absolute knowledge, control and discipline their populations by "sanctioning the knowledge-claims [what is true and false, good and bad, right and wrong] and practices [who can speak and what procedures need to be met to be heard] of the human sciences: medicine, psychiatry, psychology, criminology, sociology, and so on" (Phillips, 1990, p. 65). His books range from an analysis of how Modernity defines mental stability and appropriate medical practices to a critique of the way prisoners and the "sexually deviant" are controlled and punished.[2] In each of these works, Foucault sought to demonstrate the power of metanarratives, what he labeled discursive formations, to define who and what will be valued and who and what will be marginalized. Such decisions, he argued, are based simply on whether one falls inside or outside the arbitrary boundaries of Modernity's knowledge claims. Discursive formations are so pervasive, in fact, that they penetrate every aspect of a society and impact on all its inhabitants. Mark Phillips (1990) elaborates:

> In workplaces, schoolrooms, hospitals and welfare offices; in the family and the community; and in prisons, mental institutions, and courtrooms, the human sciences have established their standards of "normality." The normal child, the healthy body, the stable mind, the good citizen, the perfect wife and the proper man—such concepts haunt our ideas about ourselves, and are reproduced and legitimated through the practices of teachers, social workers, doctors, judges, policeman. The human sciences attempt to define normality; and by establishing the normality as a rule of life for us all, they simultaneously manufacture—for investigation, surveillance, and treatment—the vast area of our deviation from this standard. (p. 66)

Thus, as Phillips (1990) eluded to, knowledge and power become inseparable for Foucault.[3] Those who define for a culture what is acceptable and appropriate (the experts and the ordained), subsequently impose order and power on the culture. "The battle for truth," writes Foucault (1980), "is not on behalf of the truth but about the status of truth." He expands:

> Each society has its regime of truth, its general politics of truth: that is the types of discourse which it accepts and makes function as true; the mechanisms and instances which enable one to distinguish true and false

statements, and means by which each is sanctioned; the techniques and procedures accorded value in the acquisition of truth; the status of whose who are changed with saying what counts as true. (*Power and Knowledge*, p. 131-132)

Consequently, while some are empowered by the metanarrative, others who do not meet the "criteria of acceptability" become oppressed and are pushed to the periphery (minorities, gays and lesbians, women, the disabled, the insane, children).[4] For this reason, Foucault explores the voices that have been silenced and denied the right of legitimacy because they have fallen outside the metanarrative. As Richard Harland (1987) claims, "Foucault identifies with the victims, not because their discourse would be more true, but because it would be no less true, and yet they are made to suffer for it." And in essential Foucault form, he is "hostile towards Modern science, not because any alternative would be more objective, but because Modern science proclaims and dismisses any alternative as less objective" (pp. 107-108).

Of course, we may still want to argue against Foucault by pointing to the lifesaving "successes" (advancements in medicine) and the positive "results" (walking on the moon) that have been met in the 20th century as proof for Modernity's claim of absolutism. But Foucault surely would have reminded us that, a discourse [metanarrative] itself furnishes the very criteria by which its results are judged successful. And certainly, as Richard Harland (1987) has observed, there has been growing skepticism that the acclaimed achievements of Modern science are, by other criteria, "somehow missing the point." In the field of Modern medicine, for example, we have repeatedly heard suspicion and critique about "the long-term implication of the 'Magic bullet' approach;" the psychological implications of the 'hygienic' approach to childbirth, patient care, and the treatment of the terminally ill; the lack of serious consideration given to the human soul and spirit during recovery; and the "moral implication of the 'human vegetable' approach to maintaining bodily functions at all costs." Ironically, Modern medical science has produced its own kind of blindness along with its own kind of visibilities" (pp. 103-104).

Rhetorical Construction of Reality

A second characteristic of Postmodernity is the view that what people know, the truths they embrace, and the realities they perceive are rhetorically constructed (sometimes referred to as "socially constructed"). "Rhetoric," does not mean simply "the art of persuasion," as defined by our discipline's founders, i.e., Aristotle, Cicero, Augustine, Bacon, Campbell, and Whately. For Postmodernists, rhetoric is, "grounded not in the quest to make truth effective, but rather in the quest to evoke truth via rhetoric" (Cherwitz, 1977, p. 219). At its deepest and fundamental sense, rhetoric is the "advocate of reality" (Brummett, 1976, p. 31) and "epistemic" (Scott, 1967, p. 15).

As argued by Lyotard and Foucault, rhetoric constructs epistemologies that supply the sciences with legitimacy. But rhetoric also shapes the way people, in their everyday lives, see their reality and existence. Language and society constructs our notions of family, love, hate, individuality, freedom, liberty, and democracy. It dictates our tastes in food, clothing, art, music, architecture, literature, and the erotic. Such ideas, therefore, are not universal, but have emerged within a particular social context, influenced by politics, economics, culture, and the Modernist metanarrative.

The Postmodernist view of reality, however, does not mean that there are no constraints placed upon our socially constructed reality; Postmodernism does not empower humans to walk through walls. Postmodernists argue, though, that discourse can create meaning and reality out of "meaningless" material. With discourse, for example, individuals can turn what has been labeled as a "wall" into something one prays to (The Wailing Wall), an object of contempt (The Berlin Wall), a sign of peace and redemption (Vietnam War Memorial), an Icon of national pride (Great Wall of China), or an object to be ignored (the walls in our homes).

An important consequence of breaking the bonds of Modernistic predetermination and viewing rhetoric as epistemic is that the possibilities for change become infinite. Since individuals no longer are committed to following absolute, *a priori* Truths, then all reality is open for debate. The philosophical alternative, argues Condit (1987), poses serious moral ramifications. "If we reify the current best principles," she writes, "we put ourselves in the position of . . . preserving an old moral order at the cost of a newer [and better contextually based code]." As Condit reminds us, "The current code may be used, as such codes historically have been used, to prevent the development of a better code" (p. 93). The Postmodern ethic demands that all codes be seen as constructs, awaiting continual reaffirmation or reform.

Intersubjectivity of Truth

If all reality is constructed by rhetoric, may one reasonably ask, is the Modernist notion of objective Truth replaced with subjective relativism? To this, Postmodernists would answer, no; societies do not operate in a state of individualized reality. Instead, objectivity, for the Postmodernist, is replaced with intersubjectivity or a collectively determined social consensus. A social consensus, for Railsback (1983), "is simply that which we no longer debate, that which we accept as a given part of our language structure, in order that we may pursue other problematic issues" (p. 363). This view of intersubjectivity, therefore, becomes diametrically opposed to the "illusion of" objectivity posited by Modernists. Thinkers like Rorty, Kuhn, and Derrida "deny that the search for objective truth is a search for correspondence to reality, and urge that it be seen instead as a search for the widest possible intersubjective agreement" (Rorty, "Philosophical Presuppositions," 1994, p. 52). "Objectivity," Rorty asserts, "is not a matter of corresponding to objects but of getting together with other subjects—there is nothing to the Modernist notion of objectivity except intersubjectivity" (p. 56). Subsequently, at any given movement, "what we know to exist in the world is a product of an evolving set of human agreements" (Wander, 1976, p. 226). Karl Popper (1959) eloquently explains how the Modernist conception of Knowledge and Truth is reconceptualized through the Postmodern lens:

> Science does not rest upon rock-bottom. The bold structure of its theories rises, as it were, above a swamp. It is like a building erected upon piles. The piles are driven down from above into the swamp, but not down to any natural or "given" base; and when we cease our attempts to drive our piles into a deeper layer, it is not because we have reached firm ground, We simply stop when we are satisfied that they are firm enough to carry the structure, at least for the time being." (p. 111)

For Popper (1959), then, society stops searching for new scientific or moralistic answers not because objective truth has been found but, rather, because consensus has been reached. However, as Thomas Kuhn (1962) has shown, consensus will be threatened by newly constructed anomalies. If a strong enough case is made for rethinking societal agreement, consensus will erode into debate and uncertainty and, with it, the illusion of Truth.

Political Agenda

The fourth characteristic of Postmodernity is its unique political agenda. Readers should not expect, however, to find clear and precise directions on "how to build a better society"; that would be a Postmodern oxymoron. Postmodernism is concerned with dismantling order, not constructing order. To create a metanarrative out of Postmodernity would be self-defeating and philosophically inconsistent. Instead, many Postmodern Philosophers (Foucault, 1965, 1973, 1977, 1978, 1980, 1981; Derrida, 1976; Baudrillard, 1975) see their role as provocateurs, purposely inviting consternation, shock, and anger in an attempt to make society think critically about power and knowledge. Detailed policies for specific social problems are outside the scope, function, and motivation of the writings of Postmodernism. Therefore, "political goals" should be recast as "possible alternatives" to Modernity and not blueprints for a Utopia. The two predominant themes found in Postmodern writings are 1) embracing the fragmented and the contextual and 2) dismantling order.

Consistent with the Postmodern view that reality is rhetorically constructed and contingent upon context, thinkers like Foucault, Derrida, Baudrillard, and Jameson (1981) embrace the "relative plural" rather than "absolute singular." These writers argue that if all knowledge is intersubjective, then no knowledge should claim "inherent" superiority. To do so oppresses equally legitimate voices simply because they have fallen outside the arbitrary borders of the dominant paradigm. Therefore, "fragmentation, indeterminacy, and intense distrust of all universal or totaling discourse becomes the hallmark of Postmodern social thought" (PRECIS, 1987, p. 9). Foucault instructs society, for example, to "develop action, thought, and desires by proliferation, juxtaposition, and disjunction," and "to prefer what is positive and multiple, difference over uniformity, flows over unities, mobile arrangements over systems. Believe that what is productive is not sedentary but nomadic" (Harvey, 1989, p. 44).

Ultimately, privileging heterogeneity is linked with social egalitarianism. "The idea that all groups have the right to speak for themselves, in their own voice, and have that voice accepted as authentic and legitimate is essential to the pluralistic stance of Postmodernity" (Harvey, 1989, p. 48). Even Huyssens (1984), a critic of Postmodernity, emphasizes the opening given in its philosophy for the understanding of differences and otherness, "as well as the liberatory potential it offers for a whole host of new social movements (women, gays, blacks, ecologists, regional autonomists, etc.)" (p. 23). Not surprisingly, then, Postmodernity and its emphasis on social equality has had profound effects on a myriad of disciplines seeking the empowerment of marginalized voices within the social order (African American Studies, Women's Studies, Cultural Anthropology, Social Planning and Design, Psychology, and Multiculturalism).

A second political agenda advocated in most of the Postmodern literature is iconoclasm, or the deconstruction of established social orders. By dismantling social orders (government, religious institutions, legal codes, gender roles), the delegitimated of a society are emancipated from their restrictive and stifling effects. As John McGowan (1991) argues, the goal of Postmodernism is to "disrupt the social hierarchy" and thereby "empower suppressed groups" (p. 17). But what makes Postmodernism more radical than its predecessors (Frankfort critical theory, Neo-Marxism, Existentialism) is that the deconstruction of power/knowledge relationships becomes a continuous process. There is no teleological end. Therefore, whatever metanarrative replaces Modernity ultimately will become the new target of Postmodernity's destructive eye, no matter how noble its goals. For any discourse that claims absolute propriety while excluding alternatives is tyrannical, according to Postmodern thinking. Postmodernity "attacks order," writes Allan Megill (1987), "not only the existing order but any order." Because all order oppresses—one is therefore "justified in opposing these orders" (p. 197).

Critique of Postmodernity

Postmodernism has invited its share of criticism from both the political left and right, scientists and artists, theists and atheists, capitalists and communists. The philosophy often is characterized as destroying without rebuilding, of destabilizing without restabilizing. Leading intellectual thinkers such as J. Searl ((1992) and I. Hassan (1987) echo the sentiments of most by claiming that Postmodernity is void of morals and leads to social bankruptcy. The most telling criticism, however, is that "Postmodernism cannot save itself from relativism" (Gill, 1994, p. 206). "If there is nothing outside language, then it is our history, our community, our hope that is abandoned" (O'Neil, 1990, p. 74). "The celebration of pluralism is one thing," expands Gill (1994), "abject relativism is another, particularly if it allows for the complete breakdown of society and the retribalization of the global village" (p. 206). Even Harvey (1989), a leading spokesperson for the cause, agrees that Postmodernism "takes matters too far" (pp. 116-117).

More than any other single Postmodern voice, Foucault has received the most concentrated and probing criticism.[5] Michael Walzer(1986), a leading commentator, sees dangerous consequences to the French philosopher's theories. He writes that Foucault's alternative to metanarratives is "the dismantling of the whole thing, the fall of the carceral city, not revolution but abolition" (p. 59). For this reason, Walzer argues, "Foucault is an anarchist, he is a moral as well as a political anarchist." But after he is finished dismantling, "what will be left?" For Foucault gives us no reason to expect that the new codes will be any better than the ones we now live with. "Nor, for that matter," Walzer concludes, "does he give us any way of knowing what 'better' might mean" (p. 61).[6]

In a review written shortly after the release of Foucault's *Power/Knowledge*, the philosopher Ian Hacking (1986) summarized the major critiques articulated by most critics of Postmodernism. Of these, the most recurring and problematic to Foucault and Postmodernity are 1) his anarchistic social tendencies; 2) solipsism, including a disbelief in the notion of "man"; and 3) his unwillingness to give society even the smallest anchor to stabilize itself, i.e., hope, love, democracy, freedom, etc. Hacking writes:

> "What is man?" asked Kant. "Nothing," says Foucault. "For what then may we hope?" asks Kant. Does Foucault give the same nothing in reply? To think so is to misunderstand Foucault's reply to the question about Man. Foucault said that the concept Man is a fraud, not that you and I are as nothing. Likewise the concept Hope is all wrong. The hopes attributed to Marx and Rousseau are perhaps part of that very concept Man, and they are a sorry basis for optimism. Optimism, pessimism, nihilism and the like are all concepts that make sense only within the idea of a transcendental or enduring subject. Foucault is not in the least incoherent about all this. If we're not satisfied, it should not be because he is pessimistic. It is because he has given no surrogate for whatever it is that springs eternal in the human breast (pp. 39-40)

The question must be asked, therefore, is Postmodernism only an exercise in intellectual masturbation—a chic, ephemeral philosophy with no practical use for improving the human condition?

Communication and Postmodernism

With Postmodernity's recontextualization of "t"ruth, contemporary thinkers are freed from the oppressive Modernist ideas of teleology, absolute Truths, and the predetermination of knowledge. This conceptual liberation has affected the way researchers in a myriad of disciplines approach the nature of reality, knowledge, and power relationships. Specifically, in the field of communication, Postmodernity has significantly shaped research in the areas of 1) empowerment and 2) epistemology.

For many communication researchers, concern for the empowerment of marginalized voices, previously silenced by metanarratives, has increasingly become an important area of study. Whether writing on women, the poor, African-Americans, Native Americans, or the elderly, references to Postmodern literature abound. Foucault, Lyotard, and others inform our discipline's social critics and critical theorists that the ability to claim inherent superiority, to express one's self, and to have that expression valued is contingent upon metanarratives and language—not *a priori*, absolute Truths. Therefore, previously unchallenged knowledge claims, made by males, first-world countries, whites, or the rich, are now decentered, and the forgotten voices of the past are now heard.

A second related research interest influenced by Postmodernity is epistemology. In scholarly journals and in classrooms, communication is being reconceptualized—ascending from a simple tool that organizes and expresses previously existing ideas, to the force that constructs social reality. With such a radical redefinition, the study of communication no longer is dependent on, or subservient to, any other discipline, whether it be science, physics, history, logic, or philosophy. Indeed, a case is often made by Postmodern communication scholars that science, physics, history, logic, and philosophy are dependent on, and subservient to, communication. For communication, Postmodernity reminds us, ultimately is responsible for constructing reality and legitimating the methods, criteria, and presuppositions used by all disciplines.

While Postmodern theorists were not the first to question the absolute status of Truth (i.e., the Greek Sophists, Giambattista Vico, Friedrich Nietzsche), or to give voice to the marginalized (i.e., Karl Marx, Frederick Douglass, Susan B. Anthony, Frantz Fanon) they have, at the very least, intensified the study of power and knowledge. Whether or not Postmodernity will have a lasting impact on our field, we can for now, borrow a page from William James and Richard Rorty, and view Postmodernity as a pragmatic success. For its presence has helped elevate our discipline to the realm of the socially significant and the intellectually essential.

References

Adorno, T., & Horkheimer, M. (1972). *Dialectic of enlightenment.* New York: Herder.

Barnes, B. (1990). Thomas Kuhn. In Q. Skinner (Ed.), *The return of the grand theory in the human sciences* (pp. 83-100). Cambridge: Cambridge University Press.

Baudrillard, J. (1975). *The mirror of production.* St. Louis, MO: Telos.

Blair C., Marsha S., Jeppeson, M. S., & Pucci, E. Jr. (1991). Public memorializing in Postmodernity: The Vietnam Veterans Memorial as prototype. *Quarterly Journal of Speech, 77,* 263-288.

Brummett, B. (1976). Some implications of 'process' on 'intersubjectivity': Postmodern rhetoric. *Philosophy and Rhetoric, 9,* 21-51.

Cherwitz, R. (1977). Rhetoric as a 'way of knowing': An attenuation of the epistemological claims of the 'new rhetoric.' *Southern Speech Communication Journal, 42,* 207-219.

Condit, C. M. (1987). Crafting virtue: The rhetorical construction of public morality. *Quarterly Journal of Speech, 73,* 79-97.

Conley, T. M. (1990). *Rhetoric in the European tradition.* New York: Longman.
Derrida, J. (1976). *Of grammatology.* (G. C. Spivak, Trans.). Baltimore: Johns Hopkins University Press. (Original work published 1967)
Durant W. & Durant A. (1963). *The story of civilization (Volume 8: The age of Louis XIV).* New York: MJF Books.
Fisher, V., Gleiniger-Neumann, A., Klotz, H., & Schwartz, H. P. (1985). *Postmodern visions: drawings, paintings, and models by contemporary architects.* New York: Abbeville.
Flew, A. (1979). *A dictionary of philosophy, revised second edition.* New York: St. Martin's Press.
Foucault, M. (1965). *Madness and civilization: A history of insanity in the age of reason.* (R. Howard, Trans.). New York: Pantheon. (Original work published 1961)
Foucault, M. (1973). *The birth of the clinic: An archaeology of medical perception.* (A. M. Sheridan Smith, Trans.). New York: Pantheon. (Original work published 1963)
Foucault, M. (1977). *Discipline and punish: The birth of the prison.* (A. Sheridan, Trans.). New York: Pantheon. (Original work published 1975)
Foucault, M. (1978). *The history of sexuality: volume 1: An introduction.* (R. Hurley, Trans.). New York: Pantheon. (Original work published 1976)
Foucault, M. (1980). *Power/knowledge: selected interviews and other writings 1972-1977.* (C. Gordon, L. Marshall, J. Mepham, & K. Soper,, Trans.) (Gordon, C., Ed.) New York: Pantheon.
Foucault, M. (1981). An interview with Michel Foucault. *Ideology and Consciousness, 8,* 10-24.
Gianmarco, V., Shinoda, P., & Kesler, D. (Eds.). (Columbia University Graduate School of Architecture, New York.). (1987). The culture of fragments: Notes on the question of order in a pluralistic world [Special issue]. *PRECIS, 6.*
Gill, A. (1994). *Rhetoric and human understanding.* Prospect Heights, IL: Waveland Press.
Hacking, I. (1981, April). The archaeology of Foucualt. In D. C. Hoy (Ed.), *Foucault: A critical reader.* (pp. 27-40). New York: Basil Blackwell Ltd.
Harland, R. (1987). *Superstructuralism: The philosophy of Structuralism and Post-Structuralism.* London: Methuen.
Harvey, D. (1989). *The condition of Postmodernity.* Oxford, England: Basil Blackwell Ltd.
Hassan, I. (1987). *The postmodern turn: Essays in postmodern theory and culture.* Columbus, OH: Ohio State University Press.
Huyssen, A. (1984). Mapping the Postmodern. *New German Critique, 33,* 5-52.
Jameson, F. (1981). *The political unconscious: Narrative as a socially symbolic act.* London: Methuen.
Kolenda, K. (1990). *Rorty's humanistic Pragmatism: Philosophy democratized.* Tampa. FL: University of South Florida Press.
Kuhn, T. S. (1962). *The structure of scientific revolutions.* Chicago: University of Chicago Press.

Lecky, W. E. (1910). *History of the rise and influence of the spirit of rationalism in Europe*. London: D. Appleton.
Lyotard, J. F. (1984). *The Postmodern condition: A report on knowledge*. Minneapolis, MN: University of Minnesota Press.
Marcuse, H. (1978). *One-dimensional man*. Boston: Beacon Press.
McGowan, J. (1991). *Postmodernism and its critics*. Ithaca, NY: Cornell University Press.
McLeod, M. (1985). Architecture. In S. Trachtenberg (Ed.), *The Postmodern moment: A handbook of contemporary innovation in the arts* (pp. 19-52). Westport, CT: Greenwood.
Megill, A. (1987). *Prophets of extremity: Nietzsche, Heidegger, Foucault, Derrida*. Berkeley, CA: University of California Press.
Miller, J. (1993). *The passion of Michel Foucault*. New York: Simon and Schuster.
O'Neill, J. (1990). Postmodernism and (Post)Marxism. In H. J. Silverman (Ed.), *Postmodernism—the philosophy and the arts* (pp. 69-79). New York: Routledge.
Ognibene, E. (1976). [Review of Wayne Booth's *Modern dogma and the rhetoric of assent and a rhetoric of irony*]. *Southern Speech Communication Journal, 42*, 81-84.
Phillips, M. (1990). Michel Foucault. In Q. Skinner (Ed.), *The return of the grand theory in the human sciences* (pp. 65-82). Cambridge: Cambridge University Press.
Pirsig, R. (1974). *Zen and the art of motorcycle maintenance*. New York: Bantam Books.
Popper, K. R. (1959). *The logic of scientific discovery*. New York: Harper and Row.
Putman, G. H. (1906). *Censorship of the church of Rome*. New York: B. Blom.
Putnam, H. (1990). *Reality with a human face*. Cambridge, MA.: Harvard University Press.
Railsback, C. C. (1983). Beyond rhetorical relativism: A structural-material model of truth and objective reality. *Quarterly Journal of Speech, 69*, 351-363.
Rorty, R. (1991). Method, social science, and social hope. In R. Rorty (Ed.), *Consequences of Pragmatism (Essays: 1972-1980)* (pp. 191-210) Minneapolis, MN: University of Minnesota Press.
Rorty, R. (1991). Philosophy as a kind of writing: An essay on Derrida. In R. Rorty (Ed.), *Consequences of Pragmatism (Essays: 1972-1980)* (pp. 90-109). Minneapolis, MN: University of Minnesota Press.
Rorty, R. (1994). Does academic freedom have philosophical presuppositions?" *ACADEME, 80*, 52-63.
Scott, R. L. (1967). On viewing rhetoric as epistemic. *Central States Speech Journal, 18*, 9-17.
Searle, J. (Fall, 1992). Rationality and realism, what is at stake? *Daedalus, Volume 122, no, 4*, 55-84.
Smart, B. (1993). *Postmodernity*. London: Routledge Press.
Toulmin, S. (1990). *Cosmopolis: The hidden agenda of Modernity*. New York: Free Press.
Walzer, M. (1986). The politics of Michel Foucault. In D. C. Hoy (Ed.), *Foucault: A critical reader*. (pp. 51-68). New York: Basil Blackwell Ltd.

Wander, P. C. (1976). The rhetoric of science. *Western Journal of Speech Communication, 40,* 226-235.

Footnotes

¹Besides Modernity's epistemology, other grand systems of thought that have found vast arrays of followers through time include Freudianism, Marxism, Darwinism, Islam, Judaism, Pantheism, Transcendentalism, Rationalism, New Age Faith Healing, and Plato's Idealism, to name a few.

²See Michel Foucault's (1965). *Madness and civilization: A history of insanity in the age of reason.* (R. Howard, Trans.). New York: Pantheon; (1973). *The birth of the clinic: An archaeology of medical perception.* (A.M. Smith, Trans.). New York: Pantheon; (1977). *Discipline and punish: The birth of the prison.* (A. Sheridan, Trans.). New York: Patheon; and (1978). *The history of sexuality: Volume 1: An introduction.* (R. Hurley, Trans.). New York: Patheon.

³Foucault believed that the link between knowledge and power was so important that his later works, he combined the two into a single word to illustrate their interdependency: "knowledge/power."

⁴Foucault, a gay man who died from AIDS, was all too familiar with the social order that made him a pariah. For more on the personal aspects of his life that had an impact on his work, see: Miller, J. (1993). *The passion of Michel Foucault,* New York: Simon and Schuster.

⁵An obvious explanation for why Foucault has been the focal point of criticism is because he was the most prolific and erudite writer of the movement. He has been characterized by both friend and foe, however, as being the most influential and sagacious French philosopher since Sartre.

⁶Foucault has very rarely given us any insights into his personal goals. In the role of the writer/provocateur, we clearly see him as an iconoclast. However, in a 1981 interview, we find a different side of the philosopher—one in which an awareness of the relationship between knowledge and power is all that is wanted. He writes:

> To give some assistance in wearing away certain self-evidentness and commonplaces about madness, normality, illness, crime and punishment; to bring it about together with many others, that certain phrases can no longer be spoken so lightly, certain acts no longer, or at least no longer so unhesitatingly, performed, to contribute to changing certain things in people's ways of perceiving and doing things, to participate in this difficult displacement of forms of sensibility and thresholds to tolerance,—I hardly feel capable of attempting much more than that. (1981, p. 11-12.)

Part 2
Theoretical Perspectives: Context and Communication Behavior

Chapter 4

Pragmatism and Context: A Matter of Pattern

Katherine L. Adams
California State University, Fresno

What counts as context? What counts as communicative behavior? How are the two related? These are the issues addressed in this special volume. The authors in this volume speak to the serious role context plays in our understanding of human communicative behavior. By serious I mean the recognition that context is not inseparable from human activity nor is it merely the container within which such activity occurs. Instead, context and human communicators "coexist and jointly define one another and contribute to the meaning and nature of a holistic event"(Altman & Rogoff, 1987, p. 24).

Scholars in various disciplines have struggled for years with describing and explaining the relationship between context and human behavior. For example, in 1942 Stephen Pepper laid out his philosophical analysis of four "world hypotheses," which he believed described numerous approaches in the physical, biological, and behavioral sciences. Pepper (1948) argued that all four could be characterized by one root metaphor which captured the unique focus of each world hypothesis. One such world hypothesis, contextualism, called attention to the dynamic and intricate role context plays in human behavior. Pepper identified its root metaphor as the historical event or, as Pepper explains, "the event alive in its present" (p. 232). This world hypothesis and similar ones, such as Dewey and Bentley's (1949) transaction approach and Altman and Rogoff's (1987) transactional world view, all place context front and center in the study of human social behavior.

However appealing such notions may be, no one social science discipline can claim consensus on how the relationship between context and human behavior should be articulated and studied. The discipline of communication is no exception. As recently as 1991, Lannamann lamented that much of interpersonal communication research, for example, is ideologically biased toward ahistorical approaches. That is, context is not seriously recognized. Three years later in a review of current trends in interpersonal communication, Knapp, Miller, and Fudge (1994) argue that while many interpersonal scholars would not deny that context is fundamental to our understanding of communication and meaning, few still agree on the nature of context and its relationship to communication and vice versa.

The various approaches to context include using it to demarcate various subareas of communication (e.g., interpersonal, small group, organizational), social and institutional settings (e.g., Thanksgiving dinners, church revivals, schools), relationship types (e.g., acquaintance, best friend, romantic), environmental characteristics (e.g., architecture, seating arrangements), and characteristics of messages (Knapp et al., 1994). They ended their review by noting that the various theoretical and methodological approaches to context are differentiated by how the relationship between communication and context is articulated. "Is context so much a part of the communication process that it is distorted when considered apart from the process . . . Or is it one of the many external and isolated sources of influence on message selection and interpretation" (Knapp et al., 1994, pp. 12-13)?

The purpose of this volume is to present to the serious student of context and communicative behavior, various answers to the question, How are context and communicative behavior related? One such perspective, pragmatics, provides some answers to this question and is the exclusive focus of this chapter. I will first introduce the pragmatic perspective, explain its fundamental assumptions about human communication, and then describe how context and communication are considered within this perspective.

The Pragmatic Perspective of Human Communication

A group of interdisciplinary scholars referred to as "The Palo Alto Group," heavily influenced by the renowned anthropologist Gregory Bateson explored the underlying premises of pragmatics in the classic book entitled *Pragmatics of Human Communication: A Study of Interactional Patterns, Pathologies, and Paradoxes.* Paul Watzlawick, Janet Beavin, and Don Jackson's (1967) work in psychotherapy and schizophrenia was driven by their fundamental belief in the identification of observable behaviors as the unit of analysis in studying human communication. The "pragmatic" aspect of human communication was the recognition that communication affects behavior (Watzlawick et al., 1967). Furthermore, they treated communication and behavior synonymously and, following Bateson, focused their attention on exploring the dynamics of emergent patterns of behavior. They believed that "[m]an's awareness of himself is essentially an awareness of functions, of relationships in which he is involved, no matter how much he may subsequently reify this awareness" (p. 28).

Watzlawick et al. (1967) grounded this perspective of human communication in the basic tenets of a metatheoretical framework called system theory. The biologist Ludwig von Bertalanffy is most often associated with this multidisciplinary and general science of "wholeness" (Littlejohn, 1996). System theory has had a broad and tremendous impact on how human communication is conceptualized and studied. Its basic philosophical tenets emerge in various applications. The pragmatic perspective is one form it takes in the discipline of communication. Before the principles of pragmatics are discussed further, it would be useful to briefly outline some of the central tenets of system theory which inform the foundation of pragmatics.

Basic Tenets of System Theory

Key themes in system theory revolve around numerous concepts, including interdependence, wholeness, nonsummativity, openness, equifinality, and hierarchical system levels. According to Rapoport (1968), a system by definition functions "as a whole by virtue of the interdependence of its parts" (p. vii). Any system, whether it be a physical (e.g., a galaxy), biological (e.g., human body), or social (e.g., a marriage), is not characterized by its elements or components but by the interdependent relationships between those elements. Thus, the most essential property of a system is "wholeness." Hall and Fagen (1968) explained that all elements of a system affect each other. Any change in one aspect of the system changes the other elements.

"Nonsummativity," the second property of a system, is closely related to wholeness. The unique character of any system is an emergent quality derived from the interdependent relationships between the elements of the system (Fisher, 1978). "The system takes on a *quality* that is separate from the individual components and cannot be described solely by information about its parts" (Fisher & Adams, 1994, p. 7).

Systems vary in their degree of "openness;" the third property of any system. No system exists in a vacuum, but in an environment, and varies in its ability to exchange energy with its environment. Closed systems such as stars, for example, are not capable of exchanging energy with their environment and over time will eventually end. Open systems, such as social systems, have more permeable boundaries with their environments than do closed systems. This permeability allows for a great deal of exchange with the environment and allows open systems to self-regulate or experience ongoing renewal. Social systems are thus capable of increased, not decreased, order and complexity (Fisher, 1978).

The overriding implication of wholeness, nonsummativity, and openness is "equifinality;" the fourth property of open systems. Open systems by their very nature are equifinal. Whereas the final state of a closed system is determined by its initial state, the final state, or outcome, of an open system is not determined by its initial state (von Bertalanffy, 1968).

Systems are embedded not only in environments but also within other systems. Systems are found within a nested "hierarchy" or "series of levels of increasing complexity" (Littlejohn, 1996). The elements of one system are nested in the next level and so on. For example, two small subsystems, such as two relational partners, interact within a larger system, a relationship. At increasingly more complex levels, systems are embedded within larger interacting systems or suprasystems such as organizations. The boundaries between the systems in the hierarchy are arbitrary because each lower level system is a part of the next systemic level.

Watzlawick et al. (1967) were instrumental in applying these tenets to the study of human communication. They shifted the study of human behavior from the individual to the relational and argued that the essence of human experience could be found in relationships or, more specifically, in patterns of relationships.

Paramount to those in the discipline of communication is the authors' placement of communication at the heart of this human experience. Communication is no longer treated merely as a tool for people to use to produce outcomes, but as a formative process in its own right (Millar & Rogers, 1976). One can easily understand why this perspective was embraced by some in the discipline of communication. The work of The Palo Alto Group was eventually taken into the discipline by people such as B. Aubrey Fisher, Edna Rogers, Frank Millar, Carol Wilder, Art Van Lear, Don Ellis, Peter Monge, and Bill Wilmot and applied to the study of social systems.

Principles and Application of Pragmatics

Five general principles of pragmatics demonstrate how the interactional view of Watzlawick et al. emerged in the field of communication. First, behaviors, or human actions, are the locus of interest. Second, the interpretation of any behavior is found in patterns of behaviors. Third, the meaning of these patterns is found in context. Fourth, people make sense of emergent patterns retrospectively. And, fifth, understanding communication involves asking, "*How* does behavior mean?" These principles reflect a particular application of system theory and the interactional approach originally outlined by Watzlawick et al. in 1967.

First, "behaviors [human actions] are the phenomena necessary for the understanding of human communication" (Fisher & Adams, 1994, p. 10). The processes of human communication are understood by focusing on observable behaviors rather than on the intrapsychic processes of individuals. These behaviors occur in time and are treated as temporal events which cannot be taken back. Watzlawick et al. (1967) hypothesized that "in an interactional situation . . . one cannot not communicate" (pp. 48-49). All communication is considered behavior, and it is recognized that behavior has no opposite; one cannot *not* behave in an interactional situation. Admittedly, some behavior may not be communicative; however, "one probably cannot avoid communicating in a social setting" (Bavelas, 1990, p. 593). Thus, communication/behavior is recognized as important in its own right. Bavelas (1988) explained that "behavior goes to other people (it does not just drop off into space). It connects people and thereby creates a new phenomenon" (p. 1).

Second, "the interpretation or definition of communicative behaviors is to be found in the patterns of how those behaviors interconnect with one another" (Fisher & Adams, 1994, p. 12). No act or message exists in a meaningful form alone, but must be considered always in a pattern of *inter*actions (Fisher, 1981). These interactions are sequences of behaviors which serve to connect individual subsystems to social systems. The pragmatic perspective accords primary importance to social interaction rather than to separate actions (Rogers, 1989). Communication is treated as a systematic whole and cannot be broken down into isolatable elements. Any element of focus is linked to others in "dynamic and mutually influencing associations and those associations help to account for change throughout the whole system" (Montgomery, 1993, pp. 209-210). Scheflen (1968) added, "It is the *relations* of the elements or events, the configuration, the pattern we are after" (p. 190).

Furthermore, these sequences of behaviors can be interpreted differently because they can be ordered or punctuated differently. "Different punctuations, or orderings of a sequence of behavior, can create different realities for interactants" (Fisher & Adams, 1994, p. 13).

Third, "the meaning or significance of the communicative patterns is discovered by recognizing that they are context-bound" (Fisher & Adams, 1994, p. 14). Gregory Bateson, whose work in combination with system theory thinking helped shape the pragmatic perspective, was unwavering in his belief that meaning is found in "the pattern which connects; that all communication necessitates context, and that without context there is no meaning" (Bateson, 1978, p. 13). Pragmatic practitioners do not treat context as a container of communication or merely as the mere environment of communication. Communication and context are inextricably linked in a reflexive relationship; that is, the context defines the emergent patterns of behavior and simultaneously is defined by those emergent patterns (Ellis, 1981; Fisher & Adams, 1994).

Given this kind of interrelationship, context does not determine individual behavior. Context is an integral aspect of behavior, and human communicators with their sensemaking capabilities do not so much react to context but act toward context. For instance, people long believed that some rooms were actually more friendly than other rooms. Based on research by Maslow and Mintz (1956) and Kitchens, Herron, and Behnke (1976) many inferred that the physical design, color, and decoration of rooms led people in them to behave differently. This research was based on what people said they did in the rooms and reports of their feelings about the rooms and others in the rooms with them. In 1976 Sue Pendell replicated the previous research, but observed only the communication that occurred in the different rooms. She discovered no difference in communication occurring in the different rooms.

Remember, open social systems are self-renewing and self-organizing; they experience a continual interchange with their environments. "Environmental interactionism" captures the notion that "people's actions are partially defined by their environment, and they simultaneously create the social meaning of their environment when they act toward it and among themselves" (Fisher & Adams, 1994, p. 96).

Fourth, "to understand communication is to 'make sense' of the communicative patterns retrospectively (that is, after they have occurred)" (Fisher & Adams, 1994, p. 15). Although individuals are prone to think that thought precedes action and thus make sense of behavior in terms of causes and effects, that is not the case. Weick (1979) explained that individuals punctuate or order sequences of action after the fact or after the events have occurred in a form of retrospective sensemaking. He argued that individuals are only able to experience the separateness of their experiences by removing themselves from the experience and directing their attention to the experience. In other words, "How do I know what I think until I hear what I have to say" (Fisher & Adams, 1994, p. 15)?

Fifth, "a pragmatic view of human communication involves asking different questions in order to acquire knowledge or understanding" (Fisher & Adams, 1994, p. 17). It follows from the first and second principles that if the focus is on interaction and not on intrapsychic processes, then new questions are called for. If messages derive their meaning from within the patterns of other messages, then "How does behavior mean?" becomes the question of interest, not "What does individual A mean by his or her behavior?" Behavior, to be meaningful socially, "involves finding how that behavior links or interconnects with other behaviors in the stream of interaction" (Fisher & Adams, 1994, p. 17). Further, any understanding of the sequence of actions is not clear until the sequence is contextualized. The social system is an open system characterized by wholeness and nonsummativity and no single behavior can be used to describe the whole system.

Finally, as mentioned above, pragmatists privilege the social system not the individual actor. The smallest social system is the interpersonal system not the intrapersonal system. Pragmatic practitioners claim as their focus the "communication properties that exist only at the dyadic system level; relational variables do not lie within interactors, but rather exist between them" (Rogers & Farace, 1975, p. 222). Further, interpersonal communication systems are embedded or nested within a hierarchy of systems. The individual is considered a subsystem of the interpersonal system and important only as a source of behaviors; he or she is not considered the same as the interpersonal system. And conversely, while larger suprasystems such as organizational and societal systems are influenced by the interpersonal systems embedded within them, they are not the same systems.

To learn about any level, one must understand how the different levels are tied together or how one level interconnects with another (Fisher, 1978). Lower levels serve to constrain the upper levels, and these suprasystems give significance to the system. Communication as patterned interaction (or relationship) continually results in a temporal form (e.g., a mother/daughter relationship), and this form is embedded in larger systems (e.g., family) and serves to provide a broader perspective from which to understand the significance of the interaction.

Nested hierarchies of systems are multi-level, interconnected systems of patterns of interaction giving rise to temporal forms which themselves become interconnected, giving rise to larger and larger sets of interactions or metapatterns and, thus, larger and larger macrostructures. All levels simultaneously influence and are influenced by the next level of patterns and metapatterns.

The pragmatic perspective of human communication is an epistemology of patterns. As stated earlier, human experience is essentially one of relationships--patterns of relationships. The epistemological shift moves from a monadic focus on individual acts, to a relational focus on forms of organization. Underlying the perspective and the research of pragmatists is their belief that these relationships are enacted over time in co-defining and co-present communicative processes. The patterns are emergent and "unfold and accumulate over time into more enduring social structurings which both characterize the relationship, and influence the relational form of future enactments" (Rogers, 1993, p. 20).

Several basic presumptions of the pragmatic view help summarize its contributions to communication theory and lay down a foundation from which to examine in detail the interrelationship between context and communication within this pragmatic perspective. First, "communication," "behavior," and "relationship" are interchangeable. Second, "formative processes of social interaction" (Rogers, 1993, p. 21) are privileged; thus, the smallest unit of analysis in an *inter*act. Third, the meaning of relationship is found in the connections *between* people. Fourth, communication is where interactants define their selves in relationship to others and simultaneously enact the ongoing character of their relationship. Sixth, these relationships are "bestowed, sustained, and transformed through communicative behaviors" (Millar & Rogers, 1976, p. 87). Put simply, "people do not relate and then talk, but they simultaneously relate in talk" (Duncan, 1967, p. 249).

One of the most specific applications of pragmatics to the study of human communication can be found in a body of work often referred to as "relational communication" or Rel/Com. Rel/Com research shifts its emphasis from the individual, or the intrapersonal, to the dyad as the most basic unit of analysis. The "formative processes of social interaction" (Rogers, 1993, p. 21) is where communication is located. More to the point:

> The unit of analysis in a transactional perspective is a minimum of two, a dyad; and the focus of analysis is on the systemic properties that the participants have collectively, not individually. The system is viewed as a joint product of behavior, a product admittedly made up of individual actions, but one that has a 'life' of its own which goes beyond the sum of its constituent parts. (Millar & Rogers, 1976, pp. 89-90)

Edna Rogers and Frank Millar, two of the most prominent Rel/Com researchers, use a spatial metaphor to capture the unfolding nature of relationships (Neuliep, 1996). In interaction, dyadic partners co-create and maintain a degree of distance between each other. They do so in cycles of offering and responding to each other's definitions of self in relation to the other. An axiom of pragmatics stipulates that these dyadic partners can respond to each other's relational definition in two ways: similarly or differently (Littlejohn, 1996). Thus, general patterns of symmetry and complementarity emerge over time. When interactants' relational definitions are accepted, the relationship is characterized by moments of complementarity; the differences between the interactants are maximized. On the other hand, when interactants' relational definitions are rejected, the relationship is characterized by moments of symmetry; the differences between the interactants are minimized because they behave in a similar manner.

The most often studied distancing dimension is control. The variable control in this case is not treated as an individual need or aspect of an interactant's behavior, but as emergent characteristics of interaction or "joint products of behavior that emerge, have 'life,' and fluctuate through the exchange of messages" (Millar & Rogers, 1976, p. 90). Control is the "process of establishing the right to define, direct, and delimit the actions of the dyad at the current moment" (Millar & Rogers, 1987, p. 120). When individual dyadic partners assert their definition of the relationship in statements such as "I will make the decision here," "I will not be treated in this manner," or "Go get the newspaper," they are said to be attempting control. These behaviors are referred to as "one-up" behaviors. "One-down" behaviors accept a partner's relational definition, for example, "Oh, okay let's go to that movie," or "Fine, let's do it your way."

Patterns of symmetrical and complementarity control vary across topics and situations. While the study of control patterns in various kinds of relationships has dominated Rel/Com research, other areas of interest do exist. For instance, Millar and Rogers (1987) have studied two other distancing dimensions: trust and intimacy.

Context and Communication within Pragmatics

What, then, has been said about the relationship between the pragmatic perspective and "context?" To begin to answer this question, it becomes necessary to return to one of the fundamental principles of pragmatics--the very essence of human experience consists of relationships and patterns of relationships (Watzlawick et al., 1967). Pragmatically, there is no such thing as a simple message or behavior. A message's interpretation must rest on other messages which serve to frame or even modify it. Without context, or what Bateson (1979) referred to as "pattern through time" (p. 15), "words and actions have no meaning at all" (p. 15) thus, without context or pattern, communication does not exist (Bateson, 1972).

Without question "context" is taken seriously in the pragmatic perspective. However, there is no single unifying statement about the exact nature of context and its role in the pragmatic perspective. Individuals such as Bateson, Watzalwick, Beavin, Jackson, Fisher, and Ellis have grappled with its conceptualization and place in pragmatics. The theme that no single behavior carries any message value or information about the interpersonal or social system unless considered in a sequence of other messages, gives rise to various pragmatic treatments of context. Below I will flush out the variations of this theme all of which have implications for the significance given context in pragmatics.

Recall the first principle of pragmatics: behaviors are the locus of interest in pragmatics. All communication is behavior, and it is the study of behavior that grounds the study of communication. Another axiom of pragmatics and a fundamental presumption of the Rel/Com research discussed earlier is that any message is comprised of two dimensions: a report (content) and a command (relational) dimension. First, any message carries content or ideas; the stuff or "what" of the message. Second, a message does not occur in a vacuum but is always said or done in a certain way. Messages always carry information about "how" to interpret the content. The relational dimension of messages is referred to as metacommunication or communication about communication. These two dimensions always exist and are inseparable (Wilmot, 1987).

Here is the first and most elementary treatment of context in pragmatics. On this level, context is the relational dimension of *a* message. "When two people are interacting, each is relating information to the other, and simultaneously each is also 'commenting' on the information at a higher level" (Littlejohn, 1996, p. 251). These comments are the offered definition of the relationship between interactants and serve to "contextualize" the content.

While behavior is the focus of pragmatics, no single behavior carries any information about the interpersonal or relational. The relational dimension of a message may inform an intertactant about how another defines the relationship, but it alone does not define the relationship. Recall the second principle of pragmatics. Only in and through patterns of behavior do interactants enact their relationships. The interpersonal/social/relational is an emergent temporal form and only found between interactants. Fisher (1981) reminds us that no behavior alone exists in any meaningful form; it must be interpreted within a pattern of behaviors. Thus, the interact is the fundamental unit of analysis in pragmatics, and patterns of interacts contextualize behavior. So, on this level, "context" emerges out of patterns of metamessages.

At this level, metamessages are not the relational definition asserted in a single message, but the emergent pattern of behaviors. A dyadic partner can assert a relational definition; however, that assertion alone is not the relationship. The relationship is found in the patterns that connect the partners. For example, consider the relational control studies discussed earlier. While a dyadic partner can assert his or her right to define and thus direct the actions of the other, that *one* behavior does not define the control nature of the relationship. Sequences of control assertions and responses must be examined to find the emergent nature of control.

For example, "dominance" and "domineeringness" are used by Millar and Rogers (1979) to distinguish between individual assertions of control and patterns of relational control. When dyadic partners assert their definition of the relationship (a one-up message) their assertion is said to be "domineering." If one partner's assertion is accepted by the other in a one-down message, this forms a complementary interact and "dominance." So one partner can be domineering, but if his or her relational definition is not accepted by the other then he or she is not dominant in that moment.

Dominance emerges in complementary patterns, and struggles between partners for dominance are found in symmetrical patterns. These patterns can vary across relationship types and topics. For instance, Millar and Rogers (1979) have shown that for some marital couples, a high incidence of domineeringness is not necessarily associated with redundant patterns of dominance. Also, relationships vary in how much partners share control (flexibility/rigidity) and their consistency of control (stability/instability) (Littlejohn, 1996).

At this level, then, context becomes "pattern through time" (Bateson, 1979, p. 15). Context is itself understood as emergent, fluid, and inseparable from patterns of behavior. Watzlawick et al. (1967) explained that "the manifest messages exchanged become part of the particular interpersonal context and place their restrictions on subsequent interaction" (p. 132). Context, as "pattern through time," or sequenced interaction, is not separate from the very processes from which it emerges. Context continually emerges out of patterned behavior offering an ongoing frame for individual behaviors *and* restricting future interaction. More specifically, patterns of behavior define context while, simultaneously, context defines message behavior (Ellis, 1981; Fisher & Adams, 1994). The implication is that context, pragmatically, is *both* emergent (follows the behavior and aids in its interpretation) and retrospective (precedes behavior and aids in its interpretation) (Knapp et al., 1994).

Actions are not only contextualized within patterns of actions; those emergent patterns of actions themselves become connected with other patterns over time. Individual acts become patterned into sequences of interaction, those sequences become patterned into other sequences which in turn become patterned into larger sequences, and so on. Metapatterns (Bateson, 1979) refer to the patterns which connect patterns. Social relationships "unfold and *accumulate* [emphasis mine] over time into *more enduring* [emphasis mine] social structurings which both characterize the relationship, and influence the relational form of future enactments" (Rogers, 1993, p. 20). Millar and Rogers (1987) speculate that these metapatterns, once identified, should help differentiate various relationship types.

These social structurings do not unfold through time in a vacuum but are embedded within a hierarchy of systems which is a "series of levels of increasing complexity" (Littlejohn, 1996, p. 45). Recall that the intrapersonal system is embedded within the interpersonal, the interpersonal within the group, the group within the organization, the organization within society, and so on. Each level is increasingly more complex. Furthermore, the boundaries between the levels are arbitrary because each system is separate and a part of each other (Littlejohn, 1996). Any system is *itself* understood within context; it "must be viewed in relation to other systems" (Fisher, 1981, p. 202).

The meaning of communicative patterns is "discovered by recognizing that they are context bound" (Fisher & Adams, 1994, p. 14). Remember, however, that form is not separate from process in pragmatics. "Process and form are two sides of a coin; they determine each other" (Littlejohn, 1996, p. 56). Those various social contexts such as relationship types, small group types, and organizations are themselves emergent and reveal themselves "more and more as complex patterns of relationship and interaction" (Watzlawick et al., 1967, p. 22). Over time these contexts may very well become reified. When this happens, form (in this case, social context) is separated from process, exists in isolation, is measurable, and is something that can be found. In essence, form appears "thinglike" (Watzlawick et al., 1967). Some even suggest that context may become so reified that it actually controls behavior (see Duranti & Goodwin, 1992). However, just because context appears reified, do not lose sight of its emergent, fluid nature. There is nothing substance-like about communicative forms because communication functions in "time and context; and the meanings, qualities, and attributes of communication are alterable over time" (Ellis, 1981, p. 218).

Individuals use context to interpret and influence their behaviors; simultaneously, those behaviors in pattern restrict and give meaning to the context. Pragmatic research necessitates detailing information about context, and Ellis (1981) scolded when he stated, "If this point had not been so neglected, it would be trivial" (p. 226). But, he added, individuals insist on conceptualizing context as an artificial entity, invariant in time, and independent of human interaction.

Weick (1979), for example, argued that the notion of "an organization" is a myth. If one goes looking for the noun "organization," he or she will search in vain. More appropriately, an organization should be considered an "organ*izing*" [emphasis mine] (p. 3). "Organizings" are emergent phenomena created out of complex layers of patterns of double interacts which in turn produce increasingly complex links, which in turn produce larger, more macro structures referred to as "networks" (Weick, 1979).

In summary, the contextual theme in pragmatics takes on three general permutations. First, at the individual level, context is the relation dimension of a message that serves to frame the content dimension. Second, at the micro-social level, context is the sequence of *patterned* relational definitions that serve to frame behavior. Third, at the macro-social level, contexts are various macro-social temporal structures that serve to frame numerous metapatterns of interaction. Furthermore, I have argued that (a) communication/behavior defines and simultaneously is defined by context; (b) understanding communicative processes necessitates recognizing multiple hierarchical levels of context; (c) context is emergent and retrospective; and (d) context is a fluid and nontangible phenomenon.

Conclusion

Many in the communication discipline have called for the serious treatment of context. Many still challenge the discipline to recognize the significant and integral role context plays in communicative processes and vice versa. In 1995, Sigman argued strongly that context as a key characteristic of communication is not "extrinsic to the communication process," (p. 81) but instead represents what Birdwhistell referred to as an "interdependent surround" (cited in Sigman, 1995, p. 81). Sigman further claimed that if research does not hold to this treatment of context, then it is not "communication" research. In an October 1995 newsletter for the Language and Social Interaction Division of the Speech Communication Association, Ray challenged division members to make the study of context a preeminent focus of their research.

As an intriguing and perplexing construct, context is perhaps both a curse and a blessing for all of us who marvel at what humans do with language. Let us go beyond the mere acknowledgment of context as a fascinating fixture in human communication, and put forth a solid effort to analyze and explicate the concept. (p. 2)

Pragmatist thinkers and practitioners have contributed to the efforts to take context seriously, but they have not been entirely successful. They are to be challenged to put forth their own solid effort toward clarifying the relationship between communication and context. Their greatest contributions still remain at the micro-social level. Here, they have argued persuasively that no behavior alone carries information about the social system. At this level, understanding social relationships as emergent patterns of behavior inherently is a study of context. Much work has been done and continues to be done at this level. However, work remains to be done in a few areas. First, at the more macro levels of social structuring, researchers have not reached the sort of contextual detail they have called for in the past. In 1985, Rogers, Millar, and Bavelas posited three required characteristics of any method used for systems-level analysis. One such requirement is that the method must have the capacity to describe system-level structurings. They went on to explain that the goal of pragmatic research "is to move toward the identification of temporal forms at second- and higher-order structurings of patterns, in an effort to investigate the consequences of interactional dynamics" (p. 183) on various relationship forms. By the authors' own admission, studies at this triadic level and beyond are few and far between. Yet, they do remind researchers that only in the investigation of "successively higher levels of patterning of patterns" (p. 183) will the "investigation of the nature of contextual interaction become a possibility" (p. 183). Two years later Millar and Rogers (1987) argued that only by using "contextual, relationally specific, comparative measures" could researchers describe how those metapatterns are formed and thus more effectively understand emergent relationship types.

Second, Rel/Com researchers have not consistently recognized the place of physical contexts in their studies of interaction. Fisher (1981) speculated that "the interactional sequences should be considered a necessary element of context (or frame of metamessages), but it is *not* sufficient (in the sense that no other elements of context exist)" (p. 202). Social contexts are obviously more germane to pragmatists. Perhaps they can look to the transactional view of human behavior (see Altman & Rogoff, 1987) to learn how the physical context can be treated as an integral part of the whole.

Knapp et al. (1994) called for individuals to explicate the nature of context from their own perspective. "Contextualizing" context will go a long way toward clarifying how context is taken seriously in several perspectives within the communication discipline, identify where perspectives overlap on the issues, identify points of divergence, and promote a more thorough understanding and empirical investigation of this pervasive and significant construct.

References

Altman, I., & Rogoff, B. (1987). World views in psychology: Trait, interactional, organismic, and transactional. In D. Stokols & I. Altman (Eds.), *Handbook of environmental psychology* (pp. 7-40). New York: Wiley.

Bateson, G. (1972). *Steps to an ecology of mind*. New York: Ballantine.

Bateson, G. (1978). The pattern which connects. *Co-Evolution Quarterly, 18*, 4-15.

Bateson, G. (1979). *Mind and nature: A necessary unity*. Toronto: Bantam.

Bavelas, J. B. (1988, February). "Notes for special session." Paper presented at the annual meeting of the Western Speech Communication Association, San Diego, CA.

Bavelas, J. B. (1990). Behaving and communicating: A reply to Motley. *Western Journal of Speech Communication, 54*, 593-602.

Dewey, J., & Bentley, A. F. (1949). *Knowing and the known*. Boston: Beacon.

Duncan, H. D. (1967). The search for a social theory of communication in American sociology. In F. E. X. Dance (Ed.), *Human communication theory* (pp. 236-263). New York: Holt, Rinehart, and Winston.

Duranti, A., & Goodwin, C. (Eds.). (1992). *Rethinking context: Language as an interactive phenomenon*. Cambridge: Cambridge University Press.

Ellis, D. G. (1981). The epistemology of form. In C. Wilder-Mott & J. H. Weakland (Eds.), *Rigor & imagination: Essays from the legacy of Gregory Bateson* (pp. 215-230). New York: Praeger.

Fisher, B. A. (1978). *Perspectives on human communication*. New York: Macmillan.

Fisher, B. A. (1981). Implications of the 'interactional view' for communication theory. In C. Wilder-Mott & J. H. Weakland (Eds.), *Rigor & imagination: Essays from the legacy of Gregory Bateson* (pp. 195-214). New York: Praeger.

Fisher, B. A., & Adams, K. L. (1994). *Interpersonal communication: Pragmatics of human relationships* (2nd ed.). New York: McGraw-Hill.

Hall, A. D., & Fagen, R. E. (1968). Definition of a system. In W. Buckley (Ed.), *Modern systems research for the behavioral scientist* (pp. 81-92). Chicago: Aldine.

Kitchens, J. T., Herron, T. P., & Behnke, R. R. (1976). Effects of visual environment aesthetics on interpersonal communication. A paper presented at the annual meeting of the Southern Speech Communication Association, San Antonio, TX.

Knapp, M. L., Miller, G. R., & Fudge, K. (1994). Background and current trends in the study of interpersonal communication. In M. L. Knapp & G. R. Miller (Eds.), *Handbook of interpersonal communication* (2nd ed.)(pp. 3-20). Thousand Oaks, CA: Sage.

Lannamann, J. (1991). Interpersonal research as ideological practice. *Communication Theory, 1*, 179-203.

Littlejohn, S. W. (1996). *Theories of human communication* (5th ed.). Belmont, CA: Wadsworth.

Maslow, A. H., & Mintz, N. L. (1956). Effects of esthetic surroundings: I. Initial effects of three esthetic conditions upon perceiving "energy" and "well-being" in faces. *Journal of Psychology, 41*, 247-254.

Millar, F. E., & Rogers, L. E. (1976). A relational approach to interpersonal communication. In G. R. Miller (Ed.), *Explorations in interpersonal communication* (pp. 87-103). Beverly Hills, CA: Sage.

Millar, F. E., & Rogers, L. E. (1987). Relational dimensions in interpersonal dynamics. In M. E. Roloff & G. R. Miller (Eds.), *Interpersonal processes: New directions in communication research* (pp. 117-139). Newbury Park, CA: Sage.

Montgomery, B. M. (1993). Relationship maintenance versus relationship change: A dialectical dilemma. *Journal of Social and Personal Relationships, 10*, 205-223.

Neuliep, J. W. (1996). *Human communication theory: Applications and case studies.* Boston: Allyn & Bacon.

Pendell, S. D. (1976). The influence of room design on small group communication. Doctoral dissertation, University of Utah, 1976. *Dissertation Abstracts International, 37*, 10A.

Pepper, S. C. (1948). *World hypotheses: A study in evidence* (2nd. ed.). Berkeley, CA: University of California Press.

Rapoport, A. (1968). Forward. In W. Buckley (Ed.), *Modern systems research for the behavioral scientist* (pp. vii-xxii). Chicago: Aldine.

Ray, G. B. (1995, October). Back to the future: The study of context in language and communication. *The LSI Gazette*, 1-2.

Rogers, L. E. (1989, April). The relational dance: The study of process and pattern. *Proceedings of the 16th annual student conference in communication*, California State University, Fresno.

Rogers, L. E. (1993). The concept of social relationship from an interactional pragmatic view. *Personal Relationship Issues, 1*(2), 20-21.

Rogers, L. E., & Farace, R. V. (1975). Analysis of relational communication in dyads: New measurement procedures. *Human Communication Research, 1*, 222-239.

Rogers, L. E., Millar, F. E., & Bavelas, J. B. (1985). Methods for analyzing marital conflict discourse: Implications of a systems approach. *Family Processes, 24*, 175-187.

Rogers-Millar, L. E., & Millar, F. E. (1979). Domineeringness and dominance: A transactional view. *Human Communication Research, 5*, 238-246.

Scheflen, A. E. (1968). Quasi-courtship behavior in psychotherapy. In W. G. Bennis, E. H. Schein, F. I. Steele, & D. E. Berlow (Eds.), *Interpersonal dynamics: Essays and readings on human interaction* (rev. ed.)(pp. 182-196). Homewood, IL: Dorsey.

Sigman, S. J. (1995). Question: Evidence of what? Answer: Communication. *Western Journal of Communication, 59*, 79-84.

von Bertalanffy, L. (1968). *General system theory: Foundations, development, applications.* New York: Braziller.

Watzlawick, P., Beavin, J. H., & Jackson, D. D. (1967). *Pragmatics of human communication: A study of interactional patterns, pathologies, and paradoxes.* New York: Norton.

Weick, K. (1979). *The social psychology of organizing* (2nd ed.). Reading, MA: Addison-Wesley.

Wilmot, W. W. (1987). *Dyadic communication.* New York: Random House.

Chapter 5

The Meaning and Use of "Context" in the Theory of the Coordinated Management of Meaning

Jonathan G. Shailor
University of Wisconsin-Parkside

What shall count as "context" in our investigations of human communication? How shall we investigate the relationship between context and communicative action? And for what purposes are we pursuing the investigation? These three questions are, I believe, the most central in helping us to develop a critical awareness of what we as researchers are doing when employ the "context" construct. In this essay, I wish to pursue the answers to these questions as they are articulated in the theory of the coordinated management of meaning, or CMM. Developed by W. Barnett Pearce, Vernon E. Cronen, and their associates, CMM is a pragmatic theory in the social constructionist tradition (Cronen, 1995; Cronen, Chen, & Pearce, 1988; Pearce, 1989; Pearce, 1992; Pearce & Cronen, 1980). Its intellectual roots include the tradition of American pragmatism exemplified by John Dewey and William James, the ordinary language philosophy of Ludwig Wittgenstein, and the systems orientation of Gregory Bateson. CMM's synthesis of these strands has produced a distinctive theory and method for exploring the relation of context to human interaction.

The basic premise of CMM is that our social realities are continually created, maintained and transformed in a reflexive process of action and interpretation. These realities include episodes, relationships, identities, organizations and cultural patterns, which CMM models as levels of meaning organized in terms of Wittgensteinian "grammars" (Cronen, 1995). Grammars consist of (a) meaning structures such as narratives and metaphors, and (b) the rules that integrate these structures and tie them to action (Cronen, 1995; Shailor, 1994). Part of the utility of CMM is that it can be used to construct sophisticated readings of the grammars at play in specific interactions, in such a way that participants gain an enlarged vision of the constraints and possibilites inherent in such conversations.

In the CMM world view, contexts can be characterized in terms of four distinctive features: (1) Contexts are not found things, but are interpretive achievements; (2) contexts are situated--they occur between particular persons at certain times and places; (3) contexts are constituted as sets of systemic relations; (4) contexts are elaborated and transformed in interaction.

In the following sections, I will discuss each of these features of context at some length, making use of a wide range of examples. Examples will include fictional and nonfictional cases of family communication, conflicted communication and (inter)cultural communication. The use of a range of examples is intentional; it will help to demonstrate the power of the theory.

Contexts are Interpretive Achievements

In CMM theory, contexts are understood as the interpretive frameworks that persons use to give meaning to their experiences; they are also the frameworks that persons use to assess and select from their alternatives for action (Pearce, 1992). "Storytelling," for example, is a framework for a particular type of interactional episode. That framework serves as a set of interpretive resources (narratives, metaphors, rules) that one can use to make sense of verbal and nonverbal acts. For example: In the context of an episode of storytelling, we would most likely make sense of the storyteller's description of a flying carpet by applying the conventional rule of suspending our disbelief. We could also use the storytelling frame to consider which alternatives for action are appropriate, practical or necessary; it is a commonly accepted rule that in an informal episode of fiction-based storytelling, audience members can occasionally interrupt to ask questions of clarification; on the other hand, it would not make sense for an audience member to interrupt in order to challenge the truthfulness of the tale.

CMM theory, then, accounts for conventional contexts that endure across times and places; however, the theory does not formulate contexts such as our storytelling episode as static templates which are appropriately or inappropriately applied and followed. Rather, CMM depicts contexts as interactional achievements--"made things," as opposed to "found things." This characterization is true to the etymological roots of the word context. The word derives from the Latin contextus, which is the past participle of contexere: "To weave together." Contexts are social fabrics that are woven together by multiple weavers using multiple strands of meaning. What is produced in this interactional weaving will often resemble earlier products; however, it will never perfectly match them. The fabric will consist of an integration of threads of meaning that have been introduced and applied by various actors. The colors, textures and patterning of those threads will complement or clash with each other in a great variety of ways. From the perspective of CMM, it is the responsibility of the researcher to describe these strands of meaning and how they have been woven. The emphasis is not upon how well the fabric matches the patterns of earlier or idealized accomplishments, but instead upon the aesthetic and pragmatic value of the pattern created at this unique moment of collaboration.

To return for a moment to our storytelling example: In her well-known account of storytelling in the the West African "bush," Laura Bohannon (1984) articulates her intention of introducing the plots, characters and themes of Hamlet to members of the Tiv tribe in order to confirm her belief that the story is "universally intelligible." Despite her best efforts, however, the story *in its telling on this occasion* becomes something different. As Bohannon speaks, the Tiv accept some strands of meaning and reject others, while contributing their own threads to the weave. For example, the concept of "ghost" does not exist for the Tiv; thus the ghost of Hamlet's dead father is rejected for something recognizable: A witch-inspired omen. Hamlet's confusion, rage and self-doubt are interpreted as signs of "bewitching," and so on. Bohannon's persistent attempts to tell the story in a way that preserves its original coherence combines with the tribe's insistence that the characters and their motivations make sense within the Tiv moral order. With each turn at talk, the collaborative re-interpretation of the story works as an emergent and developing frame for each new twist of the plot. According to CMM, these qualities of context as collaborative and emergent are not limited to episodes of storytelling or intercultural contact: they are central aspects of context construction in all conversations.

This characterization of context as a collaborative, open-ended achievement implies at least three implications for method. *First:* Since contexts are always unique constructions, they should be studied as such. Analysts should not make the mistake of reading conversations as *only* more or less adequate enactments of standardized rules, scripts and so on. *Second:* Since actors contribute varied interpretive strands to any conversation, the analyst should recognize the distinctiveness of individual actors' contributions. *Third:* The "weave" of a conversation is a patterned combination of threads of meaning; thus the interwoven nature of the conversational fabric should be acknowledged and explored.

CMM often describes this process in part in terms of the "serpentine model," in which the action of Person A is the most recent move in an emerging context with Person B. Person B interprets that move and selects a course of action compatible with her understanding. The action performed by Person B elaborates or transforms the emerging weave of contextual relations. Person A makes her interpretation of the emerging context and formulates a meaningful response on that basis ... and so on. It is important to note at this point that CMM does not limit the idea of "context" to the immediately preceding utterance, nor to the conversation in isolation. Both the emerging conversation and a broader pattern of relevant conversations are taken into account (this point will be discussed more fully under the third characteristic of context, below).

Contexts are also interpretive achievements in the sense that they are co-constructed by the theorist and the persons who are being studied. This does not necessarily mean that the researcher and the people in her study are literally co-researchers. What it does mean is that the researcher is not an objective observer who "discovers" the "actual" interpretive frameworks utilized by her social actors. The researcher is herself a social actor who participates in the contextual (re)construction. This assumption precludes an objectivist notion of "accuracy" as a criterion for a good analysis of context, and instead suggests other criteria: responsiveness to actors' meanings, elegance, pragmatic value, and ethical adequacy. CMM theory holds that the duty of the theorist is to provide interpretations that are designed to improve understanding and to contribute to the improvement of people's lives.

Contexts are Situated

This characteristic is closely related to the first. Contexts are collaborative achievements which are formed within particular constraints of person, time and place.

Take, for example, the context established by the Public Conversations Project ("PCP") of the Family Institute of Cambridge, Massachusetts (Becker, L. Chasin, R. Chasin, Herzig, & Roth, 1995; L. Chasin, R. Chasin, Herzig, Roth, & Becker, 1991; Roth, L. Chasin, R. Chasin, Becker, & Herzig, 1992). Since 1989, the PCP has been developing and practicing a model for public conversations on controversial issues. The model includes criteria for understanding the differences between "debate" and "dialogue." According to the PCP, debates occur in a threatening atmosphere, and are often framed within a "dominant discourse" that circumscribes talk within narrow, easily identified boundaries. Such discourse is frequently polarized into two competing positions. Persons speak from a position of certainty, with the intention of defending their own territory and attacking others' positions. Their audience is often their own constituency, and sometimes the undecided middle. Advocacy and win-lose argument are the preferred forms of talk, and the discourse often leads to self-perpetuating cycles of antagonism. Dialogue, on the other hand, takes place in an atmosphere of safety; it involves the open exchange of views within an atmosphere of mutual respect. In dialogue, persons address each others as individuals. They tell stories about how they came to their current beliefs. Also, they express their uncertainties, and are open to discovering new information and unsuspected connections. Differences may come to be understood as sources of insight, rather than stumbling blocks.

The PCP story is one of a transformation from one context for discussion ("debate") to another ("dialogue"). In the PCP literature, these contexts are represented as clearly distinct, and the shift from debate to dialogue an achievement which occurs in a regular and predictable manner. From a CMM perspective, this "story told" is quite likely to differ in some interesting ways from the "story lived." The reason for this is that as any established contextual grammar enters a particular, situated interaction, it structures that interaction to a limited extent, blending and coordinating with other grammars in ways that are not fully predictable.

In one PCP session which I arranged and facilitated, several persons met at my home in order to discuss "gay and lesbian lifestyles." Three of the participants were Christian heterosexuals who believed that homosexuality is a sin, and three of the participants were homosexuals who were concerned about the Christians' characterization of their sexuality. All of the participants went through a thorough orientation prior to the actual meeting, and they appeared to have successfully co-constructed a context for "dialogue." At the meeting, the participants began by effectively performing "dialogue": speaking from personal experience, addressing others respectfully, and so on. Then one participant ("Gregory") began to shift the frame by bringing up references to "scientific evidence" of the dangers associated with homosexual activity, and by arguing that we ought to explore the evidence objectively and fearlessly. At first the shift was not obvious, since Gregory cheerfully framed his remarks as personal expressions of "curiosity" and "concern." As he continued, however, the lesbian participants in particular became angered by his way of speaking. They sensed that their very identities were being framed as "illegitimate," and in response, they went on the attack, not only questioning Gregory's reasoning and evidence, but also his morality. As a result, the context of "polarized debate" was developed and reinforced.

What is remarkable about this event is that despite very clearly stated intentions and very carefully made preparations, the desired context was only partially brought into being, and a very undesirable context emerged. The reason is simple, but profoundly important: Each of the participants brought his/her own identity and experiences to the "interactive moment" in which the context was produced. As an academic, conservative Christian and anti-homosexual activist, Gregory framed "dialogue" not so much as an event based on "human understanding and therapy," but more as "the open sharing of knowledge and information" (his own words). The lesbian women were both progressives, one involved in community work, the other in higher education. As lesbians with many years of facing hatred and intolerance, both subtle and overt, they looked for an exchange that would first and foremost demonstrate respect for each participant's life choices. They interpreted Gregory's remarks as hostile attempts to deny their very right to exist. As a heterosexual male academic, I heard Gregory's remarks as provocative, but not as threatening; thus, I did not attempt to interrupt or reframe them. As a result, the context which was produced that evening--part "dialogue," part "debate"--was in a very significant sense the nonsummative product of individual identities and expectations.

The Public Conversation Project's thorough guidelines for "preparing participants for a journey into the new" are much like other prefabricated constructions of context: They are traces of a history of practice, and their substantialization in situated interactions will always be both more and less than what we envision. In the case of the PCP, the grammar of "the new conversation" will always be an emergent one, woven together with the identity and experiences of the facilitators who adopt it, and combined with the histories and unique expectations of the discussants. The consequence is not chaos, but complexity, and a broader range of concerns than is often expressed in studies of communication-in-context.

What guidelines does CMM offer us for taking into account these "broader concerns"? I will address this issue in the remaining sections.

Contexts are Sets of Systemic Relations

Cronen, Pearce and Harris (1982) have argued that "the structure of the transpersonal systems that individuals form specifies the contexts within which they act" (p. 70). In the previous section, I used a case study of a public dialogue as an indicator of some of the constituents of such transpersonal systems. In this section, I would like to make a more comprehensive review of some of the more formal elements of CMM theory as they apply to the investigation of communication contexts.

CMM states that contexts consist of multiple levels of meaning which are created, maintained, negotiated and transformed in patterns of conversation. These meanings do not exist "in the heads of individuals," but in the talk and nonverbal expressions of persons in interaction. Meanings may include speech acts, episodes, relationships, identities, family myths, organizational stories, and cultural narratives. CMM analyses offer interpretations of these levels of context, and explanations of the ways in which contexts are reflexively reconstituted in specific interactional sequences.

In my study of communication patterns in dispute mediation, for example, I show how the context of any given mediation session is actually a transpersonal system made up of the meanings created in interaction by disputants and mediators (Shailor, 1994). In that analysis, I use the theoretical constructs of "narrative" and "rule" to create an "experience-near" interpretation of the meanings at play. For each participant in the interaction, I conduct a three-stage analysis:

(1) Use the CMM Levels as a Heuristic Device to Tease Out the Layers of Narrative Spoken by Each Person.

What story does she tell about the episode "How we came to mediation?" What story does she tell about her *relationship* with the other disputant and other relevant persons? How does she construct her *identity*? Do *family myths, organizational stories,* or *cultural narratives* come into play? Finally: How does the person tie these narrative strands together?

In the case of "Peter and Anne," a young couple fell into a pattern of angry fighting, culminating with Anne's obtaining a restraining order for Peter, which resulted in his being removed from their apartment. A judge approved the order on the condition that the couple attend mediation, and then return to court for further review. In the mediation session, Peter framed this sequence as the story of "Anne's betrayal," a detailed series of events in which Anne's actions are interpreted as attacks and cold-blooded manipulations, and his own actions are explained as necessary acts of self-defense. His story of the relationship mirrors the structure of "Anne's betrayal," excluding all other aspects of their relationship. Peter's autobiographical narrative is a story of rehabilitation, of "getting his life back together."

(2) Infer Rules That Tie the Actors' Narratives to Each Other, and to the Actors' Sense of Requirements for Action.

How do the actors' narratives inform one another? Do any express oppositional meanings? Do any narratives work as context for the others? As Peter speaks his narratives, it becomes clear that the relationship narrative serves as a *higher order context*, one that frames Peter's autobiography. This fact is much more than a logical nicety: it has serious consequences for action. He repeatedly argues that he cannot begin to make a new life for himself until he has disengaged from the relationship in a manner that will restore his sense of dignity and honor. These integrated narratives inform a regulative rule (rR), or rule for action, that Peter uses throughout the mediation:

> rR: In the context of "getting on with his life," Peter is obligated to make demands of Anne that will exact retribution and restore his self-esteem.

(3) Analyze the Reflexive Reconstitution of Actors' Meanings in Specific Moments of Interaction.

How do actors' meanings play into patterns of interaction? How does the interplay of meanings and actions work to reestablish or transform contexts? At this stage of the analysis, I summarize repetitive patterns and also conduct fine-grained analyses of specific moments of interaction. The focus is on reciprocal chains of influence between persons, meanings and actions. In the case of Peter and Anne, I show how Anne links her family history of abuse with her sense of being "endangered" by Peter. Anne also constructs an autobiographical narrative as a former victim who is now establishing her career. In this context, a continued relationship with Peter counts as dangerous and unwanted. These family, relationship and autobiographical contexts inform her efforts to avoid making any agreements in mediation that might compromise her physical or economic security and define her as a "victim."

How do these meanings play into specific moments in the dispute mediation? One repeated pattern is that Peter makes a demand: for example, that Anne pay for the rent during the two weeks that he was prevented from living in the apartment due to the restraining order. This demand makes sense, of course, within the subsystem of contextual meanings that Peter has assembled. Anne interprets this demand within her subsystem of meanings, and finds it unacceptable. Her refusal to meet Peter's demand is a confirmation of his construction of her as his persecutor, which obligates him to continue to press for retribution by looking for concessions on other issues. Anne, determined not to play the victim, continues to refuse. The knotted contextual system that Anne and Peter bring to mediation is perpetuated, in part because the mediators construct their own "neutrality" as a directive to relay messages with little or no attempt to reframe them.

The ways in which contextual systems are developed in interaction is a special concern in CMM theory. In the next section of the paper, I will summarize some of the more important theoretical issues.

Contexts are Elaborated and Transformed in Interaction

In a 1985 article entitled "Between Text and Context: Toward a Rhetoric of Contextual Reconstruction," rhetorician Robert J. Branham and CMM theorist W. Barnett Pearce argued that:

Every communicative act is a text that derives meaning from the context of expectations and constraints in which it is experienced. At the same time, contexts are defined, invoked, and altered by texts. Particular communicative acts simultaneously depend upon and reconstruct existing contexts (p. 19).

What counts as "text" and what counts as "context" is a mattter of the punctuations made by social actors in particular interactive moments. If, for example, I speak of my personality as the natural outcome of my family history, my autobiography is the text for which my family myth functions as context. My family story is the frame through which my self-concept is to be interpreted. If, however, at another point in time I speak of my developing self-understanding as the source of a new interpretation of my family life, then family is the text for which autobiography serves as context.

This definition of text/context relations can be understood in relation to our discussion of contexts as sets of systemic relations: All elements in an interactional system--actions, episodes, relationships, identities, family myths, organizational stories, cultural narratives, and so on--co-exist in patterns of reciprocal, mutually influential relationship. All elements are mutually defining, thus potentially both text and context for all the others. In actuality, the form of particular text/context relations is achieved in moments of social interaction. As we will see, these socially constructed articulations of text/context relations have important consequences for the ongoing evolution of meaning and action. In the following paragraphs, I will discuss three common patterns of reflexive relationship: charmed loops, subversive loops, and strange loops.

Two or more levels of meaning take the form of a *charmed loop* when their relationship is *transitive;* that is, both (or all) levels can serve equally well as context for the other(s) (Cronen, Johnson, & Lannamann, 1982, p. 103). As social actors use one level, then another as a context marker, no problematic differences or confusions in meaning result. Consider a relationship in which actions taken to further the career interests of an individual also serve to deepen the relationship. Here the contexts of autobiography and relationship are mutually supportive; privileging one as context rather than the other does not entail a change in meaning. Unfortunately, charmed loops are not always happy ones--they can just as easily be pernicious. Consider the charmed loop expressed by Carol Freeman as she discusses her understanding of contemporary race relations with social historian Studs Terkel (1992):

You're looking at generations of black males that have been raised by women. We have not had the men to raise men. We have been doing the best we can, but sometimes we've made a mess of it. The black men have so often been put down in this society; they just disappear (p. 35).

In Freeman's construction of the world, there is a consonance between (1) the troubled *identity* of the black male, (2) the absence of a father figure in the black *family,* and (3) The position of the black male in contemporary United States *culture.*

The transivity of these levels of meaning can be shown by writing three constitutive rules (cR), or rules for meaning in the CMM format:

cR 1. In the context of a black family that is missing a strong father figure, the black child's identity formation counts as insecure.

cR 2. In the context of an insecure black male identity, a black family counts as lacking a strong father figure.

cR 3. In the context of contemporary United States culture, the black male's identity counts as insecure.

As we can see in this example, the writing of the formal rules helps us to clarify the logical entailments that tie levels of context together.

Some charmed loops constitute "stable hierarchies," where one level of meaning clearly serves as a higher order context for others. We have already seen the example in which Peter's understanding of his relationship with Jane serves as a higher order context which constrains the development of his identity. In Peter's construction of context, he cannot get on with his life until he has successfully renegotiated the meaning of the relationship.

The concept of the stable hierarchy can sometimes alert us to important structural differences in individuals' contextual constructions. Consider a pair of tennis partners. After their first game, in which Lucinda is badly beaten, she is nonetheless eager to play again, while her partner Maria is not. One possibility is that Lucinda has framed the episode in terms of her hopes for a developing relationship. If meeting again is what is important, and tennis is the only apparent pretext, then another bad tennis game is a legitimate option. On the other hand, it may be that Maria has framed both the interaction and the relationship in terms of her identity as an expert tennis player (i.e., one who needs a challenge in order to consider a game worth playing). With "expert tennis player" the higher order context, Maria may feel prohibited from agreeing to another game, and may even feel indifferent about the relationship.

A second form of context-text relation is the *subversive loop*. In this situation, the social actor constructs an "irreparable breach" between text and context. One way of creating this "non-relation" is to define a context "for which no text is appropriate or sufficient." In the context of the Buddhist conception of *shunyata*, which asserts the inherent emptiness of all forms, all expressions of experience are considered illegitimate. On a more mundane level, a "moment of silence" declared at the opening of a school day defines any noticeable verbal or nonverbal actions as unfitting. Like many charmed loops, subversive loops can have significant social consequences.

In Marsha Norman's play 'Night, Mother (1983), the character Jesse constructs a bleak Saturday evening episode: she has decided that she is going to settle her affairs with her mother, and then kill herself. Her decision to do this has been carefully worked out over a period of weeks, if not months or years. For Jesse, her ritualized suicide is the one great meaningful act of her life; in the face of a lifetime of suffering, lies and confusion, it is the first clear assertion of her autonomy. Although Jesse's mother feels compelled to stop her by whatever means necessary—persuasion, protest, prevention—no action that her mother can conceive of makes sense within the context Jesse has established.

Part of the terrible irony of this situation is that the mother is unaware that she is a powerful collaborator in the contextual constructions that Jesse uses to legitimate her suicide. For example, the mother has for many years framed Jesse's epilepsy as a shameful condition that must be hidden from as many people as possible. Of course cultural level meanings are also implicated: There is a strong tendency in American culture to frame epilepsy and similar conditions as bizarre, frightening, and to be avoided.

Another kind of subversive loop is created when a person creates a text which denies the validity of any context which might make it interpretable" (Branham & Pearce, 1985, pp. 24-25). Husserl (1962; 1965), the founder of modern phenomenology, argues that the pure experience of a thing can only be achieved through an epoche, or phenomenological reduction, which involves the methodical removal of all elements of subjective awareness--in other words, the elimination of any social context that might be used to interpret the observed object . In a demonstration of this process, Giorgi (1990) reproduces a transcript of an interview between a psychologist and a restaurant manager. The irony of this demonstration is that it can easily be read as evidence of the impossibility of context-free descriptions of experience. The transcript includes no descriptions of facial expressions, vocal characteristics, body movements, clothing, or the environment, thus implying that verbal expressions are more important than nonverbal ones. Of course, the transcript also has a beginning and an end, effectively punctuating experience in a way that makes it more amenable to some interpretations than to others.

Whether or not one holds the philosophical position that context-free expression is possible, dedicated scientists, artists and others continue to create texts that deny their own interpretability.

The third type of context-text relation is the *strange loop,* where two or more levels of meaning exist in an *intransitive* relationship to one another; at some point in a progression of events, a change of context entails a change of meaning. One form of strange loop is that of a pragmatic paradox. Consider the episode in which a parent who is chastizing a child orders the child to make eye contact, as a sign of respect ("Look at me when I'm speaking to you!"). The child complies with a direct gaze, which the adult interprets as insolence: "Don't look at me like that!" The recipient of these commands is placed in a double bind: in order to obey the parent, she must disobey. The sequence also places the parent in a double bind: in order to elicit the child's respect, she utters a command which is bound to elicit a sign of disrespect. This paradox might be sustained within a broader set of contextual relations in which the parent feels unsure about the legitimacy of her authority, and/or insecure about her ability to discipline her child. One source of

Figure 1
A strange loop in the form of a pragmatic paradox

1. Parent's Contextual Patterning

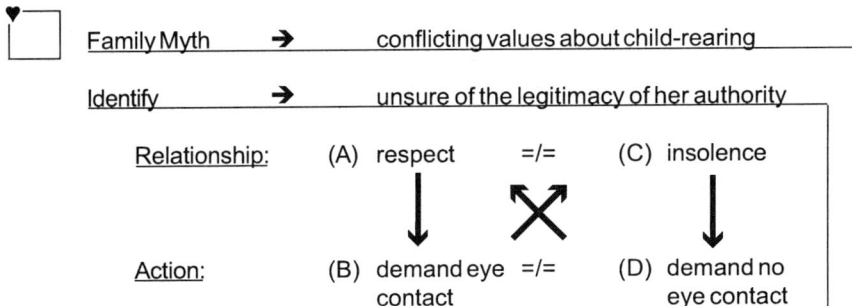

2. Child's Contextual Patterning

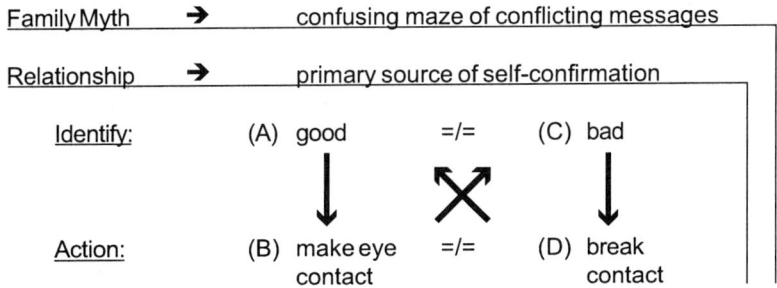

Key:

——————————— means "in the context of"

——————————— means "stable hierarchy"

♥☐ means "charmed loop"

→ means "entailment"

=/= means "mutually exclusive alternatives"

this insecurity may be related to role conflicts and arguments about "proper child-rearing" that the mother is having with the child's father or grandmother.

One way of representing these contextual patterns is through drafting diagrams like those in *Figure 1*. The first diagram, which represents the strange loop as experienced by the *parent*, is to be read as follows: "In the reciprocal causal contexts (charmed loop) of family conflict and a parent unsure of her authority, (A) a parent-child relationship characterized by respect is desirable, but elusive. As a means of creating the desired context, (B) the parent demands that the child make eye contact with her. The demand is met by the child, but the parent's fundamental sense of insecurity is only aggravated, and (C) the eye contact is therefore interpreted as a sign of insolence. (D) In this context, the parent demands that the child look away in order to show proper respect. This, too, is unsatisfactory, in part because the kind of respect that is most worth having cannot be coerced.

The second diagram, which represents the strange loop as it might be experienced by the child, is to be read as follows: "In the context of a confusing maze of conflicting messages from family members, the child's relationship with *this* parent counts as relatively stable, and thus a particularly important source of self-confirmation. In these contexts, (A) a confirmation of self as "good" is desirable, but elusive. As a means of creating the desired context, (B) the child obeys the parent's command to make eye contact. This angers the parent, which must mean the child is being "bad." The parent reverses the command, and the child, still hungry for approval, obeys. Of course, this interaction elaborates the contextual system that is already in place: the child's confusion about what kind of behavior is acceptable in this family, her dependence upon her mother to show her support in the midst of this confusion, and her fundamental insecurity about whether or not she can be a "good" girl.

The contextual layers outlined in *Figure 1* are *not* to be read as the cognitive operations of individual minds. Neither are they simple readings of public meanings. They are instead interpretations of the ways in which socially constructed meanings are being experienced at particular locations in space/time.

Conclusion

To conclude this essay, I wish to recapitulate the basic argument by revisiting the three questions with which we began:

What shall count as "context" in our investigations of human communication?

In CMM theory, contexts are sets of systemic relations composed of persons, meanings and actions. Contexts are not "found things"; they are continually evolving interpretive achievements. These temporary and shifting patterns of socially constructed meanings-in-action are subject to constraints of person, time and place. Finally, researchers do not "observe" contexts; they offer interpretations which are in effect expansions of contextual systems.

How shall we investigate the relationship between context and communicative action?

In this chapter I have proposed a three-step process of investigation compatible with CMM theory. First, the investigator should use the CMM concept of *levels of meaning* to tease out each person's construction of episodes, relationships, and identities (in all cases); as well as family myths, organizational stories, and cultural patterns (in some cases). In the study in which I made use of this method, I modeled these levels of meaning as narratives: cogent stories summarizing actors' sense of their parts in the unfolding nature of events.

The second step of this investigative method involves inferring *rules* that connect narratives to each other, and to the actors' sense of requirements for action. Constitutive rules (meaning rules) are used to reconstruct connections between levels of meaning, while regulative rules (action rules) are used to model links between meaning and action.

The third step of the method requires the analyst to explore the *reflexive reconstitution of actors' meanings* in specific moments of interaction. CMM models possible relationships between layers of meaning and action in terms of charmed loops, stable hierarchies, subversive loops and strange loops.

For what purposes are we pursuing the investigation?

People who work with CMM in order to study communication contexts are usually interested in two things. The first interest is to create a sophisticated interpretation of the constraints and possibilities inherent in particular instances of situated interaction. The second interest is to help people improve their lives. Elsewhere I have defined oppressive communication as a pattern of contextual relations that degrades, disables or deprives the people who co-create it. Empowering communication consists of a pattern of meanings-in-action that ennoble, ennable or enrich the participants (Shailor, 1993). CMM theorists are committed to exploring the ways in which we create empowering contexts, and transform oppressive ones.

References

Becker, C., Chasin, L., Chasin, R., Herzig, M., & Roth S. (1995). From stuck debate to new conversation on controversial issues: A report from the Public Conversations Project. In K. Weingarten (Ed.), *Cultural resistance: Challenging beliefs about men, women, and therapy* (pp. 143-163). Binghamton, NY: Hayworth Press.

Bohannon, L. (1984). Shakespeare in the bush. In E. Angeloni (Ed.), *Annual Editions: Anthropology 84/85* (pp. 62-66). Guilford, CT: Dushkin Publishing Group.

Branham, R. J., & Pearce, W. B. (1985). Between text and context: Toward a rhetoric of contextual reconstruction. *Quarterly Journal of Speech 71:* 19-36.

Chasin, L., Chasin, R., Herzig, M., Roth, S., & Becker, C. (1991). The citizen clinician: The family therapist in the public forum. *American Family Therapy Association Newsletter*, Winter, 36-42.

Cronen, V. E. (1995). Coordinated management of meaning: The consequentiality of communication and the recapturing of experience. In S. J. Sigman (Ed.), *The consequentiality of communication* (pp. 17-65). Hillsdale, NJ: Lawrence Earlbaum Associates, Inc.

Cronen, V. E., Chen, V., & Pearce, W. B. (1988). Coordinated Management of Meaning: A critical theory. In Y. Y. Kim & W. Gudykundst (Eds.), *International intercultural annual: Vol. 12. Theories of intercultural communication* (pp. 66-98). Beverly Hills, CA: Sage.

Cronen, V. E., Johnson, K. M., & Lannamann, J. W. (1982). Paradoxes, double binds, and reflexive loops: An alternative theoretical perspective. *Family Process 21:* 91-112.

Cronen, V. E., Pearce, W. B., & Harris, L. M. (1982). The coordinated management of meaning: *A theory of communication*. In F. E. X. Dance (Ed.), Human communication theory (pp. 61-89). New York: Harper & Row.

Giorgi, A. (1990). Phenomenology, psychology and common sense. In G. R. Semin & K. J. Gergen (Eds.), *Everyday understanding: Social and scientific implications* (pp. 64-82). Newbury Park, CA: Sage.

Husserl, E. (1962). *Ideas: General introduction to pure phenomenology* (W. R. Boyce Gibson, Trans.) New York: Collier Books.

Husserl, E. (1965). *Phenomenology and the crisis of philosophy*. (Q. Lauer, Trans.). New York: Harper and Row.

Norman, M. (1983). *'Night, mother*. New York: Hill and Wang.

Pearce, W. B. (1989). *Communication and the human condition*. Carbondale, IL: Southern Illinois University Press.

Pearce, W. B. (1992). *Interpersonal communication: Making social worlds*. New York: HarperCollins.

Pearce, W. B., & Cronen, V. E. (1980). *Communication, action and meaning: The creation of social realities*. New York: Praeger.

Roth, S., Chasin, L., Chasin, R., Becker, C., & Herzig, M. (1992). From debate to dialogue: A facilitating role for family therapists in the public forum. *Dulwich Centre Newsletter, No. 2*, 41-48.

Shailor, J. G. (1994). *Empowerment in dispute mediation: A critical analysis of communication*. Westport, CT: Praeger.

Shailor, J. G. (1993, June). Embodied practices, engaged researchers, empowering research. Paper resented at the conference on Inquiries in Social Construction, Durham, NH.

Terkel, S. (1992). *Race: How blacks and whites think and feel about the American obsession*. New York: The New Press.

Chapter 6

Theories of Culture, Communication and Context

Bradford 'J' Hall
University of New Mexico

Recently (Hall, 1992), I examined the assumptions of three prominent theoretical perspectives in regards to culture and communication. In addition, I explored how these assumptions would inform and direct research on the process of acculturation. In this chapter, I build upon that earlier work by explicitly considering the nature and role of context within each of the three theoretical perspectives.

The three perspectives to be discussed include: traditional, coordinated management of meaning (CMM), and the ethnography of communication. The term traditional refers to a variety of social scientific perspectives that, though distinct in specific directions and concerns, are internally consistent enough in basic assumptions to be considered one perspective. Although each of the above perspectives draws on work outside of the communication discipline, in order to better focus the comparative discussion desired for this chapter, these perspectives will be discussed largely in terms of how they are manifested in the work of communication scholars.

Before explicitly discussing the concept of context, I will briefly review some of the primary and distinctive assumptions of each perspective in regards to culture, communication and their general research goals. This review is meant to assist the reader in understanding the different visions of context that will be discussed later. However, the reader should remember that, as with any brief review of a theoretical perspective, a variety of nuances will not be completely identified and discussed and the interested reader is encouraged not only to consult the earlier review noted above, but also the many original sources noted throughout this chapter.

Following this review, a general discussion of how context is understood and treated in each of these perspectives will be given. Finally, a specific communication behavior, ingratiation, will be used as a focal point for understanding how the perspective specific notions of context discussed would be used to understand communication behavior in general.

Traditional Perspective

The traditional or social scientific perspective is modeled after work in the natural sciences and is directed toward predicting causal relationships among variables. Culture is the key independent variable in this approach. Gudykunst and Ting-Toomey (1988) define culture as "a script or a schema shared by a large group of people" (p. 30).

Two aspects of the above definition reflect fundamental aspects of the way culture is conceived in the traditional perspective, the notions of script and group. Culture is viewed as a type of script for life made up of values, beliefs, attitudes, and the multitude of other nonbiological parts of human existence (Klopf, 1991). Ultimately, however, culture is operationalized and treated as essentially shared group membership. If two people from one ethnic group are found to have differing values, they are still considered to be members of the same culture, whereas shared values, but differing group membership would justify classifying them as belonging to two different cultures. Certainly, a shared value, meaning, act, and so forth, is seen as an element of culture, however these component parts are subservient to shared group membership. It is generally taken for granted that those who share a group membership are members of the same culture. It is assumed that different group membership necessitates a different life script and, therefore, what is important in deciding if two people share a particular culture is not their beliefs about how the world works, but their recognized membership in a racial, ethnic, national, etc., group. Thus the term "international communication" is often used within this perspective synonymously with intercultural communication. Indeed, Gudykunst (1986) argues that intercultural communication can be seen as one kind of intergroup communication.

The script aspect of the traditional conceptualization of culture plays a more important role when the relationship between culture and communication is being explained. Culture is treated as an internalized script or guide which functions as an independent variable, causing group members to generally act or communicate in certain ways.

Communication within the traditional perspective has generally been viewed as "an intentional, transactional, symbolic process" (Gudykunst & Ting-Toomey, 1988, p. 20). However, the notion of intentionality is not a settled one, as can be seen in a recent change in work by Porter and Samovar (1988; Samovar & Porter, 1995). In their 1988 definition of culture, Porter and Samovar define communication as "intentionally" coded, whereas in their 1995 definition they note the concern over intentionality and then drop it from their definition in order to allow communication to take into account the inadvertent sending of messages, such as an American showing the sole of his or her foot to a Saudi without even realizing that such an action is meaningful.

However, regardless of the angle taken on intentionality, the communication process within the traditional perspective is basically seen as a stimulus/response model. The stimulus is the message encoded by a sender through some channel to a receiver which is then decoded (the response) and generally results in some feedback. Samovar and Porter (1995) note that in communication "the message, a representation of the internal state, must pass from one individual to another" (p.

29). Although the notion of a message necessarily being the representation of an internal state again seems to imply the existence of source intentionality in communication, the more important aspect for our understanding is that communication is taken to be effective in the traditional perspective when the decoder accurately understands the internal state of the encoder (Gudykunst & Kim, 1984). Thus, any communication may be viewed as having a correct meaning, the internal mental state of the encoder.

The research goals of the traditional perspective follow a three step path, prediction, control and effectiveness. Prediction is desirable mainly because it affords for greater control and thus greater effectiveness. For example, a researcher might study culture and non-verbal styles in order to make a causal link between the culture and a particular non-verbal style or behavior. Based on this information, one might be able to predict problem areas that a 'stranger' might encounter when interacting with host nationals, and thereby take steps to help alleviate (control) these problems, thus improving the effectiveness of the encounter.

The fundamental question dictating the work of the traditional perspective in regards to human action is "why?" It is assumed that if one really knows *why* a person acted a certain way and if part of that reason is related to their group membership, then the actions of not only that person, but all group members can be generally predicted, thus allowing for greater effectiveness and control of intercultural encounters.

Coordinated Management of Meaning (CMM) Perspective

The Coordinated Management of Meaning, or CMM perspective views both culture and communication in radically different ways than those noted within the traditional perspective. The CMM perspective takes its lead from the seminal work of Pearce and Cronen (1980) and is a perspective explicitly and inherently concerned with issues relevant to intercultural communication as it seeks a multicultural input in order to find a culturally independent way of understanding the communication process (comparing the incommensurate).

Culture from the CMM perspective emphasizes the ongoing lived experience of its members, with culture constantly being recreated through the interaction of its members. Cronen, Chen, and Pearce (1988) maintain that cultures are both coevolving and polyphonic. In other words, culture (or social reality) is an ongoing creation of the everyday activities of its members and, though generally shared, contains diverse, but harmonious, expressions of lived experience. Culture within the CMM perspective is a school of thought or philosophical orientation (Pearce, Stanback, & Kang, 1984; Pearce & Cronen, 1980) which constitutes a socially constructed world (Pearce & Kang, 1988). Pearce and Kang note that culture is used in a synonymous manner with the idea of social reality or a given set of beliefs about how the world operates, and that cultures are given substance through communication.

In contrast to the traditional perspective, culture is not one of many variables in a system, but is *the* overriding social system or reality encompassing all systems of a social nature. From this perspective, culture becomes a viable topic on its own, rather than just a variable among many used to explain some other phenomenon. Indeed, culture is not a means for organizing and interpreting some world out there, but is the taken-for-granted organization and interpretation which *is* our social world. Culture is the emic grammar in which we punctuate our actions and interactions as humans. Emic, rather than etic, in that the grammar is not some underlying truth of the social world that exists separate from persons' communicative practices, but a very local creation of those practices.

Even though in the CMM perspective culture is all pervasive (being synonymous with social reality), it is not some powerful transcendent force separate from single individuals. Persons, not cultures, are posited as the only powerful and enduring entities (Pearce & Cronen, 1980). The CMM perspective is immanentist in nature and views culture as residing in the heads of individuals and constantly being recreated in the daily activities of those individuals (Cronen et al., 1988). In this sense, every communication encounter is to some extent intercultural (Pearce et al., 1984).

Pearce and Cronen (1980) maintain that communication is the process by which persons co-create and co-manage social reality. Communication, then, is an omni-potent source of all that is social. One cannot choose whether or not to communicate, rather communication is inherent in being "human" (Pearce & Kang, 1988). Pearce and Kang further elaborate by saying that communication "is the generic term for the processes of interpreting one's own and others' actions, and for performing actions that will be interpreted" (p. 25). Communication, therefore, is action versus a tool or vehicle for action. Meanings can best be said to be made in particular communication encounters.

Communication is not morally vacuous or completely relative, rather it is accountable and open to critique based on its paramount role as liberator (Cronen et al., 1988). The ultimate good or ultimate function of communication is to allow for the freedom of creatively extending seminal ideas and for the freedom of going beyond old ideas to new ones. Of course, communication can not only liberate, but can also bind or imprison. It is how communication functions in regards to these two opposite processes that provides the major basis for critique in the CMM perspective. Indeed, "efforts opposed to the intrinsically liberating character of communication strike at the heart of what it means to be human" (Cronen et al., p. 93). Thus, the notion of communication as liberator allows for a meaningful critique of incommensurable social realities.

The CMM perspective takes as its major goals interpretation and critique (Cronen et al., 1988). The goal of interpretation tends to take as its focus the production of particular episodes, both in terms of the rules used for producing and understanding them and their negotiated, reflexive features. But it is the goal of critique that plays the subsuming role for CMM. Cronen et al. maintain that critique aimed at enhancing human life is a fundamental responsibility of any social science and that one's guiding principles for critique should be the same as for interpretation.

Thus, the underlying question driving the CMM perspective in regards to human action is "how?" It is assumed that if one really knows *how* people get on in life in particular cases, that people will be liberated from cycles of communication that are dysfunctional or undesirable.

Ethnography of Communication

The ethnographic perspective described in this chapter is one that has grown out of work by Hymes (1962), Geertz (1973), and Philipsen (1992) and explicitly seeks to discover and describe the communicative particularities of a cultural community. The ethnographic perspective has tended to focus on culture as a system of meanings and ideals. Philipsen (1989) has defined culture as "a historically transmitted system of symbols, meanings, premises, routines, and rules..." (p. 260). Unlike the traditional perspective that would see a given "act" and its attendant meaning(s) as culture or the CMM view that culture is the individual's social reality, culture in the ethnographic perspective is the intersubjective resources available for generating a given meaning or meanings from an observed act. This system of resources operates at the level of "common sense" and enables members to act, feel and think in collectively appropriate ways.

Group labels may be used in the ethnographic perspective, but these are in reference to communities that have been or are being studied in regard to their shared codes. The focus is not on the "individual qua group" or even the group per se, but on discovering a system of symbols and meanings which in part constitutes the group as a distinctive cultural entity. Group membership is not the basis of culture, rather culture is the foundation for group membership.

Culture provides the person with a sense of place in one's social world. This sense of place is invoked and constituted through community specific ways of speaking, thus facilitating a sense of shared meaning and a coordination of action among members (Philipsen, 1989). In addition, cultural changes are not new, independent creations, but are transformations linked to and intelligible with the past. In learning of a person's culture, the researcher is learning what it means to think, feel, and act as particular types of persons (Basso, 1990).

Within the ethnographic perspective, culture is not viewed as the property of an individual, nor one group of individuals set in time; rather, culture transcends individuals both in time and space and is, therefore, not reducible to single individuals (Philipsen, 1987). Culture exists by convention and, though dynamic in nature, it is not fully dependent on a particular individual or set of individuals. Thus, culture resides not in the heads of individuals as understood by the CMM perspective, but between people. It has an intersubjective reality.

Carbaugh (1990) reasons that "communication is the primary and situated social process of meaning-making, which occurs in particular forms and yields multiple outcomes" (p. 19). Communication is, therefore, posited in a similar manner in ethnographic research as in that of CMM. It is viewed as necessarily constitutive of that which is meaningful in the world, be that persons, relationships, institutions, and so forth. However, communication is not sufficiently so, such that communication by itself without reference to the intersubjective realities of setting, positioning, etc., cannot change the social world.

One highlighted function of communication within the ethnographic perspective is that of the communal function or in other words to provide a means whereby individuals experience a subjective sense of shared identity or community membership (Philipsen, 1989; Hall 1988/89). Every meaningful communicative act can be seen in terms of what it includes and what it excludes. This process of inclusion and exclusion exists at a very micro, intra-community level as well as at a more macro, inter-community level.

Philipsen (1989) maintains that to communicate is to "produce messages so as to create an intended meaning" (p. 258). Indeed, any communicative *act* versus behavior is an act with intent in light of the social situation (Philipsen, 1987). This type of intention is more of a social than a personal possession in that it depends less on the so-called sender of a message than on the receiver and it resides less in the internal workings of an individual mind than in the social conventions of a community. Thus, a behavior that is recognizable within a given community as meaningful and oriented to as purposeful in regards to that meaning, regardless of what is going on inside the sender's head, can rightly be referred to as intentional.

The driving forces behind the bulk of ethnographic research are the goals of description and explanation (Philipsen, 1989). Philipsen explains that ethnography is concerned with developing a "theory of description." In juxtaposition to the traditional approach, which would only see description as a forerunner to theory making, ethnographers strive to develop an ever finer framework for discovering the distinctive communication patterns of any particular community. The descriptive framework also provides a means for intelligible comparison and conversation between communities marked by different ways of speaking by establishing comparison points with universal significance (though these comparison points have an inherently open texture in light of each new community studied). These comparison points along with universal theses regarding communicative conduct provide a backdrop for delineating the nature and scope of cultural variation in communicative conduct.

The overarching question of work done within the ethnography of communication perspective is that of "what?" What is it that people are doing from their own perspective and what is the system of meaning that people use in producing and interpreting what they are doing? In answering such questions, we can better understand *what* it means to be a member of a particular community and better deal with the consequences that arise from membership in a world saturated by membership.

I will now overview how each of these three perspectives would define context and give an exemplar of each. Then I will take a communication behavior and try to explain how context would play a different role in the study of this behavior from the three perspectives.

Context

Traditional Perspective

Context from the traditional perspective refers to the situation in which the communicators find themselves. Over recent years the complexity with which this situation is described has increased (Gallois, Giles, Jones, Cargile, & Ota, 1995). This move is reflected not only in explicit theories, but in textbooks. For example, Samovar, Porter and Jain's 1981 text implies the importance of situation, but does not deal directly with "context" or have it in their index. Later texts by Samovar and Porter (1991, 1995) move from describing context as setting and environment to identifying and elaborating on four elements that they maintain make up the context: place, occasion, time, and number of participants. This increasing recognition of the importance of context and efforts to incorporate it can be seen throughout work within the traditional perspective.

Regardless of the level of complexity with which the context or situation is depicted within the traditional perspective, it inevitably functions as an independent variable triggering certain actions, attributions, and so forth. Sometimes this causal role is explicitly positioned as an independent variable. At other times, it is just assumed. An example of both of these approaches may be seen in Gudykunst and Nishida's (1984) examination of individual and cultural differences on uncertainty reduction. Specifically, they generate hypotheses about how attitude similarity, culture (operationalized as nationality), culture similarity and self-monitoring as independent variables would influence such dependent variables as attributional confidence, attraction, and non-verbal expressives in initial interactions. Each hypothesis ends with the tag "in initial interactions." Initial interactions thus become the context or general situation with which all respondents are presented, based on the assumption that having this context noted in the questionnaires will influence the respondents' answers in predictable and comparable ways.

In its most simplistic form within the traditional perspective, context in this research would only be "initial interactions." For example, there is no discussion in the Gudykunst and Nishida (1984) study as to where this interaction takes place, when it takes place, the number of people involved or their social roles, or if the person would expect to have an ongoing relationship with the person they are being introduced to and so forth. It is considered a safe assumption that with random selection people will make assumptions about those things and others that would balance the responses out.

A somewhat more complex and systematic view would posit the context as not only consisting of "initial interactions," but also each of the independent variables. Thus, when a respondent is asked how they would behave when introduced to a stranger from another country who has been introduced as having similar attitudes, it adds the independent variables as part of the causal context. This type of a perspective was recently illustrated in some theoretical work by Gallois et al. (1995). These authors explicitly note the importance of context and argue that they take it more into account than most theories. Their theory is intended to deal with both a sociostructural context and an immediate social context. For example, their lead in and articulation of their fourth proposition is as follows:

> Contextual factors, including important cultural values are important to social and personal identity:
>
> Proposition 4: Many members of collectivistic cultures are more likely to show higher dependence on their ingroup and its sociolinguistic markers than members of individualistic cultures (p. 140).

In a later effort to include immediate situation into their theory, they present their proposition 9, "In formal and status-stressing situations, many speakers are likely to converge to the sociolinguistic markers and behaviors of the dominant group (p.142)." Gallois et al. (1995) also soften the hard causal sense found in many traditional perspectives through the use of "many members" or "many speakers." However, with either the Gudykunst and Nishida (1984) or Gallois et al. examples many of the questions about the context noted earlier are still left open and, thus treated as inconsequential for the current research goals. Efforts to more fully take into account contextual concerns through this "context as independent variable" approach tend to have one of two outcomes. One is that the propositions, axioms, etc., become very layered with dependent possibilities such as Gallois et al.'s proposition 15B:

> When recipients perceive their interlocutors' behavior to be counterattuned (divergent) or badly attuned, in terms of their own or their group's perceived or stereotyped communication style, or when they perceive it to depart from a valued communication norm, especially when they attribute to their interlocutor high effort, high choice, and malevolent intent, recipients are likely to evaluate their interlocutors' behavior negatively (as hostile, unattractive, and so forth) (p. 146).

A second outcome is that the number of propositions or axioms begins to explode in order to try to cover all the many possibilities such as one finds in Gudykunst's (1995) formulation of Anxiety/Uncertainty Management Theory which has 94 axioms. These two outcomes are inherent in an approach which seeks to isolate the causal impact of various contextual features.

In summary, the main messages in regards to context from the traditional perspective are: one, context functions solely as an independent variable; two, context may be broken down into various, largely independent parts that may be analyzed for effect in isolation from other parts of the context; and three, contextually determined actions can be understood out-of-context via such devices as the manipulation of hypothetical questions ("If you met a stranger from Japan, how would you act?") in surveys.

Coordinated Management of Meaning (CMM) Perspective

From the CMM perspective context is the specific formulation of culture as it pertains to ongoing communicative acts. All communicative acts or series of acts are performed within a set of expectations and constraints that may be viewed as culture or social reality. The specific set of expectations and constraints which exists at any one time may properly be referred to as the context (Branham & Pearce, 1985).

The relationship between communication and context is one of reflexivity. Contexts provide the interpretive frame through which behavior is made meaningful and communication is made possible. However, at the same time communication both creates and sustains the given context. In this sense contexts are not seen as objective properties of a situation, such as those proposed by Samovar and Porter (1995), open to observation by a well placed camera, but rather are internalized beliefs/understandings of the way the world works that are relevant in specific encounters. Thus, contexts are always peculiar to specific social encounters and may be seen as essentially a set of beliefs which change and are changed by the encounter.

These beliefs are hierarchically organized into various levels of abstraction (Cronen, Pearce, & Tomm, 1985; Cronen et al., 1988). Although the exact labeling and content of these levels may vary from study to study, there are typically five key levels that are considered in CMM research.

The first level, often referred to as the speech acts level, deals with the specific messages seen as possible in this encounter, such as praise, threat, or rejection. The second level is episodes. Episodes refer to patterns of actions which are perceived as meaningful to the participants in the interaction, such as, going on a date, visiting mom and dad, or negotiating a business deal. The third level deals with the perceived nature of the relationship of the focus person to other relevant individuals. For example, a person may see the relationship as one of victim/aggressor, advisor/advisee, or co-adventurers on a journey. This level may be divided into many other levels with each of these levels referencing a different, but particular relationship as perceived by the interactants. A fourth level may be termed autobiographical or life scripting. This level has to do with one's beliefs about one's own course or place in life. For example, a person may see him or herself as a hard worker, a sacrificing parent or a good joke teller. Finally, a fifth level deals with larger group (family, community, ethnic, national, etc.) conceptions of how the world does and should work. For example, what constitutes an ideal family, how people build trust, or why the government works the way it does. Each of these levels of belief or context may serve as a lens through which the other is understood. Therefore, my belief about what episode we are involved in may inform the way I see our relationship, or my beliefs about the nature of employees may guide the way I see myself within a particular organization and the way I see myself may influence the range of speech acts I see as possible. Context is thus a set of embedded beliefs with each having the possibility of framing the way another level of beliefs is perceived.

These contexts/beliefs may be seen as producing one of three possible patterns of human interaction (Branham & Pearce, 1985). These patterns are called loops and constitute three primary patterns of interaction: charmed, subversive and strange. The charmed loop gives the impression of being the most stable. In charmed loops, each of the levels of context work together in such a way that the appropriateness of each level is supported by the other levels. Thus, on many American television shows such as *Perry Mason*, we see society's system of law as encouraging justice and fair play. This view empowers the lawyer to seek the truth and to fight for its establishment in court. Such empowerment creates an expectation for the lawyer to engage in episodes which may otherwise have been beyond the call of duty for a lawyer (such as detective work on who the real killer is) and later in the court room to be aggressive in dealing with those who seek to hide the truth. This view also explains the losing lawyer's sense of gratitude to Perry Mason when he wins the case and reveals who is truly guilty. In other sorts of disputes, the loser would not be expected to display gratitude. This cycle reinforces a sense that all is right in the world, authorities are doing good and discontents are speaking nonsense.

The second pattern is the subversive loop. It is perhaps the least explained of the three loops and not surprisingly so as it refers to actions which are not perceived as appropriately understood by any context. Thus, the judge knowingly releases the guilty criminal, yet the judge is perceived as good and fair, or the criminal who is known to hate police officers helps one pick up some spilt papers with no hidden agenda. In short, one is left without an explanation because whichever direction one turns the explanation is denied, thus resulting in the ineffable. Explaining this loop is difficult because it explicitly denies the ability of any context to account for the communicative behavior. The idea here is a recognition that there are things which may be experienced, but not expressed.

The third pattern, or strange loop, is one of seeming paradox. These loops start out one direction, but by following the pattern of reasoning established at the start, the original meaning is reversed. This sort of loop may be found in the bumper sticker "Question Authority." If I follow the direction given by the sign and question authority, I may in turn be led to question the right to question authority as authorized by the sticker. This questioning of the question authority admonition may result in me being obedient to authority, which in turn legitimizes the advice on the sticker which advises me to question authority again and the whole process starts over. A frequently used example in the CMM literature is of a person who says, "I am drunk, so I cannot drink." Then after not drinking, they say I don't drink so I'm not a drunk so it is okay if I drink. Then after drinking they again come to the conclusion that they are a drunk and so they cannot drink and so on.

An excellent example of the use of context from the CMM perspective is found in the Cronen et al. (1985) case study of a family involved in a therapy program. In this case the parents shared a certain understanding (or context) of the way the world worked. This "family myth" constituted the fifth or most abstract level of context described above. In short, this context or belief was that the world is made up of worthy and worthless individuals and that one established one's worth by being right. Thus, the primary goal in life was to be right. Attendant to this idea was the belief/context that all differences in opinion inherently implied a judgment that one of the ideas was more right. There was no notion of differing ideas both being right in their own way. This family myth provided a frame for interpreting the life-scripting level, such that if there was a disagreement, the self was either worthy or worthless, depending on how much more right he or she was than the other. At the relationship level of context, there was the belief that a spouse must be a worthy person in order to be a worthy spouse and that a person who destroys the worth of his/her spouse is worthless. At the episode level there was the belief that differing ideas immediately initiate a test of who is right, and that acting upon the other person's ideas is a concession that one is wrong and, therefore, worthless. These levels resulted in beliefs at the speech act level which dictated that a person must attack any differing idea in order to be worthy, yet if a spouse is about to concede, then s/he must end the episode or else be shown to be worthless for having destroyed the worth of the spouse.

This context resulted in a strange loop which involved a frequent cycle of conflict that would go something like the following. The husband and wife would disagree strongly, the husband would take a more and more forceful position until the wife would be about to concede. Instead of conceding, though, she would begin to cry which signaled to the husband that she couldn't take it any more so he (with her agreement) would terminate the disagreement episode without ever having made a decision. The therapist's first take was that the crying was a sign of weakness, and, therefore, taught her to be more assertive. This, however, only confounded the problems.

The resolution to this problem was enacted when the therapist realized what was happening and created a strange loop pattern that legitimized a new way of framing their interaction (or context). In brief, the therapist identified the nature of the above cycle of conflict and warned against trying to change it as it worked so well (a decision was made, but no one had to be worthless). This created a problem for the couple as it showed that their way of perceiving the world was wrong, as it didn't allow for a decision of who was right or wrong to be made. At the same time it emphasized how necessary such a decision was. This, of course, made them wrong (worthless) and the therapist right (worthy). Over the coming weeks, the couple ignored the therapist's advice to leave the pattern unchanged, and working on their own, attacked the therapist's perspective. In so doing, they created alternative ways of determining who was right (and worthy) that involved knowing when to empower others. A key trigger in this process was changing which level of context was allowed to frame other levels. When their speech act level of context was made primary (impossible to have one person be right as neither could concede without destroying the worth of the other), the assumptions of the family myth (always one person right) fell apart and had to be restructured, which eventually changed the entire context. Cronen et al. (1985) argue that this is an example of how context and communication behaviors enjoy a reflexive relationship, with each changing and being changed by the other.

Ethnography of Communication

The ethnography of communication explicitly recognizes that all meaningful acts are situated within a context (Carbaugh, 1990). Meaning can never be separated from context. The context may be implicit, but if there is meaning, there is a context. At its most fundamental level, this context would best be understood as a system of communication by which meaning is generated and understood within a group (Caroll, 1988).

Work by Katriel and Philipsen (1981) on understanding the meaning of named, recurring types of communicative activities illustrates how the illumination of context is inescapably part of the ethnography of communication's approach to understanding. Katriel and Philipsen attend to what may be viewed as two interwoven types of context, discursive and social. The discursive context refers to the specific system of symbols which allows for the meaningful interpretation of a social activity. The social context refers to broader, conventionally understood categories, such as types of people, episodes, settings, and so forth, that are necessary and sufficient to account for meaningful interaction within a particular community.

The discursive context maps out the symbolic domain of any communicative activity. It does this through the systematic search for paradigmatic and syntagmatic relationships between natively named activities and other natively perceived concepts/categories. These relationships form patterns of co-occurrence and alternation that allow group members to share meaning and coordinate actions in a world that would otherwise be chaotic nonsense. For example, Katriel and Philipsen (1981) look at the symbolic domain or patterns which bring sense to the term "communication" in at least some American communities. They find that communication is associated with such symbols as "working," "relationships," and "growth." Thus, it is sensible to talk about *working* on your *relationships* through *communication* or attributing the lack of *growth* in a relationship to the lack of *communication*. Other ideas were shown to be culturally nonsensical. Thus, one does not encourage the growth of a relationship by *playing* at communication, nor does one hear that a relationship *died* because of too much communication.

This may all sound like common sense, and it should if you are communicatively competent within the community being referenced. If it wasn't *common sense*, it wouldn't allow members to share meaning and coordinate action. This point is often clearer when one is not a member of the community being studied. For example, Basso (1990) posits several comments which are simply common sense to the western Apache, such as, "The land is always stalking people. The land makes people live right" (p. 100). A nonmember may easily be perplexed by such a comment. However, Basso goes on to elaborate a system of communication which accounts for such comments and to talk about how his work was used in court cases to help others understand one Native American perspective on the land. Readers unfamiliar with the western Apache community generally see how this information is both useful and interesting, often failing to see that it too is just simply "common sense." It just happens to be the common sense of a different community from their own. This common sense is, of course, just one particular formulation of context. Chances are that it was Katriel's Israeli background that helped her to hear the cultural nature of the use of "communication" in everyday life in the United States. For, although small talk may be a very recognized form of communication, when one has to work on her or his relationship, culturally it does not make sense to say, "What you need is more small talk."

The social context refers to all the socially accessible knowledge relevant to understanding the communication activity under consideration. Typically, ethnographies use etic analytical frameworks to guide their discovery of the social context (see Carbaugh & Hastings, 1992; Fitch, 1991; Spradley, 1979). Perhaps the most well known of these is Hymes' (1972) SPEAKING framework. It is, however, not the only one and I do not mean to imply by reviewing it that no other aspects of context may be studied. Still the Hymes framework does show the type of things typically considered in analyzing the social context from an ethnographic perspective. A brief overview of Hymes SPEAKING framework follows. *Setting* includes both physical and psychological elements. *Participants* refers to the types of social actors involved from the perspective of the community members. *Ends* points toward the social activity accomplished (or what is perceived to be potentially accomplished) in doing such an activity. *Act* substance refers to the content of what is conveyed in the activity and act sequence refers to any significant ordering of that content. *Key* or tone encourages the researcher to look at the appropriate moods or emotions associated with the activity in question. *Instrumentality* refers to the mode of delivery or channels through which people may participate in the activity. *Norms* of interpretation and production reference the socially appropriate connections between the other components noted above. Therefore, given certain types of participants, should there be certain types of behaviors? Or should certain types of ends only be pursued in certain types of settings? Finally, *Genre* refers to the nature of the activity and the episode of which it may be part. Remember the key from the ethnography of communication viewpoint is the adequacy with which the framework allows for an account of the production and interpretation of meaning that resonates with the community in question.

Katriel and Philipsen (1981), use aspects of the above framework to help make explicit the cultural assumptions surrounding a particular way of using the term communication and the nature of the social world created by its use. In doing so, they demonstrate how "communication" is a ritualistic process that involves the correct ordering of certain communicative steps, the violation of which may justify the claim that there has been a communication breakdown or a lack of communication. They also help to explain and demonstrate how the use of the term communication influences the context. For example, if I comment in this community that a particular couple needs to start communicating, another person may immediately assume that the couple is having a relationship problem.

The recognition that communication and context change each other is common to both the CMM and ethnography of communication perspectives.

However, there are some subtle differences in the way this change is framed. The CMM perspective posits communication and context as mutually dependent (Cronen & Shuter, 1983; Pearce et al., 1984), whereas the ethnography of communication posits this relationship as interdependent (Philipsen, 1989). The CMM perspective subtly underscores a causal nature to the relationship, which emphasizes the way people are bound by communication and context, thus leading to the goal of liberation. The ethnography of communication perspective assumes a simultaneously constraining and enabling nature to the relationship which emphasizes choice and communal consequences, thus leading to a goal of understanding shared meaning. Given the necessary connection between context and meaning noted earlier, the entire ethnography of communication endeavor may thus be seen as a quest for context.

One final point in regards to context and intercultural communication as viewed from the ethnographic position is articulated in detail by Katriel (1995). She notes that intercultural communication should be seen as involving context*s*, rather than *an* "intercultural context." This focus on multiple contexts is grounded in the idea noted above that a context enables and constrains. When two or more interactants come from different cultural backgrounds, they each operate with different system constraints and so forth, such that an interaction is more profitably understood as actually involving two or more contexts.

Three Applications of a Single Case

In order to better compare the three perspectives on context and communication behavior, one specific type of communication behavior will be considered from all three perspectives with particular attention paid to the role context would play in understanding the communication behavior. The behavior to be considered is ingratiation. There is nothing inherently better about ingratiation than other possible communication behaviors for a comparison such as this. Any communication behavior should be just as good as any other for such a comparison, but I have recently been doing some reading on this subject and thought it would provide an interesting comparison point. Obviously what follows is not an attempt to do three actual studies of ingratiation, but an attempt to show how context would typically be considered in a study of ingratiation from the different perspectives.

Traditional

Given the broad topic of ingratiation, one might make an initial decision to limit the context based on researcher interest to a particular type of setting, such as ingratiation in a business organization or, even more specific, ingratiation during meetings marked by conflict. One of the first steps in the traditional perspective would then be to review past literature on this topic. Some of the key objectives of this review would include, establishment of a concise definition of ingratiation and its possible forms, identification of what independent variables make up the relevant context in which ingratiation is likely to occur, identification of what dependent variables are affected by the context of ingratiation, identifying a theory which may connect all these variables in a principled way, and formulating guidelines for how to best measure ingratiation and other relevant variables.

For example, Liden and Mitchell (1988) explicitly borrow a definition of ingratiation by Wortman and Linsenmeier (1977), "behaviors employed by a person to make himself more attractive to another" (p. 573). They argue for this definition over many competing ones on the basis that it is less limiting. Thus, the determination of what constitutes ingratiation is seen as objective and grounded in researcher expertise, not context. Context is only used to limit the setting and, thus, the extent of the literature review.

The next step is to identify the variety of independent variables that have been found to be positively associated with ingratiation, for example, a gregarious personality, high self-monitoring, low degree of tenure in an organization, desire to be liked, autocratic boss, one's gender, perceived risk, perceived gain, low self-esteem, attractiveness of the target, perceived power of the target, and so on. The possible variables are extensive. Then, using a general theory, such as social exchange theory (Roloff, 1981), the researcher tries to show why the variables are connected in the way they are. The theory may suggest new, as yet untested variables or it may be used to develop a specific theory of ingratiation which justifies the testing of only a few "key" variables. Regardless of these specific decisions, these variables are assumed to constitute the relevant context for the occurrence of ingratiation as defined by the researchers. Researchers may make a similar move with dependent variables. In this case, the researchers treat ingratiation as a context and try to determine what outcomes may be predicted by ingratiatory behavior.

Finally, researchers from within the traditional perspective must determine how ingratiation and the other variables are to be measured. This measurement typically implies a way to reduce the defined variable into a number that allows for statistical analysis. For example, Kumar and Beyerlein (1991) devised a questionnaire for measuring ingratiatory behaviors in organizations. They asked subjects to respond to statements such as, "Offer to help your supervisor by using your personal contacts" (p. 623) on a five point Likert type scale with one indicating the subject never does it, two, seldom does it, three, occasionally does it, four, often does it and, five, almost always does it. Again, the most explicit context in this approach is the simple setting "organizations." However, in the above question the type of help envisioned and the nature of personal contacts might make a big difference in one's response.

The questionnaires would then be administered and the researchers would see if the proposed connections between variables was rejected, partially rejected, or not rejected (supported). The reasons for the various findings would then be discussed. This means that, contrary to the CMM or ethnography of communication perspectives which only report "contexts" which they can support, the proposed context (or independent variable) may in fact be rejected as a part of the predictive context. Thus, in a particular study, one may find that the perceived power of the target is not a predictive variable of ingratiation. Typically, however, the researcher is able to come up with reasons why the data did not fully support the theory and why the theory and the contextual feature should still be preserved.

Context, then, would primarily be used as an initial boundary setter for the research. Context would be given greater detail later on through the implicit assumption that the variables which the researcher found based on a literature review or general theory of behavior constitute the relevant context. Context involves a one-way relationship with communication behaviors, which the objective researcher as an expert understands better than anyone else.

Coordinated Management of Meaning (CMM) Perspective

Although there are many differences between how the CMM perspective and the traditional perspective would approach this research task, two differences that have implications for the way context and its relationship to communication behavior are understood will be reviewed. The first stems out of the idea that context and communication are social creations which are mutually dependent on each other. This assumption makes futile the effort to treat ingratiation as some real thing, independent of communication, which can be accurately defined, objectively measured and used as an etic comparison point across communities. If ingratiatory messages are dependent on the context for their existence, yet simultaneously are part of what constitutes the context, the effort to measure ingratiation outside of that context through a questionnaire does not make sense. Further, since the nature of the context is changed by the existence of ingratiation, the idea of using context as a stable predictor of ingratiation also lacks credibility.

Second, the above points lead to a natural difference in the scope of what is being studied. The traditional perspective accepts that ingratiation is a thing out there that can be measured and which is caused in predictable ways by contexts which are easily manipulated. Such an assumption leads to studies that seek and assume a high degree of generalizability. CMM, on the other hand, tends to focus on very specific situations and encounters. Given the nature of context from the CMM perspective as explained earlier, each encounter/situation involves a unique, ongoing contextual refiguring that must be analyzed in a way open to that uniqueness. Thus, CMM proponents would be unlikely to study ingratiation as a broad concept, but would more likely conduct a detailed study of a particular encounter or set of related encounters in which the natively perceived resource of "ingratiation" is used or debated.

For purposes of example I will select a specific encounter reported by a student which she perceived as ingratiation. This student claimed that she ingratiated herself to a professor the other day while visiting with him. After responding to her initial question, the professor began talking about some of his research and she said that, although she really didn't care all that much about the research and found it rather boring, because she knew this person was on her thesis committee she smiled and nodded a lot, asking some questions and pretending to be really interested. Now that we have a specific encounter with which to deal, the first step would be to lay out the different levels of context for those involved in the interaction.

At the societal or broadest level of context the student appears to be working under three constitutive rules: one, that professors have power over students; two, that people in power often make judgments based on their impression of the person rather than on their impression of the person's work; three, people in general like to see themselves as interesting and competent and like best those who confirm that self perception. The professor, on the other hand, also appears to be working with three broad constitutive rules: one, graduate students are novices who aspire to be like their professors; two, professors have the responsibility to help graduate students achieve this goal by being a mentor; three, a mentor must lead the way, which requires that the mentor communicate to the protege what s/he has accomplished and how it was done.

These societal rules frame the next level or life-scripting level, which could contain an image for the student such as I am not really interested, but I am a smart student who knows how to avoid trouble. For the professor, this level may contain images such as I am interesting, insightful and impressive. Given the two levels above, the third or relationship level would include for the student a recognition of being largely at the mercy of the professor and a need to make the professor feel good about her and her academic interests. Whereas, for the professor the relational level would be grounded in the idea that he is more knowledgeable and experienced than this person and admired for that expertise. The next level is that of the episode, which in one sense is an informal teacher/student discussion. However, given the context identified above, this meeting seems to be perceived by the student as largely a brag session for the professor and an opportunity to show how dedicated a student she is. Whereas for the professor, it is an advice giving time, in which he is expected to demonstrate expertise and dispense wisdom on areas of mutual interest. Finally, at the speech acts level of context the student sees this as a time to engage in ingratiation, while the professor perceives this as a time to expound on his knowledge to an interested novice.

The context elaborated above creates a sort of strange loop for both interactants. The professor wants to be seen as competent and interesting, and feels that telling the student in great detail about his work is how to do this, yet the more he talks the less interesting he is seen. The student on the other hand, wants to be evaluated highly by the professor, but is not really very interested in what he has to say. She feels she must pretend to be interested, but the more she pretends to be interested, the longer she has to stay and engage in an activity with which she does not want to be involved. The more she pretends to be involved and interested in what he is saying, the greater the perceived risk in freely speaking her opinions of what he is talking about.

This constraining loop would likely be evaluated by CMM researchers in a negative light because it limits rather than liberates the communication possibilities of the interactants. Indeed, one can see how the very nature of talk seen as ingratiating creates and recreates positions of power which are often perceived as unbreakable. Liberation from such a loop would necessarily involve a reconfiguration of the context described above. Such a reconfiguration would require a change in communication patterns.

Ethnography of Communication

The ethnographic perspective is dedicated to understanding the forms and functions of communication from the perspective of particular communities. Thus, it is unlikely that a set definition of ingratiation found in scholarly literature would be viewed as sufficient for an ethnographic study. Rather, an incident within a community which highlights the importance or meaning of a concept for that community is more likely to lay the foundation for the study. For example, take the following exchange recorded by Hall and Valde (1995):

1. D: *All* these *ni*::ce letters.
2. J: What a *bun*ch of BROWN-NOSERS
3. (mutual laughter)
4. D: Hey! She's new, just *try*ing to get off to a good start (p. 391).

One of the first things to notice in this exchange is that the term ingratiation is not used. Because the ethnographic perspective is concerned with native perceptions, native terms are also used. If one is a member of the speech community in which brown-nosing is a common and/or meaningful label for a type of communication, this exchange makes ready sense. The extent to which the notion of brown-nosing fits with the academic notion of ingratiation is not typically one of primary concern from this perspective, although at times ethnographies can be used as a test of universal theses.

One difference between the ethnographic approach to this exchange and the CMM approach is that instead of being concerned with just this particular incident, ethnographers would typically be focused on the communal sense associated with this type of talk. Thus, although the reference to brown-nosing in this exchange is informative in and of itself, it is mainly of interest because of what it tells us about the way a group of people go about making sense of the world. One of the key issues, then, would be an initial understanding of the boundaries of this group or speech community. Although speech communities are in the long run determined by the sharing of rules for meaningful interaction, the exchange above indicates quite a diverse speech community. For example, the exchange was in reference to a contest which had employees of different organizations writing in to justify why their place of work deserved a party. In addition, the exchange was produced for a mass audience and the term brown-nosing was not treated as if it needed any explanation. This would seem to indicate that community would likely consist of a wide range of organizational members within that region.

The primary task of the ethnographer of communication would be to understand the native meanings and norms associated with the type of talk referenced as brown-nosing. One culturally interesting item that Hall and Valde (1995) pointed out about the above exchange was that, given the nature of the contest and other social norms within that community, it would seem expected that the letters would say nice things. However, the use of the term brown-nosers and the subsequent response to it suggests that something is not right here. In other words, being nice may in fact be perceived as not a nice thing to be. Understanding such culturally subtle nuances as when it is not nice to be nice, is grounded in community specific common senses. These common senses are the contexts from which meaning is inseparable. Thus, the ethnographer may be seen as engaged in a quest for understanding all the possible contexts in which brown-nosing has meaning.

Although there are many ways in which this may be approached from an ethnographic perspective, the pattern followed by Katriel and Philipsen (1981) and noted earlier regarding discursive and social contexts provides one useful example.

One of the first steps would be to map out the discursive context within which brown-nosing makes sense. Based on participant observation, review of member generated documents, and interviews, the ethnographer would try to find as many similar terms as possible. In this case, these may include terms like buttering up, schmoozing, sucking up or kissing ass. Part of the consideration here is to understand to what extent these terms are interchangeable. The ethnographer would also consider terms or concepts that were perceived by members as contrasting (sincerity, being straight and hard work) and co-occurring (boss, teacher, reward). By doing so, the researcher is able to identify brown-nosing in a system of meaning. This system would begin to reveal how brown-nosing is understood within the community.

A second type of context to be considered is the social context. For example, what sort of social interactions are necessarily associated with the concept of brown-nosing? Hall and Valde (1995) found that social relations were either of a competitive or remedial nature. If brown-nosing is enacted, it is perceived as a competitive move, but if it is reflected upon, there is an implied need for remediation. In order to help ensure that the researcher does not overlook important contextual features, a framework such as the one noted above by Hymes (1972) is often used. Such a framework helps to ensure that a wide range of categories is considered. In addition, it is also valuable for identifying patterns of action. For example, perhaps certain types of participants (P) are associated with certain types of settings (S) or ends (E) and so forth. Indeed, it is often the interrelationships of the component parts of a framework which prove to be most insightful. Indeed, Hall and Valde found that participants who engage in act sequences associated with brown-nosing are evaluated differently depending upon the perceived setting. As these community specific patterns of action are understood, the researcher and readers can better understand different ways of living a life and identify potential trouble spots when members of different speech communities interact with each other.

Conclusion

Context has been shown to play a distinctive role in each of the three perspectives discussed above. For the traditional perspective, it plays the role of a predictive variable which can be readily manipulated by the researcher. In the CMM perspective context is a hierarchically related set of social rules which inevitably function as a constraint on communication and, therefore, may always be critiqued and hopefully reconfigured in ways which continually allow for greater freedom of communication. Indeed, it is through communication that context is created. The ethnography of communication also recognizes context as a constraint, but focuses primarily on the possible shared meanings and coordinated actions that are made possible through the tension between what may and may not be sensibly or appropriately connected. Communication may transform the nature of the context, but it must do so in ways which are sensible with previous contextual understandings. Finally, both of these latter perspectives recognize that a given encounter may involve multiple contexts.

References

Basso, K. (1990). *Western Apache language and culture*. Tucson, AZ: University of Arizona Press.

Branham, R. J., & Pearce, W. B. (1985). Between text and context: Toward a rhetoric of contextual reconstruction. *Quarterly Journal of Speech, 71*, 19-36.

Carroll, R. (1988). *Cultural misunderstandings*. Chicago: University of Chicago Press.

Carbaugh, D. (1990). Toward a perspective on cultural communication and intercultural contact. *Semiotica, 80*, 15-35.

Carbaugh, D., & Hastings, S. O. (1992). A role for communication theory in ethnography and cultural analysis. *Communication Theory, 2*, 156-164.

Cronen, V. E., Chen, V., & Pearce, W. B. (1988). Coordinated management of meaning: A critical theory. In Y. Y. Kim & W. B. Gudykunst (Eds.), *Theories in intercultural communication* (pp. 66-98). Newbury Park, CA: Sage.

Cronen, V. E., Pearce, W. B., & Tomm, K. (1985). A dialectical view of personal change. In K. Gergen & K. Davis (Eds.), *The social construction of the person* (pp. 203-224). New York: Springer-Verlag.

Cronen, V. E., & Shuter, R. (1983). Forming intercultural bonds. In W. B. Gudykunst (Ed.), *Intercultural communication theory* (pp. 89-118). Beverly Hills, CA: Sage.

Fitch, K. (1991). The interplay of linguistic universals and cultural knowledge in personal address: Colombian *Madre* terms. *Communication Monographs, 58*, 255-272.

Gallois, C., Giles, H., Jones, J., Cargile, A., & Ota, H. (1995). Accommodating intercultural encounters: Elaborations and extensions. In R. Wiseman (Ed.), *Intercultural communication theory* (pp. 115-147). Thousand Oaks, CA: Sage.

Geertz, C. (1973). *The interpretation of cultures*. New York: Basic Books.

Gudykunst, W. B. (1986). *Intergroup communication*. London: Edward Arnold.

Gudykunst, W. B. (1995). Anxiety/uncertainty management (AUM) theory: Current status. In R. Wiseman (Ed.), *Intercultural communication theory* (pp. 8-58). Thousand Oaks, CA: Sage.

Gudykunst, W. B., & Kim, Y. Y. (1984). *Communicating with strangers: An approach to intercultural communication*. New York: Random House.

Gudykunst, W. B., & Nishida, T. (1984). Individual and cultural influences on uncertainty reduction. *Communication Monographs, 51*, 23-36.

Gudykunst, W. B., & Ting-Toomey, S. (1988). *Culture and interpersonal communication*. Newbury Park, CA: Sage.

Hall, B. J. (1988/89). Norms, action, and alignment: A discursive perspective. *Research on Language and Social Interaction, 22*, 23-44.

Hall, B. J. (1992). Theories of culture and communication. *Communication Theory, 2*, 50-70.

Hall, B. J., & Valde, K. (1995). *Brown-nosing* as a cultural category in American organizational life. *Research on Language and Social Interaction, 28*, 391-419.

Hymes, D. (1962). The ethnography of speaking. In T. Gladwin & W. Sturtevant (Eds.), *Anthropology and human behavior* (pp.15-53). Washington D.C.: Anthropological Society of Washington.

Hymes, D. (1972). Models of the interaction of language and social life. In J. J. Gumperz & D. Hymes (Eds.), *Directions in sociolinguistics: The ethnography of communication* (pp. 35-71). New York: Holt, Rinehart & Winston.

Katriel, T. (1995). From "context" to "contexts" in intercultural communication research. In R. Wiseman (Ed.), *Intercultural communication theory* (pp. 271-284). Thousand Oaks, CA: Sage.

Katriel, T., & Philipsen, G. (1981). "What we need is communication": "Communication" as a cultural category in some American speech. *Communication Monographs, 48*, 302-317.

Klopf, D. (1991). *Intercultural encounters* (2nd edition). Englewood, CO: Morton Publishing.

Kumar, K., & Beyerlein, M. (1991). Construction and validation of an instrument for measuring ingratiatory behaviors in organizational settings. *Journal of Applied Psychology, 76*, 619-627.

Liden, R. C., & Mitchell, T. R. (1988). Ingratiatory behaviors in organizational settings. *Academy of Management Review, 13*, 572-587.

Pearce, W. B., & Cronen, V. E. (1980). *Communication, action, and meaning: The creation of social realities*. New York: Praeger.

Pearce, W. B., & Kang, K. (1988). Conceptual migrations: Understanding "Travelers' Tales" for cross-cultural adaptation. In Y. Y. Kim & W. B. Gudykunst (Eds.), *Cross-cultural adaptation* (pp. 20-41). Newbury Park, CA: Sage.

Pearce, W. B., Stanback, M. H., & Kang, K. (1984). Some cross-cultural studies of the reciprocal causal relation between communication and culture. In S. Thomas (Ed.), *Communication theory and interpersonal interaction* (pp. 3-10). Norwood, NJ: Ablex.

Philipsen, G. (1987). Lecture in Speech Communication 590. University of Washington, Spring Quarter.

Philipsen, G. (1989). An ethnographic approach to communication studies. In B. Dervin, L. Grossberg, B. J. O'Keefe, & E. Wartella (Eds.), *Rethinking communication* (pp. 258-268). Newbury Park, CA: Sage.

Philipsen, G. (1992). *Speaking culturally: Explorations in social communication.* New York: State University of New York Press.

Porter, R., & Samovar, L. (1988). Approaching intercultural communication. In L. Samovar & R. Porter (Eds.), *Intercultural communication: A reader* (5th ed., pp. 15-31). Belmont, CA: Wadsworth Publishing Company.

Roloff, M. E. (1981). *Interpersonal communication: The social exchange approach.* Beverly Hills, CA: Sage.

Samovar, L., & Porter, R. (1991). *Communication between cultures.* Belmont, CA: Wadsworth Publishing.

Samovar, L., & Porter, R. (1995). *Communication between cultures* (2nd ed.). Belmont, CA: Wadsworth Publishing.

Samovar, L., Porter, R., & Jain, N. (1981). *Understanding intercultural communication.* Belmont, CA: Wadsworth Publishing Company.

Spradley, J. P. (1979). *The ethnographic interview.* New York: Holt, Rinehart, & Winston.

Wortman, C. B., & Linsenmeier, J. (1977). Interpersonal attraction and techniques of ingratiation in organizational settings. In B. Staw & G. Salancik (Eds.), *New directions in organizational behavior* (pp. 133-178). Chicago: St. Clair Press.

Chapter 7

Social Contexts for Communication: Communicative Power as Past and Present Social Consequences

Bernard Guerin
University of Waikato

Communication can be defined to include almost all the behaviors of most animals or it can be restricted to specific human behaviors. While the latter strategy is usually more productive, especially for research, it occasionally is worthwhile looking at a slightly bigger picture. In this paper I wish to look at human communication in a broad sense from a behavior analysis framework, although what I will say is by no means unique to behavior analysis, and the material I will draw upon comes from many disciplines. Behavior analysis works by analysing behaviors in context and studying the events that follow any activity that make it more likely to occur again in that context or in a similar context. This is why behavior analysis has always been a strongly contextual analysis: the activities and the "motivations" for those activities are all immeshed in the situational context.

Perhaps the most important point for a behavior analysis that is missed in other studies of communication is that it looks at what events happen after a behavior occurs (and this is any activity, including thinking and remembering) and at how those events affect future occurrences of similar behaviors. The point is to look at what affects what, or who influences whom, and how these events affect similar activities in the future. One older definition of communication captures some but not all of such an analysis: "Who says what, through what channels...of communication, to whom, with what results" (Smith, Laswell, & Casely, 1946, p. 121). But the term "results" here has usually meant only the effect on the listener or audience, a persuasive effect for example, not the more inclusive context of adding how the listener's activity affects the likelihood that the speaker will act in similar ways in similar contexts in the future. That is what the broader behavior analysis picture can add to communication studies. Behavior analysis can provide a fully social, contextual analysis of communication, without the vague terminologies of postmodernist approaches (e.g., Leeds-Hurwitz, 1995), while remaining as a natural science (Guerin, 1994a, 1996).

Differences and Similarities between Behavior Analysis and Traditional Studies of Communication

Behavior analysis does not invalidate previous research but, on the whole, talks about it in a different way (Andresen, 1992). The major guiding assumption I have already mentioned, that the effects of one activity and its outcomes on future activity in similar situations are studied intensively. So a concerted effort is made to measure the history of a person's responding in the contexts under study. This means that some constructs such as "desire," "need," "purpose," and "anticipation" disappear, not because the phenomena referred to are not real but because a further question is asked: what is the previous history that produced or (socially) constructed such needs or desires in such situations? For example, if I "need" to tell a friend about my new job then there is a question of what has happened previously when I have told similar friends about my life events that leads me to "need" to tell them now. Likewise, having a "perspective" when speaking or listening means having a history in those types of situations (cf. Graumann & Sommer, 1989).

The same relentless back-questioning also occurs for one commonly stated goal of communication: that communication "expresses," "conveys," or "reports" something. For behavior analysis, however, there is no such thing as an innocent report or expression--one merely expressed (cf. Rosaldo, 1982). We need to analyse the effects of previous "expressings" that have led to the current activity. This is probably what Kellermann (1992) meant by commenting that communication is always purposeful or strategic, except that the words "purpose" and "strategy" lead behavior analysts to look for previous effects when doing similar activities. Both viewpoints suggest that communicating is always about a speaker getting something done (Guerin, 1996), and in cases where someone "merely" reports that there is a cat in the room, or they "merely" express their feelings, doing so still changes the behavior of listeners in ways that shape those sorts of expressing and reporting.

The behavior analysis position also entails that future events cannot affect what we do now--not directly anyway. What happens tomorrow cannot affect what I am doing now, although my talking about tomorrow's events can certainly change my current activities. So now the question becomes one of what has happened in similar situations in the past when I have thought or talked to myself about future events; what events happened previously that leads me now to think about future events? I hope it can be seen that closely studying the history of what has happened in the past with any type of activity is important in a behavior analysis-whether that be talking to oneself, talking to neighbors, or going for a jog in the park.

One of the most interesting findings in recent behavior analysis, which again is not a new finding but is now being talked about and studied in new ways, is that when people begin talking about events, they can change their activities without needing an actual history with the events talked about (Hayes & Wilson, 1993). If I tell you that Martha has some really funny stories about her childhood and that you should talk to her sometime, I might change your activity even though you have never had a history of talking with Martha. However, notice that there are still some very relevant histories here: your history of listening to me and of doing what I tell you, and your history of knowing about Martha and about funny stories. In the past, the effects of doing what I tell you have been such that you might talk to Martha following what I tell you.

The speaker-listener situations I have been writing about so far have been very simple ones. When we come to study human interactions, as all communication researchers will know, things are not so simple. We must study activities such as specific voice inflections in a particular community which only occur when older males talk to young males, and then only in situations in which the older men are instructing the boys and not otherwise interacting with them. Piecing together how such a specific situation has come about will be difficult with any type of analysis, and behavior analysis is no exception.

To begin analysing such complexities, it is useful to focus on three aspects of the same relations: what activities are happening, in what situations do they occur, and what effects happen now (and have happened in the past) in similar circumstances. Theoretically, it is a mistake to try and separate these three aspects (Guerin, 1996; Lee, 1994, 1995). If I only speak with a particular accent when talking to certain people and not others, this contextualizing happens precisely because the effects which lead me to do this again (called, by definition, reinforcing effects) have only occurred when talking to those people and not to others. The contextualizing only happens because the effects have been specific to that context in the past and only when doing that particular activity. So the three aspects of contingent relations really form an indivisible unit.

The behavior analysis view, despite wide misunderstanding (corrected by Andresen, 1992, for example), therefore comes close to recent conversational approaches (Edwards,1994; Edwards & Potter, 1993; Gumperz, 1982; Hilton, 1995; Psathas, 1995) by emphasizing the mutual influence of speaker and listener as a single unit of analysis, and by treating all communicating as actively doing something rather than "merely" expressing or reporting something (Billig, 1991; Shotter, 1993). It differs from self-presentation and impression management positions (e.g., Baumeister & Hutton, 1987) only because it asks further questions about why self-presentation needs to occur at all: What are the events that have occurred in the past which make it happen now (cf. Jellison & Gentry, 1978); why should we self-present and manage impressions; what has happened in the past?

While theoretically we should not separate context, activity and the past and present effects of that activity in that context, in practice and in research it is useful to do so. In presenting this paper, therefore, I am going to separate the three aspects to make the presentation easier. I will first review some of the contexts in which people learn to communicate differentially, followed by some of the research on what consequences of communicating might change the future activities of both speakers and listeners, and finally, some more about the activities that occur in communicating which have not been covered to that point.

Contexts for Discriminating

Behavior analysis is not, of course, the first position ever to study contextual discrimination of communication. I will be reviewing many areas of social psychology, sociolinguistics, psycholinguistics and communication studies which have found that people communicate in certain ways only with certain audiences or listeners, or act differently when there is no audience at all. For example, in an excellent framework proposed for studying communication, Bell (1984) suggested that we can consider five types of audiences or listeners, which he termed speakers (listening to oneself), addressees, auditors, overhearers, and eavesdroppers. With the exception of the last, speakers will have been shaped to verbalize differently for each type of audience. He also argued, in line with a behavior analysis approach, that specific topics and stylistic effects only occur in certain settings because they are associated with (behavior analysis would say because they have a past history with) certain audiences. Bell's idea was that by specifying the context--that is, the type of audience--we could predict how people will communicate. We will come back to this later, but notice that Bell has left out the consequences from the audience. One of the three aspects of contingent relations has been hidden.

Ede and Lunsford (1984) suggested a similar type of scheme when discussing the audiences for someone writing: A writer might address an audience of self, friend, colleague, critic, mass audience, or some future audience. They also suggested that during the writing activity a writer might "invoke" (cf. Baldwin & Holmes, 1987; Guerin, 1990) audiences, such as self, friend, colleague, critic, mass audience, future audience, past audience, or anomalous audiences, without those audiences actually needing to be present.

With this in mind, I wish first to review some studies finding that people act differently when they "expect" (that is, have had their activities shaped differentially in the past) an audience of any sort, followed by studies of expecting specific audiences which seem important in producing specific behaviors, including a quick look at "imaginary" audiences.

Expecting an Audience at All

Following Zajonc (1960), there have been a large number of studies conducted under the rubric of "cognitive tuning sets" which present experimental participants with a personality description and tell them either that they will transmit that description to an audience (transmitter set) or else that they will receive further information (receiver set). The typical findings of such studies (Guerin & Innes, 1989) are: that transmitters produce descriptions that are more coherent, unified, complex, and with more polarized judgments; that these unified descriptions lead to attribution errors and use of general traits; that the transmitters prefer to listen to supportive information, reject inconsistent information, and come to believe the description more; that transmitters remember more and process the information more carefully (more attending and verbalizing about it); and that transmitters try to look good, look consistent, and avoid looking foolish (Moore, 1974). Most of these effects are strongest when the expectation of an audience is given before participants read the descriptions, but results have also been found for post-message effects. Mazis (1973) also found that transmitters were less receptive to novel information, and Brock and Fromkin (1968) found that transmitters were less receptive to discrepant information. Powell (1974) found that transmitters generated more arguments consistent with their own view and less arguments that were inconsistent.

The results of these studies suggest that people have been shaped in their histories to speak about the descriptions of others in a particular way when expecting an unspecified audience. In line with what I wrote earlier, social psychologists have studied these findings but talked in terms of "needs" and "desires." For example, in this case we might (Boudreau, Baron, & Oliver, 1992) apply the epistemic motivation model of Kruglanski (Freund, Kruglanski, & Shpitzajzen, 1985; Kruglanski & Mayerless, 1987) which suggest two motivations: a need for structure and a fear of invalidity. The need for structure revolves around using (Kruglanski calls it "freezing") names or labels for objects when required to deal with them quickly (cf. Horne & Lowe, 1996; Wilkinson, Dube, & McIlvane, in press). Because this involves naming, verbal behavior, and equivalence relations it is called a "cognitive" need. The fear of invalidity refers to expected consequences of negative evaluation from other people. The idea seems to be that if participants have a history of being evaluated negatively by an audience then they are said to have a fear of invalidity.

I have mentioned Kruglanski's motivation model because it has some features that will re-occur throughout this paper. Most models of motivation end up referring to two sources of contingencies (Guerin, 1994a), one of which seems to emanate from the person, and one which seems to emanate from our social groups. In the present case, the need for structure seems to come from the individual's cognitive (verbal) system, and the fear of invalidity from the social environment. Likewise, Dillard and Witte (1993; Prentice, 1987) argue that persuasion can be instrumental or symbolic--one to do with the individual, one to do with a social reference group; Ajzen and Fishbein (1980) argue for an effect of personal beliefs and an effect of social norms; traditional social psychology talks about informational and normative influences. A behavior analysis would agree with all these versions of two sources excepting that the individual "needs" would be analysed back to a history with the physical environment or with a different type of social effect (many of the "individual motivations" are, in fact, social, Guerin, 1994a).

Two contradictory tests have been published which look more closely at the effects of cognitive tuning sets. Hoffman, Mischel, and Baer (1984) argued that when expecting to communicate with an audience (transmitter condition), participants would exacerbate the effects of using traits or verbal names--more global traits about the person described would be produced (also Jeffery & Mischel, 1979). Based on Kruglanski's model, Boudreau et al. (1992) predicted that when transmitting, participants would use less names or global traits because there would be less tendency to categorize, as Kruglanski's model apparently would predict.

Both groups of authors found the results they predicted. Hoffman et al. (1984) found more use of global traits when transmitting and Boudreau et al. (1992) found less traits when transmitting, especially with an expert or a peer as opposed to a child. The latter authors suggested a minor procedural difference to account for the discrepant results but it is also likely that the latter authors used a more evaluative procedure--they told participants that they were doing a "test of their ability to accurately predict" (p. 448). Thus the "anticipated consequences" from a future audience might have been heightened for the participants in Boudreau et al. (1992).

In some similar interesting studies, Higgins and his colleagues have found that actually writing the impression formed from the descriptions read changed the speaker's later verbalizing. Higgins and Rholes (1978), for example, had participants read a message that was biased or not and then either wrote down their impressions or not. Those who actually wrote down their impressions were more biased two weeks later (also McCann & Hancock, 1983). Higgins, McCann and Fondacaro (1982) found that speakers were more likely to stick to facts if an expected listener had been given different information.

Guerin and Innes (1989) have questioned this result, however. They pointed out that, depending upon subtle changes to the consequences of the situation, the opposite prediction could be made. If the transmitters were to present information to an audience which would evaluate them strongly, and provide consequences contingent upon their evaluation, then transmitters would be expected to stick closer to the information when the listeners had the same information. If listeners have the same information then they can check up on the participants more easily. This means that subtle differences in procedures could have brought about different results in this area. Similar differences will be pointed out later in this paper, between making causal attributions to an audience that can make the speaker accountable or not (Slugoski, Lalljee, Lamb & Ginsburg, 1993; Tetlock, 1985) and whether new or old information is presented.

In a closely related study, Gilovich (1987) had participants read information about a person and then write their summary for a second group of participants to read (second-hand information). It was found that the latter readers made more extreme judgments from this second-hand information. Gilovich showed that the first participants had left out situational information and provided more traits or dispositional information. Inman, Reichl and Baron (1993) found the same result, but also found the same when the original writers were forced to leave in the situational information. So it looks like the second-hand readers did not weigh the situational information much, even when it has been transmitted. So expecting to transmit to an audience seems likely to have been a context for presenting only more global trait information. That is, verbal summary information is used more than verbal descriptions of facts. It will be argued later that the former is more socially defensible than the latter when the audience has similar information at hand, and thus avoids punishing consequences.

There are other research areas which have looked at the contexts for changing behavior when expecting an audience. Research on social facilitation suggests what we have seen already: That an audience makes verbal "self-control" over behavior more likely (increased "self-awareness") and more social conformity to general norms that an audience might be likely to hold the speaker accountable for (Guerin, 1993). Once again we find the situation of one motive which seems to come from the individual and one which seems to come from the social environment.

Effects of Particular Audiences

There has been other research in which speakers have expected to face audiences with particular attitudes or characteristics. While every person with whom we have a history of interacting will shape a mutual repertoire (see "common grounds" later), the research on specific audiences has looked at the more general cases. Only in applied areas such as clinical therapy might we be interested in specific audiences (how this particular man and this particular woman communicate). The question for research is usually whether people "in general" have similarly shaped histories.

Expecting audiences with a particular view or opinion. The area of anticipatory attitude change has participants expecting to present or write their attitudes or opinions for an audience which they know has specific views on the issues. It has been found many times that under such general conditions, most (college student) participants bias their presented views towards that of the audience (Cialdini & Petty, 1981; Manis, Cornell, & Moore, 1974; Newtson & Czerlinsky, 1974; Schramm & Danielson, 1958; Zimmerman & Bauer, 1956). If the expected presentation to the audience is cancelled then the speakers' reported attitudes return to their pre-intervention baselines (Hass & Mann, 1976).

It was pointed out after much of this research had been done that the research had only used expected audiences with extreme views on the various issues: participants were told, for example, that the expected audience was a strong anti-abortion group. It could be, therefore, that participants changed their views to become more moderate (and therefore defensible) rather than more extreme and biased. Cialdini, Levy, Herman, and Evenbeck (1973) tested this and found evidence that, indeed, participants moved to the middle of evaluation scales rather than biasing towards the extreme views of their expected audience. These results have been replicated by Hass (1975) amongst others.

Cialdini, Levy, Herman, Kozlowski, and Petty (1976) placed the issue of audience expectation in a more motivational (history of consequences) framework and called the effects "strategic shifts." In their experiment they again found moderation but only for a low "reward" condition: when there was high involvement by the participants (high "reward" condition) they did not moderate their attitudes, participants gave their own extreme views. This suggests that consequences outside of the experimental situation were influencing the outcome and previous research succeeded in changing reported attitudes when the issue was of no other consequence to the participants. It therefore looks as if participants are shifting towards a socially defensible position, and are acting strategically with respect to the consequences of their whole situation.

The mediating role of consequences was further supported by the experiment of Gaes and Tedeschi (1978) who managed to find strategic shifts even under high involvement conditions. This was done, however, by introducing further consequences into the experimental situation: The experimenter reminded participants about the conditions and expressed concern to them about the experiment. So local social consequences were introduced and attitude shifts were found even in a high involvement condition. Also manipulating consequences, Moore (1974) had participants expect to meet the audience who was high status relative to the participants but did not get attitude shifts. A second experiment did find anticipatory attitude change, however, when the audience was given power over the participants which meant that they could enact consequences.

This area of research therefore looks like it is manipulating different situational consequences in a speaker/expected audience interaction. Whether or not such effects will be found seems to depend upon the consequences brought to bear on participants. Under very general conditions, however, and with low involvement from the participants, attitude shifts are usually found when participants expect to talk to an audience with a particular attitude or opinion. When more specific consequences are made contingent upon presenting a particular viewpoint, other attitude shifts are found.

Gender. There is evidence that both men and women speak differently to audiences of men and women. Lakoff (1973, 1975) has even argued that women are so low in power in western societies (at least) that they have been shaped into using a special feminine style of speech (also Tannen, 1990, 1992). While some (Ng & Bradac, 1993) have argued against these views, there is good evidence for many speech differences (Thorne & Henley, 1975). Wolfson (1984) showed that for the giving of compliments there were different rates given to men and women, and there is other evidence that society differentially evaluates (shapes) the speech of men and women (Henley & Kramarae, 1991). Carli (1990) found that females who spoke tentatively were more influential with males than with females. Using a fairly weak manipulation and dubious measures, Grace (1951, 1952a, b) found very weak effects of knowing the audience's gender characteristics.

The role of consequences in producing these gender differences comes in the many suggestions that such differences are indicative of power differences in current society (e.g., Eckert & McConnell-Ginet, 1992; Gallois, 1994; Kramarae, 1990; Labov, 1990; Wolfson, 1984). What this means is that males can have more effects or consequences on females than vice versa. Therefore, in situations of communicating, different patterns of context-dependent activities are shaped for males and females. This means that communicating itself is not the important thing, it is the power to apply contingent consequences to communicating that is important, and this is differential between the genders in our society. I will discuss this point later in this paper, that consequences and histories of consequences are the "power" behind audiences, words, and communicating activities (e.g., Ladegaard, 1995).

Language community or speech community. In the presence of speakers of one's own language, speaking that language is heavily reinforced (which only means that it is likely to occur again in that context or similar ones). In the case of language usage, both Kellermann (1992) and Skinner (1957) point out that such discriminatory behavior is usually automatic: it is not verbally governed, subject to awareness or private verbalizing, or controlled, except perhaps when learning a second language (Schmidt, 1990, where "consciousness" means verbally-governed contingencies).

Some of the effects of this are very subtle. Beebe (1981) has shown how for bilinguals and for speakers of dialects, very subtle and immediate code-switching (Heller, 1988) can occur when speaking to different audiences or to someone fluent in both codes. In these cases, it is both the listener and the situation that controls the particular code used, as also in the case of diglossia when two separate verbal repertoires are used with different situational functions (Hudson, 1992). For example, in a classic study, Ervin-Tripp (1964) found more Japanese word intrusions and English syntax problems when Japanese women were interviewed by a Japanese-American interviewer than with a Caucasian-American interviewer. Again, the situation is controlling the set of words with automatic (Kellermann, 1992) or contingency-governed shifts.

Specifically trained audiences. There is one very nice example of two specifically trained audiences controlling separate sets of codes. Silverman, Anderson, Marshall, and Baer (1986) trained children to respond with different repertoires to two audiences. The audiences were puppets which asked the children questions and reinforced certain responses. Probes run by having a trainer-puppet ask questions from the other repertoire found that the repertoires were functionally separate, as has been found in young children previously (Guess, 1969; Guess & Baer, 1973; Lamarre & Holland, 1985). When some responses for one audience were taught with a new audience, it was found that whole repertoire generalized to the new audience (Silverman et al., 1986).

Auditors and overhearers. Bell (1984) and Clark (e.g., Schober & Clark, 1989) have argued that different categories of listeners shape different behaviors of speakers, or at least, that addressees (persons directly addressed) shape behavior that does not generalize to auditors and overhears. The studies finding this will be reviewed below, but it should be noted that the consequences from addressees, auditors, and overhearers listening to a speaker are likely to be very different.

Children, foreigners and persons with intellectual disabilities. DePaulo and Coleman (1986) found that when women were speaking to children they were clearer, simpler, more attention-maintaining, and had longer pauses. Speech to persons with intellectual disabilities was very similar, especially the repetitiveness of the talk, but it was even more babyish and there were fewer and shorter pauses. They also found that speech to foreigners was more repetitive but otherwise similar to speech directed towards normal adults. When talking to sophisticated foreigners, however, DePaulo and Coleman's (1986) participants were shaped more by the actual conversation: they used fewer devices for clarifying, simplifying and maintaining attention.

There are many other examples of talking to foreigners and the problems of adjusting to whole new systems of audience shaping. Gallois and Callan (1991), for example, give many cases where speaking to someone of another ethnic origin leads to problems of miscommunication.

In an early series of experiments, Spradlin and Rosenberg (1964) had college students interview people with high or low levels of intellectual abilities. Their participants used a larger number of different words and longer responses with the higher level people. They reported, however, that the effects only occurred in the first five minutes. Likewise, Spradlin (1985) reported an early study in which college students interviewed persons with intellectual disabilities who had been labelled as having high or low verbal skills. However, this labelling had little effect and the college students adjusted (their behaviors were shaped) very quickly to the abilities of the real person present, coming quickly under the immediate control of the interviewee. This suggests that while there might be general repertoires which generalize to specific audiences, direct interacting will shape a new way of communicating very quickly. We will later look at Clark's research on building common ground between people in conversation.

Status. Many studies have manipulated the status of their audiences and measured changes in participants' actions. It was mentioned earlier that the study by Moore (1974) did not find differences, despite status differences, until the audience was given some power of consequences over the participants. Thus it seems that it is not status per se but the power to give consequences that differentiates responding in the presence of unequal status persons (cf. Ladegaard, 1995).

Cansler and Stiles (1981) and Stiles, Waszak, and Barton (1979) found that in mixed-status dyads, the higher status member was more presumptuous. To test this they used a measure of presumptuousness developed by Stiles (1978), which rates different types of interaction as to their presumption. Similarly, Chiasson and Hayes (1993) found that freshmen talked twice as much and initiated twice as much when in homogeneous groups than when in mixed status groups.

There have also been studies on social class differences in communication which are relevant here. In a thorough review of these studies, Higgins (1976) suggested that social class differences in communication are real, but that they are very difficult to measure and there are lots of problems with the research area. Ervin-Tripp (1976) pointed out some of her findings on giving directives to other persons, and the subtle mitigations for status and other social variables. The research on politeness (see below) also suggests subtle changes with status differences.

In-groups and out-groups. For a long while, close groups have been known to be important to human functioning (Cooley, 1902; Tönnies, 1957/1887; Turner, Hogg, Oakes, Reicher, & Wetherall, 1987). From a behavior analytic perspective, Guerin (1994a) suggested that the reason for this is that close human groups shape the behavior of members in ways that do not usually occur with other parts of the physical environment. Our activities can be maintained for a long time by the groups to which we belong without us necessarily having to reciprocate to the behavior of other group members.

Such generalized social consequences (Guerin, 1995a; Sahlins, 1965; Yamagishi & Cook, 1993) produce some interesting properties from which arise the properties of in-group and out-group directed behaviors (Turner et al., 1987). For example, Mackie, Gastardo-Conaco, and Skelly (1992) ran a study in which participants received a message from an in-group or an out-group member with or without knowing the position advocated by that member. When receiving an in-group message without knowing what the in-group member was actually advocating, the participants processed more; that is, they paid more attention to the message contents and had more verbal behavior about those messages. Thus listeners act differently if receiving an in-group or an out-group communication.

Bell (1984) suggested that reference groups not physically present can shape the behavior of speakers (Cooley, 1902). This occurs because the previous history of shaping is controlling the behavior rather than the more immediate, local conversational contingencies. In line with this, Youssef (1993) found that her results depended upon wider societal norms and cultural events in which her children participants were immersed.

Most of the behaviors which are sensitive to (are operants for) audience consequences, and which will be discussed in the section below on communication activities, show strong sensitivity to in-group audiences and (sometimes) out-group audiences. These include: the accommodation to style; and the shaping of verbal content discussed as social constructions or social representations (Abrams, Wetherall, Cochrane, Hogg, & Turner, 1990; Gergen, 1985; Moscovici, 1984). With the accommodation literature for example, Milroy and Milroy (1992) have explicitly linked socio-economic class effects in style accommodation to the weak ties in social networks or in-groups.

Finally, many authors (e.g., Guerin, 1994b; Maass, Salvi, Arcuri, & Semin, 1989) have found that the effects for level of abstractness in verbs and adjectives are sensitive to in-group audience characteristics. Guerin (1994b) found that when writing about their own gender, both males and females used less abstract language when writing about undesirable behaviors and more abstract language when writing about desirable behaviors. There were no complementary out-group effects, however, as has often been the case with in-group/out-group research (Hewstone, 1989).

Friends and strangers. Many pieces of evidence show strong differences between friends and strangers as both listeners and speakers, although in some cases this might be the same as in-group and out-group differences. Wolfson (1988) suggests that there was a "bulge" in the data such that there was more solidarity-establishing speech among status-equal friends and acquaintances than either intimate friends or strangers. Her evidence for this came from the use of compliments and invitations. She suggested that interactions with both intimates and strangers have more certainty than with acquaintances, for whom some negotiation is required.

Boxer (1993), however, gives evidence for the opposite in the case of indirect complaints. On a "social distance" scaling there was more indirect complaining to intimates and to strangers. Her research still shows that the dimension is important, though. It should hopefully be clear now that "certainty" in interacting with intimates and strangers means the certainty of consequential outcomes: we expect (prior history again), and most often have available, regularly shaped consequences from strangers and intimates, albeit very different consequences in both cases. We get only a few general effects from strangers and many different strong effects from intimates, but both of these are certain; whereas with acquaintances there needs to be more contextually negotiated exchange or shaping of consequences, and these are less certain.

Such notions were also present in Guerin's (1995b) findings that participants reported that they would use different sorts of influence tactics on friends and strangers. With a prior network of reciprocal consequences already in place for friends, people reported being more likely to use assertiveness and exchange tactics of influence with friends than with strangers.

Another closely related study was that by Brown and Garland (1971) on face-saving behaviors. They had participants in a situation of saving face after finding out they had not done well at singing, with experimental conditions of different types of audiences and whether they would meet the audience afterwards. It was found that most face-saving occurred with audiences of close friends and strangers whom they would meet later, and less with both acquaintances and with strangers whom they would not meet later.

Effects on listeners from speakers who are friends or strangers has been reported by Lewis and Gallois (1984). Their participants watched videos of two friends or strangers giving messages that contained refusals, disagreements, or negative feelings. Participants reported that they thought disagreements were better than refusals which were in turn better than negative feelings. They also reported that it was better when friends disagreed than when strangers did, and when a friend refused it was seen as less socially skilled and more hurting than when a stranger refused.

Finally, different social relations other than the broad friend/stranger distinction will, of course, shape different behaviors, but these need to be studied intensively in their specific contexts (Spencer-Oatey, 1993). Dunn and Cowan (1993), for example, found that Japanese women had different influence strategies for friends and their bosses at work.

Multiple audiences. There has been research on the effects of multiple audiences: some research on how having two audiences present interferes with clear communication; and other research on how well people can send a message to one person while not sending to another person who is also present, that is, how they can have an effect on one person without having that same effect on another person present (Bell, 1984, 1991; Fleming, 1994; Tracy & Coupland, 1991).

Fleming, Darley, Hilton, and Kojetin (1990) asked people to write essays containing false information but to do this so as not to fool their friends. Their participants managed to fool strangers while their friends picked up on the deception. Fleming et al. (1990; Fleming, 1994) related this research to prisoners of war who are forced to make propaganda messages on mass media, who manage to present the message while making it clear to people back home that they are being forced to do so.

Clark and colleagues have done nice research on two types of listeners: addressees and eavesdroppers. Their speaker participants had to get a message across to an addressee (identifying photos of city landmarks) without letting an eavesdropper understand what was going on (Clark & Schaefer, 1987). Their participants were successful in doing this. Schober and Clark (1989) took the procedure further, by having someone (eavesdropper) listen to two people talking about a problem. They found that even if the eavesdropper heard everything that was said between the two problem-solvers, if they were not an addressee then they were not able to "understand" everything that transpired. This study will be discussed later in the context of additional studies by Clark showing that "common ground" between two interactants is built up throughout conversations; that being able to refer back to an earlier part of a conversation easily is a real advantage in conversation that an eavesdropper cannot as readily utilize.

Finally, some of the same sorts of ideas present in Fleming (1994) and the work of Clark has been discussed within linguistics by Fill (1986), who called such effects "divided illocution." By this it was meant that there could be multiply addressed audiences at any time. I might say something to one student "knowing" that another student listening will also be affected in a different way by the same words.

Imaginary audiences. For behavior analysis, verbalizing can occur even in the absence of a listener, and such private events (they cannot otherwise be seen) can occur for any audience that has been shaped (Skinner, 1957). Such a view is compatible with the "private speech" research that suggest that private speech arises originally as a social event (Diaz & Berk, 1992), and Bell's (1984) suggestion that speakers can use style to initiate events, but only with reference to an absent audience. Such views come from the earlier writings of Mead (1924/1925, 1934) and Cooley (1902). We can clearly have imaginary conversations, and Bauer (1958) suggested that reference groups or in-groups commonly make up this secondary audience. Thus, again, it is the consequences which afford contextual control to the particular audiences.

Some research along these lines has been started by Baldwin and Holmes (1987; Baldwin, Carrell, & Lopez, 1990), and related research on self-editing by Hyten and Chase (1991). The research on private speech, of course, is well developed (Diaz & Berk, 1992).

Consequences for Speakers and Listeners

Through the material we have covered so far, we have seen that different audiences shape the different activities of speakers because of the consequences for those speakers in the past with similar audiences in similar contexts. As mentioned at the beginning, the activities, the audiences (the context), and the consequences go together as functional units and cannot really be separated. This section will look at some of the common consequences that are functional in communication situations, but I will again focus on more general ones because researchers do not usually study the singular or particular consequences of two unique individuals. The two sections here will also separate the consequences for speakers from the consequences for listeners, although, once again, these will always form functional units that determine whether one or both interactants will be affected and whether they will ever interact again.

Consequences from Audiences Shaping the Speaker

Consequences have been the part of functional units (contingencies) that has been studied least in traditional social psychology, communication studies, and sociolinguistics. Some examples were shown in the previous section of how the consequences were relegated to "needs" and similar constructs. It was also suggested that two sources of consequences are commonly suggested: one supposedly emanating from the individual and one from a generalized social source.

I wish to point out briefly that I think the "needs" and the "two sources" are closely related, and this shows how the "needs" approach is not completely off the mark, just a bit vague in terminology. I have argued elsewhere that when a close community (in-group, speech community, social network) has evolved, it works by setting up a unique system of support such that members can have their actions supported (reinforced) by that group without having to reciprocate for long periods of time (Guerin, 1994a, 1995a). If we want something from the physical environment, on the other hand, we have to act immediately and directly ourselves. If I "want" a banana, for example, to obtain it from the environment I would have to walk and find a banana tree (or worse, plant one and wait some years!) and then pick one. In a community system, I only have to ask someone to bring me a banana or walk to the shop and pay for one. I either can reciprocate the favors gradually over time, or, reciprocate in some way which is totally unrelated to bananas, trees and walking, such as paying money which I earn by doing something else altogether (Durkheim, 1933/1893).

There are different types of reciprocity which determine exactly what you can have others do for you in different social contexts. Families and intimates usually give lots over a long period without requiring immediate reciprocation, whereas borrowing even two items from a neighbor within a day might need to be negotiated with more immediate reciprocation on your part. In all, the dynamics of such reciprocal systems is complex (Amato, 1993; Farber, 1989; Litwak & Szelenyi, 1969; Peterson, 1993; Sahlins, 1965; Wellman & Wortley, 1989; Williams, 1995; Yamagishi & Cook, 1993).

For our present purposes, what this means is that a large number of human actions seem to occur without any consequences, or at least any immediate and obvious consequences, especially among friends and in-groups. If a stranger asks me the time, I tell them without immediate or obvious reinforcement. The supporting consequences for my action come from being a member of that, in this case societal, community and I use that community in similar ways to the stranger on a very regular basis. In times of war or scarce resources, however, such communities break down (Hart, 1986; Turnbull, 1973).

It is not surprising to me therefore that a "desire" for social identity, a "fear of invalidity," and a "need" for affiliation appear regularly in the literature, along with distinctions between instrumental and symbolic (i.e., generalized social consequences) needs, and individual and social norm factors (Ajzen, & Fishbein, 1980; Dillard & Witte, 1993; Prentice, 1987). The literatures on symbolic, reference group, and social norm motivations are problematic, however, not because they are wrong, but because the generalized social consequences that give rise to these "needs" are not obvious and are diffused through large communities and through time. To researchers, such "social motivators" sometimes seem to be regulated by magic, and sometimes that is exactly what does regulate the social community consequences (Evans-Pritchard, 1976). But we miss this most important source of "power" if we ignore past and present consequences as determinants of activity, even when those consequences are diffuse and generalized and we cannot readily see or measure them.

Common consequences for speakers. Guerin (1991) reviewed many experimental manipulations used in social psychology to locate typical patterns of consequences, because, as mentioned immediately above, it often looks as if there are no consequences determining generalized patterns of actions. It was found that there were two major manipulations used in social psychology, evaluation and anonymity, and several other common manipulations: expected future interaction with the other interactant, having to give an explanation, status, being made responsible for another person, being dependent upon another person, reversibility of your actions, and having real consequences rather than just verbal consequences applied.

Some of this research was also reviewed by Tetlock (e.g., 1985) as "accountability": the idea that actions change dramatically when someone is made "accountable" for their actions. I hope it can be seen that accountability is a mixture of several, very general social community consequences. If I am accountable for my actions then I am usually subject to evaluation with contingent social approval or disapproval, or sometimes more specific consequences depending upon the particular context. Being held accountable also usually means future interaction with the "accountant" and having to explain your reasons for acting. Such experimentally manipulated consequences seem "lumpy" compared to experimental research in behavior analysis, but this lumpiness is also present in real life.

As would be predicted from a behavior analysis point of view, such a manipulation of several generalized consequences lumped together produces strong changes in behavior, and Tetlock has conducted an impressive series of experiments demonstrating this. For example, following an earlier section of this paper, Tetlock found strategic attitude shifts using accountability as the manipulation (Tetlock, Skitka, & Boettger, 1989). Participants who were made accountable also generated more pre-emptive self-criticisms (to lessen the consequences if the criticisms were to made by someone else afterwards), and when committed to a position they showed more "defensive bolstering." Cvetkovich (1978) found that when made accountable there was a shift to verbal self-editing and making judgments that could be easily stated with reasons (were defensible). It was suggested that the participants were "talking to themselves" as if talking to the person to whom they were accountable.

Some more specific consequences for speakers arise from other studies (cf. Graumann & Herrmann, 1989). We have already seen that friends and strangers seem to shape different behaviors (e.g., Brown & Garland, 1971), and this probably reflects different consequences. A person who is a member of your close group has many and varied ways to influence your behaviors, which is not the case for strangers. So we would expect many different consequences to be used in both cases (Guerin, 1995b). We would expect strangers to rely on consequences which are possible in the immediate environment, which is one reason that physical force is common, and friends to rely on longer term exchanges or the force of coalitions with other members of the close groups. Just imagine how you might get either a close friend and a stranger to tie your shoe-lace for you. How would you get it done in each case?

Other strategies have been shown to shape speakers' activities, such as listeners being responsive and showing understanding of what a speaker is saying. This has been studied in many ways. Clark and Schaefer (1989) point out that evidence of understanding can come from a listener giving continued attention, initiating the next and relevant contribution, giving acknowledgements, giving other sorts of demonstrations of understanding, and open displays. Kraut, Lewis, and Swezey (1982), for example, found that giving feedback kept events understandable. Davis and Holtgraves (1984; also Davis & Perkowitz, 1979) also found that listener responsiveness played a large role, especially when the responses were content-related.

As to the question of what are "relevant" responses or contributions to conversation, Clark and Schaefer (1989) pointed out that adjacency pairs would ordinarily be evidence for a speaker that a listener has understood and is tracking their conversation. Adjacency pairs are statements that form a pair that almost always follow each other: an answer follows a question or a summons; compliance or refusal follow a request; acceptance or rejection follow requests, proposals invitations, apologies and thanks; agreement or disagreement follow assessment and compliments; greetings follow greetings; and farewells follow farewells. Correctly responding with an adjacency pair should shape a speaker's activity. In a very similar list to that of Clark and Schaefer (1989), Higgins, Fondacaro, and McCann (1981) argued that for listeners to support (shape or maintain) a speaker's actions they should take the speaker's characteristics into account, determine the speaker's intent, take context into account, pay attention and be ready for message, try to understand the message, and provide feedback about their understanding.

The speech accommodation area of research shows that under many, but not all, conditions, when a speaker converges in style to that of the listener they are rated more highly. Once again, two reasons have been given for this, one reflecting a generalized social consequence and one an individual consequence. The social reason reflects the in-group or speech community support that is given, the idea being that if a speaker shows "solidarity" by speaking in a similar style then the listener will reinforce that behavior. The individual reason reflects that speech is probably more understandable to listeners if the speaker has a similar style. Therefore, the speaker is reinforced for converging because listeners have tended to understand better in the past, and we have seen immediately above that this is an important consequence in conversations.

On the subject of generalized social consequences, Bell writes (1984, p. 162), "Grossly described, the accommodation model hypothesizes that speakers accommodate their speech style to their addressee in order to win approval," while later (p. 199), he sets out the more "individual" convergence-for-clarity idea, "In concentrating on approval seeking as a reason for style shift, accommodation theory has often overlooked a more transparent motivation: a speaker's desire to be understood...one or both parties will be under strong pressure to converge for the sake of mere intelligibility." For example, Shockey (1984) reports that when she moved from the United States to England she changed some pronunciations because she was better understood that way.

There is evidence for both generalized social and individual sources of consequences, however, and we do not have to decide between the two reasons (Buller & Aune, 1992; Putman & Street, 1984). Speech accommodation theory has presented good evidence for in-group functions of convergence and also divergence, as well as other reasons for accommodation (Coupland, 1980, 1984). Recent efforts have looked at the strength of in-group membership using a measure of ethnolinguistic vitality (Giles & Johnson, 1987).

On a more molecular level, Tannen (1989) suggests several involvement strategies for narrative and dialogue that will reinforce speakers if present, based on sound or meaning. Sound can be used to shape listener involvement through rhythmic patterns, through repetition and variation, and through stylistic figures of speech. Meaning can be used to shape listener involvement through patterns such as indirectness, ellipsis, tropes, dialogue, imagery, and narrative structures. Using topics that are highly involving will also secure the listener's attention. This is especially apparent in the literature on rumors and gossip because the highly involving topics are anxiety provoking and this presumably secures the listener's attention (Difonzo, Bordia, & Rosnow, 1994; Esposito & Rosnow, 1984; Kimmel & Keefer, 1991; Rosnow, 1988; Rosnow, Yost, & Esposito, 1986; Walker & Blaine, 1991).

Finally, some speech is supported not for anything that takes place within a dialogue, but because speaking itself supports a social community which in turn supports many other unrelated, but reciprocated, activities. Chatting intermittently to a neighbor might only have consequences for the speaker when an emergency arises and they can ask that neighbor to help (Litwak & Szelenyi, 1969). Such talk has been called "phatic communion" by Malinowski (1923) and it probably serves several functions, albeit indirect (see Coupland, Coupland, & Robinson, 1992, for a good review).

The mitigation of consequences. It is not only the functional consequences for speaking that are important but also the actions required to mitigate those consequences and control, shape, or socially negotiate consequences in the more local and immediate context. Such strategies have been discussed as "autoclitics" by Skinner (1957; Catania, 1973; Smith, 1983) and in sociolinguistics and social psychology as "mitigations" (Ng & Bradac, 1993), "equivocal communications" (Bavelas, Black, Chovil, & Mullett, 1990), and pragmatics (Levinson, 1983).

Methods used to modify the consequences of interactions include:
1. Disclaimers (Hewitt & Stokes, 1975), which can be found even with children (Bennett, 1990);
2. Hedges (Holmes, 1989);
3. Apologies (Blum-Kulka, & Olshtain, 1984; Holmes, 1984; Ohbuchi, Kameda, & Agarie, 1989);
4. Politeness (Brown & Levinson, 1987; Clark & Schunk, 1980; Fraser, 1990; Holmes, 1993; Holtgraves & Yang, 1990; Nwoye, 1992; Pan, 1995);
5. Deference or respect (Fraser & Nolen, 1981);
6. Presenting explanations or reasons for your conduct (Hagiwara, 1992; Hamilton & Hagiwara, 1992; Innes & Gilroy, 1980; Langer & Abelson, 1972).

Such strategies will depend upon the exact relations between the two persons and the situation: that is, all the audience variables discussed in the earlier section of this paper. For example, Ervin-Tripp (1976) provides good examples on giving directives and the common mitigations required when there are status differences and other social variables, and Tannen (1986, 1990) gives good examples of the miscommunications that can arise from people who have shaped by different audiences when they try to use ineffective mitigation strategies on each other. Other examples are given in Chapter 12 of Skinner (1957).

What Shapes Listening Behavior?

Consequences from speakers and others. We now come to the question of what keeps a listener listening. We have had some answers to this already: phatic communion; and, from the discussion earlier about rumors, it is clear that listeners can often learn about something (have a repertoire shaped) through their listening, and in turn, they can use this to get the attention of another listener. Weiss, Lombardo, Warren and Kelley (1971) found that being able to speak in reply showed reinforcing properties. That is, listeners would do something (which could be paying attention) in order to be able to speak in reply.

In their role-model approach to communication, Higgins et al. (1981) have suggested that in order to reinforce a listener's listening activities, speakers should: take the listener's characteristics into account, convey the truth as they see it, try to be understood by being coherent and comprehensible, give neither too much nor too little information, be relevant, and produce an appropriate message for the context and for the effect they are to have on the listener.

Such a list is very close to the classic lists of Grice (1975, 1978), that conversationalists should be cooperative in the following ways:

1. Maxim of quantity
   Be as informative as possible for the situation
   Do not be more informative than necessary
2. Maxim of quality
   Do not say what you think is false
   Do not talk about things for which you do not have evidence
3. Maxim of relevance
   Be relevant
4. Maxim of manner
   Avoid obscurity
   Avoid ambiguity
   Avoid unnecessary verboseness
   Be orderly

Briefly then, to shape your listener's listening, it is suggested that you give just the right amount of information that is true and relevant to the context and to do so in an efficient and sensible manner.

Implications of how audiences view speakers. We can get further clues about what reinforces listening behaviors by considering studies in which listeners have rated speakers on evaluative dimensions. Those speakers rated as more positive are probably acting in ways which reinforce and maintain listening, although this evidence is indirect as self-reports.

In a nice series of studies, Ng has looked at how speakers are rated in terms of influence (Brooke & Ng, 1986; Ng, Bell, & Brooke, 1993; Ng, Brooke, & Dunne, 1995). In interpersonal settings, those speakers who take more turns and speak more are considered more influential. If speakers are frequently interrupted then they are rated as more influential, especially if they hold their ground against the interruptions. If the style of proactive, involving dissent, making offers, or replying, then speakers are rated as more influential. If the style is passive, involving consent, reacting, and requesting, the speakers are considered less influential. Also on ratings of influence, Canary, Brossman, Brossman, and Weger (1995) found that those speakers using complex arguments were rated by listeners as more effective. Guerin (1995b) found that strictly logical arguments were reported as not good for use on friends.

Social situations and social relationships, of course, modify the ratings by listeners. Holtgraves (1986) found that the type of situation changed listeners' judgments about the politeness of a speaker. If there was a threatening situation then indirect replies (evasive) were more likely to happen and were rated as more polite than irrelevant replies (also found by Clark & Shunk, 1980). Mills and Jellison (1968) found that listeners (readers) rated that they agreed more with a talk when they thought that the speaker had given the talk to a group that were similar to the speaker. As would also be expected, social identity or in-group membership changes the ratings of listeners. Studies in speech accommodation have asked listeners to rate speakers along evaluative dimensions and then provided in-group information, for example, the speaker might have an accent similar (in-group) to the listener's (Giles & Johnson, 1987). Many dimensions can be affected in this way, including attractiveness, perceived supportiveness, intelligibility, and interpersonal involvement (Bourhis, Giles, & Lambert, 1975; Gallois, Callan & Johnstone, 1984; Giles, Coupland, & Coupland, 1991).

Lastly, looking at ratings of those speakers considered to be boring, Leary, Rogers, Canfield, and Coe (1986) had their participants verbally rate many situations of boredom. They found that the most boring speakers were said to be egocentric and with banal behaviors. A further study of boring speakers showed that they used fewer disclosures and edifications (expressions of objective information), and used more questions and acknowledgements.

Studies of participants and observers. A final research area to review consists of studies which compare participants in an interaction to observers of that interaction. Monahan (1995), for example, reports studies which have found that participants rate other participants more positively than do observers (also excellent research by Benoit, Benoit, & Wilkie, 1995). As we have come to expect, two sources of motivation were suggested: First, that participants might be more concerned with self-presentation than observers, and second, that participants, as opposed to observers, have a heavier "cognitive load" (meaning they have many concurrent verbal tasks which might conflict) and therefore spend less time on impression formation. Observers have the luxury of putting more thought into their judgments during an interaction because they are not so engaged as participants. Guerin (1995b) also suggested this as a difference between attempting to influence a single person, face-to-face, and attempting to influence a group of people. Specifically, people in a group can perform activities that a single person is too busy to do.

The attention of observers, as opposed to participants, differs not only in the time available but also in what they are observing. Storms (1973) and Taylor and Fiske (1975) found that participants and observers focussed on different events during conversations because of their placement and seating. This led to their making different attributions about who was most influential in a conversation. If participants and observers were shown videos of the others' point of view, the attributions were reversed.

It has already been mentioned that some writers have suggested differences between addressees and auditors as two types of listeners (Bell, 1984; also Fleming,

1994). The studies of Clark and colleagues, presented earlier, show how someone merely observing (eavesdropping) on a conversation does not understand, and cannot do, tasks that an addressee can (Clark & Schaefer, 1987; Schober & Clark, 1989; Wilkes-Gibbs & Clark, 1992).

Activities of Speakers and Listeners

We now come to the final aspect of the contingent relations among audience contexts, contingent consequences, and the activities of speakers and listeners. Some of the following studies have already been mentioned above because when studying the audience consequences which can modify the activities of a listener or speaker, researchers have naturally chosen activities which can be easily modified (in the old behavior analysis terminology, they are activities which are operants).

Types of Communication Activities Affected by Audiences

Many of the activities in conversation which can be affected by audiences have been mentioned in passing. Most speech behaviors are included here, including the language used, the dialects and code-switches. Many stylistic variables have been mentioned already: accent, gestures, phonology, syntax, grammar (an autoclitic), repetition, rhythm, verbal imagery, particular words, speech markers, tropes and figures of speech, abstractness of verbs and adjectives, utterance length, turn taking, speech rate, vocal intensity, pausing, and posture. All these can be modified by the consequences from an audience (Bell, 1984; John-Lewis, 1986; Romaine, 1982).

The content of speech, or the semantics, can also be modified by audience consequences (Dines, 1980). This includes the amount of self-disclosure, jokes, phatic communications, the clarity and relevance of what is said (Grice, 1975), the various mitigation strategies, expressed attitudes and opinions (anticipatory attitude change), and rumors. I have also mentioned that the abstractness of verbs and adjectives can be changed by audience consequences (De Poot & Semin, 1995; Brown & Fish, 1983; Guerin, 1994b; Maass et al., 1989; Semin & Fiedler, 1988, 1989, 1991, 1992). The conclusions from this research seem to be that the use of more abstract verbs and of adjectives leads listeners to the impression that what is being talked about is more permanent and more likely to be repeated in the future (Maass et al.).

A long research tradition with in-group membership shows that the groups to which we belong can determine the content of what we say (Abrams, Wetherall, et al. 1990; Farr & Moscovici, 1984; Gergen, 1985; Guerin, 1992a, 1994c, 1995c, 1995d; Moscovici, 1984; von Cranach, Doise, & Mugny, 1992). Social constructionism and social representation positions advocate that we learn much of what we know through the groups to which we belong. Once again, two "motivations" have been given for this: that we go along with our groups to win social approval (generalized social consequences), and also that knowledge gained from group membership helps us make sense of unfamiliar things and events (Guerin, 1995c; Moscovici, 1984).

It has been argued in more specific ways that particular types of speech content differ in how they affect audiences. Guerin (1994d) argued that attitude and belief statements have different consequences for speakers: If the audience is such that you are relatively influential then belief statements will be stronger for persuasion or getting attention than attitude statements ("War kills people" vs. "I don't like war"); if the audience is relatively strong or the speaker is challenged, however, then attitudes are easier to defend than beliefs ("I don't care what arguments you make, I still don't like war"). Such a situation shows the social negotiation that occurs, that is, the shaping and mitigation of consequences between speakers and listeners (Guerin, 1994c), with the content of speech not just the stylistics. Guerin (1994d) also suggested that consistency between attitudes, beliefs and behavior would also be determined by whether the particular audiences reinforced consistency or not.

The same idea, of how speech content is shaped, applies to research on anticipatory attitude change, which was dealt with earlier in this paper, and also to the work of Papageorgis (1963). Papageorgis followed the design of Bartlett (1932) and had participants pass on messages to others. He found that messages with qualifications lost those qualifications as they were remembered over time. Further, unqualified messages had more impact on the participants (cf. Bavelas et al., 1990). It has also been suggested that, at least in some contexts, abstract and very general speech content is accepted by listeners more readily (Boudreau et al., 1992; Guerin, 1994d; Hoffman et al., 1984; Street, 1994)

A further "speech content operant" was suggested by Silver, Cohen and Crutchfield (1994). They argued that different types of messages have different "social risk" involved, meaning that the consequences differ for these different types of messages. The presentation by speakers of either ideas or negative evaluations are the most risky to communicate, the first one because they can be criticized easily, the second because people do not like negative evaluations. Presenting data or positive evaluations, on the other hand, is less risky for a speaker. In their research, Silver et al. (1994) have found some evidence for these ideas, which also depended upon the relative status of the participants. Their experiments found that more data/fact messages were used and less ideas were generated in status differentiated than status undifferentiated groups.

Different Goals of Speakers

Many of the activities found in the studies that have been discussed depend upon the "goal" of the speaker, that is, what sorts of things-that-can-be-done-to-listeners have been reinforced in the past. The cognitive tuning set literature outlined earlier pointed out that the two experimental conditions traditionally used differed in their expected goals: receiver groups expected to receive more information and not to transmit; while transmitter groups expected to have to tell another group of people their impression of the target person. Often it was never adequately explained to the receiver group what their role would eventually be (Guerin & Innes, 1989). Both groups, therefore, could have had multiple goals:

presenting themselves well to an audience for social approval, presenting themselves consistently and coherently, and presenting a description that the audience could evaluate easily or remember easily. In each case, knowing the goals of the speaker, or their history of speaking, would better predict what they do than just the fact that they were a transmitter or a receiver.

The point, then, is that the goals will predict the behaviors used, but the goals are only reports of actions that have been reinforced in the past. We have already seen that in most cases this leads to conceptualizing two goals: a seemingly individual goal and a generalized social goal of remaining part of that group. This leads to the same distinctions between the instrumental and symbolic goals, normative and informational goals, or the rational and generalized social (often called irrational when they are not obvious) goals that we have seen a few times now (Dillard & Witte, 1993; Freund, Kruglanski, & Shpitzajzen, 1985; Kellermann, 1992; Monahan, 1995; Prentice, 1987; Tracy, 1991).

Finally, the research on social influence tactics, to be covered in more detail below, shows that some different effects occur when the goal of the influencer is changed (Erez & Rim, 1982; Fung, 1991; White, 1988; Yukl, Guinan, & Sottolano, 1995).

"Understanding" by the Listener

I have already discussed some of the activities of listeners, those that are consequential for speakers. Other writings have more about what we mean when we say that a listener "understands" a speaker and therefore reinforces what was said (Schoneberger, 1990). For Skinner (1957, 1989), listener understanding meant that the listener was able to repeat back what a speaker said, could respond appropriately, or "knew" (presumably, could verbalize) about the current controlling variables in the situation.

This view was criticized by Parrott (1984; Hayes & Hayes, 1989) for, amongst other reasons, the vagueness of what "responds appropriately" means. In a general way, whatever the listener does is responding appropriately (cf. Guerin, 1996). If it is restricted to mean that the listener reinforces the speaker then this becomes a weird situation in which a listener only "understands" when they do exactly what the speaker "wants." Parrott (1984) suggested instead that understanding by listeners might entail having perceptual and covert verbal responses, and organizing words and objects into relational networks, that is, behaving as if the speaker's content were part of the listener's history. In this vein, Schoneberger (1990) suggested that a listener's understanding involves verbal behavior having control of the listener's behavior as if the stimuli referred to were either present or in the listener's history.

In line with this, some studies have found differences between listening and speaking skills. Brilhart (1965), for example, reported that speaking was not correlated with listening skills, although the results were not particularly clear. Higgins et al. (1981, p. 292) present other evidence and suggest that: "More generally, speaking (production) and listening (comprehension) require different types of information processing" (p. 293). I have already mentioned studies which find that children's speaking and listening repertoires are functionally independent for some time (Guess, 1969; Guess & Baer, 1973; Lamarre & Holland, 1985).

Common Ground between Conversants

We can also look at the activities which are shared between speaker and listener and which come to "exist" during an interaction, as speakers and listeners affect each other's verbal repertoires as if objects were present or as if the listener had a history with that object. The best work on this is that done by Clark and colleagues, which has been mentioned earlier in this paper. Clark's goal was to outline the "common ground" built up between speakers and listeners as a conversation continued, and the effects of such common ground (also Wilkes-Gibb & Clark, 1992; Krauss & Fussell, 1989). For example, when someone enters an already happening conversation, there are elements that they will not understand without the immediate history of that conversation. [These are the influences, I believe, that Schoneberger (1990) and Parrott (1984; Hayes & Hayes, 1989) have talked about in a behavior analysis context.]

As a conversation continues, common ground is "accumulated" and both parties can refer back in a short form to that content (Clark & Brennan, 1991; Clark & Murphy, 1982). That is, a mutual history is shaped. Such common ground can come from memberships in similar communities, physical co-presence (when they both see something happen), or linguistic co-presence (they both heard something or had conversed on a topic earlier). In one of Clark's many intriguing experiments, Issacs and Clark (1987) had experts and novices talk about a problem. Both adjusted (their behaviors were shaped) quickly to the different levels of expertise and changed proper names, descriptions, and perspectives to match. The experts supplied specialized knowledge to make the communication easier, and novices acquired this knowledge as the conversation continued. Wilkes-Gibb and Clark (1992) had "directors" talk about the same problems to two participants. The talk quickly developed common ground which was referred to in abbreviated forms by participants. When a second participant who had not been party to the formative talk joined in, the short forms were ineffective.

Many studies have varied whether speakers and listeners have common ground or not and find that the conversants either shift to common ground or have less effective communications (e.g., Rosenberg & Cohen, 1966). Foddy (1978) found that students used common ground when with appropriate others in communication. Feffer and Suchotliff (1966) found that participants who were better at taking another's role could communicate word associations to a listener quicker and with fewer clues. Rosenberg, Spradlin, and Mabel (1961) had pairs of males with intellectual disabilities, who were either high or low in verbal abilities, interact. They found that same-ability pairs were more vocal and used more gestures. Mixed-ability pairs had almost zero rates of interaction. Triandis (1960) found that if his participants used similar abilities then they were better at a communication task involving those abilities.

In a long series of experiments, Krauss and colleagues had subjects try and convey an answer to themselves (at a later time), a friend, or a stranger. They did better with themselves and some of the evidence is that they also do better conveying information to friends, who share common ground (Fussell & Krauss, 1989a, b, 1992; Krauss, 1987; Krauss, Dushay, Chen, & Rauscher, 1995; Krauss, Vivekananthan, & Weinheimer, 1968). When writing for themselves they used more idiosyncratic and low frequency words. When participants shared referential information they were quicker, especially if there was feedback (Krauss & Weinheimer, 1964, 1966). They also showed that participants often assumed that others shared common ground and made mistakes (false consensus effects) because of this (Fussell & Krauss, 1992).

Slugoski et al. (1993) conducted an experiment that is relevant here in which participants were told that the person they would communicate with either lacked or had some knowledge (common ground). They found that speakers made salient the relevant information about which they thought the listener was ignorant. Speakers did not do this if they thought listener had the common ground knowledge.

Anderson and Boyle (1994) found that when starting a new topic in conversation, common ground is very important and people find this out by different methods. They found that the use of a question the most effective and most common. For example, when changing to a new topic the speaker might initiate with, "Do you remember Bill? Well, he..." In this way the common ground is carefully evaluated by the listener's response and the conversation mutually shaped or socially negotiated.

Finally, many areas of research have also looked at how communication is less effective when people come from widely differing groups or audiences. This is the focal issue for miscommunication research across ethnic origins, gender, and other common social membership groups (Coupland, Giles, & Wiemann, 1991; Gallois & Callan, 1991; Hall, 1992; Tannen, 1990, 1992).

Influence and Compliance Gaining

A common activity between speaker and listener is that of influencing the other to do something. Social influence strategies have been studied in many ways, and a brief outline is given here.

Taxonomies of influence. Many schemes have been put forwarded or researched to categorize the many influence (Mulholland, 1994) and social influence strategies used by speakers (Buss, Gomes, Higgins, & Lauterbach, 1987; Falbo, 1977; Friedlander & Schwartz, 1985; Kellermann & Cole, 1994; Kipnis, Schmidt, & Wilkinson, 1980; Marwell & Schmitt, 1967; Rule & Bisanz, 1987; Schriesheim & Hinkin, 1990; Yukl & Falbe, 1990).

Kellermann and Cole (1994), for example, sorted through sixty-four strategies which had been proposed, while Littlepage, Van Hein, Cohen, and Janiec (1993) compared three common measures. Most commonly, about six influence strategies appear: assertive or emotional appeals, logical or rational influence, upward appeals, coalitions, ingratiation, and exchanges (e.g., Schriesheim & Hinkin, 1990). Questionnaires built upon such influence tactics, and other methods, have been used to study influence on audiences in many contexts: organizations (Ansari & Kapoor, 1987; Deluga, 1991; Erez, Rim & Keider, 1986; Kipnis & Schmidt, 1988; Kipnis et al. 1980; Krone, 1992; Schriesheim & Hinkin, 1990; Yukl & Falbe, 1990); personal relationships (Buss et al. 1987; Cowan, Drinkard, & MacGavin, 1984; Dunn & Cowan, 1993; Falbo & Peplau, 1980); therapy situations (Ward, Friedlander, Schoen, & Klein, 1985); with children (Haslett, 1983); and in other influence situations (Falbo, 1977; Marwell & Schmitt, 1967; White & Roufail, 1989).

Such influence attempts are under many contextual controls, most of which have been mentioned in passing through this paper. For example, Dunn and Cowan (1993) found that Japanese women had different strategies for their friends and their bosses, while Cowan et al. (1984) found that participants used different tactics for friends and parents. Situations of influencing subordinate ineptness in organizations lead to different tactics than disciplining (Ansari, 1989; Goodstadt & Kipnis, 1970). Yukl and Tracey (1992) found that tactics had different effectiveness in different work situations, and that tactics were changed when dealing with superiors or subordinates (Yukl, Falbe & Youn, 1993; Yukl, et al. 1995). The types of organization, how participatory they are for workers, also affect the use of upwards and downwards tactics (Krone, 1992).

Gender differences have also been found in influence attempts, both that whether the listener to be influenced is male or female changes the tactics used, and also that male and female influencers report using different tactics (Ansari, 1989; Carli, 1990; Eagly, 1983; Eagly & Carli, 1981; Koberg, 1985; White, 1988; White & Roufail, 1989). Some discrepancies have been found in this literature but this is not surprising because all such effects will depend upon the histories of the participants, and these gender context histories will vary widely across societies and groups within societies. White and Roufail, for example, found similar lists of tactics reported by males and females, but the frequencies of reported use were different. In an interesting meta-analysis, Eagly and Carli found that the size of the influence effect in research depended upon the gender of the experimenter: male researchers obtained larger differences, while there were no gender differences in studies conducted by women.

Finally, influence tactics have also to found to be dynamic within specific influence attempts. Studies by White and Roufail (1989) and Yukl, Falbe and Youn (1993) found that participants reported using different social influence strategies for their first choice and their last resort at influence.

Principles of influence strategies. Much less has been written about the basis or principles for social influence strategies, to help tie this area to communication studies. Burgoon (1990) suggested four principles that speakers can use to get some influence with listeners, or at least get their attention: Fear appeals, intensity of speaking, opinionation, and obscenities. Each of these utilizes events which are likely to motivate listeners.

In behavior analysis terms, what I suggest is happening is a version of Premack's Principle--that a high probability response can be used to "motivate" a low probability response if they are made contingent (Guerin, 1994a). If people are already, for many common reasons, likely to act so as to avoid a fearful verbal story (fear appeal), then the speaker can make a low probability response (the one they "want" to induce) contingent upon the removal of the fear-inducing story. Similarly, the already existing attention to, and general reaction against, obscenities can be utilized to make a less probable response more likely. Elsewhere, Arno (1980) has shown how rumor is similarly used in a group as a method of social control, and the same type of "Premacking" can be found in that report. Guerin (1994c) suggested that social representations can also be utilized to negotiate influence with other people, and Guerin (1992b) makes a similar interpretation for social control through ritual and taboo.

Another attempt at proposing principles to account for influence was made by Guerin (1995b), who used two factors--group diffusion of responsibility and generalized social consequences--as the bases for predicting reported influence attempts over individuals or groups, and influence attempts over friends or strangers. On the first factor, it was argued that influence tactics of assertion and ingratiation would work better with single individuals than groups because such tactics need to be shaped or socially negotiated as the influence attempt proceeds. Any attempt on a group would also be diffused (Latané & Darley, 1970), meaning that the consequences would be divided between the group members rather than apply to each. It was argued that logical or rational arguments, on the other hand, would not be diffused through a group because their import would apply equally to all members if the arguments were sound.

On the second factor, it was argued that assertive, ingratiating, and exchange tactics require a prior network of members of a close social group who have a "web of consequences" (cf. Simmel, 1955) already in place, whereas sound logical arguments again should work regardless. This means that tactics of assertion, ingratiation, and exchange would be more prevalent with friends than strangers, whereas logical arguments would be prevalent with both. Tactics of coalitions or upwards appeal more obviously depend upon having a social group to rely upon, in line with the findings of minority group studies (Moscovici, 1976; Moscovici & Mugny, 1983). Some evidence in line with these predictions was found by Guerin (1995b) although the tactics were only imaginary self-reports. So we cannot really say that there is strong evidence for these predictions yet.

Argument and Reasoning. Many researchers have looked more closely at how people make arguments in conversation, by analysing the content of conversations (e.g., Antaki, 1988; Billig, 1991; Edwards, 1994; Edwards & Potter, 1993; Hilton,

1995; Psathas, 1995; Schönbach, 1990; Shotter, 1993; Tannen, 1984; Van Dijk, 1983). As we have been finding throughout this paper, these attempts show the strategic nature of communication-how it gets things done for the communicator (Kellermann, 1992). As Haslett writes, "Strategic communication occurs when actors utilize their knowledge of what is appropriate in order to maximize the likelihood of achieving some goal." (Haslett, 1990, p. 143). Fleming (1994) calls this "Tactical communication."

The reports about arguments in conversation present excellent examples of socially negotiating consequences. Antaki and Leudar (1992) found that attributions, far from being individual cognitive reports, were mainly used to make arguments: to justify peoples' claims or counter-argue against other arguments. "Causal attributions turn out to look like argumentative claim-backings" (Antaki & Leudar, p. 181). In a similar way with their participants, Frazer and Cameron (1989) found that beliefs and even contradictions (cf. Guerin, 1994d, on consistency as socially controlled) were changed with different audiences and situations. Changes were made in social negotiation (shaping) with particular audiences, and mitigated if the consequences were harsh.

Schönbach (1990) found many strategies to give accounts to other people and to repair those accounts when they are challenged. His participants used concessions, excuses, justifications, and refusals to negotiate with the listeners. Brown and Van Kleck (1989) also have hypotheses about how repairs to conversations are made, a research topic well conceptualized by Schegloff, Jefferson, and Sacks (1977).

An even bigger list of conversational strategies was compiled from the discourse analyses of Van Dijk (1983). He found (pp. 398-400) that common conversational strategies with his participants were: Generalization, example-giving, contrast, apparent concessions, explanations, specifications, denials, corrections, emphasis, avoidance, repetition, stating negative consequences, specifying perspectives, presupposition, implication, mitigation, suggestion, exaggeration, vagueness, indirectness, blaming the other, ignorance, distance, and displacement. Many of these have already been mentioned when dealing above with actions that can be modified by audience consequences. For example, Tannen (1989) gives a good coverage of the role of repetition in conversation.

Other suggestions come from the data of Canary et al. (1995). They used a coding scheme of argument structures and found that those people using complex arguments were seen as more effective. It has already been mentioned that Guerin (1995b) argued that logical arguments had special properties because they could be used on groups of people without the consequences being diffused. If the arguments are sound then they could affect all people in the group, or large mass crowds, equally. It would be predicted that people speaking to large groups would, for this reason, use less assertion tactics such as threats and rely more on logical arguments, unless they had a social network in place already.

Conclusions

Hymes (1974) argued that sociolinguistic researchers need to look at variables of situational factors, setting, participants, ends, act, key, instrumentalities, norms, and genre. In reviewing the social contexts for communication we have covered all these, albeit under different names sometimes. We have seen that there are many human activities that are shaped by listeners who provide contingent consequences to speakers, that listeners do this if appropriately shaped by speakers, and that both speakers and listeners can maintain conversation for longer periods without reinforcement if they are part of a close group with multiple reciprocities. The major social contexts for communicating are identical to the major social contexts for negotiating consequences through other people. As Bell (1984) wrote, certain contexts such as topic and setting only have style effects because they are associated with discriminative audiences, or to put it in behavior analysis terms, certain contexts such as topic and setting only have style effects because in the past the audiences have differentially provided consequences contingent upon certain stylistic actions of the speakers. In a library we speak softly because in the past we have been praised for being quiet or have been punished for being noisy.

When we take the behavior analysis formulation to the real world, the principles stay the same but the analysis becomes more complex. I have tried to show how some reduction of complexity is possible by artificially separating the activities, the contexts, and the past and present consequences of acting in those contexts. Once these are analysed, the major dynamics of social communication have been covered. Much of the literature from social psychology, sociolinguistics, and communication studies has been organized easily into such a framework in this paper, including the many audience contexts, consequences and communication activities.

Throughout this paper, there have been three general points which re-occurred, and these remain to be summarized now.

1. The first general point is that the consequences of communicating are often generalized social consequences. These are difficult to identify in practice but are so ubiquitous that social science researchers have assumed either that there were no consequences maintaining the activities they have been studying, or else they have labelled them as generic "needs." In social psychology experiments, for example, the consequences used in manipulations are fairly "lumpy," usually combining several social consequences, but this is also the way things are in real life (Guerin, 1991).

In sociolinguistics, the generalized social consequences were originally assigned to the words themselves or to the style, as if just saying a word or using a style would automatically and always cause someone to change their actions. This is the charge that Bell (1984) brings against traditional sociolinguistics, such as that of Labov: why should just saying a word or using a style change someone's actions? Bell (1984) then argued that it is the type of audience that leads to the changes. But the same criticism Bell uses against traditional sociolinguistics can be, and already has been, made against Bell's use of the audience: why should just being with a certain type of audience (addressee, auditor, overhearer, eavesdropper) lead to a change in activities? Ladegaard (1995) argued that we must look to the power relations between people to find the real answer to what brings about changes in actions through speaking and listening.

Behavior analysis mirrors Ladegaard's (1995) reasoning except that the nature of "power" is spelt out more clearly. In behavior analytic terms, the "power" is the prior history and current arrangement of contingent consequences in a certain setting or with certain audiences. Actions change when consequence are applied contingently, and if this occurs in a particular setting or with a particular audience then those actions will be more likely to re-occur in the future in those settings or with that same audience if reinforced, and re-occur less if punished. This also mirrors the arguments of Bourdieu (1991) and Foucault (1982), that it is the power behind words that is important, not the words themselves. The same applies to audiences (Bell, 1984); it is the power (consequences) of the audience that is important, not the audience per se.

2. The second general point to summarize is that while prior histories of consequences with certain kinds of audiences influence current activities, some studies have shown that the local, current contingencies readily took control of behavior despite the history (DePaulo & Coleman, 1986; Issacs & Clark, 1987; Spradlin, 1985). This shows that the immediate consequences in such situations have a stronger role than previous shaping, that is, self-control (which is part of our history) is not as strong as we believe in real social situations. The immediately possible consequences can be weighed (as in Matching Law weights, Guerin, 1994a) more heavily when in real conversations.

3. The final general point to come out of this review is the consistent reporting of two major types of "motivators": an individual one and a social one; instrumental and symbolic; informational and normative. This crops up in Dillard and Witte's (1993) discussion of Prentice (1987), in Kruglanski's epistemic motivations (Freund et al. 1985), in Monahan (1995), and in the model of Ajzen and Fishbein (1980). We also find, for example, that Tannen (1986) refers to the same needs: "We need to get close to each other to have a sense of community, to feel we're not alone in the world. But we need to keep our distance from each other to preserve our independence, so others don't impose on or engulf us" (p. 17). The play between these two "needs" drives the people in her book. But the behavior analysis position pursues further back-questioning, as to why we "need" independence, and of why we "need" a sense of community.

It has been suggested (Guerin, 1992b, 1994a) that the individual "needs" actually refer to the contingent relations between the individual and the physical environment (or more direct social relations in many cases), while the community "needs" refer to the difficult to observe generalized social consequences which arise through membership in reciprocating social groups. A major problem with the "needs" approach is that the two "needs" are not in fact static: they are the very social negotiating of the contingent relations that form our social communication activities, and calling them "needs" seems to imply non-dynamic relations and a lack of prior history. The full context of activities, consequences, and the situations in which those consequences have occurred in the past needs to be mapped out to make a full analysis of the communicating activities of humans.

References

Abrams, D., Wetherall, M., Cochrane, S., Hogg, M. A., & Turner, J. C. (1990). Knowing what to think by knowing who you are: Self-categorization and the nature of norm formation, conformity and group polarization. *British Journal of Social Psychology, 29*, 97-119.

Ajzen, I., & Fishbein, M. (1980). *Understanding attitudes and predicting social behavior.* Englewood Cliffs, NJ: Prentice-Hall.

Amato, P. R. (1993). Urban-rural differences in helping friends and family members. *Social Psychology Quarterly, 56*, 249-262.

Anderson, A. H., & Boyle, E. A. (1994). Forms of introduction in dialogues: Their discourse contexts and communicative consequences. *Language and Cognitive Processes, 9*, 101-122.

Andresen, J. T. (1992). The behaviorist turn in recent theories of language. *Behavior & Philosophy, 20*, 1-19.

Ansari, M. A. (1989). Effects of leader sex, subordinate sex, and subordinate performance on the use of influence tactics. *Sex Roles, 20*, 283-293.

Ansari, M. A., & Kapoor, A. (1987). Organizational context and upward influence tactics. *Organizational Behavior and Human Decision Processes, 40*, 39-49.

Antaki, C. (Ed.). (1988). *Analysing everyday explanation: A casebook of methods.* London: Sage.

Antaki, C., & Leudar, I. (1992). Explaining in conversation: Towards an argument model. *European Journal of Social Psychology, 22*, 181-194.

Arno, A. (1980). Fijian gossip as adjudication: A communication model of informal social control. *Journal of Anthropological Research, 36*, 343-360.

Baldwin, M. W., Carrell, S. E., & Lopez, D. F. (1990). Priming relationship schemas: My adviser and the Pope are watching me from the back of my mind. *Journal of Experimental Social Psychology, 26*, 435-445.

Baldwin, M. W., & Holmes, J. G. (1987). Salient private audiences and awareness of the self. *Journal of Personality and Social Psychology, 52*, 1087-1098.

Bartlett, F. C. (1932). *Remembering.* Cambridge, England: Cambridge University Press.

Bauer, R. A. (1958). The communicator and the audience. *Journal of Conflict Resolution, 2*, 67-77.

Baumeister, R. F., & Hutton, D. G. (1987). Self-presentation theory: Self-construction and audience pleasing. In B. Mullen & G. R. Goethals (Eds.), *Theories of group behavior* (pp. 71-87). New York: Springer-Verlag.

Bavelas, J. B., Black, A., Chovil, N., & Mullett, J. (1990). *Equivocal communication.* London: Sage.

Beebe, L. M. (1981). Social and situational factors affecting the communicative strategy of dialect code-switching. *International Journal of the Sociology of Language, 32*, 139-149.

Bell, A. (1984). Language as audience design. *Language in Society, 13*, 145-204.

Bell, A. (1991). Audience accommodation in the mass media. In H. Giles, J. Coupland & N. Coupland (Eds.), *Contexts of accommodation: Developments in applied sociolinguistics* (pp. 69-102). New York: Cambridge University Press.

Bennett, M. (1990). Children's understanding of the mitigation function of disclaimers. *Journal of Language and Social Psychology, 130*, 29-37.

Billig, M. (1991). *Ideology and opinions: Studies in rhetorical psychology*. London: Sage.

Blum-Kulka, S., & Olshtain, E. (1984). Requests and apologies: A cross-cultural study of speech act realization patterns (CCSARP). *Applied Linguistics, 5*, 196-213.

Boudreau, L. A., Baron, R. M., & Oliver, P. V. (1992). Effects of expected communication target expertise and timing of set on trait use in person description. *Personality and Social Psychology Bulletin, 18*, 447-451.

Bourdieu, P. (1991). Authorized language. In P. Bourdieu (Ed.), *Language and symbolic power* (pp. 107-116). London: Polity Press.

Bourhis, R. Y., Giles, H., & Lambert, W. E. (1975). Social consequences of accommodating one's style of speech: A cross-national investigation. *International Journal of the Sociology of Language, 6*, 55-72.

Boxer, D. (1993). Social distance and speech behavior: The case of indirect complaints. *Journal of Pragmatics, 19*, 103-125.

Brilhart, B. L. (1965). The relationship between some aspects of communicative speaking and communicative listening. *Journal of Communication, 15*, 35-46.

Brock, T. C., & Fromkin, H. L. (1968). Cognitive tuning set and behavioral receptivity to discrepant information. *Journal of Personality, 36*, 108-125.

Brooke, M. E., & Ng, S. H. (1986). Language and social influence in small conversational groups. *Journal of Language and Social Psychology, 5*, 201-210.

Brown, B. R., & Garland, H. (1971). The effects of incompetency, audience acquaintanceship, and anticipated evaluative feedback on face-saving behavior. *Journal of Experimental Social Psychology, 7*, 490-502.

Brown, P., & Levinson, S. (1987). *Politeness: Some universals in language use*. Cambridge, England: Cambridge University Press.

Brown, R., & Fish, D. (1983). The psychological causality implicit in language. *Cognition, 14*, 237-273.

Brown, R., & Van Kleck, M. H. (1989). Enough said: Three principles of explanation. *Journal of Personality and Social Psychology, 57*, 590-604.

Buller, D. B., & Aune, R. K. (1992). The effects of speech rate similarity on compliance: Application of communication accommodation theory. *Western Journal of Communication, 56*, 37-53.

Burgoon, M. (1990). Language and social influence. In H. Giles & W. P. Robinson (Eds.), *Handbook of language and social psychology* (pp. 51-72). New York: John Wiley.

Buss, D. M., Gomes, M., Higgins, D. S., & Lauterbach, K. (1987). Tactics of manipulation. *Journal of Personality and Social Psychology, 52*, 1219-1229.

Canary, D. J., Brossman, J. E., Brossman, B. G., & Weger, H. (1995). Toward a theory of minimally rational argument: Analyses of episode-specific effects of argument structures. *Communications Monographs, 62*, 183-212.

Cansler, D. C., & Stiles, W. B. (1981). Relative status and interpersonal presumptuousness. *Journal of Experimental Social Psychology, 17*, 459-471.

Carli, L. L. (1990). Gender, language, and influence. *Journal of Personality and Social Psychology, 59*, 941-951.

Catania, A. C. (1980). Autoclitic processes and the structure of behavior. *Behaviorism, 8*, 175-186.

Chiasson, C., & Hayes, L. J. (1993). The effects of subtle differences between listeners and speakers on the referential speech of college freshmen. *The Psychological Record, 43*, 13-24.

Cialdini, R. B., Levy, A., Herman, C. P., & Evenbeck, S. (1973). Attitudinal politics: The strategy of moderation. *Journal of Personality and Social Psychology, 25*, 100-108.

Cialdini, R. B., Levy, A., Herman, C. P., Kozlowski, L. T., & Petty, R. E. (1976). Elastic shifts of opinion: Determinants of direction and durability. *Journal of Personality and Social Psychology, 34*, 663-672.

Cialdini, R. B., & Petty, R. E. (1981). Anticipatory opinion effects. In R. E. Petty, T. M. Ostrom, & T. C. Brock (Eds.), *Cognitive responses in persuasion* (pp. 217-235). Hillsdale, NJ: Erlbaum.

Clark, H. H., & Brennan, S. E. (1991). Grounding in communication. In L. B. Resnick, J. M. Levine, & S. D. Teasley (Eds.), *Perspectives on socially shared cognition* (pp. 127-149). Washington, DC: American Psychological Association.

Clark, H. H., & Murphy, G. L. (1982). Audience design in meaning and reference. In J.-F. Le Ny & W. Kintsch (Eds.), *Language and comprehension* (pp. 287-299). Amsterdam: North Holland.

Clark, H. H., & Schaefer, E. F. (1987). Concealing one's meaning from overhearers. *Journal of Memory and Language, 26*, 209-225.

Clark, H. H., & Schaefer, E. F. (1989). Contributing to discourse. *Cognitive Science, 13*, 259-294.

Clark, H. H., & Schunk, D. H. (1980). Polite responses to polite requests. *Cognition, 8*, 111-143.

Cooley, C. H. (1902). *Human nature and the social order.* New York: Scribner.

Coupland, J., Coupland, N., & Robinson, J. D. (1992). "How are you?": Negotiating phatic communion. *Language in Society, 21*, 207-230.

Coupland, N. (1980). Style-shifting in a Cardiff work-setting. *Language in Society, 9*, 1-12.
Coupland, N. (1984). Accommodation at work: Some phonological data and their implications. *International Journal of the Sociology of Language, 46*, 49-70.
Coupland, N., Giles, H., & Wiemann, J. M. (Eds.). (1991). *"Miscommunication" and problematic talk*. London: Sage.
Cowan, G., Drinkard, J., & MacGavin, L. (1984). The effects of target, age, and gender on use of power strategies. *Journal of Personality and Social Psychology, 47*, 1391-1398.
Cvetkovich, G. (1978). Cognitive accommodation, language and social responsibility. *Social Psychology, 41*, 149-155.
Davis, D., & Holtgraves, T. (1984). Perceptions of others: Attribution, attraction, understandability, and memory of their utterances. *Journal of Experimental Social Psychology, 20*, 383-408.
Davis, D., & Perkowitz, W. T. (1979). Consequences of responsiveness in dyadic interaction: Effects of probability of response and proportion of content-related responses on interpersonal attraction. *Journal of Personality and Social Psychology, 37*, 534-550.
Deluga, R. J. (1991). The relationship of upward-influencing behavior with subordinate-impression management characteristics. *Journal of Applied Social Psychology, 21*, 1145-1160.
DePaulo, B. M., & Coleman, L. M. (1986). Talking to children, foreigners, and retarded adults. *Journal of Personality and Social Psychology, 51*, 945-959.
De Poot, C. J., & Semin, G. R. (1995). Pick your verbs with care when you formulate a question! *Journal of Language and Social Psychology, 14*, 351-368.
Diaz, R. M., & Berk, L. E. (Eds.). (1992). *Private speech: From social interaction to self-regulation*. Hillsdale, NJ: Erlbaum.
Difonzo, N., Bordia, P., & Rosnow, R. L. (1994). Reining in rumors. *Organizational Dynamics, 23*, 47-62.
Dillard, J. P., & Witte, K. (1993). Possessions theory of persuasion: An examination of its basis and range. *Communication studies, 44*, 188-199.
Dines, E. R. (1980). Variation in discourse-"and stuff like that". *Language in Society, 9*, 13-31.
Dunn, K. F., & Cowan, G. (1993). Social influence strategies among Japanese and American college women. *Psychology of Women Quarterly, 17*, 39-52.
Durkheim, E. (1933/1893). *The division of labour in society*. New York: Macmillan.
Eagly, A. H. (1983). Gender and social influence. *American Psychologist, 38*, 971-981.
Eagly, A. H., & Carli, L. L. (1981). Sex of researchers and sex-typed communication as determinants of sex differences in influenceability: A meta-analysis of social influence studies. *Psychological Bulletin, 90*, 1-20.
Eckert, P., & McConnell-Ginet, S. (1992). Think practically and look locally: Language and gender as community-based practice. *Annual Review of Anthropology, 21*, 461-490.

Ede, L., & Lunsford, A. (1984). Audience addressed/ audience invoked: The role of audience in composition theory and pedagogy. *College Composition and Communication, 35*, 155-171.

Edwards, D. (1994). Script formulations: An analysis of event descriptions in conversation. *Journal of Language and Social Psychology, 13*, 211-247.

Edwards, D., & Potter, J. (1993). Language and causation: A discursive action model of description and attribution. *Psychological Review, 100*, 23-41.

Erez, M., & Rim, Y. (1982). The relationship between goals, influence tactics, and personal and organizational variables. *Human Relations, 35*, 871-878.

Erez, M., Rim, Y., & Keider, I. (1986). The two sides of the tactics of influence: Agent vs. target. *Journal of Occupational Psychology, 59*, 25-39.

Ervin-Tripp, S. (1964). An analysis of the interaction of language, topic, and listener. *American Anthropologist, 66*, (6) Part 2, 86-102.

Ervin-Tripp, S. (1976). Is Sybil there? The structure of some American English directives. *Language in Society, 5*, 25-66.

Esposito, J. L., & Rosnow, R. L. (1984). Cognitive set and message processing: Implications of prose memory research for rumor theory. *Language and Communication, 4*, 301-315.

Evans-Pritchard, E. E. (1976). *Witchcraft, oracles, and magic among the Azande.* Oxford, England: Clarendon Press.

Falbo, T. (1977). Multidimensional scaling of power strategies. *Journal of Personality and Social Psychology, 35*, 537-547.

Falbo, T., & Peplau, L. A. (1980). Power strategies in intimate relationships. *Journal of Personality and Social Psychology, 38*, 618-628.

Farber, B. (1989). Limiting reciprocity among relatives: Theoretical implications of a serendipitous finding. *Sociological Perspectives, 32*, 307-330.

Farr, R. M., & Moscovici, S. (Eds.). (1984). *Social representations.* Cambridge, England: Cambridge University Press.

Feffer, M., & Suchotliff, L. (1966). Decentering implications of social interactions. *Journal of Personality and Social Psychology, 4*, 415-422.

Fill, A. F. (1986). "Divided illocution" in conversational and other situations-and some of its implications. *International Review of Applied Linguistics, 24*, 27-34.

Fleming, J. H. (1994). Multiple-audience problems, tactical communication, and social interaction: A relational-regulation perspective. *Advances in Experimental Social Psychology, 26*, 215-292.

Fleming, J. H., Darley, J. M., Hilton, J. L., & Kojetin, B. A. (1990). Multiple audience problem: A strategic communication perspective on social perception. *Journal of Personality and Social Psychology, 58*, 593-609.

Foddy, M. (1978). Role-taking in a communication task. *Personality and Social Psychology Bulletin, 4*, 388-392.

Foucault, M. (1982). The subject and power. *Critical Inquiry, 8*, 777-795.

Fraser, B. (1990). Perspectives on politeness. *Journal of Pragmatics, 14*, 219-236.

Fraser, B., & Nolen, W. (1981). The association of deference with linguistic form. *International Journal of the Sociology of Language, 27*, 93-109.

Frazer, E., & Cameron, D. (1989). Knowing what to say: The construction of gender in linguistic practice. *Sociological Review Monograph, 36,* 25-40.

Freund, T., Kruglanski, A. W., & Shpitzajzen, A. (1985). The freezing and unfreezing of impressional primacy: Effects of the need for structure and the fear of invalidity. *Personality and Social Psychology Bulletin, 11,* 479-487.

Friedlander, M. L., & Schwartz, G. S. (1985). Toward a theory of strategic self-presentation in counseling and psychotherapy. *Journal of Counseling Psychology, 32,* 483-501.

Fung, S. S. K. (1991). The effects of power, relationship, and purpose in gaining compliance. *Contemporary Social Psychology, 15,* 44-52.

Fussell, S. R., & Krauss, R. M. (1989a). The effects of intended audience on message production and comprehension: Reference in a common ground framework. *Journal of Experimental Social Psychology, 25,* 203-219.

Fussell, S. R., & Krauss, R. M. (1989b). Understanding friends and strangers: The effects of audience design on message comprehension. *European Journal of Social Psychology, 19,* 509-525.

Fussell, S. R., & Krauss, R. M. (1992). Coordination of knowledge in communication: Effects of speakers' assumptions about what others know. *Journal of Personality and Social Psychology, 62,* 378-391.

Gaes, G. G., & Tedeschi, J. T. (1978). An evaluation of self-esteem and impression management theories of anticipatory belief change. *Journal of Experimental Social Psychology, 14,* 579-587.

Gallois, C. (1994). Group membership, social rules, and power: A social-psychological perspective on emotional communication. *Journal of Pragmatics, 22,* 301-324.

Gallois, C., & Callan, V. J. (1991). Interethnic accommodation: The role of norms. In H. Giles, J. Coupland, & N. Coupland (Eds.), *Contexts of accommodation: Developments in applied sociolinguistics* (pp. 245-269). New York: Cambridge University Press.

Gallois, C., Callan, V. J., & Johnstone, M. (1984). Personality judgements of Australian Aborigine and white speakers: Ethnicity, sex and context. *Journal of Language and Social Psychology, 3,* 39-57.

Gergen, K. J. (1985). The social constructionist movement in modern psychology. *American Psychologist, 40,* 266-275.

Giles, H., Coupland, J., & Coupland, N. (Eds.). (1991). *Contexts of accommodation: Developments in applied sociolinguistics.* New York: Cambridge University Press.

Giles, H., & Johnson, P. (1987). Ethnolinguistic identity theory: A social psychological approach to language maintenance. *International Journal of the Sociology of Language, 68,* 68-99.

Gilovich, T. (1987). Secondhand information and social judgment. *Journal of Experimental Social Psychology, 23,* 59-74.

Goodstadt, B., & Kipnis, D. (1970). Situational influences on the use of power. *Journal of Applied Psychology, 54,* 201-217.

Grace, H. A. (1951). Effects of different degrees of knowledge about an audience on the content of communication. *Journal of Social Psychology, 34,* 111-124.

Grace, H. A. (1952a). Effects of different degrees of knowledge about an audience on the content of communication: The male audience. *Journal of Social Psychology, 36,* 83-88.

Grace, H. A. (1952b). Effects of different degrees of knowledge about an audience on the content of communication: The comparison of male and female audiences. *Journal of Social Psychology, 36,* 89-96.

Graumann, C. F., & Herrmann, T. (1989). *Speakers: The role of the listener.* Philadelphia: Multilingual Matters.

Graumann, C. F., & Sommer, C. M. (1989). Perspective structure in language production and comprehension. In C. F. Graumann & T. Herrmann (Eds.), *Speakers: The role of the listener* (pp. 35-54). Philadelphia: Multilingual Matters.

Grice, H. P. (1975). Logic and conversation. In P. Cole & J. L. Morgan (Eds.), *Syntax and semantics 3: Speech acts* (pp. 41-58). New York: Academic Press.

Grice, H. P. (1978). Some further notes on logic and conversation. In P. Cole (Ed.), *Syntax and semantics 9: Pragmatics* (pp. 113-128). New York: Academic Press.

Guerin, B. (1990). Gibson, Skinner, and perceptual responses. *Behavior & Philosophy, 18,* 43-54.

Guerin, B. (1991). Anticipating the consequences of social behavior. *Current Psychology: Research and Reviews, 10,* 131-162.

Guerin, B. (1992a). Behavior analysis and the social construction of knowledge. *American Psychologist, 47,* 1423-1432.

Guerin, B. (1992b). Social behavior as discriminative stimulus and consequence in social anthropology. *The Behavior Analyst, 15,* 31-41.

Guerin, B. (1993). *Social facilitation.* Cambridge, England: Cambridge University Press.

Guerin, B. (1994a). *Analyzing social behavior: Behavior analysis and the social sciences.* Reno, NV: Context Press.

Guerin, B. (1994b). Gender bias in the abstractness of verbs and adjectives. *Journal of Social Psychology, 134,* 421-428.

Guerin, B. (1994c). Using social representations to negotiate the social practices of life. *Papers on Social Representations, 3,* 177-183.

Guerin, B. (1994d). Attitudes and beliefs as verbal behavior. *The Behavior Analyst, 17,* 155-163.

Guerin, B. (1995a). Generalized social consequences, ritually reinforced behaviors, and the difficulties of analysing social contingencies in the real world. *Experimental Analysis of Human Behavior Bulletin, 13,* 11-14.

Guerin, B. (1995b). Social influence in one-to-one and group situations: Predicting influence tactics from basic group processes. *Journal of Social Psychology, 135,* 371-385.

Guerin, B. (1995c). The use of group views when giving opinions about unknown, group-salient or neutral items. *Journal of Social Psychology, 135,* 57-61.

Guerin, B. (1995d). Some recent and future developments in the study of social representations. *Japanese Journal of Experimental Social Psychology, 34*, 205-212.

Guerin, B. (in press). How things get done: Socially, nonsocially; with words, without words. In L. Hayes & P. Ghezzi (Eds.), *Investigations in behavioral epistemology*. Reno, NV: Context Press.

Guerin, B., & Innes, J. M. (1989). Cognitive tuning sets: Anticipating the consequences of communication. *Current Psychology: Research & Reviews, 8*, 234-249.

Guess, D. (1969). A functional analysis of receptive language and productive speech: Acquisition of the plural morpheme. *Journal of Applied Behavior Analysis, 2*, 55-64.

Guess, D., & Baer, D. M. (1973). An analysis of individual differences in generalization between receptive and productive language in retarded children. *Journal of Applied Behavior Analysis, 6*, 311-329.

Gumperz, J. J. (1982). *Discourse strategies*. Cambridge, England: Cambridge University Press.

Hagiwara, S. (1992). The concept of responsibility and determinants of responsibility judgment in the Japanese context. *International Journal of Psychology, 27*, 143-156.

Hall, G. A. (1992). Aspects of conversational style-Linguistic versus behavioral analysis. *The Analysis of Verbal Behavior, 10*, 81-86.

Hamilton, V. L., & Hagiwara, S. (1992). Roles, responsibility, and accounts across cultures. *International Journal of Psychology, 27*, 157-179.

Hart, K. (1986). Heads or tails? Two sides of the coin. *Man (N.S.), 21*, 637-656.

Haslett, B. (1983). Preschoolers' communicative strategies in gaining compliance from peers: A developmental study. *Quarterly Journal of Speech, 69*, 84-99.

Haslett, B. (1990). Developing strategic communication. In J. P. Dillard (Ed.), *Seeking compliance: The production of interpersonal influence messages* (pp. 143-160). Scottsdale, AZ: Gorsuch Scarisbrick Publishers.

Hass, R. G. (1975). Persuasion or moderation? Two experiments on anticipatory belief change. *Journal of Personality and Social Psychology, 31*, 1155-1162.

Hass, R. G., & Mann, R. W. (1976). Anticipatory belief change: Persuasion or impression management? *Journal of Personality and Social Psychology, 34*, 105-111.

Hayes, S. C., & Hayes, L. J. (1989). The verbal action of the listener as a basis for rule-governance. In S. C. Hayes (Ed.), *Rule-governed behavior: Cognition, contingencies, and instructional control* (pp. 153-190). New York: Plenum Press.

Hayes, S. C., & Wilson, K. G. (1993). Some applied implications of a contemporary behavior-analytic account of verbal events. *The Behavior Analyst, 16*, 283-301.

Heller, M. (Ed.). (1988). *Codeswitching: Anthropological and sociolinguistic perspectives*. New York: Mouton de Gruyter.

Henley, N. M., & Kramarae, C. (1991). Gender, power, and miscommunication. In N. Coupland, H. Giles, & J. M. Wiemann (Eds.), *"Miscommunication" and problematic talk* (pp. 18-43). London: Sage.

Hewitt, J. P., & Stokes, R. (1975). Disclaimers. *American Sociological Review, 40*, 1-11.
Hewstone, M. (1989). *Causal attribution: From cognitive processes to collective beliefs.* Oxford, England: Basil Blackwell.
Higgins, E. T. (1976). Social class differences in verbal communicative accuracy: A question of "Which question?" *Psychological Bulletin, 83*, 695-714.
Higgins, E. T., Fondacaro, R., & McCann, C. D. (1981). Rules and roles: The "communication game" and speaker-listener processes. In W. P. Dickson (Ed.), *Children's oral communication skills* (pp. 289-312). New York: Academic Press.
Higgins, E. T., McCann, C. D., & Fondacaro, R. (1982). The "communication game": Goal-directed encoding and cognitive consequences. *Social Cognition, 1*, 21-37.
Higgins, E. T., & Rholes, W. S. (1978). "Saying is believing": Effects of message modification on memory and liking for the person described. *Journal of Experimental Social Psychology, 14*, 363-378.
Hilton, D. J. (1995). The social context of reasoning: Conversational inference and rational judgment. *Psychological Bulletin, 118*, 248-271.
Hoffman, C., Mischel, W., & Baer, J. S. (1984). Language and person cognition: Effects of communicative set on trait attribution. *Journal of Personality and Social Psychology, 46*, 1029-1043.
Holmes, J. (1984). Hedging your bets and sitting on the fence: Some evidence for hedges as support structures. *Te Reo, 27*, 47-62.
Holmes, J. (1989). Sex differences and apologies: One aspect of communicative competence. *Applied Linguistics, 10*, 194-213.
Holmes, J. (1993). New Zealand women are good to talk to: An analysis of politeness strategies in interaction. *Journal of Pragmatics, 20*, 91-116.
Horne, P. J., & Lowe, C. F. (1996). On the origins of naming and other symbolic behavior. *Journal of the Experimental Analysis of Behavior, 65*, 185-241.
Holtgraves, T. (1986). Language structure in social interaction: Perceptions of direct and indirect speech acts and interactants who use them. *Journal of Personality and Social Psychology, 51*, 305-314.
Holtgraves, T., & Yang, J-N. (1990). Politeness as universal: Cross-cultural perceptions of request strategies and inferences based on their use. *Journal of Personality and Social Psychology, 59*, 719-729.
Hudson, A. (1992). Diglossia: A bibliographic review. *Language in Society, 21*, 611-674.
Hymes, D. H. (1974). *Foundations in sociolinguistics: An ethnographic approach.* Philadelphia: University of Pennsylvania Press.
Hyten, C., & Chase, P. N. (1991). An analysis of self-editing: Method and preliminary findings. In L. J. Hayes & P. N. Chase (Eds.), *Dialogues on verbal behavior* (pp. 67-81) Reno, NV: Context Press.
Inman, M. L., Reichl, A. J., & Baron, R. S. (1993). Do we tell less than we know or hear less than we are told? Exploring the teller-listener extremity effect. *Journal of Experimental Social Psychology, 29*, 528-550.

Innes, J. M., & Gilroy, S. (1980). The semantics of asking a favor: Asking for help in three countries. *Journal of Social Psychology, 110,* 3-7.
Issacs, E. A., & Clark, H. H. (1987). References in conversation between experts and novices. *Journal of Experimental Psychology: General, 116,* 26-37.
Jeffery, K. M., & Mischel, W. (1979). Effects of purpose on the organization and recall of information in person perception. *Journal of Personality, 47,* 397-419.
Jellison, J. M., & Gentry, K. W. (1978). A self-presentation interpretation of the seeking of social approval. *Personality and Social Psychology Bulletin, 4,* 227-230.
John-Lewis, C. (Ed.). (1986). *Intonation in discourse.* London: Croom Helm.
Kellermann, K. (1992). Communication: Inherently strategic and primarily automatic. *Communication Monographs, 59,* 288-300.
Kellermann, K., & Cole, T. (1994). Classifying compliance gaining messages: Taxonomic disorder and strategic confusion. *Communication Theory, 4,* 3-60.
Kimmel, A. J., & Keefer, R. (1991). Psychological correlates of the transmission and acceptance of rumors about AIDS. *Journal of Applied Social Psychology, 21,* 1608-1628.
Kipnis, D., & Schmidt, S. M. (1988). Upward-influence styles: Relationship with performance evaluation, salary, and stress. *Administrative Science Quarterly, 33,* 528-542.
Kipnis, D., Schmidt, S. M., & Wilkinson, I. (1980). Intraorganizational influence tactics: Explorations in getting one's way. *Journal of Applied Psychology, 65,* 440-452.
Koberg, C. S. (1985). Sex and situational influences on the use of power: A follow-up study. *Sex Roles, 13,* 625-639.
Kramarae, C. (1990). Changing the complexion of gender in language research. In H. Giles & W. P. Robinson (Eds.), *Handbook of language and social psychology* (pp. 345-361). New York: John Wiley.
Krauss, R. M. (1987). The role of the listener: Addressee influences on message formulation. *Journal of Language and Social Psychology, 6,* 81-98.
Krauss, R. M., Dushay, R. A., Chen, Y., & Rauscher, F. (1995). The communicative value of conversational hand gestures. *Journal of Experimental Social Psychology, 31,* 533-552.
Krauss, R. M., & Fussell, S. R. (1989). Other-relatedness in language processing: Discussion and comments. In C. F. Graumann & T. Herrmann (Eds.), *Speakers: The role of the listener* (pp. 105-121). Philadelphia: Multilingual Matters.
Krauss, R. M., Vivekananthan, P. S., & Weinheimer, S. (1968). "Inner speech" and "external speech": Characteristics and communication effectiveness of socially and nonsocially encoded messages. *Journal of Personality and Social Psychology, 9,* 295-300.
Krauss, R. M., & Weinheimer, S. (1964). Changes in reference phrases as a function of frequency of usage in social interaction: A preliminary study. *Psychonomic Science, 1,* 113-114.

Krauss, R. M., & Weinheimer, S. (1966). Concurrent feedback, confirmation, and the encoding of referents in verbal communication. *Journal of Personality and Social Psychology, 4,* 343-346.

Kraut, R. E., Lewis, S. H., & Swezey, L. W. (1982). Listener responsiveness and the coordination of conversation. *Journal of Personality and Social Psychology, 43,* 718-731.

Krone, K. J. (1992). A comparison of organizational, structural, and relationship effects on subordinates' upward influence choices. *Communication Quarterly, 40,* 1-15.

Kruglanski, A. W., & Mayerless, O. (1987). Motivational effects in the social comparison of opinions. *Journal of Personality and Social Psychology, 53,* 834-842.

Labov, W. (1990). The intersection of sex and social class in the course of linguistic change. *Language Variation and Change, 2,* 205-254.

Ladegaard, H. J. (1995). Audience design revisited: Persons, roles and power relations in speech interactions. *Language and Communication, 15,* 89-101.

Lakoff, R. (1973). Language and woman's place. *Language in Society, 2,* 45-80.

Lakoff, R. (1975). *Language and woman's place.* New York: Harper Row.

Lamarre, J., & Holland, J. G. (1985). The functional independence of mands and tacts. *Journal of the Experimental Analysis of Behavior, 43,* 5-19.

Langer, E. J., & Abelson, R. P. (1972). The semantics of asking a favor: How to succeed in getting help without really dying. *Journal of Personality and Social Psychology, 24,* 26-32.

Latané, B., & Darley, J. M. (1970). *The unresponsive bystander: Why doesn't he help?* New York: Appleton-Century-Crofts.

Leary, M. R., Rogers, P. A., Canfield, R. W., & Coe, C. (1986). Boredom in interpersonal encounters: Antecedents and social implications. *Journal of Personality and Social Psychology, 51,* 968-975.

Lee, V. L. (1994). Organisms, things done, and the fragmentation of psychology. *Behavior & Philosophy, 22,* 7-48.

Lee, V. L. (1995). What is the psychological unit? *Behaviour Change, 12,* 98-108.

Leeds-Hurwitz, W. (Ed.). (1995). *Social approaches to communication.* New York: The Guilford Press.

Levinson, S. C. (1983). *Pragmatics.* Cambridge, England: Cambridge University Press.

Lewis, P. N., & Gallois, C. (1984). Disagreements, refusals, or negative feelings: Perception of negatively assertive messages from friends and strangers. *Behavior Therapy, 15,* 353-368.

Littlepage, G. E., Van Hein, J. L., Cohen, K. M., & Janiec, L. L. (1993). Evaluation and comparison of three instruments designed to measure organizational power and influence tactics. *Journal of Applied Social Psychology, 23,* 107-125.

Litwak, E., & Szelenyi, I. (1969). Primary group structures and their function: Kin, neighbors, and friends. *American Sociological Review, 34,* 465-481.

Maass, A., Salvi, D., Arcuri, L., & Semin, G. R. (1989). Language use in intergroup contexts: The linguistic intergroup bias. *Journal of Personality and Social Psychology, 57,* 981-993.

Mackie, D. M., Gastardo-Conaco, M. C., & Skelly, J. J. (1992). Knowledge of the advocated position and the processing of in-group and out-group persuasive messages. *Personality and Social Psychology Bulletin, 18,* 145-151.

Malinowski, B. (1923). The problem of meaning in primitive languages. Supplement to C. K. Ogden & I. A. Richards (Eds.), *The meaning of meaning* (pp. 146-152). London: Routledge and Kegan Paul.

Manis, M., Cornell, S. D., & Moore, J. C. (1974). Transmission of attitude-relevant information through a communication chain. *Journal of Personality and Social Psychology, 30,* 81-94.

Marwell, G., & Schmitt, D. R. (1967). Dimensions of compliance-gaining behavior: An empirical analysis. *Sociometry, 30,* 350-364.

Mazis, M. B. (1973). Cognitive tuning and receptivity to novel information. *Journal of Experimental Social Psychology, 9,* 307-319.

McCann, C. D., & Hancock, R. D. (1983). Self-monitoring in communicative interactions: Social cognitive consequences of goal-directed message modification. *Journal of Experimental Social Psychology, 19,* 109-121.

Mead, G. H. (1924/1925). The genesis of the self and social control. *International Journal of Ethics, 35,* 251-277.

Mead, G. H. (1934). *Mind, self, and society from the standpoint of a social behaviorist.* Chicago: University of Chicago Press.

Mills, J., & Jellison, J. M. (1968). Effect on opinion change of similarity between the communicator and the audience he addressed. *Journal of Personality and Social Psychology, 9,* 153-156.

Milroy, L., & Milroy, J. (1992). Social network and social class: Towards an integrated sociolinguistic model. *Language in Society, 21,* 1-26.

Monahan, J. L. (1995). Information processing differences of conversational participants and observers: The effects of self-presentation concerns and cognitive load. *Communications Monographs, 62,* 265-281.

Moore, J. C. (1974). Audience effects in a communication chain: An instance of ingratiation. *Personality and Social Psychology Bulletin, 1,* 58-61.

Moscovici, S. (1976). *Social influence and social change.* London: Academic Press.

Moscovici, S. (1984). The phenomenon of social representations. In R. M. Farr & S. Moscovici (Eds.), *Social representations* (pp. 3-69). New York: Cambridge University Press.

Moscovici, S., & Mugny, G. (1983). Minority influence. In P. B. Paulus (Ed.), Basic group processes (pp. 41-64). New York: Springer.

Mulholland, J. (1994). *Handbook of persuasive tactics: A practical guide.* London: Routledge.

Newtson, D., & Czerlinsky, T. (1974). Adjustment of attitude communications for contrasts by extreme audiences. *Journal of Personality and Social Psychology, 30,* 829-837.

Ng, S. H., Bell, D., & Brooke, M. (1993). Gaining turns and achieving high influence in small conversational groups. *British Journal of Social Psychology, 32,* 265-275.

Ng, S. H., & Bradac, J. J. (1993). *Power in language: Verbal communication and social influence.* London: Sage.

Ng, S. H., Brooke, M., & Dunne, M. (1995). Interruption and influence in discussion groups. *Journal of Language and Social Psychology, 14,* 369-381.

Nwoye, O. G. (1992). Linguistic politeness and socio-cultural variations of the notion of face. *Journal of Pragmatics, 18,* 309-328.

Ohbuchi, K., Kameda, M., & Agarie, N. (1989). Apology as aggression control: Its role in mediating appraisal of and response to harm. *Journal of Personality and Social Psychology, 56,* 219-227.

Pan, Y. (1995). Power behind linguistic behavior: Analysis of politeness phenomena in Chinese official settings. *Journal of Language and Social Psychology, 14,* 462-481.

Papageorgis, D. (1963). Bartlett effects and the persistence of induced opinion change. *Journal of Abnormal and Social Psychology, 67,* 61-67.

Parrott, L. J. (1984). Listening and understanding. *The Behavior Analyst, 7,* 29-39.

Peterson, N. (1993). Demand sharing: Reciprocity and the pressure for generosity among foragers. *American Anthropologist, 95,* 860-874.

Powell, F. A. (1974). Cognitive tuning and differentiation of arguments in communication. *Human Communication Research, 1,* 53-61.

Prentice, D. A. (1987). Psychological correspondence of possessions, attitudes, and values. *Journal of Personality and Social Psychology, 53,* 993-1003.

Psathas, G. (1995). *Conversation analysis: The study of talk-in-interaction.* London: Sage.

Putman, W. B., & Street, R. L. (1984). The conception and perception of noncontent speech performance: Implications for speech-accommodation theory. *International Journal of the Sociology of Language, 46,* 97-114.

Romaine, S. (Ed.). (1982). *Sociolinguistic variation in speech communities.* London: Edward Arnold.

Rosaldo, M. Z. (1982). The things we do with words: Ilongot speech acts and speech act theory in philosophy. *Language and Society, 11,* 203-237.

Rosenberg, S., & Cohen, B. D. (1966). Referential processes of speakers and listeners. *Psychological Review, 73,* 208-231.

Rosenberg, S., Spradlin, J. E., & Mabel, S. (1961). Interaction among retarded children as a function of their relative language skills. *Journal of Abnormal and Social Psychology, 63,* 402-410.

Rosnow, R. L. (1988). Rumor as communication: A contextualist approach. *Journal of Communication, 38,* 12-28.

Rosnow, R. L., Yost, J., & Esposito, J. L. (1986). Belief in rumor and likelihood of rumor transmission. *Language and Communication, 6,* 189-194.

Rule, B. G., & Bisanz, G. L. (1987). Goals and strategies of persuasion: A cognitive schema for understanding social events. In M. P. Zanna, J. M. Olsen, & C. P. Herman (Eds.), *Social influence: The Ontario symposium, Volume 5* (pp. 185-206). Hillsdale, NJ: Lawrence Erlbaum.

Sahlins, M. D. (1965). On the sociology of primitive exchange. In M. Banton (Ed.), *The relevance of models for social anthropology* (pp. 139-236). London: Tavistock.

Schegloff, E., Jefferson, G., & Sacks, H. (1977). The preference for self-correction in the organization of repair in conversation. *Language, 53,* 361-382.

Schmidt, R. W. (1990). The role of consciousness in second language learning. *Applied Linguistics, 11,* 129-158.

Schober, M. F., & Clark, H. H. (1989). Understanding by addressees and overhearers. *Cognitive Psychology, 21,* 211-232.

Schönbach, P. (1990). *Account episodes: The management or escalation of conflict.* New York: Cambridge University Press.

Schoneberger, T. (1990). Understanding and the listener. *The Analysis of Verbal Behavior, 8,* 141-150.

Schramm, W., & Danielson, W. (1958). Anticipated audiences as determinants of recall. *Journal of Abnormal and Social Psychology, 56,* 282-283.

Schriesheim, C. A., & Hinkin, T. R. (1990). Influence tactics used by subordinates: A theoretical and empirical analysis and refinement of the Kipnis, Schmidt, and Wilkinson subscales. *Journal of Applied Psychology, 75,* 246-257.

Semin, G. R., & Fiedler, K. (1988). The cognitive functions of linguistic categories in describing persons: Social cognition and language. *Journal of Personality and Social Psychology, 54,* 558-568.

Semin, G. R., & Fiedler, K. (1989). Relocating attributional phenomena within a language-cognition interface: The case of actors' and observers' perspectives. *European Journal of Social Psychology, 19,* 491-508.

Semin, G. R., & Fiedler, K. (1991). The linguistic category model, its bases, applications and range. In W. Stroebe & M. Hewstone (Eds.), *European review of social psychology* (Vol. 2, pp. 1-30). New York: John Wiley.

Semin, G. R., & Fiedler, K. (1992). *Language, interaction and social cognition.* London: Sage.

Shockey, L. (1984). All in a flap: Long-term accommodation in phonology. *International Journal of the Sociology of Language, 46,* 87-95.

Shotter, J. (1993). *Cultural politics of everyday life.* Buckingham: Open University Press.

Silver, S. D., Cohen, B. P., & Crutchfield, J. H. (1994). Status differentiation and information exchange in face-to-face and computer-mediated idea generation. *Social Psychology Quarterly, 57,* 108-123.

Silverman, K., Anderson, S. R., Marshall, A. M., & Baer, D. M. (1986). Establishing and generalizing audience control of new language repertoires. *Analysis and Intervention in Developmental Disabilities, 6,* 21-40.

Simmel, G. (1955). *Conflict & The web of group-affiliations.* New York: The Free Press.

Skinner, B. F. (1957). *Verbal behavior.* Englewood Cliffs, NJ: Prentice Hall.
Skinner, B. F. (1989). The behavior of the listener. In S. C. Hayes (Ed.), *Rule-governed behavior: Cognition, contingencies, and instructional control* (pp. 85-96). New York: Plenum Press.
Slugoski, B. R., Lalljee, M., Lamb, R., & Ginsburg, G. P. (1993). Attribution in conversational context: Effect of mutual knowledge on explanation-giving. *European Journal of Social Psychology, 23,* 219-238.
Smith, B. L., Laswell, H. D., & Caselt, R. D. (1946*). Propaganda, communication and public opinion.* Princeton, NJ: Princeton University Press.
Smith, T. L. (1983). Vargas on the autoclitic. *The Analysis of Verbal Behavior, 2,* 11-12.
Spencer-Oatey, H. (1993). Conceptions of social relations and pragmatics research. *Journal of Pragmatics, 20,* 27-47.
Spradlin, J. E. (1985). Studying the effects of the audience on verbal behavior. *The Analysis of Verbal Behavior, 3,* 6-10.
Spradlin, J. E., & Rosenberg, S. (1964). Complexity of adult verbal behavior in a dyadic situation with retarded children. *Journal of Abnormal and Social Psychology, 68,* 694-698.
Stiles, W. B. (1978). Verbal response modes and dimensions of interpersonal roles: A method of discourse analysis. *Journal of Experimental Social Psychology, 36,* 693-703.
Stiles, W. B., Waszak, C. S., & Barton, L. R. (1979). Professional presumptuousness in verbal interactions with university students. *Journal of Personality and Social Psychology, 15,* 158-169.
Storms, M. D. (1973). Videotape and the attribution process: Reversing actors' and observers' points of view. *Journal of Personality and Social Psychology, 27,* 165-175.
Street, W. R. (1994). Attitude-behavior congruity, mindfulness, and self-focused attention: A behavior-analytic reconstruction. *The Behavior Analyst, 17,* 145-153.
Tannen, D. (1984). *Conversational style: Analyzing talk among friends.* Norwood, NJ: Ablex Publishing.
Tannen, D. (1986). *That's not what I meant! How conversational style makes or breaks relationships.* New York: Ballentine Books.
Tannen, D. (1989). Talking voices: Repetition, dialogue, and imagery in conversational discourse. New York: Cambridge University Press.
Tannen, D. (1990). *You just don't understand.* New York: Ballentine Books.
Tannen, D. (Ed.). (1992). *Gender and conversational interaction.* Oxford, England: Oxford University Press.
Taylor, S. E., & Fiske, S. T. (1975). Point of view and perceptions of causality.*Journal of Personality and Social Psychology, 32,* 439-445.
Tetlock, P. E. (1985). Accountability: The neglected social context of judgment and choice. *Research in Organizational Behavior, 7,* 297-332.

Tetlock, P. E., & Boettger, R. (1989). Accountability: A social magnifier of the dilution effect. *Journal of Personality and Social Psychology, 57,* 388-398.

Tetlock, P. E., Skitka, L., & Boettger, R. (1989). Social and cognitive strategies for coping with accountability: Conformity, complexity, and bolstering. *Journal of Personality and Social Psychology, 57,* 632-640.

Thorne, B., & Henley, N. (Eds.). (1975). *Language and sex: Difference and dominance.* Rowley, MA: Newbury House.

Tönnies, F. (1957/1887). *Community and society.* East Lansing, MI: Michigan State University Press.

Tracy, K. (Ed.). (1991). *Understanding face-to-face interaction: Issues linking goals and discourse.* Hillsdale, NJ: Erlbaum.

Tracy, K., & Coupland, N. (Eds.). (1991). *Multiple goals in discourse.* Philadelphia: Multilingual Matters.

Triandis, H. C. (1960). Cognitive similarity and communication in a dyad. *Human Relations, 13,* 175-183.

Turnbull, C. M. (1973). *The mountain people.* London: Jonathan Cape.

Turner, J. C., Hogg, M. A., Oakes, P. J., Reicher, S. D., & Wetherall, M. (1987). *Rediscovering the social group: A self-categorization theory.* Oxford, England: Basil Blackwell.

Van Dijk, T. A. (1983). Cognitive and conversational strategies in the expression of ethnic prejudice. *Text, 3,* 375-404.

von Cranach, M., Doise, W., & Mugny, G. (Eds.). (1992). *Social representations and the social bases of knowledge.* Bern: Hogrefe & Huber.

Walker, C. J., & Blaine, B. (1991). The virulence of dread rumors: A field experiment. *Language and Communication, 11,* 291-297.

Ward, L. G., Friedlander, M. L., Schoen, L. G., & Klein, J. G. (1985). Strategic self-presentation in supervision. *Journal of Counseling Psychology, 32,* 111-118.

Weiss, R. F., Lombardo, J. P., Warren, D. R., & Kelley, K. A. (1971). Reinforcing effects of speaking in reply. *Journal of Personality and Social Psychology, 20,* 186-199.

Wellman, B., & Wortley, S. (1989). Brothers' keepers: Situating kinship relations in broader networks of social support. *Sociological Perspectives, 32,* 273-306.

White, J. W. (1988). Influence tactics as a function of gender, insult, and goal. *Sex Roles, 18,* 433-448.

White, J. W., & Roufail, M. (1989). Gender and influence strategies of first choice and last resort. *Psychology of Women Quarterly, 13,* 175-189.

Wilkes-Gibbs, D., & Clark, H. H. (1992). Coordinating beliefs in conversation. *Journal of Memory and Language, 31,* 193-194.

Wilkinson, K. M., Dube, W. V., & McIlvane, W. J. (In press). A crossdisciplinary perspective on studies of rapid word mapping in psycholinguistics and behavior analysis. *Developmental Review.*

Williams, H. A. (1995). There are no free gifts! Social support and the need for reciprocity. *Human Organization, 54,* 401-409.

Wolfson, N. (1976). Speech events and natural speech: Some implications for sociolinguistic methodology. *Language in Society, 5*, 189-209.

Wolfson, N. (1984). Pretty is as pretty does: A speech act view of sex roles. *Applied Linguistics, 5*, 236-244.

Wolfson, N. (1988). The bulge: A theory of speech behavior and social distance. In J. Fine (Ed.), *Second language discourse: A textbook of current research* (pp. 21-38). Norwood, NJ: Ablex.

Yamagishi, T., & Cook, K. S. (1993). Generalized exchange and social dilemmas. *Social Psychology Quarterly, 56*, 235-248.

Youssef, V. (1993). Children's linguistic choices: Audience design and societal norms. *Language in Society, 22*, 257-274.

Yukl, G., & Falbe, C. M. (1990). Influence tactics and objectives in upward, downward, and lateral influence attempts. *Journal of Applied Psychology, 75*, 132-140

Yukl, G., Falbe, C. M., & Youn, J. Y. (1993). Patterns of influence behavior for managers. *Group & Organization Management, 18*, 5-28.

Yukl, G., Guinan, P. J., & Sottolano, D. (1995). Influence tactics used for different objectives with subordinates, peers, and supervisors. *Group & Organization Management, 20*, 272-296.

Yukl, G., & Tracey, J. B. (1992). Consequences of influence tactics used with subordinates, peers, and the boss. *Journal of Applied Psychology, 77*, 525-535.

Zajonc, R. B. (1960). The process of cognitive tuning in communication. *Journal of Abnormal and Social Psychology, 61*, 159-167.

Zimmerman, C., & Bauer, R. A. (1956). The effect of an audience upon what is remembered. *Public Opinion Quarterly, 20*, 238-248.

Author Note

I wish to thank my friends at Kieo University, Auburn University, and West Virginia University for their many kindnesses which allowed me the time and peace to sort out these materials and ideas. Jim and Merle Owen have made very helpful suggestions which improved the paper. This was generously supported by a Research Fellowship from the Japan Foundation and a Waikato University School of Social Sciences Research Grant.

Chapter 8

Communication as History and Evolution: Comparing Contextualism and Symbolic Interactionism

Dennis C. Alexander
University of Utah

As the title suggests this essay will examine some commonalties and differences between Contextualism and Symbolic Interactionism. Before I start I must first identify which "brand" of symbolic interactionism I come from. It has been noted that symbolic interaction is a term covering several differing points of view (Meltzer, Petras, & Reynolds, 1975). This discussion is a reflection of the Chicago School of symbolic interaction. The school is highlighted in the writings of Blumer (1969) as well and the traditional scholars such as Mead, Dewey, Cooley and so on. The conceptions of Pepper and his exponents provide the basis of the contextual side of this discussion.

Both contextualism and interactionism are reactionary to the larger paradigm of covering law or positivism in the social sciences. Each perspectives seeks to explain human behavior in ways which avoid the mechanistic view. The mechanistic view is characterized by a strict and linear causal relationship of behavior. Mechanism's explication in psychology and communication was the form of experimental research. This essay offers the caveat that no perspective is more valued than another. Instead, any given perspective encourages differing ways of explaining phenomena. The preferences of this author and this text are toward methods other than positivism. To that end I shall not argue that one perspective is right. I shall compare the explanatory powers of contextualism and interactionism as applied to communication.

The Root Metaphors

Hayes (1993) notes that the early influences of contextualism (Pepper, 1942) came from the writings of James, Dewey, Mead, Cooley and others. Toward the end of his essay he asks the question, "What happened to American Pragmatism?" His answer is that psychology turned toward the empirical approach of experimental research. In offering this answer, Hayes ignored the fact that American Pragmatism never went away, it just became useful in fields other than psychology. What was originally called pragmatism has given way in sociology and communication to the label symbolic interactionism. The genesis of contextualism and symbolic interactionism was the writers of the American pragmatic movement. Contextualism and symbolic interactionism place slightly different "spins" on the writings of the pragmatists. The different spins are evident in the root metaphor that each adopted. A root metaphor is a means of defining something by saying what it is most like. The metaphor becomes a way of helping others understand the concept under investigation. When someone tastes alligator for a first time, many of the person's companions ask what it tastes like. The answer, of course, is that it tastes like chicken. The "tastes like" is a means of explaining alligator for those without direct experience. So too in academia, we offer many explanations by metaphorical comparisons.

The contextualists have often used the metaphor of history to explain what they mean. They see people situated in a place in time. How a person behaves is a reflection of the past experiences and events which surrounds the person. Pepper (1942) wrote of the contextual metaphor being a historical event. The event is a "spatial and temporal confluence of people, settings, and events" (Altman, 1986, p.27). History is not a stale body of facts. Instead, history is active and interpretative. The spatial and temporal nature of history is to emphasize both place and activity. The confluence of people, settings, and events is a dynamic process.

For the interactionist, the root metaphor is evolution. Human activity is seen as a growing experience which is constantly on the move toward some unknown state. Evolution has a historical trace, but its import is the nature of what a phenomenon is becoming. While evolution is also processual, the process is a movement or flux in what is coming rather than a focus on what has passed. In writing about Darwin's concept Mead states, "it is an evolution of form, of the nature, and not an evolution of the particular animal or plant (1956, p.10)." Mead suggests evolution is about the discovery of form and how form changes rather than the historical permutations of a given thing. Evolution as metaphor for interactionism encourages an analysis of forms or nature of communication rather than what a person said.

Contextualism as History

Although history may be discussed in several ways, I find four specific claims about history in the literature of contextualism. First, history is "embedded in time, space, culture, and the local tacit rules of conduct" (Rosnow & Georgoudi, 1986, p. 6). The first implication of history is that people must be examined in their past milieu. People and their actions are understood within a context of time, when did it happen; space, where did it happen; culture, in what social locale did it occur; and local tacit rules, what were the norms of behavior. The force of the implication is that the examination of people situated in a historical setting is an enriching explanation of why people behave as they do. The contextual theorist is interested in human behavior that is both past and localized. The history metaphor encourages more than a time orientation, it demands setting and culture. When a person did something is only a part of the story. The location and the rules of conduct also apply in contextual analysis.

Secondly, people operate within "nets of interrelated causal factors" (Rosnow & Georgoudi, 1986). Beyond the assumption that people act in time, space, and culture, the contextualist sees a causation that is more complex than in positivism. The contextualist is still interested in causal explanations but causation is a complex web or net. The causal factors that lead someone to behave are not so easily broken down into the three assumptions of linear causality. Those assumptions are: 1. A cause must precede an effect, 2. a cause must be contiguous to an effect, and 3. a cause must be necessary and sufficient to produce an effect. Now those criteria are gone and in their place is a web of causal factors which are only partially known. This element of a historical metaphor means that we seldom know all that motivates people to act as they do. It is also argued that the net of causality is bi-directional. The influence of behavior may come from multiple feedback loops: A person tries one thing and is not satisfied with the outcome; accordingly, the person tries other alternatives to see which outcome is most satisfactory. History now has memory. The memory of past activities is part of the explanation of future behaviors. We are not only acted upon by multiple forces but we remember what happened the last time we acted in a similar manner.

Thirdly, the history metaphor encourages a person oriented interpretation. Sarbin (1993) argues that the construct of an historical act places a dual emphasis on history as time and act as a person doing. The argument is advanced on the grounds that people make sense of their histories by telling stories. The story has a narrative form of beginning, middle, and ending. The emphasis on personal narrative makes a good deal of intuitive sense. We often tell each other stories to demonstrate a particular event in our lives. In media, stories may be as short as a 20-second commercial or as long as a four-hour epic motion picture. Both the commercial and the movie are trying to make a personal sense. The story is told to demonstrate a point or explain why a certain behavior appeared warranted. Such history is person centered. The events are a backdrop for personal action.

The fourth claim of history is that people are related. Altman (1993) argues that people's behavior can be seen as a dialectical experience. The dialectic in this case is a tension between a totally private behavior and a totally public behavior. Altman views the dialectic as a continuum. We move between private and public behaviors along the continuum. I might close the door to my office while working on this chapter. In that way I am creating a space which is more private, and I am attempting to exclude the casual visit of a student. In another view of my writing this chapter, it is very public in that I am hoping to write something that other people will find informative. The two ways of looking at my one set of behaviors are placed in relation to other individuals. Historically, we operate in worlds populated by others. Altman's question is not are we related to others, but in what ways are we related.

History as metaphor for contextualism is more than a view of our past. It specifically demands explanations of current behaviors which are lodged in another time and place, a net of causality, a person orientation, and a view of relatedness to other. The history metaphor becomes a rich and complex explanation of human behavior.

Interactionsim as Evolution

As with the history metaphor of contextualism, the evolutionary metaphor of symbolic interactionism carries several implications. Here I shall focus on four that seek to draw the distinctions between contextualism and symbolic interactionism.

The first implication specifies that self is a social product. While contextualism sees self as imbedded in a culture with implicit rules, symbolic interaction sees the self as wholly an entity that arises in a social environment. Mead (1956) notes that the "self is essentially a social structure, and it arises in social experience" (p. 206). The present tense of the verb arises is important to Mead; he views the self as always possessed with the current state of things. When a self reflects on past experiences it is to better understand what is now going on. This view of self in present is a contrast to the contextualist. Self is not so much a product of past experiences, instead the self uses past to evaluate the present. The self is in the process of interacting with others and those interactions will be formative of future behaviors. The self as social product is a dynamic view which invests the self with a great deal of reflectivity for the purposes of future actions.

A second implication of the evolutionary metaphor is that meaning is in the interaction. Mead's view of meaning is that it is not a personal element but something that exists outside the individual. Meaning arises in the give and take between individuals. Mead's conceptual position on meaning is linked to communication. He argues that meaning occurs in the actions of one person using significant symbols to which another individual must react with significant symbols and these actions are related to a social object (p. 163). The threefold relationship (act of one, act of another, and social object) constitutes the matrix of meaning. The phrase used by many communication people "shared meaning" is not understandable from an interactionist point of view. Meanings are in the interaction rather than in people. Shared meaning only makes sense if meanings are in people. This distinction of meaning is crucial to the evolutionary metaphor. Meanings are created, maintained, and changed within the communicative behaviors of people. The meaning grows in the relationship and alters itself as the relationship is altered. The meaning of friendship that Terry and I have at a point in time is different than the meaning that Laura and I hold. The meaning is closely linked to the talk of people and the talk of different people produces different meanings.

Third, actions in human group life are based on meanings. What we have come to know between people provides the resource of how we act. "The human individual confronts a world that he must interpret in order to act instead of an environment to which he responds because of his organization" (Blumer, 1969, p.

15). People are not reactive to their situations but interactive. The lack of a specific human reaction to an event is what creates the ambiguity of things. One person sees a violent movie such as "Pulp Fiction" and hates the level of inhumanity portrayed while another praises the intricate and clever dialogue. Each is drawing upon a reserve of meaning from interaction rather than some organismic response of the human being. Our actions are evolutionary. How we act toward something today might be quite different from a later point in time because we have had more interaction or an alteration of meaning. To turn the phrase another way, the interactionist sees little of human behavior that is predictable. Just when we think we know someone and how that person will react to a situation, the person draws on a different set of interactions and interprets the event differently than in past times.

The fourth implication of the interactionist's evolutionary metaphor is that relationships grow and change. Although two people are friends, their friendship will not be the same in two years as it is today. Any roles we take, one to another, start as fairly traditional and move to being more unique role behaviors. The concept is known as role sets (Faules & Alexander, 1978). All roles are known in relation to other roles. For instance, to have a teacher we need students, wife to husband, politician to voter, and so it goes. In any role set we start by behaving in terms that society teaches us. So the first day in class the teacher is very teacher-like and the students are very student-like. However, as the term goes along the teacher and students begin to rely more and more on their meanings and less and less on the social prescriptions. The same teacher may teach the same course once a year, but each time the course is taught a different ending occurs in terms of the relationship between teacher and students.

Interactionism views the world as sets of coordinated behaviors between people. The coordination gives rise to self, meaning, ability to act, and change within the relationship. These elements are best thought of as an evolutionary process. The symbolic interactionist took the work of Darwin and found a like model for human behavior.

Applying the Metaphors to Communication Analysis

Both contextualism and interactionism emphasize the use of qualitative methods for analysis. The use of interviews, participant and non-participant observation, journals, and ethnographies are common research practices for these scholars. The difference of the two views is much like looking through the two ends of binoculars. When one looks through the small lens out through the large lens (the typical method), the object of observation is brought into close view and much of the surroundings are omitted. When one looks through the large lens out through the small lens (the atypical method), one sees the object of observation at a distance and seemingly surrounded by a variety of elements. So it is with contextualism and interactionism in the study of human communication. Interactionism encourages the close-up view where the object is in immediate sight.

Contextualism encourages the longer view with more of the surrounding space occupied by important elements. Neither view is more correct, rather the two views serve different purposes for the analyst. As children we often enjoyed looking through the binoculars both ways, it was only our parents who kept telling us to use them in only one way. As analysts of communication, we need to resist the "parental" voices of our discipline who tell us to use our methods in only one way. As a point of demonstration, I shall use two studies in which I participated. I also choose two different areas of communication to indicate that contextualism and interactionism are not bound to a particular setting of communication.

Friends Research in Interpersonal Communication

Several communication researchers have been interested in the communicative practices of friends. In 1981, Alexander and Newell reported a study of friends in which the symbolic interactionist findings fell into two categories. The analyses of friends' talk suggested that friends spend a good deal of time in talk that is related to "being friends" and "doing friends." In the being friends category we discovered that friends spend talk time in telling each other how unique their friendships are, helping each other make sense of their joined behaviors, and reinforcing each other's feelings as positive. In these ways friends carve out special places for the friendships to reside. The places make one pair of friends different from all others, and hence the friends find their relationship to be special. Moreover, the sense-making function in being friends is the expression of meaning from the interactionist point of view. The friends are not interested in a private interpretation of how to "read" an event, instead they want confirmation of the interpretation from the significant other. The sense- making is the creation, maintenance, and change of meaning in a friendship. The reinforcing function within being friends serves the friendship in verifying the human-ness of the people. Within the role of friends the people are saying that each other's self is valuable and worthy of praise.

A contextualist could have taken these same exemplars of friends talking and reached different conclusions. The conclusions would be guided by the metaphoric lens. The unique talk may be seen as an analysis of how each person is culturally and spatially different. The emphasis is on the individual and the things that individual brings to the relationship. The analysis would then move to how the two people find in each others history the elements of mutual understanding. The sense-making is now a view of how to relate current topics of communication to past conversations. Sense- making of the contextualist becomes the reliance on past events to predict future events within the web of causality. The reinforcing nature of the talk is analyzed with a view of behavioral reinforcement. Reinforcing talk becomes the positive "strokes" to keep the pair of friends in an ongoing relationship.

In doing friends we analyzed the friends' talk for what it accomplished in the relationship. Because of their time together friends use a variety of key phrases which are only understood by them. One friendship pair used the phrase "let's go for a ride" to mark a place where their talk would be intimate and private. The phrase came from a period of time when the friends were in high school and driving was a means of getting away from parents and siblings who might listen in on their conversations. Ten years after the high school years, they figuratively went for drives to discuss items of intimacy. The interactionist interpretation of this behavior is that friends create selves located in roles that allow them to signal changes of topic. The contextualist could look at the same behavior and find that the significance is in the linked behavior of ten years.

Making space and making time are two other important elements in doing friends. Friends spend a fair amount of time finding places to talk. Many of our relationships are space bound: we talk with people at work, we talk with spouses in our kitchens and bedrooms, we talk to our parents in their homes, and so forth. Friends do not occupy such space, in fact, most spaces in which friends talk serve some other primary function. You and your friends at work find times to do friendly talk as opposed to the business of work. A friend talking in another's kitchen is mindful of spouses and children. The lack of friends' space means that friends talk about space and negotiate the talk of friendliness in space which have other primary interests. For our symbolic interaction analysis, making space became an expression of inventing the role of friend in relation to location. We saw the talk as not only the past restrictions on places of talk but how the friends could find new places of talk. The contextualist could see these routines as friends restricted by the "local tacit rules" for interaction. The contextual analysis stresses the ways in which the rules have come to govern the talk of friends.

Making time is closely related to making space in that it occupies a goodly amount of friends' talk time. The difference is that time is seen as a limited commodity. The amount of time friends talk limits the amount of time for talk in other role sets. More often friends lament that it is other role sets that take up the time, and friendships create lower priority demands. Spouse talk and children-parent talk have higher demand characteristics. So friends talk about the time for talk. As interactionists we saw this element as strain in the relationship. The focus on finding time to talk was often couched in terms of how other demands had to take priority. The ranking of important times for talking places a diminished emphasis on the friendship as important. The feeling is that because the amount of time for talking is diminished the relationship is diminished. This concept of quantity closely follows the truism of, "if you are having trouble talking to the other person, communicate more." Of course increasing the quantity of something that is stressful usually increases the stress. Friends appear to make a different move in making time, they stress the quality of the time more than the amount. The contextualist looking at making time may see that time like many other resources in friendship is part of the web of causality. One can not explain friendship talk without linking it to other competing forms of relational talk.

The last element we analyzed in the doing of friends talk was how taboo topics were handled. Any friendship has certain topics which are off limits. In one of our friendship pairs, a husband was the taboo topic. Each of the friends was back at the university after many years. The one woman was a traditional housewife who did not hold a job outside the home and had raised three children. The other woman was a single parent whose children were teenagers and she worked to support the family. These two quickly became fast friends from school. The single parent could not resist a periodic shot at the friend. The jibes usually dealt with his lack of involvement in his family or similar issues. The topic took on taboo proportions. Each knew that it was a tender spot in their talk and yet it came up from time to time. The pair's routine for working out of the taboo area was to start with a self deprecating line and a laugh. The other friend would then deny the deprecation and offer the friend a positive statement. Our interactional analysis of this routine suggested that the error was a slip and the repair was face-saving work much as Goffman (1959) describes. The pair would use the taboo topics to engage in face work which would strengthen a person's self view. The face work became a means of promoting the friend into a position of self worth. It was not so much about the husband as it was about telling the woman she was valued and need not create an identity linked to only one other person. A contextual analysis of the taboo topic "work" may focus on the meaning a person holds for the conversation. The jibe at the husband carries different meanings for the wife or the single parent. The single parent may see a chance to speak for independence, but the wife sees the opportunity to speak for marital support. In each meaning, the person's relatedness to significant others becomes a principal means of creating the meanings held by each.

In each area of the friends' talk, interactionism and contextualism "read" the events or exemplars differently. The analyses offer differing explanations of the same behaviors. The difference of explanations would lead to different conclusions about the friends' talk. The same difference could be shown in other communicative settings. The next section of this essay examines a political communication event.

Political Communication Research

In our analysis of the 1992 Vice Presidential Debate, we took the position that Gore was more presidential in his role of debater than Quayle (Tiemens, Alexander, & Sillars, 1993). Our analysis of the debates used the concepts of decorum and incumbency to define presidential. Survey research prior to the debate showed that although the Clinton-Gore ticket was the challenger in the presidential campaign, they led the incumbent ticket in the polls. The Bush-Quayle strategy took on the traditional role of the challenger by adopting an attack strategy in the debate and other public appearances. In the opening statement of the debate, Quayle attacked the character of Bill Clinton on four abstract issues. Quayle never explained the abstract issues but returned again and again in the debate to the idea of whether or not Clinton would keep his word or could be trusted to do what was right. Although Quayle did not directly mention Clinton's infidelity, the trust issue became a code for questioning Clinton both as a presidential candidate and as a person. The many issues introduced and the attack character of the Quayle presentation made him appear in the role of challenger. By contrast, Gore was focused on what the Clinton-Gore agenda could do. He seldom attacked President Bush instead opting to talk about a general problem the American people faced and how Clinton-Gore could solve it. Interesting in Gore's presentation was the use of the pronoun "we" to create a meaning of Clinton-Gore being a united team. The lack of challenge to Bush and the ability to solve problems made the incumbent role better fit Gore.

A contextualist analysis of the content of the debate would have focused more on the history of what was said. Given that Quayle had a poor debate showing in 1988, the contextual analysis could focus on how the content of 1988 differed from 1992. The question would address what web of causes led Quayle to the attack and how he responded to the poll's report of Clinton leading Bush. The analysis would have turned more on the surrounding issues of the presidential debates and how the third-party candidate, General Stockton, debated; or how the moderator, Hal Bruno, asked the questions. Clearly, the role of incumbent versus challenger would not be as central as it was to our analysis.

Our analysis not only assessed the role of presidential in terms of incumbency but also examined the decorum of the two candidates. Throughout the debate, Quayle was shown in brief close-up shots while the close-up shots of Gore were of much longer duration. Based on visual theory we concluded that the difference of close-ups made Quayle appear disjointed and scattered—a visual meaning for the audience that closely paralleled his content. Gore's longer close-ups created a meaning of coherent dedication to issues. His persona became steady and passionate in the long, close visual presentations. Beyond the visual, Quayle had the habit of uncomfortably giggling and laughing at various points. We counted 30 incidents of Quayle giggling or laughing. The television audience saw 26 of these giggling incidents on the television screen. The giggles made Quayle appear uncomfortable in the debate situation. This situation reinforced an image of Quayle as less than presidential. His decorum was that of a worried youngster rather than the Vice President of the United States articulating the positions of the administration. Conversely, Gore appear at ease in his role of debater. His presentation was personable and far less wooden than his critics had led the viewing public to expect. The meanings constructed from the differences of the performances made the decorum sense of presidential role appear to favor Gore more than Quayle. The public perception of who looked presidential was more in tune with Gore.

The contextualist could examine the performances of the two vice presidential candidates and come to slightly different points of analysis and conclusions. More emphasis would be placed on their past behaviors and how those performances related to the current displays of behavior. The questions could have focused more on how Quayle and Gore were related to the candidacy of the their political parties. A question of the public to private set of behaviors that revealed a level of intimacy to Bush or Clinton would be an intriguing question for the contextual analyst. The contextual analyst might also ask questions about the past rules of debate and how these candidates adhered to or violated those rules.

The interactionist and contextualist could take the same videotape records of this political event and ask quite different questions about what and how the event occurred. Both points of view would have reason to claim legitimate conclusions.

Conclusions

Why should you and I be interested in the fact that interactionism and contextualism can offer differing conclusions about communicative events? I can think of three important reason. First, the more we understand the fine points of a perspective the more coherent our analysis. With a growing number of qualitative perspectives, we must isolate the issues of each perspective and then "be true to our school." The "being true" does not negate another point of view, instead it creates clarity. The implications of a perspective can serve as an outline of critical issues for one particular analysis. Whether contextualism, interactionism, feminism, pragmatism, or cultural analysis, the issues in qualitative research are not as much how were data collected as how were data analyzed. The mere fact that one selects one data point over another begins the act of interpretation. It is important for the analyst and reader to both recognize why that data point was selected.

Secondly, the more we understand others' points of view, the more tolerant we may become of alternative perspectives. Rather than privileging one point of view, the embracing of difference becomes a means of inclusion and strength. When contextualists asked where American Pragmatism went, they implicitly admitted that a single dominant paradigm of one discipline blinded them from what was still there and being practiced in disciplines which allowed competing paradigms. From a political standpoint, we in the humanities and social sciences need to be inclusive to gain strength within the academy. When state legislatures are the asking question, "what have you done for me lately?" Our answer should be that we are educating the state's citizenry in being able to approach a problem from multiple methods of solution. If we answer that we are teaching the one and only way, we run the risk of finding people who will not support that one avenue to success.

Lastly, understanding both an interactional and a contextual analysis leads to the research tradition of "triangulation." To see a problem from multiple points of view is to better understand the problem and the solution. Research textbooks call for triangulation as a means of providing richer explanations of a phenomenon. To return to the binocular metaphor, we need to look from both ends. The two views provide a deeper understanding of the human condition, in this case, communication. We must best serve our students by continually looking through both ends of the binoculars and resist the voices of authority who tell us there is only one set of lenses.

References

Alexander, D. C., & Newell, S. E. (1981). Negotiating the role of friend. In G. Ziegelmueller & J. Rhodes (Eds.), *Dimensions of argument: Proceedings of the second summer conference on argumentation* (pp. 643-662). Annandale VA: Speech Communication Association.

Altman, I. (1986). Contextualism and environmental psychology. In R. L. Rosnow & M. Georgoudi (Eds.) *Contextualism and understanding in behavioral science: Implications for research and theory* (pp. 25-46). New York: Praeger.

Altman, I. (1993). Dialectics, physical environment, and personal relationships. *Communication Monographs, 60,* 26-34.

Blumer, H. (1969). *Symbolic interactionism: Perspective and method.* Berkeley, CA: University of California Press.

Faules, D. F., & Alexander, D. C. (1976). *Communication and social behavior: A symoblic interaction perspective.* Reading, MA: Addison-Wesley.

Goffman, E. (1959). *Presentation of self in everyday life.* Garden City, NY: Doubleday Anchor Books.

Hayes, S. C. (1993). Analytic goals and the varieties of scientific contextualism. In S. C. Hayes, L. J. Hayes, H. W. Reese, & T. R. Sarbin (Eds.), *Varieties of scientific contextualism* (pp. 11-27). Reno, NV: Context Press.

Mead, G. H. (1956). *George Herbert Mead on social psychology: Selected papers* (edited by A. Strauss). Chicago: University of Chicago Press.

Meltzer, B. N., Petras, J. W., & Reynolds, L. T. (1975). *Symbolic interaction: Genesis, varieties, and criticism.* London: Routledge & Kegan Paul.

Pepper, S. C. (1942). *World hypothesis: A study in evidence.* Berkeley, CA: University of California Press.

Rosnow, R. L., & Georgoudi, M. (1986). The spirit of contextualism. In R. L. Rosnow & M. Georgoudi (Eds.), *Contextualism and understanding in behavioral science: Implications for research and theory* (pp. 3-24). New York: Praeger.

Sarbin, T. R. (1993). The narrative as the root metaphor for contextualism. In S. C. Hayes, L. J. Hayes, H. W. Reese, & T. R. Sarbin (Eds.), *Varieties of scientific contextualism* (pp. 51-65). Reno, NV: Context Press.

Tiemens, R. K., Alexander, D. C., & Sillars, M. O. (1993). On being "presidential": The Quayle-Gore Debate. In R. E. McKerrow (Ed.), *Argument and the postmodern challenge* (pp. 398-404). Annandale, VA: Speech Communication Association.

Chapter 9

Vygotsky's Contextualism: Cultural Historical Psychology

Tom Whelan
Communication Consultant
Boulder City, Nevada

Introduction

Consciousness is reflected in the word like the sun is reflected in a droplet of water. The[spoken] word is...related to consciousness like a living cell is related to an organism, like an atom is related to the cosmos. The meaningful word is a microcosm of human consciousness (Vygotsky, 1987, p. 285).

An important task for scholars of any discipline is to relate research from other fields to their own subject matter. Our understanding of human communication can be enhanced by reviewing, analyzing and interpreting related research from a great number of sources in other sciences.

One Soviet psychologist whose work bears directly upon an understanding of human communication, and whose approach is inherently contextual, is Lev Semyonovich Vygotsky (1896-1934). Vygotsky produced a considerable body of critical, speculative and empirical work on spoken language genesis and concept formation in human beings, and he developed a contextual psychology which is philosophically cultural, qualitative, developmental, holistic and integrated.

Vygotsky's psychological scholarship is often collectively referred to as "Cultural-Historical Theory." Although Vygotsky was working toward a theory, he died of tuberculosis at age 37, leaving the theory-building process unfinished. More accurately, Vygotsky set the philosophical and metatheoretical foundation for a cultural-historical approach to psychology, and he completed the preliminary stages of theory building.

In this chapter, I provide an overview of what I will call *Vygotsky's Cultural-Historical Psychology* beginning with metatheory, then theory, the relationship between thinking and speech and empirical methodology. Within each of these sections, I summarize Vygotsky's central ideas and discuss the role these ideas play in his psychology. I ask the reader to keep in mind that Vygotsky's psychology is extensive and subtle, and by summarizing Cultural-Historical Theory into a book chapter I risk oversimplifying his ideas. Please read his own words.

Cultural Historical Psychology

Metatheory

For The Continental Europeans, philosophy establishes a discipline's metatheory–the context within which theories are developed from the disciplines' perspective. Consistent with the Continental European approach, Vygotsky worked throughout his career to integrate psychology's body of knowledge and establish a disciplinary metatheory which he referred to as "General Psychology." I will explain what Vygotsky means by a "General Psychology." and then explicate the guiding principle for his own work–the "cultural-historical" approach.

Vygotsky's early ideas on psychological reform were first expressed in his 1924 presentation at the Second All Russian Psychoneurological Congress. Beginning with the conference paper, "Methodology of Reflexological and Psychological Research" and, later that year, the published article, "Consciousness as a Problem of the Psychology of Behavior," Vygotsky began the disciplinary critique that would form the basis of his scholarship.

In 1924, reflexologists considered themselves a separate science from psychology, viewed all animal behavior as reflexes, and ignored consciousness as a subject matter. Disagreeing with these boundaries, Vygotsky (1979) commented on reflexology's potential value to the psychology discipline, adjusted their methodology to include reflex *systems* vs. *aggregates*, and criticized their limited focus by calling for the integration of the reflexological paradigm with the concept of human consciousness.

Vygotsky often commented on the psychology discipline's condition and direction. His concerns about the discipline culminated in a major work, *The Historical Meaning of the Crisis in Psychology,* completed in 1927. In *Crisis*, Vygotsky analyzes the psychology discipline and delineates guidelines for developing a unifying psychological metatheory.

> In this paper of approximately 140 pages Vygotsky analyzed the psychological currents of his time, traced to what extent they were compatible or incompatible with the goals of psychology as he saw them, and sought to find materials for a future methodology (Van der Veer & Valsiner, 1991, pp. 142-143).

By "methodology" Vygotsky means a set of shared assumptions, concepts and interpretive strategies, and a philosophy of methods for posing and seeking answers to psychological questions–equivalent to what American social scientists would call "metatheory."

Vygotsky referred to this unifying metatheory as a "general psychology," and he began *Crisis* by establishing grounds for his claim.

> He began the paper by observing the lack of unity and consistency in psychology's research findings. Researchers from different schools had

produced facts that seemed to have little in common. It was hard to see, for instance, how to reconcile the psychoanalytic image of man with Pavlov's theory of the higher nervous activity. It seemed impossible to combine Gestalt psychology's ideas with those of Watson's behaviorism. In short, to Vygotsky psychology seemed a hodgepodge of unrelated or contradictory research findings without any unifying idea whatsoever (Van der Veer & Valsiner, 1991, p. 143).

Vygotsky envisioned "general psychology" not only as a unifying metatheory, but also as a psychology subdiscipline comprised of scholars whose task was studying and developing theoretical unity.

In Vygotsky's view it would be the task of general psychology to evaluate the findings unearthed in the different research domains, to consider whether they could be reconciled, and to design a consistent theoretical framework. Psychology does not need new fact-finding, Vygotsky argued, but shared concepts or ways to interpret the gathered facts (Van der Veer & Valsiner, 1991, p. 143).

Along with his call for establishing theoretical unity through a general psychology subdiscipline, Vygotsky pointed out some of psychology's fundamental problems creating the crisis. One fatal flaw of psychology was circular explanatory models which stemmed from the discipline's lack of philosophical self-reflection. Vygotsky referred to reflexological and mentalistic models to illustrate this circularity.

For example, reflexologists view all behavior as reflexes, and the nervous system becomes both the source and the theoretical explanations for reflexes. Similarly, mentalists refer to a theoretical construct of consciousness to explain the phenomenon of consciousness. Consequently, subject matter and explanatory principle are identical.

Vygotsky argues that a theoretical explanation of psychological phenomena must come from another reality stratum of which consciousness is a function. This metatheoretical insight supports Vygotsky's positions on a cultural-historical explanation of uniquely human consciousness.

...the distinction between the subject of study and the explanatory principle is probably the most important epistemological contribution made by Vygotsky in his early psychological papers. The implicit conclusion is that if consciousness is to become a subject of psychological study, some other layer of reality should be referred to in the course of the explanation...Socially meaningful activity, then, may serve as such a layer and as an explanatory schema (Kozulin, 1990, pp. 83-84).

The Cultural-Historical Approach

Along with critiquing the discipline and arguing for a general psychology, *Crisis* served as a springboard for the next phase in Vygotsky's thinking–the cultural-historical approach–which guided his psychological scholarship for the remainder of his career. Because the term *cultural-historical* does not translate precisely, and because Vygotsky uses this term in a specific way, I will clarify this metatheoretical concept.

Vygotsky conceives of *cultural-historical* as a holistic, integrated concept. In this sense, the terms culture and history cannot be viewed in isolation–culture is historical, and history is cultural. In order to understand Vygotsky's intended meaning, the terms must first be differentiated, then reintegrated and conceived of holistically as a single concept.

For Vygotsky, *culture* represents the collective totality of human social experience and consciousness. This social context expresses the current level of biological evolution and societal development. Fundamentally, cultural influence on individual development is experienced through interaction with other individuals who are also experiencing the dynamic cultural milieu. The "individual" within this context is an interdependent player who assimilates the cultural consciousness through a complex web of spoken interpersonal interaction. Vygotsky (1978) states,

...the social dimension of consciousness is primary in time and in fact. The individual dimension of consciousness is derivative and secondary (p. 30). [And] In a broad sense, speech is the source of social behavior and consciousness (p. 29).

Vygotsky uses the term *history* to represent human individual development.

To study something historically means to study it in the process of change; that is the dialectical method's basic demand. To encompass in research the process of a given thing's development in all its phases and changes– from birth to death–fundamentally means to discover its nature, its essence...(Vygotsky, 1978, p. 65).

Individual development is also viewed within the phylogenetic scope which includes both biological evolution and cultural history. Thus, Vygotsky not only situates the individual within the cultural milieu, but along the culture's historical time line as well.

Human beings make use not just of physically inherited experience: throughout life, an individual's work and behavior draw broadly on the experience of former generations, which is not transmitted at birth from parent to child. We may call this historical experience (Vygotsky, 1979, p. 13).

Vygotsky believed the individual can only be understood within a universal context, and the term *cultural-historical* became, for Vygotsky, a metatheoretical perspective which guided his own theoretical and empirical work.

Theory

Consistent with his own prescribed guidelines, Vygotsky began with a philosophical grounding (dialectic philosophy), analyzed and critiqued the psychology discipline to determine a productive direction, and then embarked on theoretical work within his proposed context. In this section, I define the term *theory*, classify the body of work which is often referred to as "cultural-historical theory," and overview the two substantive areas of Vygotsky's theoretical position--human phylogeny and ontogeny.

A meaningful discussion of cultural-historical "theory" first requires a comparison of the term *theory* as it is predominantly used in American social science versus the way Vygotsky uses the term. Contemporary American social science is grounded in the empiricist/positivist tradition. Although theorists disagree about subtleties, in general, empiricist theories can be defined as systematic, symbolic explanations of phenomena, comprised of lawful statements about the relationships among observed facts (Kaplan, 1964).

Empiricist social science theories are modeled after theories in the physical sciences and are subjected to the same evaluation criteria. Stephan Hawking (1988) summarizes the essential criteria from the empiricist position.

> ...a good theory...satisfies two requirements: it must accurately describe a large class of observations on the basis of a model that contains only a few arbitrary elements, and it must make definite predictions about the results of future observations (p. 9).

The empiricists' preoccupation with Hawking's second criterion–prediction–arose from historical attempts to account for planetary and stellar movements. The eventual success of these predictive efforts in physics influenced social scientists to adopt the prediction criterion in an effort to legitimize the developing behavioral science disciplines (Dubin, 1978).

More recently, most behavioral science theorists have recognized the unique nature of behavioral phenomena and now distinguish between theories in the physical and social sciences. According to Dubin (1978), theories of human behavior often address only *one* of two possible theoretical goals.

> Theories of social and human behavior address themselves to two distinct goals of science: (1) prediction and (2) understanding...[T]hese are separate goals and...the structure of theories employed to achieve each is unique...In the usual case of theory building in behavioral sciences, understanding and prediction are not often achieved together...[and] each goal may be attained without reference to the other (p. 19).

Dubin (1978) defines theoretical prediction as the ability to anticipate system *outcomes*, and understanding refers to knowledge about interaction *processes*. While much of twentieth century American social science emphasizes prediction, understanding has become an increasingly legitimate theoretical goal.

Because of his alignment with Continental European philosophy, Vygotsky's "theorizing" is roughly consistent with the goal of understanding that Dubin (1978) describes. For Vygotsky and the Continental Europeans, however, theory building is *not* a rigorous, hypothetico-deductive, covering law approach to systematizing knowledge about phenomena. Thus, the term "theory" when applied to Vygotsky's work can be confusing for American Scholars.

Vygotsky's conception of "theory" more closely resembles the way the term is used in critical theory, hermeneutics and phenomenology where "theory" refers to a philosophical perspective, its application method, and the work that arises from applying that philosophical perspective to any aspect of human life. From Vygotsky's viewpoint, philosophy, metatheory, theory and methodology interrelate in a comprehensive, integrated psychological system; thus, his "theory" is the collective body of critical, speculative, and empirical work that he produced from the cultural-historical perspective between approximately 1927 and his death in 1934.

Vygotsky envisions psychology's task as the understanding of human individual consciousness viewed from the cultural-historical perspective. For Vygotsky, consciousness arises through two distinct developmental lines–*natural* and *cultural*–which account for different aspects of human consciousness. The natural developmental line accounts for the lower psychological processes; whereas, the cultural line accounts for the higher psychological processes.

The categories Vygotsky considers within this theoretical framework include *natural phylogenic* development, *cultural history*, *natural ontogenic* development, and *cultural ontogenic* development. Although Vygotsky focuses on cultural ontogenic development, the foundation for this focus comes from his attention to the other categories. In the following discussion, I overview these foundational categories.

The Lower Psychological Processes

For Vygotsky, the individual develops lower psychological processes [LPPs], such as physical sensory perception, early practical intelligence and kinesthetic awareness, independent of social interaction. For example, the human infant's sight and crude hand/eye coordination mature spontaneously, initially independent of any aid or influence by others. At the lower psychological process level, humans share analogous anatomical, physiological and psychological structures with other animals, differing from animals in degree. Vygotsky argues that biological evolution accounts for the origins of these processes (Vygotsky, 1978; Vygotsky, 1987).

Natural Phylogenic Development.

Phylogeny can be defined as the transformation of species or lineages over time. Regarding phylogeny, *natural* development refers to biological evolution, specifically human biological evolution, and Vygotsky relied on Darwin's evolutionary theory to support this phylogenetic aspect of his work.

For Vygotsky, the greater part of human phylogenesis had been explained by Charles Darwin. He was well acquainted with Darwin's writings and repeatedly praised him for his theory of evolution, which provided the key to our understanding of animal behavior (Van der Veer and Valsiner, 1991, p. 191).

More important than Darwin's particular theoretical conclusions, Vygotsky views Darwin's work as a metatheoretical and methodological model for psychology's preliminary task.

The key to biology was found in evolution, in the idea of the natural development of living forms. Just as biology began with the *origin of forms*, so too, psychology should begin from the *origin of individuals*...(Vygotsky, 1993, p. 154).

Vygotsky calls this type of analysis Darwin performed the "causal-genetic" approach because Darwin discovered a unifying concept [evolution] and, applying this concept, traced an immensely diverse array of facts to their common origin. Vygotsky contrasts Darwin's analysis with classification systems based upon superficial, phenotypic similarities. For example, dolphins and fish shared the same taxonomic classification until Darwin's approach led scientists to categorize dolphins as mammals based upon subtle, internal characteristics. Because psychologists often rely on superficial, phenotypic observations for fact finding, Vygotsky enthusiastically endorses the causal-genetic approach for studying psychological phenomena as well (Vygotsky, 1993).

Although Vygotsky praises Darwin's method and account of the evolutionary process, he disagrees with Darwin regarding the relationship between homo sapiens and other animal species. Darwin proposes a linear relationship between humans and other animals. "...the mental faculties of man and the lower animals do not differ in kind, although immensely in degree" (Darwin, 1981, p. 186).

Applying Hegel's law of the transformation of quantity into quality, Vygotsky, unlike Darwin, believes that humans differ from other animals, not only in degree, but also in kind. Regarding the lower psychological processes, Vygotsky agrees that humans differ from animals only quantitatively; however, the human capacity for higher psychological processes–which arose culturally, not biologically–qualitatively distinguishes humans from other species (Vygotsky, 1978).

Thus, debating with his contemporaries about the implications of evolutionary theory for psychology, Vygotsky accepted a hereditary basis for human anatomy, physiology and lower psychological processes, but he revised Darwin's thesis regarding the phylogenesis of higher psychological processes.

The Higher Psychological Processes.

Higher psychological processes [HPPs] are a direct product of social interaction. Vygotsky believes these processes originate in the cultural knowledge base and arise through spoken interaction within the family, community, and in modern Western culture, within social institutions such as educational systems. HPPs include such processes as voluntary attention, mediated memory, abstraction, and synthesis–in general, conceptual thinking. Regarding HPPs, humans differ from animals in kind and *cultural history* refers to the time period during which these processes emerged and developed among homo sapiens (Vygotsky, 1978).

Cultural History

Cultural history refers to the development and passing on of cultural knowledge since the beginning of tool use, cooperative labor and spoken language. Basing his conclusions upon Engels' work, Vygotsky postulates that biological evolution's impact on lower psychological processes has been minimal since the onset of the cooperative labor culture. However, the onset of culture has vastly transformed the human capacity for higher psychological processes (Vygotsky, 1978).

Comparing 20th century Europeans with indigenous peoples, Vygotsky speculates about the long-term transformation of HPPs. The historical transformation of HPPs occurs through the creation of *cultural tools* which can be defined as auxiliary stimuli, based upon signs, that mediate psychological processes and change the psychological structure of behavior. Cultural tools, Vygotsky argues, are invented by, and simultaneously transform, the human intellect (Vygotsky, 1978).

For example, Vygotsky distinguishes between natural and mediated memory.

[Natural memory] is characterized by the nonmediated impression of materials, by the retention of actual experiences as the basis of mnemonic (memory) traces...This kind of memory is very close to perception, because it arises out of the direct influence of external stimuli...From the point of view of structure, the entire process is characterized by a quality of immediacy...On the contrary, other types of memory belonging to a completely different developmental line coexist with natural memory. The use of notched sticks and knots, the beginnings of writing and simple memory aids all demonstrate that even at early stages of historical development humans went beyond the limits of psychological functions given to them by nature and proceeded to a new culturally-elaborated organization of their behavior...We believe that these sign operations are the product of specific conditions of *social* development (Vygotsky, 1978, p. 39).

Vygotsky (1978) argues that mediating sign operations change the psychological structure of memory:

> Even such comparatively simple operations as tying a knot or marking a stick as a reminder change the psychological structure of the memory process. They extend the operation of memory beyond the biological dimensions of the human nervous system and permit it to incorporate artificial, or self-generated, stimuli which we call *signs*. This merger, unique to human beings, signifies an entirely new form of behavior (p. 39).

This change in psychological structure, originating culturally through the introduction of mediating sign operations, transforms the memory process from a perception-bound, concrete function to an abstract, higher psychological function.

> The central characteristic of elementary functions [LPPs] is that they are totally and directly determined by stimulation from the environment. For higher functions, the central feature is self-generated stimulation, that is, the creation and use of artificial stimuli which become the immediate causes of behavior (Vygotsky, 1978, p. 39).

Thus, as mediating operations such as writing systems, mathematics and technologies become more elaborate, these cultural tools change the structure of higher psychological functions and ultimately transform human consciousness.

Cultural Ontogenic Development

Cultural ontogenesis is the thrust of Vygotsky's Cultural-Historical Psychology. After distinguishing humans from other animals and comparing modern with previous cultures, Vygotsky then addresses the origins of uniquely human consciousness in the individual.

Vygotsky believes that psychologists need to identify and study both zoosemiotic and anthroposemiotic aspects of human behavior that function in human consciousness. For Vygotsky, the higher psychological processes represent the species specific aspect of human consciousness.

During the 1920s and 1930s, two general schools of psychological thought were competing for disciplinary dominance. Representative of these schools, in Vygotsky's opinion, were the Wundtians and the reflexologists. Wundtian psychologists studied human consciousness but lacked a biological foundation, and the reflexologists provided a compelling account of biologically based behavior and the lower psychological processes but focused only on behaviors and structures that humans share with other animal species.

During the 1920s, Vygotsky became dissatisfied with reflexology's theoretical assumption that all human behavior develops passively through biological maturation.

> Among all these [reflexological] principles we find not even one psychological law of human behavior that would express the relationship or interdependence of phenomena that would characterize the uniqueness of human behavior (Vygotsky, 1979, p. 5).

Vygotsky believes that reflexology conflates biological and cultural development by attributing all behavioral development to physical maturation and passive responding to environmental stimuli. Vygotsky argues that this theoretical stance prevents the possibility for understanding uniquely human consciousness.

> ...maturation per se is a secondary factor in the development of the most complex, unique forms of human behavior. The development of these behaviors [higher psychological processes] is characterized by complicated, qualitative transformations of one form of behavior into another (or, as Hegel would phrase it, a transformation of quantity into quality). The conception of maturation as a passive process cannot adequately describe these complex phenomena (Vygotsky, 1978, p. 19).

According to Vygotsky (1978, 1986, 1987, 1993), the psychological processes are structured hierarchically with the lower processes forming a foundation for the higher ones. This hierarchical development is sequential, transformational and cumulative. The lower processes emerge first and dominate during infancy as the developing anatomical and physiological structures set a biological foundation for further psychological development. Vygotsky refers to this biological maturation process as the *natural* developmental line.

However, the onset of speech qualitatively transforms the child's psychology, creating an opportunity for *culture*-based social influence along an initially distinct developmental line. This qualitative consciousness shift produced by speech acquisition initiates HPP development.

In general, the child's ensuing higher psychological development involves the intersection and merging of natural and cultural developmental lines.

> ...the most significant moment in the course of intellectual development, which gives rise to the purely human forms of practical and abstract intelligence, occurs when [cultural] speech and [natural] practical activity, two previously completely independent lines of development, converge (Vygotsky, 1978, p. 24).

This merging of social speech with natural intelligence creates the capacity for verbal thinking, opens the door for higher processes, and initiates the concept formation process.

Through his cultural-historical work, Vygotsky attempted to account for uniquely human consciousness by tracing the biological evolution of lower psychological processes, the historical transformation of cultural psychological structures, and the ontogenesis of higher psychological processes. He believed that the nature of human consciousness qualitatively distinguishes humans from other animals, that uniquely human behaviors arise from social, not biological, reality, and his perspective emanates from the spoken word and the relationship between higher thinking and speech.

Thinking and Speech

Vygotsky began his work on thinking and speech by stating what he believed to be the fundamental psychological problem and by demonstrating why this fundamental problem remains unresolved.

> The first issue that must be faced in the analysis of thinking and speech concerns the relationship among the various mental functions, the relationship among the various forms of the activity of consciousness. This issue is fundamental to many problems in psychology. In the analysis of thinking and speech, the central problem is that of *the relationship of thought to word* (Vygotsky, 1987, p. 43).

Vygotsky (1987) argues that psychological research regarding thinking and speech, however, assumes an unvarying relationship between these two mental functions.

> Traditionally...the connections among the mental functions...have simply been accepted as a given. The reason for this becomes apparent only when we become aware of an important tacit assumption...that has become part of the foundation of psychological research. This assumption (one that was never clearly formulated and is entirely false) is that the links or connections among the mental functions are constant and...do not have to be considered...(p. 43).

According to Vygotsky, this research perspective arose because theories regarding the phenomena of thinking and speech either assume one of two extreme positions or oscillate between the two positions from an intermediate point. The first position which Vygotsky calls *identification* conflates thinking and speech assuming only a mechanical difference between them.

> If we begin with the claim made in antiquity that thought is "speech minus sound," we can trace the development of the...tendency to identify [conflate] thinking and speech...through to the contemporary American psychologist or the reflexologist. These psychologists view thought as a reflex in which the motor component has been inhibited. Not only the resolution of the problem of the relationship of thought to word but the very statement of the issue itself is impossible within these perspectives. One cannot study the relationship of a thing to itself (Vygotsky, 1987, p. 44).

The other extreme position treats thinking and speech as two distinct but only superficially connected mental functions. According to Vygotsky, this position is typified by the phenomenologically based Wurzburg School which arose in opposition to psychological associationism, a tradition that conflates thinking and speech.

Because the Wurzburg scholars sever thinking and speech, Vygotsky believed their perspective was an improvement over conflating these functions because they were at least in a position to consider the relationship between the functions.

> Perspectives...that begin with the concept that thinking and speech are independent of one another, are obviously in a better position to resolve the problem. Representatives of the Wurzburg school...attempt to free thought from all sensory factors, including the word. The link between thought and word is seen as a purely external relationship...Within this framework, it is indeed possible to pose the question of the relationship between thought and word and to attempt a resolution (Vygotsky, 1987, p. 44).

Vygotsky argues, though, that this type of approach also fails to uncover the relationship between thinking and speech because *verbal thinking*-the primary phenomenon arising from *both* the internal and external interrelationship between thinking and speech-is reduced into *disconnected elements that no longer reflect the unified whole.*

> Verbal thinking is partitioned into...the elements of thought and word and these are then represented as entities that are foreign to one another. Having studied the characteristics of thinking as such (i.e. thinking independent of speech) and then of speech isolated from thinking, an attempt is made to reconstruct a connection between the two, to reconstruct an external, mechanical interaction between two different processes (Vygotsky 1987, p. 44).

Elemental or reductionistic analyses fail, Vygotsky (1986) argues, because the qualities associated with the reduced elements differ from the qualities of the unified whole. Vygotsky draws an analogy from chemistry to illustrate this argument:

> [Analyzing] complex psychological wholes into *elements*...may be compared to the chemical analysis of water into hydrogen and oxygen, neither of which possesses the properties of the whole and each of which possesses properties not present in the whole. The student applying this method in looking for the explanation of some property of water-why it extinguishes fire, for example-will find to his surprise that hydrogen burns and oxygen sustains fire...Psychology winds up in the same kind of dead end when it analyzes verbal thought into its components, thought and word, and studies them in isolation from each other...[The] original properties of verbal thought have disappeared. Nothing is left...but to search out the mechanical interaction of the two elements in the hope of reconstructing, in a purely speculative way, the vanished properties of the whole (p. 4).

Because the investigator is forced to speculate about the interaction between elements in order to account for the original phenomenon, this analysis produces generalization instead of explanation.

> Rather than providing an explanation of the concrete characteristics of the whole that we are interested in, it subordinates this whole to the dictates of more general phenomena. That is, the integral whole is subordinated to the dictates of laws which would allow us to explain that which is common to all speech phenomena or all manifestations of thinking, to speech and thinking as abstract generalities...The internal relationships of the unified whole are replaced with external mechanical relationships between two heterogeneous processes (Vygotsky, 1987, p. 46).

Vygotsky illustrates the limitations of elemental analysis common to speech research by referring to the areas of phonetics and semantics. These two research areas exemplify the decomposition of speech into the elements sound and meaning. Phoneticists study sound isolated from meaning which produces only a generalized theoretical understanding of vocalization and ignores the species specific aspects of human speech and consciousness.

> Divorced from thought, sound loses all the unique features that are characteristic of it as the sound of human speech, the characteristics that distinguish it from other types of sound that exist in nature...That which is specific to this particular form of sound has remained unexplored. As a consequence, this research has not been able to explain why sound possessing certain physical and mental characteristics is present in human speech or how it functions as a component of speech (Vygotsky, 1987, p. 46).

Whereas phoneticists study meaningless sound, semanticists research soundless meaning in the form of concepts. When applied to the development of the child's speech and verbal thinking, the study of concepts in isolation from speech creates the illusion that thought and speech develop independently and unite in only an external, mechanical way.

Vygotsky suggests that the severing of thinking and speech by the Wurzburg school and the isolation of meaning from sound by classical semantics and phonetics illustrate the limitations of reductionistic or elemental analyses regarding thinking and speech.

> This type of analysis provides no adequate basis for the study of the multiform concrete relations between thought and language that arise in the course of the development and functioning of verbal thought in its various aspects...It leads us...into serious errors by ignoring the unitary nature of the process under study. The living union of sound and meaning that we call the word is broken up into two parts, which are assumed to be held together merely by mechanical associative connections (Vygotsky, 1986, p. 5).

In sum, the research problem central to understanding higher psychological processes, particularly concept formation, requires investigating the developmental relationship between thinking and speech. Research approaches that conflate or reduce these functions are inadequate. Conflating the functions prevents stating the problem, and *elemental* analysis reduces the phenomenon of verbal thinking into parts that no longer reflect the qualities of the unified whole. Therefore, Vygotsky proposes an alternative approach to studying thinking and speech.

Analysis Based Upon Units

Vygotsky views thinking and speech as two developmental lines that become "inextricably intertwined" in verbal thinking. He often refers to the relationship between these functions using the metaphor of a *knot* which *ties* the lines together. Whereas conflating thinking and speech ignores the knot that ties these functions and elemental analysis cuts the knot then speculates how it should be retied, Vygotsky attempts to unravel the knot by observing its development.

As an alternative to identification or reduction, Vygotsky substitutes a holistic partitioning of phenomena using what he calls an analysis based upon *units*.

> In contrast to the term "element," the term "unit" designates a product of analysis that possesses all the basic characteristics of the whole...The key to the explanation of the characteristics of water lies not in the investigation of its chemical formula but...in its molecule and its molecular movements. In precisely the same sense, the living cell is the real unit of biological analysis because it preserves the basic characteristics of life that are inherent in the living organism (Vygotsky, 1987, p. 46).

Vygotsky suggests that thinking and speech, instead of functioning independently, developmentally unite in word meaning.

> ...meaning is an inseparable part of the word; it belongs not only to the domain of thought but to the domain of speech. A word without meaning is not a word, but an empty sound...One cannot say of word meaning what we said earlier of the elements of the word taken separately. Is word meaning speech or is it thought? It is both at one and the same time; it is a *unit of verbal thinking* (Vygotsky, 1987, p. 47).

More specifically, Vygotsky argues the unit *word meaning* captures the relationship between *communication*, the initial and primary function of human speech, and *generalization*, a fundamental operation in verbal thinking.

> ...the initial and the primary function of speech is communicative. Speech is a means of social interaction, a means of expression and understanding. The mode of analysis that decomposes the whole into its elements divorces the communicative function of speech from its intellectual function...However, in the same sense that word meaning is a *unit of thinking*, it is also a unit of both these speech functions (Vygotsky, 1987, p. 48).

In addition to capturing the communicative aspect of speech, Vygotsky argues that word meaning encompasses the *generalizing* property of thought which is embodied in the spoken word and functions in uniquely human communication.

> The word does not relate to a single object, but to an *entire group or class of objects*. Therefore, every word is a concealed *generalization*. From a psychological perspective, word meaning is first and foremost a generalization (Vygotsky, 1987, p. 47).

This generalized reflection of reality, made possible through the meaningful word, contributes to the qualitative developmental shift from lower psychological processes based upon sensation and perception to higher psychological processes based upon verbal thinking.

> [The meaningful word's] reflection of reality differs radically from that of immediate sensation or perception...This qualitative difference is primarily a function of a *generalized reflection of reality*. Therefore, generalization in word meaning is an act of thinking in the true sense of the word (Vygotsky, 1987, p. 47).

This generalized reflection of reality functions intellectually in uniquely human communication.

> ...social interaction...is impossible without meaning. To communicate an experience or some other content of consciousness to another person, it must be related to a class or group of phenomena...[and] this requires generalization. The higher forms of mental social interaction that are such an important characteristic of [homo sapiens] are possible only because–by thinking–[humans reflect] reality in a generalized way (Vygotsky, 1987, pp. 48-49).

In sum, as opposed to conflating or reducing thinking and speech into elements, Vygotsky addresses the phenomenon verbal thinking using an analysis based upon units. For Vygotsky, the unit *word meaning* captures the fundamental qualities of both thinking and speech. Because thinking and speech unite in word meaning, verbal thought development can be monitored by observing transitions in the intellectual operations which create, maintain and ultimately transform word meaning. Thus the development of word meaning is a thread that can be used to trace an individual's movement through the process of concept formation.

Methodology

> [We are] presented with the task of studying the development of concept formation, the task of studying how this process is causally and dynamically determined...[And what] unifies all these investigations is the idea of development, an idea that we attempt to apply in our analysis of word meaning as the unity of speech and thinking (Vygotsky, 1987, p. 51).

The relationship between thinking and speech is fundamental to Vygotsky's account of concept formation. Developmentally, this relationship exhibits interdependence, dynamism and congruent movement where the initially separate, later interacting and eventually converging lines evolve concurrently toward greater intellectual capacity.

> The basic fact we encounter in a genetic analysis of the *relationship* between thinking and speech is that this relationship is not constant. The quantitative and qualitative significance of this relationship changes in the course of development (Vygotsky, 1987, p. 101).

At the heart of concept formation is the child's increasing sophistication with the spoken word.

> In this research, we [want] to clarify the role of the [spoken] word–that is, the nature of its functional application–in the process of concept formation (Vygotsky, 1987, p. 127)...It is through the word that the child voluntarily directs his attention on a single feature, synthesizes [this with other] isolated features, symbolizes the abstract concept, and operates with it as the most advanced form of the sign created by human thinking (Vygotsky, 1987, p. 159).

Vygotsky used a specific application of the *functional method of double stimulation*, developed by his student Sahkarov (1930), to study the role of the spoken word, word meaning and the relationship between speech and thinking in concept formation.

In this method, two sets of stimuli are applied: one set functions as the object of activity and the other functions as sign means [psychological tools] that aid the subject in organizing and completing a task or problem. The task and object(s) of the subject's activity are presented at the outset and remain constant. The means are introduced incrementally.

Sahkarov describes the functional method of double stimulation:

> There is a collection of figures [usually wooden "blocks"] of different shapes, colors, height and planar dimensions...this collection is a motley, unorganized whole: it is irregular and unsymmetric. Different attributes occur an unequal number of times. The collection is based on four experimental concepts associated with test words [nonsense words], which are written on the bottoms of the figures, not visible to the child [subject]. One concept embraces all tall and large figures ["lag"]; the other, all tall and small ["mur"]; the third, all short and small ["cev"]; and the fourth, all short and large ["bik"]. The experiment is done as a game. The figures are [randomly] arranged on a game board...One of them is turned [over] and its name...is read aloud. According to the rules of the game, the child must [then identify and] remove all the toys that have the same name as the [turned over] model and place them in a special field...without turning them over...After each such attempt, the experimenter turns over [one]

new figure, revealing [a] mistake, which is either among the removed figures...or among the figures not removed...Thus, the principle of the experiment is that the series of objects is given to the child immediately as a whole, but the series of words is given gradually, and the nature of the double stimulation continually varies. After each such change we obtain the child's free response, which enables us to assess the changes that have taken place in the child's psychological operations as a consequence of the fact that the series of objects now contains a new element from the verbal series...Of course, the task can be correctly accomplished only if the experimental concepts that underlied the test words have been formed (Van der Veer & Valsiner, 1991, p. 261).

As the researcher turns over blocks [models] throughout the experiment, s/he observes the process through which the subject generalizes the model/word to refer to a group of objects. Vygotsky (1987) explains:

The stimulus-sign or word constitutes the variable. The task is the constant. This makes it possible to study how the subject uses the sign as a means of directing his intellectual operations. Depending on how the word is used, depending on its functional application, we are able to study how the process of concept formation proceeds and develops (p. 128).

In sum, the functional method of double stimulation enables the researcher to observe both the process through which a word's meaning develops as well as the changes in intellectual operations which underlie a word's usage. As a result of empirical work conducted along with Sahkarov, Kotelova and Paskovska, Vygotsky developed an account of the complex developmental process from the beginning of verbal thinking through true conceptual thinking, then verified and modified his account through observations of children in a variety of settings. Detailed accounts of this work on speech development and concept formation can be found in *Thinking and Speech* (Vygotsky, 1987) and *Thought and Language* (Vygotsky, 1986), and an historical-critical analysis can be found in the dissertation *Scientific and Everyday Concepts: An application of Vygotsky's Work to the Speech Theory of Human Communication* (Whelan, 1993, University of Denver).

Conclusion

I chose to write about Vygotsky in this book about contextualism for two reasons. I believe that Vygotsky's *Cultural Historical Psychology* can serve as a highly developed model for contextual thinking and I am convinced that Vygotsky has a great deal to offer the discipline of speech communication.

As a model for contextual thinking, Vygotsky's approach illustrates 1) an internally consistent flow among philosophy, metatheory, theory and method, 2) an emphasis on subtle, qualitative analysis, 3) a developmental process orientation, 4) a holistic unit of analysis, and 5) a broad sweeping conceptualization of the cultural-historical context. In fact, if Vygotsky were alive today, it would not surprise me if he considered Punctuated Equilibrium and the Big Bang in his ontogenic account of intellectual development.

In this summary of Cultural Historical Psychology, I included those aspects of Vygotsky's approach that illustrate the contextual nature of his thinking. I was unable to include his fascinating account of concept formation and scientific and everyday concepts, his work on abnormal psychology and learning disabilities or his discussions on childhood development of perception, memory, emotions, imagination and the will. However, I provided the philosophical grounding for further exploration in these and the many other areas of Vygotsky's inquiry and I hope that I have piqued your interest.

Norris Minnick, in the introduction to Volume 1 of Vygotsky's Collected Works, points out that many international scholars are convinced that Vygotsky was not only ahead of *his* time, but "...his ideas and insights are in many respects considerably ahead of our time...[and] his influence on the development of psychology and the social sciences has not been nearly as considerable as it must be" (Vygotsky, 1987, p. 34).

Vygotsky repeatedly points out that the place he left us is not an ending but a beginning. He conducted his work in the spirit of providing psychology with a new direction, founded on a sound consideration of various theoretical perspectives and based on an interplay among the biological, psychological and social contributions to development. Vygotsky offers the same heuristic potential for the speech communication discipline as he does for psychology.

Clearly, Vygotsky saw himself as a visionary, hoping to steer social science in a more productive and meaningful direction, and always reaching well beyond the scope of his own lifetime.

> In conclusion, we would like to indicate that our aim has by no means been some sort of exhaustive and final resolution of the questions we have posed. Rather, this is simply an introduction to boundless areas of research–and only that...(Vygotsky, 1993, p. 208).

References

Darwin, C. (1981). *The descent of man, and selection in relation to sex.* Princeton, NJ: Princeton University Press.

Dubin, R. (1978). *Theory Building.* New York: MacMillan Publishing Company.

Hawking, S. (1988). *A brief history of time: From the big bang to black holes.* New York: Bantom.

Kaplan, A. (1964). *The Conduct of inquiry: Methodology for behavioral science.* San Francisco: Chandler Publishing Company.

Kozulin, A. (1990). *Vygotsky's psychology: A biography of ideas.* Cambridge, MA: Harvard University Press.

Van der Veer, R., & Valsiner, J. (1991). *Understanding Vygotsky: A quest for synthesis.* Cambridge, MA: Blackwell.

Vygotsky, L. S. (1978). *Mind in society: The development of higher psychological processes,* M. Cole, V. John-Steiner, S. Scribner, & E. Souberman (Eds.). Cambridge, MA: Harvard University Press.

Vygotsky, L. S. (1979). Consciousness as a problem of the psychology of behavior. *Soviet Psychology,* 17, 5-35.

Vygotsky, L. S. (1986). *Thought and language* (A. Kozulin, Ed. and Trans.). Cambridge, MA: MIT Press.

Vygotsky, L. S. (1987). *The collected works of L. S. Vygotsky, Volume 1: Problems of general psychology.* In R. W. Rieber & A. S. Carton (Eds.). New York: Plenum

Vygotsky, L. S. (1993). *The collected works of L. S. Vygotsky, Volume 2: The fundamentals of defectology.* In R. W. Rieber & A. S. Carton (Eds.). New York: Plenum.

Whelan, T. (1993). *Scientific and everyday concepts: An application of Vygotsky's work to the speech theory of human communication.* Unpublished doctoral dissertation, University of Denver, Colorado.

Chapter 10

Cognitive Representation of Rhetorical Situations

Gary Cronkhite
Indiana University

Situations are Nature's way of keeping our experiences from being interminably repetitive.

Actually, that is not my thesis. It is an adaptation of Woody Allen's definition of "time" as being "Nature's way of keeping everything from happening at once." But more than that, it is a recognition of the fact that situations are infinitely variable in our natural environment, so if one were to attempt to represent all the situations we encounter, it would be somewhat akin to attempting to respond to the exam item from Hell: Describe the Universe and give two examples. I am not going to attempt that. Instead, I am going to describe how we represent situations cognitively, and advocate the definition of situation represented cognitively as "An ad hoc category of needs and constraints operant at a particular time and place." The perception of a situation, by this definition, is accomplished by operation of a cognitive schema by which environmental elements are analyzed, endowed with meaning, and stored. But more of that later.

Some Definitions and Intent of the Chapter

Magnusson, in the introduction to his edited volume, Toward a Psychology of Situations (1981), discusses the "environment" as including that which is perceptible and imperceptible at any given moment. The "actual situation" he defines as that which is available for perception at a given time and place, whereas the "perceptible situation" is that part of the actual situation that is perceived at that moment. It is the cognitive representation of the momentary "perceptible situation" I wish to describe here. Magnusson notes there have been many attempts to characterize both the environment and actual situations. I am aware of attempts to describe at least actual situations in terms of their dimensions, sets of categories, and exemplars, for example, including numerous such attempts in the discipline of communication, notably in the study of "compliance-gaining strategies" and "credibility," for example. I am going to simplify my life here by not attempting any such heroic endeavor. Moreover, I am not going to attempt to review all the variations on this theme even within the discipline of communication, and certainly not within the social sciences in general. I simply believe such attempts to be hopeless in view of the fact that, for example, a given situation may involve a rabbi, a priest, an elephant, a flagpole, a long-distance runner, a chance social encounter ... and any number of other elements far too numerous to mention. It is beyond my comprehension that one could aspire to construct a typology that would include all such variations. I am also not going to attempt to review all the literature relating to situations. That is, this chapter is not intended as a literature review, it is intended as an analytic piece. For the reader looking for a literature review, I recommend the volume edited by Magnusson, to which I have referred. Its date of publication suggests it may be outdated, but I think not. In my own literature search I found little study and discussion of situation in the past decade. What appears to have happened is that the interest of those who might have focused on situations has turned instead to schemata and scripts. There are literally hundreds of publications to be found in the literature of the social sciences if one enters the term "schema" into a literature search.

Human Adaptability to Situations

One constantly reads that this, that, or the other characteristic is the crucial element separating humans from other organisms, and I hesitate to play that game, but it does seem true that insects do not have any variety of perceived situations to which they must adapt. The bee whose genetic job description is to find food for the hive basically does that all its brief life. It does that job very well, and communicates the location of food quite explicitly, but it does so with a single-mindedness that is not useful in any other situation. Humans who do their jobs with such ability, alacrity, and persistence are difficult to find, but humans are generally adaptable to a variety of pursuits. Whether the hard-wired specialists, the insects, or the Jack-of-all-trades humans will ultimately prevail in the evolutionary contest is far from being decided at this report. Humans, of course, are convinced we are the ultimate expression of survival of the fittest, but exactly what we are fittest for is not yet clear. It may not be survival of nuclear holocausts or environmental disasters, whereas insects may go on about their genetically specified tasks with little concern about such matters. But it is clear humans are fittest for perceiving a variety of situations.

The GOALS/GRASP Model As a Cognitive Schema for Situations

What I am going to argue here is that the description of a procedure for analyzing situations proposed by Cronkhite and Liska (1980), Cronkhite (1984), and Liska and Cronkhite (1995), which we termed the GOALS/GRASP Model and originally applied to choices among prospective communicators, is in fact useful as a general model of the schema we use to analyze and represent situations. It is a procedure, not a typology. It is akin to an algorithm, a part of a program for dealing with any given situation, not a location with parameters for identifying and storing all situations. If it were to be software for a computer to deal with, it would be among the *instructions* for dealing with incoming data, not *places* to store data. It would be a program file, not a data file.

GOALS is an acronym for Goals Operant and Achievable in Light of the Situation. Of course we all have goals ranging from those involved in our long-term life scripts to those that are merely momentary, such as stepping onto the curb instead of tripping over it. But GOALS are a subset of all such far-reaching or momentary goals; they are those that are salient at the moment and appear reasonably achievable under the circumstances. GRASP is also an acronym, for Goal-Relevant Aspects of the Situation Perceived. These aspects are those characteristics of the situation that seem likely to hinder or facilitate achievement of the aforementioned GOALS. The intersection of these GOALS and GRASP focuses our attention on the characteristics of the environment and the actual situation and produces the perceived situation. Those of you who are familiar with the GOALS/GRASP Model as described in the publications cited in the previous paragraph will recognize this as the right-hand side of the model described there. We have come to realize that whatever object of choice is represented on the left-hand side, be it a potential communicator, a compliance-gaining strategy, or some other communication variable, the GOALS/GRASP part of the model remains a schema for processing situations.

Those of you who are especially perceptive regarding semantic distinctions or logical inconsistencies may have realized I am using the term "situation" as part of my description of a schema for processing situations, and that is decidedly circular. The term "situation" as represented by the "S" in GOALS and GRASP refers to the *actual* situation, as defined by Magnusson, as all the aspects of the situation available for perception, but not necessarily perceived. That is the input to the GOALS/GRASP schema. Once processed cognitively, the output of the process is the *perceived* situation, endowed with meaning in terms of the relevant GOALS that may be achieved within it and in terms of the GRASP that may facilitate or deter the achievement of those goals. This perceived situation has been represented cognitively in terms of the GOALS/GRASP schema and is ready for storage and later retrieval, if necessary, by activation of this schema.

This schema may be applicable to the perception of all the situations humans encounter, but I am not going to make such a grandiose claim. Rather, I want to limit the situations to which this model is applicable to *rhetorical* situations. Bitzer (1968) has described the Rhetorical Situation as one motivated by an exigency that can be resolved by a rhetorical act. In the present terms, this exigency consists of a set of GOALS that are somehow constrained by GRASP so they require a rhetorical (or communicative) act in order to achieve them. It is from the intersection of the GOALS and GRASP that spring the criteria for choosing among the available rhetorical/communicative acts.

Of What Do the GOALS and GRASP Consist?

I have said these perceived situations are ad hoc categories. I need to explain whence come the GOALS and GRASP, I want to describe the perceptibilia on which they are based, and I want to speculate about the brain mechanisms that may be involved.

Perceived Situations as Ad Hoc Categories

There have been numerous attempts to describe general perceptual categories in terms of their outer limits, their dimensions, and exemplars that define the centers around which they are organized. These approaches all assume we carry perceptual categories with us and apply them to the phenomena we encounter. I will not dispute that assumption, but I believe there is another approach that may be more useful for my purpose here. Consider this exercise:

What do the following have in common: Pets, a ring of keys, a photo album, children, business papers, and warm clothes? The answer: They constitute a category of things to take out of a burning house in the winter. They form an *ad hoc* category, one that really has no outer limits, dimensions, or exemplar, and one a person would construct on the spur of the moment, not something one would carry about in one's mind. I believe we persistently make lists, mentally or on paper, of things we need to do or things we need to take, and it may be there are underlying dimensions or categorical limits or exemplars on which these are based, but I am going to leave it to someone who is more compulsive to identify those categories/situations. For my part, I believe we construct perceived situations on an ad hoc basis.

That is not to say such construction is disorganized or random. Rather, it is based on the schema I have described. We rapidly list our GOALS, probably usually at a tacit rather than an explicit level, then assess the GRASP that constrain or facilitate those GOALS, and then choose the strategies for satisfying the GOALS in spite of the constraints or taking advantage of the facilitating elements. The burning house is only partly a communication situation, but one would probably communicate very quickly with one's spouse and children, so communication is involved. The specific strategies chosen would depend on one's priorities. I expect getting the children out would be high on one's list of GOALS, and the GRASP would involve the location and extent of the fire and the availability of exits. For me the pets would come next, and then things that are irreplaceable and of great sentimental value. I might well find myself standing outside with less than adequate clothing and no car keys, but I would have made the choices involved on the basis of my rapid assessment of the GOALS and GRASP.

This approach was suggested to me by Lawrence Barsalou of the University of Chicago in a lecture in the Cognitive Science Colloquium series here at Indiana University in September, 1995. What Barsalou was arguing for was a concept he termed "perceptual symbols." While I do not agree with his use of the term "symbols," his description of them is consistent with what I will speculate are "Brain Impulse Interaction Patterns" created by ad hoc categories that constitute situations. Barsalou stated explicitly that his "perceptual symbols" are *not* physical pictures or mental images; rather they are records of the brain state that accompanied the perception or cognition. As I will note later, that is exactly characteristic of my "Brain Impulse Interaction Patterns." But let us put that on hold for the moment.

Types of GOALS and GRASP

The GOALS and GRASP that constitute this scheme for processing situations may each be of at least four types: Physical, economic, social, and psychological. Achieving physical pleasure and avoiding physical pain are certainly GOALS to be considered in many actual situations, as are economic advancement, pleasant social interactions, and maintenance of psychological well-being. As a matter of fact, it would be easy to substitute Maslow's hierarchy of goals here, so long as one keeps in mind we are referring to an actual and likely momentary situation. Each of these four types may also serve as GRASP; avoiding physical pain may be constrained or enhanced by economic considerations, or vice versa, and the economic GOALS my be constrained or enhanced by social and/or psychological GRASP. It is almost necessarily a balance of such considerations that define the perceived situation.

Suppose we consider an example. A young man has as GOALS attending school, supporting his family, spending time with his family, and maintaining consistency among his values. In order to attend school and support his family, he must work two jobs, but this puts at risk his physical well-being as well as his ability to spend time with his family, which in turn puts his psychological consistency among his values in jeopardy. In a conflict such as this, what appear as GOALS must do double-time as mutually constraining GRASP. That is why parallel universes were invented.

Perceptibilia of Actual Situations

What characteristics of actual situations are available for perception, as input to the GOALS/GRASP scheme that converts them into perceived situations? The easy answer is any discriminable aspect of the environment available to the human senses. The longer and more difficult answer, for me at least, is available in Gibson's (e.g., 1950, 1966) concepts of the stimulus array, ecological discrimination, and human affordances. My review of these concepts is contained in Cronkhite (1984), pages 57-68. Such a review seems beyond the limitations of this present chapter, but I do feel inclined to a brief summary. Gibson's thesis is that an organism's perceptual apparatus has evolved so as to register those aspects of the environment that have survival significance for it. He describes the extensive information available in the stimulus array, and contends there is limited need for perceptual construction given such a rich array. He points out that an organism that persistently constructed its perceptions of the environment independently of the actual environment would come to no good end, in an evolutionary sense. But many aspects of the environment are only useful to a given species given its "affordances," those aspects of the environment it is capable of manipulating. Other aspects of the environment are not useful for that species, because they are not manipulable. Thus humans, given the way they are equipped, have little use for perceiving aspects of the environment such as the infrared and ultraviolet ranges of the spectrum, but there is a great deal of survival value in their perceiving rapidly approaching solid objects, especially if they have teeth, claws, or bumpers. The clearest category of phenomena humans seem genetically equipped to perceive and manipulate are symbols.

Gibson was especially interested in visual perceptibilia, but in my review I also described perceptibilia of objects, space, time, movement, change, events, physical causality, social causality, intention, people, speech, and writing. If I were to repeat that discussion here, however, I would be doing to some extent what I have vowed not to do: Attempting to describe the characteristics of actual situations. Instead I will leave it to the interested reader to consult the chapter, "Perception and Meaning," in which I am afraid I have attempted exactly that.

But the GOALS/GRASP Model of a schema that converts actual situations to perceived situations is consistent with the Gibsonian approach. Gibson's point was that organisms have developed perceptual abilities that are of survival value to them. My point here is that the GOALS/GRASP schema calls our attention to those aspects of actual situations that constrain or facilitate our GOALS, and makes it possible for us to make choices among strategies that are in what we believe, at least, to be our own best interests. One can only hope that these choices have survival value in that they contribute to the survival and propagation of an individual's genes. Whether survival and propagation of that individual's genes are in the best interest of the human species is another issue, and one that will be decided by a higher court.

Physiological Mechanisms and Processes

Simplistically it can be said there are basically two approaches to human cognitive processing at a physiological level: The neural pathways explanation and the wholistic explanation that relies on some analogy with holographic storage and retrieval. I will return in a moment to the suggestion that this is a simplistic dichotomy. Let me first describe the two explanations to which I refer.

The older explanation relied on the notion that a given experience, or stimulus, makes its way into the Central Nervous System by means of neural pathways, travelling along neurons and bridging synapses between neurons. Successive similar stimuli followed similar pathways, and learning occurred as the bridges between the neurons were reinforced so the most often-repeated stimuli found certain pathways easier to follow than others. Successive stimuli then stimulated existing pathways into the cortex, producing memories. New sensory inputs, in conjunction with the stored memories, produced motor excitations which issued into external motor responses. I told you this was going to be simplistic. To be fair, however, these were not necessarily represented as single stimuli; they could be stimulus complexes.

Originally it seems to have been Pribram (1971) who noticed the similarities between certain things the brain does and some characteristics of holographic storage and retrieval. Probably we have all experienced holograms and, perhaps beyond that, the experiences possible with the technology of virtual reality. The characteristics of psychophysiological processing that seem difficult to explain by the neural pathways model are:

(1) *Specific* memories do not seem to be lost when portions of the associative cortex are removed or damaged. This is also true when holographic film is cut into pieces. The resolution of the hologram may be reduced, but the information necessary to reproduce the entire image seems to be contained in every part of the holographic film, unlike photographic film, and unlike what one would expect based on the neural pathways model.

(2) The human brain has amazing storage capacity, as does holographic film. This was always a problem for the neural pathways model, since each memory required a separate neural pathway. This storage capacity is achieved because each holographic "memory" is stored, not as a separate pathway, but as a wave-interference pattern, of which there is an almost infinite variety.

(3) Retrieval of memories in the human brain is essentially instantaneous; there does not appear to be time for a stimulus to search through the billions of pathways before finding a match. This is also true with holographic storage. The activation of a given wave-interference pattern will produced resonance of similar wave-interference patterns instantaneously. At a much less complex level, one can observe a similar phenomenon when one tuning fork is struck and exposed to an array of tuning forks of different frequencies. Any tuning fork capable of the same frequency will resonate in sympathy with that one which has been struck.

Since Pribram's original advocacy of the holographic-storage explanation, there have been incredible advances in the technologies of digital storage in a variety of media, advances that seem to render the holographic explanation almost primitive. The important characteristics of the explanation remain, however; it is now just much easier to see how more wholistic storage and retrieval may be possible without reliance on individual neural pathways. However, there is no question that information is transmitted to the brain by means of specific neural pathways. What has changed are the explanations of what happens once it gets there. Moreover, it seems clear the wholistic model is best applied to the associative cortex, and there are many specialized modules within the brain that perform rather specific functions. Thus we must adopt a rather limited wholism. With respect to communication abilities in particular, it seems clear Brocca's and Wernicke's areas in the left hemisphere of right-handed adults are primarily responsible for speech production and comprehension, respectively, and while much of language is produced and comprehended in the left hemisphere, many language-related capabilities, including comprehension of metaphor and various kinds of humor, are seriously deficient when there is damage to the right hemisphere. Thus the dichotomy with which I began this section was indeed simplistic.

But what has this to do with the GOALS/GRASP schema? Very simply, each actual situation we encounter is converted by the GOALS/GRASP schema into a perceived situation, which is stored in the brain as something analogous to a wave-interference pattern—something I am going to term a "Neural Impulse Interaction Pattern"—and experienced as a memory.

The Mind Is What the Brain Does

A visual wave-interference pattern is created when two beams of light intersect one another, or when a light beam is projected through a very tiny slit. A practically infinite number of such patterns can be created by a beam of a single frequency in this way. But this is the technology based on light waves, and wholistic storage and retrieval can be created in many different media. It could be that the simultaneous arrival of multiple neural impulses from each of the various senses—odors, sights, sounds, and touches—create neural impulse interaction patterns that define a given situation/event in memory, later to be reactivated by a similar set of simultaneous neural impulses, as when all the tuning forks of a given frequency are activated by the activation of that frequency. It is clear that perceived situations are stored and recalled (1) in such amazing detail and number that the method and medium of storage must have amazing capacity, (2) in some way that makes it possible for them to be stored redundantly throughout large areas of the associative cortex rather than in specific locations, and (3) in some way that makes it possible for them to be recalled instantaneously without mental searching.

But the experiences we have when we recall situations obviously bear no relation to these neural impulse interaction patterns (henceforth, for economy, NIIPs) or whatever other means of storage and retrieval may be making such recollections possible. But neither does the three-dimensional hologram that one can walk behind and around, that changes perspective depending on the angle at which it is viewed, bear any apparent relationship to the means and medium by which it is stored. Full-size holograms are available for viewing in several museums of natural history—notably at the Sensorium in San Francisco, for example. They have also appeared on the covers of several issues of Natural Geographic, one a skull and another a globe of the world, that I recall. But easier to access than that, you may well have one in your wallet, on your Visa card. Mine contains an eagle, which changes color, perspective, and appears to fly depending on the angle of the light source. The problem here may be that we have grown accustomed to the fact that the negatives and slides from which our photographic experiences are created actually *resemble* those experiences. That is not true of holographic film. Looking at it, its appearance is murky, foggy, and contains none of the image it is capable of recreating when shot through with a laser beam. Moreover, a piece of the holographic film is capable of creating the entire image, unlike photographic film, and it contains a much greater amount of information.

Consider a CD or CD-Rom. What looks like a shiny medallion created for the pleasure of a primitive chieftain bears no relationship to the auditory and visual experiences it is capable of producing through speakers, headphones, on a computer screen, or by means of virtual reality goggles.

The point here is that we have come to realize the means and media by which experiences are stored need bear no apparent re-semblance to the experiences themselves. Thus it should come as no surprise that perceived situations bear no resemblance to the means by which they are stored in the brain, whether those means consist of neural impulse interaction patterns or something of which scientists have not yet dreamt. The solution to the ages-old brain-mind conundrum seems to be this: The experiences of the mind are created by the brain. As I mentioned Barsalou as having said, these mental storage phenomena, whether NIIPs or something else, are neither physical pictures nor mental imagery. They are records of the brain state that accompanied the perception or cognition.

I would like to explore this speculation a bit further. It is almost certain that these brain states occur in the internuncial neurons. These are neurons that do not transmit either sensory impulses to the sensory projection areas or motor impulses to their respective end-organs, although they occupy a major portion of the cortex. It seems apparent their function is associative. Now imagine that numerous neural impulses from the various senses pass simultaneously through these neurons, accompanied by interoceptive impulses from memory, and kinesthetic impulses that define the states of the motor mechanisms. If one assumes that a change of mere nanoseconds in the appearance time of one or more of these impulses would create a different and unique NIIP, then a practically infinite number of unique NIIPs would be possible. Moreover, my physiological psychology professor, Peter Grossman, who departed the University of Iowa for the University of Chicago about the same time I left for the University of Illinois, was devoted to the proposition that the brain is an electrochemical organ more than it is merely a transmitter of electrical impulses. If we specify that the concatenation of neural impulses arrives under the influence of a specific electrochemical state at that internuncial location, then the number of possible unique NIIPs is drastically multiplied. We tend not to think of rapid, subtle changes in electrochemical states, because those most of us observed in chemistry class were not particularly rapid or subtle. But deep-sea organisms have been video-taped producing dramatic light shows using electrochemical transformations almost too transient for the human eye to observe. The lowly squid is one of the most amazing performers in this regard, communicating with other squid solely by means of these electrochemical changes. I cannot demonstrate that here, but if you are interested I urge you to view the "Communication" episode of the "Trials of Life" series produced by Turner Broadcasting and the BBC. It will probably be available in your local and/or university library.

The point I want to emphasize is that neural impulse interaction patterns, consisting of such concatenations of impulses at a given nanosecond under the influence of a specific electro-chemical field, have all the potential characteristics of wave-interference patterns, including instantaneous retrieval if the brain state is duplicated later, almost limitless storage capacity, and redundant storage throughout the associative cortex.[1]

Deja Vu and the Recall of Perceived Situations

When I was searching the research literature for recent material dealing with situations, and found little, and then found a surfeit of publications dealing with schemata and scripts, it occurred to me that the deja vu experience might yield something of interest, since that experience can be considered an instance in which a previously experienced situation is recalled so incompletely or at such a low level of awareness that it hovers tantalizingly out of the grasp of explicit recall. One thinks, "I've done this before," but cannot even quite define what "this" might be. In fact, there are more such articles than I care to count, but most of them make use of the "Deja vu all over again" formula that I thought Flo Conway, Jim Siegelmann, Carl Carmichael, and I invented in Waikiki during the 1985 convention of the International Communication Association. But probably not. What I thought was an original formula is now a cliche, unfortunately surviving on life support. The titles are mostly some form of "Deja Vu All Over Again In the Stock Market ... Medical Malpractice ... Academic Dishonesty ... etcetera."

About four research studies have been devoted to the deja vu experience, but have unearthed little. Still, it may be a way into conceptualizing relations among perceived situations. It could be that in the deja vu experience the presently perceived situation, converted into its own NIIP, resonates minimally with elements of a stored neural impulse interaction pattern. The resonance may be only due to some similar background music, or a shared odor, those being two physical phenomena that are often reported as eliciting long-lost memories, or similarity on some of the other myriad dimensions situations may share. Whatever the resonance, it is not adequate to elicit the entire stored experience. It is similar to the "tip-of-the-tongue" phenomenon; this is the "tip-of-the-brain" phenomenon.

Now *if*—and this remains largely conjecture—the deja vu experience is produced by two NIIPs overlapping minimally, might that experience be considered to be at the *minimal* end of a continuum of overlap that produces at that end only tacit recall at a very low level of awareness, but at the opposite end, where *maximal* overlap occurs, quite *explicit* recall of which the individual is quite aware? At the explicit end of the continuum, one is tempted to say "This is *exactly* what happened to me last week." Of course, the match is not "exact," because no two situations are identical, but they may be close enough for government work, and no two neural impulse interaction patterns are identical either.

If this is the case, then it can be truly said that the perceived situation is an ad hoc category, there being no dimensions on which NIIPs can be characterized, the recalled situation is similarly an ad hoc category, and the similarities between them are ad hoc constructions.

But whether or not perceived situations are stored and retrieved as NIIPs, it still appears reasonable to characterize situation-matching as an enterprise that occupies a continuum from minimal to maximal overlap. If this theory of overlapping NIIPs being responsible for situation-recall turns out to be correct, it may also explain the puzzle over "coding" in short-term memory to prepare present perceptions for storage in long-term memory. The concept of "coding" in short-term memory was difficult before the advent of schemata and scripts, and it has never been satisfactorily explained or even defined. Coding has been discussed in terms of features, dimensions, and categories the present perception may have in common with conceptions in long-term memory, but detailing such commonalities has been another exercise in "describing the universe and giving two examples."

Situation Perception is Pattern-Recognition Writ Large

In this present conceptualization, the operation of coding in short-term memory would consist of the NIIP representing current input continuing to resonate briefly, while NIIPs from long-term memory that resemble the input NIIP resonate concurrently in empathic concert. This simultaneous resonance would cause the input NIIP to become a part of each of the long-term NIIPs, being coded in terms of whatever similarities caused the top-down NIIPs to resonate. Those similarities might consist of common features, dimensions, categories, or mere coincidence such as both situations having involved Mill Creek. Or whatever.

The geometric theorem that the square of the hypotenuse of a right triangle is equal to the sum of the squares on the other two sides will forever remind me of the spire of the Catholic Church at the corner of Eleventh and Grand Streets in Pueblo, Colorado, because at the time I was puzzling over that theorem in my geometry class I was also looking out the classroom window at that spire and realized that theorem could be used to calculate the height of the spire without climbing it. Aristotle's distinction between artistic and inartistic ethos will forever remind me of an episode in which I crossed the Pentacrest at the University of Iowa on my way from Donald Bryant's class in classical rhetoric on my way to my office. In the present terms, both these associations can be explained as the simultaneous resonance of otherwise unrelated NIIPs.

If this simultaneous resonance is interrupted by the advent of some compelling external stimulation, or if attention is shifted at this crucial moment, and the requisite resonances do not occur, the phenomenon of backward masking will be observed, in which case the original situation will not be subject to conscious, deliberate recall. It will be stored, but will be recalled only coincidentally, when some NIIP is activated with which it shares similarities of time, place, or other characteristics.

This explanation applies not only to situations, by the way. It should apply equally well to the perception of more specific stimuli and to the recognition of stimulus patterns to which we do not apply the term "situation."

Events Versus Situations: The Situation Is Everything Else

One might ask at this point: Could we not say you are discussing "events" just as much as "situations?" I would have to say yes. I have given this matter considerable thought, and have concluded what is one person's event is just part of another's situation. One can observe this at any convention at which the results of social scientific studies are presented. After the paper is read reporting the findings, it is almost de rigueur for someone in the audience to ask, "But doesn't this depend on the situation?" Of course it does, and the speaker who is not entirely naive will just say so and then call on someone else. But as one observes many reports of many studies at many conventions in many disciplines, one is driven inexorably to the conclusion that *the situation is just everything else.* The situation is just whatever the present study is not focused upon, and what is the variable of choice for one investigator is just part of the situation for another. In life outside conventions, whatever one is focused on at the moment is the event; the situation is just background noise *for that observer.* Some other aspect of the situation may be the event for another observer with different GOALS and GRASP. I do not propose to unravel this complicated relationship between events and situations here. I'll leave this for someone else.

GOALS/GRASP, Criteria, Strategies, and Scenarios

As I have said, the actual situation is converted by the GOALS/GRASP schema into a perceived situation. One can think of it as a cognitive script, in which perceivers are instructed to assess their GOALS, imagine what GRASP might facilitate or prevent their GOALS-achievement, and create the perceived situation on that basis. The perceived situation then becomes the output. But attached to the perceived situation are criteria for choosing among available strategies for dealing with that situation, some of which may be communication strategies for dealing with the exigencies of which Bitzer wrote. So far I have been describing only the right-hand side of the GOALS/GRASP Model as it has been diagrammed elsewhere (Cronkhite & Liska, 1980; Cronkhite, 1984; Liska & Cronkhite, 1995). The model as originally described and diagrammed was intended to describe the process of choosing among potential communicators, although it was once presented as a model of the process of choosing among compliance-gaining strategies (Cronkhite & Liska, 1982). That application, unfortunately, was presented in a research report on a convention program and, like so many good ideas presented at conventions, it died not with a bang but a whimper.

Nevertheless, it might be possible to resuscitate the general idea of the 1982 presentation. If one imagines the available strategies, including communication strategies, arrayed in a list, each strategy being assessed in terms of the strategy criteria attached to the perceived situation produced by the application of the GOALS/GRASP schema, one has the framework for converting the GOALS/GRASP Model into a general theory of the cognitive process on which message selection is based.

However, such an ambitious project is going to have to await another paper. Here, I want to discuss how strategy scripts may attach themselves to the perceived situation. It is natural that as the actual situation is converted into a perceived situation, alternative means for dealing with the GRASP in order to achieve the GOALS would become part of the same cognitive construction. It seems likely this is done by means of scenarios, imaginative scripts in which alternative strategies are evaluated in terms of criteria. I contend that these strategies are constructed on an ad hoc basis, as a part of the perceived situation, although they are surely based on previous experience, so they are not ad hoc in the sense of being purely imaginative. The criteria against which they are tested are also to some extent ad hoc, because they are criteria that are applicable *given the situation*, but I think they are based on certain considerations applicable across situations. Obviously the question of whether they will achieve the GOALS given the GRASP is a primary consideration, and that question will be answered on an ad hoc basis simply because the GOALS and GRASP are ad hoc. But some considerations seem generalizable, even though they will have to be modified from one situation to another.

Probably each of us has a preferred list of such considerations. Mine comes from Janis and Mann (1977). They list (1) utilitarian gains and losses for self, (2) utilitarian gains and losses for others, (3) self-approval and disapproval, and (4) social approval or disapproval. Those four categories seem to me to be adequately broad that they can probably subsume most of the specific criteria that will be attached to the perceived situation and applied via scenarios to prospective strategies. I would add something I have termed "Consequences for Cognitive Consistency," because I believe people act so as to maintain consistency among their beliefs, attitudes, and previous behavior, including previous verbal commitments, in ways that are not completely captured by the third and fourth categories of Janis and Mann.

Some will argue, I expect, that these criteria and the strategies to which they are applied are not part of the perceived situation generated by the GOALS/GRASP schema, but I consider them to be because recalling the perceived situation will inevitably recall the strategy scripts one used or considered using in dealing with that situation, and if one is called upon to justify actions taken or considered, the criteria will be used in such justification. And the criteria are inseparable from the GOALS/GRASP. Also, although the strategies are constructed to apply specifically to the perceived situation, they can be categorized for our purposes, just as the GOALS and GRASP were categorized: They will fall into the categories of physical, economic, social, and cognitive strategies. The first three seem quite transparent, but cognitive strategies need some elaboration. Most of the theories of opinion dynamics seem to describe such strategies. We may change our opinions, including our most basic values, come to perceive others differently, adjust our expectations, rationalize our past behaviors to reduce cognitive dissonance, and come to misperceive the relationships among apparently contradictory beliefs within our belief systems, all to deal with perceived situations that cannot be otherwise resolved.

All this will be analyzed by means of the GOALS/GRASP schema, with the strategy scripts tested by means of imaginative scenarios against the derived criteria, all generating neural input that will linger in short-term memory long enough to become part of the neural impulse interaction pattern by which the brain will store that perceived situation in long-term memory to be reactivated by another similar situation or by something that triggers thoughts of this perceived situation. The trigger may be some small part of the set of GOALS, GRASP, criteria, strategy scripts or scenarios that formed a part of this neural impulse interaction pattern.

Conclusion

Obviously, this paper has not been a report of original research or a review of research literature dealing with situations. The reader who still hungers for such a review after consulting the Magnusson volume might do well to check that by Argyle, Furnham, and Graham (1981), and then the myriad studies centered upon the concepts of schema and scripts, as developed by Schank and Abelson (1977). Closest to home in terms of discipline and topic, the interested reader might want to consult Duck (1993), which contains chapters by Peter Anderson, Charles Berger, and others dealing with scripts and schemata in the analysis of interpersonal relationships. Dealing with the concept of schema more generally are Hirschfeld and Gelman (1994), Kamppinen (1993) and the series in which it occurs, Studies in Cognitive Systems, and Light and Butterworth (1993), for example.

Instead, this paper is concerned with how the concept of situation might be analyzed. It began with definitions of "actual" and "perceivable" situations per Magnusson, although it could certainly have taken other definitions as starting points. It would then have been a very different piece. The etymological definition of "situation" as "a place with its surroundings that is occupied by something" would have led to terminal vagueness, and the same can be said for the Oxford English Dictionary specification that it can be used to describe "any state of affairs in which one finds oneself," both cited in Argyle et al. (1981). Those writers settle upon the definition of a social situation as "the sum of the features of a social occasion that impinge on an individual person [p. 3]." They then undertake to review the research that could be brought to bear on such a broadly defined construct, and report research of their own.

I have eschewed those approaches, and have instead presented a schema/script, the GOALS/GRASP Model, which I believe is descriptive of the procedure one uses in the cognitive processing, storage, and retrieval of situations, a schema/script by which actual situations are processed into perceived situations. My concern has been narrowed somewhat, although admittedly not enough, by my focus on *rhetorical/communication* situations. I have suggested that the situations in which we ought to be interested are *ad hoc* categories constructed to deal with the exigencies of the moment, which makes unnecessary the description of every situation one might encounter in terms of categories defined by borders, dimensions, and exemplars. I have speculated regarding possible Central Nervous System mechanisms used to register situations, code them in short-term memory, and store them in long-term memory. The mechanism I have chosen for my speculation I have described as a Neural Impulse Interaction Pattern, and have tried to explain how such a mechanism might account for the CNS characteristics of near-infinite storage capacity, instantaneous retrieval, and redundant storage throughout the associative cortex. Along the way I have noted why it is that such brain states produce experiences that bear no resemblance to themselves—why, that is, that we do not more directly experience our brains at work. Finally, I have suggested that the strategy scripts for dealing with situations are actually part of the GOALS/GRASP schema itself, constructed by applying criteria that spring from the intersection of GOALS and GRASP to potential strategies by means of mentally rehearsed scenarios.

While there are certainly other aspects of situations, the GOALS/GRASP schema and its Neural Impulse Interaction Pattern constitute the master schema and NIIP to which all situations are initially referred. It has been a long and winding road. Even if we have not reached a common destination, or have parted ways at some point, I hope you have enjoyed the ride.

References

Argyle, M., Furnham, A., & Graham, J. A. (1981). *Social situations.* Cambridge, United Kingdom: Cambridge University Press.

Bitzer, L. F. (1968). The rhetorical situation. *Philosophy and Rhetoric, 1,* 1-14.

Cronkhite, G. (1984). Perception and meaning. In C. C. Arnold & J. Bowers (Eds.), *Handbook of rhetorical and communication theory* (pp. 51-229). Boston: Allyn and Bacon.

Cronkhite, G., & Liska, J. (1980). The judgment of communicator acceptability. In M. Roloff & G. Miller (Eds.), *Persuasion: New directions in theory and research* (pp. 101-139). Beverly Hills, CA: Sage.

Cronkhite, G., & Liska, J. (1982, November). *The GOALS/GRASP procedure for analyzing situations as an alternative to situational taxonomies in the prediction of strategy selection.* Paper presented at the meeting of the Speech Communication Association Convention, Louisville, KY.

Duck, S. (Ed.). (1993). *Individuals in relationships.* Newbury Park, CA: Sage.

Gibson, J. J. (1950). *The perception of the visual world.* Boston: Houghton Mifflin.

Gibson, J. J. (1966). *The senses considered as perceptual systems.* Boston: Houghton Mifflin.

Hirschfeld, L. A., & Gelman, S. A. (Eds.). (1994). *Mapping the mind: Domain specificity in cognition and culture.* Cambridge, United Kingdom: Cambridge University Press.

Janis, I. L., & Mann, L. (1977). *Decision making: A psychological analysis of conflict, choice, and commitment.* New York: Free Press.

Kamppinen, M. (Ed.). (1993). *Consciousness, cognitive schemata, and relativism: Multidisciplinary explorations in cognitive science.* Boston: Kluwer Academic.

Light, P., & Butterworth, G. (Eds.). (1993). *Context and cognition: Ways of learning and knowing.* Hillsdale, NJ: Lawrence Erlbaum.

Liska, J., & Cronkhite, G. (1995). *An ecological perspective on human communication theory.* Ft. Worth, TX: Harcourt Brace.

Magnusson, D. (Ed.). (1981). *Toward a psychology of situations: An interactive approach.* Hillsdale, NJ: Lawrence Erlbaum.

Pribram, K. H. (1971). *Languages of the brain: Experimental paradoxes and principles in neuropsychology.* Englewood Cliffs, NJ: Prentice-Hall.

Schanck, R. E., & Abelson, R. P. (1977). *Scripts, plans, goals, and understanding.* Hillsdale, NJ: Lawrence Erlbaum.

Footnote

[1] I have used the term "interaction pattern" here because neural impulses are not wave forms and may or may not produce *interference* patterns. On the other hand, neural impulses converging in an electrochemical environment may produce extremely complex interference patterns. I am just hedging my theoretical bet here by using the more general term "interaction."

Chapter 11

An Impersonal Basis for Shared Interpretations of Messages in Context

Robert E. Sanders
University at Albany, SUNY

It is true by definition that messages[1] (i.e., symbolic objects) are produced in contexts and interpreted accordingly (i.e., acquire communication values[2] relative to those contexts). But unless we are careful, pursuing that idea can open Pandora's box – and we have not been careful. As a consequence a range of problems has arisen that it is my intention to address in the body of this paper, focusing especially on the problem of interpretation as the hub around which the others revolve.

It seems obvious and innocent enough to say that the interpretation of a symbolic object depends on its context. This is one way of stating the point that the standard or conventional interpretation of a symbolic object may have to be adjusted or replaced to "fit" the context in which it is produced (e.g., along the lines of Grice's, 1975, Cooperative Principle). It also captures a key point that has been stressed in Pearce and Cronen's work on "The Coordinated Management of Meaning" (Cronen, Pearce, & Xi 1989/90), and by Schegloff (1988, 1995) in a number of his analyses: The interpretation of symbolic objects is context-specific and cannot be known before the fact on the basis of conventions, rules, etc.

But consider what this could involve if taken to an extreme uncritically, without attention to the specifics of how interpretations in context are formed. We could say that the same symbolic object can occur in different contexts, and that for any new context in which the symbolic object is situated, it acquires a new interpretation (e.g., as when Shakespeare's portrayal of Shylock in *The Merchant of Venice* is situated in the context of post-Holocaust discourse about anti-Semitism, or Plato's arguments against democracy in the context of the actions of anti-democratic governments in this century). But if so, what happens to "old" interpretations that apply in other contexts, and is there anything about these assorted interpretations (past, present, possible future) that carries over from one context to another? And most importantly, how is it decided in any instance what a symbolic object's context is, and whose decision is it?

In brief, the issue here that I intend to pursue and resolve is this. On one hand, to insist that symbolic objects have no meanings before the fact, only situated interpretations, makes it problematic and unresolvable how it can be the case that symbolic objects get interpreted in a reliably uniform way from one person to the next in identifiable contexts (at least within the confines of, for lack of a better word, a common culture). On the other hand, to take the contrary view that symbolic objects have base meanings from which their situated interpretations derive, seems overly restrictive of the range of situated interpretations, and in some cases the novelty of situated interpretations, that symbolic objects evidently have. Formulations of the basis for the situated interpretation of utterances and nonverbal displays I previously devised (Sanders, 1987) appear to be unduly restrictive in just that way. I will proceed by first demonstrating that the position that symbolic objects have no meanings before the fact collapses of its own weight. I will then go on to introduce a "logic" by which situated interpretations derive from the base meanings of symbolic objects, linked to my previous formulations, but revised so as not to artificially delimit the range or novelty of situated interpretations.

A "Magical Kingdom": Contextualized Symbolic Objects Without Base Meanings

On the premise that symbolic objects can be apprehended in an indefinite number of contexts and interpreted in an indefinite number of ways, the following line of argument is possible:

- If symbolic objects are always produced in a context and are interpreted accordingly; and
- if there are an unlimited number of possible contexts in which a symbolic object can be placed, and therefore an unlimited number of possible interpretations a symbolic object can have; and
- if it is "in the eye of the beholder" what the context of a symbolic object is, and therefore what its interpretation is "now"; then
- interpretations are entirely personal rather than communal matters.

The upshot of that reasoning is that individuals could have no assurance that their interpretation of a symbolic object is the same as anyone else's, either of their own symbolic objects that they produce or of others' symbolic objects that the individual apprehends. In addition, one would have to deny that a symbolic object has *any* interpretation out of context, and therefore also deny that there is some interpretation of a symbolic object that is privileged as its "conventional" or "base" meaning (perhaps in order to reject the political implications; e.g., Lemke, 1995), from which any situated interpretations derive and by which they are constrained.

If all of this were so, we would have to conclude that it must be rare if not impossible for communication to actually happen (in the sense of just achieving understanding, let alone securing the intended response). Despite evidence to the contrary all around us, this is a conclusion that postmodernists entertain seriously, at least in terms of achieving "real" communication and "real" understanding. And Pearce and Cronen's (1980; also Cronen, Pearce, & Xi, 1989/90) work on the "Coordinated Management of Meaning" rests on precisely the idea that a particular symbolic object can be situated in any of several possible contexts at once and thus have any of several distinct interpretations in any instance, which they take at least to the point of maintaining that achieving communication (understanding) is inherently problematic.

But I contend that something is plainly wrong if we let our reasoning take us very far down this road. While Pearce and Cronen's work provides an important corrective to our field's tendency to take the achievement of communication as assured (i.e., the achievement of understanding), at least among persons with a shared language and culture, it flies in the face of ordinary experience to consider the interpretation of symbolic objects as necessarily a "personal" matter. The high proportion of communication successes we each experience personally on an average day should be enough to carry this point. If that is not enough, consider that a technologically developed mass society such as ours could not exist economically or politically without a high degree of reliability (success) in communicating, in order to have achieved the high degree of coordination needed among the diverse, widely distributed activities of members (e.g., the level of coordination needed among pilots, flight attendants, mechanics, various other ground personnel, passengers, passengers' families, friends, or colleagues, taxi services, etc. for all to assemble at the time and place needed, and perform as needed, for even a single flight of a single airline to depart with its ticketed passengers as scheduled).

What has to be wrong with the reasoning above is that either or both of the two intermediate premises must be defective: either (1) there are not an unlimited number of contexts, and possible interpretations, of a symbolic object; and/or (2) what the context of a symbolic object is in any instance, and thus its interpretation, is not "in the eye of the beholder" – both are constrained in a systematic way. The solution I will develop below is built on the second of those two propositions, though this has the effect of also endorsing a qualified version of the first. In sum, my thesis is that:

- the possible interpretations of a symbolic object are in principle open-ended, depending on its context; **but**
- a symbolic object's context and its interpretation (the object's communication value) are relatively unequivocal in any instance, and thus interpretations of a symbolic object are not open-ended in practice; **therefore,**
- there are general, systemic constraints on defining contexts and interpreting symbolic objects that arise in part from "base meanings" of symbolic objects, and in part from the way the interpretations of component symbolic objects in some larger whole have been adjusted to cohere with each other, **so that**
- the problem of achieving uniform interpretations that Pearce and Cronen address is relatively specialized, and when it occurs, it is generally evident to the people involved that on that occasion they are faced with some such problem.

(Of course, exactly what the term "context" refers to here needs close attention, but this is something that is best handled in a later section, in defending the claim below that a symbolic object's context is relatively unequivocal in any instance. For now, "context" can be understood broadly, mirroring Pearce and Cronen's, 1980, view, as any of a variety of frames within which symbolic objects can be situated, from specific episodes to interpersonal relationships to personal biographies and so on.)

Pandora's Box

The point of the analysis in this section is to show that symbolic objects must have a conventional or base meaning in their own right, from which context-dependent (situated) interpretations are derived. It is a straightforward matter to go forward from there to show that there is a principled relationship between base meanings, contexts, and situated interpretations. On that basis we can posit that context-dependent interpretations are derived from general principles that interconnect symbolic objects with certain properties (base values) and contexts with certain properties. It is with reference to such general principles proposed below that the context, and interpretation, of a symbolic object cannot be "in the eye of the beholder."

That symbolic objects must have a base meaning in their own right can be demonstrated by first not assuming this, and thereby opening Pandora's box deliberately by closely tracing what then derives from the proposition that an object's communication value is context dependent. For this purpose it is convenient to state this core proposition as the following general formula (from Searle, 1969, pp. 35-41):

(1)   X counts as Y in Context C

(1')   Symbolic object X has communication value Y in Context C

Consider that this formula has practical force not only for the **addressed** (the one to whom the symbolic object is presented) as to how occurrences of X should be interpreted in context C. It also has practical force for the **agent** (the one who produces the object) as to what particular vehicle (X, the symbolic object) would have the communication value he/she intends within the context in which the object will be produced and apprehended.

For the agent, (1) has a practical force in relation to an intention to produce a symbolic object such that it will receive a certain interpretation in the context of interest, as expressed by either or both (1a) and (1b):

(1a)   In order to achieve communication value Y in Context C, do X

(1b)   In order for X to count as having communication value Y, situate it in Context C

(1a) applies when one intends to achieve Y, the context is given, and it is optional what X will be; (1b) applies when one intends to achieve Y, doing X is given, and it is optional what the context will be. But both (1a) and (1b) presuppose that

An Impersonal Basis for Shared Interpretations of Messages

Context C exists, prior to and independent of doing X and producing Y. This need not be the case, indeed cannot be the case, if we take a social constructionist (or radical ethnomethodological or postmodernist) perspective. Instead, from that perspective a context could only exist in and through the actions in which persons engage. In that case, the practical force of (1) becomes (1c):

(1c) In order to be in Context C, achieve communication value Y by doing X

However, (1c) is still ambiguous as to whether Context C exists prior to and independently of doing X to count as Y, as in ($1c_1$) below, or whether Context C comes to exist as a result of doing X to count as Y ($1c_2$):

($1c_1$) In order to invoke Context C, achieve communication value Y by doing X

($1c_2$) In order to produce Context C, achieve communication value Y by doing X

The difference between these is that ($1c_1$) assumes that a social order that comprises a range of possible contexts has separate, independent existence, so that the use of X to express Y invokes one or another of those contexts; ($1c_2$) captures the potential for the social order to be changed, for contexts to be altered or created, by the use of X to express Y. However, as consequential as this difference is, pursuing it further here is unnecessary.

For the addressed, the force of (1) is a directive to interpret occurrences of X as occurrences of Y, but it is ambiguous whether this means that X **should** be interpreted as Y **because** it occurs in Context C, or it means that **if** X **is** interpreted as Y, then X **is therefore** in Context C, the domain or limiting condition of that interpretation.

(1d) When X occurs in Context C, then count it as having communication value Y

(1e) When X counts as having communication value Y, then situate it in Context C

Note however that (1e), similar to (1c), is ambiguous as to whether context C exists independent of and apart from, or as a product of, producing Y by doing X:

($1e_1$) When X counts as having communication value Y, then Context C is in force

($1e_2$) When X counts as having communication value Y, then construct its context as C

The following examples illustrate that all of these formulations are valid (setting aside the issues reflected by ($1c_{1-2}$) and ($1e_{1-2}$)). If so, this means that not only can an interpretation depend on what the context (independently) is, as in (1a), (1b) and (1d), but the context can depend on what the interpretation is, as in (1c) and (1e). Under this latter circumstance, the position that symbolic objects have no base (general, standardized or conventional) meaning before the fact, only interpretations in context, results in a logical absurdity. We locate ourselves in a "magical kingdom" in which symbolic objects that have no meaning out of context, and contexts that do not exist except with reference to the meanings of symbolic objects, somehow take tangible form in relation to each other.

Two Illustrations of The Dependence of Interpretation on Context

To simplify matters for purposes of illustration, "context" in the examples below consists of the interactional sequence in which a symbolic object is included (leaving aside whether nominally extrinsic personal, relational, institutional, or socio-cultural contexts are a different matter).

Schegloff (1995) – in the course of an argument that it is the aspect of turns at talk as actions that must be considered primary, not the informational aspect – analyzed part of a telephone conversation between "Debbie" and "Nick." Debbie evidently knew that Nick was intending to buy a waterbed, and after conversational preliminaries said, "u- guess what I've-(u-) wuz lookin' in the paper:.- have you got your waterbed yet?" Nick's answer was that yes, he had. Yet Debbie re-asked that same question three more times in succession and got the same answer each time (first, "Oh really? Already?"; then "Are you kidding?"; and third, "Oh no but you h- you've got it already?"). Schegloff's interest was what Debbie's question means, considering that its three reiterations came after it was already answered: "[I]t is not implausible that, if the first of Debbie's response was hearably "surprise," the second could be checking out whether this is not just more teasing by Nick [following prior teasing at the conversation's start]. But then what is the *third* about...?" (p. 189) The issue Schegloff raised is what is also of interest here: The interpretation of what is essentially the same question has to be different each time Debbie asked it insofar as each time she asked it the context had changed – in this case the sequential context. Thus, where the initial utterance of that question is evidently understood and responded to in terms of its conventional, semantic (informational) meaning, as a request for information, the fact that once the question was asked and answered, a sequential context existed where reiteration of the same question made it problematic, and in Schegloff's analysis a mistake, to interpret it again in the same way.

A second illustration of the dependence of interpretation on context involves experimental results I obtained in a test of principles of relevance that figure prominently in the main section of the paper below (Sanders, 1987). The experiments were performed to find whether naive respondents changed their preference among alternate possible interpretations of a particular utterance in the predicted direction, if the conversation leading up to that utterance changed in a specific way. Hence, along the same lines as Schegloff's data above, we have the same utterance in different sequential contexts.

In the final experiment in the series, respondents were presented with one of three versions of a conversation between two male college students, D and K.

Respondents were asked to rate the "correctness" of each of five alternate interpretations of the final utterance. Each conversation began with the same utterance, a question D addressed to K: "I've been trying to figure out what Sally [K's sister] would like for her birthday." Each conversation ended with the same question, the test utterance, asked by K of D: "Would you consider something like perfume or jewelry for her? Something feminine?" Between those common starts and endings, the conversations differed as follows. The first conversation was about Sally's relative youth and her interests: this would be her 15th birthday and K said she was more interested in "dancing" than "reading." At that point D said "Well, there goes my idea of giving her some kind of book." and K asked "Would you consider something like perfume or jewelry for her? ..." Of five alternate interpretations of that last question, respondents preferred "K is asking D to indicate any interest in that gift idea." The second conversation was about K's resistance to D's buying Sally a gift, and concern that she might form a childish crush on D. At that point, D said, "She'll be 15. Anyway, we're pals, her and me. We talk sometimes when I'm waiting on you, walk to the park once in awhile; you know." and K asked "Would you consider something like perfume or jewelry for her?..." From among the same five alternate interpretations as were presented with the first conversation, respondents preferred "K is probing whether D has a romantic interest in Sally." The third conversation was about K's evident disinterest or antipathy regarding Sally, which K justified by saying that as Sally grows up he should not be involved in her business. At that point, D said "...I'm betting you can't handle her being a better athlete than you. As if that changes the fact that she's your sister." and K asked, "Would you consider something like perfume or jewelry for her?..." From among those same five alternate interpretations, respondents in this condition preferred "K is putting Sally down."

Two Illustrations of the Dependence of Context on Interpretation

Both Schegloff (1988/89) and Clayman and Whalen (1988/89) analyzed a brief televised interview that Dan Rather, of CBS News, conducted live with then-presidential candidate George Bush. Both analyses focused on the public perception that the interview had degenerated into a "brawl," and examined what had occurred during the interaction to produce that assessment. If we consider an "interview" to be one context within which talk occurs and symbolic objects are interpreted, and a "brawl" (an undisciplined argument, in this case) to be a different context, then this represents an instance where the situated interpretations of component symbolic objects had the effect of changing the context. Both Schegloff and Clayman and Whalen gave particular attention to the "standard" protocol for turn-taking in news interviews, and the way in which the turn-taking protocol in this particular interaction deviated from that. The standard protocol is that the interviewer has a claim to the floor until and when a question is asked, and then it is the interviewee's turn at speaking for the purpose of answering the question. In practice, this protocol allows interviewers to introduce prefatory material of indefinite length before asking a question. This prefatory material may serve such innocent purposes as to clarify the question, present to the audience the background issue from which the question arises, delimit for the interviewee what an answer should address – or the strategic purpose of contextualizing the question in such a way that no matter what answer the interviewee gives, its interpretation will have been "unfairly" prejudiced. In the Bush-Rather interview, Rather's questions were about Bush's role in the so-called Iran-Contra affair (where government officials had "illegally" funded weapons for Nicaraguan insurgents by entering into a secret arms deal with the government of Iran). But Rather was not simply asking Bush about whether he had had a role and if so, what it was; he was presenting Bush, and the viewers, with evidence that Bush had been involved and asking him to comment. Bush reacted to Rather's choice of topic and mode of questioning by interrupting Rather's prefatory statements, which implicated Bush in that affair before the question had been asked, and disputed what Rather was in the process of saying. This had the effect of changing the situated interpretation of Rather's utterances from "question-prefaces" to the conventional meanings of what he was saying based on form and content, making allegations of wrongdoing. The former is consonant with the context of a news interview, the latter arguably is not. Bush's "intrusions" into Rather's prefatory statements also had the effect of changing the situated interpretation of his own utterances from "answers" to "counter-attacks" and "challenges." As the "interview" progressed, Rather's utterances progressively changed in form from question-prefatory to assertions and counter-statements that "debated" what Bush was saying. Thus, given interpretations of the symbolic objects produced by Bush and Rather as not questions and answers but accusations and counter-attacks – on the basis of their form and content, as well as their discrepancy from the "standard" turn-taking protocol – the "context" of the interaction was changed from televised interview to televised "brawl."

Goffman (1967), in an explication of what he termed "character contests" (pp. 239-258), used as one illustration a scene from a novelette (W. Sansom, *The Cautious Heart*) about an encounter between a barroom piano player and some young customers. As the piano player stopped to take a break, one of the youths said "Ain't you gonna play s'more, fellah?" and when the answer was "In a moment" the youth replied "Not too long then, fellah." Arguably, even without what transpired subsequently, the youth's admonitory response was enough to change the context, in the following sense. If we say that in the context of a service establishment customers are empowered to request services within the "menu" of choices provided by management, then the youth was empowered to ask whether the piano player would resume playing. But because the terms and conditions under which services are provided is the discretion of management, the youth was not empowered to question or direct the piano player about the duration of the interval that would occur before playing resumed. For the youth to have done so deviates from those conventions, with the consequence that unless the conventional order were reestablished, the institutional context would effectively have been altered: The context would have been changed from a service encounter within a service establishment to a "character contest" in a public arena (between service provider and customer) or worse. The ensuing episode depicts the failure of the service provider (both management and piano player) to reestablish the conventional order, and for a direct confrontation to evolve. The piano player returned to play at management request, to try curbing the growing rowdiness of the youths ("...as I went to the piano, [they] saw that their orders has been obeyed. You could almost feel them spreading themselves. So I began to play the dimity notes of *Humoresque* to put them back a little."). This led to a direct confrontation:

> As my tinkling established itself, one of them sauntered across ... and stood above me. He simply stated, as an order, the name of a disc-hit. Apart from this plain rudeness, a pianist's biggest bugbear is to be asked for another tune when he is already playing – so I gritted my teeth and tried to close my ears. He nudged my right arm off the notes with his elbow and said simply; 'mush.' And repeated, louder, his request. (Goffman, 1967, pp. 251-252)

Hence, the context was changed as was also the case in the Bush-Rather interview, given the interpretations of symbolic objects in this interaction, based on their form and content (their conventional meanings) and their discrepancy from the conventional order in the context originally in force.

Base Meanings, Contexts, and Situated Interpretations

The bi-directional relationship above between situated interpretations and contexts – where situated interpretations of symbolic objects can derive from context, or contexts can be changed or perhaps created based on the situated interpretation of symbolic objects – logically entails that there have to be starting points regarding both interpretation and context independent of and prior to the situated occurrence of symbolic objects. Symbolic objects have to have base meanings that may or may not have to be adjusted in some context, to arrive at situated interpretations. Persons' actions and interactions have to be produced from the outset with reference to a "conventional" context that may turn out does or does not accord with, and thus may or may not be altered by, what symbolic objects get produced and how they are interpreted. (These conventional contexts for present purposes can be equated with social institutions as defined by the prototypes for enacting role-identities they comprise and the conventional practices and procedures that constitutes them, institutions ranging from formal organizations, to such informal organizations as the family, support groups, and the like, to transitory entities that involve ceremonies and rituals; see Sanders, 1995a.) Beyond that, there has to be a basis for the interpretation of situated symbolic objects that is sensitive to the conventional context that is in force initially, but also allows for the possibility that interpretations could be discrepant from the conventional context and thereby change it.

I have previously developed formal characterizations of the base meanings of symbolic objects and of contexts, and the way they interact to derive situated interpretations of symbolic objects and/or changed contexts (Sanders, 1987, 1995b, forthcoming). But beyond summarizing that work below with reference to the issues here, I need to take it further on two fronts: the analysis of the base meanings of symbolic objects and the notion of situated interpretations (what I previously referred to as "specific interpretations") needs to be broadened so that it corresponds more to the range of interpretations that particular symbolic objects can receive, and does not rule out novel interpretations; and of course, the notion of "context" needs to be refined (a) so that it is explicit what a conventional context consists of, and how it can be modified or replaced insofar as situated interpretations of symbolic objects in that context are discrepant from it, and (b) so that my previous work applies as much as possible to the broad range of what have been identified as social contexts over and above particular interactions.

The Theoretical Foundation: Situated Interpretations of Symbolic Objects

The end result of the following presentation is a "systemic," impersonal basis for interpreting situated symbolic objects that establishes that the symbolic object's context is not "in the eye of the beholder," and that interpretation is (as common experience shows) a communal rather than a personal matter. The following summary of my previous work starts as I did then, with attention to the situated interpretation of utterances, and afterwards broadens that to the situated interpretation of symbolic objects.

The starting point was to reason as follows. Given at least three distinct systems of language meaning, and rules or principles of interpretation for each, that have arisen in linguistic semantics and language pragmatics – propositional content, illocutionary force (speech acts), and conversational implicature; and given that in general an utterance has two, and often all three of those types of meaning at the same time; what basis do interpreters have for selecting among those types of an utterance's meaning which to focus on and respond to in a particular instance? I now realize that this way of stating the question seems to delimit artificially the range of situated interpretations an utterance can have, to rule out that situated interpretations can be novel, and to prevent consideration of objects that become symbolic and have interpretations only in context. These deficiencies are addressed after the following synopsis.

My answer to that original question in brief was that the preferred interpretation in a given instance – what I have termed here the "situated interpretation" but originally termed the "specific interpretation" – is that one among an utterance's possible meanings that is most relevant to what has preceded the utterance in question, in terms of interpreted symbolic objects, or what follows it, at a given juncture in the unfolding discourse or dialogue. I formulated two kinds of principles of relevance, which I will refer to here as practical relevance and substantive relevance.

There is a single, generic principle of practical relevance, but different principles of substantive relevance for propositional content, illocutionary force, and conversational implicature, respectively. With regard to practical relevance, the generic principle is this: a possible meaning of an utterance, U, is relevant if a focus on that meaning of U constitutes progress, or is an incremental move, towards resolution of the discourse or dialogue. Regarding the second kind of principle of relevance, relevance is a matter of shared features of one or another of the possible (types of) meaning of the utterance, U, and some other interpreted component(s) of the discourse or dialogue (hereafter Component$_{dd}$), as follows. For propositional content, relevance is a matter of commonalties between the semantic features of U and the semantic features of Component$_{dd}$. For illocutionary force, where U counts as some act, A, relevance is a matter of meeting any of three conditions: U is relevant to Component$_{dd}$ if (a) Component$_{dd}$ is (functionally) a request that A be done, (b) Component$_{dd}$ is an act reciprocal to A (to which I now add: or is the other pair part of an adjacency pair with A), or (c) Component$_{dd}$ constitutes felicity conditions for A. For conversational implicature, where U breaches a maxim and implicates some proposition, and an implicature is a proposition predicated on a subjective state of the speaker (e.g., the speaker believes that p, the speaker regrets that p, etc.), then U is relevant to Component$_{dd}$ if Componentd$_d$ expresses or is predicated on a subjective state of the speaker that is approximately the same as the subjective state on which the implicature of U is predicated.

On this foundation, the notion that one or another of U's possible meanings is "most relevant," and focusing on that as the situated interpretation, makes a situated interpretation the product of an estimate of subjective probability, as follows. First, the "most relevant" of U's possible meanings, and therefore its situated interpretation, is the one that achieves both practical and substantive relevance. Further, one of the possible meanings of an utterance is "most relevant" substantively, under the following conditions. Let Component$_{dd}$ be a segment of the discourse or dialogue comprising either a single utterance or two or more contiguous utterances. When Component$_{dd}$ is a single utterance, a possible meaning of U is relevant to it if that other utterance has a situated interpretation that meets a condition stated in one of those principles of relevance. If U is relevant to different, non-contiguous, single utterances in the discourse or dialogue by one or more of those principles, then pending empirical examination of a variety of factors that might mitigate this, it was assumed that one of the possible meanings of U is "most relevant" to the other utterance that is physically "closest" or most proximate to U in the string of utterances forming the discourse or dialogue. When Component$_{dd}$ is a segment of two or more utterances, such segments are defined, or bounded, by having a common basis of relevance among the situated interpretations of their constituent utterances (their "ground of coherence"). A possible meaning of U is relevant to such a segment if the ground of coherence (the basis of relevance) within that segment is the same as the one by which U would be relevant. When U is relevant to two or more Components, then the "most relevant" among its possible meanings is the one that is relevant to the segment that is most physically proximate and/or most extensive (again, pending empirical investigation of the effect of mitigating factors, as well as the relative weights of the proximity versus extent of Components$_{dd}$).

As was noted in a previous section, experiments designed to test these principles did show that changing the antecedents of the target utterance in a way that changed which of its possible meanings was "most relevant" resulted in shifts as predicted among respondents as to which among alternative interpretations they favored.

On the prior foundation, I extended this approach to the interpretation of nonverbal displays (Sanders, 1985, 1987). Like utterances, nonverbal displays generally have alternative possible (conventional) meanings, though they generally are stipulated for each display rather than derived from a system of rules as in the case of utterances. One or another of these alternative possible meanings of a nonverbal display can be "most relevant" at a given juncture to some Component$_{dd}$ of the discourse or dialogue, just as for utterances. In brief, nonverbal displays can either be conventional ways of outwardly exhibiting internal states (especially emotions, but also bodily sensations), or they can be conventional indicators of some social condition, relationship, attitude, etc. Given a nonverbal display that conventionally exhibits any of a constellation of inner states, its "most relevant" meaning is as an exhibition of that inner state for which there is a (conventional) proximate cause in a prior Component$_{dd}$. Given a nonverbal display that conventionally indicates the existence of some social condition, relationship, attitude, etc., then again, its "most relevant" meaning is to indicate that social condition, relationship, or attitude for which there is either a conventional proximate cause or that has been directly expressed in some prior Component$_{dd}$.

It was stated above that a given utterance, U, can be relevant to a Component$_{dd}$ that precedes it in the discourse or dialogue, or follows it. Consider that interpreters progress through a discourse or dialogue over time, during which it "unfolds" to them incrementally (whether listening to or reading a univocal discourse, or listening to, reading, or participating in a dialogue). At the juncture when they first encounter an utterance, U, interpreters have only the preceding Components$_{dd}$ to which U might be relevant, and so a situated interpretation will initially be a function of just its antecedents. However, as the discourse or dialogue continues to unfold, U may turn out to also be relevant to Components$_{dd}$ that follow it, and may be "most relevant" to some later Component$_{dd}$ than to a prior one. In that case, the situated interpretation of U is subject to being changed over time, from what was warranted at the juncture at which it was first encountered to what might be warranted at later junctures. The potential fluidity of U's interpretation over time is an empirical fact that an adequate theory of situated interpretation has to capture, but that fact does not in itself indicate that situated interpretations have an unprincipled or personal basis.

The potential fluidity of U's situated interpretation has a further consequence of central importance to the thesis here. Again, while U is first interpreted on the basis of its relevance to prior Components$_{dd}$ of the discourse or dialogue, it may be re-interpreted on the basis of its relevance to subsequent Components$_{dd}$. This can be restated to say that as new Components$_{dd}$ are added to an unfolding discourse or dialogue, they can have the effect of warranting a re-interpretation of prior Components$_{dd}$. A classic example is Henny Youngman's joke, "Now take my wife – please." The expression "Now take X" is conventionally used as a truncated form of "Now take X, for example," and "take" is a colloquial substitute for "consider." However, to follow "Now take X," on that reading, with "please," and end the utterance is, minimally, odd or discrepant. The oddness of that pairing is reduced, however, if "take" is reinterpreted from a colloquial substitute for "consider" X to a more literal usage, to "remove" X. Thus, it is possible for the base meanings of prior components enable their re-interpretation to increase or create relevance to later ones, especially when this can be done more readily to achieve coherence than by adjusting the interpretation of later components to cohere with the way prior ones were interpreted.

As developed in the section below on "Context," this bi-directional influence that components of discourse and dialogue can have on their situated interpretations provides a foundation for explaining how situated interpretations of symbolic objects can occur that are discrepant from the apparent context and warrant modifying or changing it.

Possible Meanings and Situated Interpretations

It is important to address the shortcoming that I previously alluded to of the formulations summarized above. The problem is that the range of possible meanings on which situated interpretations are based seems too narrow. As I noted at the outset, one of the important gains in work most notably by Pearce and Cronen (e.g., Cronen, Pearce, and Xi, 1989/90) and Schegloff (1988, 1995) is finding that utterances can have meanings on the basis of their context (personal, interpersonal, relational, sequential, etc.) that it seems the utterances cannot be projected to have just on the basis of relevant systems of rules, either semantic rules or the constitutive rules of speech acts, before the fact. Yet the principles I have formulated depend on singling out as a situated interpretation the "most relevant" among alternative possible meanings of an utterance before the fact. A second, corresponding, problem is that much work in conversation analysis indicates that a symbolic object (an artifact with a distinct, specifiable interpretation) can consist of materials that seem to have no particular meaning at all before the fact, but do have an interpretation in the sequential contexts in which they occur, such as brief pauses, the hesitation phenomena and "yes but" structures that mark dispreferred turns (Pomerantz, 1984), or Schegloff's (forthcoming) finding that certain repeats confirm that an allusion was made and that the other correctly formulated it.

But generally these apparent problems in the approach I have taken are just that, apparent problems. They arise from my having failed to fully develop and adequately pursue certain distinctions. First, I have not given adequate attention to the fact that "context" often has an influence on meaning and interpretation twice, independently, in many cases, though "context" in the first instance may involve different matters than "context" in the second. In addition to the influence of context in terms of situated interpretations, as summarized above, context also has a bearing, a prior and independent one, on what the possible meanings of an object are.

Consider first that two of the three types of possible meaning of utterances, above, have a situated aspect, they depend on context. The illocutionary force of an utterance (on Searle's, 1969, analysis; but also see Sanders, 1987, and Schegloff, 1995) depends on what the specifics are of the social circumstances in which the utterance was produced: The same utterance may have the illocutionary force of a promise or a threat, for example, depending on the relationship between speaker and hearer, and their respective values towards the matter being promised or threatened. The matter implicated by an utterance, if any, depends on the way in which the utterance meets the "demand" in the local moment.

In both cases, however, there are conventional procedures and rules that specify what features of the context and what features of the utterance to take into account to arrive at what its illocutionary force is or what it implicates. These meanings are "fixed" in that local environment, not fluid; they behave like the semantics of utterance before the fact. It is a separate matter which of those possible meanings to focus on in the local moment, what its situated interpretation is, now depending on which is most relevant to other interpreted components of the discourse or dialogue.

Consider, for example, the interaction between Nick and Debbie (above) analyzed by Schegloff (1995). The interpretation that Schegloff proposed of Debbie's questions is that they are "pre-tellings" ("guess what I've-(u-)wuz lookin' in the paper:.-have you got your waterbed yet?" followed by first, "Oh really? Already?"; then "Are you kidding?"; and third, "Oh no but you h- you've got it already?"), to which Nick should respond with "Why are you asking?" Evidently, Debbie had seen an ad for a waterbed in the paper, and wanted to tell Nick about it (as indicated by her initial "guess what-I've-(u-)wuz lookin' in the paper:-"). One might think that these questions could not have as a possible meaning that they implicate the speaker's want for the hearer to ask why the speaker is asking, except in the specialized sequential context in which their repetition has that import. And while it is true that they could only have that import in this sequential context, that is not enough to make that meaning their situated interpretation in that context. To repeat the same question when it has already been asked and answered implicates, on the basis of the Cooperative Principle (especially the maxim of quantity), that the speaker has some reason for conspicuously repeating the question about which the hearer should ask. Hence, this meaning of Debbie's question can be accounted for as a possible meaning "before the fact" of the larger interaction in which it occurs, a conversational implicature that may or may not be relevant.

This implicature is just one of the possible meanings that Debbie's questions could have (as opposed to the semantics of the questions, or their illocutionary force as, perhaps, pre-complaints or negative assessments through expressed disbelief about Nick's having already bought a waterbed), and so it remains an open question whether the interpreter should focus on it. That this is a separate question is evident from the fact that Nick did not focus on and respond to that implicature, he repeatedly focused on and responded to the semantics of Debbie's questions instead. While Schegloff seems to "blame" Nick for this, he overlooks why Nick may have responded as he did. If we say that the implicature is predicated on Debbie's subjective state of a desire to be asked, or to be authorized to tell, what she has to report, then the implicature is relevant to a single prior expression of the same subjective state, expressed through her use of a conventional way to express a desire to tell something ("guess what..."), and it is also relevant to an expression of the same subjective state afterward through Debbie's going on anyway to tell about the ad she saw after Nick's third "failure" to ask her. In terms of principles of relevance, there is only a weak basis at that point in the interaction (a single prior Component$_{dd}$, a phrase) for focusing on that implicature at the time Debbie asked her questions, but a stronger one for doing so afterwards. In contrast, there is a strong basis for focusing on the semantics of Debbie's questions at the time she asked them: this exchange seems like a continuation of the prior one between Nick and Debbie, when Debbie seemed confused after Nick answered the phone about "who is this," with Debbie focused on getting the information right, and Nick teasing her about it, over several turns at speaking.

Of those three types of possible meaning considered above, implicatures are the source of the broad range of situated interpretations, including novel interpretations, that have been cited to object to saying that symbolic objects have "base meanings" before the fact. Utterances that violate a conversational maxim can, in certain environments, implicate that a certain matter is so, and thus have an interpretation that it might never have otherwise, before or since. For example, a question about where some friend, Bill, is, might be answered by saying "I saw a yellow Volkswagen parked at Susan's this morning" (where Bill drives a yellow Volkswagen). The utterance, "I saw a Yellow Volkswagen parked in front of Susan's this morning" does not seem, in any sense, to have as a possible meaning before the fact what it served to communicate in the example above, "I think Bill could be at Susan's." I have shown (Sanders, 1987) that there is a systematic basis for inferring what utterances implicate, rooted in the knowledge structures of the persons involved, moreso than Grice (1975) considered. I also considered, in addressing the situated interpretation of nonverbal displays, that they too can breach the "Cooperative Principle" and "conversationally implicate" matters that their conventional possible meanings otherwise do not.

Recently, I developed the analysis further (Sanders, forthcoming). From examining certain interactional data, it is evident that symbolic objects can be meaningful, have situated interpretations and be responded to, not simply as components of the interaction, but as components of the activity in which interacting persons are engaged. Many interactions, for example service encounters, are undertaken as a means of carrying out some task, and it is the task rather than the interaction per se that constrains the possible resolutions of the interaction, the matters that are be dealt with, and possibly sequencing (if not at the level of each component turn, then at the level of larger structural units). Persons can produce symbolic objects that are functional with reference to that task or activity, but yet not the most direct (simplest, most economical) way of fulfilling that function. Any such objects thereby task-implicate some thought, affect, disposition, or agenda that the person must have to have "deviated" in that particular way from what would directly satisfy task requirements. This makes it possible to account for the "promotion" of behaviors that ordinarily have no conventional meaning to the status of a symbolic object. For example, if a person waiting tables in a restaurant occupies him- or herself with an incidental task, such as putting napkins away, that may or may not be meaningful: It depends on whether the wait-person's involvement with that task creates a "deviation" from the most direct way of providing service to one's table, and thus task-implicates a thought, affect, disposition, or agenda by the wait-person.

Such task-implicatures can apply not only to behaviors, but aspects of speaking as well. For example, as two children were somewhat at odds about how they would work together in building a house from a set of Legos blocks, or if they would, one of them got possession of a base on which to build the house, and (using a first person singular rather than plural pronoun) said "(And now) I'm going to make the h<u>ou</u>se (on it)." The response of her partner, Lorraine, was "Okay °then°, y<u>ou</u> make the h<u>ou</u>se. (.) And I'll get the fl<u>ow</u>ers ready." (Sanders & Freeman, 1995; Sanders, forthcoming). This response, specifically its inclusion of a repetition of her partner's utterance, does not breach a conversational implicature (e.g., it does not provide more or less information than needed). However, with reference to the task, it is an unnecessarily elaborated way to express concurrence. But the "unnecessary" elaboration resulted in a verbal parallelism that can be said to task-implicate that Lorraine's agenda was to preserve joint effort, by counting her partner's and her undertakings as equal components of a division of labor on a single project.

Hence, the possible meanings of a symbolic object "before the fact" includes more than just the narrow set of conventional meanings that the object has. These possible meanings have to be considered to include an object's illocutionary force, and more to the point here, implicatures – conversational implicatures or task-implicatures. It is with reference to implicatures that we can say that the range of what an object can mean is open-ended and may involve novel meanings.

At the same time, "context" influences the meanings of symbolic objects at this level in a way that, in and of itself, opens the door to the logical dead-end I have set out to avoid. Objects only have a given force, or implicate some matter, in a specific context; what the context is in a given instance may be constructed by what the force of a given object is considered to be, or what it is taken to implicate. Moreover, the interrelation of context and meaning at this level does not resolve the questions of what basis people have for focusing on one rather than others among an object's possible meanings. The solution was and is to consider such "context-specific" meanings such as implicatures to be possible meanings that are the "input" to principles of relevance. In doing this, the open-endedness we are otherwise faced with about what an object can mean, and what the object's context is, can be avoided. This is pursued in the following sections.

Context

The notion of "context" applied in this paper has shifted back and forth between what seem to be two quite distinct ideas. The common denominator in these two ideas is that a context is a "frame" within which only a subset of possible symbolic objects are relevant, and in terms of which component symbolic objects are interconnected; however, in some cases this involves the sequential interrelation among symbolic objects in a discourse or dialogue (as in much of my theoretical work, Schegloff's, 1995, work, etc.) whereas in other cases this involves the conventions for activity, rights and obligations, within social institutions (as in the barroom incident above extracted from Goffman, 1967). My concern here is to reconcile these, and to do so in such a way as to capture the potential for the situated interpretation of symbolic objects to modify or change the context.

First, the basis above for the situated interpretation of utterances and nonverbal displays (symbolic objects) is principles of relevance, and the meaning relations among sequentially ordered components of a single "text" (a discourse or dialogue). It seems a direct and unremarkable use of the term "context" to rephrase the statement thus: principles of relevance base the situated interpretation of symbolic objects on their relationship to the situated interpretations of other symbolic objects in the (sequential) context of the discourse or dialogue. But a single "text," a discourse or dialogue, is a singular, relatively narrow kind of context, especially compared with the variety and range of contexts identified by Pearce and Cronen (1980).

But consider that many other kinds of context that have been cited can also be represented as a sequential progression of components. If one represents the context of a symbolic object as the personal relationship between speaker and hearer, then the empirical reality of that relationship lies both in the sequential progression within particular interactions, but the sequential progression of interactions from one to the next, where a whole interaction might be registered relatively completely regarding its components and their sequential progression (who said what, in what manner, in the big fight), or as an unstructured cluster of selected components (when a birthday was forgotten, or an anniversary was celebrated with dinner and dancing) or reduced to a single "symbolic object." Along these lines, I analyzed the political collapse of Communist governments in Eastern Europe in 1989 as the culminating event in a sequential progression of social and political events starting with Gorbachev's ascendancy to power in the Soviet Union in 1985 (Sanders, 1992). The analysis was that following Gorbachev's ascendancy to power, citizens of affiliated countries could project possible sequences of events to follow, depending on whether Gorbachev was a figurehead, a genuine reformer, a sign of Soviet ineffectuality in the face of U.S. pressures, and so on. On that basis, actual progressions of events functioned as symbolic objects that conformed to one or another of those projected sequences, invalidating some and confirming others, until all but one had been discredited – that Communist governments had become impotent in the face of opposition pressures from outside and inside their borders. These projected sequences thus functioned as contexts for interpreting political and social events in precisely the same way that the unfolding sequential progression of a discourse or dialogue functions as a context for the situated interpretation of utterances and especially nonverbal displays.

Of course, none of this applies to institutional contexts, which seem to involve something quite different. Let us consider a social institution as a conventional framework for undertaking certain activities, within which the possible role-identities of members/participants are prescribed in terms of their specific rights and obligations for engaging in those activities. Thus, taking "family" as a social institution, we can consider it a framework for undertaking certain activities (generally, raising and caring for children) within which members have specific rights and obligations for engaging in those activities. Viewed in this way, social institutions can be said to provide contexts for the interpretation of symbolic objects by providing "models" or prototypes of what takes place (in terms of what artifacts are produced as well as what they "count as," their situated interpretations) and how components are interconnected within that frame. Symbolic objects that occur within a social institution presumed to be in force, then, are interpreted in terms of their correspondence to the components of such prototypes. The question now is, how then is it possible for symbolic objects within such contexts to be interpreted in a way that is discrepant from them, and to thereby warrant modifying or replacing that context?

Consider that no matter how the context of symbolic objects is formulated, whether as a conversation, a personal relationship, or a social institution, component symbolic objects are produced sequentially, and accordingly, subject to being interpreted in terms of their relevance to other components of the sequence they are in. In that case, it is readily apparent how symbolic objects can receive situated interpretations in a particular instance, based on the sequential progression in which they occur, that may either be consonant with or discrepant from what is included in the "model" or prototype of the social institution presumed to be in force. For example, suppose that someone casually passes by a university's swimming pool, and observes a group of individuals line up along the edge of one end of the pool, and then all dive in and swim parallel to each other towards the opposite end. These activities, both the components and the sequence, conform to the "model" or prototype of a swim meet (a race), and the observer might well infer that that is the social context in force. However, suppose that when they reach the middle of the pool, the swimmers stop and begin treading water. This event, this symbolic object, is clearly discrepant from the presumed social context in force, unless the swimmers had a "false start" and will have to go back and begin again. If this does not happen next (a restart), the discrepancy is likely to be sufficient to warrant abandoning the presumption of the social context, though the observer may then be unable either to interpret the components of the sequence observed or to formulate what the social context might be. Suppose, however, someone on the side of the pool then tosses to one of the swimmers a ball as used in the game of water polo, and the swimmers form a large circle and begin tossing it to each other. These additional components of the sequence have meanings that can be adjusted against the meanings of prior components to produce situated interpretations of those symbolic objects commensurate with the social context of a water polo pre-game drill or practice.

Knowing What the Context Is

The concern at the outset of this paper, and the central issue to be addressed, is how do we know what a symbolic object's context is, and who decides? We can now restate this question as having two parts: (1) How do we know what the components and boundaries are of the sequence of which the symbolic object is a component? (2) How do we know what the institutional context is within which the symbolic object is produced? Insofar as there is an impersonal basis for coming to know what the context is in both senses above, then it is not "in the eye of the beholder" what the context is, or how a component symbolic object should be interpreted.

There are several overlapping indicators of the boundaries and components of a sequence within which a symbolic object is interpreted. The two most basic ones are these. First, the component symbolic objects that comprise a sequence are contiguous to each other in time and space, with contiguity a relative measure depending on the social institution and/or the identities, physical proximities, and communications media of the ratified participants. Second, a sequence comprises those symbolic objects that occur contiguously and progressively in time and space, whose base meanings can be adjusted against each other to result in mutually relevant situated interpretations, i.e., a coherent whole. In addition, third, the component symbolic objects of a sequence are all produced by the same agents, who serve as ratified participants in an interaction, and/or have role-identities within the social institution in force. And, fourth, the component symbolic objects are all produced within the physical and social boundaries of a single medium and/or an institution (from a service establishment to a government).

As to how we know what the social institution in force is (at least initially), there are three primary, intersecting factors. First, most social institutions are defined in part by the physical location, equipment and furnishings, and the like in which agents are situated. Second, social institutions are defined in terms of the role-identities claimed by those assembled in the particular place and time involved. Third, social institutions are defined in terms of the activities undertaken by the people assembled.

I do not mean to suggest that it is an "objective," factual matter what the context of a symbolic object is, in terms of the sequence of which it is a part and any social institution that might be in force. Rather, it is generally a decidable matter, on grounds that are shared among members of a community, and a negotiable or discussible matter when there is disagreement (where disagreement is often registered initially by conflicting interpretations of the same symbolic objects). In the majority of cases, it is relatively unequivocal. Symbolic objects are produced that are components of a sequence according to all four of the criteria above, and whose situated interpretations are consistent with the prototype of the social institution presumed to be in force (e.g., the engagement of patients with staff and physicians in medical settings). Of course, there are cases where it is far less clear cut. For example, citizens of a country may project that there is a sequential progression in political events in terms of which they interpret them, but those events are not uniformly produced by the same agents (or even by any apparent agent) and they do not uniformly occur within the frame of a particular social institution. But the uncertainty this produces as to the boundaries and components, and even the reality, of the sequence – and thus the situated interpretation of its alleged components – does not result in some kind of interpretive anarchy. It results in public debate (at least in our society). Arguably, the 1992 presidential election rested in precisely such a debate, specifically, whether economic events and associated political events during President Bush's term formed a sequential progression whose trajectory was a negative, dissipative one.

Obviously, there are a number of details and intricacies I have glossed in this analysis, but there is an adequate foundation here to support the central claim stated at the outset. Granted that symbolic objects occur in context and are interpreted accordingly, it is a mistake to reason from there that situated interpretations are open-ended and essentially personal. Of course, to avoid this, one has to accept that (a) there are base meanings, and conventional contexts, that constrain the situated interpretation of symbolic objects and (b) there is a systematic basis for assigning situated interpretations to symbolic objects on the basis of their sequential and institutional contexts. But given the analysis in the body of this paper, neither of these assumptions is antithetical to the proposition that the interpretation of symbolic objects is context-specific, nor do these assumptions entail that any particular base meaning of a symbolic object, or set of institutional conventions, is privileged in any instance.

References

Clayman, S. E., & Whalen, J. (1988/89). When the medium becomes the message: The case of the Rather-Bush encounter. *Research on Language and Social Interaction, 22*, 241-272.

Cronen, V. E., Pearce, W. B., & Xi, C. (1989/90). The meaning of "meaning" in the CMM analysis of communication: A comparison of two traditions. *Research on Language and Social Interaction, 23*, 1-40.

Goffman, E. (1967). *Interaction ritual: Essays on face-to-face behavior.* New York: Anchor Books.

Grice, H. P. (1975). Logic and conversation. In P. Cole & J. L. Morgan (Eds.), *Syntax and semantics 3: Speech acts* (pp. 41-58). New York: Academic Press.

Lemke, J. L. (1995). *Textual politics: Discourse and social dynamics.* London: Taylor & Francis.

Pearce, W. B., & Cronen, V. E. (1980). *Communication, action, and meaning: The creation of social realities.* New York: Praeger.

Pomerantz, A. (1984). Agreeing and disagreeing with assessments: Some features of preferred/dispreferred turn shapes. In J. M. Atkinson & J. Heritage (Eds.), *Structures of Social Action* (pp. 57-101). Cambridge: Cambridge University Press.

Sanders, R. E. (1985). The interpretation of nonverbals. *Semiotica, 55,* 195-216.

Sanders, R. E. (1987). *Cognitive foundations of calculated speech: Controlling understandings in conversation and persuasion.* Albany, NY: SUNY Press.

Sanders, R. E. (1992). The role of mass communication processes in producing upheavals in the Soviet Union, Eastern Europe, and China. In S. S. King & D. P. Cushman (Eds.), *Political communication: Engineering visions of order in the socialist world* (pp. 143-162). Albany: SUNY Press

Sanders, R. E. (1995a). A neo-rhetorical perspective: The enactment of role-identities as interactive and strategic. In S. J. Sigman (Ed.), *The consequentiality of communication* (pp. 67-120). Hillsdale, NJ: Erlbaum.

Sanders, R. E. (1995b). The sequential inferential theories of Sanders and Gottman. In D. P. Cushman & B. Kovacic (Eds.), *Watershed research traditions in human communication theory.* Albany, NY: SUNY Press.

Sanders, R. E. (forthcoming). The production of symbolic objects as components of larger wholes. In J. O. Greene (Ed.), *Message production: Advances in communication theory.* Mahwah, NJ: Lawrence Erlbaum.

Sanders, R. E., & Freeman, K. (1995). *Children's neo-rhetorical participation in peer interactions.* Paper presented at the Children and Social Competence: An Interdisciplinary Conference, University of Surrey, England.

Schegloff, E. A. (1988). Presequences and indirection: Applying speech act theory to ordinary conversation. *Journal of Pragmatics, 12,* 55-62.

Schegloff, E. A. (1988/89). From interview to confrontation: Observations of the Bush/Rather encounter. *Research on Language and Social Interaction, 22,* 215-240.

Schegloff, E. A. (1995). Discourse as an interactional achievement III: The omnirelevance of action. In S. Jacoby & E. Ochs (Eds.), *Research on Language and Social Interaction: Special Issue on Co-Construction* (Vol. 28, pp. 185-211).

Schegloff, E. A. (forthcoming). Confirming allusions: Toward an empirical account of action. *American Journal of Sociology.*

Searle, J. R. (1969). *Speech acts: An essay in the philosophy of Language.* London: Cambridge University Press.

Footnotes

[1] The term "message" lacks technical precision despite its widespread use and familiarity. First, it is ambiguous, used to refer either to a physical artifact that has a communication value, or to what the artifact communicates – i.e., either to the

artifact that receives an interpretation, or the interpretation it receives. Second, beyond this ambiguity, the term is empirically suspect (Sanders, forthcoming). The term "message" implies a self-contained unit of communication that in and of itself makes known something that was within the person who produced it to communicate. In principle, this is impossible: People cannot produce artifacts that in and of themselves have some particular communication value, and thus reliably express whatever the person's "message" might be. The artifacts that persons produce are components of larger wholes that each have a communication value in combination with other objects that form the whole. The thesis here is that the "context" in which artifacts are produced and interpreted is this larger whole (composed of other such artifacts) of which the particular artifact is a component. Hence, I will refer in this paper to the symbolic objects, the artifacts, that people produce, and concern myself with how they acquire a communication value among other objects that collectively form the whole (a discourse, an interaction).

[2] By "communication value" of a symbolic object that is produced and interpreted in the course of a particular communication event, I am referring to what it contributes to the completion of that event either in terms of its content or social function. This can involve an object's representational meaning, its illocutionary force, its instrumental utility in carrying out a task or coordinating effort, etc. Although an object's communication value is generally tied to its interpretation, this is not always so. A symbolic object may have an interpretation but little or no communication value (e.g., a pun), or not have an interpretation but have a communication value anyway (e.g., "oops").

Chapter 12

Context's "Culture": Speech

Frank E. X. Dance
University of Denver

René Descartes, it has been remarked, made things awkward for us all by his division of the human being into two classes of substances: thinking substances or *minds* and extended substances or *bodies*. This essay suggests that it is the spoken word that serves to suture up the Cartesian incision and restore the integrity of the human being. It is the spoken word that bonds the mental with the physical, thought with its bodily expression. It is as difficult to attribute corporeality to thought as it is to deny corporeality to thought's spoken expression. It is the spoken word that humans have used and continue to use to create culture and thus to contexture context.

Terms used in this essay are tied to a taxonomy originally developed for a Speech Theory of Human Communication (Dance, 1982). In the next paragraph I will narratively frame some of those taxonomic terms. A partial taxonomy is referenced at the end of this essay and the whole taxonomy may be found in Dance, 1982.

We are bombarded by **stimuli**. Of the stimuli to which we are exposed some gain our attention and play a part in shaping our relationship to our internal and external lives, serve to inform us. The taxonomic definition of **information** is one based upon statistical information theory and the work of Claude Shannon and his explicators (Shannon & Weaver, 1964). **Communication**, at its most generic, is an activity shared in by all living organisms. The fundamental activity of communication, that without which there simply is no communication, is interaction. This general meaning of communication makes it difficult to claim communication as a realistic academic domain. Communication without the delimiter of *human* communication, simply means too much. At this, its most general level, communication is an activity funded by information and not unique to human beings (Dance, 1970). The information of which communication at this level consists is composed of **signs** that announce that of which the signs(s) are themselves a part. Signs, in this usage, are usually natural and unlearned. Thunder is a sign of the dissipation of heat in the atmosphere. Human infant vocalization, such as the birth cry, announces that of which it is itself a part. Although infant vocalization lets us know the affective state of the infant—comfort, pain, contentment, pleasure—it (vocalization) has never been reported to serve as an infant's conceptual commentary on third world economics or the part played by context in human communication. **Vocalization** is prior to speech and in its initial state is reflexive and reveals affect. **Speech** requires neurological and motor planning and is teleological and thus intentional.

In general the discipline variously known as "speech," or "speech communication," or some other *nom du jour* has been adult-centered with relatively little consideration being given to infants, children, or developmental spoken language theory. Mine has always been a developmental perspective. I have also always considered the biological and physiological sub-stratums of speech and spoken language (Dance, 1967). I believe that this is also true of Vygotsky as is evidenced in his discussion of the pre-thought roots of speech and the pre-speech roots of conceptualization (Vygotsky, 1934,1987, pp.101-120). (Within the taxonomy used in this essay Vygotsky's "speech" is the same as the taxonomy's "spoken language.") Kozulin (1990, p. 153) ,when discussing this initial blending says, "This moment signifies a switch from a natural track of development to a cultural one."

In his introduction to his translation of the first volume of Vygotsky's collected works, Norris Minick meticulously indicates how Vygotsky's essays on *Thinking and Speech* were not originally produced by Vygotsky in the order in which they appear in print (Vygotsky,1987, pp. 17-36). The arrangement of the essays and papers and presentations in their current printed order came after the fact of the order of their original creation. I mention this since there are a few (most likely *very* few) readers who will recognize in this essay echoes of other of my writings. After over forty years of thought on the topics covered here I can now begin to organize my work in a more developmentally coherent manner. I welcome this opportunity to try and do so.

Although the concept of *bio-culture* enjoys neither great currency nor great acceptance, I would like to suggest that there are indeed both genetic and biological realities that act to predispose creating a uniquely human culture. John L. Locke (1993) espouses a theory of *biolinguistics* which considers the role played by vocalization and speech. Lieberman (1972) and Locke are unusual in this respect since many linguists and psycholinguists seem to exclude the role played by voice and speech in language. The position suggested by a decision that the proper study of linguistics can proceed without a central role for speech implies a doctrine of modal equipotentiality–that any mode (auditory, visual, gestural, et al.)–can equally serve the needs of the ontogenesis and practice of a language. My own view is that speech provides the primary mode for the ontogenesis and practice of language and that an holistic understanding of language is impossible without factoring in its being spoken.

In biology a specially prepared nutrient medium, such as agar, is used for growing tissue cells or other living matter, for growing a "culture." In like manner I am suggesting that considering human anatomy and physiology as the Petri dish, speech is the nutrient medium or base used for growing first spoken language and subsequently human culture.

Obviously human culture is the creation of human beings and human beings carry a genetic heritage. There are intra-uterine biological occurrences that have an impact on the neonate's cultural and social identity. Unfortunately we are all too familiar with negative examples of such intra-uterine events as fetal alcoholism and fetal drug addiction. Other happenings of positive or at least neutral weight also exist. Obviously a nutritious diet during pregnancy produces certain health predispositions in the fetus and neonate. Suppose the mother is on a particular diet (a diet unique to a given culture perhaps), may this diet not be transmitted to the fetus as an unconscious and unstated dietary appetite? How about all we have heard and read concerning acoustic conditioning of the fetus? The fetus normally senses sound at the end of the second or the beginning of the third trimester although visual stimulation awaits birth (Dance, 1979; Locke, 1993, p.25). The presumption is that the fetus' sound sense acuity does not stagnate during the final three months of gestation but continues to operate and to further develop. In fact fairly recent studies even indicate that there may be fetal learning of some elements, such as the cadence, of specific languages.

> Neonates do not merely prefer the resonance properties of their mother's voice. They also seem to prefer her vocal movements in effect–as we adult observers think of it–the *language* that she spoke when they were still in the womb. Jacques Mehler and his colleagues.have found that at four days of age, babies born in Paris of French speaking women prefer the sound of French to Russian. Babies whose mother spoke a different language during pregnancy lack this preference for French over Russian; indeed, they give little evidence that they even disciminate these languages (Locke, 1993, p. 39).

The fetus comes to birth with a history of acoustic experience and it may well be that the infant's fetal acoustic experience forecasts some cultural proclivity.

One important genetic precursor of human culture dwells in the uniqueness of the human speech mechanism. The anatomical and physiological evidence is compelling that the human double-bent tube and associated oro-pharyngeal structures working together with cortical areas is unique to the species and supports the wide range, flexibility, and syntactical creativity of human utterances. Convincing arguments exist for the position that this unique anatomical/physiological structure is not simply overlaid on other more life essential and primitive functions but rather is a structure designed to perpetuate and extend the human species even though the structure, in some formidable ways, is inimical to individual survival. As has been adequately demonstrated by Crelin and others the human speech mechanism puts the individual at greater risk of aspiration of foreign objects and resultant asphyxiation than does the corresponding structures in other mammalian forms. Only human beings seem to have need for the Heimlich Maneuver (Crelin, 1987; Dance, 1989; DuBrul, 1976, 1977; Routhier, 1979). The received interpretation of Darwinian evolution and selection of the fittest suggests that over time species reduce repetition and retain those aspects of their being that seem most beneficial for survival rejecting those qualities that work against survival. Human beings have moved from locomotion on four limbs to locomotion on two limbs, reducing redundancy and allowing further specialization of arm and hand usage. The refinement of the forelimbs freed the head and mouth from food gathering and food preparation as well as defense/offense requirements. The upright gait also allowed for additional cranial volume for brain development (Dance, 1964). So far the evolutionary development of the human being conforms to the Darwinian posture.

But how does one account for the species abandoning the general horizontal mammalian oro-pharyngeal structure in favor of the bent double tube, retracted tongue, descended larynx, loss of epiglottal lock, vertical structure that actually places the species in a greater risk position than the structure already in place? Certainly such a change wouldn't be just for the sake of general communication needs since such general communication needs are satisfactorily met by the mammalian horizontal structure. Mammals other than humans communicate, interact. In fact they seem to communicate quite satisfactorily in terms of their needs. So how can we make sense of this human adaptation? There must be a value added to balance and surpass the risk involved. The value added appears to be something other than communication. What then? Well, what else seems to set humans apart from their evolutionary companions? *Ratio*. Conceptual thought. Mentation. Higher mental processes. Perhaps it is worthwhile considering that human speech has an intimate, obviously correlational and perhaps causal, relationship with human mentation. But how (Dance and Zak-Dance, 1996)?

The newborn human infant reflexively vocalizes and then with practice and development begins to exert some voluntary control over vocalization. According to Riccillo (1994), the initial volitional control may be demonstrated in the suppression of sound rather than the expression of sound.

The initial reflexive vocalization, the initial birth cry and the vocalizations which follow the birth cry but precede the exertion of voluntary control over vocalization may well serve as an acoustic trigger to conceptualization (ATC). The ATC hypothesis was first presented in Dance (1979). The original paper considers the various senses available to the infant and examines whether any one or a combination of the available senses may better serve the inception and facilitation of conceptualization. Based upon the examination of the available sensory pathways and the overall sensorium, the hypothesis suggests that the infant's initial vocalizations or cries, utilizing the oral-aural pathways, introduce the infant for the first time to contrast. The infant hears its own vocalizations (A) as mediated by blood, flesh, and bone prior to the sounding of the utterance in acoustic space and then (B) some part of the sounded utterance returns to the infant through its ears thus affording a contrast between (A) and (B). The force of the hypothesis is in its attribution to the oral-aural utterance(s) of the development of contrast in the infant. As a side comment it should be noted that in the absence of an oral-aural stimulus other sensory pathways would be utilized but such utilization is indicated to be delayed and more heavily dependent upon expert adult assistance when compared to the oral-aural pathway.

Contrast is of the essence of mentation. There is no up without a down, no right without a wrong, no self without an other. Contrast is crucial. Since all conceptualization, mentation, and higher mental processes rely upon contrast, upon differentiation, the individual birth of contrast in the individual is central to individual conceptual development. Individual conceptual development is central to the titre of mentation in all cultural and social groupings since all such groupings are composed of individuals.

Contrast, differentiation, are essential for the initiation of symbolization and continuing development and refinement of the individual ability to create and use symbols. One pivotal difference between a sign and a symbol resides in a sign being part and parcel of that of which it is a sign, and in a symbol being completely other than, different from, that which it symbolizes. In the day to day world at the end of night a lightening in the Eastern sky is a sign of the rising of the sun and the lightening is itself a part of the sunrise. However nothing about the words "dog," hund," "perro," "canus," or "gai " is other than arbitrarily and culturally associated with the widely distributed, highly variable, domesticated four-legged mammal closely related to the common wolf. Human speech is responsible for creating symbols through speech's role in the creation of a human appreciation and use of contrast. Thus in considering the role of speech in the ontogenetic movement from sign to symbol development could occur as follows: Speech, volitional human sound-making, provides the oral-aural experience leading to the infant's initial perception and utilization of contrast. The infant's perception and utilization of contrast leads to the infant's incipient decentering and proto-symbolization. Decentering refers to being able to take the conceptual point of view of another. Empathy, a word in more common use, refers to sharing another's emotional or affective stance while decentering is concerned with perceptual and/or conceptual perspective taking. Human infants are born egocentric, with themselves as the center of their experience. The human infant's growing into the ability to take the conceptual perspective of another tracks the human infant's development from vocalization to speech to spoken language. The very beginnings of the ability to decenter depend on contrast, on differentiation of self from other. These "very beginnings" I refer to as incipient decentering. Prior to the development of "true symbols," protosymbols develop.

> Though on the surface often indistinguishable from true symbols, protosymbols lack the intentional act by which a vehicular form is taken to represent a referent. Nevertheless protosymbols are extremely important in the genetic process of symbolization; protosymbols may be transformed into true symbols by progressive differentiation of vehicle and referential meaning (Werner & Kaplan, 1963).

Although I believe this to be an important passage I also consider it fairly opaque. Here's my gloss on it.

The developing infant moving into childhood sometimes utters sounds that appear to constitute a symbol (an intentionally arbitrary referential utterance such as using "dog" to refer to the family pet) but in reality there is no intent (Werner and Kaplan's 'intentional act') on the part of the child to use that utterance (the "vehicle" to which Werner and Kaplan allude) but the utterance may be simply imitative of the sound(s) made by others in the child's immediate milieu when the animal is present. So the emerging child's "dog" is more a sign than a symbol but is not a pure sign. It is not totally a part of the thing which it announces. The child's "dog" is beginning to move away from sole identification with the animal in the presence of the animal. The path to differentiation of the utterance from the animal and the animal's presence is beginning to be trod by the child. When that differentiation is complete, when the utterance is totally independent of the animal but can voluntarily be used to refer to the animal whether the animal is present or not and whether the animal is the family pet or not, then we are either at or close upon the advent of a true symbol. It is interesting to consider the possible parallels between the proto-symbol/symbol dyad and Vygotsky's (1978) spontaneous/scientific concept dyad. Both dyads involve the user's ability to apply decentering and intent.

Ontogenetically the infant finds itself having to create symbols and symbol-using ability while at the same time living in a world suffused with already extant symbols. The infant is surrounded by symbol-using others. By decentering to these symbol-using others while at the same time forming the ability to construct and use its own symbols, the infant is moving from infancy to childhood while continuing a refinement of decentering. Incipient decentering, within the nurturing spoken language milieu, eventuates in the infant's (*infans = lacking the ability to engage in spoken language*) passage to childhood and competence and performance of symbolization (Dance, 1983). The fusion of genetically determined speech with culturally acquired language produces a qualitatively new and uniquely human phenomenon termed spoken language.

What we have tracked is the movement from the fetus to childhood through pre-natal experience, to vocalization, to speech (which is genetic), to the joining of speech with language (which is social/cultural), to the child's acquisition of the rudiments of spoken language. The symbol, once developed and integrated into spoken language (around 18 months of age) augments ever more refined and controlled decentering and precise symbolization on the part of the human child. Pavlov's schema of the three signal systems provides another window through which these processes may be viewed (Dance, 1967).

We have also delineated the role played by speech in the creation of the symbol. Human language is composed of systematized (using syntax and/or grammar) signs and symbols. Once having had its birth in the spoken word, a symbol can be transferred to any other vehicle such as writing, signing, architecture, music, mathematics, food, and on and on and on. As much or more could yet be said as has been said in this essay. An exhaustive consideration of the role of spoken language in culture and context would involve discussing the full significance of the ability to decenter, the role of the symbol in the development of choice and thus of intentionality, the necessity and role of choice and intentionality in the creation of human values and ethics, and the functions, levels, and forms of spoken language including the relationship between speech and thought.

Human culture is generated through human spoken language. Human culture is preserved in human spoken language and its surrogates. The Cartesian incision mentioned at the beginning of this essay is drawn together by the spoken word and the complete human being uses spoken language in the creation of culture. Human culture is passed on through human spoken language and its surrogates. Since we are dealing with human beings born into an already extant culture it is clear that spoken language and culture interact from the earliest moments in the creation and interpretation of context. Any given context is interpreted through the culture(s) in which it is situated. The same context (e.g., a kitchen, a physician's office, a school) affects communication differently with the languages of the participating cultures. Contexts are subsets of culture. Context, as culture, has its home in spoken language.

Taxonomy

Here are some definitions held to throughout this essay. These definitions are part of a taxonomy developed specifically for a speech theory of human communication. They are presented here since the development of this essay's argument pretty much follows the definitional schema. When citations from others are used and that usage differs from the taxonomic usage, I will point out this difference in usage and show the taxonomy's terms that may be used for the same concepts being discussed.

Stimulus: A unit of sensory input, either internal or external, which rouses the organism, incites to action.

Information: A perceived selection from available stimuli, a process resulting in the reduction of uncertainty. The selection may be either accidental or purposive. Information is that which is acted upon in communication.

Communication: Acting upon information. Limited to organisms. The original act is an interact between the organism and an informing stimulus (which may take place within the organism and then may be extended between and among participating organisms.) The informing aspect of the stimulus differentiates the communicative act from a simple reflex or stimulus/response mechanism. The organisms may or may not be human organisms. At this level neither intent nor success is implicit in the concept of communication. At this level the information communicated is constituted of sign(s).

Sign: A stimulus announcing that of which it is a part. A sign is concrete and fixed regardless of context. A sub-set of signs are signals which have acquired their sign characteristics through the process of pair-wise conditioning. Signs may be processed by a variety of analyzers such as olfactory, gustatory, tactile, visual, kinesthetic/proprioceptive, and auditory. One means of stimulation of the auditory analyzer is through vocalization.

Vocalization: The oral production of sounds by an organism which may or may not be human. Humans have available the quality of vocalization also present in other than human animals. Humans, however, have, in addition to the widely distributed capacity of general vocalization, a species specific and additional vocalization capacity which is termed speech.

Speech: The human, genetically determined, species specific individual activity consisting of the voluntary production of phonated, articulated sound through the interaction and coordination of peripheral effector organs as a group as well as the speech-specific neural structures and pathways (Dance, 1979). The human capacity for speech leads to the inception of the symbol.

Symbol: A stimulus whose relationship with that with which it is associated is a result of the decision or arbitrary agreement of human user(s). Symbols are learned, abstract, and anthroposemiotic. Symbols, which become significant symbols when agreed to by more than one person (Mead, 1982) are a primary element of human language.

Language: The culturally determined, syntactic, systematization of signs and/or of symbols. When speech fuses with language the result is spoken language.

Spoken Language: The fusion of genetically determined speech with culturally determined language. The fusion is uniquely human and thus primitive and minimum to a speech theory of human communication.

Human communication involves the acting upon of information by humans. The unique way in which humans act upon information so as to communicate is through spoken language and its derivatives (such as writing and symbolic gestures or gesture systems). Thus **Human communication** is a derived rather than a primitive term within the speech theory of human communication. Another example of an important, derived term composed of two primitive terms, is **speech communication** – acting upon information through uniquely human speech.

References

Crelin, E. S. (1987). *The human vocal tract: Anatomy, function, development, and evolution.* New York: Vantage Press.

Dance, F. E. X. (1964). Speech communication in the Soviet Union: The phylogenesis of speech according to Frederick Engels. *The Speech Teacher, xiii* (2), 114-118.

Dance, F. E. X. (1967). Speech communication theory and Pavlov's second signal system. *The Journal of Communication,* XVII (1), 13-24.

Dance, F. E. X. (1970). The concept of communication. *The Journal of Communication,* XX (2), 201 210.

Dance, F. E. X. (1979). The acoustic trigger to conceptualization. *Health Communication and Informatics*, 5 (4), 203-213.
Dance, F. E. X. (1982). A speech theory of human communication. In F. E. X. Dance (Ed.), *Communication theory: Comparative essays* (pp.120-146). New York: Harper and Row.
Dance, F. E. X. (1983). The role of speech in symbol formation. In John I. Sisco (Ed.), *The Jensen lectures: Contemporary communication studies* (pp.44-49). Tampa, FL: University of South Florida.
Dance, F. E. X. (1989). *The uniqueness of human speech*. Paper delivered as visiting scholar in the department of Speech Communication. Cinncinnati, OH: University of Cincinnati.
Dance, F. E. X., & Zak-Dance, C. C. (1996). *Speaking your mind: Private thinking and public speaking* (2nd Edition). DuBuque, IA: Kendall/Hunt Publishing.
DuBrul, E. L. (1976). Biomechanics of speech sounds. In S. R. Harnard, H. D. Steklis, & J. Lancaster (Eds.), *Origins and evolution of language and speech* (pp. 631-642). New York: Annals of the New York Academy of Science.
DuBrul, E. L. (1977). Origins of speech apparatus and its reconstruction in fossils. *Brain and Language*, 4, 365-381.
Kozulin, A. *(1990). Vygotsky's psychology: A biography of ideas*. Cambridge, MA: Harvard University Press.
Lieberman, P. (1972). *The speech of primates*. The Hague, Netherlands: Mouton.
Locke, J. L. (1993). *The child's path to spoken language*. Cambridge, MA: Harvard University Press.
Mead, G. H. (1922). A behavioristic account of the Significant Symbol. *Journal of Philosophy, XIX*, 157-163.
Riccillo, S. C. (1994). Phylogenesis: Understanding the biological origins of intrapersonal communication. In D. R. Vocate (Ed.), *Intrapersonal communication: Different voices, different minds* (pp. 33-56). Hillsdale, NJ: Lawrence Erlbaum Associates Publishers.
Routhier, M. (1979). *A critical analysis and examination of the issue of speech as an overlaid function*. Doctoral dissertation, University of Denver.
Shannon, C. E., & Weaver, W. (1964). *The mathematical theory of communication*. Urbana, IL: The University of Illinois Press.
Vygotsky, L. S. (1934,1987). *The collected works of L. S. Vygotsky*. R. W. Rieber and A. A. Carton (Eds.). Translated and with an Introduction by Norris Minick. New York: Plenum Press.
Vygotsky, L. S. (1978). *Mind in society: The development of higher psychological processes*. In M. Cole, V. John-Steiner, S. Scribner, & E. Souberman (Eds.). Cambridge, MA: Harvard University Press.
Werner, H., & Kaplan, B. (1963). *Symbol formation*. Cambridge, MA: JohnWiley and Sons.

Chapter 13

The Behavior-Context Interface in Interethnic Communication[1]

Young Yun Kim
University of Oklahoma

Issues of ethnicity and ethnic identity engender some of the most volatile responses in many contemporary societies. Hardly any day passes without reports of some new incidents of interethnic conflict. In the United States, wide-ranging views are voiced on the historically-embedded interethnic relations–from the pronouncement of Louis Farrakhan during his recent visit to Iran: "You can quote me: God will destroy America at the hands of the Muslims" (*Time*, February 26, 1996, p. 12), to President Clinton's call for reconciliation and unity in his recent University of Texas address: "Long before we were so diverse, our nation's motto was *E Pluribus Unum*—out of many, we are one. We must be one—as neighbors; as fellow citizens; not separate camps, but family" (*Weekly Compilation of Presidential Documents, 31*, October 23, 1995, p. 1851).

Reflecting the potency of interethnic issues is the extensive amount of academic attention that has been given by social scientists to them for the past several decades. Their efforts have resulted in a rich body of academic insight, although one that lacks cohesiveness and integration. Because most investigators have tended to limit their investigations to the particular research domain of the respective disciplines, no unified or general theory is available at this time that can adequately represent the person, the group, the society, and the relationships among them, all within one explanatory system.

True, there are theories pertaining to psychological experiences of individuals, on the one hand, and to the societal order, on the other. What is lacking is a connecting link that would enable social scientists to relate person to person, person to groups, and groups to the wider social order. Indeed, calls have been made for the interdisciplinary integration of the field. Blalock (1982), for instance, has pointed out the serious need to provide a "big picture" or "theoretical roadmap" in this complex and often divergent field. Such calls have been followed by efforts for developing multi-dimensional models that incorporate explanatory factors drawn from more than one disciplinary perspective.

Among them is the work by Tajfel and his associates (Tajfel, 1974; Tajfel & Turner, 1986), whose theory of social identity and intergroup relations take into account the structural conditions of the society such as its minority-majority status. Subsequent developments of Tajfel's theory have continued the original interdisciplinary tradition. The speech accommodation theory (Giles & Smith, 1979) and the ethnolinguistic identity theory of intergroup behavior (Giles & Johnson, 1987), for example, explain the "convergent" and "divergent" language behaviors of individuals, incorporating the structural/situational and psychological factors. The speech accommodation theory has since been broadened and revised into communication accommodation theory (Gallois, Franklyn, Giles, & Coupland, 1988; Gallois, Giles, Jones, Cargile, & Ota, 1995). Here, the authors emphasize the role of the situation (such as the degree of intergroup salience, dependence, and solidarity) and individual factors (such as social and personal identity) in constraining both speaker behavior and receiver attributions. The authors also emphasize the importance of interpersonal and intergroup salience in explaining the progress of a two-person intergroup interaction and the decisions the interactants make about their convergent and divergent communication strategies.

Related synthesizing efforts have been made in the area of ethnolinguistic identity and intergroup behavior. Clément and Noels (1991), for example, have examined situational norms, along with individuals' identity choice, in explaining the development of bilingualism. Situational norms include the extent to which the social milieu encourages or opposes both of the identities involved ("language institutional equality"), the language status in the minority individual's home town, and the historical evolution of the minority ethnolinguistic status. (For additional integrative approaches to intergroup behaviors, see Bourhis, 1979; Brewer & Miller, 1984; De Vos, 1990a, 1990b; Hewstone & Giles, 1986; and Van Dijk, 1987, among others.)

Toward Interdisciplinary Integration

The present work is a continuation of these efforts. It strives to move a step further toward a yet more comprehensive account for the way ethnicity is played out in social interaction. It builds on the existing disciplinary and interdisciplinary insights and attempts to offer a more broadly based model of interethnic relations. To do so, this investigator takes a **communication perspective** that focuses on the message and the surrounding circuit. This communication message focus, in turn, allows integration of the more conventional disciplinary foci such as the person, the group, and the society, all of which operate in the communication activities of processing and generating messages. As such, this approach to interethnic relations is closely aligned with the "social matrix" perspective of Ruesch and Bateson (1968), in which communication is viewed as the very substance of all things social. In their words,

> problems of communication seem to be of only secondary interest to the student of [human] behavior....But communication does not refer to verbal, explicit, and intentional transmission of messages alone; as used in our sense, the concept of communication would include all those processes by which

people influence one another....all actions and events have communicative aspects, as soon as they are perceived by a human being....Where the relatedness of entities is considered, we deal with problems of communication; when entities are considered in isolation from one another, problems of communication are not relevant (pp. 5-6).

Definitions

The word, **ethnicity**, is a foundational term for this work and needs to be examined closely. It was first employed in the 1930's and 1940's in terms of national and cultural origin (Nash, 1989, p. 1). Today, ethnicity is commonly associated with not only cultural and national origin, but racial, religious, and linguistic origins as well (Gordon, 1981; Nash, 1989; Smith, 1981). In the sociological tradition, ethnicity has been used primarily as a label to designate a social **group** and to distinguish it from other social groups, based on such indicators as race, religion, language, national origin, or combinations of them. In this group-level definition, ethnicity becomes the "objective" character, quality, or condition of belonging to a social group as well as an individual's membership in an ethnic group. Most of the sociological discussions of ethnicity have employed ethnicity or ethnic group in a domestic context. This is the way, for instance, sociologists such as Glazer and Moynihan (1975) have investigated the phenomenon of ethnic "stratification" in the United States.

Cultural approaches to ethnicity emphasize the common life patterns, practices, and symbols, which collectively connote a kind of temporal continuity or common "tradition" linking its members to a common future (Hsu, 1971; Nash, 1989). Some of the recent ethnographic studies in communication have taken such approaches, including the studies investigating communication patterns of American Indians (Wieder & Pratt, 1990), African Americans (Daniel & Smitherman, 1990; Kochman, 1981, 1986), and some of the mainstream American communities (Carbaugh, 1990; Philipsen, 1989). Like sociological approaches, cultural approaches view ethnicity primarily as a group-level phenomenon which, in essence, can be described in terms of its core, defining the group's life patterns by including language, behavior, norms, beliefs, myths, and values, as well as the forms and practices of social institutions. These cultural patterns of ethnicity comprise **ethnic markers** (Nash, 1989), that is, symbolic (e.g., emblems such as flags, crosses, anthems, folk songs, folk gestures and movements, folk dances, and decorative objects) and physical/material features (e.g., skin color, dress, and food). Such ethnic markers represent within-group commonalities and between-group differences in the individuals' backgrounds.

In contrast, psychological studies have defined ethnicity primarily in terms of the "subjective"–often "unconscious" and "irrational" (or emotional) identification of individuals with an ethnic group and not with other groups, that is, the identity experienced by the group members. Social identity theory of intergroup behavior (Tajfel, 1974, 1978, 1982; Turner, 1975), for instance, has served as a basis for many experimental studies (e.g., Giles & Bourhis, 1976; Giles & Saint-Jacques, 1979), and has provided a systematic explanation of the way ethnic and other group identities are played out in individuals. The theory postulates that an individual's personal identity is based, in part, on membership in significant social categories along with the value and emotional significance attached to that membership.

In this regard, **ethnic identity** subsumes the related concept, **ethnic identification**—or a conscious act of identifying oneself with one's ethnic group—as well as the attributes of the ethnicity (group characteristics). Although often viewed as distinct phenomena, ethnicity and ethnic identity are empirically inseparable. They are two aspects of the same phenomenon, as the collective (ethnicity) and the individual experiences of it (ethnic or ethnolinguistic identity) mutually define each other. Whether strong or weak, some degree of inseparable relationship exists between an ethnic group and its members, and the concept that ties the individual member to the group is ethnic identity. Some scholars view ethnicity as the manifestation of a "primordial" tie that is embedded in the deep core of personhood. Yinger (1986), for instance, sees ethnic attachment as a "genuine culture" that forms the person's "basic identity" during the earliest periods of socialization, serving as a source of ethnic group strength. For De Vos (1990a), ethnic identity is rooted in "the emotionally profound 'self'-awareness of parentage and a concomitant mythology of discrete origin" (p. 14). It provides "a sense of common origin--as well as common beliefs and values, or common values" and serves as the basis of "self-defining in-groups" (De Vos, 1990b, p. 204).

Interethnic communication, then, is presumed to occur whenever the psychological orientation taken by at least one interactant is based on ethnicity and ethnic identity (Collier & Thomas, 1988). As documented extensively in studies of social identity theory, intercultural interactants tend to see themselves and their interaction partners in light of the respective cultural group membership (Brewer, 1986; Brewer & Miller, 1984; Gudykunst, 1988a, 1988b; E. Ross, 1978; Tajfel, 1974; Turner & Giles, 1981).

Of course, the impact of ethnicity in shaping identities and interethnic communication behavior varies from situation to situation. Ethnicity can be critical, totally insignificant, or have a whole range of effects in between. Such varied levels of salience of the role of ethnicity and ethnic identity in communication encounters can be viewed in terms of the **intergroup-interpersonal continuum** (e.g., Brown & Turner, 1981; Tajfel, 1970; Tajfel, 1982; Turner & Giles, 1981). As Tajfel and Turner (1986) noted:

> At one extreme ... is the interaction between two or more individuals which is fully determined by their interpersonal relationships and individual characteristics and not at all affected by various social groups or categories in which they respectively belong. The other extreme consists of interactions between two or more individuals (or groups of individuals) which are fully determined by their respective memberships of various

social groups or categories, and not at all affected by the individual personal relationship between the people involved (p. 8).

An Organizing Scheme

The present communication approach is grounded in a general systems perspective, particularly of "open systems" (Bertalanffy, 1975/1955; Ford & Lerner, 1992; Rapoport, 1975). The general systems methodology emphasizes structural-functional interdependence of various elements of a given system and its environment. It is grounded in the idea that counters the commonly presumed notion of dualistic split between the individual and the social, between the objective and the subjective, and between cause and effect. This worldview recognizes the human world not as a world of separate opposites but as a dynamic "living" entity in which all seeming opposites are inseparable and the boundary line between them unreal.

Context-Behavior Interface

This integrative and harmonizing systems logic shapes the present view that human communication is co-constituted by the individual and the social, the behavior enacted and the context that "surround s" it. Consistent with the pragmatics of communication articulated by Watzlawick, Beavin, and Jackson (1967), the systems view emphasizes that "all communication practices point beyond themselves to (and derive their meaning from) sets of contexts" (Cronen, Chen, & Pearce, 1988, p. 67). In Bateson's (1972) words, "...without context, there is no communication" (p. 402), and in Givón's (1989) metaphor, "A picture is not fully specified unless its frame is also specified" (p. 2).

As such, the present systems approach counters the reductionist assumptions that underlie many of the existing models in which a given phenomenon is conceived as being linked together by a set of one-directional cause-and-effect relationship. In this methodological tradition, the variable-analytic studies have generated numerous narrow conceptions of interethnic communication by "plugging" a set of "independent" variables into a regression equation to predict an "effect" on one or more "dependent" variables. The resulting picture is of crisscrossing and fragmented chains of causation, exemplified in the common occurrence of variables (such as prejudice) treated by certain researchers as independent variables, while the same variables are treated by others as dependent variables. Relatedly, the propositions of one theory or model do not necessarily add up, or bear a coherent relationship, to the propositions of another theory or model. This variable-analytic approach is at least partly responsible for the considerable fragmentation of the field of interethnic relations and the failing of cross-fertilization of common issues, concepts, definitions, and research findings.

The present systems approach begins to address such lack of conceptual cohesiveness in the field. It does so by treating all contextual forces operating in a given communication event as arising through and being sustained and altered by behavior, and vice versa. Predictability in a communication event is explored by identifying what Bateson (1972) refers to as the "redundant patterns" in the action/interaction and in the context (p. 399). Using Bateson's metaphor, the present approach can be compared to the way we try to select a piece for a given position in a jigsaw puzzle by looking at all of the identifiable patterns holistically.

An Integrative Model

Based on the above considerations, this investigator approaches interethnic communication in its most general and simplest form. This approach is taken so that isomorphic patterns among various existing concepts across disciplines can be "seen" without being prematurely restricted by specificity or confused by complexity. It focuses on a system of a single person communicating interethnically, although implicitly present in this single-person system is one or more people with whom the person communicates. A model of this **basic communication system** is depicted in Figure 1.

Organized as a hierarchical arrangement made out of a progression of multiple levels of context, the model serves as an organizing framework in the form of a **multilayered transactional matrix** represented as a set of circles. Each level acts as a meta-level context, to the sub-level(s) embedded within it (cf. Givón, 1989; Ruben, 1975), as depicted in Figure 1. The model highlights the **interfaces** of the contextual forces surrounding a particular enactment of interethnic behavior. Although temporality is built into the reality of any communication system, we artificially stop the action for the sake of examining and analyzing it cross-

Figure 1.
Context-behavior interface in interethnic communication: An organizing scheme.

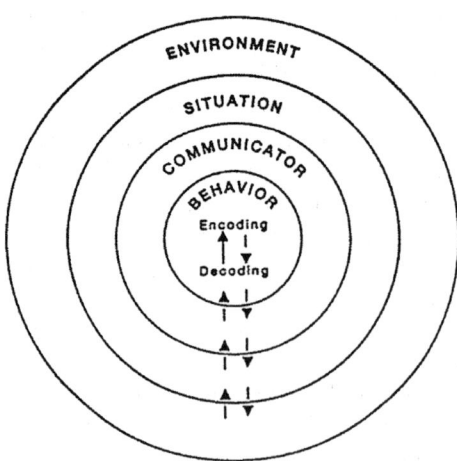

sectionally—rather like stopping a motion picture so that we can study one frame at a time.

At the core of this matrix are the activities of encoding and decoding **behavior**. These activities are viewed as the "stuff" of the communication process, that is, the "what" and "how" of the messages sent and received. At the same time, the conditions that surround this communication process comprise the **context**, that is, "covert factors" (Von Raffler-Engel, 1988) that "surround" the communication behavior.

The first layer of the context is the **communicator**—the densest locus of structure that guides, and is guided by, the communicator's encoding and decoding activities. At this level, we are interested in what is traditionally called the "mind" that organizes and processes incoming verbal and nonverbal information into forms of meaningful messages. Next comes the **situation**, that is, the immediate social milieu. This milieu is created when the communicator interfaces with one or more persons, either face-to-face or through various mediating channels from point-to-point channels such as computer, fax, telephone, and letter, to other more public channels including radio, television, and newspapers. Beyond the situational level is the larger social milieu, which is referred to here as the **environment**. This environmental context includes many sub-levels—from the suborganizational, organizational, and community levels to the larger milieus of regional, national and international levels.

Together, the behavior and the context co-constitute a communication system, in which we deal with sequences that resemble a kind of reciprocal relationship of "stimulus-and-response" rather than the linear, one-directional "cause-and-effect." Note that the three levels of context (and the many sublevels thereof) are sets of "gradation, continuum and non-discreteness" (Givón, 1989, p. 5), unlike in descriptions that have assumed that categories are discrete. Because one level acts as the meta-level and/or the sub-level in this approach, the present scheme needs to be viewed as one of "mapping" or a "rigorous metaphor" (Bateson, 1972, p. 404). This scheme is designed to serve as a simplified, yet integrative, approximation of the dynamics of interethnic communication. It provides the grounding, sensivity, and integration needed to generate an interwoven system of interpretation and explanation that closely approximates the reality it represents.

The layers represented here generally correspond to a group of concepts that have served as frequent objects of inquiry across disciplines, as explained in the following four sections.

The Behavior

The communication behavior consists of various encoding and decoding activities involved in social interactions. It includes what Ruben (1975) refers to as *personal communication* or "private symbolization," that is, all the internal mental activities that occur in individuals that dispose and prepare them to act and react in certain ways in actual social situations as well as the actual actions and reactions themselves. As such, the term, "behavior," is not limited to externalized, observable verbal and nonverbal symbolizations. It includes the internal mental activities involved in the information processing as well.

Various encoding and decoding patterns have been investigated in socialpsychology, sociolinguistics and communication. A great deal of information is available on patterns of communication behavior that are relevant to understanding the dynamics of interethnic encounters. This section identifies some of the prominent concepts.

Decoding

A widely investigated aspect of decoding is the **categorization** of information about or from outgroup members. The term, **stereotyping**, is a more popularized term for the same phenomenon. Studies of social cognition, ethnic identity, and intergroup behavior have documented extensively that people tend to perceive outgroup members based on simplistic and categorical manners, and that such decoding is closely associated with **depersonalization** or **de-individuation** (Tajfel, 1970), that is, to stereotype them as "undifferentiated items in a unified social category" and, thus, to perceive them not as individuals but as "group representatives" (Turner, 1982, p. 28). According to Oddou and Mendenhall (1984), simplistic categorization is also characterized by a cognitive tendency to **accentuate differences** or de-accentuate similarities between one's own group and an outgroup.

Along with categorization and related concepts, **bias in attribution** has been identified as a conspicuous feature of intergroup decoding (Jaspars & Hewstone, 1982). This notion comes from attribution theorists such as Heider (1958) who proposed that the behavior of a person could be causally linked to the actor's personality, to the environment, or to a combination of both. Subsequent research has shown a tendency for people to underestimate the importance of situational causes in making inferences about others' negative behavior, an effect labeled the "fundamental attribution error" by L. Ross (1977). The fundamental attribution error becomes what Pettigrew (1979) calls the **"ultimate attribution error"** when this involves a positive bias toward one's group and a negative bias toward outgroup members. These phenomena have been found to be particularly significant in interethnic situations, as have been articulated in social identity theory.

Gumperz' (1978) conversational analysis of interethnic conversationsbetween English speakers and Asian Indians demonstrates the power that biasedinterethnic attribution has to bring about serious consequences of "communication breakdowns." Similarly, Hopper (1986) coins the term **Shiboleth schema** based on a biblical tale to illustrate the tendency of **prejudicial listening**, a tendency to interpret dialectic differences as being defective and, therefore, being an object of hostility and discrimination. Volkan (1992) adds to this observation a psychoanalytic explanation of biased interethnic attribution based on the notion of **projection**, a tendency that leads to ego-defensive reactions such as feelings of inferiority or superiority, avoidance, suspicion, and paranoia. Kim (1991) calls such biased cognitive responses an element of **intergroup posturing**.

These and related concepts in the literature are counterbalanced byother concepts with opposite meanings such as **particularization** and **decategorization** (Billig, 1987). Langer (1989) uses a more global term, **mindfulness**, to refer to a pattern of perception and thought that seeks a finer cognitive discrimination and more creative ways of interpreting messages about and from outgroup members. Other terms such as **personalization** (Kim, 1992), **individuation** (Kim, 1995), and **differentiation** (Brewer & Miller, 1988) are employed to refer to the style of decoding that is more complex, refined, and less biased.

Encoding

An extensive amount of attention has been given to encoding behavior,particularly to language behavior, in sociolinguistic and social psychological studies. Based on speech accommodation theory and social identity theory, Giles, Bourhis and Taylor (1977) examine **convergent and divergent behavior** in relation to a perceived threat to one's ethnic identity and to the nature of power relationships between one's own ethnic group and that of the other. (See, also, related studies including Giles, Mulac, Bradac, & Johnson, 1987; Giles & Smith, 1979). A concept associated with divergent behavior is the **overt expressions of communicative distance** (Lambert, 1979; Lukens, 1979; Peng, 1974) or **border rituals** (Volkan, 1992), which concern the way speakers manipulate linguistic and other speech variants, either to increase or to decrease the psychological distance between themselves and others.

Yet other studies have documented various forms of **prejudiced talk** (Van Dijk, 1987) with varying degrees of emotional intensity and explicitness from the subtle expressions such as "you people" to more blatant uses of **ethnophaulism** reflected in derogatory and dehumanizing ethnic labels, jokes, and "hate speeches" (Allen, 1983; Gadfields, Giles, Bourhis, & Tajfel, 1979; Kirkland, Greenberg, & Psyzcynski, 1987; McConahay & Hough, 1976; Van Dijk, 1987). Similar observations have been made regarding **nonverbal expressions of prejudice** as well. Feldman (1985), for instance, suggests that conflicts are expressed, often covertly and subtly, through a wide range of nonverbal behaviors from arrogant or angry voice tone, physical distance, avoidance of eye contact, and frozen facial expressions, to forms of extreme hatred and aggression such as spitting, cross-burning, rioting, and acts of violence.

Countering these and related concepts is the potentially useful notionof **message complexity** that has been developed in constructivist approaches to communication (Delia, 1976). According to Applegate and Sypher (1988), a more sophisticated message behavior of this type generally requires speakers to recognize another person's perspectives and to exploit communication as a means of negotiating the definition of social situations between persons. Complex message behavior is reflected in **person-centered messages** (Applegate & Delia, 1980; Burleson, 1987; Applegate & Sypher, 1988) that contain a quality responsive to the aims and behavioral styles of one's interactional partner, and the topic or content of a message being communicated, as well as that which seeks to enhance interpersonal relationships or create positive interpersonal identities. In addition, Kim (1992), expanding on Hall's (1976, 1983) studies of cross-cultural differences in patterns of interpersonal **synchrony**, argues that the practice of "mirroring" and "complementing" communication styles helps create a harmonious and cooperative interpersonal milieu.

Associative-Disassociative Behavior Continuum

The above concepts depicting specific aspects of encoding and decoding naturally fall along a bipolar continuum of **association** and **dissociation**. As such, associative and dissociative behaviors are viewed not as two mutually exclusive categories but as varying in the degree of associative or dissociative meaning being communicated. Behaviors that are closer to the associative end of this continuum facilitate the communication process by increasing the likelihood of mutual understanding, cooperation, and the "coming-together" of the involved persons into a constructive relationship. Comparatively, behaviors at the dissociative end tend to contribute to misunderstanding, competition, and the "coming-apart" of the relationship.

Table 1 summarizes these concepts in terms of association and dissociation. A person's communication behavior is associative when it involves decoding patterns that are particularized, decategorized, personalized, and differentiated,

Table 1. Elements of associative and dissociative interethnic communication behavior.

	Association	Dissociation
Decoding	Particularization	Categorization
	Decategorization	Stereotyping
	Personalization	Depersonalization
	Differentiation	Projection
	Accentuating Similarities	Accentuating Differences
	Mindfulness	Ultimate Attribution Error
		Communicative Distance
		Intergroup Posturing
Encoding	Convergence	Divergence
	Person-Centered Message	Prejudiced Talk
	Personalized Communication	Ethnic Labels
	Mirroring/Complementing	Ethnophaulism
		Body Rituals
		Nonverbal Expressions of Communicative Distance/Prejudice

fully engaged, and that emphasize similarities and not just differences. An associative encoding behavior is one that shows convergence toward the behavioral style of the other person, that sends out verbal and nonverbal messages that are personalized (or person-centered) and that mirror and/or complement the verbal and nonverbal styles of the other person. Conversely, a communication behavior is dissociative when it is based on a categorical, stereotypical, and depersonalized perception and projection, that accentuates differences. A dissociative behavior also tends to involve inaccurate and negative attributions (ultimate attribution errors) and to show psychological distance (communicative distance) and intergroup posturing. It is reflected in divergent verbal and nonverbal encoding behavior such as prejudiced talk, name-calling and other ethnophaulic verbal expressions, as well as body rituals and facial expressions that indicate various negative emotions from indifference and arrogance to extreme hatred.

The Communicator

We now move to the first layer of communication context, the communicator. As previously noted, the communicator serves as the most immediate context for specific encoding and decoding behaviors. The communicator is examined below in terms of the relatively stable psychological attributes, or routinized patterns in one's personality structure (Givón, 1989).

Cognitive Structure

One of the psychological attributes of the communicator often examined in studies of interethnic relations is the degree of **cognitive complexity**. This factor is responsible for the way the communicator processes information (Applegate & Sypher, 1988; Delia, 1976; Kelly, 1955). Individuals of high cognitive complexity have been observed to use more refined, personalized, associative verbal messages. Comparatively, low cognitive complexity is linked to erroneous generalizations, biased attributions, psychological distancing, impersonality, ignorance, and stereotype-based expectancies (Allport, 1954; Brewer & Miller, 1988; Gudykunst & Lim, 1986; Hamilton, Sherman, & Ruvolo, 1990; Tajfel & Turner, 1986).

A related view has been provided by those who explain individualdifferences in intergroup attitude in terms of the role of **category width** (Detweiler, 1986). Studies indicate that the narrow categorizers tend to make more negative and confident attributions about outgroup members. Low cognitive complexity is also linked to an **authoritarian personality** (Adorno, Frenkel-Brunswik, Levinson, & Sanford, 1950), which reflects the decoding pattern of a simplistic, rigid categorization of people and ideas.

Identity Strength

Ethnic identity, or ethnolinguistic identity, has been extensively investigated in social psychological and sociolinguistic studies of intergroup relations. It is a focal phenomenon in many conversational analysis studies (e.g., Gumperz & Cook-Gumperz, 1982), bilingualism (e.g., Bourhis, 1979; Clément & Noels,

1991; Landry & Allard, 1991; J. Ross, 1979), intergroup behavior (e.g., Giles & Johnson, 1987; Lambert, 1979; Turner & Giles, 1981). Several characteristics of the communicator's identity vis-à-vis his or her ethnicity are viewed to be linked to encoding and decoding behavior.

In particular, **ethnic commitment** (Giles & Johnson, 1986), **psychological distinctiveness** (Bourhis, Giles, Leyens, & Tajfel, 1979), or **ingroup loyalty** (Brewer & Miller, 1988; Brown & Turner, 1981), has been found to facilitate dissociative decoding patterns such as biased attribution, psychological distance, and divergent behavior. In addition, the **insecurity** (Kim, 1989) the communicator feels in his/her ethnicity, **status anxiety** (De Vos, 1990a, 1990b), and **perceived threat** (Bourhis et al.) have been identified as being related to divergent intergroup behavior, experiences of marginality (Taft, 1977), as well as hostility and aggression (Berkowitz, 1962), outgroup discrimination (Brewer & miller, 1984, 1988), and stereotyping (Francis, 1976) of outgroup members.

Group Bias

Closely related to the strength of one's commitment and sense of security in one's identity is the degree of intergroup bias that is frequently reflected in a form of **prejudice**. The prejudice one holds is generally known to be negative toward outgroups and positive toward one's own group (Billig, Condon, Edwards, Gane, Middleton, & Radley, 1988; Brewer & Miller, 1984; Milner, 1973). Other similar terms have been used as well, such as **ingroup favoritism** (Kim, 1989), **ethnocentrism** (Brewer & Campbell, 1976; Pettigrew, 1979; L. Ross, 1977), **intergroup hostility** (Turner, 1982), **discrimination** (Smitherman-Dolnaldsen & Van Dijk, 1988), and **racism** (Essed, 1991; Van Dijk, 1987, 1991; Volkan, 1992). These terms commonly imply beliefs and feelings about ingroups and outgroups that are irrational and unjustifiable. In extreme cases, of course, people permit themselves to engage in severe dissociative behaviors, including various forms of violence we witness today around the world, from street riots and kidnapping to acts of war (Volkan, 1992).

Related Concepts

Concepts that counter the above communicator attributes are **intercultural identity** (Kim, 1988; 1995, in press) and its correlates such as **integration identity** (Berry, 1970; Berry, U. Kim, & Boski, 1988; Phinney, 1993), **multicultural person** (Adler, 1982), **double-swing** (Yoshikawa, 1986), **humanocentrism** (Gittler, 1974), and **moral inclusion** (Opotow, 1990). Each of these concepts reflects the vital component of a level of intellectual and emotional maturity that allows an outlook of intergroup accommodation. Two additional concepts of personality, **openness** and **strength**, have been proposed as important to the communicator's psychologicial resources for meeting the challenges of communicating with outgroup members and for the development of an intercultural identity (Kim, 1988, in press). These two broad concepts consolidate other more specific concepts that have been employed in research such as patience, flexibility, sensitivity, receptivity, and sociability.

The above concepts describe some of the more prominent aspects of thecommunicator–cognitive structure, identity strength, group bias, and related attributes. Together, they offer a tentative psychological profile of the communicator whose encoding and decoding behaviors are likely to be associative or dissociative.

The Situation

Next to the communicator is the situation of the interethnic encounter itself, when two or more people interact with one another, knowingly or not. The interaction can occur face-to-face or via mediating channels. The situation defines the immediate physical or social surrounding in which a particular social encounter takes place. The situation is defined by physical settings such as home, neighborhood, workplace, bank, classroom, or airport. The situation may be one in which someone makes simple, passing observations of people on the street, listens to a record album, or engages in a serious dialogue with a colleague. In addition, the situation can be defined as the participants themselves—the nature of their relationship. Each encounter presents a unique set of circumstances created by the interfacing of the interactants.

Key situational factors emphasized in social psychological studies areidentified below in relation to their importance in understanding associative and dissociative encoding and decoding behavior.

Interethnic Heterogeneity

By definition, an interethnic encounter presents a level of heterogeneity, particularly in the interactants' ethnic characteristics (Sarbaugh, 1988). The inherent **difference** that communicators bring to an interethnic encounter presents at least some degree of challenge. Research indicates, for instance, an added anxiety (Stephan & Stephan, 1985), uncertainty, and lack of attributional confidence (Gudykunst, 1988b) stemming from cultural and linguistic differences between interactants. Miscommunication occurs frequently due to differences in the interactants' language competencies and styles (Banks & Baker, 1991; Gass & Varonis, 1991).

Heterogenous encounters are also likely to increase the **incompatibility** of interests and values between the interactants, accentuating their feeling of psychological distance and inhibiting their ability to form consensus or seek common goals. While not all ethnic differences are incompatible, sociolinguistic and communication studies have examined some distinct features of communication behavior that are correlated with interethnic conflict. Gumperz (1978), for example, has focused on interethnic difference in the linguistic pragmatic features of verbal messages that contribute to communication "breakdowns" in key social situations such as job interviews. Others have analyzed cultural differences in the way conflict is experienced and managed in different ethnic groups (e.g., Kochman, 1981, 1986; Ting-Toomey, 1986, 1988).

Interethnic Salience

Closely related to ethnic heterogeneity, the notion of ethnic salience has received close attention in the literature. Ethnic salience is defined here as the degree to which the interactants'are self-conscious of each other's ethnic identity. Interethnic salience, thus, gives the encounter an "intergroup" character, which is accompanied by dissociative encoding and decoding behaviors (such as stereotyping, biased attribution, intergroup posturing, and verbal and nonverbal behaviors of divergence and communicative distance). Ethnic salience is mainly a function of the **distinctiveness** of ethnic markers present in a given encounter, such as distinct physical and behavioral features and conspicuous speech patterns (Worchel, 1979, p. 272). Often, some of the more obvious but superficial differences (e.g., skin color and speech accents) block the communicators from "seeing" less conspicuous similarities between them.

Studies have observed that ethnic salience is primarily a function of the **ethnic composition** in the immediate and larger social milieu relative to the ethnic composition of the encounter itself (Brewer & Miller, 1988, p. 174). For example, the encounter between a Japanese and an African-American in a predominantly African-American community is likely to present a strong ethnic salience. On the other hand, the same two people's encounter would entail a weaker interethnic salience if it were to take place in a community where both groups are more or less equally represented. The so-called **solo effect** (Taylor, Fiske, Etcoff, & Ruderman, 1978) illustrates this observation.

Interaction Structure

Social encounters operate according to some form of structure that organizes the way interactions are carried out. The interaction structure provides each communicator with "guidelines" for encoding and decoding. One such structural guideline is provided by a **superordinate goal** that transcends each party's own interests most clearly exemplified in situations of military combat units, sports teams, natural disasters and epidemics. Research has shown that the presence of such a goal provides a climate of interdependence and mutuality facilitating associative behaviors while discouraging prejudice (Worchel, 1986). Brewer and Miller (1988) argue that associative behaviors such as personalized decoding, rather than stereotypical categorization, is more likely to occur when the interaction is structured to promote an **interpersonal** and **cooperative** orientation rather than a **task-oriented** and **competitive** one.

An additional interactional condition that clearly influences the interethnic communication process has been identified in the relative status positions of interactants. The term, status, is employed here broadly, whether in the symbolic sense of "importance," "worth," and "respectability," or in the practical sense of formal position and control. The role of relative status positions has been examined in terms of an **asymmetric power structure** (Brewer & Miller, 1984), or **power differentials** (Sachdev & Bourhis, 1985, 1987). Studies with the "minimal intergroup situation" (e.g, Brewer, 1979; Turner, 1978) have generally indicated that differential treatment of groups by the experimenter increases interethnic conflict in the form of unfavorable discrimination against outgroup members. Other studies (e.g., Sachdev & Bourhis, 1985, 1987) report a significant increase in unfavorable outgroup discrimination when the perceived power differentials are greater, particularly among those who hold equal or superior positions.

The conditions reviewed here provide insights into the interactionsituation and its potential influence on the encoding and decoding patterns. Collectively, these conditions provide a profile of the immediate milieu where communicators engage in associative or dissociative behaviors. Such insights provide a basis on which a multicultural classroom, for example, can be designed and managed to facilitate a harmonious milieu for cooperative learning and socializing.

The Environment

As previously discussed, social psychological studies have studied interethnic relations focusing primarily on the first two levels of communication context–psychological and situational. In this section, some of the key concepts characterizing the environmental context discussed primarily in sociological literature are identified. Each of these conditions are relevant to various sublevels of the social environment from the national (and international) environments to neighborhoods and organizations. Directly or indirectly, these conditions influence, and are influenced by, all other conditions of the commmunication system we have discussed so far.

Institutional Equity/Inequity

One of the environmental factors crucial to understanding many of the contemporary incidents of interethnic conflict is the history of the interethnic relations. Particularly crucial in this regard is the **history of subjugation** of one ethnic group by another. Often, subjugation has taken the form of political, economic, or cultural domination through slavery, colonization, or military conquest. As Tagil (1984) argues, ethnic conflict can be explained based on the principle of "ethnoregionalism" in historical and geographical contexts. In this view, interethnic conflict is a conflict concerning the rights of an ethnic group to influence or control development within a certain state or region. Members of a historically subjugated group are likely to feel they have the right to live on or possess territory that the group has traditionally claimed as its own. Any historical injustice from the viewpoint of such a group cannot be easily erased from the collective memory, contributing to dissociative behavioral tendencies in contemporary interethnic encounters.

Many historical accounts have been written on the topic of colonizationand the subsequent influences on interethnic discrimination and mistrust. In the case of the West Indies immigrants living in England, for instance, the "imperial mythology" and the hegemonic tendencies of Whites against non-White immigrants have been observed to be prevalent today (cf. Rex, 1976; Richmond, 1986; Stone, 1985). Likewise, influences of subjugation history on contemporary interethnic power relationships can also be found in many other societies, including the situations of Native Americans and Blacks in the United States, Koreans in Japan, Palestinians in Israel, and French-speaking Canadians in Quebec.

The contemporary institutional inequity is reflected in patterns of the **stratification** of ethnic groups by socioeconomic class. Some have argued that capitalistic economic systems exploit ethnic minorities (cf. Wolpe, 1986). Hechter (1975) uses the term, **internal colonialism**, to explain a structural (or institutionalized) discrimination in the division of labor imposed on the "peripheral regions" (such as ethnic minorities) of a country, so that core or dominant regions keep for themselves the major manufacturing, commercial, and banking roles and delegate to the peripheral regions the least profitable kinds of work. Walker & Pettigrew (1984) theorized that, under an inequitable societal condition, subordinate groups' ethnic actions express their comparative feelings of dissatisfaction, or **fraternalistic relative deprivation**, along with claims to social parity over the political, economic, social, and cultural structures of the society (Baker, 1983; Blalock, 1982). Rigid socioeconomic stratification along ethnic lines are also emphasized in Tajfel's (1978) social identity theory of intergroup relations. Tajfel places particular emphasis on structural conflicts of interest between social groups as a critical determinant of "category salience" in intergroup interaction.

Interethnic inequity is often reflected in the **laws and rules** of a given society. Laws and rules mirror the majority of the citizens' acceptance as a form of the status quo ("the way things are"). Changes in institutional inequity in a given society accompany changes in the laws or other judicial actions. Societies such as the United States and Canada have undergone a significant transformation toward an increasing equity among its majority and minority groups. There has been a series of legal actions such as the U.S. Supreme Court's 1954 ruling against racially segregated public schools. Many of these formal barriers persist, as demonstrated by the continuing patterns of intense racial discrimination in housing. Yet enough progress has been made in some institutions, notably in education and employment, to introduce a second generation set of less formal obstacles to ethnic minority inclusion (Pettigrew & Martin, 1989).

Closely associated with the interethnic equity in the laws and rules of a society or subsociety is its "mainstream" cultural and political **ideology**. The ideology of a given social system is mirrored in its **official language policies** (such as monolingualism and bilingualism) and by mainstream institutions such as the government, mass media, and educational system. **Mass media practices**, in particular, have been examined for the stereotypes and prejudices they carry to the public (Corea, 1990; Van Dijk, 1987, 1988, 1991; Wilson & Gutierrez, 1985).

Some societies may legitimize discriminatory actions against certain minority groups, while other societies may prohibit and even punish such actions. Each of the often used terms such as "assimilationism," "pluralism," "integrationism," and "separatism," as well as popular expressions such as "racist society," "institutional racism," "ethnic purge," "ethnic genocide," "melting pot," "ethnic mosaic," "tossed salad," and "political correctness" represents a certain ideological view. Western European nations (Australia, Britain, Canada, France, Germany, the United States, and Switzerland) have expanded a range of language and cultural programs to promote "multiculturalism" while providing opportunities for learning the mainstream culture and language (Ireland, 1994). Comparatively, largely monoethnic non-Western societies have had a long-standing governmental policy to segregate foreigners and ethnic minorities from the natives. In Japan, for example, few foreign-born residents have been granted citizenship and relevant political rights. Such exclusionary policy applies even to the approximately 700,000 Koreans in Japan whose families have been born and have lived in the country over several generations (Williams, 1992).

Institutional inequity in a given society may be intensified in times of **stress** (Volkan, 1992), that is, when the society undergoes certain challenging circumstances caused by economic hardship, shortage of resources, or involvement in an international crisis. Olzak and Nagel (1986) and Olzak (1987) observe that such environmental stress tends to intensify competitive intergroup relations. Others have argued that, under stressful circumstances, more than the usual level of dissociative interethnic behaviors are enacted (Stone, 1985; Volkan, 1992).

Ethnic Group Strength

In addition to the overall structural inequity in an environment that involves a communicator, the literature suggests a linkage between the collective strength of the communicator's ethnic group, political and otherwise, to his or her associative or dissociative interethnic communication behaviors. As the ethnic group becomes stronger in its relative status or power, the communicator's relative status in a given interethnic encounter is likely to become stronger as well. In turn, an increased ethnic group strength tends to change the condition of the power differential between interaction partners. A stronger ethnic group is further likely to encourage the maintenance of ethnicity and ethnic identity in the individual and discourage assimilation into the society at large (Breton, Isajiw, Kalbach, & Reitz, 1990; Kim, 1988, in press).

The linkage between ethnic group strength and associative or dissociativecommunication behavior is empirically supported by a recent study of Greek and Italian ethnic groups in Australia. Gallois and Pittam (1991) report that adolescents in the well-organized Greek community place more emphasis on their ethnic identity and maintaining their heritage than their Italian counterparts whose community is less cohesive. The study also shows that Greek-Australian adolescents place less emphasis on adapting to the dominant Australian culture at large.

Sociologists have provided further explanations of differential ethnicgroup strengths according to evolutionary stages. Clarke and Obler (1976), for example, theorize that ethnic action evolves in a three-stage development: (1) the initial stage of the **economic development** which occurs upon arrival of the group until they become an integral part of the permanent economy; (2) the second stage of community building, or the development of community **leadership** and **institutional resources** used to assert the group's interests; (3) the third stage of **aggressive self-assertion** that develops into the group's conventional use of the existing political system. As an ethnic group grows from its initial, economic adjustment stage to the later stages of community building and political self-assertion, it increasingly shows a collective strength with which it may manipulate its cultural identity or ethnicity for the benefit of the group's interests. Breton (1964), Keyes (1981), and Marwell, Oliver and Prahl (1988) have articulated similar views on the developmental process of ethnic groups and their increased political mobilization to assert and protect their collective interests.

Crucial to the developmental process of ethnic groups are the functions of **ethnic communication systems** including ethnic media and community organizations such as churches and social clubs. As Marwell et al. (1988) observe in their theory of the "critical mass," the potential for organizing a group depends on the social ties in the group through which collective actions are made possible. Development of ethnic media are crucial to the information gathering and dissemination throughout an ethnic community, facilitating and maintaining the group's collective identity. In this process, the ethnic media act as the group's spokesperson and liaison to the larger society (Kim, 1988, in press).

A similar social psychological concept, **ethnolinguistic vitality** or "objective ethnolinguistic vitality" (compared with the "subjective ethnolinguistic vitality" concept discussed previously), has been extensively investigated as an important characteristic of ethnic group strength (cf. Giles et al. 1977; Giles, Rosenthal, & Young, 1985). This phenomenon has been assessed by Giles, et al. (1977) based on: (1) the status of a language in a community; (2) the absolute and relative number of its locuters (demographic characteristics); (3) the institutional support (e.g., governmental services, schools, mass media) for the language. Linking this concept to intergroup relations theory (Tajfel, 1974) and speech accommodation theory (Giles, 1977; Giles & Smith, 1979), Giles et al. (1977) theorized that the vitality of an ethnic language, in conjunction with the interactants' power differentials, influences their convergent or divergent speech behaviors. For example, a speaker who perceives the subordinate position of his or her group as illegitimate would be more likely to diverge from the speech patterns of the interaction partner.

Another social psychological explanation was provided by Blalock (1982) supporting the present theoretical linkage between subordinate group strength and interethnic conflict. In explaining the motivational basis of taking actions in interethnic conflict situations, Blalock presented two key concepts—Subjective Expected Utilities (SEU) and Subjective Probability (SP). Blalock views individuals as "rational" actors who enact behaviors based on SEU and SP, Blalock proposed that ethnic individuals will make behavioral choices if: (1) they attach subjective values to the goals or outcomes of a certain behavior (such as avoiding or engaging in conflict); (2) if their subjective utility associated with the behavior is high (i.e., a behavior will be enacted if it involves a high subjective probability). Applying these two conditions to interethnic encounters, we can infer that, when there is a disagreement or conflict of interest in an encounter, the communicator whose ethnic group strength is greater is more likely to engage in dissociative encoding and decoding behaviors as such actions are perceived to be desirable (or higher in SEU) and effectual (or higher in SP).

Interethnic Contact

Research has examined the environmental conditions for interethnic communication in terms of the extent of contact between different ethnic groups. Arrangements such as integrated schools and neighborhoods in urban centers allow for maximum contact and interaction, while others such as ethnic neighborhoods and certain exclusive social clubs provide the least amount of **interaction potential** in one's personal network (Kim, 1986, 1987). Since segregated settings do not allow opportunities for communication, they have been viewed to negatively contribute to interethnic relations by cementing any existing hostility or prejudice (Worchel, 1979). Frequent contact, on the other hand, has been viewed to provide opportunities for reducing conflict and promoting understanding, as postulated in the contact hypothesis (Amir, 1969).

This linkage between **segregation** and conflict, or between contact and reduced conflict, has been a main theoretical source for the proponents of school and neighborhood integration. Relatedly, a recent phenomenological study by Lanigan (1988) identifies **"isolational polarization"** in poor, urban centers. An example of this phenomenon, according to Lanigan, is the growth and development of the Black Muslim movement in the United States:

> Under the dissident, and eventually estranged, leadership of Malcolm X, the militancy of the Black Muslims reached what may be called the "crisis level" of isolational polarization. The followers of Malcolm X preferred to be left alone and were willing to kill those who would interfere with their desire for privacy. (p. 13)

The picture provided by research, however, is not so straightforward. Research has shown that, at least in the short run, intergroup contact is just as likely to heighten conflict as it is to reduce it. Worchel (1979), for example, reported that, in some cases, integrated apartment buildings led to a decrease in favorable racial attitudes. Although it appears that contact alone may not be a sufficient condition for conflict reduction, it is likely to reduce conflict in the long run. Similarly, segregation is likely to increase interethnic conflict in the long run, as it discourages ethnic groups from reducing their stereotypical perceptions and ingroup biases. A more definitive theoretical insight can be obtained only through longitudinal studies of perceptual, attitudinal, and behavioral changes over time.

The conditions of institutional inequity, subordinate group strength, and interethnic contact discussed above influence (and are influenced by) the

Table 2. Dimensions, factors, and indicators of the context of interethnic communication.

Dimensions	Factors	Associated Concepts
The Communicator	Cognitive Structure	Cognitive Complexity
		Category Width
	Identity	Ingroup Loyalty
		Psychological Distinctiveness
		Identity Security/Insecurity
		Intercultural Identity
		Openness/Strength
	Bias	Predjudice
		Ingroup Favoritism
		Ethnocentrism
		Hostility
		Discrimination
		Racism
The Situation	Interethnic Heterogeneity	Cultural/Behavioral Difference
		Cultural/Behavioral Compatibility
	Interethnic Salience	Distinctiveness of Ethnic Markers
		Solo Effect
	Interaction Structure	Superordinate Goal
		Interpersonal/Cooperative Orientation
		Power Differential
The Environment	Institutional Equity	History of Subjugation
		Internal Colonialism
		Ethnic Stratification
		Fraternalistic Relative Deprivation
		Laws/Rules
		Cultural Ideology
		Language Policy
		Media Practice
		Environmental Stress
	Ethnic Group Strength	Economic Development
		Leadership/Institutional Resources
		Collective Self-Assertion
		Ethnic Communication System
		Ethnolinguistic Vitality
	Interethnic Contact	Interaction Potential
		Segregation/Contact

intermediary-level situational conditions—ethnic heterogeneity, ethnic salience, and interaction structure. These macro-environmental conditions provide a tentative profile of an environment that facilitates or hinders the associative (or dissociative) interethnic behaviors of each communicator. *Table 2* summarizes the key concepts associated with each of the three layers of the context of interethnic communication—the communicator, the situation, and the environment. These contextual factors are inseparably linked to associative and dissociative communication behaviors (encoding and decoding).

Conclusion

In this essay, various concepts, theories, and research findings salient in the social science literature and pertinent to understanding and explaining interethnic communication have been incorporated into a multilayered, interactive model (Figure 1). This model and the constituent dimensions and factors (Tables 1 and 2) offer an organizing scheme for integrating the rich and often disjointed theoretical and empirical insights that are currently available. Grounded in the systems methodology, the present model depicts interethnic communication in a matrix of hierarchically arranged factors of the behavior and the context that are linked in reciprocal functional relationships.

The model is a "generic" one in the sense that the constituent dimensions and factors are universally applicable to all interethnic communication events. Of course, each encounter presents a unique circumstance in which some factors in the model may be of greater relevance and play a more prominent role than others. Even a single factor, such as a personality attribute of the communicator, may be so powerful as to overshadow every other force operating in a given encounter. Such would be the case when two individuals respond to an identical set of situational and environmental conditions in vastly different manners. What the present model offers, then, is an analytic framework according to which we can survey the entire "field" of a given interethnic encounter systematically and comprehensively. The dimensions and factors identified in the model illuminate, and direct our attention to, specific behavioral and contextual factors that **potentially** influence, and are influenced by, the associative or dissociative communication behavior. Once we examine all of the constituent dimensions and factors in a specific interethnic encounter, we can zero in on those factors that are most salient and significant to understanding and explaining that event.

In addition to guiding our analysis, the model serves as a framework for pragmatic action. It suggests various ways to achieve specific patterns of behavior, situation, and environment that we desire. For instance, we can infer from the model that, by changing certain existing conditions in the environment, we can help facilitate associative communication behaviors among individuals. Conversely, by facilitating associative behaviors, we can expect to improve the conditions of interethnic relations in an organization, community, and ultimately society at large. We can expect further that, when a situation is such that all involved parties aspire to a common goal, they are likely to engage in more associative behaviors.

More work is needed to refine and elaborate the present model. Improvements can be made on this mapping so as to describe and explain the infinitely varied ways in which interethnic communication is enacted with greater consistency, specificity, and realism. Questions also need to be raised about the long-term role of associative or dissociative communication behavior. While we generally prefer associative behaviors to dissociative behaviors, we must recognize that dissociative behaviors are desirable and even necessary for "forcing" a change in the existing rules of interethnic communication and bringing about a more equitable long-term relationship between individuals and groups. The "problem" of interethnic conflict and dissociative communication may be little more than a function of a particular ideological viewpoint, a lack of tolerance for ambiguity, or short-sightedness (Ruben, 1978). As much as dissociative behavior can serve as a destabilizing force in human systems, it may serve as a crucial force for a defense against their stagnation, detachment, and entropy. The "problematic" interethnic communication, indeed, offers opportunities for new learning and growth of all sides involved. At least in the United States, interethnic conflict experiences clearly have brought the society to new stages of self-awareness and a broadened democracy despite the many temporary stresses and pains that such experiences have introduced (Himes, 1974).

Determinations as to whether a conflict is good or bad may not need to be based on how it feels to social scientists, a particular ethnic person or group, or even to the public at large. Instead, they must be assessed based on what functions a conflict serves for the evolutionary change in the communicator, the situation, the society, and even the international community as a whole. This theoretical placement of conflict in the context of long-term adaptation and change in communication systems can be particularly profitable for the purpose of developing social and personal mechanisms for building communities of diversity. The growth-facilitating nature of problematic communication experiences also offers profound implications for a long-term transformation of individuals in multiethnic societies as well (Kim, 1988, 1995, in press; Kim, Lujan, & Shaver, 1996).

With these and related issues remaining to be explored, the present model is offered as a step forward in the continuing movement toward greater comprehensiveness and realism in understanding and exlaining interethnic relations. As such, the model makes the point of looking at the entire field of interethnic communication, where the behavior meets the context as two correlatives of a single reality.

References

Adler, P. (1982). Beyond cultural identity: Reflections on cultural and multicultural man. In L. Samovar & R. Porter (Eds.), *Intercultural Communication: A reader* (3rd ed., pp. 389-408). Belmont, CA: Wadsworth.

Adorno, T. W. (1950). *The authoritarian personality*. New York: Harper.

Adono, T., Frenkel-Brunswik, E., Levinson, D., & Sanford, R. (1950). *The authoritarian personality*. New York: Harper.

Allen, I. (1983). *The language of ethnic conflict: Social organization and lexical culture*. New York: Columbia University Press.

Allport, G. (1954). *The nature of prejudice*. Reading, MA: Addison-Wesley.

Amir, Y. (1969). Contact hypothesis in ethnic relations. *Psychological Bulletin, 7*(5), 319-342.

Applegate, J., & Delia, J. (1980). Person-centered speech, psychological development, and the context of language usage. In R. St. Clair & H. Giles (Eds.), *The social and psychological contexts of language* (pp. 245-282). Hillsdale, NJ: Lawrence Erlbaum.

Applegate, J., & Sypher, H. (1988). A constructivist theory of communication and culture. In Y. Kim & W. Gudykunst (Eds.), *Theories in intercultural Communication* (pp. 41-65). Newbury Park, CA: Sage.

Baker, D. (1983). *Race, ethnicity and power*. Boston, MA: Routledge.

Banks, S., Ge, G., & Baker, J. (1991). Intercultural encounters and miscommunication. In N. Coupland, H. Giles, & J. Wiemann (Eds.), *"Miscommunication" and problematic talk* (pp. 103-120). Newbury Park, CA: Sage.

Bateson, G. (1972). *Steps to an ecology of mind*. New York: Ballantine Books.

Berkowitz, L. (1962). *Aggression: A social psychological analysis*. New York: McGraw-Hill.

Berry, J. (1970). Marginality, stress & ethnic identification in an acculturated aboriginal community. *Journal of Cross-Cultural Psychology, 1*, 239-252.

Berry, J., Kim, U., & Boski, J. (1988). Psychological acculturation of immigrants. In Y. Kim & W. Gudykunst (Eds.), *Cross-cultural adaptation: Current approaches* (pp. 62-87). Newbury Park, CA: Sage.

Bertalanffy, L. (1955/1975). General system theory. In B. D. Ruben & J. Y. Kim (Eds.), *General systems theory and human communication* (pp. 6-32). Rachelle Park, NJ: Hayden Book.

Billig, M. (1987). *Arguing and thinking: A rhetorical approach to social psychology*. New York: Cambridge University Press.

Billig, M., Condon, S., Edwards, D., Gane, M., Middleton, D., & Radley, A. (1988). *Ideological dilemmas*. Newbury Park, CA: Sage.

Blalock, H. (1982). *Race and ethnic relations*. Englewood Cliffs, NJ: Prentice-Hall.

Bourhis, R. (1979). Language in ethnic interaction: A social psychological approach. In H. Giles & B. Saint-Jacques (Eds.), *Language and ethnic relations* (pp. 117-141). New York: Pergamon.

Bourhis, R., Giles, H., Leyens, J., & Tajfel, H. (1979). Psychological distinctiveness: Language divergence in Belgium. In H. Giles & R. St Clair (Eds.), *Language and social psychology* (pp. 158-185). Oxford, England: Blackwell.

Breton, R. (1964). Institutional completeness of ethnic communities and the personal relations of immigrants. *American Journal of Sociology, 70*(2), 193-205.

Breton, R., Isajiw, W., Kalbach, W., & Reitz, J. (1990). *Ethnic identity and equality: Varieties of experiences in a Canadian city.* Toronto: University of Toronto Press.

Brewer, M. (1979). Ingroup bias in the minimal intergroup situation: A cognitive-motivational analysis. *Psychologicla Bulletin, 86,* 307-324.

Brewer, M. (1986). The role of ethnocentrism in intergroup conflict. In S. Worchel & W. Austin (Eds.), *Psychology of intergroup relations* (2nd ed., pp. 288-304). Chicago: Nelson-Hall.

Brewer, M., & Campbell, D. (1976). *Ethnocentrism and intergroup attitudes: East African evidence.* New York: John Wiley & Sons.

Brewer, M., & Miller, N. (1984). Beyond the contact hypothesis: Theoretical perspectives on desegregation. In N. Miller & M. Brewer (Eds.), *Groups in contact: The psychology of desegregation* (pp. 281-302). New York: Academic Press.

Brewer, M., & Miller, N. (1988). Contact and cooperation: When do they work? In P. Katz & D. Taylor (Eds.), *Eliminating racism* (pp. 315-326). Newbury Park, CA: Sage.

Brown, P., & Turner, J. (1981). Interpersonal and intergroup behavior. In J. Turner & H. Giles (Eds.), *Intergroup behavior* (pp. 33-65). Chicago: University of Chicago Press.

Burleson, B. (1987). Cognitive complexity. In J. McCrosky & J. Daley (Eds.), *Personality and interpersonal communication* (pp. 305-349). Beverly Hills, CA: Sage.

Carbaugh, D. (Ed.). (1990). *Cultural communication and intercultural contact.* Hillsdale, NJ: Lawrence Erlbaum.

Clarke, S., & Obler, J. (1976). Ethnic conflict, community-building, and the emergence of ethnic political traditions in the United States. In S. Clarke & J. Obler (Eds.), *Urban ethnic conflicts: A comparative perspective* (pp. 1-34). Chapel Hill, NC: University of North Carolina Press.

Clément, R., & Noels, K. (1991, August). *Ethnolinguistic vitality, language and identity.* Paper presented at the 4th International Conference on Language and Social Psychology, Santa Barbara, CA.

Collier, M., & Thomas, M. (1988). Cultural identity: An interpretive perspective. In Y. Kim & W. Gudykunst (Eds.), *Theories in intercultural communication* (pp. 99-120). Newbury Park, CA: Sage.

Corea, A. (1990). Racism in the American way of media. In J. Downing, A. Mohammadi, & Sreberny-Mohammadi, A. (Eds.), *Questioning the media: A critical introduction* (pp. 255-266). Newbury Park, CA: Sage.

Cronen, V., Chen, V., & Pearce, W. (1988). Coordinated management of meaning: A critical theory. In Y. Kim & W. Gudykunst (Eds.), *Theories in intercultural communication* (pp. 66-98). Newbury Park, CA: Sage.

Daniel, J., & Smitherman, G. (1990). How I got over: Communication dynamics in the black community. In D. Carbaugh (Ed.), *Cultural communication and intercultural contact* (pp. 25-40). Hillsdale, NJ: Lawrence Erlbaum.

De Vos, G. A. (1990a). Self in society: A multilevel, psychocultural analysis. In G. A. De Vos & M. Suárez-Orozco (Eds.), *Status inequality: The self in culture* (pp. 17-74). Newbury Park, CA: Sage.

De Vos, G. A. (1990b). Conflict and accommodation in ethnic interaction. In G. A. De Vos & M. Suárez-Orozco (Eds.), *Status inequality: The self in culture* (pp. 204-245). Newbury Park, CA: Sage.

Delia, J. (1976). A constructivist analysis of the concept of credibility. *Quarterly Journal of Speech, 63*, 66-83.

Detweiler, R. (1986). Categorization, attribution and intergroup communication. In W. Gudykunst (Ed.), *Intergroup communication* (pp. 62-73). London: Edward Arnold.

Essed, P. (1991). *Understanding everyday racism.* Newbury Park, CA: Sage.

Feldman, R. S. (1985). Nonverbal behavior, race, and the classroom teacher. *Theory into Practice, 24*, 45-49.

Ford, D. H., & Lerner, R. M. (1992). *Developmental systems theory: An integrative approach.* Newbury Park, CA: Sage.

Francis, E. (1976). *Interethnic relations.* New York: Elsevier.

Gadfields, N., Giles, H., Bourhis, R. Y., & Tajfel, H. (1979). Dynamics of humor in ethnic group relations. *Ethnicity, 6*, 373-382.

Gallois, C., Franklyn, A., Giles, H., & Coupland, N. (1988). Communication accommodation in intercultural encounters. In Y. Kim & W. Gudykunst (Eds.), *Theories in intercultural communication* (pp. 157-185). Newbury Park, CA: Sage.

Gallois, C., Giles, H., Jones, E., Cargile, A., & Ota, H. (1995). Accommodating intercultural encounters: Elaborations and extentions. In R. L. Wiseman (Ed.), *Intercultural communication theory (pp. 115-147).* Thousand Oaks, CA: Sage.

Gallois, C., & Pittam, J. (1991, May). *Ethnolinguistic vitality in multicultural/monolingual Australia: Perceptions of Vietnamese and Anglo-Australians.* Paper presented at the annual conference of the International Communication Association, Chicago, IL.

Gass, S., & Varonis, E. (1991). Miscommunication in nonnative speaker discourse. In N. Coupland, H. Giles, & J. Wiemann (Eds.), *"Miscommunication" and problematic talk* (pp. 121-145). Newbury Park, CA: Sage.

Giles, H. (1977). Social psychology and applied linguistics: Towards an integrative approach. *ITL: Review of Applied Linguistics, 33*, 27-42.

Giles, H., & Bourhis, R. (1976). Voice and social organisation in Britain. *Communication Monographs, 43*, 108-114.

Giles, H., Bourhis, R., & Taylor, D. (1977). Towards a theory of language in ethnic group relations. In H. Giles (Ed.), *Language, ethnicity and intergroup relations* (pp. 307-348). London: Academic Press.

Giles, H., & Johnson, P. (1986). Perceived threat, ethnic commitment, and interethnic language behavior. In Y. Kim (Ed.), *Interethnic communication* (pp. 91-116). Newbury Park, CA: Sage.

Giles, H., & Johnson, P. (1987). Ethnolinguistic identity theory: A social psychological approach to language maintenance. *International Journal of the Sociology of Language, 68,* 69-99.
Giles, H., Mulac, A., Bradac, J., & Johnson, P. (1987). Speech accommodation theory: The first decade and beyond. In M. McLaughlin (Ed.), *Communication yearbook 10.* Newbury Park, CA: Sage.
Giles, H.. Rosenthal, D. A., & Young, L. (1985). Perceived ethnolinguistic vitality: The Anglo- and Greek-Australian setting. *Journal of Multilingual and Multicultural Development, 6,* 253-269.
Giles, H., & Saint-Jacques, B. (Eds.). (1979). *Language and ethnic relations.* New York: Pergamon Press.
Giles, H., & Smith, P. (1979). Accommodation theory: Optimal levels of convergence. In H. Giles & R. St. Clair, *Language and social psychology* (pp. 45-65). Oxford, England: Blackwell.
Gittler, J. (1974). Cultural pluralism in contemporary American society: An analysis and a proposal. *International Journal of Group Relations, 4*(3), 322-345.
Givón, T. (1989). *Mind, code and context.* Hillsdale, NJ: Lawrence Earlbaum.
Glazer, N., & Moynihan, D. (1975). *Ethnicity: Theory and experience.* Cambridge, MA: Harvard University Press.
Gordon, M. (1981). Models of pluralism: The new American dilemma. *Annals of the American Academy of Political and Social Science, 454,* 178-188.
Gudykunst, W. (Ed.). (1988a). *Language and ethnic identity.* Clevedon, England: Multilingual Matters.
Gudykunst, W. (1988b). Uncertainty and anxiety. In Y. Kim & W. Gudykunst (Eds.), *Theories in intercultural communication.* Newbury Park, CA: Sage.
Gudykunst, W., & Lim, T. (1986). A perspective for the study of intergroup communication. In W. Gudykunst (Ed.), *Intergroup communication* (pp. 1-9). Baltimore, MD: Edward Arnold.
Gumperz, J. (1978). The conversational analysis of interethnic communication. In E. Ross (Ed.), *Interethnic communication* (pp. 13-31). Athens, GA: The University of Georgia Press.
Gumperz, J., & Cook-Gumperz, J. (1982). Introduction: Language and the communication of social identity. In J. Gumperz (Ed.), *Language and social identity* (pp. 1-21). New York: Cambridge University Press.
Hall, E. (1976). *Beyond culture.* New York: Anchor Books.
Hall, E. (1983). *The dance of life.* New York: Anchor Books.
Hamilton, D., Sherman, S., & Ruvolo, C. (1990). Stereotype-based expectancies: Effects on information processing and social behavior. *Journal of Social Issues, 46*(2), 35-59.
Hechter, M. (1975). *Internal colonialism: The Celtic fringe in British national development, 1536-1966.* Berkeley, CA: University of California Press.
Heider, F. (1958). *The psychology of interpersonal relations.* New York: Wiley.

Hewstone, M., & Giles, H. (1986). Social groups and social stereotypes in intergroup communication: A review and model of intergroup communication breakdown. In W. Gudykunst (Ed.), *Intergroup communication* (pp. 10-26). London: Edward Arnold.

Himes, J. (1974). *Racial and ethnic relations.* Dubuque, IA: William C. Brown.

Hopper, R. (1986). Speech evaluation of intergroup dialect differences: The shibboleth schema. In W. Gudykunst (Ed.), *Intergroup communication* (pp. 127-136). London: Edward Arnold.

Hsu, F. (1971). *The challenge of the American dream: The Chinese in the United States.* Belmont, CA: Wadsworth.

Ireland, P. (1994). *The policy challenge of ethnic diversity.* Cambridge, MA: Harvard University Press.

Jaspars, J., & Hewstone, M. (1982). Cross-cultural interaction, social attribution and inter-group relations. In S. Bochner (Ed.), *Cultures in contact* (pp. 127-156). Elmsford, NY: Pergamon.

Kelly, G. (1955). *The psychology of personal constructs.* New York: W. W. Norton.

Keyes, C. (1981). The dialectic of ethnic change. In C. Keyes (Ed.), *Ethnic change* (pp. 3-30). Seattle, WA: University of Washington Press.

Kim, Y. Y. (1986). Understanding the social context of intergroup communication: A personal network theory. In W. Gudykunst (Ed.), *Intergroup communication* (pp. 86-95). London: Edward Arnold.

Kim, Y. Y. (1987). Facilitating immigrant adaptation: The role of communication. In T. Albrecht & M. Adelman (Eds.), *Communicating social support* (pp. 192-211). Newbury Park, CA: Sage.

Kim, Y. (1988). *Communication and cross-cultural adaptation: An integrative theory.* Clevedon, England: Multilingual Matters.

Kim, Y. (1989). Interethnic conflict: An interdisciplinary review. In J. Gittler (Ed.), *The annual review of conflict knowledge and conflict resolution* (Vol. 1, pp. 101-125). New York: Garland.

Kim, Y. (1991). Intercultural communication competence. In S. Ting-Toomey & F. Korzenny (Eds.), *Cross-cultural interpersonal communication* (pp. 259-275). Newbury Park, CA: Sage.

Kim, Y. (1992). Synchrony and intercultural communication. In D. Crookall & K. Arai (Eds.), *Global interdependence: Simulation and gaming perspectives* (pp. 99-105). New York: Springer-Verlag.

Kim, Y. (1994). Interethnic communication: The context and the behavior. In S. Deetz (Ed.), *Communication yearbook 17* (pp. 511-538). Newbury Park, CA: Sage.

Kim, Y. (1995). Identity development: From cultural to intercultural. In H. B. Mokros (Ed.), *Information and behavior, Vol. 5. Interaction and identity* (pp. 347-369). New Brunswick, NJ: Transaction.

Kim, Y. (in press). *Becoming intercultural: An integrative theory of communication and cross-cultural adaptation.* Thousand Oaks, CA: Sage.

Kim, Y., Lujan, P., & Shaver, L. (1996, May). *"I can walk both ways": Identity integration of American Indians in Oklahoma*. Paper presented at the annual conference of the International Communication Association, Chicago.

Kirkland, S., Greenberg, J., & Pysczynski, T. (1987). Further evidence of the deterious effects of overheard DELs: Derogation beyond the target. *Personality and Social Psychological Bulletin, 13*, 126-227.

Kochman, T. (1981). *Black and white styles in conflict*. Chicago: University of Chicago Press.

Kochman, T. (1986). Black verbal dueling strategies in interethnic communication. In Y. Kim (Ed.), *Interethnic communication: Current research* (pp. 136-157). Newbury Park, CA: Sage.

Lambert, W. (1979). Language as a factor in intergroup relations. In H. Giles & R. St. Clair (Eds.), *Language and social psychology* (pp. 186-192). Baltimore, MD: University Park Press.

Landry, R., Allard, R. (1991, August). *Ethnolinguistic vitality and substractive identity*. Paper presented at the 4th International Conference on Language and Social Psychology, Santa Barbara, CA.

Langer, E. (1989). *Mindfulness*. Reading, MA: Addison-Wesley.

Lanigan, R. L. (1988). *Phenomenology of communication: Merleau-Ponty's thematics in communicology and semiology*. Pittsburgh, PA: Duquesne University Press.

Lukens, J. (1979). Interethnic conflict and communicative distance. In H. Giles & B. Saint-Jacques (Eds.), *Language and ethnic relations* (pp. 143-158). New York: Pergamon.

Marwell, G., Oliver, P., & Prahl, R. (1988, November). Social networks and collective action: A theory of the critical mass. III. *American Journal of Sociology, 94*(3), 502-534.

McConahay, J., & Hough, J. (1976). Symbolic racism. *Journal of Social Issues, 32*, 23-45.

Milner, D. (1973). Racial identification and preference in "black" British children. *European Journal of Social Psychology, 3*, 281-295.

Nash, M. (1989). *The cauldron of ethnicity in the modern world*. Chicago: University of Chicago Press.

Oddou, G., & Mendenhall, M. (1984). Person perception in cross-cultural settings. *International Journal of Intercultural Relations, 8*, 77-96.

Olzak, S. (1987). Causes of ethnic conflict and protest in urban America, 1877-1889. *Social Science Research, 16*, 185-210.

Olzak, S., & Nagel, J. (Eds.). (1986). *Competitive ethnic relations*. New York: Academic Press.

Opotow, S. (1990). Moral exclusion and injustice. *Journal of Social Issues, 46*(1), 1-20.

Peng, F. (1974). Communicative distance. *Language Sciences, 31*, 32-38.

Pettigrew, T. (1979). The ultimate attribution error: Extending Allport's cognitive analysis of prejudice. *Personality and Social Psychology Bulletin, 5*, 461-476.

Pettigrew, T., & Martin, J. (1989). Organizational inclusion of minority groups: A social psychological analysis. In J. Van Oudenhoven & T. Willemsen (Eds.), *Ethnic minorities: Social psychological perspectives* (pp. 169-200). Berwyn, PA: Swets North America.

Philipsen, G. (1989). Speech and the communal function in four cultures. In S. Ting-Toomey & F. Korzenny (Eds.), *Language, communication, and culture* (pp. 79-92). Newbury Park, CA: Sage.

Phinney, J., & Rosenthal, D. (1992). Ethnic identity in adolescence: Process, context, and outcome. In G. Adams, T. Gullota, & R. Montemayor (Eds.), *Adolescent identity formation* (pp. 145-172). Newbury Park, CA: Sage.

Phinney, J. (1993). Multiple group identities: Differentiation, conflict, and integration. In J. Kroger (Ed.), *Discussions on ego identity* (pp. 47-73). Hillsdale, NJ: Lawrence Earlbaum.

Rapoport, A. (1975). Modern systems theory—An outlook for coping with change. In B. D. Ruben & J. Y. Kim (Eds.), *General systems theory and human communication* (pp. 33-51). Rachelle Park, NJ: Hayden Book.

Rex, J. (1976). Racial conflict in the city: The experiences of Birmingham, England from 1952-1975. In S. Clarke & J. Obler (Eds.), *Urban ethnic conflict: A comparative perspective* (pp. 132-163). Chapel Hill, NC: University of North Carolina Press.

Richmond, A. (1986). Racial conflict in Britain. *Contemporary Sociology, 9*(2), 184-187.

Ross, E. L. (Ed.). (1978). *Interethnic communication*. Athens, GA: University of Georgia Press.

Ross, J. (1979). Language and the mobilization of ethnic identity. In H. Giles & B. Saint-Jacques (Eds.), *Language and ethnic relations* (pp. 1-13). New York: Pergamon.

Ross, L. (1977). The intuitive psychologist and his shortcomings: Distortions in the attribution process. In L. Berkowitz (Ed.), *Advances in experimental social psychology* (Vol. 10, pp. 174-220). New York: Academic Press.

Ruben, B. D. (1975). Intrapersonal, interpersonal, and mass communication processes in individual and multi-person systems. In B. D. Ruben & J. Y. Kim (Eds.), *General systems theory and human communication* (pp. 164-190). Rochelle Park, NJ: Hayden Book.

Ruben, B. D. (1978). Communication and conflict: A system-theoretic perspective. *Quarterly Journal of Speech, 64*, 211-232.

Ruesch, J., & Bateson, G. (1968). *Communication: The social matrix of psychiatry*. New York: W. W. Norton.

Sachdev, I., & Bourhis, R. (1985). Social categorization and power differentials in group relations. *European Journal of Social Psychology, 15*, 415-434.

Sachdev, I., & Bourhis, R. (1987). Status differentials and intergroup behavior. *European Journal of Social Psychology, 17*, 277-293.

Sarbaugh, L. (1988). *Intercultural communication* (2nd ed.). New Brunswick, NJ: Hayden Books.
Smith, A. (1981). *The ethnic revival in the modern world*. Cambridge, England: Cambridge University Press.
Smitherman-Donaldson, G., & Van Dijk, T. (Eds.). (1988). *Discourse and discrimination*. Detroit, MI: Wayne State University Press.
Stephan, W., & Stephan, C. (1985). Intergroup anxiety. *Journal of Social Issues, 41*(3), 157-175.
Stone, J. (1985). *Racial conflict in contemporary society*. Cambridge, MA: Harvard University Press.
Sumner, G. (1906). *Folkways*. Boston: Ginn.
Taft, R. (1977). Coping with unfamiliar culture. In N. Warren (Ed.), *Studies in cross-cultural psychology* (Vol. 1, pp. 121-153). New York: Academic Press.
Tagil, S. (Ed.). (1984). *Regions in upheaval: Ethnic conflict and political mobilization*. Stockholm: Esselte Studium.
Tajfel, H. (1970). Experiments in intergroup discrimination. *Scientific American, 223*(2), 96-102.
Tajfel, H. (1974). Social identity and intergroup behavior. *Social Science Information, 13*, 65-93.
Tajfel, H. (Ed.). (1978). *Differentiation between groups: Studies in the social psychology of intergroup relations*. New York: Academic Press.
Tajfel, H. (Ed.). (1982). *Social identity and intergroup relations*. Cambridge, England: Cambridge University Press.
Tajfel, H., & Turner, J. (1986). The social identity theory of intergroup behavior. In S. Worchel & W. Austin (Eds.), *Psychology of intergroup relations* (2nd ed., pp. 7-17). Chicago: Nelson-Hall.
Taylor, S., Fiske, S., Etcoff, N., & Ruderman, A. (1978). Categorical and contextual bases of person memory and stereotyping. *Journal of Personality and Social Psychology, 36*, 778-793.
Ting-Toomey, S. (1986). Conflict communication styles in black and white subjective cultures. In Y. Kim (Ed.), *Interethnic communication: Current research* (pp. 75-88). Newbury Park, CA: Sage.
Ting-Toomey, S. (1988). Intercultural conflict styles: A face-negotiation theory. In Y. Kim & W. Gudykunst (Eds.), *Theories in intercultural communication* (pp. 213-235). Newbury Park, CA: Sage.
Turner, J. (1975). Social comparison and social identity: Some prospects for intergroup behaivor. *European Journal of Social Psychology, 5*, 5-34.
Turner, J. (1978). Social categorization and social discrimination in a minimal group paradigm. In H. Tajfel (Ed.), *Differentiation between social groups* (pp. 101-140). New York: Academic Press.
Turner, J. (1982). Towards a cognitive redefinition of the social group. In H. Tajfel (Ed.), *Social identity and intergroup relations* (pp. 15-40). Cambridge, England: Cambridge University Press.

Turner, J., & Giles, H. (Eds.). (1981). *Intergroup behavior*. Chicago: University of Chicago Press.

Van Dijk, T. (1987). *Communicating racism: Ethnic prejudice in thought and talk*. Newbury Park, CA: Sage.

Van Dijk, T. (1988). How "they" hit the deadlines: Ethnic minorities in the press. In G. Smitherman-Donaldson & T. van Dijk (Eds.), *Discourse and discrimination* (pp. 221-262). Detroit, MI: Wayne State University.

Van Dijk, T. (1991). *Racism and the press*. New York: Routledge.

Volkan, V. (1992, December). Ethnonationalistic rituals: An introduction. *Mind & Human Interaction, 4*(1), 3-19.

Von Raffler-Engel, W. (1988). The impact of covert factors in cross-cultural communication. In F. Poyatos (Ed.), *Cross-cultural perspectives in nonverbal communication* (pp. 71-104). Lewiston, NY: C. J. Hogrefe.

Walker, I., & Pettigrew, T. (1984). Relative deprivation theory: An overview and conceptual critique. *British Journal of Social Psychology, 23*, 301-310.

Watzlawick, P., Beavin, J., & Jackson, D. (1967). *The pragmatics of human communication*. New York: Norton.

Wieder, D., & Pratt, S. (1990). On being a recognizable Indian among Indians. In D. Carbaugh (Ed.), *Cultural communication and intercultural contact* (pp. 45-64). Hillsdale, NJ: Lawrence Erlbaum.

Williams, J. (1992, January 5). Race and Japan: A cross-cultural journey. *Washington Post Magazine*, pp. 11-28.

Wilson, C., & Gutierrez, F. (1985). *Minorities and media*. Beverly Hills, CA: Sage.

Wolpe, H. (1986). Class concepts, class struggle and racism. In J. Rex & D. Mason (Eds.), *Theories of race and ethnic relations* (pp. 110-130). New York: Cambridge University Press.

Worchel, S. (1979). Cooperation and the reduction of intergroup conflict: Some determining factors. In W. Austin & S. Worchel (Eds.), *The social psychology of intergroup relations* (pp. 262-273). Monterey, CA: Brooks/Cole.

Worchel, S. (1986). The role of cooperation in reducing intergroup conflict. In S. Worchel & W. Austin (Eds.), *Psychology of intergroup relations* (2nd ed., pp. 288-304). Chicago: Nelson-Hall.

Yinger, J. (1986). Intersection strands in the theorisation of race and ethnic relations. In J. Rex & D. Mason (Eds.), *Theories of race and ethnic relations* (pp. 20-41). New York: Cambridge University Press.

Yoshikawa, M. (1986). Cross-cultural adaptation and perceptual development. In Y. Kim (Ed.), *Cross-cultural adaptation: Current research* (pp. 140-148). Newbury Park, CA: Sage.

Footnote

[1]This paper is a reframed and expanded version of an earlier work, "Interethnic communication: The context and the behavior," published in *Communication yearbook 17* (see Kim, 1994).

Part 3

Context and the Applied Analysis of Communication Behavior

Section 1
Evolutionary Context and the Applied Analysis of Communication Behavior

Chapter 14

Signs of the Apes, Songs of the Whales: Human Communication in Evolutionary Context

Jo Liska
University of Colorado, Denver

It is now politically correct to view animal behavior as interesting, even important, but still irrevocably distinct from human action (Savage-Rumbaugh & Lewin, 1994, p. 21).

The evolutionary unity of humans with all other organisms is the cardinal message of Darwin's revolution for nature's most arrogant species (Gould, 1981, p. 324).

Introduction

The thesis advanced is that comparative analysis of the semiotic capabilities and behavior of other species is potentially useful for illuminating the evolutionary context in which human communication arose. The search for continuities in semiogenesis across phyla is not without controversy, and some of the controversies take the form of conceptual, definitional, and methodological disagreements, which will be analyzed in the course of this discussion. Further, advantages and limitations of the comparative approach are examined.

Like all living organisms, we humans are products of a bioevolutionary context – our anatomy, physiology, and even our behavior has been shaped by a complex, everchanging interaction of environmental (ecological) conditions. Modern humans are the only surviving representative of an evolutionary experiment in hominids; all others extinguished for reasons about which we can only speculate, the most obvious that they encountered contextual changes to which they failed to adapt. So all of the humans we encounter belong to a single species – Homo sapien sapien. Why did our line survive while all others failed? Again we can merely speculate and such speculation generally focuses on capabilities frequently offered as unique to our species, e.g., cooperative hunting, tool use and manufacture, culture, and language, especially language.

It would be unreasonable to deny such attributes as tool technologies and symbolic behavior a central role in our success (at least as defined in terms of distribution and prolific reproduction) as a species, for with these capacities humans changed the course of their own evolution, as well as the evolution of other species, by modifying their environmental context rather than merely reacting to it. Indeed, the human capacity to modify the environment is foundation to the belief (illusory though it may be) that we can CONTROL the enviornment thus subjugating it rather than being subjugated by it. But we did not arrive at this point without considerable help from our ancestors, who laid the foundation for the capabilities we so take for granted. Nor does it appear that we have a monopoly on such capabilities as tool use, culture, and language. So, while language is frequently offered as the last bastian of human uniqueness, recent research on the semiotic abilities of dolphins, whales, elephants, and various species of nonhuman primate suggest that advanced semiotic abilities are not the exclusive domain of Homo sapiens. Further, research exploring apes' capacity for acquiring at least the fundamentals of human language systems leads to the conclusion that these linguistic capabilities must have been present prior to the chimpanzee-hominid split of some five million years ago. Given the significance attached to human semiotic abilities, and given that humans engage their world through a complex web of symbols, it is important to explore the evolutionary foundations on which human communication was constructed.

What evidence can be offered to provide some reasonable perspective on semiogenesis? The argument advanced here is that comparison of a variety of nonhuman species' semiotic abilities is an important source for understanding the extent to which human semiotic abilities are unusual, as well as suggestive of the evolutionary underpinnings that laid the foundation for the emergence of language. Similar to Griffin's (1983, 1991) suggestion that communication provides a window through which we can peer into the minds of ourselves and other species, investigation of the semiotic behavior of extant nonhuman animals may allow us to more clearly see the reflection of our semiotic past.[1]

Cross-species Comparisons: An Overview

Although human behavior is human behavior, not chimpanzee nor rat behavior, an understanding of the principles that underlie the evolution and behavior of both diverse and similar species can provide valuable information with important implications for [hu]man (Rajecki, 1983, p. 23).

The basic question is: WHAT CAN WE KNOW ABOUT HUMAN COMMUNICATION BASED ON NONHUMAN ANIMAL COMMUNICATION? Or, put another way, are data from other species acceptable as evidence for understanding the evolution of human communication/language? For some the answer appears to be yes, for others the answer is no. For example, Bastian (1968) and Tanner and Zihlman (1976) argued that linguistic communication is the result of specialized modifications of nonlinguistic communication, and that to understand the latter will further efforts to understand the former. Tanner (1981) wrote that "The present challenge is rather to hypothesize how the cognitive and affective-social capacities underlying the nonverbal communication system of the ancestral apes could provide a base from which the human capacity for symbolic thought, language, and culture could evolve" (p. 129). Eibl-Eibesfeldt (1983) offered some insight on the requirements of cross-species comparisons:

> Single movement patterns, whole strategies of social interactions, learning processes, perceptive and cognitive processes, as well as the results of complex behavioral interactions such as social structure, rank order, and the like, can all be investigated by the comparative approach, but one must always compare categories of the same type and the same level of complexity. The comparison of patterns of expressive behavior in humans and animals (expressive movements, rituals) reveals a number of general principles regarding the evolution of these behaviors. (p. 44)

This stance is in direct contradiction to those who believe that linguistic communication is qualitatively different from nonlinguistic communication. Tooby and DeVore (1987), for example, claimed that "language is different from other animal communication systems in that it allows the exchange of model-based information referring to cause-and-effect categories" (p. 210). Savage-Rumbaugh and Lewin (1994) report comments made by Iain Davidson at a Wenner-Gren Conference:

> Humans are different from apes, and all the 'chimpology' in the world won't tell us anything of interest; chimps [aren't] representational thinkers, therefore we [can't] learn anything useful about language by looking at apes; training chimps to do tricks might be interesting in itself, but it is irrelevant to events in the past; and if you want to learn anything about language origins, the only place to look is at the archeological record; psychologists behave as if prehistoric evidence doesn't matter; finally, the archeological evidence suggests that human language arose very recently, within the last 100,000 years – so much for chimpology (pp. 26-27).

Lennenberg (1968) has offered a number of comments critical of the comparative method and the evidence used in support of that method. He argued that those who believe that comparative studies of animal communication will highlight the origins of human language operate with a continuity theory, which specifies that the evolution of language proceeded via a straight line from animal systems to human language. The alternative, and the one that Lennenberg advocates, is the discontinuity theory, which suggests that the antecedents of language are simply not obvious. Yet those antecedents may become quite obvious as we gather more data on the sign systems of other species. Given current data, eliminating one alternative in favor of the other would be premature. Consequently, we might rephrase the question thusly: TO WHAT EXTENT, AND UNDER WHAT CONDITIONS,

ARE DATA FROM OTHER SPECIES ACCEPTABLE AS EVIDENCE REGARDING THE DEVELOPMENT OF HUMAN COMMUNICATION?

Cross-species Comparisons: Closely Related Species

Moreover, tool behaviors and symbolic communication are by no means unique to our species; both can be studied in wild and captive chimpanzee populations (Bradshaw & Rogers, 1993, p. 277).

For reasons we may never fully know or understand, the parent stock of primates that was our common ancestor with chimpanzees (our closest living relative), divided, maybe many times, and took different paths. One group ventured out of the forest to exploit the edges of the woodland/savannah, new territory resulting from climatic changes associated with drier conditions. The processes of evolution continued as those groups drifted further apart, the accumulation of those evolutionary processes evident in modern humans and extant chimpanzees.[2] Those differences notwithstanding, humans and chimpanzees, along with other more distantly related primates (e.g., gorillas, orangutans, and old and new world monkeys), shared a long history, which is evident in a set of qualities characteristic of primates: grasping hands, with nails (instead of claws), and an opposable thumb, visual sensitivity to color and overlapping visual fields, long periods of postnatal development characterized by dependency upon the mother, long lives, low rates of reproduction, large and complex brains, and complex social networks on which individual survival depended (Jolly, 1985).

Darwin alluded to behavioral similarities between humans and other species in his book THE EXPRESSION OF EMOTIONS IN ANIMALS AND MAN (1871). Since that time, data gathered in studies of primate behavior have consistently challenged long held beliefs of human uniqueness, e.g., tool use and manufacture, cooperative hunting, food sharing, self-recognition and awareness, foresight and planning, and language. Moreover, recent advances in genetics have facilitated rather precise comparisons of evolutionary relationships among primates, as well as the timing of speciation among primates. Those data indicate that humans share with chimpanzees some 98-99 percent of genetic material, with an estimated split from a common ancestor occuring about 5 million years ago, a mere blip in evolutionary time. Modern Homo sapiens arose some 100,000 years ago with speech probably in place by that time (Lieberman, 1992). Indeed, "the driving force that produced modern human beings may have been the evolution of speech adapted for rapid communication" (Lieberman, 1992, p. 21).

There is no doubt that extant chimpanzees and modern humans live vastly different lives. Chimpanzees are far more tied to the natural world than are humans, who live in a world – symbolic and technological – largely of their own creation. Chimpanzees forage for their food, dependent upon seasonal variations in food sources, whereas humans, especially in industrialized nations, depend upon large commercial farms technologically enhanced to overcome seasonal variations to grow food that is then typically procured at a local market. Chimpanzees travel within a rather well-defined and limited territory, while humans can venture to almost any part of the planet. Chimpanzees engage in social interaction limited to their immediate troop-mates, while humans can access people in all reaches of the globe via such communication devices as television, the telephone, fax machines, and e-mail. Chimpanzees do not build cities, guns, or atomic weapons, travel by rail, auto, or plane, cultivate land, or manufacture goods, but they do use and manufacture rudimentary tools, live in hierarchically organized societies, engage in cooperative hunting and organized warfare, forge friendships and alliances, and coordinate these and other activities via a rich system of vocal and visual communication signs. And these abilities are fundamental building blocks upon which elaborated communication systems – languages – and technology are built.[3]

Further, the roots of human communication are evident in the semiotic system of our cousins the chimpanzees. Gestures such as hugging, kissing, and begging are similar in both structure and function in both chimpanzees and humans. A number of facial expressions (e.g., fear, and anger) are shared, and body positions indicating fear, anger, and dominance are so similar as to be easily understood by members of both species. "It is hardly surprising, therefore, that a more or less unconscious recognition of these capacities, while realizing that apes' naturally elicited vocalizations nevertheless do markedly differ from our own, has led people for hundreds of years out of curiosity to try to train apes to communicate with us" (Bradshaw & Rogers, 1993, p. 323).

Armed with this evidence, Tanner (1981) argued in favor of using nonhuman primates, and especially chimpanzees, as the ancestral model of human behavior. Tanner wrote that the evidence "together strongly support the idea that relatively sophisticated cognitive and communicatory capacities already existed in the ape population ancestral to the living African apes and to humans" (p. 110). Later she explained that:

> These studies are significant because they demonstrate (1) that chimpanzees think in a manner humans consider to be intelligent and (2) that chimpanzees can learn to use aspects of human language in two-way communication with humans. We understand their abilities in our terms – conceptualization, referential communication, symbol using. They can do things that, when we do them, we describe in these terms. The simplest explanation for their behavior is that they do think and that they are capable of learning rudiments of linguistic systems devised by humans. If not, then a very complex explanation is necessary. (p. 121).

Wrangham (1987) argued that no extant ape provides the "best model"; rather, data gathered from all species of great ape provide the most reasonable way to identify fundamental behavioral patterns that constitute the "ancestral suite." He explained that:

> The principle of the analysis is that because humans and the three living species of African apes are derived from a common ancestor (CA), the

probability of a given behavior occurring in the ancestor can be judged from its distribution in the four descendants. If it occurs in all four species, it is likely (though not certain) to have occurred in the CA because otherwise it must have evolved independently at least twice. If the four species differ with respect to a particular behavior, nothing certain can be said about the CA. The aim, accordingly, is to distinguish between aspects of hominoid social organization which are shared, and therefore phylogenetically conservative, and those which are variable (p. 53).

Ape Language Projects

Following this logic, a number of researchers set about teaching various forms of language to apes to see what, if any, cognitive and semiotic capabilities humans shared with apes, and therefore must have been present in our common ancestor. Early research focused on vocal language, but the studies were abandoned when it was discovered that chimpanzees did not have the vocal anatomy necessary to produce human sounds. Since that time visuospatial languages have been used including sign languages (e.g., Fouts, 1973; Gardner & Gardner, 1969; Gardner, Gardner, & Van Cantfort, 1989; Patterson, 1978), a plastic chip language (Premack, 1971; Premack & Premack, 1983), and a computer language called "Yerkish" developed by Duane Rumbaugh (1977). The conclusions based on these studies have created considerable controversy, with most of the controversy centered on the extent to which the signing abilites of the apes involved in these projects constitutes "real language" (e.g., Dance, 1977; Sebeok, 1968). Debate has focused on a number of issues including (1) whether the use of a sign system necessarily implies understanding the representational force of those signs; (2) the extent to which the sign combinations reflect grammar or syntax (Terrace, 1983); (3) the extent to which sign manipulation can be explained by what is termed the Clever Hans phenomenon (e.g., Sebeok, 1979; Sebeok & Umiker-Sebeok, 1980; Sebeok & Rosenthal, 1981), which suggests that sign manipulation on the part of nonhuman animals is merely the result of subtle cuing by the human caregivers; and (4) the extent to which the acquired sign system is used communicatively and rhetorically; that is, to share information or affect the behavior of another.

Language. Simon (1983) wrote that "Washoe's learning of some ASL (American Sign Language) initiated what now seems to be an endless definitional dispute over 'language.' The charges and rebuttals revolve around the necessary and/or sufficient conditions of language and whether nonhumans could possibly ever satisfy these conditions" (p. 98). Miles (1983) claimed that "The problem lies in the conception of language as a single 'thing.' Defining language is like trying to identify an elephant while holding only its tail or trunk" (p. 45).

Minimally, language may be defined as a set of symbols that can be arranged and rearranged according to a set of rules (grammar or syntax) by which meaning is created, derived, and recreated. To elaborate somewhat, language consists of multiple representations of reality and the routines or programs for encoding and decoding the information contained in those representations. Reynolds (1981) defined language as a system of social action. He wrote that language is "an interaction process whose major function is not the transmission of information but social coordination implemented through the induction of belief in the minds of listeners" (p. 213).

Since the basic unit of language is the symbol, we must address the question WHAT IS A SYMBOL? In common parlance a symbol has come to mean any sign that stands for something else, its significate. So, the sign of the cross "symbolizes" Christianity, the American flag "symbolizes" democratic principles, and a raised right fist "symbolizes" the Black Power movement. This definition is too broad to be useful for comparing communication signs across species, cultures, and time. Peirce (1940) and Morris (1938) wrote of a type of sign that bears an arbitrary relationship to its significate. I am using the term "symbol" to refer to that type of sign. Symbols do not occur in nature, they are created. We may conceive of two levels of symbols: Proper symbols, which are used to name objects and people, and conceptual symbols, which refer to abstract concepts and have no external referents. The distinction between the two is important because, "The accquisition and use of proper symbols can be explained in terms of operant and/or classical conditioning. The acquisition and use of conceptual symbols, however, requires postulating a schema, concept, or 'internal mediating response'" (Liska, 1994a, p. 171). Proper symbols allow one to name aspects of reality, whereas conceptual symbols allow one to CREATE reality. (For an elaborated discussion of this distinction see Liska, 1987, 1993b, 1994b.)

Syntax. Terrace (1983) has discounted the strings of signs produced by apes in language acquisition projects on the grounds that such combinations do not reflect understanding of grammatical rules. His observation was that those sign combinations are best explained as "sequences of contextually related signs." It is also generally true even of humans that USING rules of grammar does not necessarily imply UNDERSTANDING or explicit awareness of those rules. Children act as if they know the rules of their language, and we assume such understanding because they are human, yet few could articulate the rules they use to construct meaningful utterances. In fact, many adults cannot describe with any proficiency the rules by which their languages are constructed. Yet, we would not take this as evidence that they were therefore not using language.

Sebeok and Umiker-Sebeok (1980) wrote:

> Throughout this introductory chapter, we have skirted the consequential issue ... – namely, is what is being taught the apes really "language"? We have done so for the simple reason that, at present, of the two related questions posed by Chomsky – "What is a human language?" and "What is a language?" – neither the first, which is open to scientific, i.e., biological, explanation, nor the second, which is not, can be finally answered. Although the debate over problems such as these is in itself of appreciable

value, there seems to be no point in adding further speculative material to the fires of contention (p. 53).

Clever Hans. The ensuing discussion by scholars from various fields focuses on the nature of language, whether species other than humans can learn language, whatever that may be, and, if not, just what it is that nonhuman species learn. For Sebeok and many of the contributors to the aforementioned volume (Sebeok & Rosenthal, 1981), the results of the ape language projects can be explained by the "Clever Hans Effect." Clever Hans was a horse who could count, as well as add and subtract numbers. His unusual abilities were the focus of great intrigue and debate among scholars and the public alike. After careful analysis of demonstrations of his counting ability, Pfungst (see Sebeok, 1979) concluded that the horse was responding to subtle nonverbal clues from his owner, Mr. von Osten, who was apparently unaware of the messages he was sending his horse. The Clever Hans Effect is a not-so-subtle way of raising questions with the integrity of the people, their methods, and their interpretations, involved in teaching language to a nonhuman species. It is a case of questioning whether these researchers are (1) seeing what they want to see given a priori dispositions, (2) setting up conditions that necessarily result in obtaining the desired responses, (3) avoiding setting up conditions that would facilitate falsification, (4) inadvertently cuing (or leading) their subjects to make the appropriate responses, and/or (5) making errors in observation and recording. These problems are not, of course, unusual to ape language projects. Indeed, they are potential problems in research with any living organism, and even with nonliving materials, as Heisenberg observed when he noted that the observer influences that which is observed. Moreover, this kind of activity – cuing – is an essential and integral part of human communication, and I suspect a part of the social interaction of many nonhuman species. Part of conversational negotiation depends upon "reading" the frequently subtle cues of others, and it is undoubtedly an important factor in determining one's communicative competence. Moreover, it is a skill that probably has considerable survival value. I recall reading that a good gunslinger – one who is still alive – especially attended to subtle changes in the direction of his opponents' gaze as an indication of when they would draw and shoot. This is an instance in which the blink of an eye could cost one their life.

Many of the ape language projects employed some form of ASL, frequently mixed with "home signs," that is signs of the experimenters' creation. Critics charged that many of the signs produced by the apes were vague, misformed, and/or difficult to interpret. Other criticisms focused on the artificial or, conversely, overly social nature of the experimental situations, the use of shaping and food rewards to initiate signing on the part of the ape subjects, and the number of stimulus repetitions required to initiate signing. Even the personality and temperament of individual apes was subject to scrutiny (e.g., Ristau & Robbins, 1979). A number of tests were suggested to off-set the potential for inadvertent cuing including double-blind procedures, careful analysis of video records of experimenters' behavior toward their subjects in and outside of training sessions, the use of multiple experimenters, and so forth. Experimenters involved in ape language projects responded by providing more data, more sophisticated experimental tests, and by codifying a linguistic system, such as Yerkish, which avoided many of the pitfalls associated with manual gestural systems. (For additional discussion of these and other criticisms and remedies see Sebeok & Rosenthal, 1981).

The appropriateness and importance of these criticisms notwithstanding, some of them seem to be differentially applied. Consider the criticism that experimenters in ape language projects may overinterpret their subjects' behavior because they fervently, but subconsciously, believe that language is not species-specific. It is equally likely that critics may question (underinterpret?) experimenters' interpretations because they hold an equally fervent but opposing view. As another example: Umiker-Sebeok and Sebeok (1980) discussed the emotional commitment evident in the trainers' relationship with their subjects and among themselves. They wrote: "It is immediately clear to an outside visitor to any of the ape 'language' projects, or to anyone who talks at length with those involved in them, that the animals are surrounded by a dedicated group of enthusiastic workers, one that constitutes a tightly knit social community with a solid core of shared beliefs and goals in opposition to outside visitors, as well as against groups elsewhere which are competing for scarce research resources" (p. 7). This sort of charge, for which they do not provide the data on which they base their interpretation, could certainly be leveled against any research team engaged in long-term projects. They went on to say: "The total dedication required for projects of this sort may partially explain why it seems to be the rule rather than the exception that the work becomes a family affair, the principle investigators – husbands and wives (e.g., the Gardners, Premacks, and Rumbaughs) – both becoming deeply involved..." (p. 8). It is interesting to note that the authors of this comment are also a husband and wife team. Does this suggest that their work suffers, or could suffer, from the sort of "groupthink" they suggest about the "families" who conduct ape language projects? Emotional and/or ego-involvement in one's research, the need to continue to secure funding, and the tendency for closely knit groups to exclude contrary opinions are probably not problems peculiar to those who work with ape language projects.

More critical to the study of language are the insights that can be gleaned from such research. Rumbaugh (1977), Savage-Rumbaugh (1986), Savage-Rumbaugh and Lewin (1994), and others (e.g., Premack, 1976) have noted that their ape subjects seem to learn best when in social situations and in close contact with their human caregivers. This seems similar to the situations humans prefer, and indeed, such conditions may have been essential in the emergence of language in evolution (e.g., Humphrey, 1976; Quiatt & Reynolds, 1993), and appears to be essential to the normal development (physical, cognitive, and social) of human children (e.g., Savage-Rumbaugh & Lewin, 1994). If this process, that is language acquisition, is to be simulated with nonhuman subjects, then comparable conditions should be established, at least in some projects.

Finally, some of the criticisms go well beyond those that would be leveled at projects investigating human language acquisition, largely, I suspect, because no one questions that humans use language, so such rigor as that expected of other species can be relaxed for humans. This is probably also a result of characterizing language in human terms (e.g., Dance, 1977) rather than attempting to describe it in a way that is not species-specific at the outset, thus inhibiting comparative research efforts. Schubert (1978) suggested that to "appraise the relative excellence of nonhuman cognitive abilities by measuring the extent to which these conform to those characteristics of our own species [is] a very unbiological approach" (p. 597).

The point I am making, and it certainly is not new, is that all of us bring to our research a set of assumptions and beliefs that can influence the way we gather, analyze, and interpret data. And, it is difficult to maintain a healthy degree of skepticism, let alone an "objective" stance, when the fruits of our labors are the sources of our livelihood and sense of self-worth. Those who study other humans share a problem with those who study other species in that they may become emotionally involved with their subjects to a greater degree than those who study inanimate objects. And I suspect there is a tendency to see the behavior of other humans as more sophisticated, more self-directed, and more self-motivated than the behavior of nonhuman species. Finally, of all the characteristics humans possess language may be the one that sets us apart from other species, and therefore it may be the most ego-involving. Menzel and Johnson (1978) wrote that:

> The study of "animal language," ... may have, if anything, tended to increase rather than decrease expectations of human chauvinism and presumed "biological superiority," especially in the popular press, where it is more and more often suggested that chimpanzees, gorillas, and perhaps dolphins may deserve special consideration based on the outcome of research projects demonstrating their similarity to humans (p. 587).

Meaning. Meaning is another central issue in the research on language acquisition in other species. One of the criticisms is that, while apes may demonstrate facility with the signs presented them, little suggests that they understand the meaning of those signs. The data offered by Savage-Rumbaugh (1986, 1990), as one example, provide compelling insight into the extent to which the meaning inherent in sign relationships is understood. She reported considerable evidence indicating that apes understand the meaning of sign relationships as evidenced by their ability to respond to and generate such abstractions as requests, share information to achieve a common goal, and make statements about objects. At least, if a chimp is asked to get a hammer and he/she does so, he/she probably has some understanding of the relationship among the object, signs specifying the request, and the appropriate response. Some would counter that this behavior can be explained by the processes of conditioning and reinforcement. A radical behaviorist would apply those explanations to the behavior of all species. Others would offer such explanations only when the "language user" was a species other than human.

A Bizarro cartoon by Dan Piraro sums up these issues nicely:

A parrot leans over to a human and says, "I just can't shake the feeling that I don't really understand language as an abstract concept, but am merely imitating syllables as a trained response."

Results. In spite of, or more likely because of, these controversies, research on the ability of other animals to acquire a human form of language continues and with some interesting results. Savage-Rumbaugh and Rumbaugh (1986) wrote that:

More than 20 years have elapsed since Project Washoe rekindled current interest in questions regarding animals' capacities for language. More than any research with children, the research with the great apes, dolphins, and sea lions has served to stimulate attention and thought regarding the components, antecedents, and dynamics of language competence. It has also served to emphasize the merits of comparative research (p. 401).

The fundamental question posed in such research is WHAT ASPECTS OF HUMAN LANGUAGE CAN OTHER SPECIES LEARN? And what has been learned is considerable. Other primate species can use signs to facilitate goal attainment, have constructed sequences of signs that are organized, if not grammatical, initiate interaction spontaneously, recognize that a sign is not the thing for which it stands, acquire signs observationally, that is without explicit training, and respond appropriately to signs (e.g., Miles, 1983; Premack & Premack, 1983; Savage-Rumbaugh, 1986; Gardner et al., 1989). Savage-Rumbaugh (1990) and Savage-Rumbaugh and Lewin (1994) reported that a young bonobo (Pan pansicus) named Kanzi, who was not engaged in any specific form of training, nevertheless acquired a number of lexigrams (words in Yerkish), apparently as a result of observing and mimicking (described as spontaneous acquisition by Savage-Rumbaugh) his adopted bonobo mother who was in language training. Further, Kanzi is reported to understand oral English, not just single words such as one might expect from one's dogs or cats, but grammatical utterances such as, "Go get the lettuce in the microwave." Finally, Kanzi appears to have some command of simple syntax, evidenced by changes in word order consistent with the order of actors and actions. For example, "Matata bite" was used when Matata initiated the action toward another. "Bite Matata" is used only when the biting is directed toward Matata by another actor. In an interview reported in DISCOVER (1991, p. 20), Chomsky responded to these latest findings saying, "If an animal had a capacity as biologically advantageous as language but somehow hadn't used it until now, it would be an evolutionary miracle, like finding an island of humans who could be taught to fly." His comment prompts another question: If language is so biologically advantageous, why should we presume humans to be the only species to use it?

A related question is WHAT ABILITIES ARE PREREQUISITE TO OR FACILITATE LANGUAGE? Again the language acquisition projects go a considerable distance toward answering this question. As with human children, apes apparently need to be exposed to language early in life. Matata, Kanzi's adopted mother, was put in language training at the age of ten. "After two years of training and thirty thousand trials, she mastered only six symbols in a limited way" (Savage-Rumbaugh & Lewin, 1994, p. 130). Given the success of Kanzi, who spontaneously picked up the Yerkish language, as well as oral English (comprehension), and other bonobos who started language training in their very early years, bonobos are clearly not incapable of learning language. The better explanation is that there is a critical period early in life in which language is most readily acquired. This is consistent with the fact that human children who are not exposed to language early in life encounter great difficulty in learning it later. Moreover, again as with human children, apes who live in an enriched social environment acquire language more easily and readily. This may explain why Washoe, who was home reared and exposed to sign language early was more linguistically facile than Nim, Terrace's chimpanzee, who was reared in a lab and exposed to an everchanging stream of trainers. Moreover, Savage-Rumbaugh has used games and social situations as a primary vehicle for training, which was not the situation for Nim.

The subjects in these studies recognize relationships of same/different, is/is not, and so forth. Evidence of planning and foresight are apparent in their use of linguistic constructions. All of these abilities appear to be requisite to or facilitative of linguistic development.

As Savage-Rumbaugh and Rumbaugh (1986) aptly put it:

> The effort has taught humankind a great deal about the basic requisites of language, about the continuua [sic] which link operant learning to the competent use of symbols, about the way in which nonverbal and verbal behaviors support the coordination of interindividual behaviors, and about apes as an advanced form of life that psychologically is not so different from us as their appearance might otherwise suggest (p. 401).

Qualifications. As revealing as these studies are of the abilities of apes, they do not, however, stand as an illustration of the evolution of language. First, while these studies demonstrate how subtle are the differences between apes and humans, those differences are nonetheless significant. Apes do not learn language with the rapidity and ease evidenced by human children, nor do they seem to have the genetically based enthusiasm for acquiring and using their nonnative sign system. Remember, however, that the emergence of language in humans appears to be the result of millions of years of evolutionary change, and apparently occurred within the 5 million or so years since our split from an ancestor we shared with extant chimpanzees. That chimps can acquire even a rudimentary form of language suggests that the foundations for its emergence are indeed ancient, not to mention the fact that the environmental conditions that prompted its emergence must have been unusual. Second, the process by which apes acquire signs is unlikely to be similar to the way in which language evolved. That is, in this case at least, ontogeny does not necessarily recapitulate phylogeny (or semiogeny). The characteristics of experimental situations and extensive and intensive training are unnecessary for the acquisition of language on the part of human children, and unlikely to reflect the process by which early humans acquired language. Third, the situation in which apes are trained, that is by another species and in that species' domain, is almost certainly not characteristic of the environment in which language emerged. Fourth, the studies to date have not focused on the ability of apes to CREATE their own symbol systems, and thus have not yielded information on that issue. It is clear that the apes involved in these projects can USE symbols; however, there is as yet no conclusive evidence that they can CREATE symbols. Of course, our belief that we are the only species to have invented symbols may simply result from the fact that we have not yet been able to decode the semiotic systems of apes, birds, elephants, whales, and dolphins. Thus it may be our limited understanding of the semiotic systems of other animals that stands in the way of finding the evidence.

Cross-species Comparisons: Distantly Related Species

Increasingly, the boundaries between ourselves and other species are being blurred, particularly with respect to tool behaviors, language, thought, and consciousness(Bradshaw & Rogers, 1993, p. 315).

Evidence from species similar to us, which similarity is rooted in a shared evolutionary history, has important implications for the study of human communication. However, the relevance of evidence derived from research on species more distantly related to humans may be acceptable as well, although some would disagree. Eibl-Eibesfeldt (1983) observed:

Again and again one reads that not much can be learned from the study of greylag geese or cichlid fishes that is relevant for understanding man, that such studies may have some aesthetic value of their own, but contribute little to the understanding of human conduct, and that if one really wants to get comparative data relevant to the understanding of man, one has to turn to nonhuman primates who are our close relatives. This view is based on the assumption that only homologies (similarities based on common ancestry) count, a view that is clearly a misconception. True, analogies tell us something different than homologies, but both certainly contain information of interest (p. 44).

A homology is similarity based upon descent from a common ancestor, while an analogy is "convergence toward a similar form among unrelated structures" (Reynolds, 1981, p. 25). Homologous relationships are of particular concern to those interested in the evolution of particular structures. Analogies inform us about the "selection pressures that shaped these structures and caused processes of behavior to develop along similar lines" (Eibl-Eibesfeldt, 1983, p. 44). Moreover, "the absence of analogies and homologies in behavior can provide us with useful information about how members of a species are unique" (p. 64). She went on to say that:

Should one, therefore, be interested in phenomena like ranking, territoriality, or mating systems, it is certainly advisable to study these in many different groups of animals, regardless of their phylogenetic relationship. The further apart they are, the better, because only then can we be sure that the regularities observed can be attributed to the more general laws of function and not derived from a genetic relationship (p. 44).

Comparison of the specialized semiotic systems of other species may suggest ways in which environmental characteristics operate on the evolution of communication systems, the relative efficacy of a variety of sensory/motor systems for transmitting information of various types, and provide further insight into the characteristics fundamental to all communication systems. The research on bird songs indicates that some species of birds learn their species' songs on the basis of observation and imitation, just as humans appear to learn the sounds of their language (Morton & Page, 1992). Also like humans, birds seem to have a genetically endowed set of restrictions on the sounds relevant to them, i.e., sounds that are species-specific (Lieberman, 1984). Humans are particularly tuned to the sounds of other humans, and birds are especially sensitive to the sounds of their own species. Moreover, their songs reflect family and regional dialects. Again, like humans, some species of birds (Marler, 1970; 1977), as well as vervet monkeys (Cheney & Seyfarth (1990), are clearly able to distinguish the identities of others on the basis of their vocal characteristics and songs/calls. Dolphins develop signature whistles that afford the identification of individuals (Tyack, 1991), and humpback and bowhead whales engage in complex songs that change over time, which songs are specific to populations/groups (Payne, 1991). These findings suggest some fundamental similarities in the functions of communication systems across diverse species in diverse environments, e.g., recognition of others as individuals, group identity, and group cohesion.

It seems that research on the communication systems of social species such as birds, elephants, dolphins, and whales, to name only a few, is a reasonable route for understanding the relationships among sociality, intelligence, and environment in the evolution of communication. As Milton (1988, p. 303) wrote "It is presumably not accidental that many animal lineages which possess relatively large brains for their body mass are strongly social and possess an unusually elaborate communication system." Consider, for example, that elephants are large brained, highly social animals with long periods of post-natal development, and long life spans, who are thought to be intelligent, are known to use tools (Chevalier-Skolnikoff & Liska, 1993), and who also have what appears to be a large repertoire of calls for interacting with other members of their species (Moss, 1988; Payne, 1986; Poole, 1987). The fact that they are only distantly related to humans in evolutionary terms does not invalidate the possibility that their communication systems may be based on principles or features that bear a striking resemblance to the principles on which human communication are based.

Rhetorical Force: A Common Denominator?

...many of [hu]mankind's most prized technological discoveries, from agriculture to chemistry, may have had their origin not in the deliberate application of practical intelligence, but in the fortunate misapplication of social intelligence (Humphrey, 1988, p. 25).

Kennedy (1992) has written that "these various features are vehicles, techniques, or rules of rhetoric, which itself is a form of energy driven by a basic instinct to survive" (p. 20). His definition of rhetoric is general enough to apply to species other than humans. He defines rhetoric as a "form of energy" found not only in language, but "present also in physical actions, facial expressions, gestures, and signs generally" (pp. 3-4). His conceptualization is so general as to include plant photosynthesis, the behavior of social insects, and such symptomatic behaviors as the noises associated with digestive processes. While one can appreciate his attempts to identify continuities in the behavior of especially our closest living relatives, he has erred by presenting a conceptualization well over-generalized, even for those of us who remain open to the notion, that when compared to other species, human capacities for communication, language, symbolic behavior, and/or rhetoric are differences in degree rather than kind (see Liska, 1993a, for a critique of Kennedy's definition). However, if one describes rhetoric as "the MANIPULATION of signs in the service of social influence" (Liska, 1993a, p. 34), then one can begin comparisons of rhetorical activity across species with the idea of identifying some universal characteristics. Similar to Jolly's (1966) and Humphrey's (1976) argument that social pressures were the forces behind the elaboration of intelligence in primates, it may be that rhetorical exigencies were the forces that drove organisms to create increasingly arbitrary signs. Note that vervet monkeys are reported to have several specific alarm calls that are not genetically transmitted, but are apparently learned by observation and imitation (Cheney & Seyfarth, 1990). Each call specifies a predator: eagle, snake, and leopard. While such labeling may be one fundamental property of language, it is probably the case that most would not call this system of alarm calls "real" language. However, these calls are communicative and have rhetorical force; that is, they are used to influence the behavior of others, and in some most interesting ways. Seyfarth, Cheney, and Marler (1980) and Cheney and Seyfarth (1991) reported instances in which vervets used an alarm call to spare themselves from attack by another, or to otherwise distract the group.

Chimpanzees are well-known for their rhetorical inclinations: they withhold, conceal, or convey inaccurate information, make false overtures at reconciliation, bluff their way to dominant positions, and so forth (de Waal, 1982, 1989; Goodall, 1986; Jolly, 1991). Other species quite distantly related to humans also appear to engage in rhetorical acts. For example, ground nesting birds such as plovers feign a broken wing to distract potential predators from their nests (Ristau, 1991). When threatened, hognose snakes engage in a dramatic ritual of bluff attack prior to feigning death (Burghardt, 1991). And I can personally testify to the persuasive impact of a bluff charge by a wild African elephant on members of their own and other species (see also Douglas-Hamilton & Douglas-Hamilton, 1975; Moss, 1988).

Engaging in rhetorical acts for establishing dominance via the use of objects and bluffs rather than counting solely on one's physical prowess clearly has survival advantages for oneself and one's genes. Deception, achieving dominance, engaging friendships and alliances, and influencing the behavior of others to facilitate their cooperation is enhanced by the ability to manipulate a system of signs. And, these abilities are currently under investigation under the rubric of "machiavellian intelligence," and "primate politics" (see, for example, Byrne & Whiten, 1988 and de Waal, 1982, 1989).

Conclusion

Linguistic facility is typically offered as a critical discriminator between humans and the rest of the animal world. Indeed, humans seem to have become highly specialized for inhabiting a world of symbols. And that specialization is offered as the reason why humans have successfully invaded almost every ecological niche on the planet, and in doing so have systematically altered those niches to suit their own whims and wiles. Yet it is becoming increasingly clear that we are not the sole inhabitants of a symbolic universe. Other species have developed semiotic codes that at least in some respects resemble those used by humans. Understanding those similarities will facilitate developing a clearer and more realistic view of our differences. If we seek to understand the distinctiveness of our own reflection, it is necessary to understand the reflections of others with whom we share this planet.

The evolutionary context in which symbolic behavior emerged is forever lost, so to understand the contextual forces that honed a species so utterly dependent upon and fascinated with symbolic realities requires examination of not just the material remains of our ancestors, but of the semiotic behavior of other species. Such investigations will yield insights into our semiotic past, as well as suggest our place among all those other species. In finding our place, we may begin to feel comfortable with our own identity as a species, and cultivate a more complete understanding of and value for the other species with whom we share the third rock from the sun.

Wilson (1992) put it thusly:

Our troubles, as Vercors said in YOU SHALL KNOW THEM, arise from the fact that we do not know what we are and cannot agree on what we want to be. The primary cause of this intellectual failure is ignorance of our origins. We did not arrive on this planet as aliens. Humanity is part of nature, a species that evolved among other species. The more closely we identify ourselves with the rest of life, the more quickly we will be able to discover the sources of human sensibility and acquire the knowledge on which an enduring ethic, a sense of preferred direction, can be built (p. 348).

References

Bastian, J. (1968). Psychological perspectives. In T.A. Sebeok (Ed.), *Animal communication* (pp. 572-591). Bloomington, IN: Indiana University Press.

Bradshaw, J., & Rogers, L. (1993). *The evolution of lateral asymmetries, language, tool use, and intellect.* New York: Academic Press.

Burghardt, G. M. (1991). Cognitive ethology and critical anthropomorphism: A snake with two heads and hog-nose snakes that play dead. In C.A. Ristau (Ed.), *Cognitive ethology: The minds of other animals* (pp. 53-90). Hillsdale, NJ: Lawrence Erlbaum.

Byrne, R., & Whiten, A. (1988). *Machiavellian intelligence: Social expertise and the evolution of intellect in monkeys, apes, and humans.* Oxford, England: Clarendon.

Cheney, D. L., & Seyfarth, R. M. (1990). *How monkeys see the world.* Chicago: University of Chicago Press.

Cheney, D. L., & Seyfarth, R. M. (1991). Truth and deception in animal communication. In C. A. Ristau (Ed.), *Cognitive ethology: The minds of other animals* (pp. 127-151). Hillsdale, NJ: Erlbaum.

Chevalier-Skolnikoff, S., & Liska, J. (1993). Tool use among wild and captive elephants. *Animal Behaviour, 45,* 209-219.

Dance, F. E. X. (1977). The rhetorical primate. *Journal of Communication,* 12-16.

Diamond, J. (1992). *The third chimpanzee.* New York: HarperCollins.

Douglas-Hamilton, I., & Douglas-Hamilton, O. (1975). *Among the elephants.* New York: Viking Press.

de Waal, F. (1982). *Chimpanzee politics.* New York: Harper & Row.

de Waal, F. (1989). *Peacemaking among primates.* Cambridge, MA: Harvard University Press.

Eibl-Eibesfeldt, I. (1983). The comparative approach in human ethology. In D. W. Rajecki (Ed.), *Comparing behavior: Studying man studying animals* (pp. 43-65). Hillsdale, NJ: Lawrence Erlbaum.

Fouts, R. S. (1973). Acquisition and testing of gestural signs in four young chimpanzees. *Science, 180,* 978-980.

Fouts, R. S. (1974). Language: Origins, definitions, and chimpanzees. *Journal of Human Evolution, 3,* 475-482.

Gardner, B. T., & Gardner, R. A. (1969). Teaching sign language to a chimpanzee. *Science, 165,* 664-672.

Gardner, R. A., Gardner, B. T., & Van Cantfort, T. E., (Eds.). (1989). *Teaching sign language to chimpanzees.* Albany, NY: State University of New York Press.

Goodall, J. (1986). *The chimpanzees of Gombe.* Cambridge, MA: Belknap Press of Harvard University Press.

Gould, S. J. (1981). *The mismeasure of man.* New York: W. W. Norton.

Gould, S. J. (1991). Of mice and mosquitos. *Natural History, 7,* 12-20.

Griffin, D. R. (1983). Prospects for a cognitive ethology. In J. de Luce & H. T. Wilder (Eds.), *Language in primates* (pp. 159-186). New York: Springer-Verlag.

Griffin, D. R. (1991). Progress toward a cognitive ethology. In C. A. Ristau (Ed.), *Cognitive ethology: The minds of other animals* (pp. 3-17). Hillsdale, NJ: Lawrence Erlbaum.
Humphrey, N. K. (1976). The social function of intellect. In P. P. G. Bateson & R. A. Hinde (Eds.), *Growing points in ethology* (pp. 303-317). Cambridge, England: Cambridge University Press.
Humphrey, N. K. (1988). The social function of intellect. In R. Byrne & A. Whiten (Eds.), *Machiavellian intelligence: Social expertise and the evolution of intellect in monkeys, apes, and humans* (pp. 13-26). Oxford, England: Clarendon Press.
Jolly, A. (1966). Lemur social behavior and primate intelligence. *Science, 53,* 501-506.
Jolly, A. (1985). *The evolution of primate behavior* (2nd ed.). New York: Macmillan.
Jolly, A. (1991). Conscious chimpanzees? A review of recent literature. In C. A. Ristau (Ed.), *Cognitive ethology: The minds of other animals* (pp. 31-252). Hillsdale, NJ: Lawrence Erlbaum.
Kennedy, G. A. (1992) A hoot in the dark: The evolution of general rhetoric. *Philosophy and Rhetoric, 25,* 1-21.
Lennenberg, E. H. (1968). Language in the light of evolution. In T. A. Sebeok (Ed.), *Animal communication* (pp. 592-613). Bloomington, IN: Indiana University Press.
Lieberman, P. (1984). *The biology and evolution of language.* Cambridge, MA: Harvard University Press.
Lieberman, P. (1992). On the evolution of human language. In J.A. Hawkins & M. Gell-Mann (Eds.), *The evolution of human languages* (pp. 21-47). Redwood City, CA: Addison-Wesley.
Liska, J. (1987). Variations in the arbitrariness of ASL: An assessment of the symbolicity of simian signs. *Human Evolution, 2,* 205-212.
Liska, J. (1993a). The role of rhetoric in semiogenesis: A response to Professor Kennedy. *Philosophy and Rhetoric, 26,*(1), 31-38.
Liska, J. (1993b). Bee dances, bird songs, monkey calls, and cetecean sonar: Is speech unique? *Western Journal of Communication, 57,*1, 1-26.
Liska, J. (1994a). Sign arbitrariness as an index of semiogenesis. In J. Wind, A. Jonker, R. Allott, & L. Rolfe (Eds.), *Studies In Language Origins,* Vol. 3 (pp. 161-177). Amsterdam: John Benjamins Publishing Co.
Liska, J. (1994b). The foundations of symbolic knowledge. In D. Quiatt & J. Itani (Eds.), *Hominid evolution in primate perspective* (pp. 233-251). Niwot, CO: University Press of Colorado.
Marler, P. (1970). A comparative approach to vocal learning: Song development in white-crowned sparrows. *Journal of comparative and physiological psychology* (Monograph Supplement, 71), 1-25.
Marler, P. (1977). The evolution of communication. In T. A. Sebeok (Ed.), *How animals communicate* (pp. 45-70). Bloomington, IN: Indiana University Press.
Menzel, E. W. Jr., & Johnson, M. K. (1978). Should mentalistic concepts be defended or assumed? *The Behavioral and Brain Sciences, 1*(4), 586-587.

Miles, H. L. (1983). Apes and language: The search for communicative competence. In J. de Luce & H. T. Wilder (Eds.), *Language in primates* (pp. 43-61). New York: Springer-Verlag.

Milton, K. (1988). Foraging behaviour and the evolution of primate intelligence. In R. Byrne & A. Whiten (Eds.), *Machiavellian intelligence: Social expertise and the evolution of intellect in monkeys, apes, and humans* (pp. 285-305). Oxford, England: Clarendon Press.

Morris, C.W. (1938). Foundations of the theory of signs. In *International Encyclopedia of Unified Science, 1* (no. 2). Chicago: University of Chicago.

Morton, E.S., & Page, J. (1992). *Animal talk.* New York: Random House.

Moss, C. (1988). *Elephant memories.* New York: Ivy Books.

Patterson, F. G. (1978). The gestures of a gorilla: Sign language acquisition in another pongid species. *Brain and Language, 5,* 72-97.

Payne, K. (1986, February). Elephant calls that humans can't hear. *Science News,* 129.

Payne, K. B. (1991). A change of tune. *Natural History, 3,* 45-46.

Peirce, C. S. (1940). Collected papers of Charles Sanders Peirce. C. Harshorne, P. Weiss, and A. W. Burks. Cambridge, MA: Harvard University Press.

Poole, J. H. (1987). Elephants in musth, lust. *Natural History, 11,* 46-53.

Premack, D. (1971). Language in chimpanzee? *Science, 172,* 808-822.

Premack, D. (1976) *Intelligence in ape and man.* Hillsdale, NJ: Erlbaum.

Premack, D., & Premack, A. J. (1983). *The mind of an ape.* New York: W.W. Norton & Co.

Quiatt, D. & Reynolds, V. (1993). *Primate behavior.* Cambridge, England: Cambridge University Press.

Rajecki, D. W. (1983). Successful comparative psychology: Four case histories. In D. W. Rajecki (Ed.), *Comparing behavior: Studying man studying animals* (pp. 67-107). Hillsdale, NJ: Lawrence Erlbaum.

Reynolds, P. C. (1981). *On the evolution of human behavior.* Berkeley, CA: University of California Press.

Ristau, C. A., & Robbins, D. (1979). Book review: A threat to man's uniqueness? Language and communication in chimpanzee. *Journal of Psycholinguistic Research, 8*(3), 267-300.

Ristau, C. A. (1991). Aspects of the cognitive ethology of an injury-feigning bird, the piping plover (pp. 91-126). In C. A. Ristau (Ed.), *Cognitive ethology: The minds of other animals* (pp. 91-126). Hillsdale, NJ: Lawrence Erlbaum.

Rumbaugh, D., (Ed.). (1977). *Language learning by a chimpanzee: The Lana Project.* New York: Academic.

Savage-Rumbaugh, E. S. (1986). *Ape language: From conditioned response to symbol.* New York: Columbia University Press.

Savage-Rumbaugh, E. S., & Rumbaugh, D. (1986). Ape-language research: Past, present and future. In E.S. Savage-Rumbaugh (Ed.), *Ape language: From conditioned response to symbol* (pp. 398-409). New York: Columbia University Press.

Savage-Rumbaugh, E. S. (1990, July). *Implications of the cognitive and linguistic abilities of the bonobo for theories of the development of hominid culture.* Paper presented at the XIIIth Congress of the International Primatological Society, Kyoto, Japan.

Savage-Rumbaugh, S., & Lewin, R. (1994). *Kanzi.* New York: John Wiley & Sons, Inc.

Schubert, G. (1978). Cooperation, cognition and communication. *The Brain and Behavioral Sciences, 1*(4), 597-600.

Sebeok, T. A. (1968). Goals and limitations of the study of animal communication. In T. A. Sebeok (Ed.), *Animal communication* (pp. 3-14). Bloomington, IN: Indiana University Press.

Sebeok, T. A. (1979). *The sign and its masters.* Austin, TX: Univiversity of Texas Press.

Sebeok, T. A., & Umiker-Sebeok, J. (1980). *Speaking of apes: A critical anthology of two-way communication with man.* New York: Plenum Press.

Sebeok, T. A., & Rosenthal, R. (1981). The Clever Hans phenomenon: Communication with horses, whales, apes, and people. *Annals of the New York Academy of Sciences.* New York: The New York Academy of Sciences.

Seyfarth, R. M., Cheney, D. L., & Marler, P. (1980). Vervet monkey alarm calls: Semantic communication in a free-ranging primate. *Animal Behaviour, 28,* 1070-1094.

Simon, T. W. (1983). Limits of primate talk. In J. de Luce & H. T. Wilder (Eds.), *Language in primates* (pp.97-111). New York: Springer-Verlag.

Tanner, N., & Zihlman, A. (1976). The evolution of human communication: What can primates tell us? In S. R. Harnad, H. D. Steklis, & J. Lancaster (Eds.), *Origins and evolution of language and speech* (pp. 467-480). New York: New York Academy of Sciences.

Tanner, N. M. (1981). *On becoming human.* Cambridge, England: Cambridge University Press.

Terrace, H. S. (1983). Apes who "talk": Language or projection of language by their teachers? In J. de Luce & H. T. Wilder (Eds.), *Language in primates* (pp. 19-42). New York: Springer-Verlag.

Tooby, J., & DeVore, I. (1987). The reconstruction of hominid behavioral evolution through strategic modeling. In W. Kinzey (Ed.), *The evolution of human behavior: Primate models* (pp. 183-237). New York: State University of New York Press.

Tyack, P. (1991). If you need me, whistle. *Natural History, 8,* 60-61.

Umiker-Sebeok, J., & Sebeok, T. A. (1980). Introduction: Questioning apes. In T. A. Sebeok & J. Umiker-Sebeok (Eds.), *Speaking of apes: A critical anthology of two-way communication with man* (pp. 1-59). New York: Plenum Press.

Wilson, E. O. (1992). *The diversity of life.* Cambridge, MA: Harvard University Press.

Wrangham, R. W. (1987). African apes: The significance of African apes for reconstructing human social evolution. In W. G. Kinzey (Ed.), *The evolution of human behavior: Primate models* (pp. 51-71). New York: State University of New York Press.

Footnotes

[1] Approaching the problem of the evolution of semiotic behavior is not an easy task largely because there is little direct evidence on which to identify the semiotic stages or phases that preceded human language. The fossil record is incomplete because sounds and gestures disappear without a trace, and the neurophysiological and soft tissue components underlying communication behavior decompose rapidly. Attempting to experimentally replicate the process raises some difficult ethical issues, and is further complicated by the fact that it is the rare human who does not learn a language.

Fossil, geological, archaeological, and genetic evidence provide insights into the possible stages of semiogenesis, the order and timing of those stages, and the environmental characteristics associated with those stages. While these are important data sources, cross-species comparisons have the potential to augment the incomplete picture those data portray.

[2] Pan paniscus, the bonobo, is believed to be more closely related to humans than is the common chimpanzee (Pan troglodytes) (see A. Zihlman, 1984, November, "Pygmy Chimps, People, and the Pundits," *New Scientist, 15,* p. 39; H. M. McHenry, "The Common Ancestor," in Susman (Ed.), *The Pygmy Chimpanzee* (pp. 201-230); Kano, T., 1992, *The Last Ape,* Palo Alto, CA: Stanford University Press. Dates for divergence of chimpanzee and bonobo are not yet clear.

We owe our ancestry to an early primate living some 60-65 million years ago, from whom radiated Old World monkeys about 40 million years ago, the New World monkeys split off approximately 30 million years ago, the first apes appeared about 25-30 million years ago, and the first hominids appeared about 5 million years ago, the time at which the ancestors of extant chimpanzees went their separate way from our ancestors, the Australopithecines (see Fagan, B.M. (1992). *People Of The Earth,* New York: HarperCollins; Fagan, B., 1990, *The Journey From Eden.* New York: Thames and Hudson; Meller, P., and Stringer, C., 1989, *The Human Revolution: Behavioral And Biological Perspectives On The Origins Of Modern Humans.* Edinburgh, Scotland: Edinburgh University Press.

[3] There is thought to be a strong relationship between the neurocognitive and motor capabilities underlying tool use and manufacture (object manipulation) and language, but especially syntax. Both require foresight and planning, organized sequences (patterns) of behavior, and so forth. For discussion see Bradshaw, J., and Rogers, L., 1993, *The Evolution Of Lateral Asymmetries, Language, Tool Use, And Intellect.* New York: Academic Press; Savage-Rumbaugh, S., and Lewin, R., 1994, *Kanzi.* New York: John Wiley & Sons, Inc.

Section 2
Social Context and the Applied Analysis of Communication Behavior

Chapter 15

The Concept of Context in Social Communication Theory

Wendy Leeds-Hurwitz
University of Wisconsin-Parkside

Introduction

To begin, a few clarifications of terms used in this chapter (or elsewhere in this book) that appear deceptively similar.

"Social communication theory" is one particular approach to the study of communication behavior. It is an outgrowth most directly of the research of Ray Birdwhistell, Dell Hymes, Gregory Bateson, and Erving Goffman. It assumes, among other things, that communication as behavior has pattern, is learned, context-bound, multi-channel and multi-functional (Leeds-Hurwitz, 1989; see also Sigman, 1987; Leeds-Hurwitz & Sigman with Sullivan, 1995).

"Social approaches" is a term coined to emphasize that a number of assumptions are shared by various approaches to the study of communication otherwise viewed as quite discrete. Among those approaches are included social communication theory, the ethnography of communication, the coordinated management of meaning, conversation analysis, ethnomethodology, and semiotics. At the very least, those who take any of the social approaches can be defined as being interested in communication as a social, rather than an individual, phenomenon, and always as being interested in some aspects of the context, though which aspects may vary considerably (Leeds-Hurwitz, 1995).

"Context" refers to everything which must be taken into account in order to understand the meaning of a particular word or behavior for the participants; as such, it is important in some transformation, some version, to everyone who studies human communication, regardless of theoretical approach. The various chapters in this book present a wide range of explanations of exactly what a variety of different approaches deem necessary to take into account as appropriate context. Only some of these are appropriately described as "social approaches."

"Context analysis" is a term used primarily by psychologists to describe one particular approach to the study of behavior that emphasizes moving beyond an individual to the larger group (Owen, 1996).

In this chapter, I will present the view of context that makes the most sense to me, as someone whose own work falls under the rubric of social communication theory.[1] Most briefly, context is whatever must be taken into account to understand the communication behavior that is the focus of study.[2] Context does not consist only of those comments immediately preceding and immediately following an utterance, but of any comments, or actions, or communicative behaviors that must be taken into account in order to fully understand the data or text that is of interest to the analyst in a roughly comparable way to how it is understood by the participants. If possible, the analyst should understand the data or text better than the participants (combining an insider's and an outsider's point of view); a fragmented, partial understanding should not be assumed to be sufficient, merely because that is what comes most easily.

Equally important to social communication theory, context is not something which can be clearly separated from the behavior or text under analysis. The two (context and behavior) are not of a different order of thing. Since each behavior forms part of the context of other behaviors, there is no inherent, essential distinction between behavior and context. The distinction is thus solely analytical: The behavior or text is that which serves as the focus of attention at a particular point in time; the context is everything which must be taken into account in order to understand the meaning it conveys to participants. Context frequently includes some or all of the following: information about when and where the text occurred; who were the participants; what was the larger event of which it was a part; what were the utterances and behaviors occurring before, after, and simultaneously with it; what were the utterances on the same or related topic occurring at other times; what related events occur at other times; and so forth. It also includes issues more clearly related to the research and the researcher, most generally omitted from explicit discussion: when and why the researcher conducted the particular study, under what conditions, for what period of time, what questions were of paramount concern at that point, what the researcher hoped to learn by the project, and so forth. Much as we may like to do so, it is inappropriate to entirely omit ourselves from our research, as if questions asked themselves and topics grew from the earth with no instigation from researchers.

In the following pages, a brief description of a particular interaction is first presented as data, then placed into several types of context, and, finally, analyzed in several different ways. This will illuminate how social communication theory would describe and analyze behavior in context by providing a concrete example.[3]

Data Extract: "Teacher Said That I'm Supposed To Do This!"

The following discussion occurred as part of a biology class. The students were eight-year-olds taking part in a "College For Kids" program, taught by a university professor. Jeremy, Kyle, Darin, Matt, Von are all students in the class; Dr. P is the teacher.

Jeremy: Can I put this together? [points to a life-size model of the human body]

Dr. P.: Yes.

Jeremy works on putting the pieces back together on the model, and Kyle comes over to help. Kyle leaves to join in another activity with the other students, but Darin comes to help, then Matt, then Von. They begin to compete for access to the model (there are too many hands and not enough room for all to reach).

Jeremy: Teacher said that I'm supposed to do this! (said loudly)

Jeremy pushes the one who is closest to the model, Von, out of his way.

Jeremy: Teacher said that I'm supposed to do this! (the same words, uttered in the same tone of voice)

Jeremy and Von play-fight, while Darin continues to work on the model. Matt leaves, Kyle returns, Von leaves. Jeremy gets up onto the table, sitting directly in front of the model in order to work on it more easily. (It is difficult to maneuver the pieces, and he has more leverage this way.) Darin leaves, Matt returns to help, Stephen joins in. At this point Dr. P. walks around the room with a handout (drawing of a grasshopper with labels for body parts missing), turns on the overhead projector, and puts on a slide with labels for the body parts. As this happens, Darin and Matt have left the model and are returning to their seats. Jeremy walks away, leaving Kyle alone still working on it. Two of the parent volunteers, Kathy and Pat, go over the model, sending Kyle to his seat, and put the remaining pieces back themselves. Kyle picks up a handout on the way to his desk.

First Context: The Research

One might well ask, so what? What does this mean? Is there anything important to be learned from this story of a child putting together a model of the human body? My answer is that by itself, this description of behavior provides little meaning; however, understood in its proper context, it has a great deal of meaning. But what is the "proper context"? The remainder of this paper is an attempt to answer that rather simple question.

It is a truism by now to say that events only make sense when viewed in their proper context. In practical terms, this most often means the boundaries of the particular small part of interaction currently under investigation are expanded to include a somewhat larger, but still immediate, context. Thus, a joke is appropriately understood within the context of the party at which it was presented, or a compliment in light of the conversation that surrounds it. It is definitely appropriate to view behavior as occurring within larger events, yet as researchers we must ask ourselves if the minimum information about the behavior we generally provide is always sufficient. What of those events which can only be understood through a context so large that it is not contained within a single day? Assuming that we as researchers can only study that which we know about, the question arises, "where do we draw the border around what we wish to study?" In other words, how much context is necessary? For me, the contextual information provided is sufficient only at the point when we know enough to understand the behavior that is our focus of study in the same way the participants understand it. Traditionally communication scholars have used a fairly narrow definition of appropriate context, and for many examples this is certainly sufficient. The problem becomes noticeable when events drawing their meaning from more than one context, or from events occurring over an extended period of time, where the participants are present but the researcher absent, remain unrecorded and unstudied.

This problem was on my mind when I observed a two-week class within a College For Kids at a midwestern university held during the summer of 1989.[4] It was my assumption that this setting, where the same children met with the same instructor, two hours each day for two weeks, for a total of 20 hours together, would provide examples of events that could only be completely understood through reference to previous events they had experienced jointly. At the same time, the period involved, two weeks, was not so long that I would have trouble being present for all of the class meetings. In this way, my knowledge of the experience as researcher would match that of the participants in the class as closely as possible.

In addition, recognizing that the larger temporal and spatial boundaries of the class would provide additional contextual material for events (the children came together a little before class began, and were still present together after it had officially ended while they waited for rides home), I wanted to be present as early as anyone else, and as late as anyone else. Toward this end, I served as one of the parent volunteers, assigned the duties of meeting the children before the instructor arrived and supervising them until their parents arrived to pick them up. As a joint decision between the instructor, the director of the program, and myself, the information that I was a researcher in addition to a volunteer was conveyed neither to the other parent volunteers nor to the children.[5]

Another problem on my mind when beginning this research was the issue of how a teacher establishes (or, more correctly, how teacher and students together jointly construct) a sense of predictable structure quickly enough so that in an educational setting lasting only two weeks the students would know what to expect and how to act quickly enough to gain something of value from the course. In a nine-month school year, at least the first two weeks are generally devoted to negotiation of this issue, but in a two-week class, the negotiated structure clearly has to be established almost immediately. Having prior experience in observing the same age students during their regular school year, I was curious to see if I could observe that process as it occurred, and to discover the extent to which that process was explicitly verbalized by the teacher and/or by the students.[6] As it turned out, the answer is related to my understanding of context.

This College For Kids setting was similar to others I know about.[7] The classes were taught primarily by university faculty or, less commonly, by well-qualified high school teachers or other members of the community, during the summer. The students were self-selected, or, more often, parent-selected. They were generally understood to be participating because they were bright and not always excited by regular classroom activities during the year.[8] (There are obviously other reasons for enrolling in the classes, from having nothing better to do during the summer, to wanting to pursue particular fields of study not available during the regular school year, but these were less frequently stated by any of the participants.) Several parents drove long distances into the metropolitan area where this College For Kids was held in order to give their children some reinforcement that learning was enjoyable, despite experiences during the school year with programs or teachers sometimes inadequately prepared to cope with bright children easily bored. The parent volunteers either had children in the class, and found it most convenient to attend class with them, or were gaining priority for their children the next summer.[9]

The particular class of concern here was a Biology class taught to eight-year-olds, from 11:30 to 1:30. It was chosen in large part because the instructor was known to be flexible, and the director of the program thought he would be willing to permit me to observe. This instructor had an additional advantage over some other possible choices since he had been with the program many years and was considered to be a good representative of what happened in the classes. There was some concern expressed that it would not be appropriate to place me with a teacher new to the program, who had not yet established a particular style within the rather loose guidelines provided by the program staff. There was also considerable interest in what I might discover through observing this particular teacher, and the hope expressed that I could clarify for new teachers what worked in the program.[10] This teacher was considered to be good at his job, and they wanted to know how to explain what constituted "good teaching" in this setting.

This eventually turned into an additional research question for me: What constituted "good teaching," in this setting, or more specifically, What did this teacher do to convey his interest in the topic to the students so that they too would understand the importance of the subject? A hidden agenda of the course was to influence elementary level students to choose science as an eventual career. The teacher wanted this course to be a positive experience for students, though no explicit comments about future career paths were made to them. Although it is never clearly stated, the majority of the classes in the College for Kids program are science courses, partly for this reason, and partly because elementary students get few hands-on science courses in their regular schools; courses in the program must be hands-on to be successful with the intended audience of young children.

Beginning with general questions is reasonable in ethnographic research, and widely recommended, but there was one drawback: not knowing what would later turn out to be a focus for study, it was necessary to document virtually everything that occurred in the class. This would have been easiest through videotaping, or at least audiotaping the sessions, but the director of the program requested that neither be used in order to minimize my impact on the class. Understanding the argument I had no choice but to agree, though it made part of my job more difficult, and undoubtedly has led to some gaps in my data. At the same time, much of what later proved to be interesting occurred at the fringes of the central activity: just before the class began, after it was officially ended, or during trips elsewhere. These peripheral events would have been difficult to videotape without heavily influencing what was occurring, and so it was perhaps just as well that I had to rely on old-fashioned notebook and pen.[11]

Second Context: The Course

The following are all of the explicit fieldnotes I have relating to the model of the human body that the students took apart in the data segment previously presented.

Monday, Day 6.

For the first time, the instructor made a comment about the model. He pointed to it standing in the left rear corner of the room while in the midst of some comments about what the class will be doing this week:

1 Dr. P: ...and sooner or later we have to take apart that person standing in the corner (gestures vaguely in the direction of the model).

A parent volunteer sitting in front of the model looked up and answered:

2 Amy: Not me!

3 Dr. P: No, you don't have to worry.

Tuesday, Day 7.

I noted several children standing in front of the model discussing it, very briefly, before class began.

Wednesday, Day 8.

The instructor had moved the model to the right forward corner of the room, on a desk in front of the door through which the children generally entered. It was impossible not to notice when entering the class that morning. The first part of class was taken up by a trip to the biology department's animal facilities; when we returned there was some discussion of differences between plant and animal cells, plant fibers, grass clippings as food for animals versus people, leading to a discussion of heart beats.

4 Dr. P.:   I'd like to begin another exercise.

He uses the model of a human body to show where the heart is located, while discussing heart beats. In response to a question by Jeremy,

5 Dr. P.:   Well, let's digress a moment.

and he begins to take the model apart. The lungs are difficult to remove.

6 Dr. P.:   We need a hammer.

7 Children: He's going to die!

Several of the children groan and shiver as the model is taken apart. Various internal organs are held up in turn: liver, gall bladder, intestines, fat. Dr. P. comments that each student should have the opportunity to take the model apart and put it back together. [It is unclear when he intends this to occur.] In response to questions, children call out the name and function of various organs, and answer questions:

8 Dr. P.:   How big is your heart?

Michael knows how big it is, as big as your fist. Kyle and Stephen sitting next to me make fists, compare their size, talk about those being the size of their hearts. Further comments on the color of blood, function of arteries and veins, then:

9 Dr. P.:   We're going to perform open heart surgery.

as he takes half the heart out (half stays in, with diagrams of the circulatory system printed on it).

10 Dr. P.:   I'd like you to feel your heart beat.

Tells them to check at the wrist, not with their thumbs, then at the neck.

One child tells a story about her father having heart surgery. Dr. P. brings out stethoscopes, describes the parts, has everyone come up to the table and get one, they push and crowd and in the process one is pulled apart. Dr. P. holds it up, saying:

11 Dr. P.:   Who has dissected a stethoscope?

They wander around the room listening to each other's pulse; he encourages this:

12 Dr. P.:   Play with it a few minutes.

After a short time, he checks that they know where to find the heart (on the left side). Dr. P. begins an exercise where they take their own pulse and graph the result on paper, it requires two attempts before most have completed the task. Dr. P. then has them run up and down the stairs in the building to increase their heart rate, and graph the result. After the stair-runners return they want to do the exercise again, and Dr. P. agrees. At this point Jeremy asks him:

13 Jeremy: Can I put this together? [points to the model]

14 Dr. P.:   Yes.

Jeremy works on putting the pieces back together on the model, and Kyle comes over to help. Then Kyle leaves to run down the stairs with the others, but Darin comes to help, then Matt, then Von. They begin to compete for access to the model (there are too many hands and not enough room for all to reach.)

15 Jeremy: Teacher said that I'm supposed to do this! (said loudly)

Jeremy pushes the one closest to the model, Von, out of his way.

16 Jeremy: Teacher said that I'm supposed to do this! (the same words, in the same tone of voice)

Jeremy and Von play-fight, while Darin continues to work on the model. Matt leaves, Kyle returns, Von leaves. Jeremy gets up onto the table, sitting directly in front of the model in order to work on it more easily. (It is difficult to maneuver the pieces, and he has more leverage this way.) Darin leaves, Matt returns to help, Stephen joins in. At this point Dr. P. walks around the room with a handout (drawing of a grasshopper with labels for body parts missing), turns on the overhead projector, and puts on a slide with labels for the body parts. As this happens, Darin and Matt have left the model and are returning to their seats.

Jeremy walks away, leaving Kyle alone still working on it. Two of the parent volunteers, Kathy and Pat, go over the model, sending Kyle to his seat, and put the remaining pieces back themselves. Kyle picks up a handout on the way to his desk.

Thursday, Day 9.

I walk in 10 minutes before class is scheduled to start, but there are already some children in the room (they have been arriving earlier and earlier). Jeremy is putting together the model again; Jennifer's brother Kevin (joining us only today, here with their mother to hear Jennifer's report) helps. Von and Dan wander over to help. At 11:30 the class formally begins with:

17 Dr. P.: Who has a report?

[The children have been encouraged to do related experiments at home, and to tell everyone the results; only a few have done so to date.] As Jennifer gives her report describing a rabbit, Jeremy, Von and Dan continue to work on the model and talk.

18 Dr. P.: Could I ask the youngsters who are dissecting the model to please be seated so we can listen to the reports?

One of the parent volunteers, Kathy, walks over to them; as they walk back to their seats, she begins to complete the model.

19 Dr. P.: You don't have to reassemble it. I'm sure someone will do that later.

[Later I noticed the model was put back together, but did not see who did it.]

Friday, Day 10.

Again I walk in early, and again Jeremy, Von and Dan are working on the model. Jeremy sits on the table with the model, as he did on Wednesday. After putting my notebook and pen down on a table, I walk over to the model. Jeremy comes towards me with the brain in his hand:

20 Jeremy: I'm the smartest person in the world.

I have him balance the brain on his head and try walking without letting it fall, he walks that way back to the model. Dan and I work on the model, with Jeremy as critic (taking out the very parts we just put in). Several parts do not fit perfectly, which is cause for some discussion. By working with them, I discover that Jeremy knows nearly all the body parts by name now, though Dan calls the liver "a second kidney." As Dan and I try to complete the model, Nathan comes over and helps us get the chest wall on (it fits badly and is difficult to attach). David and his father come in.

21 David: Some people do it every day.

As Nathan and Dan finish closing up the model, Jeremy has moved to the nearby sink and is playing with the water. Today everyone stops playing and sits down in time for the formal beginning of class. An hour later, after they have dissected frogs and are cleaning up, David puts the head of the model on backwards, and many of the children crowd around laughing.

The Concept of Context in Social Communication Theory

First Analysis: Immediate Interactional Concerns

This interaction involves a full-sized model of the human body standing in a corner of the room made available for viewing before and after class, and for touching, should anyone have been bold enough, during the first week, but I have no notes on anyone actually touching it or otherwise obviously interacting with it that week. (As it was very close to my seat, I assume I would have noted any special interest on the part of the students.) Just as I noted its presence, so I assume others did as well. Since there were plenty of other things to notice during the few minutes available to general surveillance of the classroom environment, this lack of obvious interest is not particularly surprising. Mating frogs caused quite a stir the first week, for example, and had the dual advantage of being alive, and leading to questions about sex.

Nearly any one day's events related to the ways in which the model played a part in the class would be comprehensible without knowledge of any further context, but only at a superficial level. Knowing what else occurred on the same day would provide additional information, certainly, but would obscure the total pattern of learning about the model that seems to have been involved here. Looking at what occurred over the entire 10-day span of the course, it is evident that the following pattern emerged:

Days 1-5: The model is physically available, although no one does anything noticeable with it; the students learn to expect it as a normal part of the surroundings. This is a case of a "non-event" having great significance in understanding an interaction, since what appears to be nothing happening actually has a specific result. The children gained at least minimal familiarity with the model during its unremarked presence for an entire week. It is unlikely most of them had previous exposure to a life-size model of the human body, and this could be a threatening object. Some time to gradually become accustomed to it was appropriate. At the same time, there were numerous other objects in the room which equally could be viewed or touched by the children, and which only sometimes became the topic of extended class discussion, or a full lesson, during the two weeks (such as a model of a plant cell, an animal cell, etc.).

Day 6: The teacher refers to the model, calling it to the attention of the children in the class; specifically he mentions that we will be taking the model apart, though no particular day is mentioned for that activity. Whether the exchange on lines 1-3 is understood as joking between adults in the context of a children's class, or as an adult who wasn't especially aware of the model's presence, it served to call the model to the specific attention of all of the students, presumably the instructor's intent. This technique of referring to topics that would be brought up later for more detailed discussion was typical of this teacher, and served as a good way to prepare the children for what was yet to come.

Day 7: The children stand in front of the model for the first time and look it over, without being prompted to do so by the teacher, though they do not touch it. It is noteworthy that they did not do this before he called their attention to the model, but that they did so afterwards. (It is of course possible that several children had stood in front of the model and discussed it during week 1, and I had not noticed or recorded them doing so. That does not change the importance of their obviously noticing it after he called it to their attention as a group.)

Day 8: Before class begins, the instructor moves the model to a more prominent position in the room; he then uses it as a prop during class. After this occurs, one of the children asks a question about it, also during the lesson, to which the teacher responds by taking it apart and labeling the various organs, though that was apparently not originally part of the lesson plan (line 5). There were other examples of topics that were presented as "available" for further discussion to the children; this seemed an effective warning system for the children: they could take note of the large list of potential topics, and specifically request further information on those of greatest interest. At the first *appropriate* moment (lines 13-14), the same child obtains permission to put the model back together, the first time a child touches the model. (Being able to choose an appropriate moment obviously both requires and demonstrates extensive knowledge of the context on the part of the child.)

The particular circumstances were important: Dr. P. was letting those who wished to do so repeat an experiment that Jeremy had already completed successfully, so this was an ideal time to work on the model. Once the first child begins working with the model, others join, and there is some pushing as they compete for access to the model. Jeremy makes an interesting choice of words, saying that he is the one "supposed to" do this. In fact, he was given permission to do it, but no one told him he was supposed to do it. It is unlikely that "supposed to" and "permission to" mean the same thing to him; presumably they are here conflated for the sake of rhetorical emphasis. At this point Jeremy, the originator of the task, sits on the table with the model while working on it. In this way he manages to maintain a closer relationship with it than the others, and keep better control of the pieces representing the internal organs. Not all the children leave the model when it is time to continue with a new topic in class, and the parent volunteers appear, ensuring that they are ready to move on to a new task with the rest of the class.

Several examples of timing are worthy of note here: Jeremy, who started working on the model, ends his part in the activity in such a way that he only missed a single exercise, a repetition of something he had already done. Kyle, who participated in the second running down stairs and only later in the effort with the model, was in the end less skillful about leaving the model before another activity had begun, and was one of those who had to be told to stop working on it; yet even Kyle noted the transition to a new exercise, and picked up the appropriate handout on the way to his seat without anyone having to call it to his attention explicitly.

Day 9: Several children begin the day by working with the model, and have to be asked to join the class when it begins; they then leave it alone most of the rest of the day. The instructor makes a specific comment about class beginning, and the need to stop working on the model; children who displayed knowledge of appropriately timing overlap between events the previous day do not display a similar ability today. The discrepancy may be due to one or both of the following factors: 1) the different skills required to control boundaries between events within the class as opposed to skills required to control the boundary between "before-class" and "class-proper," and 2) the different attention granted a peer (the child giving a report on an experiment performed at home, in this case) as opposed to the teacher.

Day 10: Again, several children begin the day working on the model, but this time they have moved beyond the simple task of taking the body parts out of the mold, naming them, and putting them back together correctly. Several pieces are for the first time manipulated in new ways: in line 20 the brain is removed, and used as a prop in a joke for a limited audience of one parent; later in the day the head is turned backwards as a joke, this time to a large audience of peers. By line 21 a comment is made which demonstrates that the activity of playing with the model has become a taken-for-granted activity in the context of the classroom: It is glossed (incorrectly) by one student to his father as something occurring every day.

Second Analysis: Pedagogical Concerns

In her excellent book on teaching children science, Eleanor Duckworth (1987) suggests that the essence of pedagogy is giving children the occasion to have wonderful ideas. Doing this requires extensive preparation on the part of the teacher, who must not only provide interesting materials, but an environment conducive to experimentation with those materials, combined with a nonjudgmental stance, so incomplete ideas are not stifled before they reach completion. If we know only the core event described at the beginning of the paper, where Jeremy asks permission to take apart the model, we might mistakenly assume that he has, with minimal if any encouragement from the teacher, come up with the idea to take apart the model. Only once we understand what has occurred over the preceding week and a half do we discover just how much preparation has gone into the encouragement of that question.

An important point is that the teacher encouraged the development of interest in the model by any of the children, not on the part of any specific child. Having taught the course more than once before, he has learned some of the likely questions, but displays less concern that the questions occur to individual children than that they are at some point verbalized by at least one child. Once any child has expressed interest in the model, it becomes a topic for discussion by the entire class. And only once we know what follows in the week after that initial request are we able to realize the entire learning curve. First, the children focus on learning the names of the body parts, and their place in the body, and work on the physical manipulation of the parts, and they work on this until they are required to stop, beginning again the next day, and again having to be told to stop; only once these essential tasks have been accomplished do they begin to explore what else can be done with the same body parts. They can now play a role in jokes, having become a taken-for-granted aspect of the environment.

In the process of taking apart the model, only a small subset of the class has worked directly with it, but they have learned what every biology teacher might wish for: the names, locations, and functions of the various internal organs of the human body. And the exercise was hardly wasted on the other students, who at the very least heard the names and functions of the various body parts, and, perhaps more significantly, learned that it is appropriate to take apart models of the human body. When next exposed to similar models in their regular classrooms, they will be more immediately familiar with them and their uses.

Third Analysis: Broader Interactional Concerns

There are other things we can learn from this case study that have less to do with the nature of learning in classrooms than with the nature of interaction in any setting. For one, it may be significant that a physical object was involved in this particular example of interaction. Perhaps there is often a need, especially with children, or especially in a classroom setting, for a physical object to serve as an "interactional peg," that is, to serve as a reminder of the topic, as an "anchor" around which discussion revolves, and to which it can readily return.[12] Adults may be more adept at using solely verbal reminders to return to topics over a period of time. By virtue of its physical presence, the model continued to pique the children's interest, and to remind them that there was something available yet to investigate. Without it, they might have dropped the subject much sooner, and moved on to one of the many other topics included within the scope of this biology class. With it, they maintained an interaction with the model until they no longer were able to learn anything new from it.

Another implication of the foregoing discussion is that context is fluid: The amount of context that must be considered to ensure a reasonable (never a complete) understanding of interaction varies in accord with the duration of that interaction. That is, on the first day, this group had only a brief history together, and there was little on which one could draw for a complete understanding of what occurred, outside of a particular segment of discourse. New topics were continually introduced because the group did not have enough of a history together to successfully refer to many old topics. (Old topics assumed to be common experiences included: a general knowledge of the requirements and assumptions of schools, a small amount of television viewing, and the common experience of interaction between parents and their children.) By the middle of the course (Day 5), a much larger context served as the pool from which information could be drawn, and all participants could reasonably be expected to share that information. A researcher thus would have to know more, and take more into account, in order to make sense of what was observed on Day 5, when the group had established a unique, shared history, than on Day 1, when it had not yet done so. By the end of the course (Day 10), the context from which meaning could be drawn was larger still, and a researcher would need to take far more into account, just as the participants would need to do. This complicates our understanding of context, and our decisions of how much context to consider when attempting to discuss meaning in interaction, but the complication in and of itself should not serve as sufficient reason to ignore the problem.

Conclusion

Because this example describes children in a classroom, it focuses on children learning something new. In this case, with the appropriate materials supplied, and minimal explicit prompting from their teacher, some of the children in the class make use of the opportunity provided to manipulate the parts of a model of a human body, learn the names for those body parts, and learn where they belong. These are all central topics in biology, ideas that a biology teacher would want to teach students; simultaneously, these are all ideas easy enough for eight-year-olds to understand, if they are sufficiently interested to make the attempt.

In this case study, the teacher can be seen to present the opportunity for learning during the first week, to bring the opportunity more directly to the attention of students at the beginning of the second week, to follow-up on the first indication that someone is interested in what he has proposed (and to noticeably deviate from the planned schedule of events) in order to let a child work with the model when it most immediately interests him. That child can be seen to move from a single initial question about the model, to considerable familiarity with the body parts, and, finally, to using the body parts as objects and in ways unrelated to their function within the body. Other children can be observed taking part in the exploration, and learning, as well.

Particular pieces of this event would have been interesting even if only one day had been observed, most especially if that day had been Wednesday of the second week, but our understanding of what happened in all its complexity would have been incomplete. Including all of the contributing interactions occurring over the course of two weeks permits us to discover much more about the content of the event: how children learn, and what teachers can do to encourage them. At the same time we uncover a generalization about the form of the event. There is a rhythm here, of first minimal, then increasing, then decreasing, involvement in a new topic. This rhythm should be apparent for most new topics, not just the one presented here, especially in groups where ongoing interactions between a stable set of group members occur. These would prominently include family, school, and work settings, although less obvious groups in other contexts would also be pertinent.

What implications for future research can we draw? By expanding the boundaries of the amount of context that needs to be taken into account for a full and appropriate interpretation of interaction, the life of the researcher is made more complicated. This is offset by the fact that the resulting interpretation is more complex and, presumably, more complete. Of course, I am not suggesting that all research which does not take into account the entire history of interactions between participants is inadequate; that would make much past research invalid and most future research particularly difficult. There are many cases where it is simply not practical to discover the complete set of interactions relevant to understanding an event in the way the participants are able to understand it, and many research questions which do not require it (the latter is, of course, more significant theoretically). Yet, at the same time, the example provided here does imply that we as researchers make deliberate choices as to the extent of the context we are willing to consider relevant. This case study demonstrates the need to make such choices consciously, basing them upon as much knowledge of the type of behavior to be studied as feasible.

In general, we should expand the amount of time and type of events we are willing to include in our data-gathering in order to improve our eventual understanding of social interaction. In this particular case, the boundaries were expanded in two ways: from a single event (one class) to include all comparable events (all classes in a particular course); and from the formal class period (11:30-1:30) to include informal class-related activities (what happened immediately before and immediately after the class). It is important to recognize that not all of the expanded context proved to be necessary. On some of the days (as during the first week) nothing much happened that was directly related to consideration of the model, and nothing that occurred after the class officially ended each day turned out to be directly relevant. Note the use of the phrase "directly relevant" here. Lots that happened was indirectly relevant, as in the particular combination of children who chose to gather around the model, which was not happenstance, but based on prior groupings of children within the class. It is impossible to predict beforehand exactly which elements of a context will prove most informative. We must therefore initially include as much contextual information as we can, since we cannot be sure what will provide important clues that permit us to interpret behavior. As we come to acknowledge the frequent intertextuality of events, we must shift our research techniques to take our new understandings into account.[13]

But what of the initial question raised by the College For Kids staff members, who wanted to know what constituted good teaching? Does this discussion of context shed any light on their concerns? I would argue that it does. The obvious connections made between different class meetings is one part of what made this teacher so effective, in that it led the children to experience their 10-day session as a coherent whole (thus answering my initial question about how a teacher works to establish a common framework for interaction, permitting teaching to occur). By introducing numerous topics briefly, and by obviously responding to what the children found most enticing out of the list of possibilities, this teacher showed his flexibility, and permitted the children to govern, if not the selection of topics, then the varying emphases placed on those topics, during the course. One part of what constitutes "good teaching" is generally recognized as getting the students interested in their material, in somehow getting them to "accept ownership" of the material (as it is sometimes phrased); this is precisely what occurred in this classroom. It was with great delight that I discovered the connection between the varying questions driving this research: the questions of how much context is required for understanding interaction, how a teacher establishes a common framework for interactions occurring specifically within a classroom, as well as what constitutes good teaching in this particular setting, have all been addressed in overlapping ways, if not answered completely.

At the same time, for the more immediate goals of this particular chapter within this book, it is to be hoped that the concrete demonstration of the overlapping issues of data, context, and analysis as manifested within one particular setting, a Biology course offered within the College for Kids, has served to adequately answer the question of what the concept of context means within social communication theory.

References

Barthes, R. (1977). The rhetoric of the image. In *Image-music-text*. London: Fontana.

Duckworth, E. (1987). *"The having of wonderful ideas:" And other essays on teaching and learning*. New York: Teacher's College Press.

Feldhusen, J., & Sokol, L. (1982). Extra-school programming to meet the needs of gifted youth: super Saturday. *Gifted Child Quarterly*, 26, 51-56.

Feldhusen, J. F., & Wyman, A. R. (1980). Super Saturday: Design and implementation of Purdue's special program for gifted children. *Gifted Child Quarterly*, 24, 15-21.

Hensel, N. (1985). A cooperative university/school district gifted program. *Roeper Review*, 7, 220-222.

Juntune, J. (1981). *Successful programs for the gifted and talented*. Hot Springs, AK: National Association for Gifted and Talented.

Leeds-Hurwitz, W. (1989). *Communication in everyday life: A social interpretation*. Norwood, NJ: Ablex Publishing.

Leeds-Hurwitz, W. (1993). *Semiotics and communication: Signs, codes, cultures*. Hillsdale, NJ: Lawrence Erlbaum Associates.

Leeds-Hurwitz, W. (Ed.). (1995). *Social approaches to communication*. New York: Guilford Press.

Leeds-Hurwitz, W., & Sigman, J., with Sullivan, S. (1995). Social communication theory: Communication structures and performed invocations, a revision of Scheflen's notion of programs. In Stuart J. Sigman (Ed.), *The consequentiality of communication* (pp. 163-204). Hillsdale, NJ: Lawrence Erlbaum Associates.

Owen, J. L. (1996, February). Context theory and consequated interaction. Paper presented to the Western States Communication Association, Pasadena, CA.

Robinson, B. (1981). College for kids. In R. E. Clasen, B. Robinson, D. R. Clasen, & G. Libster (Eds.), *Programming for the gifted, talented, and creative*. Madison, WI: University of Wisconsin-Madison Extension.

Seeley, K. R., Katz, E. & Linder, T. W.. (1981). The university as a community resource for gifted: The university for youth. *Gifted Child Quarterly*, 25, 112-115.

Sigman, S. (1987). *A perspective on social communication*. Lexington, MA: Lexington Books.

Footnotes

[1] Obviously, at other times, for other purposes, I have labeled my work as falling under the rubric of either the ethnography of communication or semiotics. I do not reject those labels now, but they are not directly relevant to what I am describing here, since I have been asked to represent social communication theory in this chapter. It is simply that I use different theoretical approaches and/or labels as they seem the most relevant to my discussion, or valuable to my analytic needs.

[2] See Leeds-Hurwitz (1989, pp. 71-99) for an extended explanation of what needs to be taken into account in order to understand context from the point of view of social communication theory.

[3] This data, although with a different analysis, has been presented to the Speech Communication Association, and the Ethnography in Education Research Forum. My thanks to participants in those conferences for their comments, especially Fred Erickson. This analysis has also benefited from conversations about the data with Yves Winkin.

[4] In addition to observing a two-week session, I also interviewed those involved in administering the program, teachers, parents, and talked more informally with students. Since the results were interesting, I then observed a second two-week session on another topic, computer programming, order to gain comparative data, the same summer. Also, for the next two summers I participated as a regular parent volunteer for additional sessions (that is, I did not take extensive fieldnotes), and continued interviewing parents and teachers, as well as talking with students. Those observations do not directly figure into my comments here, but clearly they have influenced my ideas.

[5] This may be a questionable decision, but I wanted to do what those running the program felt most appropriate. It became quite obvious during the session that I did not always behave like a volunteer (I took extensive notes during class, for example, though none of the other parent volunteers did), but this seemed to cause little concern or question from parents or from children (much to my surprise).

[6] The most interesting results of my prior experiences observing students in more traditional classrooms are documented in Leeds-Hurwitz (1989).

[7] Some descriptions of similar programs may be found in Feldhusen and Sokol (1982), Feldhusen and Wyman (1980), Hensel (1985), Juntune (1981), Robinson (1981), and Seeley, Katz, and Linder (1981). Colleges for Kids were first developed

in Wisconsin by Beecham Robinson in 1980, spreading from UW-Parkside to other UW campuses. My thanks to Beecham Robinson for discussing the history of the program with me.

[8]This aspect of the program is uncommon; comparable programs generally are intended only for children specifically identified as "gifted." The original goal of the first College for Kids at UW-Parkside was specifically to meet the perceived needs of gifted students during the long summer months away from a formal education setting. The main advantages to the lack of explicit selection practiced at the university where I made my observations are: 1) A wider potential audience, and 2) no time need be spent on selection criteria, or ensuring that appropriate children are not being left out inadvertently. At the same time, it should be noted that the implicit message of the title is clear to most parents: Only unusually bright children should be sent to "college" while they are still in elementary school.

[9]As an incentive to attract the large numbers of volunteers necessary to make the teachers' jobs easier, the program grants priority registration to children whose parents had volunteered the previous summer. Since there was always more demand for spaces than could be met by the small program, this was effective. I attended several of the registration days for the program, and spoke with many parents about their motives for enrolling their children in these classes.

[10]I discussed my research with the teacher in the class, and shared my field notes (several hundred pages) at the end of each week (the delay was due to the time necessary to turn my notes into a typed manuscript), as well as a draft of my analysis of the data. His response: "Now I know what a stage magician feels like after his tricks have been exposed."

[11]Yves Winkin suggests that perhaps it is significant that some of the most interesting interactions occurred during liminal stages, that is, between named events rather than during them (personal communication, December 1989). This implies that researchers should pay particular attention to what occurs immediately prior to and immediately following what they think they're studying, in case the same holds true across many types of events.

[12]This concept of interactional pegs or anchors is worthy of more attention than it has been granted here or elsewhere; useful comments may be found in Barthes (1977) on the role of captions as anchors to the visual images they accompany.

[13]See Leeds-Hurwitz (1993) for a discussion of the concept of intertextuality as well as for references to the literature on the topic.

Chapter 16

The Researcher in Communication: The Primary Research Position

Robyn Penman
Communication Research Institute of Australia

There are a number of new theoretical developments in communication that share a concern with context, in its complex sense. But while they all reflect the intellectual heritage of contextualists like Pepper (1942), they go well beyond that heritage in at least two important and interrelated ways in their treatment and understanding of communication

First, as Vern Cronen (1995) points out, in these new theoretical developments in communication "context returns to its original Latin source as a *verb* meaning to weave together. Thus context and utterance reflexively evolve and inform one another" (p. 225). This is in contrast to a more simplistic treatment, in which the context of an utterance is no more than its surrounds; i.e., something was said in a certain context, or situation. In this simplistic treatment the meaning of an utterance or text is seen, at most, to be partially dependent on the context of the saying or reading. But, in the more complex sense in which context is taken in its verb form, meaning arises from the mutual interplay of context and utterance. Our understanding of communication, and in communicating, is contextually bound.

Second, the way in which knowledge is conceived of is radically transformed in these new developments in communication. These new developments directly acknowledge the contextually bound and humanly constructed nature of social knowledge. Indeed, in recognising the interdependency between context and utterance you are inexorably led to the recognition that that all knowledge is generated in context; specifically in the context of communicating.

The recognition of the socially constructed nature of knowledge—and all that implies about the reflexive relationship between context and 'text'—is in stark contrast to the intellectual tradition of the past three centuries. Over this era of Modernity, scholars of all kinds have been preoccupied with the search for knowledge that transcended themselves and their time. They believed that there is an objective, immutable, base to knowledge in the real world just waiting to be found or discovered. All it required was the right reasoning process and a 'pure' truth could be found. In short, they were concerned with a search for knowledge 'out of context', as it were. But when it is recognised that there is no 'pure' truth to be found independent of the human world in which the finding is being done, new questions about how and what we know need to be asked.

These interrelated concerns with context in its complex sense and the social construction of knowledge have radical implications for how we undertake research in communication. As various writers have argued, any form of contextualist thinking is antithetical to conventional scientific methodology (e.g., Gergen, 1982; Leeds-Hurwitz, 1995). So the question we need to ask is what method can be compatible with this new way of thinking. This is the aim of this chapter: to explore what it can mean to do communication research in a way that recognises the contextually bound and humanly constructed nature of social knowledge and in a way that recognises that our knowledge of communication arises out of communicating. But before moving forward into new territory, it will help to look back to see how and why conventional research methods are not appropriate for our new understanding of communication. In taking this look backward, I also want to draw out the link between research methods and conceptions of communication.

Looking Backwards: Communication As Unproblematic

In this look backward, we need to go to the dawn of the Enlightenment in the 17th century. It was there that the foundations for the past three centuries of Modernity were laid and it was there that our mainstream conceptions of communication and research methods were also laid.

Toulmin's (1990) historical analysis of the rise (and fall) of modernity shows how much the founders of Modernity strove to remove themselves from their time and their humanity. The major contributor to this movement, Descartes, was convinced that we could build a secure, permanent body of human knowledge using rationally validated methods that relied on working from formal logic, with general principles and abstract axioms. And it is this that Toulmin argues provides the basis for "the deeper meaning of the term 'scientific method'" (p. 81). 'Scientific method' was developed to generate 'pure,' context-free and universal truths.

In order to be able to pursue the context-free questions of Cartesian rationalism, the philosophers of the day made four major moves (Toulmin, 1990). First they moved from the oral to the written. With this move, public arguments before audiences became unacceptable as a means for discovery or confirmation. Instead, the soundness or validity of an argument could only be demonstrated as a series of written chains of statements with internal consistency. To quote Toulmin, "formal logic was in, rhetoric was out" (p. 31).

Second, they moved from the particular to the universal. It was no longer acceptable to explore the implications of specific cases; all examination had to be based on comprehensive, universal principles of general theory by which particulars could be rationally linked together.

Third they moved from the local to the general. In this move, ethnographic and historical information was discarded as irrelevant to true philosophical enquiry and in doing so a whole realm of context-related questions became irrelevant. Instead, the goal was to develop abstract, generalised axioms to cover all manner of things.

Fourth, they moved from the timely to the timeless. In this move, concern with transient human affairs was put into second place. The concern was not with factors that held good in different ways at different times, but with the timeless principles that held good at all times in all places.

The pursuers of context-free and universal truths, however, had a problem—language (or communication in a broader sense). This problem can best be seen in the arguments of the British scholars that heralded the start of the Empiricist school and whose arguments still influence many areas of communication research today. The core of their arguments rested on the proposition that there was a great division between the material and the immaterial, and only material things mattered. It was only to the material that the rational principals had to be applied, not the immaterial. And in this great division, communication was classed as inessential or immaterial—it did not count (Shepherd, 1993).

For those thinkers, the need to class communication as immaterial was critical to the maintenance of their other arguments. Particularly for the 'linguistic radicals' in England, the conception of language as an ever-moving stream, a medium of innovation, and a source of great uncertainty was abhorrent (Davies, 1987). You could not build a secure, permanent body of human knowledge using rationally validated methods that relied on working from formal logic, with general principles and abstract axioms with something as uncertain as ordinary human language.

For example, Hobbes in the *Leviathan* urged that we had to purge language of all ambiguity, expel metaphor, outlaw new phrasings and reduce it to a rational system of signs. Wilkins, a compatriot of Hobbes, went even further. He argued that natural languages were just too treacherous to be tolerated—the meanings kept on changing and betraying the speaker/listener. Wilkins wanted to destroy the very nature of language in which words referred to things other than themselves and make the words the things themselves. Making the words the things themselves would ensure understanding, eliminate contention, and ensure the pathway to pure knowledge was achievable (Davies, 1987).

Fortunately they could not quite achieve the destruction of 'natural language', nor eliminate the inherent uncertainties of communication. But they did the next best thing. They asserted it did not matter. The search for pure knowledge would go on by asserting that language (and by implication communication) was immaterial to the search; words did not count. We have the heritage of that view in such twentieth century phrases as "actions speak louder than words" and in the childhood saying of "sticks and stones will break my bones but names will never hurt me" (although, curiously, that childhood saying was usually uttered in my childhood just when the words did 'hurt').

This conception of language as neutral, transparent and non positional, however, was most apparent in the forerunner of the British empiricist tradition, John Locke. It was John Locke who sealed the fate of communication-as-immaterial for three centuries. As Shepherd (1993) argues, "Words, to Locke, were insubstantial and untrustworthy nothings" (p. 87). What mattered were individuals and their ideas. But Locke was confronted with a problem when he tried to develop his social theory of liberalism; he had to have some mechanism to connect the individual and their ideas to society. He resolved this problem by making words the vehicles for carrying individuals' ideas from one to the other, but in themselves the words were empty. Thus was born the modern view of communication as a conduit (see Reddy, 1979); communication was no more than the means for the conveyance of ideas in words. It was the ideas that counted, not the transmitter or vehicle for the words.

Unfortunately too much of modern day communication studies still reflects the conventional wisdom of the past three centuries: that communication is immaterial; it is merely a trivial vehicle for something far more important. This 'wisdom' is reflected in arguments about the need to investigate how messages can be best 'shaped' and manipulated in order to best 'transmit' the ideas they 'contain' and to bring about desired effects on others. It is a choice for what Krippendorff (1993) calls message-driven research; research that focuses on the messages (words or texts) and their effects. It is also a choice for undertaking research that will lead to generalised, abstract, and context-free knowledge. And as Krippendorff goes on to argue, it is likely to remain a popular choice because "people in positions of authority are all too eager to embrace deterministic reality constructions that can offer them the prospect of forcing predicability and controllability onto others" (p. 40).

We can still find numerous examples of this type of research, with its concomitant trivialising assumptions about communication, in any number of communication journals today. For example, in the two 1993 issues of the *Journal of Communication* on "The Future of the Field—Between Fragmentation and Cohesion" I found that, of the forty eight articles, only four were clearly advocating a view of communication as foundational to our being (Penman, 1994).

As Toulmin (1990) argues, despite all the intellectual developments in the last half of this century, rationalism, and its concomitant empiricist methodology, dies hard. Nevertheless, it is dying. There have been too many intellectual moves away from rationalism for it to continue to exist in the mainstream for much longer. Indeed from Toulmin's point of view, we have got to the stage where we now only have two choices: "The choice is one between *facing* the future, and so asking about the 'futuribles' open to us, or *backing* into it with no such horizons or ideas" (p. 203). Having faced the past to see the context for where we are, let us now face the future for a new means of communication research.

Looking Forward: Communication As The Problematic

In facing the future, we need to deny the rationalist tradition that treats communication as immaterial and to conversely assert that communication is foundational to our being, it is material and it does matter (Sless, 1991). As many recent authors who have made this move argue, there is a general transformation underway in the humanities and social sciences based on the recognition of the role communication plays in constructing our lives (e.g., Craig, 1993; Gergen, 1982; Penman 1988; 1992). When we start treating communication as the essential problematic of concern; when we start studying communicating and not communication (Dervin, 1993); and when we recognise that we construct our reality in our communicating (Krippendorf, 1993), then we have left the domain of rationalism altogether and turned to face the future.

This radical change in understanding arises from a re-consideration of the very nature of language, the means by which we engage in our social world. At the heart of language is an arbitrary stand-for relation between a word and the thing named. This stand-for relation is such that the relationship between language (the word) and the world (the thing) is ineffable (Wittgenstein, 1953). When these philosophy of language arguments are couched in a communication perspective, we do not just use language; we are actively involved in a communication process that generates meaning. It is this active involvement that the Rationalists had to deny in order for their project to continue. But, it is not necessary to deny it if you are prepared to enter a more uncertain, but challenging, world.

Because of the nature of language, every time we act to represent our knowledge in language we are at the same time bringing it about. This constitutive process is perhaps more obvious when we deal with communication as our problematic. Communication has self-generating capacities, and these capacities arise out of the very interaction of participants, not out of the properties of their external environment. So, in this sense, every act of communication involves participation.

What is important for our purposes here is recognising that the self-generating properties of communication exist in all forms of communicating, including our communication research practices. In undertaking research into communication we are at the same time participating in the very same process we are researching. Within a constructionist's framework, this participation is unavoidable. In this vein, our knowing from our research practices is as much constitutive as it is representational (e.g., see Penman, 1992; Gergen, 1985).

Communication creates the social world, for both the researcher and the other participants in the process. But, the nature of the participation is variable. And, it is here that I want to introduce a major distinction that will lie at the heart of the argument to follow: that between primary and secondary positions.

The notion of positionality is contained in various theoretical arguments which recognise the reflexive relationship between 'text' and 'context'. For example, Shotter (1984) proposes the grammatical notion of a 'person' to capture a sense of position. When we give accounts of communicative activity we can do so from one of three positions: the first (I), second (you) or third (she, he, it) persons. Accounts in the first person are from the position of actor in the process. Accounts in the second person are addressed to the other actor in the process. Accounts in the third person take the position of observer of both the first and second persons. Each person's position, then, provides a different viewpoint of the action and one more or less removed from it.

Sless (1986) has similarly argued that the concept of position is critical to our understanding of communicating. He argues that there are two basic positions a person can take in the process, as well as a successive number of removed positions. In any communicative process one is either an 'author' or 'reader' of a text—there is no independent objective position. But, you could be a reader or author second, third or more removed.

Neither Sless (1986) or Shotter (1984), however, are suggesting there is a direct linear relationship between position and the nature of the account of communication. Instead both evoke a different, and the same, metaphor—that of landscape. As describers of the human social landscape, we can take various positions in that landscape and what we see is dependent on where we are standing: "as the position (s)he occupies changes so does the scene, and as certain views become visible, others disappear" (Sless, 1986, p. 31). The landscape is an elastic one; wherever we stand, we change the shape of the landscape around us.

There is, in fact, no complete landscape; no complete and unalterable view of communication. Instead, there are an infinite array of understandings of the communicative landscape in which we find ourselves or, more accurately, project ourselves. It is this notion of position, and its consequences that ultimately denies the possibility of 'objective' knowledge. All inquiries into the nature of communication are interventions, not neutral observations. In the very act of inquiring into communication from within the communication landscape, we are intervening in that landscape (Penman, 1988).

Wherever we stand as researchers, we change the shape of the landscape about our position. Although this change is unavoidable, different changes have different implications for how we understand.

Primary research involves direct participation in the conversation, in the communication process; whereas, secondary involves a removed position. Primary research explicitly acknowledges our reflexive position in the research process (see Steir, 1995), whereas secondary research ignores it, and sometimes even denies it. Secondary research from a removed (and often far removed) position is the only one possible for a conventional scientist/researcher. While there is nothing inherently wrong with a removed position, it is not the one I want to pursue here. Instead, I want to concentrate on what it means to engage in primary research in communication. In this type of research we are participating directly in conversations with others and it is these conversations that are the generative source, as it were, for our consequent understandings.

But in this type of primary participative research we are, in the very act of entering the process, changing it. In a broad sense, any act of participation in communicating brings about change in understanding; in the act of projecting into the future with our conversations, we are always changing our understandings. So, in this view, change is inevitable—for both the researcher and the other participants.

The inevitably of change is one of the more problem-laden implications of research within a constructionist's framework. In the very act of participation we are influencing what we set out to know. Such a recognition brings with it a moral responsibility that cannot be ignored (Penman, 1992). This moral responsibility leads us onto the next arena of exploration of what it means to be a primary researcher —what *should* (with all the moral implications that entails) we be doing in practice? What counts as good communicating in this view? What is good for the participants in the process?

Without Neutrality Or Truth, What Is Good?

The means whereby we engage in primary research cannot be the means used for traditional scientific 'discovery'. In that traditional approach we would need to research at a distance from a neutral, objective position. And in that traditional approach we would use objective notions of truth to make judgements. But neither neutral positions or objective truth standards are available to us here. Such methods and standards negate the very concept of participation. So how can we participate, if not neutrally, and how can we know we are doing it well, if not truthfully?

In order to talk about this, I need to introduce another concept—a concept of a different way of knowing. Because it is only out of this different way of knowing that the question can be approached. You will recall at the beginning of this chapter that I discussed four major moves that the rationalists had to make to conduct their project. One of these moves was from the particular to the universal. As part of that move a new form of moral philosophy came about. It was concerned not with particular case studies in context, but with the comprehensive general principles of ethical theory (Toulmin, 1990). Now we need to reverse that move and go back to the primary concern of Aristotle in the *Nichomachean Ethics* where he argued that the good has no universal form, regardless of the subject or situation (Toulmin, 1990). Understanding how we can participate well, then, requires us to reconsider 'good' knowing in a different, contextualised way.

John Shotter (1990, 1993) has called this different way of knowing a "knowing of the third kind." Taking Ryle's distinction between 'knowing that' (facts or theoretical principles) and 'knowing how' (technique), he adds this third kind that he calls 'knowing from' (1990, p. 12). This knowing of the third kind is a form of practical knowledge, but it is practical knowledge of a moral order. Shotter (1993), drawing on Vico, Vygotsky, and Mead, emphasises the social context of this moral knowing; it is knowing that comes from our relations with others. To quote from Shotter:

> ...it is knowledge of a *moral* kind, for it depends upon the judgements of others as to whether its expression or its use is ethically proper or not—one cannot just have it or express it on one's own, or wholly within oneself. It is the kind of knowledge one has *only from within a social situation* ...and which thus takes into account (and is accountable to) the others in the social situation... (p. 7)

Moral knowing is about doing; it is about doing with other people. Moral knowing does not exist independently of a social situation, it is brought about within it.

A parallel argument is made by Hans-Georg Gadamer (1989), drawing directly on the Aristotelian tradition. Gadamer's major philosophical concern was with elucidating the hermeneutical nature of the human sciences and human experience generally. From his hermeneutical stance he argued that the pursuit of pure knowledge—in which the interpreter is alienated from the interpreted—is incompatible with moral knowledge. "For moral knowledge, as Aristotle describes it, is clearly not objective knowledge—i.e., the knower is not standing over against a situation that he merely observes; he is directly confronted with what he sees. It is something that he has to do." (p. 314). This view of moral knowing then negates the mainstream philosophical concept of morality as being in the realm of abstract, reasoned principle. For Gadamer, moral knowledge is in the domain of the full human experience.

Gadamer (1989) goes on to argue that moral knowledge is never knowable in advance like knowledge that can be taught: we do not possess moral knowledge in such a way that we already have it and then apply it to specific situations. For Gadamer, then, the conventional twentieth century concept of ethics as a list of imperatives or injunctions does not reflect moral knowledge; moral knowledge is always immanent in practice.

The point that both authors make that is important to the argument here is that moral knowing is not something we know independent of ourselves or our social living, and it is not something that can be learnt as a set of ethical rules and then applied; rather we act into our morality. This has important implications for how we can go about assessing what makes a good conversation or, equivalently, good primary research. From the position of morally knowing, it is not possible to specify a set of generalised injunctions or ethical belief statements and then use them to assess a good conversation; rather we can only act into this moral knowing.

But I need to emphasise here that I am not saying all of our communicative practices are morally 'correct' or otherwise. To say this would be to fall back into a limited conventional view of morality. Instead, I am saying that all communicative practices, by virtue of them being communicative, have a moral element, a moral dimension. In the very process of acting into communicating we are acting into some moral order or another. We are, to return to Gadamer (1989) and Shotter (1990, 1993), bringing about a moral knowing in our communicating.

So, as participating researchers what we have available to us is this third way of knowing; a knowing of the moral kind. This third way of knowing is not available outside of the process of communicating; it is not a way of knowing available from a removed position. Moral knowing is unique to participation.

This then leads me to change the question of 'what counts as good?'. Such a question implies a static view of a participative process; it also implies the possibility of an abstract set of principles by which judgements can be made. Given this, perhaps it is better to simply ask how can we participate well in the process of knowing of the third kind? This is a question about ways, not ends.

Participating Well In The Process

Here I want to argue that the best way, or the good way, focuses on the process itself, not on any arbitrarily defined effects of the process. Indeed, within the conceptual framework I am writing in, it is not possible to base any form of judgement or evaluation outside of communicating. That would assume some external standard, or some objective reality. And, in the very assumption of that outside reality or standard, we would be denying the human agency that created it. Instead we need to base our judgement on the very characteristics of the process we are engaged in. I am suggesting as a general principle that participating well affirms the very features of the process being participated in. Two important features are a) it is a process that goes on, and b) goes mutually.

Future Orientation

In orienting to the practice of communicating our focus as researchers is on the constructive activities between people; it on those "elusive moments of human communicatings" (Dervin, 1993, p. 53). I have found Dewey's (1981) pragmatic arguments about how we can understand these elusive constructive moments most useful here. For Dewey it is not the antecedent phenomena or the precedents that are critical to this understanding but the consequent phenomena and the possibilities for future action. In Dewey's framework, 'anticipation is more primary than recollection, projection more than a summoning of the past, the prospective more than the retrospective" (Rogers, 1994, p. 41).

But I would like to extend Dewey's argument further here. Rather than just saying that the prospective is more important than the retrospective. I would like to also argue that one precludes the other, at least when doing primary research. You cannot be looking back–to study antecedents–while you are looking forward–to understand possibilities–within the same communication process. This would be like trying to row a boat with two rowers with their backs to each other. Just as it would be impossible for them to move, so would it be impossible for a primary researcher to move if they started to look backwards; while still in participation.

So in looking at the elusive, constructive moments, as both participants and as researchers, we can choose to look forward or backward. But to look backward, always loses the moment; the momentum of conversations is forward. In looking forward we are presented with the unfolding of options and the closing off of others as the constructive activity proceeds.

As participating researchers, then, we need to be oriented towards the momentary order of possibilities, the permissions or affordances, that are offered as conversation proceeds. Similarly, we need to be oriented to what options are closed as we proceed, and how we can go on regardless. This is a view from within the process; within the practice of communicating. It is an orientation to going on, and generating the means to do so (hopefully well). It is a view oriented to future solutions or possibilities, not to past 'causes' of problems.

Primary research then is about the study of possibilities, not the study of regularities. The study of regularities requires attention to antecedent conditions, whereas our concern here is with the consequent. But while we can talk about the study of possibilities, we have a problem in practice. In practice, the possibilities are always there before us, always imminent, but never in actuality. So you cannot directly 'study' these possibilities. Instead what is open to us is what cannot be done, what cannot (or is unlikely to) happen. In other words, possibilities are indicated from the constraints experienced and the pathways closed.

It is our sensitivity to the constraints experienced and the potential pathways closed that allow us to work well, or otherwise, in primary research. It is also our capacity to move the conversation forward into new and different pathways that means we are participating well. I perhaps need to reiterate this last point in a different way. I do not think it is enough, as some have argued, simply to keep the conversation going (e.g., Rorty, 1980). Conversations can go round in circles and can go backwards, often in weird paradoxical loops and often seemingly forever. What is important, is that the conversation goes forward, not just onward.

Mutuality

This participatory process is a mutual affair; it is something that goes on between people. To participate well, this mutuality also needs to be affirmed. But, we need to consider here exactly what can be meant by mutuality.

For some, mutuality means equal contribution (e.g., Habermas in McCarthy, 1984). This presumes a whole range of contextual factors, including equality of capacities, powers etc, and I do not think we have to make these assumptions. Instead I would like to suggest that mutuality can simply mean that all participants are able to make some contribution, but not just any contribution. Their contribution should be to the joint development of the methods by which new understandings and changes are brought about.

This particular point about mutual contribution to the method of bringing about new understanding is important and needs elaboration. In various forms of secondary research, participants, at best, are expected simply to consent to the method imposed by the researcher. It is the researcher who knows best how to discover what the researcher wants. Indeed this knowledge of the so-called 'proper' means of discovery (or recovery) is what distinguishes a conventional researcher from her/his participants.

On the other hand, in primary research, while the researcher usually brings a range of conversational tools or methods to the process, these tools of invention are there for the offer of all to choose and use. It is the range of conversational tools that primary researchers bring to the process which distinguish them from other participants, not the use of so-called proper methods of discovery. But, like all the other participants in the process, the researcher must still negotiate the use of their offerings.

The nature, as well as the range, of the conversational tools is important. Drawing on Bennett's (1985) arguments, we need ways of talking with our participants that keeps our participatory process sensitive and accountable to human experience and, by implication, keeps our experiences open. A similar theme is reflected in Klaus Krippendorff's (1989) essay on the ethics of communication. He argues that we have a major social imperative: "in communicating with others, maintain or expand the range of choices possible" (p. 93). It is in this maintenance or expansion of the choices offered that we enable the people with whom we are participating to go forward.

Conclusions

Theory Out Of Practice

I have said that we need to affirm the future orientation and mutuality of our communicating if we are to participate well in knowing of the third kind. But to end the argument, and the practice, there leaves it incomplete or too open. While there are some very good communicating reasons for incompleteness and openness, there are also are some very good reasons for closure, however temporary (Penman, 1992). It is both the reasons for and the nature of the closure in all conversations that help to round out the argument here.

I think we all recognise this need for closure in conversations. It happens whenever we wonder such things as "why did she say that?" or "why did the conversation go the way it did?" When we think we have an answer we have a momentary understanding. But it is only momentary. As the conversation proceeds, the context for understanding changes and so too does the understanding. The answer to "Why did she say that?" often later becomes, "Oh, she meant this, not that."

My colleague, David Sless (1986), has poignantly captured this momentary, changing nature of understanding: "Understanding is the dead spot in our struggle for meaning: it is the momentary pause, the stillness before incomprehension continues...Thus understanding is a temporary state of closure" (p. i).

To understand, to provide temporary closure, is to step away from the participation, if only for the moment. And once we are outside the process we are making a different type of assessment, a different type of judgement. For Dewey (1981), making judgments outside the process are akin to the aesthetic experience, not the moral. It is an aesthetic quality that rounds out an experience into completeness and unity; it is a momentary understanding of the pattern, structure and coherence of an experience.

But this aesthetic judgement can only be made to use Dewey's words from the consumer's standpoint, not the producers. This parallels in many significant ways the arguments of Bakhtin (Morson & Emerson, 1989; Holquist & Liapunov, 1990). In Bakhtin's account, all text or lived experience contains a hero (sometimes present and sometimes implied) and ethics (or morals) belong to the hero and her actions. Aesthetics on the other hand belong to the author or beholder of the hero and her actions.

As researchers, we find ourselves in this authorial role whenever we want to understand, to make sense of our experience of participating. In this authorial role we are brought into a narrative frame out of a direct participating one. It is in this narrative frame we make our judgements, but the judgements, according to Dewey and Bakhtin, are aesthetic ones. We act to provide coherence and a sense of 'harmony' to the experience that we have participated in. But while understanding or generating the narrative as author is done in the aesthetic mode, it still has moral import (Holquist & Liapunov, 1990).

As primary researchers we take these narratives back to the participating process. They are in fact part of our conversational tools, our offerings to the mutual process for consideration. It is in these offerings in the process that the moral import is experienced. When we are back in the conversation, when we have moved back into the primary participation position, we are one of the 'heroes.' We act morally into the conversation.

So here we are, once again, having moved in and out, and back to participation. That is ultimately where we live our experience and that is where we enact our moral knowing. As participating researchers we can make moral offerings in our practice, along with all other participants. All offerings are up for mutual negotiation within the process; not outside of it. The judgements we make outside are in the aesthetic dimension; the work we do inside is moral work.

Within this framework, we can see that these aesthetic judgements resemble what others have called 'theories.' They are certain accounts of practices made from a position outside of a practice yet, nevertheless integrally tied to practice. Indeed, as Margolis (1989) has argued, we could see that theory is a certain advanced and necessary form of practice. Craig and Tracy (1995) have argued similarly in their development of an argument for a grounded practical theory of communication. Within their perspective theory is seen as a "rational reconstruction of practices for the purposes of informing further practice and reflection" (p. 248). The major difference between their argument and that being proposed here, is that I am not assuming or requiring a 'rational' reconstruction; simply an aesthetically coherent one.

Nevertheless, both my own arguments and those of Craig & Tracy (1995) point to the need to go beyond participation; to bring theory out of and back into the practice of communicating. The aim of this 'theorising,' though is not one of determining eternal and unchanging things. It is more "a matter of knowing how to move in the patterns of communication in which we live, of finding our way about and of acting wisely" (Pearce, 1994, p. 7).

Primary Before Secondary

Finally, to end this chapter, I wish to assert that primary research is just that—primary. It is only in primary research that we can genuinely understand the act of communicating. It is only in primary research that we realise we are involved as persons in the construction of a mutual social reality, not as objective observers of someone else's. It is only in primary research that we recognise the real reflexivity in our position as researchers of the process we are always in. But most importantly, it is only primary research that allows us to deal with primary "data"–real, empirical data in the real, communicating world.

When Barnett Pearce commented on an earlier version of this paper, he related a very pertinent argument of Vern Cronen's that I would like to use here–an argument about the result of secondary research. 'Empirical data', according to Vern, has undergone an ironic shift. It is now taken to mean marks on a questionnaire that stand for something, such as attitudes, that are in the heads of people. But these attitudes are only inferred not observed, and hence are not empirical. We have also shifted the notion of the independent variable from we who act into a situation, to something that we manipulate and then observe. When all of the shifts are pointed out, the notion that conventional empirical research is actually secondary research is obvious–as is its inadequacies to deal with real practical problems in the communicating world.

It is these real practical problems in the communicating world that give us our direction for future research. To use Toulmin's (1990) phrase, we need to be asking about the 'futuribles open to us'. It is in communicating about these futuribles with fellow participants in our social world, that we gather our primary research data and that we, at the same time, bring about the possibility for change in that world.

Acknowledgments

The arguments in this paper were generated with many conversational partners, some in participation and some in imagination. I particularly want to thank Barnett Pearce for his constructive constructionism, John Shotter for pointing to a way, Eero Riikonen for his therapeutic insights, and my colleagues David Sless, Art Shulman, David Rogers and Sue Turnbull for their continual offerings.

References

Bennett, W. L. (1985). Communication and social responsibility. *Quarterly Journal of Speech, 71,* 259–288.

Craig, R. (1993). Why are there so many communication theories? *Journal of Communication, 43* (3), 26–33.

Craig, R. T., & Tracy, K. (1995). Grounded practical theory: The case for intellectual discussion. *Communication Theory, 5* (3), 248-272.

Cronen, V. (1995). Practical theory and the tasks ahead for social approaches to communication. In W. Leeds-Hurwitz (Ed.), *Social approaches to communication* (pp. 217-242). New York: Guilford Press.

Davies, T. (1987). The Ark in flames: Science, language and education in seventeenth-century England. In A. Benjamin, G. Cantor, & J. Christie (Eds.), *The figural and the literal: Problems of language in the history of science and philosophy* (pp. 1630–1800). Manchester, England: Manchester University Press.

Dervin, B. (1993). Verbing communication: Mandate for disciplinary invention. *Journal of Communication, 43*(3), 45–54.

Dewey, J. (1981). *The philosophy of John Dewey*. (J. McDermott, Ed.) Chicago: Chicago University Press.
Gadamer, H-G (1989). *Truth and method* (2nd Edition). New York: Crossroad.
Gergen, K. (1982). *Toward transformation in social knowledge*. New York: Springer-Verlag.
Gergen, K. (1985). The social constructionist movement in modern psychology. *American Psychologist, 40,* 266–275.
Holquist, M., & Liapunov, V. (Eds.) (1990). *Art and answerability: Early philosophical essays by M. M. Bakhtin*. Austin, TX: University of Texas Press.
Krippendorff, K. (1989). On the ethics of constructing communication. In B. Dervin, L. Grossberg, B. O'Keefe, & E. Wartella (Eds.), *Rethinking communication: Volume 1: Paradigm issues* (pp. 66–96). Newbury Park, CA: Sage.
Krippendorff, K. (1993). The past of communication's hoped-for future. *Journal of Communication, 43*(3), 34–44.
Leeds-Hurwitz, W. (1995). Introducing social approaches. In W. Leeds-Hurwitz (Ed.), *Social approaches to communication* (pp. 3-22). New York: Guilford Press.
Margolis, J. (1989). *Theory and practice*. Paper presented at the Tenth Annual Discourse Analysis Conference, Temple University, Philadelphia.
McCarthy, T. (1984). *The critical theory of Jürgen Habermas*. Cambridge, England: Polity Press.
Morson, G., & Emerson, C. (Eds.) (1989). *Rethinking Bakhtin: Extensions and challenges*. Evanston, IL: Northwestern University Press.
Pearce, W. B. (1994). *On "changing the universe": Two ideas and the future of the discipline*. Paper presented at 1994 Institute for Faculty Development: Communication Theory and Research Conference, Hope College, Holland, MI.
Penman, R. (1988). Communication reconstructed. *Journal for the Theory of Social Behaviour, 18,* 391–410.
Penman, R. (1992). Good theory and good practice: an argument in progress. *Communication Theory, 2*(3), 234–250.
Penman, R. (1994). What can the study of communication mean? *Communication News, 7*(3), 6-8.
Pepper, S. (1942). *World hypotheses: A study in evidence*. Berkeley, CA: University of California Press.
Reddy, M. (1979). The conduit metaphor. In A. Ortony (Ed.), *Metaphor and Thought* (pp. 284-324). London: Cambridge University Press.
Rogers, D. (1994). *Dewey on experience: Implications for contemporary communication theory*. Unpublished Masters Dissertation, Charles Sturt University, Bathurst, Australia.
Rorty, R. (1980). *Philosophy and the mirror of nature*. Oxford, England: Blackwell.
Shepherd, G. (1993). Building a discipline of communication. *Journal of Communication, 43,* 83-91.
Shotter, J. (1984). *Social accountability and selfhood*. Oxford, England: Blackwell.
Shotter, J. (1990). *Knowing of the third kind*. Utrecht, The Netherlands: ISOR

Shotter, J. (1993). *Cultural politics of everyday life*. Toronto, Canada: University of Toronto Press.
Steir, F. (1995). Reflexivity, interpersonal communication, and interpersonal communication research. In W. Leeds-Hurwitz (Ed.), *Social approaches to communication* (pp. 63-87). New York: Guilford Press.
Sless, D. (1986). *In search of semiotics*. Totowa, NJ: Barnes & Noble.
Sless, D (1991). Communication and certainty. *Australian Journal of Communication, 18*(3), 19–31.
Toulmin, S. (1990). *Cosmopolis: The hidden agenda of modernity*. Chicago: University of Chicago Press.
Wittgenstein, L. (1953). *Philosophical investigations*. Oxford, England: Blackwell.

Section 3
Conversational Context and the Applied Analysis of Communication Behavior

Chapter 17

Context and Conversational Processes[1]

Robert E. Nofsinger
Washington State University

Think of the context of any conversation as a set of resources which the participants use to make sense of what is going on at the moment. Certain background understandings shared by the participants as to the kind of communication episode they expect to take part in, who they are and what their respective parts in the interaction might be, what constraints operate on their communicative behavior, what potential outcomes are anticipated, and so on, may be useful contextual elements. In addition, patterns of interaction among the participants, changes in those patterns, and other displays by participants of their current understanding of the ongoing episode are important sense-making resources. Goodwin and Duranti (1992) provide a discussion of several possible dimensions of context as well as an historical review of the concept. Drew and Heritage (1992) discuss the approaches to context of discourse analysis, speech act theory, and conversation analysis. They also compare certain formal contexts to informal ones.

Thinking of context as a list of potential interpretive resources poses a serious problem both for conversational participants and for analysts of conversation: The list of potential resources is open-ended. That is, participants presumably share a very large (and unknown) number of background understandings with varying (and changing) degrees of relevance to the conversation in which they are engaged. In addition, conversations often comprise many interactive patterns, cues, and participant practices—also with different degrees of usefulness as sense-making resources. Finally, participants themselves exhibit a variety of characteristics (including gender, age, and ethnicity), any of which might or might not be important to the ongoing interaction (see Sacks, 1972; and Schegloff, 1992, on the analytical problem posed by the application of collections of social categories to societal members). Yet participants usually do not seem overwhelmed by having to deal with an excess of contextual riches; they have ways of locating just which resource(s) might be usefully relevant at the moment. Analysts, too, need some way of determining which of the indefinitely many contextual elements they should employ when analyzing some segment of conversation. The approach to context employed by conversation analysts is to focus on what the participants themselves are demonstrably orienting to in the ongoing interaction (Beach, 1995; Heritage, 1984; Schegloff, 1987).

Relevance for Participants

Conversation has been found to be persistently and contextually organized by the participants as they display what it is they are doing at the moment and how they understand what has already occurred (Heritage, 1984; Zimmerman, 1988). This orderliness, and other aspects of routine interaction, are not produced for analysts (researchers), but occur "*independently* of social scientific inquiry" (Beach, 1990, p. 217; see also pp. 234-237). As active agents, participants in the *first* instance work to make sense of each other's talk and to reveal *for each other* what sense they have made of it. In making their interaction accountable (describable, explainable) to each other, they observably orient to certain contextual resources as being momentarily relevant. This helps overcome the potential problem of dealing with an unmanageable set of interpretive resources: Participants collaboratively manage which resources are to be taken as relevant context. Since participants have methods for invoking context (see, for example, Mandelbaum, 1990/1991; Nofsinger, 1989; Zimmerman, 1992), analysts can approach the study of context by investigating which resources are demonstrably relevant to participants and the methods participants use to demonstrate such relevance. This focus on interactional details distinguishes conversation analysis from other social-science approaches (Beach, 1990). If something is considered "meaningful," it must be because the *participants* have oriented to it as such; "relevant" means relevant to *them* (Schegloff, 1987). Adopting this as a methodological constraint reduces the list of contextual elements available for analysis to those which the participants *demonstrate* are relevant to them. This provides the analyst with a data-based rationale for construing context in certain ways or selecting certain resources for study.

Intrinsic Context

Context is, indeed, a major factor participants use to make sense of each other's communicative actions. But not only is each speaker's talk shaped by the context in effect at that moment, each additional contribution to the ongoing interaction also renews that context (Heritage, 1984). Most conversational turns follow a prior turn and are recognized as having the status of some communicative or social action by virtue of being seen as responsive to that prior talk. Each new turn is not only interpreted in the context of the prior turn, it is treated as having been constructed so as to be relevant to that prior turn (unless the new turn is designed to discourage such an assumption). Each new turn thus demonstrates its speaker's understanding of the prior turn and the context of which that prior is a part. This serves to confirm, extend, modify, or replace that context. Conversational context, according to Beach (1995), "is continually and intrinsically re-achieved as participants display their understandings of specific moments of conversational involvement" (p. 124). As viewed by conversation analysts, context is *intrinsic* to the interaction: It is constructed within and by that interaction. This contrasts with the view that context is extrinsic to the interaction (or separate from it) and is imposed on participants or "received" by them from outside. A basic assumption here is that even outside factors, such as previously established plans, the social or business status of participants, background knowledge of participants about each other, and so on, will be made relevant during the course of the conversation by the contexting work of participants. As this happens, participants display for each other—and secondarily for the analyst—which resources they are orienting to as contextually relevant at that point.

An exchange of views on conceptualizing and analyzing context (and other matters, as well) appears in a lengthy special section of *Research on Language and Social Interaction*, edited by Robert Hopper (1990/91). The section features papers by ethnographers, conversation analysts, and others who discuss methodological issues and analyze interactional data. Several conversation analysts respond to a contrasting (extrinsic) view of context in which the analyst (an ethnographer, in this case) uses extensive background knowledge of the participants' culture, social status, life situation, and so on, to interpret and analyze the talk (Moerman, 1988). In particular, Mandelbaum (1990/91) demonstrates how a detailed analysis of the organization of participants' communicative behaviors can produce a different insight into the interaction—and one more sensitive to participants' actual displays toward each other—than an analysis based on outside factors. Beach (1990/91) discusses the uncertainties surrounding how cultural and other background knowledge becomes known to the researcher and whether it can be convincingly shown to apply to some particular moment of ongoing talk. Relying on the actual and specific details of interaction focuses the analyst's attention on the processes through which participants engage their situation and each other. Thus, according to this view, context is not only limited to what is relevant to the participants, it is also regarded as intrinsic to and constructed by way of the interaction itself.

Sequential Position as Context

One extremely powerful concept of conversational context is that of an utterance's sequential position. In general, participants interpret a turn at talk by using the prior turn as the relevant context. This occurs not only when the current speaker is answering a prior question, or has, in some other way, been specifically selected to speak (a type of context that we shall consider shortly). It also occurs following turns that do not require any specific sort of response, or that are addressed to participants generally, rather than to someone specific. A method for *achieving* that prior turn as context for one's utterance would be for a listener to self-select as next speaker as early as is proper, thus obtaining the sequentially next position. In Data Segment 1, participants are conversing during dinner. Lines 1-6 involve coordinating the serving of food, but in line 7, L delivers (to everyone) some news about her son.

Data Segment 1 [FWD 4:22 (simplified)][2]
01   C: Great. (1.2) Plea:se: (.) go ahead 'n'
02   (1.2)

```
03    F:      I'll hold this.
04            (0.8)
05    (C):    (mhm?)
06            (4.2)
07    L:      T'day was Aaron's last day at McDonald's la:n [d (.) an]d=
                                                          [         ]
08    F:                                                  [ Oh:::   ]
09    L:      =they gave him a cake
```

The news in line 7 is that Aaron has worked his last day at a local restaurant. L continues right on to deliver some even more remarkable news (line 9): They gave Aaron a cake. F (line 8) produces an elongated "oh" that overlaps the end of L's "la:nd" and the beginning of her "and." Other participants then contribute appreciative comments (shown in Data Segment 3). L's line 7, up to the short untimed pause marked as (.), provides an important context for F's "Oh:::" and allows F to be heard as marking the receipt of new information, and possibly even evaluating that news (perhaps expressing sympathy). F achieves this context for her "Oh:::" by precisely placing it at the point where L's turn might have ended: after "la:nd" (or possibly after "McDonald's"). Furthermore, F maximizes the likelihood that no other utterance will intervene between her turn and L's by starting a bit early (assuming that she projected L's turn to end after "la:nd"), slightly overlapping L. The result is that F gives her utterance the context it needs to be heard as a response to the news. As it turns out, F overlaps well before the end of L's extended turn when L continues in line 9.

This is one type of sequential-positioning context, a very local kind. A turn placed just after a prior turn may be heard as occasioned by and responsive to that prior. Jefferson (1978) describes how even multi-component turns—specifically stories—can be occasioned by a prior turn. Note in the data segment above how F's turn might maintain the context set up by L: that some news has been delivered (and that Aaron's job has ended). So F's turn is context-shaped by L's, but also renews some of the context displayed by L. Another type of sequential-positioning context—an adjacency pair—is even stronger than the one just examined.

An adjacency pair is a sequence of two communicative actions (two speakers' turns) in which the first speaker's turn creates a strong and fairly specific expectation that the second speaker must produce a certain action (or one of a small set of actions) in return (Schegloff & Sacks, 1973). Common examples of adjacency pairs include greeting-greeting, invitation-acceptance (or -refusal), and question-answer. The first action in the pair provides context for the second action, but in this case the context can last over the course of several turns. Data Segment 2 shows three adjacency pairs: a request-agreement (lines 1 and 6), and two question-answer sequences (lines 2-3 and 4-5).

Data Segment 2 [Sacks, 1992, p. 529]
```
01   A:   Can I borrow your car?
02   B:   When?
03   A:   This afternoon.
04   B:   For how long?
05   A:   A couple of hours.
06   B:   Okay.
```

In each pair, the first turn has special relevance for the second. This can be most clearly seen in the case where the second turn in the pair is not sequentially positioned next to the first turn (lines 1 and 6). An important contextual element for B's "Okay" is the first action of the adjacency pair (line 1). A's "Can I borrow your car" is a request that creates the expectation that B should either agree or refuse. This context is still relevant five turns later, where B may be heard to agree to loan the car to A. Modifications of the initial request that are negotiated between lines 1 and 6 (for example, that B needs the car for a relatively short period of time) also become part of the context of B's "Okay." That is, B may be heard as agreeing to loan the car only for a few hours that afternoon. Other arrangements of adjacency pairs produce other versions of this slightly less local type of context. Still broader groupings of interaction can also provide conversational context, especially the ongoing activity that participants are engaged in.

Activity Type as Context

Participants may be exchanging conversational actions in pursuit of some larger communicative endeavor. They may, for example, be producing suggestions, counter suggestions, invitations and acceptances as part of "making plans." We can call this endeavor an *activity type*. As Levinson (1992) explains, the way participants use language depends upon what activity type they are engaging in. To put it another way, people use language in certain ways to enact certain activity types. Accordingly, the particular activity type in progress is a context for individual actions, action pairs, and other participant practices. This is the *activity context* for these interactional behaviors. Note that these same practices constitute that activity context. The relationship between the context and the behaviors being contexted is a reciprocal one.

It may be that participant expectations prior to the actual opening of conversation help to establish an activity context for the talk. For example, the very fact of calling an emergency number (e.g., 911) sets up an interpretation by the answering dispatcher that emergency business is to be transacted, even before the caller actually speaks (Zimmerman, 1992). And the entry of a person into a physician's examining room (a person not recognizable as medical staff) may begin to build the context for a physician-patient interview (Robinson, 1995). But such activity types are by no means established by preconversation expectations. As the interaction itself begins, participants' expectations begin to be confirmed, modified, or disconfirmed. Answerers at 911 numbers routinely identify themselves as speaking for an emergency service, and if the emergency nature of the call is not made clear in the first exchange of talk, they check out the status of the caller and refer nonemergency matters elsewhere (Zimmerman, 1992). In Robinson's (1995) study of British physician-patient interaction, physicians initiate several preliminary sequences before beginning (or allowing the patient to begin) the medical interview. The actual interview context is constructed by such preliminary participant work as a greeting sequence, an identity-check sequence, and a business-determination sequence (among others). The participants create the activity context through their conduct in the interaction. They display for each other (and thereby for the analyst) which resources they deem relevant and how they will proceed (for example, what constraints they will observe).

For each activity type, there are constraints on what sorts of actions may be used to build it and on the ways in which participants should interpret each other's conduct (Levinson, 1992). This provides a continual updating of the activity context as each new action by a participant is evaluated as to whether it is properly a part of the activity-so-far, or indicates a participant's orientation to some other activity. Producing an action that is not well fitted to the ongoing activity type can result in the activity context being renegotiated. For example, Jefferson and Lee (1981) discovered that the giving of advice by a troubles-telling recipient (to the person telling the trouble) resulted in the rejection of that advice by the troubles-teller. A resumption of the troubles-telling often resulted. This seemed to occur even when the troubles-telling had progressed to a stage where the nature of the trouble had been revealed and advice about it might be a logical next step. The authors concluded that the reversal in conversational identity from speaker (teller of the trouble) to recipient (of the advice) created an ambiguity between the activity types of troubles-telling and service encounter (Jefferson & Lee, 1981, pp. 410-411). That is, in a troubles-telling the teller is primarily a speaker and the other participant is primarily a recipient. But in a service encounter, the initial requester of the service (speaker) loses that conversational identity and becomes a recipient of the service being provided—advice, in this case. So when the troubles-teller's coparticipant "turns the tables" on the teller, transforming him or her into an advice recipient, the action of giving advice is oriented to as not normal for a troubles-telling. Activity contexts, then, are created and maintained on an ongoing basis within the interaction. Participants maintain and extend the context by orienting to the activity-so-far, but may renegotiate that context by introducing elements of another activity type. Again, there is a reciprocal relationship between a context and the actions that constitute it. This is an important rationale for viewing context as intrinsic to the interaction.

Characterizing a Context

Even though conversation analysts try to discover what elements of an interaction the participants are treating as relevant, participants and analysts may not name, describe, or otherwise characterize a context in the same way. For example, when participants later report on what they were doing in a particular conversation, they may characterize the occasion or activity type with a folk or vernacular name or description. This characterization may or may not reflect the underlying interactional dynamics to which they oriented at the time (and which are of interest to analysts). The communication event from which Data Segment 1 is excerpted has been described by the participants as a "farewell dinner." Several families of friends have gathered together to say goodbye to a family that is moving to another city and to wish them well in their new location. Everyone present (or at least every adult) knows that this is the stated purpose of the dinner. And participants do seem to orient to this background understanding as being shared by all and as intermittently relevant to the ongoing talk. For example, the guests of honor mention having eaten at a restaurant in a distant city (the city to which they are moving, although they do not actually say this). They also refer to a family not previously mentioned in the conversation and indicate that the husband has almost the same name as one of the guests present: "Wo- I wonder what our *s*:ellers: middle initial is. It's Don Wilson." These utterances are designed with no explanation of the relevance of that restaurant (in that distant city) and no explanation of what has been sold to them (a house) that makes it appropriate to refer to the Wilsons as "our sellers." Through these matter-of-fact references, the guests of honor display that they take for granted that the other participants can supply the interpretive resources required to make sense of this talk (cf. Hopper, 1981). And the other participants do, indeed, orient toward these and similar references as normal. This pattern can be noted in Data Segment 3 (an extension of Data Segment 1).

Data Segment 3 [FWD 4:22 (simplified)]
```
07    L:     T'day was Aaron's last day at McDonald's la:n [d (.) an]d=
                                                         [        ]
08    F:                                                 [ Oh:::  ]
09    L:     =they gave him a cake=
10    ( ):   =•hhh [hh
                   [
11    (A):           [( [  )
                        [
12    D:               [Oh did the [y:.
                                   [
13    (L):                         [heh heh heh [ heh
                                                [
14    D:                                        [Gr [eat.
                                                   [
15    F:                                           [Isn't that ni:ce.
16           They (must uv) appreciated your work then.
```

When L delivers the news about Aaron (lines 7 and 9), she reports two items that might ordinarily call for an explanation or account. The cake, perhaps, is explained by the occasion of Aaron's last day at work, and L's mentioning it can be seen as an expression of pride in her son's work. But a person's last day at work (reported in line 7) is itself an event that might well deserve an explanation in this setting. The following comments rely on this assumption—that one cannot tell friends who do not know the background, "today was my child's last day of work," and naively expect that they will not inquire about it.

In designing her utterance, L displays a reliance on other participants knowing *why* Aaron will no longer be working at McDonald's. She orients to the presumably shared background understanding (that Aaron is moving away with his family) as being a momentarily relevant context. The other participants who respond in this segment also orient to this report about Aaron as being adequately contexted (in effect, already explained). Instead of focusing on line 7, they respond (lines 10, 12, 14, and 15-16) to the report of Aaron being honored with a cake. (And no one, for example, asks why Aaron is leaving McDonald's.) The activity type as the participants have characterized it—a farewell dinner—seems to be the context that allows this smooth exchange regarding Aaron's situation. But aside from the informational issue of knowing why they are talking about Aaron leaving McDonald's, is a "farewell" dinner fundamentally any different from a "welcome the travelers back" dinner, or a "celebrate the end of the football season" dinner? Indeed, are such activities fundamentally different from a casual, nondinner conversation?

A related aspect of the participants' dinner conversation (or perhaps a coexisting activity) is their coordination of passing and serving the food. They would likely not have later reported that they had communicatively "organized the food service," but throughout this dinner event, they did just that (e.g., lines 1-6 of Data Segment 1). The two kinds of talk, stories related to moving away, and utterances coordinating the serving of food, are woven together effortlessly. Data Segment 4 (an extension of Data Segment 3) shows another instance of this.

Data Segment 4 [FWD 4:22 (simplified)]
```
15   F:                         Isn't that ni:ce.
16        [They (must uv) app]reciated your work then.=
          [                   ]
17   (C): [ (         ) hot.  ]
18   D:   =(All right t') put it down on the table Cindy?
19   C:   Yes. Go right ahead.
20   A:   ( ) right after I clocked out ((Aaron tells the cake story))
```

Somewhat in the background, and overlapping the first part of F's line 16, C apparently cautions someone about hot food or a hot dish (line 17). Latched onto the end of line 16, D then asks C about putting a dish down on the table and C answers the question (lines 18-19). The very next turn is Aaron beginning to tell the story of being given the cake. So another part of the context for at least some of the talk around the dinner table would seem to be the food and the food-related behaviors of the participants. As in the case of participants' orientation to the "farewell" aspect of the dinner, this orientation to the momentary configuration of the food service is internal to the dinner and constructed by the behaviors of the participants. And it, too, seems primarily relevant to the informational aspects of the conversation: What is being talked about, what does he mean by that message, to whom does she refer, and so on. In a sense, characterizing an activity according to shared background understandings of what the participants' purpose is, why they are the relevant people to participate, what they are going to talk about, what they in fact did talk about, and the like, puts the focus of inquiry on the "content" of the activity. While this has some degree of importance, especially to the participants, conversation analysts are first interested in the process: How is this sort of activity carried out, how do communicative actions get coordinated and turns taken, and how do the participants organize their interaction? Such an analysis requires that activities (and other aspects of interaction) be characterized in technical terms, rather than in everyday "folk" parlance.

Lerner (1995) warns us that activities distinguished from each other in vernacular terms may not be different procedurally (p. 128). That is, they may be based on the same interactional processes. For example, "farewell" dinners, "celebrate the end of the football season" dinners, and even "organize the food service," or "talk about our day," or "gossip" conversations may well be organized by the same interactional system. Participants' vernacular characterizations of their activities may obscure this important commonality of process. At the same time, a vernacular characterization (Lerner's example is "classroom interaction," p. 128) may categorize as one activity type what are, upon analysis, distinguishably different interactional processes. One way to focus on the processes of communication is to treat the process itself—the interactional system—as the context (Schegloff, 1987).

Interactional System as Context

In order that the idea of context be of maximum use to analysts investigating the processes by which participants organize their interaction (the primary endeavor of conversation analysis), Schegloff (1987, 1992) proposes an additional criterion for something to be designated as context. Not only must it be observably relevant to the participants, but it must also "issue in [some] consequence for the shape, form, trajectory, content, or character of the interaction..." (1992, p. 111). In other words, since conversation analysts focus in some way on the interactional procedures employed by participants, a technical characterization of context should indicate how that context is consequential for those procedures. Schegloff (1987, 1992) calls this requirement *procedural consequentiality*. From this point of view, the interactional system itself is the context of interest.

The turn-taking system for conversation as described by Sacks, Schegloff, and Jefferson (1978) is one such context. Technically, "mundane conversation" is interaction that is organized by that turn-taking system. In this system, the participants locally manage the transition from one speaker to the next (even when "next" speaker is the same speaker continuing). They do this at the point where the current turn unit is projected to end (the transition relevance place, or TRP), and they do it via one of three turn allocation practices. These are: current speaker selects next (where the current speaker directs the first part of an adjacency pair to another participant); any listener self-selects (where a listener starts talking and thus becomes next speaker); and current speaker continues (where the current speaker produces an additional turn unit) (Sacks et al., 1978). The "farewell dinner" conversation is organized by just this system, and so are most casual, everyday conversations among friends—even though the participants might vernacularly characterize them as being a variety of different activities. An example of a different (nonconversational) context viewed at this systemic level would be the broadcast news interview. The activity context of an interview differs from that of mundane conversation not because the interview is (for example) about a political election campaign and the everyday conversation is about friends moving to another city, but rather because the constraints that organize the interactional identities of interviewer and interviewee are different from those that organize the conduct of participants in mundane conversation (Greatbatch, 1988). These are different contexts because they are based on (somewhat) different underlying interactional systems. Other broadcast "talk shows" might be different from news interviews in their underlying systems. See, for example, Nofsinger (1995) for a look at a televised product demonstration program. Another example (hypothetical in the sense that these kinds of events have not been extensively studied) would be the differences between informal conversations and public meetings. A public hearing might have a similar interactional-systemic context to a meeting of a state legislature (or student senate, etc.), in the sense that the presiding officer selects each next speaker and other participants may only indicate that they wish to be called upon. The interactional system of that same public hearing would likely be a very different context from a family or neighborhood discussion (even if the discussion were about the same issues on the agenda of the public hearing). To the extent that a discussion involved processes of listener self-selecting as next speaker, current speaker selecting (questioning, challenging, thanking) another participant who then becomes next speaker, and so on, analysts might judge it to have a similar context to mundane conversation. Note that this type of context—the interactional system—is also intrinsic to the interaction.

Conclusion

In summary, conversation analysis focuses on the study of actual, situated, occasioned, participant-organized interaction—interaction in context and as context. From this perspective, context is conceptualized as those interpretive resources which are demonstrably relevant to the participants and invoked by their own conduct; which are thus intrinsic to the conversation; and which have procedural consequences for how participants carry out their interaction. The methods of this perspective are especially useful for investigating talk and other interactional behaviors contexted by way of their sequential position within the ongoing interaction, or in terms of the activity type of which they are a part, or by the underlying organizational system that participants orient to in enacting their business. But these interactional behaviors must not be thought of only as contexted or "in context." They also create context or do contexting work. The relationship between conversational behavior and conversational context is reciprocal.

References

Atkinson, J. M., & Heritage, J. C. (Eds.). (1984). *Structures of social action: Studies in conversation analysis.* Cambridge, England: Cambridge University Press.

Beach, W. A. (1990). Orienting to the phenomenon. In J. A. Anderson (Ed.), *Communication yearbook 13* (pp. 216-244). Newbury Park, CA: Sage Publications.

Beach, W. A. (1990/91). Searching for universal features of conversation. *Research on Language and Social Interaction, 24,* 351-368.

Beach, W. A. (1995). Conversation analysis: "Okay" as a clue for understanding consequentiality. In S. J. Sigman (Ed.), *The consequentiality of communication* (pp. 121-161). Hillsdale, NJ: Lawrence Erlbaum.

Drew, P., & Heritage, J. (1992). Analyzing talk at work: An introduction. In P. Drew & J. Heritage (Eds.), *Talk at work* (pp. 3-65). Cambridge, England: Cambridge University Press.

Goodwin, C., & Duranti, A. (1992). Rethinking context: An introduction. In A. Duranti & C. Goodwin (Eds.), *Rethinking context: Language as an interactive phenomenon* (pp. 1-42). Cambridge, England: Cambridge University Press.

Greatbatch, D. (1988). A turn-taking system for British news interviews. *Language in Society, 17,* 401-430.

Heritage, J. (1984). *Garfinkel and ethnomethodology.* Cambridge, England: Polity Press.

Hopper, R. (1981). The taken-for-granted. *Human Communication Research, 7,* 195-211.

Hopper, R. (Ed.). (1990/91). Special section: Ethnography and conversation analysis after *Talking culture. Research on Language and Social Interaction, 24,* 159-387.

Jefferson, G. (1978). Sequential aspects of storytelling in conversation. In J. Schenkein (Ed.), *Studies in the organization of conversational interaction* (pp. 219-248). New York: Academic Press.

Jefferson, G., & Lee, J. R. E. (1981). The rejection of advice: Managing the problematic convergence of a "troubles-telling" and a "service encounter." *Journal of Pragmatics, 5,* 399-422.

Lerner, G. H. (1995). Turn design and the organization of participation in instructional activities. *Discourse Processes, 19,* 111-131.

Levinson, S. C. (1992). Activity types and language. In P. Drew & J. Heritage (Eds.), *Talk at work* (pp. 66-100). Cambridge, England: Cambridge University Press.

Mandelbaum, J. (1990/91). Beyond mundane reason: Conversation analysis and context. *Research on Language and Social Interaction, 24,* 333-350.

Moerman, M. (1988). *Talking culture: Ethnography and conversation analysis.* Philadelphia: University of Pennsylvania Press.

Nofsinger, R. E. (1989). Collaborating on context: Invoking alluded-to shared knowledge. *Western Journal of Speech Communication, 53,* 227-241.

Nofsinger, R. E. (1991). *Everyday conversation.* Newbury Park, CA: Sage Publications.

Nofsinger, R. E. (1995). Micromanaging expert talk: Hosts' contributions to televised computer product demonstrations. In B. R. Burleson (Ed.), *Communication yearbook 18* (pp. 345-370). Thousand Oaks, CA: Sage Publications.

Robinson, J. D. (1995). *Working to begin the medical interview: Verbal and non-verbal communication during the opening of British physician-patient interaction.* Unpublished manuscript, University of California at Los Angeles.

Sacks, H. (1972). An initial investigation of the usability of conversational data for doing sociology. In D. Sudnow (Ed.), *Studies in social interaction* (pp. 31-74). New York: Free Press.

Sacks, H. (1992). Lecture 1 [Spring 1972]. In H. Sacks, *Lectures on conversation* (Vol. 2, G. Jefferson, Ed.). Cambridge, MA: Blackwell.

Sacks, H., Schegloff, E. A., & Jefferson, G. (1978). A simplest systematics for the organization of turn taking for conversation. In J. Schenkein (Ed.), *Studies in the organization of conversational interaction* (pp. 7-55). New York: Academic Press.

Schegloff, E. A. (1987). Between micro and macro: Contexts and other connections. In J. C. Alexander, B. Giesen, R. Munch, & N. J. Smelser (Eds.), *The micro-macro link* (pp. 207-234). Berkeley, CA: University of California Press.

Schegloff, E. A. (1992). On talk and its institutional occasions. In P. Drew & J. Heritage (Eds.), *Talk at work* (pp. 101-134). Cambridge, England: Cambridge University Press.

Schegloff, E. A., & Sacks, H. (1973). Opening up closings. *Semiotica, 7,* 289-327.

Zimmerman, D. H. (1988). On conversation: The conversation analytic perspective. In J. A. Anderson (Ed.), *Communication yearbook 11* (pp. 406-432). Newbury Park, CA: Sage Publications.

Zimmerman, D. H. (1992). Achieving context: Openings in emergency calls. In G. Watson & R. M. Seiler (Eds.), *Text in context* (pp. 35-51). Newbury Park, CA: Sage Publications.

Footnotes

[1] My thanks to Wayne Beach and Jeff Robinson for helpful suggestions and detailed comments on an earlier version of this paper. That version was presented at the 67th Annual Meetings of the Western States Communication Association, Pasadena, CA, February 16-20, 1996.

²The basic transcribing notations used in the data segments are as follows: (1.2) indicates silences timed to tenths of a second. (.) indicates short, untimed silences. (C) indicates transcriber doubt about who spoke. (All right t') indicates transcriber doubt about what was said. ( ) indicates talk that was not transcribable. =indicates segments of talk latched onto each other, with no pause or "beat" between them. Three vertically aligned square brackets indicate overlapping talk. Colons in the talk indicate a stretched or lengthened sound. Transcriber comments are enclosed in double parens. For a more comprehensive explanation of transcribing notation, see Atkinson and Heritage (1984, pp. ix-xvi), or Nofsinger (1991, pp. 167-169).

Chapter 18

Contingency Analysis Applied to the Pragmatics and Semantics of Naturally Occurring Verbal Interactions[1]

Ullin T. Place
University of Wales Bangor

I. Contingency Analysis and the Three-Term Contingency

Contingency analysis is a technique for analyzing the relation between a living organism and its environment based on a generalized version of Skinner's (1969) concept of the "three-term contingency." It can be applied to the analysis of any sequence of events in which a single individual interacts with its environment or, as in the case of social behavior, in which two or more individuals interact with each other. I shall try to show that it is particularly valuable when applied to the analysis of naturally occurring verbal interactions, such as conversations and business transactions.

II. Bringing together Two Conceptual Schemes

In developing a contingency analysis of verbal interactions, I propose to bring together concepts derived from two different research traditions:
(1) contemporary *behavior analysis*, as it has developed in the wake of Skinner's book *Contingencies of Reinforcement* which appeared in 1969, long after most psychologists and students of language had ceased to pay attention to what he had to say on such matters,
(2) the research tradition within ethnomethodological sociology known as "*conversation analysis*," founded by the late Harvey Sacks and his two principal lieutenants, Emmanuel Schegloff and Gail Jefferson.

III. Concepts from Behavior Analysis

From contemporary behavior analysis comes the concept of a *contingency* analyzed, following Lindsley (1964), as a relation between three "terms":
(A) a set of *Antecedent* conditions which call for
(B) some *Behavior* to be emitted or omitted by an organism (the 'owner' of the contingency), and
(C) the actual or anticipated *Consequences* of so behaving.[2]

Two kinds of Antecedents are distinguished:
(A1) *discriminative stimuli* or signs which alert the organism to the presence or availability of a particular contingency (behavior-consequence relation),[3] and
(A2) *establishing conditions* (Michael, 1982), such as an aversive (unpleasant) stimulus or a state of food deprivation, which give to subsequent events their reinforcing (incentive) or disinforcing (disincentive) properties as the case may be.[4]

This distinction between discriminative stimuli and establishing conditions corresponds both to the traditional distinction within Psychology between *cognition* and *motivation* and to the distinction within linguistics and semiotic between the *semantic* properties of an utterance whereby it *refers* the listener to objects and situations both inside and outside the listener's current stimulus environment, and the *pragmatic* properties of an utterance whereby it constrains the listener's response.

We can similarly distinguish two kinds of Behavior:
(B1) the *emission*, and
(B2) the *omission* of what Skinner, somewhat misleadingly,[5] calls a *response*.
Likewise, Consequences are classified as:
(C1) *reinforcing*, if the propensity to repeat the same behavior on similar occasions in the future is strengthened, or
(C2) *disinforcing* (Harzem & Miles, 1978), if it is weakened.
Use is also made of:
(a) Skinner's (1957) distinction between a *mand*, interpreted as the utterance of an imperative or interrogative sentence which specifies its own reinforcement, and a *tact*, interpreted, as I have proposed elsewhere (Place, 1985), as the utterance of a declarative or information-providing sentence the propensity to emit which is maintained by distinctive *unspecified* verbal reinforcers (the so-called "back-channels" or "response tokens" of the discourse and conversation analysts), and
(b) the distinction he draws in 'An operant analysis of problem solving' (Skinner 1966/1969/1988) between *contingency-shaped behavior* in which the organism's behavioral propensities are shaped or honed by past experience of the *immediate* consequences of behaving in that way in one's own case, and *rule-governed behavior* in which behavior is controlled by a verbal specification of the relevant antecedent – behavior – consequence relation.

IV. Concepts from Conversation Analysis

From conversation analysis comes the concept of the *sequence* divided into
(A) the *Pre-sequence* or preliminary formalities,
(B) the *Main-sequence* in which the business is transacted, and
(C) the *Post-sequence* or concluding formalities.
These are themselves sub-divided into
(i) *turns* in which one person speaks and the other(s) provide(s)
(ii) *response tokens*, which are either
    (a) *continuers* which maintain the speaker in turn, or
    (b) *terminaters* which acknowledge the completion of the speaker's turn and allow the listener to take over.

An *adjacency pair* may be defined as an utterance followed by an appropriate response token, or two successive turns in which the second is the response demanded by the first. Examples of such pairs are Request/Compliance, Question/Answer, Offer/Acceptance, Greeting/Return Greeting, but also Opinion/Agreement, News/Surprise, Joking/Laughter and Troubles/Sympathy.

Preference organization is the term used for the phenomenon whereby listeners systematically avoid giving offence to speakers, or try to minimize the offence when it is unavoidable.

V. Contingency Analysis Applied to Non-Verbal Interactions

We have seen that contingency analysis is a technique for analyzing any sequence of events involving the behavior of one or more living organisms in which the relationship between successive events is construed in terms of the concept of the three-term contingency in its generalized form, consisting of Antecedent, Behavior and Consequence. Although it is applicable to any sequence of events involving the behavior of an organism, it is particularly useful as a tool for the analysis of naturally occurring social interactions between two or more organisms. When applied to the analysis of an interactive sequence, each event is classified, where appropriate, in three different ways:

(a) as *Antecedent* with respect to the behavior of the agent whose behavior constitutes the *next* event in the sequence,

(b) as *Behavior* on the part of the agent whose behavior constitutes the event in question and

(c) as *Consequence* with respect to the behavior of the agent whose behavior constitutes the immediately preceding event in the sequence.

This is illustrated in Table 1.

Table 1. *Contingency analysis of non-verbal behavior*

EVENT	CONTINGENCY ANALYSIS		
Agent	*The noisemaker*	*The baby*	*The mother*
(1) Someone makes a noise.	Behavior	Antecedent	
(2) The baby wakes up and cries.	Consequence*	Behavior	Antecedent
(3) The mother picks up the baby and gives it a bottle.		Consequence/ Antecedent	Behavior
(4) The baby goes back to sleep.		Behavior	Consequence

*In most cases of this kind, this consequence will not impinge on the noisemaker's subsequent behavior unless it is drawn to his or her attention by those more immediately concerned with caring for the baby; but in that case the effective consequence as far as the noisemaker is concerned is the carer's protests rather than the baby's waking up.

A similar analysis of interactive sequences such as this was proposed by Jones and Gerard (1967) in the shape of what they call the "social contingency model" of social interaction. On the evidence of their citation of Skinner (1953) in this connection, it would seem that Jones and Gerard's use of the term "contingency" is suggested by Skinner's use of the term in his earlier writings. However their use of the term differs from Skinner's in that for them a contingency is a complete interactive sequence involving two participants; whereas on Skinner's usage each response that is consequated by one's partner in the interaction constitutes a different contingency with its own distinctive antecedents and consequences.[6] This means:
(a) that we can think of each contingency as being 'owned' by the individual relative to whose behavior the contingency is defined, and
(b) that the same sequence of events constitutes a different set of contingencies for each of the participants in an interaction which together constitute that individual's distinctive standpoint with respect to that sequence of events.
This enables us to capture the sense in which an interaction is viewed from a different standpoint by each participant without in any way compromising the objectivist epistemology (Place, 1993) which is the foundation of the behaviorist position and the source of its strength.

VI. Contingency Analysis Applied to the Pragmatics of Verbal Interactions

The example of the baby waking up illustrates the application of contingency analysis to an interactive sequence all of whose constituent events are constituted by non-verbal behavior on the part of the three participants. To illustrate the application of contingency analysis to verbal interactions and in order to show at the same time where the idea of contingency analysis comes from, I have set out on Table 2, in the same format as Table 1, four examples of short verbal interactions which are derived from a series of diagrams which Skinner (1957) uses in his book *Verbal Behavior* to explain his concepts of "mand" and "tact." Three of them are taken from Chapter 3 on the Mand and the fourth from Chapter 5 on the Tact.

VII. Some Principles of Contingency Analysis as Applied to the Pragmatics of Verbal Interactions

Pragmatic Principle 1 - Verbal Behavior is Contingency-Shaped.

If we apply Skinner's (1966/1969/1988) distinction between contingency-shaped and rule-governed behavior to the case of verbal behavior itself, we see that verbal behavior is predominantly contingency-shaped rather than rule-governed. We sometimes work out what we are going to say to someone on the basis of an estimate of the probable consequences of saying one thing rather than another, but this applies only occasionally, and then only to the initial moves in the sequence. Once the sequence has been initiated the swift reaction that is normally required does not permit this kind of "rule-governed" approach. This means

Table 2. Contingency analysis of verbal behavior – Skinner's examples.

		Speaker	*Listener*
(1)	Skinner (1957) Figure 1, p. 38		
	S: *Bread, please.*	Behavior	Antecedent
	L: *passes* the bread.	Consequence/Antecedent	Behavior
	S: *Thanks.*	Behavior	Consequence/Antecedent
	L: *Don't mention it.*	Consequence	Behavior
(2)	Skinner (1957) Figure 2, p. 39		
	L: stands in S's way.	Antecedent	Behavior
	S: *Step aside* + threat	Behavior	Consequence/Antecedent
	L: steps aside	Consequence/Antecedent	Behavior
	S: withdraws threat	Behavior	Consequence
(3)	Skinner (1957) Figure 3, p. 39		
	L: attracts S's attention	Antecedent	Behavior
	S: *What's your name?*	Behavior	Consequence/Antecedent
	L: *Lester*	Consequence/Antecedent	Behavior
	S: *Thank you*	Behavior	Consequence
(4)	Skinner (1957) Figure 6, p. 85		
	Telephone request	Antecedent	
	S: looks for L	Behavior	
	S: sees L	Consequence/Antecedent	
	S: *Telephone for you*	Behavior	Antecedent
	L: goes to phone + *Thanks*	Consequence	Behavior

(a) that all spontaneous verbal behavior is contingency-shaped, shaped, that is, by the response token that the listener supplies as an immediate consequence of its emission by the speaker, and
(b) that speakers are for the most part unaware of receiving these verbal reinforcers or "continuers", as the conversation analysts call them, things such as the head nods, *Mmhmm*s, etc, as is the listener largely unaware of supplying them.

Pragmatic Principle 2 - Verbal Behavior Consequated at Sentence Completion

The unit of verbal behavior which is "consequated," i.e., the unit of behavior which attracts a response token from the listener as its immediate consequence, is the sentence. In other words a sentence has to be completed before the appropriate reinforcer or disinforcer is received from the listener. This is illustrated in Table 3 which presents an excerpt from the transcript of a recording which I made in the Office of the Leeds University Philosophy Department in October 1985 of an interaction between Mrs Penny Ewens, then a mature student in her second undergraduate year, and the Senior Departmental Secretary, Mrs Rose Purdy. A complete transcript of this recording, together with a detailed contingency analysis of the data, has been published (Place, 1991) as Chapter 5 of Hayes and Chase (Eds.) *Dialogues on Verbal Behavior*.

Table 3. The Party 10/85

Penny:	it's *just* this bus'ness of (.) th' *party* [for the *first* y:e:ars. ↑ [↑	01
Rose:	[ye:(s) yes	02
Penny:	=*I* won't (.) be *i*:n tomorrow mo:rning. ↑	03
Rose:	no=	04
Penny:	=I've *left* a *notice* on the *board*. ↑	05
Rose:	yeah.=	06
Penny:	=and there's a *note* for them °of the money. ↑	07
Rose:	who wants to pick it up?= ↑	08
Penny:	=we:ll (.) the:'re on that li: [st. [↑	09
Rose:	[oh the're °all on that *list*.= ↑	10
Rose:	= (.) and any-any of these people [can *have* it, (.) can they.= [↑ ↑	11
Penny:	[yes:: (.)	12
Penny:	=I *do*:: know John's girl friend *knows* about it.= ↑	13
Penny:	=*bu*(t) *she's* not *free* at the same time as *them* tomorrow.= ↑	14
Penny:	=so:th't *lots* of people *know* about it,= ↑	15
Rose:	=anan the:'re goin(g) to *get* the shoppin(g) *ou*[t of it. (.) I see= ↑ [↑	16
Penny:	[yes (.)	17

In this excerpt I have marked the points at which the speaker completes a sentence with a vertical arrow in the line below. You will see from this that, in general, the listener places her response, whether it is a continuer such as *yes* or *no* or a terminator such as the initiation of a question, very precisely at the point where the speaker's sentence becomes syntactically complete. There are 15 such sentence completions in this section of the transcript. Of these 11 are immediately followed by a response from the listener. In a further case (lines 11 and 12) the listener's response anticipates the completion of the speaker's sentence at a stage when it is quite clear what the completion is going to be. Of the eleven responses six are reinforcers in the form either of a confirmation, an expression of agreement or an acknowledgement of comprehension (5 *yes* or *yeah*, 1 *no*), two are questions asking for clarification or confirmation of the current speaker's understanding of the previous speaker's utterance, one is an echo of the previous speaker's sentence followed by a request for confirmation, one is a sentence emitted in reply to one of those questions and one is an unsolicited elaboration of some background information. In only four cases is there no response from the listener to the completion of a sentence by the speaker:

(1) on lines 10-11 where there is no apparent response from Penny when Rose completes the sentence *the're all on that list* which echoes Penny's immediately preceding sentence *the're on that list*, and can, perhaps, be regarded simply as a response to that sentence rather than a sentence in its own right,

(2 & 3) on lines 13-15 where Penny engages in the extraordinary piece of self-directed reasoning which makes up her final three sentence turn and which, apart from its conclusion, is ignored by Rose, presumably because she is only interested in the conclusion and not in the tortuous mental process by which the conclusion is reached, and

(4) on lines 16-17 where Penny's *yes* occurs halfway between the completion of Rose's sentence *and they're going to get the shopping* and the completion of its extension *out of it*; this response can be seen either as a delayed reaction to the first sentence-completion or as an anticipation of the second (extended) sentence-completion at a stage when its form can be confidently predicted, or possibly as both.[7]

Pragmatic Principle 3 - It is Words and Phrases that are Repeated - Not Sentences

Although sentences are the units of verbal behavior which are consequated, they are not, as Chomsky (1957, etc) has repeatedly pointed out, the units of verbal behavior that are repeated as a consequence of reinforcement. What are repeated on subsequent occasions are the individual words, phrases and sentence frames which make up the sentence, and the gist of stories, arguments, etc. of which it forms part.

Pragmatic Principle 4 - Sentences on a "Win-Shift/Fail-Stay" Contingency

At the level of sentence construction, verbal behavior is on a "win-shift/fail-stay" contingency (Olton & Schlosberg, 1978), one in which if your utterance is reinforced by the listener's response you do not repeat yourself, you move on to the next sentence. You only repeat yourself at the time if you fail to get a response first time. Even then, the sentence you construct is invariably slightly different in intonation, if not in other ways, from your first attempt.

Pragmatic Principle 5 - Discourse Type on a "Win-Stay/Fail-Shift" Contingency

At the level of discourse type, on the other hand, verbal behavior is on a "win-stay/fail-shift" contingency. This is illustrated in a study by Gail Jefferson (1981) in which she points out that news-telling behavior on the part of a speaker is maintained by expressions of interest and surprise such as *Really?*, *Did you?*, *You did?*. Clearly what is maintained here is not the propensity to repeat the individual news items, but the propensity to continue producing new items that the listener has not heard before. After all, news is only news if you haven't heard it before.

Pragmatic Principle 6 - Reinforcers of Mands are specified: Reinforcers of Tacts are Unspecified

A 'verbal reinforcer' is a response on the part of the listener which acts as a reinforcing consequence with respect to the immediately preceding sentence emitted by a speaker. Verbal reinforcers in this sense are of two kinds:

(a) *specified verbal reinforcers* such as the behavior of answering a question or complying with a request which provides the reinforcing consequence for what Skinner calls "a mand", in other words, a sentence which specifies the behavior on the part of the listener which, if emitted, will reinforce the emission of the mand by the speaker;

(b) *unspecified verbal reinforcers* by which is meant the reinforcing consequences of a tact or information-providing sentence whose emission is reinforced by what conversation analysts call a "response token," a verbal reinforcer such as an expression of gratitude, sympathy, agreement, comprehension or surprise which is not specified by the sentence which it consequates.

Pragmatic Principle 7 - The Intra- and Extra-Episodic Effects of Continuers and Terminaters

Unspecified verbal reinforcers may be sub-classified as:

(a) *continuers* whose effect is mainly intra-episodic in that they serve to maintain on-going verbal behavior on the part of the current speaker;

(b) *terminaters*, as we may call things such as clapping or saying *Thank you* when someone finishes speaking, whose reinforcing function is purely extra-episodic, that is to say, their function is to strengthen the speaker's propensity to emit similar utterances on relevantly similar occasions in the future.

Pragmatic Principle 8 - Reinforcement of Verbal Behavior is Response Specific

The reinforcement of verbal behavior is *response specific*; that is to say, each type of sentence utterance or "speech act" has its own characteristic form of reinforcement which is peculiar to verbal behavior of that kind. This is the phenomenon known to conversation analysts as the "*Adjacency Pair*". It is illustrated on Table 4.

Two points need to be made in connection with this table in the light of comments made by Dr. Paul Drew:[8]

Table 4. Adjacency Pairs.

	Speech Act Type		Reinforcer
(a)	MANDS		SPECIFIED
	(i)	*In S's self-interest*	
		S orders	L obeys
		S requests	L complies
		S applies	L permits
	(ii)	*In L's interest*	
		S invites	L accepts
		S offers	L accepts
(b)	TACTS		UNSPECIFIED
	(i)	*Narrative*	
		News telling	Expressions of surprise
		Joke telling	Laughter
		Troubles talk	Expressions of sympathy
	(ii)	*Informative*	
		Instructing	Expressions of comprehension
		Directing	Expressions of gratitude
		Opinion-stating	Expressions of agreement

(1) As the expression is used by conversation analysts, "adjacency pair" is usually restricted to the relationship of some kind of *mand*, to use Skinner's term, and its specified (intended) reinforcement. On Table 4 the expression has been extended so as to include the relationship between the different varieties of *tact*, to use *one* of the senses in which Skinner uses that word (Place, 1985), and the different kinds of reinforcer in the form of response tokens which, though unspecified in the utterance which they consequate, are nevertheless specific to the type of speech act to which they respond.

(2) Table 4 should not be regarded as in any sense an exhaustive summary of the constraints which an utterance places on the response which it evokes from the listener. By restricting attention to the reinforcing consequences of utterances, it tends to conceal the fact that disinforcing consequences of utterances, though less common than reinforcing ones, are equally adapted to the nature of the speech act to which they are responding. Both positive disinforcers, such as the refusal to comply with a request or an expression of disagreement, and negative disinforcers, such as the listener's failure to supply the expected response within the conventionally established time limits, are constrained by the nature of the utterance to which the listener is responding or failing to respond, just as much as it is in the case where the response is a reinforcer.

Table 5. Contingency analysis applied to semantic content

(a)	*Instruction:*	*The baby minder*	
	If the baby cries,	Antecedent	
	give it a bottle,	Behavior	
	and it will go back to sleep.	Consequence	
(b)	*Narrative (Sacks, 1972):*	*The baby*	*The mother*
	The baby cried.	Behavior	Antecedent
	The mommy picked it up.	Consequence	Behavior

Pragmatic Principle 9 - Preference Organization - Moderating and Avoiding Listener's Anger

Motivated presumably by the fear of arousing the speaker's anger, the vast majority of the speaker's utterances are appropriately reinforced by the listener. For the same reason, when the listener withholds reinforcement for whatever reason, listeners tend to avoid or minimize the speaker's anger by such devices as copious apologies, excuses or postponing their admission that they are unable or unwilling to comply. This is what is known to conversation analysts as "preference organization".

VIII. Contingency Analysis as Applied to the Semantics of Verbal Interactions

According to the principle of 'Behavioral Contingency Semantics' (Place, 1983; 1992a) or plain 'Contingency Semantics' as I am now inclined to call it, sentences exercise discriminative stimulus control over the behavior of (i.e., are "understood" by) listeners, in so far as they "specify" or "depict" one or more terms of a contingency which is "owned" by the listener in the sense that the behavior which has the consequences and is called for by the antecedent conditions is either

(a) behavior to be emitted by the listener, as in the case of the *instruction* to the baby minder in example (a) on Table 5, or

(b) behavior on the part of an individual with whom the listener is able to *identify*, as in the case of a *narrative* such as the child's story discussed in a paper by Sacks (1972) as set out under (b) on Table 5.

IX. Principles of Contingency Analysis as Applied to the Semantics of Verbal Interactions

Semantic Principle 1 - Presenting Listener's Contingencies as a Condition for Comprehension

In order for a listener or reader to understand and thereby perform the behavior prescribed in a set of instructions, the speaker/writer must present the antecedent conditions, the behavior to be performed and the consequences to be expected in the form and in the order in which they will be encountered by the listener/reader. Where instructions are presented verbally, the listener has the opportunity to ask questions which will have the effect of inducing the instructor to fill any gaps or correct defects of order as they present themselves to the listener. Two such questions appear in the transcript presented on Table 3. Writers of instructions, where the reader has no opportunity to ask such questions, need to take special care to ensure that the reader's contingencies are described in the form and in the order in which they will confront the reader. It seems that failure to follow this simple principle of putting oneself in the reader's shoes is a major source of communication breakdown and the failure to make effective use of complex and expensive equipment.

Semantic Principle 2 - Contingency Identification and Narrative Preference

The individual's narrative preferences, in whatever medium the narratives are presented, will depend on the ease with which he or she can identify with the contingencies of the individuals, particularly the hero/heroine, depicted in the story.

Semantic Principle 3 - Completion of Contingency Specification - A Constraint on Turn-Taking

When a speaker is telling a story, the listener cannot take over the turn until all three terms of the reported contingency have been specified. If a speaker omits one of the terms, the listener is constrained to ask a question which will evoke the missing term, and thus ensure that the speaker completes his or her turn before taking over. Take for example the story laid out on Table 6 which comes from a paper by Local, Kelly, and Wells (1986).
Now perform the following thought experiments[9] in each of which a different contingency term is removed:

Table 6. Contingency completion and narrative turn taking

N:	So when he went,	Antecedent
	I just stuck them bits of cardboard behind	Behavior
	and it works great	Consequence

	A thought experiment	
Thought Experiment:		Invites the question
(i)	*I just stuck them bits of cardboard behind and it works great.*	*What made you do that?*
(ii)	*So...he went and it works great.*	*What made the difference?*
(iii)	*So when he went I just stuck them bits of cardboard behind.*	*So, what happened?*

Semantic Principle 4 - The Speaker's Preference for own Contingency Rehearsal

Not only does the semantic content of an utterance determine how easily the listener can relate what the speaker is saying to his or her own contingencies and thereby understand what is being said, the same principle also controls the speaker's utterance. Thus, the reinforcement of a speaker's verbal behavior is maximized in so far as:
(a) the behavior is frequently reinforced by continuers supplied by the listener;
(b) the speaker is able to rehearse his or her own contingencies or those of his or her family and friends without sacrificing the frequency of continuers supplied by the listener (interpreted as evidence of the listener's interest in what is being said).

Semantic Principle 5 - Speaker's Own Contingency-Presentation - A Barrier to Communication

In business transactions, such as the example of the arrangements for the party which we have already looked at on Table 3, difficulties and misunderstandings arise because the initiating speaker formulates what she wants the listener to do in terms of her own contingencies - the antecedent conditions prompting the speaker to make the request - rather than in terms of the contingencies as they present themselves to the listener.

Semantic Principle 6 - Taking Turns at Own Contingency-Rehearsal in Casual Conversation

In casual conversation participants tend to take turns to rehearse their own contingencies and receive the appropriate continuers. These, however, are unlikely to be forthcoming unless the listener can easily identify with and thus maintain interest in the speaker's contingencies.

Semantic Principle 7 - Friendship as a Willingness to Share Each Other's Contingencies

A friend is someone with whose contingencies one can readily identify and thus listen to without becoming bored, thereby failing to supply the necessary verbal reinforcers, and who, by the same token, can listen to one's own rehearsal of one's own contingencies without becoming bored by them.

X. Conclusion: Towards an Applied Conversation Analysis

In attempting to integrate the conceptual schemes of behavior analysis and conversation analysis, Skinner's concept of the three-term contingency (antecedent, behavior and consequence) has been used to analyze both the pragmatics of the interaction between the participants in a conversation and the semantic content of what is said. How productive that attempt has been and what the future holds for such an enterprise is for the reader to judge.

For the writer two results stand out, one from the pragmatic analysis, the other from the semantic. From the pragmatic analysis there emerges a conception of the process which Skinner (1981) refers to as "selection by consequences" which is much richer and more subtle than that which springs to mind, if the paradigm case of a reinforcing consequence is the delivery of a food pellet and that of a disinforcing consequence an electric shock. What adds this new dimension to our understanding of the process whereby behavior is shaped by its consequences is the discovery that different types of speech act demand correspondingly different types of reinforcing and disinforcing consequence. That discovery emerges as soon as we begin to examine the kind of detailed study of naturally-occurring verbal interactions which the conversation analysts have shown us how to do in the light of Skinner's concept.

From the semantic analysis the most striking result is the discovery that a major obstacle to interpersonal communication is the fact that a contingency is unique to the individual whose behavior constitutes its defining middle term. This means that in a verbal interaction the interests of speaker and listener are in conflict. What is a reinforcing consequence for the speaker is to be able to rehearse her own contingencies, while receiving the kind of reinforcing consequences for so doing that only an attentive and interested listener can provide. What is a reinforcing consequence for the listener is to hear from the speaker either a specification of reinforcing consequences for behavior which she (the listener) has emitted or can easily and comfortably emit or the specification of similar consequences for behavior emitted by someone else with whose contingencies she can readily identify. How that conflict of interests gets reconciled as the turn passes from speaker to speaker in the course of a conversational exchange is what gives the study of conversation its peculiar fascination.

But the study of conversation is not just intrinsically fascinating. Although the art of conversation is a typical contingency-shaped skill acquired through practice rather than verbal instruction, it seems reasonable to suppose that the better we understand how it works, the better we shall be at giving practical advice, to ourselves as well as to others, on how to communicate effectively. Conversation analysis, as it has been practiced hitherto, has paid little attention to the possibility of its practical application. Behavior analysis with its roots in a tradition which emphasizes experimental manipulation and control is much more alert to such possibilities. May it not be that the greatest benefit to be derived from bringing the two research traditions together in the way suggested here will be the development of an applied conversation analysis?

XI. References

Chadwick-Jones, J. K. (1989). Baboon charades. *The Psychologist, 2,* 58-61.

Chomsky, N. (1957). *Syntactic structures.* The Hague: Mouton.

Harzem, P., & Miles, T. R. (1978). *Conceptual issues in operant psychology.* New York: Wiley.

Jefferson, G. (1981). The abominable *Ne?*. University of Manchester, Department of Sociology, Occasional Paper No.6.

Jones, E. E., & Gerard, H. B. (1967). *Foundations of social psychology.* New York: Wiley.

Kantor, J. R. (1959). *Interbehavioral psychology.* Bloomington, IN: Principia Press.

Keller, F. S., & Schoenfeld, W. N. (1950). *Principles of psychology.* New York: Appleton-Century-Crofts.

Lindsley, O. R. (1964). Direct measurement and the problems of retarded behavior. *Journal of Education, 47,* 62-81.

Local, J. K., Kelly, J., & Wells, W. H. G. (1986). Towards a phonology of conversation: turn-taking in Tyneside English. *Journal of Linguistics, 22,* 411-437.

Michael, J. (1982). Distinguishing between discriminative and motivational functions of stimuli. *Journal of the Experimental Analysis of Behavior 37,* 149-155.

Olton, D. S., & Schlosberg, P. (1978). Food-searching strategies in young rats: Win-shift predominates over win-stay. Journal of Comparative and Physiological Psychology, 92, 609-618.

Place, U. T. (1983). Skinner's *Verbal behavior* IV - How to improve Part IV, Skinner's account of syntax. *Behaviorism 11,* 163-186.

Place, U. T. (1985). Three senses of the word "tact". *Behaviorism 13,* 63-73.

Place, U. T. (1991). Conversation analysis and the analysis of verbal behavior. In L. J. Hayes & P. N. Chase (Eds.), *Dialogues on verbal behavior: Proceedings of the first international institute on verbal relations* (chap.5, pp. 85-109). Reno, NV: Context Press.

Place, U. T. (1992a). Behavioral contingency semantics and the correspondence theory of truth. In S. C. Hayes & L. J. Hayes (Eds.), *Understanding verbal relations: Proceedings of the second and third international institutes on verbal relations* (chap. 5, pp. 135-151). Reno, NV: Context Press.

Place, U. T. (1992b). The role of the ethnomethodological experiment in the empirical investigation of social norms, and its application to conceptual analysis. *Philosophy of the Social Sciences 22*, 461-474.

Place, U. T. (1993). A radical behaviorist methodology for the empirical investigation of private events. *Behavior and Philosophy, 20*, 25-35.

Place, U. T. (1996). Linguistic behaviorism as a philosophy of empirical science. In W. O' Donohue & R. Kitchener (Eds.), *The philosophy of psychology* (chap. 9, pp. 126-144). London: Sage.

Sacks, H. (1972). On the analysability of stories by children. In J. J. Gumpertz & D. Hymes (Eds.), *Directions in sociolinguistics: The ethnography of communication* (pp. 329-345). New York: Holt, Rinehart and Winston.

Skinner, B. F. (1938). *The behavior of organisms: An experimental analysis.* New York: Appleton-Century.

Skinner, B. F. (1953). *Science and human behavior.* New York: Macmillan.

Skinner, B. F. (1957). *Verbal behavior.* New York: Appleton-Century-Crofts.

Skinner, B. F. (1966/1969/1988). An operant analysis of problem solving. In B. Kleinmuntz (ed.) *Problem solving: Research, method and theory.* New York: Wiley. Reprinted as Chapter 6 of Skinner, B. F. *Contingencies of reinforcement: A theoretical analysis.* New York: Appleton-Century-Crofts. Reprinted with peer comments and a reply in A. C. Catania & S. Harnad (Eds.), *The selection of behavior. The operant behaviorism of B. F. Skinner: Comments and consequences* (pp. 218-236). Cambridge: Cambridge University Press.

Skinner, B. F. (1969). *Contingencies of reinforcement.* New York: Appleton-Century-Crofts.

Skinner, B.F. (1981). Selection by consequences. *Science, 213*, 501-504.

Wahler, R. G., & Fox, J. J. (1981). Setting events in applied behavior analysis: Toward a conceptual and methodological expansion. *Journal of Applied Behavior Analysis, 14*, 327-338.

Footnotes

[1] Earlier versions of this paper were presented at the Annual Conference of the Experimental Analysis of Behaviour Group, Leeds, April 1988, in a symposium on 'Problems and Methods in Recording, Transcribing and Analyzing Naturally-Occurring Verbal Interactions' at the Annual Convention of the Association for Behavior Analysis, Philadelphia, PA, May 1988, at Temple University's Tenth Annual Conference on Discourse Analysis, Philadelphia, PA, March 1989, at a Conference on 'Conversation, Discourse and Conflict', Trinity College, Dublin, March 1989, with peer commentary by L. V. Baker, P. Drew, J. Schwieso and J. Rae, at the Annual Conference of the History and Philosophy of Psychology Section of the British Psychological Society, Lincoln, March 1989, and at the Cambridge Center for Behavioral Studies, Cambridge, MA, March 1991.

The author wishes it to be known that its inclusion in this collection should not be construed as an endorsement of the doctrines of the late Stephen C. Pepper which, as a professional philosopher, he regards as profoundly misguided, both with respect to the nature of and criteria for the truth of a proposition (Place 1992a) and with respect to the nature of the causal relation and the methods by which the existence of such relations is determined (Place, 1996). On the other hand, this repudiation of Pepper's epistemology should not be construed as implying any lack of sympathy for the emphasis in this volume on the importance of context for the understanding of behavior in general and linguistic behavior in particular.

[2] I am personally indebted to Dr. Ogden Lindsley of the University of Kansas for introducing me to this way of formulating the three-term contingency, when I visited him in Kansas City in 1965. However, Dr. Lindsley (personal communication) is reluctant to take the credit for its introduction. Moreover, in his published account of what he calls the "operant behavior equation" (Lindsley 1964 p.68), he uses the terms "antecedent" and "consequence", together with "movement" instead of "behavior" and "arrangement" as a fourth element corresponding to the scheduled relation between behavior and consequence.

[3] There is reason to think that this way of construing the function of discriminative stimuli which, as I am reliably informed by Dr. Evalyn Segal, is now widely accepted amongst behavior analysts derives from the work of J. R. Kantor.

[4] Michael's concepts of "establishing condition", "establishing stimulus", and "establishing operation" would seem to have two sources. The concept of an "establishing operation" comes from Keller and Schoenfeld's (1950 p. 269) discussion of motivation where it refers to procedures such as depriving a rat of food which is said to establish a "hunger drive." Another source is J. R. Kantor's (1959) concept of "setting factors" which has been widely adopted by behavior analysts in the form of Wahler and Fox's (1981) "setting events." I prefer Michael's formulation because it brings out much more clearly the contrast between the discriminative and motivating functions of antecedent events and states of affairs.

The terms "disinforcement" and "disinforcer" referring to a consequence which tends to weakens the organism's propensity to emit a response, in the way that the terms "reinforcement" and "reinforcer" refer to a consequence which tends to strengthen it, was proposed by Harzem and Miles (1978).

[5] From the outset, Skinner (1938) insisted that, in contrast with respondents (involuntary reflexes) which appear only when elicited by the appropriate stimulus, operants are spontaneously "emitted" by the organism. They come under the "control" of discriminative stimuli in whose presence they are subsequently reinforced. Once this "stimulus control" has been established, Skinner allows us to say that stimulus "evokes" a response; but until this stage is reached, the term "response" is, strictly speaking, inappropriate.

⁶I am indebted to an article on the social behavior of baboons by J. K. Chadwick-Jones (1989) for drawing my attention to Jones and Gerard's work in this area.

⁷I am indebted to Dr. John Rae for drawing my attention to the inadequacy of my treatment of this point in an earlier version of this paper in the comments which he made on it at the Lincoln Conference of the History and Philosophy Section of the British Psychological Society in March 1989.

⁸When responding to an earlier version of this paper at the Lincoln Conference of the History and Philosophy of Psychology Section of the British Psychological Society in 1989.

⁹For a discussion of the rationale behind the use of this kind of 'ethnomethodological' thought experiment as a way of throwing light on social norms in general and those governing verbal behavior in particular, see Place (1992b).

Section 4

Rhetorical Context and the Applied Analysis of Communication Behavior

Chapter 19

Rhetorical Contexts and Scholarly Inquiry

Jeanine Czubaroff
Ursinus College

The second half of the twentieth century has witnessed a renaissance in rhetorical studies based on renewed interest in symbolic modes of action and nondemonstrative modes of proof. One result of this renaissance, as we move into the twenty-first century, is that for many the term "rhetoric" calls to mind not deceptive discourse, but an area of study and a unique perspective on human communication. I will argue in this essay that this rhetorical perspective is fundamentally contextualist in the sense that it views communicative interactions as complex, relational, situated actions. After explaining what I mean by the "rhetorical perspective", I apply the perspective to a recent scholarly conflict between behavior analysts and some of their critics. I conclude by summarizing some of the principles common to the rhetorical perspective and social, interpretive approaches to study of communicative action (see, Leeds-Hurwitz, 1995).

The Rhetorical Perspective

Rhetoric is traditionally recognized as instrumental or influential discourse, that is, discourse deliberately formulated to deepen, modify, shape, or change persons' perceptions, beliefs, values, and/or actions (see, Bryant, 1965; Cooper, 1989; Hart & Burkes 1972; Hauser, 1986). Within an instrumental perspective, the most fundamental evaluative question a rhetorical critic may ask of a particular rhetorical act is, Did it accomplish its intended influence? This, of course, is the question of effectiveness. As a discursive mode of influence aimed at modifying persons' beliefs and actions, rhetoric is fundamentally concerned with meanings, that is, with perceptions, feelings, valuations, judgments, beliefs, or, in sum, with "consciousness." Rhetoric assumes that human beings are "reasoning" beings, that is, that they tend to act on the basis of their perceptions, beliefs, and feelings about their communication situations (see, Trenholm, 1989, Chapter 1).

Lloyd Bitzer (1968), the first to characterize systematically the components of the rhetorical situation, described the situation as "a complex of persons, events, objects, and relations presenting an actual or potential exigence which can be completely or partially removed if discourse is introduced into the situation and so constrains human decision or action as to bring about the significant modification of the exigence" (p. 6). For Bitzer, the "rhetorical situation" is a construct of the instrumental dynamics at the heart of human communication aimed to influence. While I find his concepts of "exigence" and "constraints" somewhat limiting, Bitzer's recognition that the constellation of elements comprising rhetorical experience constitute a dynamic "situation" is important, and I build on that recognition.

The prototypical rhetorical situation within which individuals frame discourse intended to influence includes a rhetor with his or her own unique consciousness or frame of reference and the audience members, each with his or her own distinctive consciousness or frame of reference. Communicative interaction and transaction occurs between the rhetor's frame of reference and the audiences members' frames of reference within the dimensions of a particular social context. Just as the rhetor in a particular sociological situation brings a self-identity, a definition of the context, and a set of goals with respect to the context, the subject matter, and the audience, so does each member of the audience. In addition to their social roles and definitions of the situation, the rhetor and audience members may share particular histories and relationships with each other. Obviously, in ongoing relationships or extended interactions, the roles of rhetor and audience may repeatedly shift.

A full sense of the complex, interactive nature of rhetorical communication emerges as one describes the constituent elements of the particular setting within which rhetor and audience interact. Persistent components of such situations include, (a) the cultural beliefs and practices which contextualize the rhetorical discourse or action; (b) the historical events, including rhetorical imperatives, which immediately motivate the rhetorical discourse; (c) the institutional setting and occasion, as well as physical setting for the discourse; and (d) the subject matter and relevant constellation of argumentation issues and voices presupposed and addressed by the discourse (see, Andrews, 1990; Hillbruner, 1966)

At the broadest level, every rhetorical discourse reflects cultural beliefs and practices, including metaphysical, political, economic, and ethical beliefs and practices. Beyond the cultural backdrop is the sequence of historical events, sometimes very personal in nature, which motivate and give meaning to the rhetorical action. Among these motivating factors are the "rhetorical imperatives" (see, Andrews, 1990), or "exigences" (see, Bitzer, 1968), including problems, needs, interests, issues, visions, or ideals which move human beings to discourse in the belief that symbolic action may mediate change in the original situation. The historical sequence of events, in turn, takes place within an institutional setting. Institutional goals, practices, norms, roles and patterns of interaction structure broad areas of human activity, including the political, economic, educational, religious, familial, and legal, providing many of the constraints rhetors must consider in framing their discourse. Often, institutional settings define prototypical rhetorical situations, for example, the political campaign stump stop, the presidential inaugural, the university classroom, or the college commencement, with accompanying genres of rhetoric, for example, the campaign speech, the inaugural address, the academic lecture, the commencement address. Audiences come to such institutional settings with expectations which the rhetor typically must meet if she or he is to effectively communicate. Finally, all rhetorical acts occur within argumentation contexts including the history of the subject and issues, and the sequence of voices involved in discussion of the subject.

The rhetorical discourse or text which is framed as a response to this complex of persons interacting in context, on the one hand, gains meaning by its embeddedness in the situation. On the other hand, once it emerges from the context, the discourse reacts back on the situation, potentially modifying the audience members' points of view, eliciting audience feedback which modifies the rhetor's point of view, or, finally, eliciting human behaviors which modify the social context itself. (Thus, for example, speeches in Congress may result in passage of a new law and the new law may prescribe new forms of behavior.) Besides the central relations between rhetor, audience, and situation, then, is a dialectical, transactive relationship between the rhetorical text or discourse and the rhetorical context or situation from which it emerges. Once complete, the rhetorical act becomes part of the ongoing context and other rhetorical acts may emerge in response to it. Time becomes a factor in the dynamic in the sense that what is past is past, what is said is said—is a communication fact which forms the efficient ground for present action.

As a communicator develops a genuinely rhetorical perspective, he or she begins to appreciate that the effective rhetor takes into consideration not only his or her own perspective, commitments, and purposes, but also the audience members' perspectives, commitments, and purposes and the commitments and purposes of the context (Hart & Burkes, 1972, p. 80). Indeed, the first thing a rhetor may need to do with an audience is negotiate the definition of situation which is to prevail. Hauser (1986) notes the critical importance of definitions of situation for humans who must act: "In defining any situation, then, we are confronted with the reality of dynamics and flux. Meanings emerge and are relative. It is important not to lose sight of this, for humans act on the basis of how they define situations. Were we unable to define a situation, we would be unable to act because it would lack meaning for us" (p. 32). Contrary to what some might assume, there are no objective definitions of social situations. What counts as an "important" event, what that event means in the context of past history and other contextual elements, what cultural practices and norms are relevant and how those norms are to be interpreted, all are relative to the individuals involved and therefore negotiable. Indeed, individuals in interaction may disagree on the relevant institutional setting for their communication. This frequently occurs among rhetors who discuss the abortion issue. Some present their cases as matters of privacy and personal ethics and others present their cases as matters of law or religion. Finally, the rhetor and audience may disagree about the relevant issues and voices. Thus, depending on the position one takes in the evolution-creationism debate, one will identify different issues (for example, freedom or environmental determinism) as critical and different spokespersons (e.g., Reverend Falwell or Professor Gould) as authoritative. While situational elements seem to be given, they are not, paradoxically, objectively given, but must be recognized and interpreted by the social actors. One function of a rhetorical act, then, is to explicitly or implicitly define the rhetorical situation to which it is a response. This naming and interpretation includes contextualizing the act in a specific culture or subculture and presupposing specific institutional goals and communication conventions.

The concept of the rhetorical situation rests on the recognition that the rhetor is relationally defined and entangled with other people and situations. Competent rhetors consider their own identities, points of view, interests, and relational and contextual purposes, their audience's identities, points of view, interests, and purposes, and the goals and requirements of the social-institutional context.[1] To give attention to one's relationships as well as to one's own immediate goals entails, especially, considering and relating one's ideas to the others' definitions of situation, needs, interests, and goals in the relationship and context (see, Wilson, Arnold, & Wertheimer, 1990, Chapter 1)[2]

A crucial variable in the rhetor-audience relationship turns on the degree of congruence or incongruence, similarity or difference between the rhetor and audience's views of the communication situation and relationship, as well as their views of the particular topic and issues at stake. If the two parties totally agree, there is little reason for persuasive/influential talk. However, if they are separated by different perceptions and judgments, there is reason for persuasive talk, for, since social reality emerges from corporate action among individuals, these differences must be negotiated. This is the fundamental rhetorical imperative.

Rhetorical theorists have developed different schemes to attempt to capture the different approaches rhetors may take to audiences which have at least somewhat different frames of reference regarding the rhetorical situation.[3] In each instance, the rhetor pursues a specific kind of relationship with the audience and differentially weighs the goal of being true to his or her own identity, frame of reference, purposes, and view of the relationship, and the goal of being open to the audience members' identities, frames of reference, purposes, and views of the relationship. At one extreme the rhetor, variously called a rhetorical reflector, conventional or conformist communicator, sacrifices (or, even fails to develop) self-identity, beliefs, and goals in favor of message congruence with more highly valued audience points of view and purposes. Conformist rhetors include individuals who, as organizational mouthpieces, celebrate institutional events without voicing any personal interpretations or judgments. Rhetors at the opposite extreme, variously labeled noble selves, expressive communicators, seducers, rapists, institutional violators, or combative persuaders, assume they have the right point of view and construction of the rhetorical situation. As a consequence, they are uninterested in, even actively disrespectful and rejecting of the audience's differing points of view. In their strong conviction they may be willing to use any persuasive means, including manipulation and deception, to achieve their communication goals. Finally, rhetors, variously called rhetorically sensitive, coactive communicators, or lovers, may approach their audiences in a spirit of mutual respect, that is, with a concern to balance expression of their own points of view and purposes with recognition and consideration of the interests, points of view, and identities of audience members. Wilson et al. (1990) express the more idealistic spirit of this approach when they assert, "To properly respect an audience enough to try to relate new ideas to their perspective is to reject personal arrogance and to see such arrogance as undermining mutually productive relationships of reciprocal respect" (p. 7). While profound mutual respect is not a necessary component of this approach, when such respect obtains, the rhetor, as lover, no longer insists on a particular message or communication goal and engages with the other in the co-creation of meaning and message.

The rhetorical perspective, in sum, assumes that human discourse aimed at influence is best understood in its relational, situational, interpersonal context. It also assumes that rhetorical competency requires contextual, relational thinking about the dynamics of rhetor, audience, situation, and communication resources.

Rhetorical Study of Science

One of the unique aspects of the recent rhetorical renaissance has been the rhetorical scholar's insistence that the construct of the rhetorical situation describes important communicative relations in all situations in which humans are attempting to influence each others' perceptions, judgments, choices, and actions. This insistence has led some scholars to examine the discursive behavior of scientists, thereby initiating the sub-field of the rhetoric of inquiry. The following analysis of the rhetorical situation surrounding the publication of an essay by behavior analyst A. Charles Catania (1991) illustrates how the construct of the rhetorical situation captures the complexity of judgments Catania had to make as a scientific rhetor and illustrates the usefulness of the construct for the rhetorical critic intent on assessing the dynamics of rhetorical interactions among scientists.

Rhetorical critics typically admonish fellow critics to begin their critical analysis by identifying a rhetorical discourse or text which seems relevant or important (see, Foss, 1989; Andrews, 1990). If we consider that the only artifacts from the ongoing flow of human communicative interaction are the symbolic and physical artifacts, this advice makes sense. Criteria of relevance or importance for the rhetorician of inquiry include the scholarly community's judgment of the intellectual merit of a rhetorical text, as well as the amount of attention or controversy generated by a discourse. A. Charles Catania's essay (1991), "The Gifts of Culture and of Eloquence: An Open Letter to Michael J. Mahoney in Reply to His Article, 'Scientific Psychology and Radical Behaviorism'" interests me not because it is an original piece of research, but because Catania managed, in the process of writing, disseminating and publishing this piece, to mobilize the behavior-analytic community to feeling and action in ways seldom achieved by individual scholars. As a rhetorician of science I was intrigued by the situation which could elicit this discourse. Thus, I examine the situation in which this rhetorical text was formulated and disseminated.

The history of Catania's piece dates to late 1989 when he read psychologist Michael J. Mahoney's essay (1989), "Scientific Psychology and Radical Behaviorism: Important Distinctions Based in Scientism and Objectivism," published in *American Psychologist*. The piece, Catania concluded, required a response. The first draft of his response began circulating among behavior analysts and friends of behavior analysts between January 5 and February 8, 1990. The second draft was distributed in April. A final draft was published in *The Behavior Analyst* (1991), an archival journal of the behavior analyst association. In all three versions, the essay is an angry defense of the behavior analytic research tradition—a classic essay from the decades long psychology guerrilla wars.

After identifying and initially examining the rhetorical artifact, the rhetorical critic attempts to reconstruct the rhetorical situation from which the text emerged (see, Foss, 1989; Andrews, 1990). The rhetor, in this case, A. Charles Catania, a behavior analyst and former student of B. F. Skinner at Harvard University from 1958 to 1961, has served the behavior analyst community for decades in such capacities as journal editor, president of division 25 of the American Psychology Association and president of the Association of Behavior Analysts. Throughout his career he has been deeply implicated in the intellectual conflicts that have dogged radical behaviorists. In correspondence, Catania (A. C. Catania, personal communication, January 5-February 8, 1990), states that his fundamental concern in the 1990 essay was to confront what he termed the "intellectual bigotry" that he observed in Michael J. Mahoney's essay. He also wanted to "turn the tide against this bigotry." Thus, his declared communication goal was one of defense and redress of the issues surrounding the merits of the radical behaviorism research program.

To identify the audience for Catania's essay is a complex task, partly because of the number of drafts involved. Again, from correspondence, it seems clear that Catania's intended audience was the community of professional psychologists of the *American Psychologist*, the main journal of the American Psychological Association (correspondence, Jan. 5-Feb. 8). The *American Psychologist* was an ideal forum for this controversy and, indeed, a series of letters to the editor responding to Mahoney's essay and Mahoney's response to his critics appeared in its October 1990 issue. For Catania this broad audience of fellow psychologists was, in many ways, the ideal audience because among them were individuals who harbored misguided views of behaviorism. While readers of the *American Psychologist* were the empowered audience in the sense that to change their views would be to move in the direction of vindicating behavior analysis in the field of psychology, one must wonder whether the audience was ideal as far as openness to change is concerned (see Cooper, 1989, Chapter 2, on the ideal audience) In addition to this intended audience, was another, actual, preview audience, namely, the behavior analysts and friends, who received copies of the first and second drafts of the essay. Catania invited these individuals to cosign his essay, and asked those who intended to sign to consider sending letters to the *American Psychologist* declaring their intention. In this fashion, he hoped to indicate broad support for his outrage and for his request for an opportunity to respond in print to the Mahoney essay. The third and final audience comprised the behavior analysts who read the essay once published in *The Behavior Analyst*. At this point, needless to say, the essay was preaching to the already convinced. For a number of reasons, the essay was never published in the *American Psychologist* (see Catania, 1991, Postscript), and, thus, the ideal audience was never addressed. Catania did, however, send the essay to Michael J. Mahoney who, in turn, responded to Catania in his written response to his critics for *American Psychologist*.

The scene which motivated Catania's essay may, as noted earlier, be described in terms of the underlying cultural structures and beliefs, the history of events leading up to and precipitating the rhetorical action, the institutional setting, and, finally, the argumentation context.

The cultural and ideological belief systems presupposed, respectively, by Catania's and Mahoney's essays, as well as by the institutional context of social science research are very diverse, including contradictory beliefs and norms. For instance, the cultural matrix included the belief systems defining the educational and research missions of higher education in America, the scientific ideology of American social science and psychology research, and the intellectual and philosophical research paradigms of behavior analysis and cognitive psychology. The more encompassing American political-ideological context included a pervasive commitment to democratic principles and cultural premises like social libertarianism, secularism, and humanism.

The history of events initiating the conception, dissemination, and eventual publication of Catania's essay included the central exigence or rhetorical imperative, namely, psychologist Michael J. Mahoney's publication in a national academic journal of an essay viewed by many behavior analysts as outrageously inaccurate and bigoted in its characterization of the behavior analytic research tradition. The broader historical context included a thirty or forty year history of controversies between radical behaviorists and various schools in psychology as well as controversy between radical behaviorists and other intellectuals (see, for example, Chomsky, 1958; MacCorquodale, 1970; Skinner, 1957, 1971; Wheeler, 1973).

A third aspect of the rhetorical situation is the institutional backdrop including the purposes, roles, norms, practices, and beliefs systems of the institutions of higher education and the American Psychology Association and psychology discipline. Particular to psychology in the twentieth century has been its institutional breakdown into "schools," that is, institutionally affiliated groups of scholars who share a research tradition. Freudian, Jungian, cognitivist, gestalt, and radical behaviorist schools have flourished, to name a few. This institutional fragmentation has profoundly affected communication among twentieth century psychologists and thus calls for consideration.

Scientific schools emerge for political and intellectual reasons. As a school, behavior analysts forged political power bases that enabled them to survive and reproduce in sometimes hostile academic environments and to foster a community that encouraged behavior analytic research. Although institutionalized school status affords real advantages to scholars, it also entails potential dangers. For example, members of one school may become isolated from other research traditions within the larger academic discipline. When a research school's isolation is accompanied by a tendency to assume a competitive orientation toward opponents, the result may be self-absorption and an aggressive-defensive stance that can militate against active engagement with outside ideas and consequent loss of the creative and critical impact these ideas may have on the research tradition (see, Hagstrom, 1965, Chapter 6; Toulmin, 1972, Chapter 4). Communication consequences of reliance upon competitive orientations often lead to a reduction in the amount of communication between parties, a dramatic increase in misunderstanding and miscommunication, ad hominem attacks, and lack of mutual influence (see, Folger & Poole, 1994; Hocker & Wilmot, 1985) The constitution of behavior analysis as a distinct research school in an academic discipline itself made up of numbers of distinct research schools has not only enabled behavior analysis to survive, but has, as we shall see, confronted behavior analysts with some of their most vexing communication challenges and problems.

The last element of the scene within which this essay emerged is the constellation of argumentation voices and issues surrounding and defining the ongoing debate about the merits of the behavior analytic research tradition. For much of its history, radical behaviorists have defined and developed their research tradition in a hostile or indifferent academic context. Central to the indifference and hostility has been controversy over radical behaviorism's conceptions of human nature, of science and its goals, and of social reality and social goals (see, Lacey, 1980; Czubaroff, 1988). Central among its presuppositions are: (a) A natural evolutionary process of selection by consequences underlies all biological, behavioral, and cultural processes; (b) human beings do not exercise significant agency because they are not shaped by ideas and conscience, but by environmental contingencies, or the consequences of their behaviors; therefore, freedom and responsibility are meaningless concepts; (c) biological/species and cultural survival are the central goals of a culture, not individual survival; (d) the goals of science are prediction and control; and (e) science and technology are the most important means for solving human social problems. In response to these premises, opponents, especially humanists and theists, have decried radical behaviorism's scientism, materialism, secularism, and anti-liberalism. In the context of decades of often bitter controversy over these premises, Mahoney published his essay in *American Psychologist* in November 1989. Nor, of course, did the argumentation stop with Mahoney and Catania. It subsequently included four letters to the editor of *American Psychologist* and Mahoney's (1990) response to his critics, "Diatribe is not Dialogue: On Selected Attempts to Attack and Defend Behaviorism."

As we consider the complex rhetorical context in which Catania found himself early in 1990, we can appreciate that his rhetorical problems and choices about how to define and respond to the rhetor-audience-situation constellation were diverse and complex. First, he had to decide how to define the rhetorical situation as it included him, Mahoney, and behaviorist and nonbehaviorists psychologists: Was Mahoney's essay friendly or hostile? Was the essay important or trivial? Was the context to be conceived narrowly, that is, as a matter of difference of opinion between Catania and a professional colleague, or broadly as a matter of honor and respect for an entire research tradition in conflict with other research traditions? Once Catania characterized his rhetorical situation, he had to grapple with practical questions of selecting an audience, clarifying a rhetorical purpose, and framing his discourse: Which segment of his audience should he address most intensively—fellow behavior analysts, Mahoney, nonbehaviorist psychologists? What should his communication purpose be—to defend, to attack, to listen, to complain? What style of address should he use—an aggressive, defensive, dispassionate style? What medium of communication should he rely upon—face to face conversation, scholarly essay, or letter to the editor? Which issues and statements in the Mahoney essay should he see as salient and which should he ignore? Over time, in the context of discussion with friends and colleagues, Catania answered these questions to his satisfaction and fashioned his essay. With this background in mind, we can examine some of the discourse.

In his essay, "Scientific Psychology and Radical Behaviorism," Mahoney (1989) argues that radical behaviorism has been scientifically dogmatic and epistemologically absolutist and suggests that different schools in psychology should engage in "open dialectical exchange". His abstract states: "The intolerance of some radical behaviorists for other views—characterized as a *scientistic* rather than a *scientific* attitude—is discussed as one possible factor in the apparent decline of radical behaviorism. Also influential may have been the impossibility of absolute objectivism in any epistemic venture, including scientific inquiry. It is concluded that traditions in science reflect a valuable legacy and that future developments in scientific psychology would be well served by open dialectical exchanges both within and among differing ideologies" (p. 1372). In response to an outpouring of radical behaviorist objections to his arguments and his insinuation that radical behaviorism was in "apparent decline" Mahoney insists, "The central intent of my article was not to initiate an offensive against radical behaviorism but, rather, to assert that Skinner's (1987) lament over the 'unfortunate effects' of humanistic psychology, the helping professions, and cognitive psychology (p. 780) on the field reflect an unnecessarily narrow definition of both science and psychology. I feel no personal animosity toward Fred Skinner: He was a positive and generous influence on my early professional development and, despite our conceptual differences, we have maintained a mutually respectful acquaintance over the years" (1990, p. 1184). Unfortunately for Mahoney, who suggested in his original essay that, "The time has come to transform ideological swords into conceptual plowshares and to risk trusting in the harvest of open dialectical exchange" (1989, p. 1376), his radical behaviorists readers did not perceive a conciliatory message. Part of the reason certainly has to do with Mahoney's problematic rhetorical choices, including an invidious distinction between "scientific psychology" and "radical behaviorism," the latter of which is variously characterized as "orthodox," "intolerant," and "scientistic," and to an undocumented charge about "the development and circulation of a list of 'banned readings,' books that faculty and students in some radical behavioral departments were instructed not to read" (1989, p. 1375). Understandably, radical behaviorists hit the ceiling on the censorship charge, feeling that they had not only been stereotyped but potentially slandered.

Mahoney acknowledges in his response to critics that his article drew a "flood of phone calls and correspondence," and that, "with rare exceptions, those responses have also been unmistakably emotional," (1990, p. 1183). One important critical response was the essay Charles Catania circulated privately among radical behaviorists and also sent to Mahoney. Catania's embattled mentality formed from years of controversy in the psychology guerilla wars, is revealed in his opening lines, "Dear Michael: I have read your paper in *American Psychologist* (Mahoney, 1989), and the extent to which it is laden with errors of fact and interpretation compels me to respond. You may wonder about my title ["The Gifts of Culture and of Eloquence: An Open Letter to Michael J. Mahoney"]. It comes from W. H. Fremantle's account of the 1860 Oxford debate over Darwin's *On the Origin of Species* (Darwin, 1892/1958, pp. 251-252)" (1991, p. 61). Catania responds point by point to the factual errors and misrepresentations noted and, on the issue of banned books, questions "is it appropriate to offer such a slanderous accusation without a shred of documentation?" (p. 66). Obviously, Catania found it impossible to respond to (let alone take seriously) Mahoney's appeal to turn "ideological swords" into "conceptual plowshares." Instead, in scathing direct address Catania comments, "I am compelled to charge you with a level of intellectual prejudice that has led you to careless scholarship and to misrepresentation" (p. 65). Mahoney appears to have been pained by Catania's open letter for in his response to his critics, he writes, "Among the critical letters ... came [one] from an old behaviorist colleague with whom I had been on a first name basis for almost 20 years. What I found in that envelope was not a letter or a personal note, however, but a sizeable manuscript titled 'An Open Letter to Michael Mahoney.' It was a direct attack on my integrity and intelligence" (1990, p. 1183).

In a postscript to his essay published in *Behavior Analyst*, Catania takes a more conciliatory (but certainly not contrite) tone. Mahoney, he writes, "refers to my open letter, and calls it 'a direct attack on my integrity and intelligence' ... Yet no where does he acknowledge even the most thoroughly documented of the misunderstandings that he has helped to perpetuate, such as his reversal of Bacon and Descartes. Despite all his rhetoric, he still seems not to have recognized that he has gotten some things wrong. Until he can do so, there seems little hope that he will be able to reconcile his views with those of contemporary radical behaviorism" (p. 72). Interesting here are the implicit conditions for more friendly relationship: (a) Acknowledgment of misunderstandings that have been perpetuated among others; (b) recognize that you have gotten some things wrong. In short, Catania requires acknowledgment of misunderstanding, a genuine effort to seek understanding and signs of mutual respect as the conditions for efforts at reconciliation. Of course, as in all relational conflicts, what counts as acknowledgment of error, apology, and genuine efforts to understand are themselves debatable matters. Reconciliation after years of bitter fighting is not easy.

In hindsight, two observations about this rhetorical situation and series of interactions seem especially salient to me.[4] First, I note the reliance upon written rather than oral, face-to-face modes of discourse. This choice, it seems to me, made it difficult for the actors to reach beyond their differences, be held genuinely accountable for their competitive assertions, and be able to encourage their partners to genuinely listen (see, Czubaroff, forthcoming). Had Mahoney appreciated the importance of demonstrating mutual respect and effort to understand and had he engaged in some informal, oral discourse with behavior analyst colleagues about his essay's conceptualization, much wasted energy and alienation might have been avoided. Once the piece was in print, anger, ill will, and polarization of positions resulted, over the weeks reaching phenomenal proportions, certainly out of line with the importance of the initial piece. Assertions and charges, once put to paper, could not be retracted, reworded, or modified. Negotiation of different data and perspectives and even rudimentary damage control became almost impossible.

Second, I observe incomplete awareness of the multiple goals and relationships among the participants in the controversy. Academic discourse, like all rhetorical discourse, is motivated by a complex blend of sometimes incompatible personal and professional goals and relational dynamics. While Catania was concerned especially to confront the "intellectual bigotry" of fellow psychologists and to defend the merits of the radical behaviorist research program, Mahoney, apparently, had his own intellectual agenda with respect to radical behaviorism and other psychology schools, including the desire to challenge radical behaviorists to leave behind what he characterized as outmoded goals and styles. Certainly, other participants in the widening circle of response in the October 1990 issue of *American Psychologist* had their own agendas. Interesting in the context of these diverse and conflicting agendas, however, is the fact that Catania and Mahoney had a history of past professional relationship—a relationship that Catania seems to have taken more casually than Mahoney, though Mahoney's stance of hurt can also be read as a defensive strategy. Nonetheless, Catania's adversarial advocacy stance made this victim move possible. Finally, it is not clear that Catania took into consideration the multiple goals of the editors of *American Psychologist*. While on the one hand, the editors most certainly could have an ideological commitment to advance non-behaviorist psychological research, they might also have initially resisted publishing the Catania essay because they felt it was in the interest of the whole profession to preserve dispassionate discourse through the control of passionate exchanges (see, Hagstrom, 1965).

In light of this analysis of the diverse points of view and goals at stake, the rhetorical critic can conjecture that for Catania to be maximally effective with the broad audience of American psychologists he would have had to couch his advocacy in terms likely to be viewed as professional and non-attacking by both the editors of *American Psychologist* and the target audience. On the other hand, Catania almost certainly (and very possibly rightly) would argue that a dispassionate, gentlemanly discourse would not have gotten the attention of his opponents, let alone have gained a sympathetic hearing. If this is the case, and if antagonistic rhetoric is counter-productive, then it would seem that scientists who represent marginal or broadly unpopular research programs must devise "non-violent," confrontational strategies analogous to the non-violent civil disobedience tactics relied upon by protestors in the public domain. Such tactics gain attention, motivate indifferent or hostile audiences to give a hearing to relatively powerless groups, and are less alienating than more aggressive tactics (see, Stewart, Smith, & Denton, 1989, Chapter 5).

The Rhetorical Perspective and Social Approaches to Communication Study

The foregoing analysis, I hope, illustrates the relational, situated nature of rhetorical discourse, including rhetorical discourse among scholars. Interestingly, many of the themes that animate the relatively new field of rhetoric of inquiry are consistent with themes central to social, interpretive approaches to human communication research. Leeds-Hurwitz (1995), for instance, argues that researchers within the social, interpretive orientation tend to be committed to the view that communication is a fundamentally "interactive" process between persons. These researchers argue that we cannot understand human communication if we focus exclusively on one or another element of the communication event (for example, on the source or the receiver). Second, notes Leeds-Hurwitz, scholars working within social, interpretive approaches focus on symbols, that is, verbal and nonverbal behaviors/ texts/ discourses. Indeed, the symbolic text, when captured in print or on film or videotape, is often the only residual artifact of communicative interactions. A third theme common to many researchers in this broad tradition is the conviction that human social reality is negotiated and constructed (rather than objectively given) in communicative interaction. The idea here is not so much that there is no "reality" outside human concepts, but that the *meaning* of our experience of our world is corporately and symbolically constructed. Needless to say, the meanings constructed are not monolithic and thus we have complex subcultures or co-cultures with their particular conceptual categories and world views. A fourth theme relates directly to the importance of culture, understood by Leeds-Hurwitz as that knowledge of norms and practices which members of a society must learn to become appropriate members of that society (p. 11). Researchers within the social, interpretive tradition recognize that all human interactions take place within cultural contexts. Implicit here, of course, is the recognition that communicative actions emerge from the interactions among individuals in socially constructive cultural contexts and thus that communicative actions can only be understood when we examine the complex web of interrelated elements.

Researchers who accept these broad themes about human communication tend, suggests Leeds-Hurwitz (1995), to view their research activity as itself socially constructed within specific cultural contexts. This view of communication research rejects the idea that researchers can be independent of the subjects they study and, instead, assumes that they are deeply implicated in the social situations they study. These researchers value highly what they call "reflexivity" in their research (see Leeds-Hurwitz, p. 14)–a provisional attitude of awareness of the multitude of other questions and assumptions that may be brought to the task of understanding a particular communication event. Finally, Leeds-Hurwitz suggests that researchers within the broad social, interpretive rubric often define wider intellectual contexts for their research findings in order to achieve some holistic understanding of human communication and the human condition.

Certainly, the rhetoric of inquiry program, at least as understood in its first decade of work, shares many of the above themes, suggesting that it is broadly social and interpretive in its orientation. In their introduction to one of the groundbreaking works of this subfield, *The Rhetoric of the Human Sciences: Language and Argument in Scholarship and Public Affairs* (1987), Nelson, Megill, and McCloskey note the focus on symbolic action, "Rhetoric of inquiry is a way of conversing about intellectual conversation–and improving its quality" (p. 5). In another early anthology of essays, *Rhetoric and the Human Sciences* (1989) editor Herbert W. Simons confirms, similarly, that the rhetorician interested in study of the communicative actions of scholars will focus on the scholars' "discursive behaviors" (p. 2). Besides sharing with the social, interpretive approaches a concern for symbolic behaviors, the rhetoric of inquiry also recognizes the fundamental social constructedness of scholarly world views and communities. For instance, Simons writes, "the Protagorean thesis that man is the measure of all things does not necessarily imply human superiority; only that in our science and mathematics, as in all else, discourse creates features of the world rather than simply providing independent proof of their existence. Variants of this constructionist position find repeated expression in this book" (p. 7). Rhetoric of inquiry emerged with the renaissance in history and sociology of science studies and thus, with history and sociology, takes as axiomatic the premise that human inquiry occurs in social-historical-cultural-ideological contexts. Recognizing the political power conferred upon scientific experts and scientific knowledge in the larger society, some rhetoricians of inquiry urge, much as does Leeds-Hurwitz (1995) in referring to a broadening of the cultural context, that rhetorical studies move beyond systematic analyses of expert discourse to critique of the current culture within which human inquiry takes place. For instance, in the Simons volume, Robert Hariman (1989) argues that the disciplinary practices and professional ideology and ideals of contemporary American universities emerged as part of broader social movements in the late nineteenth century favoring the power and ascendance of the middle class. He writes, "The rhetoric of inquiry must develop a cultural critique. The first step here is to recognize that disciplinary knowledge is an apparatus of the disciplinary system—or, in Louis

Althusser's (see Hariman essay, 1989, p. 225) terms, that it is an 'ideological state apparatus'—and so avoid replicating the willed political incapacities of positivism." It is perhaps worth noting that Hariman goes on to lament that much of the work of American rhetoricians of inquiry has failed to undertake such cultural critique (see also, Nelson, in Megill et al., 1987). Finally, rhetoric of inquiry has a profoundly reflexive view of its own activity. The rhetorician of science sees scholars as actively engaged in constructing knowledge and, perforce, sees him or herself as engaged in constructing views of knowledge and inquiry, views which, at most, may be edifying, but certainly will not be conclusive or exhaustive. Simons (1989) confirms the self-reflexive and even ironic character of the rhetoric of inquiry when he notes, "Like the foregoing epigraph about epigraphs, a rhetoric about rhetoric cannot avoid doubling back upon itself; cannot avoid its own rhetoricity. This adds another dimension to all rhetorical analysis" (p. 4). The case is clear, I believe, that rhetoric of inquiry shares many of the presuppositions of social, interpretive approaches to human communication research.

References

Althusser, L. (1971). *Lenin and philosophy* (B. Brester, Trans.) (p. 132). New York: Monthly Review Press.

Andrews, J. R. (1990). *The practice of rhetorical criticism* (2nd ed.). New York: Longman.

Bitzer, L. (1968). The rhetorical situation. *Philosophy and Rhetoric, 1,* 1-14.

Branham, R. J., & Pearce, W. B. (1985). Between text and context: Toward a rhetoric of contextual reconstruction. *Quarterly Journal of Speech, 71,* 19-36.

Bryant, D. C. (1965). Rhetoric: Its functions and its scope. In M. Natanson & H. W. Johnstone, Jr. (Eds.), *Philosophy, rhetoric, and argumentation* (pp. 32-62). University Park, PA: Pennsylvania State University Press.

Brockriede, W. (1972). Arguers as lovers. *Philosophy and Rhetoric, 5* (1), 1-11.

Catania, A. C. (1991). The gifts of culture and of eloquence: An open letter to Michael J. Mahoney in reply to his article, "Scientific psychology and radical behaviorism." *The Behavior Analyst, 14,* 61-72.

Chomsky, N. (1958). Review of *Verbal behavior* by B. F. Skinner. *Language, 35,* 1, 6-58.

Cooper, M. (1989). *Analyzing public discourse.* Prospect Heights, IL: Waveland Press.

Czubaroff, J. (1988). Criticism and response in the Skinner controversies. *Journal of the Experimental Analysis of Behavior, 49,* (2), 321-329.

Czubaroff, J. (Forthcoming). The public dimension of scientific controversies. *Argumentation.*

Folger, J. P., & Poole, M. S. (1984). *Working through conflict: A communication perspective.* Dallas, TX: Scott, Foresman, & Co.

Foss, S. K. (1989). *Rhetorical criticism: Exploration & practice.* Prospect Heights, IL: Waveland Press.

Hagstrom, W. O. (1965). *The scientific community.* New York: Basic Books.

Hariman, R. (1989). The rhetoric of inquiry and the professional scholar. In H. W. Simons (Ed.), *Rhetoric in the human sciences*. London: Sage.

Hart, R. P., & Burks, D. M. (1972). Rhetorical sensitivity and social interaction. *Speech Monographs, 39*, 2, 75-91.

Hauser, G. A. (1986). *Introduction to rhetorical theory*. New York: Harper & Row.

Hillbruner, A. (1966). *Critical dimensions: The art of public address criticism*. NY: Random.

Hocker, J. L., & Wilmot, W. W. (1985). *Interpersonal conflict* (2nd ed.). Dubuque, IA: William C. Brown.

Lacey, H. (1980). Psychological conflict and human nature: The case of behaviourism and cognition. *Journal for the Theory of Social Behavior, 10* (3), 131-155.

Leeds-Hurwitz, W. (1995). "Introducing social approaches," in *Social approaches to communication*. New York: Guilford Press, 3-20.

MacCorquodale, K. (1970). On Chomsky's review of Skinner's *Verbal behavior*. *Journal of the Experimental Analysis of Behavior, 13*, 83-99.

Mahoney, M. J. (1989). Scientific psychology and radical behaviorism: Important distinctions based in scientism and objectivism. *American Psychologist, 44* (11), 1372-1377.

Mahoney, M. J. (1990). Diatribe is not dialogue: On selected attempts to attack and defend behaviorism. *American Psychologist, 45* (10), 1183-1184.

Nelson, J. S., Megill, A., & McCloskey, D. N. (Eds.). (1987). *The rhetoric of the human sciences: Language and argument in scholarship and public affairs*. Madison, WI: University of Wisconsin Press.

O'Keefe, B. J. (1988). The logic of message design: Individual differences in reasoning about communication. *Communication Monographs, 55*, 80-103.

Simons, H. W. (1976). *Persuasion: Understanding, practice, and analysis*. Reading, MA: Addison-Wesley.

Simons, H. W. (1985). Chronicle and critique of a conference. *Quarterly Journal of Speech, 71*, 52-64.

Simons, H. W. (Ed.). (1989). *Rhetoric in the human sciences*. London: Sage.

Skinner, B. F. (1957). *Verbal behavior*. New York: Appleton-Century-Crofts.

Skinner, B. F. (1971). *Beyond freedom and dignity*. New York: Alfred A. Knopf.

Stewart, C. J., Smith, C. A., & Denton, R. E., Jr. (1989). *Persuasion and social movements* (2nd ed.). Prospect Heights, IL: Waveland Press.

Toulmin, S. (1972). *Human understanding*. Oxford: Clarendon Press.

Trenholm, S. (1989). *Persuasion and social influence*. Englewood Cliffs, NJ: Prentice Hall.

Wheeler, H. (Ed.). (1973). *Beyond the punitive society: Operant conditioning: Social and political aspects*. San Francisco: W. H. Freeman & Co.

Wilson, J. F., Arnold, C. C., & Wertheimer, M. M. (1990). *Public speaking as a liberal art* (6th ed.). Boston: Allyn and Bacon.

Footnotes

[1] Specification of rhetorical competency or rhetorical effectiveness is a challenging task. Since rhetoric is fundamentally instrumental, the tendency is to assume that a rhetorically competent or effective individual achieves some kind of intended goal. However, the goals of a rhetor may be multiple and complex. For instance, the rhetor may have an ideal personal goal, but also many secondary goals, which temper how s/he goes about attempting to realize the personal goal. These underlying goals include relational goals with respect to the audience members, and context-driven goals. For instance, a debater's personal goal may be to win a debate. In addition, however, the debater may wish to honor his or her own convictions, may wish to maintain a relationship with the opponent by demonstrating respect for the opponent's point of view, and may wish to support achievement of the institutional goals (for instance, in a law court, discovery of the truth). The rhetor must weigh the relative importance of these multiple goals, and may, depending on the weighting, frame a discourse which makes winning the debate difficult. Rhetorical competency and effectiveness, then, involve careful thought about all the goals in a situation, careful prioritizing of these goals, and formulation of the discourse goal in light of the constellation of values.

[2] A major suspicion about rhetoric has to do with the need for the rhetor to relate or "adapt" ideas to the audience members' frames of reference. Perhaps some of this concern may be allayed if we distinguish—admittedly only provisionally—between discursive adaptation whose goal is greater clarity and understanding between the speaker and audience points of view and discursive adaptation which intends to identify the operative elements of an audience's point of view in order to selectively formulate the message in ways that will be most pleasing and cogent to the audience. The concern in this latter case is not with clarity or understanding, but with proof and persuasion. There is not necessarily anything wrong with this latter form of adaptation as long as the rhetor is open about his/her persuasive intent. Audiences are rightly ambivalent, however, about persuaders who do "audience analyses" with no interest in understanding the audience's point of view and experiences, but merely to identify convenient symbolic hooks and terms to enable them to influence the audience. Audiences are also rightly suspicious of persuaders who are not open about their motivations and strategies. Perhaps the operative difference here is that in the first mode of adaptation the rhetor is concerned to understand the audience's point of view in order to meaningfully relate his or her own ideas to the audience's frame of reference. In the second mode, the rhetor is concerned to use what he or she knows about the audience to achieve a self-centered goal with respect to that audience.

[3] I am thinking here of H. W. Simon's (1976) framework of coactive, combative and expressive strategies of communication, Branham and Pearce's (1985) model of rhetors conforming to or challenging situational definitions, B J O'Keefe's (1988)

distinction between expressive, conventional, and rhetorical message design logics, Hart and Burke's (1972) concepts of the rhetorical reflector, the noble self, and the rhetorically sensitive communicator and W. Brockriede's (1972) distinction between the arguer who engages in rape, seduction, or love.

[4]As a rhetorical critic I am sensitive to the fact that in describing any rhetorical act I impose my own definition of the rhetorical situation and, in my judgments, I bring to bear my own conception of rhetorical competency and effectiveness. This became particularly clear to me in discussions with Catania about the Mahoney essay.

It may also be worth noting that over the twelve years of my engagement with the behavior analytic community, I moved from a more distant, dispassionate stance to one of engagement and participation. Perhaps this change occurred when Catania invited me to cosign his letter, or perhaps at a dinner in Atlanta. Whenever—gradually I crossed the line from being an unconcerned, disengaged observer to being a participant, and, finally, a "friend." Nor was I dismayed by the progressive involvement. For, as Simons (1985) notes, friendship may be the ideal form of relationship for academicians. Friendship implies mutual respect, openness, and effort to understand the other's point of view. Academic friendship entails commitment to finding grounds for thoughtful self-criticism (see also, Wilson, Arnold, & Wertheimer, 1990).

Chapter 20

Narrative and Context: Communication's Milieu

Deborah S. Ballard-Reisch
Barbara C. Thornton
University of Nevada, Reno

"Each of us is a singular narrative, which is constructed continually and unconsciously by, through, and in us—through our perceptions, our feelings, our thoughts, our actions and not least, through our discourse, our spoken narrations" (Sacks, 1985 in Fredricks–Fitzwater, 1991, p. 13).

Historically, classical rhetoricians and literary critics argued that the most appropriate methods for analyzing rhetorical and literary acts were those that arose from the historical, social and political context within which the act took place (Sereno & Mortensen, 1970). As the field of communication has broadened as a discipline to focus not only on discourse in public arenas but private venues as well and as the field has become more strongly linked with social sciences, this awareness of the importance of context in framing rhetorical acts has been overtaken by more empirical, rational approaches to inquiry which seek generalization of results across situations (Mumby, 1993). With the reemergence of interest in a contextual approach to social science inquiry, we in the field of communication have a unique opportunity to reclaim our historical tradition through a reexamination of the importance of context when viewing rhetorical acts in personal, private and public spheres. Classically, rhetoric was viewed as both arising from a context and as an attempt to change the context in which the act occurred (Fisher, 1989). Rhetorical scholars have long been aware of the mutual impact of act and context; they viewed rhetorical acts as attempts to respond to something in the environment in a teleological way (Brockreide, 1970; Littlejohn, 1978).

Our purpose in this chapter is to suggest that the use of narrative theory, as a contextual approach to the study of human communication, offers unique insight into the dynamic, integrative relationship between communication and context and, indeed, communication's milieu! In order to advance this thesis, we will present an overview of the nature of contextualism. We will then examine the relationship of narrative theory to contextualism. Finally, we will discuss the insights both contextualism and narrative theory have to offer the study of human communication.

On Contextualism

Steven Pepper (1942) advanced four "root metaphors" or philosophical world views, underlying theory development and research in the behavioral sciences. World views are not only composed of our knowledge and concepts but also of our attitudes, values and opinions; they are strong forces in determining how we think, make decisions, behave and define events" (Sue, 1991, p. 300). While Pepper explicated the organicism, formism, mechanism and contextualism metaphors, his book was primarily a treatise on the importance of contextualism. He argued that "root metaphors" reflect specific views of the world and are therefore perspectives within which theory, research, and day-to day living take place. Central to the contextualist root metaphor is the notion of a "transitory historical situation" which posits that social reality is constructed and carried out within a constantly changing environment. Pepper and Rosnow & Georgoudi (1986) view environment as an integral part of social reality and action, an active, changing element of an act, as well as a patterned, rule–governed frame within which behavior is enacted. This behavior occurs within a contemporaneous historical situation marked by patterns and rules which are constantly undergoing change. Thus, contextualism is a broad perspective that organizes facts, relationships and the human condition.

A contextual approach to the study of human communication holds that all human behavior is best understood as embedded within historical, social, political, relational and personal contexts which impact human action and which are impacted by the acts that occur in conjunction with them. Context is defined as "the set of circumstances that surround a particular event" (Rosnow & Georgoudi, 1986, p. 5). It is an integral part of human behavior to the extent that a change in the context directly affects human behavior and a change in behavior affects the context (Shotter, 1983). In short, as Rosnow and Georgoudi conclude "an act or event cannot be said to have an identity apart from the context that constitutes it; neither can a context be said to exist independently of the act or event to which it refers" (p. 6). From a contextual perspective, acts and contexts mutually define, modify and influence one another.

Characteristics of a Contextual Approach to Human Communication

Contextualism enriches the study of human communication particularly because it takes into account all of the environmental factors that affect us. History, values, as well as change and chaos are some of the importance considerations of this perspective for the study of communication and other human behavioral sciences.

1. Contextualism Sees or Explores Behavior as Embedded Within Context.

The basic assumption of contextualism is that all human activity is "rigorously situated within a socio-historical and cultural context of meanings and relationships" (Rosnow & Georgoudi, 1986, p. 4). As Bateson (1972) concluded, the meaning of an event is contained in its relationship to the context. To illustrate, two seemingly opposite views of "fact" can both be true, depending on their context. For example, while this chapter was being written, in 1995, President Clinton and the Republican Congress were in the midst of a budget conflict. Returning together in the President's plane from the funeral of Israel's Prime Minister, Yitzhak Rabin, Republican leaders had expected to discuss the budget with the President, as it had been the leading national agenda item before Rabin's murder. This discussion did not take place. Immediately after the trip, Republican Speaker of the House Newt Gingrich suggested that representatives of his party had been slighted by the President, because this discussion did not occur on the plane, and admitted that he was retaliating for this perceived lack of courtesy by escalating the budget crisis.

President Clinton indicated amazement at Speaker Gingrich's view. He had been, he said, grieving for his friend, Rabin, and felt that the return trip to the United States was not the appropriate time (or context) to discuss political affairs of state. Both sides felt righteous about their point of view as each came from a different perception of context in forming their views or their "truths " of this situation.

2. Contexts are Multiple and Nested.

A second important element is the nested nature of contexts. Acts are situated not only within historical, social and political contexts (*macro* contexts) but also relational and personal contexts (*micro* contexts). The nature of these multiple contexts can either reinforce one another, creating a strong pattern of behavioral expectations with clear rules of conduct, or they can be inconsistent and work in opposition to one another leading to ambiguity and lack of clarity regarding appropriate behavior.

The current national debate over welfare can be used to illustrate the significance of multiple contexts. Based on statistics, conservatives in Congress take the perspective that women on welfare tend to have more children and therefore, receive higher welfare payments. They view this as an indication that mothers on welfare are encouraged and, in fact, rewarded for having more children. From a *macro* level perspective, these statistics are viewed as indication of an economic trend that many feel should not be supported. Consequently, these conservatives advocate restricting welfare payments and limiting the amount of time a woman can receive welfare, after which the woman is expected to get a job and support herself and her child.

This *macro* view of the situation, (more and more women are having babies while on welfare, costing taxpayers more and more money) does not consider the *micro* level view of individual women. Focusing on employment, this view fails to take into consideration the related issues that *would* make employment possible for these women including their needs for job training and education, employment opportunities, the availability of affordable, quality daycare, birth control, financial support from the fathers of their children, personal support from their families, etc.

If the child's father is absent, if the woman has no supportive family, if she has little or no education or job training, if she is uninformed about birth control and its effective use, and perhaps most importantly, if she doesn't have access to quality, affordable daycare for her children, she is forced to work long hours, often at multiple jobs, just to make ends meet, while her children are home alone, supervising one another or totally unsupervised. These contextual conditions dramatically increase the likelihood of early pregnancy, drug use, delinquency, etc. for her children and further enmeshment in the cycle of welfare.

A second *micro* level context is illuminated in the reality of a 13-year-old boy growing up in the inner city, trying to finish high school while living with an unemployed, alcoholic mother. If the drugs, gangs and violence in the neighborhood are not enough, he also has to worry about his next meal. His reality is based on an entirely different dynamic still unaccounted for in the *macro* level view. Without looking at all the contextual dynamics at the *micro* level of people's lives, a *macro* level perspective on the issue of welfare has little chance of accomplishing its goals.

3. Contexts are Dynamic, On–going and Ever-Changing; Consequently, Acts That Occur in Context are Reframed as Contexts Change.

Contextualism, as a system view, sees change as a continuous process, one in which, "tensions among shifting biological, psychological, cultural and historical influences are resolved only to generate further tensions" (Steenbarger, 1991, p. 288). As Gluck (1994) indicates, standards respond to social change and are usually a product of lengthy national dialogue. Since public debate is itself an American value, this debate has been able to continually enlarge our definition of our country, as well as of our values, to acknowledge the bad and the good, and to recognize earlier versions of American history or the history of its sub-groups, some of which have been ignored. For example, slavery was not seen as evil by many individuals prior to and during the Civil War; in more recent times most people see it as wrong. Again, it is only through a contextual world view that we take these factors into account.

Contextualism provides an understanding of the setting in which values can be advocated and understood from an historical perspective. Given the continuously changing nature of contexts, every experience, every behavior, every communication event is subject to revision and reinterpretation (Gergen & Gergen, 1988; Rosnow & Georgoudi, 1986).

> ...behavior occurs in context and must be studied, as such, for context gives behavior its meaning (i.e., its function)—the whole is primary, the elements are derived as abstractions or constructs. The meaning of

behavior emerges from the ever-evolving historic context...as the present becomes the past for subsequent behavior... (Morris, 1988, p. 299)

For example, in the 1940's and 1950's textbooks as well as "Cowboy and Indian" movies often presented the American Indian as cruel, ignorant and evil, a perspective clearly reflective of the Euro-American view. With more cultural sensitivity and in a different time frame, recent fictional and nonfictional treatises and cultural works have presented Native Americans from a perspective that is more consistent with their experiences of Euro-American expansionism. Similar comparisons can be made to the portrayal of veterans of the Vietnam conflict during and immediately after the war and those made in television and movies toward the end of the 1980's and early 1990's. As these examples indicate, when views of the context change, so does the narrative.

On the Pervasiveness of Narrative

While contextualism offers us a framework for viewing acts as arising within a "transitory historical situation" that gives the act its meaning, narrative theory is the vehicle utilized to explore people's perceptions and interpretations of those contexts. In arguing for the pervasiveness of narrative, Polkinghorne (1988) advances that "the history of narrative begins with the history of [hu]mankind, there does not exist, and never has existed, a people without narratives" (p. 14). "All forms of human expression and communication from epic to architecture, from biblical narrative to statuary" (Fisher, 1989, p. 5) from oral to written language, from pictures to gestures (Polkinghorne), come within the purview of the narrative. As Gerbner (1986) concluded, there is no more "telling word than story to distinguish human action . . . . Homo sapiens live in a world erected, experienced, and conducted largely through many forms and modes of story telling" (p. 254). Perceptions of context communicated narratively are inherent on both a cultural (see Mumby, 1993) and personal level (Sterk & Sterk, 1993). It is through communication that people share their "stories about" their behavior and the world in which they live (see Fisher, 1989). It is the narrative, then, that must be studied and analyzed, but this must be done within context.

Public stories function on a cultural level to formulate, communicate and modify the fabric of the culture itself (Mumby, 1993). The dynamic relationship between communication and culture is illustrated by Gerbner (1986) who states that "communication is interaction through messages. Messages are formally coded symbolic or representational patterns of some shared significance in a symbolic context called culture. Culture itself may be conceived as a system of messages through which we define and regulate social relationships" (p. 252). Bormann (1972) refers to stories that are "chained out" in the culture linking members of the culture together through a common perspective. These story chains connect people in the context of beliefs, attitudes and values shared to varying degrees among individuals.

An example of a story chain that functions on a cultural level involves the American folk myth commonly referred to as the "American Dream." This is grounded in the belief that America is the land of opportunity and that "anyone who works hard enough can achieve their goals". For a more elaborate discussion of American folk mythology, see Polanyi (1985). The notion of "hegemony" has been expanded in recent years to include the assimilation and active integration of disparate stories into larger folk myths of the dominant culture (Clair, 1991). For example, when an individual excels beyond all odds and achieves success, prominence or status, particularly if s/he has had to overcome significant disadvantages, s/he is held up as an example that the "American Dream" is alive and well. Ross Perot, Amy Tan, Clarence Thomas, Oprah Winfrey, Bill Clinton, and Michael Jordon serve as contemporary examples. In reality, those who achieve often do so because of extraordinary opportunities or the intervention of others, dynamics that are not available, for whatever reason to others who are striving to excel.

Unfortunately, rather than being the "road map" to success the cultural myth heralds, these individual success stories become a mechanism for invalidating and disconfirming the stories of others who are not privileged by such serendipitous opportunities and who cannot on their own successfully overcome the odds and excel beyond reasonable expectations. The success stories advance the myth of the "American Dream" and silence and invalidate the stories of those who cannot achieve it. In her synthesis of the American story, Polanyi (1985) articulates this cultural story:

> An adult must know and must be able to take it, to withstand pain, to know that he has a future and that the future is better than the past. Knowing about the world allows the person to plan and if he plans correctly (chooses what to do realistically), he will have what he wants and be able to satisfy his own needs. If he does not plan correctly, understand what an adult must, then he will not have what he wants and may not be able to satisfy his own needs. Therefore, not having is proof of the fact of not being an adult since an adult has what he needs and can do what he must do in order to satisfy those needs (p. 134).

Note the implications of the above story: Men are adults; adults get what they need; if men do not get what they need, they do not understand; because they do not understand and cannot meet their needs, they are not adults. In other words, men who excel do so because they are competent; men who do not excel are deficient. Women are not included at all in this story.

On an interpersonal level, stories function to link individuals to one another through the development of relationships and, on a personal level, narratives validate self concepts, promote self awareness and reinforce, alter or change one's view of the world (see Polanyi, 1985; Sterk & Sterk, 1993). "Individuals are not structured as much as continually constructed in social exchange through their stories and the stories of others" (Steenbarger, 1991, p. 289). MacIntyre (1984) concluded that because human beings understand their own lives in terms of narratives, narrative is appropriate for understanding the actions of others. At all points, the context of the story is vital to the narrative. Watzlawick, Beavin, and Jackson's (1967) text *Pragmatics of Human Communication*, offers a classic example of the relational impact of personal stories. The authors recount the stories of the wife and husband who each explain their behavior as a reaction to the behavior of the other. "In explaining their frustrations, the husband will state that withdrawal is his only defense against her nagging, while she will label this explanation a gross and willful distortion of what "really" happens in their marriage: namely that she is critical of him because of his passivity. Stripped of all ephemeral and fortuitous elements, their fights consist in a monotonous exchange of the messages "I withdraw because you nag" and "I nag because you withdraw" (p. 56).

On the Appropriateness of Narrative

The argument that we advance in this paper is that the application of narrative theory to the study of human communication illuminates people's perceptions of the contexts within which they live and behave. We agree with Fisher (1989) that the process of communication is the process of telling our stories in context and conclude as he did that "all forms of human communication need to be seen fundamentally as stories" (Fisher, 1987, p. xi). By focusing on all communication as "storied" we emphasize the grounded nature of human behavior. People express their perceptions of context and their understanding of their own and others' behavior through stories (the narrative). Stories locate people in history, time and space. Gerbner (1986) argued that "meaning comes from the symbolic context of mind and culture in which they are embedded and through which all human meaning emerges" (p. 251). Shotter (1986) puts it more strongly arguing that we see the world through our accounts of it.

When faced with the stories of others, there are three ways we can choose to respond. We can accept their stories (confirmation), validating both the storytellers and their perspectives; we can reject their stories (disconfirmation), disagreeing with their perspectives and their stories, or rejecting/negating their stories, disregarding them as if we had never heard them (Watzlawick et al., 1967). The responses we choose to make to the stories of others have significant implications. When we confirm the stories, we create identification and consubstantiality (Burke, 1969). The implications of disconfirmation and rejection are division (Burke, and separation. To paraphrase Polanyi, (1985) stories are rooted in what the storyteller knows to be true, and when a story is shared with someone who does not share the presuppositions about the world as expressed in the story, the implication is that the storyteller does not really know what s/he is talking about. She concludes, "When you talk to people who can't understand you, your story gets lost and what happens is that the people you are talking to know you are not one of them" (p. 145).

By taking a contextual approach to the study of human communication, a variety of stories (narratives) can be validated. As Polanyi (1985) concluded, there is only one world, "but a thousand views of it. Each view coherent, self-consistent, limiting in some respects, a blessed relief in others" (p. 145). Rather than a linear view of reality that privileges certain perspectives, contextualism accepts a relational perspective of behavior and reality based on pluralism and diversity (Steenbarger, 1991). We believe through analyses of stories in context, we may gain insight into the dynamic relationship between context and act, as well as a fuller understanding of the "world" in which we live.

As with contexts, narratives function on both *micro* (intrapersonal, interpersonal, small group) and *macro* (social, political, cultural) levels. Individually, the narrative enables people to make sense of their own lives within the context of the culture in which they live (Fisher, 1989; Sterk & Sterk, 1993). Culturally, narratives serve to give cohesion to shared beliefs and to transmit values (Barthes in Polkinghorne, 1988). On the fundamental level, the narrative paradigm views human beings as storytellers who construct and reconstruct the experiences of their lives through the generation and dissemination of their stories.

The premises of the narrative paradigm, summarized from Fisher (1989) are:
1) people shape, create and tell stories to meet their own ends;
2) they communicate, make decisions, and take action for 'good reasons' (rationality);
3) the conceptualization of 'good reasons' is affected by, among other things, history, biography, culture, and character;
4) rationality is determined by the storyteller's "inherent awareness of what constitutes a coherent story" (narrative probability), and the practice of testing whether stories are faithful to both the storyteller's and listener's experience (narrative fidelity);
5) we continuously construct and reconstruct the world we live in on the basis of the stories we choose to use to make sense of our experiences;
6) on both cultural and interpersonal levels, stories are tested for accuracy, intelligibility and a good fit with reality (p. 5).

Polanyi (1985) expands upon this notion and illuminates the contextually grounded nature of storytelling when she concludes that "a proper storyteller" is "one whose stories are received as normal and reasonable contributions to a conversation already underway ... whose points do not ignore generally accepted truths about the nature of things, but which, rather, relate to them in some fashion" (p. 1). Thus, she perceives stories as constructions that have meaning to both the listener and the storyteller and that are imbedded within a context of shared, expected, commonplace understandings.

A Note on Orality

Scholars often think of stories in contemporary times as a written medium. It is important to remember when talking about the narrative, that much communication, even in current times is oral. Ong (1982) reports that certain basic differences have been discovered between the ways of managing knowledge in primarily oral cultures and cultures that are deeply affected by writing. Contextual awareness of story telling is sensitive to whether the story is written or oral. Ong sees differences between oral and written cultures and between primary oral cultures and secondary oral cultures. The former are cultures without written language and the latter are cultures with written language that also have a residual oral culture operating within them.

Learning in oral cultures usually occured through the achievement of close, empathetic and communal identification. Oral cultures use stories, proverbs and relationships to make sense of the world (Sample, 1994). Sample argues that about half of the people in the United States come from oral cultures and two-thirds of the people of the world are primarily oral. He contends that American schools are often unequipped to work within these oral contexts finding that people in these traditions are bucolic, redneck or primitive. He also sees the intellectual community viewing people who rely primarily on oral cultures as not capable of critical, informed thinking. "They are 'common' or 'average' we say, when we really mean vulgar and this in its pejorative sense" (p.7).

Scholars studying orality, are also aware of electronic orality such as television, the computer, e-mail and the web (Sample, 1994). These media do not promote the closeness and dialogic components of orality that were discussed previously, but must be studied in their own right in terms of context and storytelling. Ours is a culture where traditional orality, literality and electronic orality are important contexts for the stories we all must strive to tell and understand.

Implications for the Study of Human Communication

It is our contention that communication cannot be effectively studied without reference to the context in which the communication act arises. Furthermore, every translation of any communication act is done through story telling whether it be a child's fairy tale, a personal conversation, a criminal trial, a political campaign, or a scientific study. Sharing and listening to people's stories and placing them in context is at the foundation of shared meaning and fundamental to quality communication. Taking a contextual approach to the study of communication, through narrative, has widespread implications for interaction on cultural, political, personal and scientific levels.

On a cultural level, as Littlejohn (1992) noted, a culture's reality is defined in terms of its meanings which arise from interaction within social groups. This paper reaffirms this view, stressing that communication can be understood only by viewing interaction in context and by realizing that contexts are continually interpreted through storytelling. Remembering that the very nature of storytelling is rhetorical, as is the nature of communication, Fisher (1989) notes that no form of communication is without its narrative perspective:

> In narrative no form of discourse is privileged over others . . . . No matter how strictly a case is argued--scientifically, philosophically or legally--it will always be a story, an interpretation of some aspect of the world that is historically and culturally grounded and shaped by human personality. (p. 42)

Culturally, politically and personally, the sharing of disparate stories can lead to a fuller, richer understanding of the contexts within which people perceive themselves and others as acting. Sharing stories and perceptions of context have the potential to prevent misinformation or conflict and increase shared meaning. Earlier in this article we mentioned the misunderstanding that arose between President Clinton and Speaker of the House Gingrich on their way back from Israeli Prime Minister Rabin's funeral; both had different perceptions of the context. Barring the possibility that either was looking for an excuse to inflame the other, sharing their agendas and becoming sensitve to context could possibly have prevented this misunderstanding. While both parties would still have been in disagreement over budget issues which needed to be resolved, this trip would not have been symbolic of that disagreement. We are not arguing that a study of context and narrative will do away with fundamental and important disagreements but that such study, and the consequent sensitivity, will enable participants in disagreements to proceed to the real (rather than contextual) issues of contention.

In the scientific arena, realizing that all research is colored by the context in which it occurs, researchers need to be aware of the "story" behind their investigation. By carefully articulating their stories at the beginning of a research project and comparing them to the stories of their subjects, researchers can assure that their proposed design and methology are appropriate for the questions they are interested in and the population of interest. Openly listening to stories can often provide new and enriched ways to view potential research and problems. Barbara Sharf's (1990) article on using a narrative approach to assessing patients' medical records, as opposed to asking the traditional open and closed questions of a medical interview, is an outstanding example of the invaluable use of storytelling in a research setting. This approach led to new data and new diagnostic possiblilites.

By becoming aware that all communication is made up of stories in context, and that stories are told through many different modalities such as oral presentations, film studies as well as scientific documents, we enlarge the realm of human interaction and the possibilities of human communication study.

Teaching Effective Story Telling

It is sometimes hard to remember, as mentioned at the beginning of this article, that the roots of the communication field lie in the teaching of effective story telling. While we can take pride in the fact that we are now a legitimate social science, we can no longer take as much pride in our abilities to advance the "arts" of communication. We still teach beginning speech classes at most of our universities, yet very few institutions dwell on the etiquette of speech-making, the credibility of both the story and the storyteller and the importance of creating a narrative that will spur a dialogic response on the part of the listener. We suggest that by focusing on interaction as stories rather than as speeches, we can more creatively deal with these problems while utilizing both old and new methods of analysis and education.

There are many approaches to effective storytelling. One that has stood the test of time is Bitzer's (1968) work on the rhetorical situation. If speakers begin to think of their stories as responses to a situation and carefully analyze 1) the nature of the exigence that compels them to speak, 2) the audience they will be addressing and 3) the constraints inherent in the situation, they will go a long way toward constructing dialogic stories.

Within this framework, speakers need to be taught how to analyze the biases and expectations of audiences; the limitations of the situation in which they are telling their stories; argument construction in terms of the use of alternative structures/approaches, argument, evidence and ethics; persuasive techniques including appeals to logos, pathos and ethos; and appropriate delivery choices including image and style.

In addition to the traditional approach to argument which we view as linear, logical and reductionistic, speakers need to be taught alternative approaches to storytelling based on both a more holistic, synthetic logic and critical thinking approach to designing and listening to stories. Mumby (1993) advances that the narrative is one of the most effective ways to look at these alternative perspectives. Critical theory (Held, 1980; Littlejohn, 1992) offers questions and challenges for the storyteller that fit nicely into a contextual and narrative perspective. Often considered post-modernistic, critical theory challenges traditional models of science and politics on the basis that they are in place in order to maintain the status quo. It also challenges the "grand" narrative of traditional science.

Two particular issues for critical theorists studying context and narrative, include power and social control. Critical theorists ask us to look at how traditional stories are loaded with words that are often political and socially motivated. They point out how difficult it is to inject new words or ideas into older models of thinking and arguing which continue to advocate the status quo. For example, words such as "diversity" and "feminism" often make supporters of the status quo uncomfortable.

Within traditional, oral and postmodern perspectives, it is necessary to keep Fisher's (1987) criteria for effective narrative in mind. An effective story needs to have narrative probability (coherence) and narrative fidelity (faithfulness) in order to be effective. The argument needs to be coherent, the material included needs to be comprehensive and the speaker needs to be credible with respect to the story s/he is telling. Communication literature is replete with how these goals should be accomplished.

Models such as Bitzer's, critical theory, and others, both modern and classical, need to be applied to both speaking and listening. It is in listening that we confirm, disconfirm or negate stories while remembering that confirmation does not necessitate nor imply agreement. Communication is only successful when individuals are able to share meaning and to come to a mutual understanding of what is being said. We need to select, attend, understand and remember. We all know how this should be done, but many people do not adhere to listening guidelines such as checking out our interpretations by using paraphrasing, reflecting, probing or supporting responses. To us in the discipline of communication these are introductory course skills; to much of the rest of the population these skills are unknown.

Utilizing and Creating Effective Collaborative Frameworks

If the political right is going to listen to the political left, if men are going to listen to women and minorities, and if Congress is going to listen to the President, we need to develop and teach new collaborative models within which dialogue can take place .

There are many collaborative models for listening to each other's stories and trying to arrive at solutions to societal problems. One of the most effective (in terms of the model itself) was the Oregon Health Decision Project, the basis for the controversial but very innovative model of healthcare that the State of Oregon designed. With the approval of the state government, citizens throughout the state met in town meetings to discuss health priorities. These discussions were facilitated by trained discussion leaders and participants were given written materials that outlined the issues and their major arguments. For example, should the needs of infants take priority over the needs of the elderly and should transplants be available to everyone? At the end of the series of meetings, the groups' recommendations were forwarded to a regional body and later to the state legislature where many of the grassroots proposals became part of the new Oregon Healthcare Plan (Hadorn, 1991).

The health decisions projects (and there were many besides Oregon), worked well and showed that citizens, given training and appropriate information, could contribute to community decision-making. Similar in form are the National Issues Forums which are also held throughout the country to study national issues.

Cooperative inquiry groups have become both a part of the problem-solving approach and a new research design. In these groups, people work together as co-researchers in an emergent, negotiated process where the people being studied are part of the study process (a form of participant research model). Effectively working in these groups takes particular skills on the part of participants such as, a desire to work in genuine collaborative settings with peers and an ability to manage the anxiety that arises when one genuinely examines both the world and our assumptions. Reason (1988) report on several successful programs.

Another model, currently institutionalized in more than 90% of the nation's hospitals is the ethics committee, designed to advise practitioners, patients and families as well as institutions about ethical issues in healthcare. These committees, primarily made up of a diverse group of professionals, tackle many of society's most serious problems. The committees that work well, are ones that utilized group development techniques and are willing to spend time to study the issues (Ross et al., 1993)

Nationally, particularly in business, we are also experiencing a focus on quality assurance projects. In these projects, possible problems are identified as are a group of people who are most familiar with the issue. The people are asked to come together as a group, to tell their stories, and to search for data necessary to solve organizational problems. At all times participants are encouraged to listen to each other and to collaboratively find data that will define the problem and to recommend possible solutions. Emotion, after the initial storytelling sessions, is often turned into action and the original problem is often found not to be the real issue. Groups that work well, are ones that have full authority to look at the organization and the issues with few, if any, constraints. Their success in some businesses has been noteworthy (Oakland, 1993).

All these projects have in common the following factors: participants actively listen to one another's narratives; they have structures in place that allow free inquiry without manipulation on the part of the members or outsiders; they ultimately use both storytelling and data to make decisions; they are consensus-building and nonadversarial. Members of groups such as these are trained to argue and persuade utilizing techniques that have proven to be reasonable and effective. Dialogic communication (storytelling) is encouraged. These programs and approaches are examples of how rational and critical dialogue can be designed to solve problems.

Conclusion

Context and narrative are interrelated components of human communication behavior. The relationship among these three concepts forms a continuous spiral. While communication is formed and arises within a specific context, it also acts to shape and modify those contexts within which it occurs. People's perceptions of the contexts within which they act are reflected in their narratives, in the stories that they tell at cultural, interpersonal and intrapersonal levels both verbally, nonverbally, and through the written word. These stories, or narratives, both implicitly and explicitly, reveal people's perspectives on how they and others act. As Mumby (1993) concludes, "narrative is a socially symbolic act in the double sense that it takes on meaning only in context and it plays a role in the construction of that social context . . ." (p. 5). By illuminating the relationships among context, narrative and communication people can learn to listen to and validate the stories of others. By teaching people how to tell stories effectively and learn to listen to the stories of others, collaborative models can be developed for individual, community, national and international problem solving. Disagreement then becomes a point of exploration and negotiation, expanding perspectives beyond individual views and striving for a new view rather than a mechanism for personal alienation and isolation.

References

Bateson, G. (1972). *Steps to an ecology of mind.* New York: Ballatine Books.
Bitzer, L. F. (1968). The rhetorical situation. *Philosophy and Rhetoric,1,* 1-14.
Bormann, E. H. (1972). Fantasy and rhetorical vision: The rhetorical criticism of reality. *Quarterly Journal of Speech. 58,* 396-407.

Brockreide, W. (1970). Dimensions of the concept of rhetoric. In K. K. Sereno & C. S. Mortensen (Eds.), *Foundations of communication theory* (pp. 25-39). New York: Harper and Row.

Burke, K. (1969). *A rhetoric of motives.* Berkeley, CA: University of California Press.

Clair, R. P. (1991, October). *Hegemony and harassment.* Paper presented at the Speech Communication Association National Conference, Atlanta, GA.

Fisher, W. R. (1987). *Human communiction as narration: Toward a philosophy of reason, value and action.* Columbia, SC: University of South Carolina Press.

Fisher, W. R. (1989). Clarifying the narrative paradigm. *Communication Monographs, 56(1),* 55–58.

Friedricks–Fitzwater, M. (1991, February). Stories, power and healing. *Sacramento Medicine.* 13+.

Gerbner, G. (1986). The symbolic context of action and communication. In R. Rosnow & M. Georgoudi (Eds.), *Contextualism and understanding in behavioral science: Implications for research and theory* (pp. 251-268). New York: Praeger.

Gergen K. J., & Gergen, M. M. (1988). Narrative and the self as relationship. In L. Berkowitz (Ed., *Advances in experimental social psychology* (Vol. 21, pp. 17-56). San Diego, CA: Academic Press.

Gluck, C. (1994). History according to whom? *The New York Times* (November 19) OP-ED, 15.

Hadorn, D. C. (1991). The Oregon priority-setting exercise: Quality of life and public policy. *Hastings Center Report, 21,* 11-16.

Held, D. (1980). *Introduction to critical theory: Horkheimer to Habermas.* Berkeley, CA: University of California Press.

Littlejohn, S. W. (1978). *Theories of human communication.* Columbus, OH: Charles E. Merrill Publishing Company.

Littlejohn, S. W. (1992). *Theories of human communication* (4th ed.). Belmont, CA: Wadsworth Publishing Company.

MacIntyre, A. (1984). *After virtue: A study in moral theology* (2nd ed.). Notre Dame, IN.: University of Notre Dame Press.

Morris, E. K. (1988). Contextualism: The world view of behavior analysis. *Journal of Experimental Child Psychology, 46,* 289-323.

Mumby, D. K. (1993). *Narrative and social control: Critical perspectives.* Newbury Park, CA: Sage Publications.

Oakland, J. S. (1993). *Total quality management: The route to improving performance (2nd ed.).* East Brunswick, NJ: Nichols Publications.

Ong, W. J. (1982). *Orality and literacy: The technologizing of the word.* New York: Methuen and Co.

Pepper S. C. (1942). *World hypotheses.* Berkeley, CA: University of California Press.

Polanyi, L. (1985). *Telling the American story: A structural and cultural analysis of conversational storytelling.* Norwood, N.J.: Ablex Publishing Corporation.

Polkinghorne, D. E. (1988). *Narrative knowing and the human sciences.* Albany, NY: State University of New York Press.

Reason, P. (1988). *Human inquiry in action: Developments in new paradigm research.* Beverly Hills: SAGE Publications.

Rosnow, R. L., & Georgoudi, M. (1986). The spirit of contextualism. In R. Rosnow & M. Georgoudi (Eds.), *Contextualism and understanding in behavioral science: Implications for research and theory* (pp. 3-22). New York: Praeger.

Ross, J. W., Glaser, J. W., Raskinski-Gregory, D., Gibson, J. M., Bayley, C. (1993). *Health care ethics committees: The next generation.* Chicago: American Hospital Publishing, Inc.

Sample, T. (1994). *Ministry in an oral culture: Living with Will Rogers, Uncle Remus, and Minnie Pearl.* Louisville, KY: Westminister/John Knox Press.

Sarbin, T. (1993). The narrative as the root metaphor for contextualism. In S. C. Hayes, L. J. Hayes, H. W. Reese, & T. R. Sarbin (Eds.), *Varieties of Scientific Contextualism* (pp. 51-65). Reno, NV: Context Press.

Sereno, K. K., & C. S. Mortensen (Eds.), *Foundations of communication theory.* New York: Harper and Row.

Sharf, B. (1990). Physician-patient communication as interpersonal rhetoric: A narrative approach. *Health Communication, 2,* 217-31.

Shotter, J. (1983). "Duality of structure": "Intentionality" in an ecological psychology. *Journal for the Theory of Social Behaviour, 13,* 19-45.

Shotter, J. (1986). Speaking practically: Whorf, the formative function of communication, and knowing of the third kind. In R. Rosnow & M. Georgoudi (Eds.), *Contextualism and understanding in behavioral science: Implications for research and theory* (pp. 211-227). New York: Praeger.

Steenbarger, B. N. (1991). All the world is not a stage: Emerging contextualism themes in counseling and development. *Journal of Counseling and Development, 70,* 288-296.

Sterk, H. M., & Sterk, K.J. (1993). Birthing: Women owning their stories. In C. Berryman–Fink, D. Ballard–Reisch, & L. Newman (Eds.), *Communication and sex role socialization* (pp. 433–461). New York: Garland Publishing, Inc.

Sue, D. W. (1991). A diversity perspective on contextualism. *Journal of Counseling and Development, 70,* 300-310.

Watzlawick, P., Beavin, J., & Jackson, D. (1967). *Pragmatics of human communication.* New York: W. W. Norton and Company.

Section 5
Cultural Context and the Applied Analysis of Communication Behavior

Chapter 21

Culture as Communication Context: Finnish Cultural Characteristics in Political Television Programs

Maili Pörhölä
Aino Sallinen
Pekka Isotalus
University of Jyväskylä, Finland

Speech communication scholars generally agree that context is a foundational factor when trying to understand the variance in human communication. For example, the goals, expectations, norms, and roles of individuals vary from one communication context to another. The way people interact, and the way they interpret and evaluate the interaction of others, is dependent upon how they perceive the environment and circumstances, as well as the social relationships of participants in a communication situation, thus, how they perceive the communication context.

Likewise, culture is understood as another substantial force in explaining the variance in communication behavior. Culture provides the means to perceive, organize, and interpret the world. Hence, culture also supplies individuals with the means to perceive, organize and interpret communication in various situations. In sum, culture has the same kind of role as context has in explaining people's cognition and behavior in interaction settings. Given that there are different levels and types of cultures and contexts, the figure becomes more complicated. Various cultures, subcultures, contexts, and subcontexts can simultaneously place even contradictory demands and constraints upon people's communication behavior.

The main goal of the present article is to discuss the nature of culture as a communication context. The focus is on the complicated interrelationships between national culture, subcultures, environmental contexts, and subcontexts. These interrelationships are illustrated by Finnish empirical data gathered both in general and in television context, particularly in the subcontext of the televised political program. Since Finland is culturally one of the most homogeneous countries in Europe, it offers an interesting basis for examining the relationship between national culture and contexts.

Cultural Conceptualization of Context

Context has multiple functions in human interaction. As an example of this multiplicity, context is seen, first, as a source of information which helps people to make sense of their social world (e.g., Berger, 1987). Second, context is seen to help interactants to develop expectancies regarding social encounters, that is, to predict what will happen in an anticipated interaction. These expectancies or schemata serve to organize contextual information and provide a basis for expectations regarding, for example, contextual strategy payoffs, situational goals, and rules of appropriateness and constraints (Spitzberg & Brunner, 1991, p. 29). Third, context gives guidelines for understanding, interpreting and evaluating one's own behavior as well as the behavior of others. It has been noticed, for example, that evaluations of communicator competence are contingent upon the social context in which the communicator is judged (Spitzberg & Brunner, 1991).

The foundational nature of context is reflected in the use of the construct as an organizing principle within the handbooks and textbooks of the communication discipline (Stamp, Vangelisti, & Knapp, 1994, p. 173). However, several scholars have emphasized their concern over the fact that despite the presumptive importance of the role of context in human interaction, there has been relatively little effort to investigate the nature of this construct (e.g., Goodwin & Duranti, 1992; Katriel, 1995; Pettegrew, 1988; Spitzberg & Brunner, 1991). Literature concerning the nature of context has been accused of being fairly fragmented and lacking in theory (Katriel, 1995, p. 271; Spitzberg & Brunner, 1991, p. 29), and a need for rigorous and relevant defining of context has been expressed (Goodwin & Duranti, 1992, p. 4-5; Pettegrew, 1988, p. 333), as well as a need for developing a typology of contexts and subcontexts (Pettegrew, 1988, p. 333).

Illustrative of the confusion concerning the ontological nature of the phenomenon, context has been conceptualized in several different ways, depending on the organizing principle. According to the review made by Stamp, Vangelisti, and Knapp (1994, p. 173) these principles include 1) the areas which broadly define the communication discipline (interpersonal, group, organizational, mass), 2) distinct social and institutional settings, 3) distinctions within a particular arena such as task/work, social, and family, 4) objects or characteristics that comprise an environment, 5) perceptions of role relationships in different settings, 6) message variables including language style, affect displays, and overt statements regarding intentionality, and 7) situational variables such as participants' understanding of their social roles, recognition of others' territorial boundaries, and knowledge of special social occasions.

By contrast, Spitzberg and Brunner (1991) propose that social contexts should be perceptually organized according to culture, type, relationship, and function. The culture mode refers to racial, national, or ethnic identifications as well as to cultural rule systems, norms, and perceptual orientations to the world. The type mode refers to typologies of setting and social context (e.g., conflicts, informal contexts, formal contexts). The relationship mode concerns the nature of interpersonal relationships. The fourth mode, function, separates contexts according to goals or objectives accomplished in an episode.

Hence, context can be approached from various perspectives. Since the goal of this article is to explore the nature of culture as context, the conceptualization of primary interest is the cultural one suggested by Spitzberg and Brunner (1991). This perspective is compared with the one that perceives context as an observable environment (see Stamp et al., 1994, p. 173). More concretely, Finnish national culture is examined as an example of culturally organized context. Television and especially political television programs are examined as environmentally organized contexts. An attempt is made to integrate these two perspectives.

Interrelationship between Culture and Context

In this chapter, a link between the constructs of context and culture is sought, and the nature of culture as context is explored. Instead of attempting to redefine context from a cultural perspective, questions concerning the cultural conceptualization of context are raised.

We first need to consider what kind of context culture is. Conceptually, it is not difficult to recognize culture as context. The definitions of culture are quite similar to those of context. For example, Gudykunst and Ting-Toomey (1988) finish their review on conceptualizations of culture by stating that culture is "a script or a scheme shared by a large group of people" (p. 30). As a synthesis of a review of research concerning the construct of communication context, Haslett (1987) considers context as "the knowledge humans have about how to interact in a specific setting" (p. 85). Further, Argyle, Furnham, and Graham (1981) define social situations – a term which seems to refer to the construct of context – as "social constructions by members of a culture or subculture" (p. 12). All of these definitions describe socially shared cognitive orientations in a very similar way.

A group considered to share a common culture may be a race, a nation, or an ethnic group. In addition, each of these may contain several subcultures. Therefore, empirically recognizing the relevant cultural context becomes difficult. For example, in literature concerning organizational communication, it is commonly agreed that each organization has its own culture and even its own subcultures and communication cultures related to these. Hence, people working in television companies may have a specific culture and corresponding communication culture, and people working for common political interests may also have a culture and a communication culture of their own, even though both of these groups share the same national culture.

The second concern in this article addresses the interactive and dynamic nature of context. It has been required that the context surrounding the communication phenomena studied should always be clearly articulated in empirical research (Goodwin & Duranti, 1992; Katriel, 1995; Pettegrew, 1988). Simultaneously, a question has been raised as to who is capable of defining the relevant context (Goodwin & Duranti, 1992; Katriel, 1995). Environmental as well as cultural contexts have been widely understood to be social facts which can be observed and defined by an outside researcher. However, this approach has been seen to be problematic, and attention has been drawn to the individual interpretations of participants made in a given context. Instead of being social facts, social contexts are seen to be co-created and negotiated by interactants. The demands of contexts are presumed to be shaped through interaction. Contextual effects are considered bi-directional: the context influences interaction, while being simultaneously determined by ongoing interaction. (See Buttny, 1985; Goodwin & Duranti, 1992; Haslett, 1987; Spitzberg & Brunner, 1991; Stamp et al., 1994.)

When interactants represent different cultures or subcultures, their understanding and interpretations of a given context may differ significantly. In this case, they may define the context in different ways, and therefore they may tend to shape substantially different kinds of communication situations through their communicative behavior. In addition, social contexts are also considered dynamic by nature. Thus, a context considered "relevant" may change when interactants move from one activity to another (Goodwin & Duranti, 1992, p. 5). This dynamic nature makes it even more difficult to define a given context.

As suggested above, context can be viewed either as an antecedent to communication or as an emergent variable. As an antecedent variable context refers to the participants' prior knowledge of the social setting in which interaction occurs. This knowledge basis provides interactants with expectations concerning the anticipated interaction. (Haslett, 1987, p. 85.)

When interactants represent different cultures or subcultures, the amount of variance in people's expectations concerning communication increases. The third concern in this article addresses these expectations. It would be interesting to know what would happen if these expectations were violated due to interactants' markedly different understanding of the demands and constraints of the given context. This question of violated contextual expectations has been addressed, amongst others, by Burgoon (1995), and Spitzberg and Brunner (1991).

According to Burgoon (1995, p. 196), communication expectancies refer first to those communicative acts which are most typical in a given culture or subculture. These predictive communication expectancies are shaped by factors which are related as much to the communication context as to the individual communicators and the relationship between the interactants. The other meaning of the construct reflects the degree to which a certain type of behavior is regarded as appropriate, desired or preferred (prescriptive). Expectancy violations, on the other hand, refer to "actions sufficiently discrepant from the expectancy to be noticeable and classified as outside the expectancy range" (p. 200).

Burgoon (1995) suggests that both the content and the valence of each culture's interactional expectancies vary along such cultural dimensions as collectivism-individualism, uncertainty avoidance, power distance, masculinity-femininity, ascription versus achievement orientations, time and activity orientation, universalism-particularism, degree of face concern, and high- versus low-context communication (p. 197). It is reasonable to assume that as the differences in these dimensions increase between cultures, the probability of expectancy violations also increases.

In the following sections, some of these critical points are approached in terms of empirical data gathered in Finnish culture. The attempt is not to find answers to all the questions raised here, but rather to illustrate and make concrete the problems arising from the cultural conceptualization of context. Hence, the basic concern of this article is what kind of role culture has in a dynamic and co-created environmental communication context.

This question will be approached by addressing Finnish national communication culture as the cultural context. Television as an environmental context is used as a mirror because of its multiplicity. Although television is a national mass media, it simultaneously forms a cross junction of different cultures (e.g., racial, national, and ethnic) as well as of different subcultures (e.g., children, music, politics). Moreover, television reflects a wide spectrum of communication contexts (e.g., public speaking, debates, dyads, formal/informal contexts). In addition, television is expected to respond to the continuously changing expectations of various audiences, which also represent several cultures and subcultures. For these reasons, television offers a dynamic, flexible and multifaceted system for observation. Political programs represent a specific subcontext of television. This subcontext, in turn, will bring an interesting addition to our study: political subculture and a series of specific communication contexts related to this subculture (e.g., political television interviews and political panel discussions).

Finnish Communication Culture

In order to familiarize the reader with the target culture, some of the communicative characteristics of Finnish culture are described first. Major findings based on a) the way Finns see themselves as communicators, b) foreigners' opinions of Finns as communicators, and c) the observed behavior of Finns in various communication contexts in the Finnish culture as well as in intercultural settings are presented next. The study is limited primarily to communication characteristics typical of public and formal encounters. This research has established a fairly uniform picture of Finns as communicators.

In Hofstede's (1980, 1983) model of cultural differences, Finland is placed high on "individualism," low on "power distance," high on "femininity" and high on "uncertainty avoidance." In comparisons based on communication patterns that predominate in the culture, it is suggested that Finland, along with other Scandinavian countries, the United States, Canada, Israel, Germany and France, for example, represents a culture characterized by low-context communication (see Hall, 1976). Characteristic of low-context communication is that "the mass of the information is vested in the explicit code," whereas characteristic of high-context communication is, in turn, that "most of the information is either in the physical context or internalized in the person, while very little is in the coded, explicit, transmitted part of the message" (Hall, 1976, p. 79). Low-context communication is used predominantly in individualistic cultures, whereas high-context communication is used predominantly in collectivistic cultures (see Gudykunst & Ting-Toomey, 1988). Empirical data gathered in Finnish culture are consistent with some of the presumptions concerning these dimensions, while in some respects, the findings are rather contradictory.

Public Speaking and Finnish Speech Culture

As typical of cultures exhibiting low-context communication, holding the floor is highly valued in Finland and the role of the speaker is respected. Speaking in public seems to be an especially demanding communication context in Finnish culture. The outcome expectations of Finns concerning oral performance are high, and appreciation of the literal mode of communication is reflected in speech culture: in public encounters Finns are highly concerned about speech processing, fluency of speech, use of correct language, and brief verbal expression. Therefore, public speakers usually prefer reading their manuscripts without engaging in extemporaneous speech. (Sallinen-Kuparinen, 1987a, p. 16.)

Moreover, in public and formal encounters Finns would rather listen than take verbal turns. They appreciate polite listening and show respect for the speaker without verbal feedback signals. Therefore, Finnish communication culture has been characterized by receiver centricity instead of emphasizing the expressive function in interaction. (Sallinen-Kuparinen, 1986, p. 184-187, 1987a, p. 17.)

High demands and outcome expectations concerning the role of the speaker and the speaker's responsibility for communication, as well as limited experience of speaking in public are displayed, for example, in high levels of physiological arousal among Finnish speakers. Heart rate levels of Finns have been reported to be substantially higher than those of Americans in public speaking contexts. (Pörhölä, 1995; Pörhölä, Isotalus, & Ovaskainen, 1993; Sallinen-Kuparinen & Pörhölä, 1986.)

Silence is highly tolerated in Finnish communication culture. According to widely held stereotypes, the Finns are portrayed as silent, timid, taciturn, shy, sullen, and introverted (Lehtonen & Sajavaara, 1985; Sallinen-Kuparinen, 1986). Similarly, self-reported data has revealed that Finns are less willing to communicate than people from most other cultures studied. However, the Finns' unwillingness to communicate does not seem to be either a function of communication reticence or of self-perceived communication competence, as it seems to be in Anglo-American cultures. The average scores for Finns have been very similar to those from the United States on both communication apprehension and self-perceived communication competence. (Sallinen-Kuparinen, McCroskey, & Richmond, 1991.)

Finns typically show a high level of communication reticence in public speaking and formal communication contexts. Previous research indicates that anxiety associated with public speaking is not only a Finnish communication characteristic but rather a universal phenomenon reflecting the specific nature of this context. Indeed, reticence related with communication in informal, interpersonal settings is moderately low among Finns, and people report enjoying interacting informally. (Sallinen-Kuparinen, 1986, 1987a.)

According to Sallinen-Kuparinen, McCroskey, and Richmond (1991), being unwilling to communicate in Finnish culture seems to be accounted for by sociocultural variables such as the role of talk in society and values placed on communication. In Anglo-American cultures, which represent low-context communication cultures, oral communication is highly appreciated with positive social evaluation as concomitant (McCroskey & Richmond, 1979, 1987; Okabe, 1983). Consequently, remaining silent is considered a problem and silent cultures are interpreted as representing a high prevalence of communication apprehension. In cultures with a high tolerance of silence, such as Finland, the same overt behavior is socially more acceptable, and the perceptions of a person's competence are not predominantly based on his or her verbal behavior (Sallinen-Kuparinen, 1987a; Sallinen-Kuparinen et al., 1991). Instead, silence in Finnish culture is largely associated with politeness, prudence, and confidence in interpersonal settings and, in many other settings, with personal strength. Instead of quantity, the quality of speech is appreciated. (Sallinen-Kuparinen, 1986, p. 184-187.) These considerations refer rather to high-context than to low-context communication culture.

Interpersonal Communication and Expressiveness in Formal Encounters

As typical of low-context communication cultures, Americans believe, according to Carbaugh (1995), that one should express oneself with very few constraints. Such rules lay the basis for great amounts of verbal communication, including speaking of one's personal experiences, thoughts, and feelings. Conversely, in Finnish communication culture, strict rules exist concerning the content of conversation. Particularly when in public with people one does not know very well, but at times even with close friends, it seems to be important to speak "properly," which includes discourse that is socially worthwhile, does not state the obvious, is non-contentious or non-conflictual, is not overstated, and reflects one's personal commitments. (Carbaugh, 1995, p. 55.)

While American rhetoric is basically argumentative and logical in nature, with confrontation carrying a positive connotation, in Finnish oral interaction the role of speaking is to contribute to the maintenance of consensus and harmony in a group and in society (Sallinen-Kuparinen, 1986, p. 188). It has been noticed that in various communication contexts Finns are considered cooperative, affirming communicators and intensive listeners by foreigners representing several other Western cultures (Hiukka, 1992, p. 12). In addition, self-reported data has revealed significantly lower levels of assertiveness and responsiveness for Finnish students than for American students (Sallinen-Kuparinen, Thompson, & Klopf, 1991). In agreement with these findings, it has been established that there are remarkable similarities in the social style of Finns and Japanese (Sallinen-Kuparinen, Thompson, Ishii, Park, & Klopf, 1991). As suggested, Japanese represent a high-context communication culture.

While the dialogical and dialectical modes of communication are suggested to be dominant characteristics of American rhetoric (Okabe, 1983, pp. 36-38), long monologues, avoidance of stating one's own opinions directly, silent approval of opposite opinions, and avoidance of openly questioning others' authority seem to be characteristic of Finnish debates and conversations (Lehtonen, 1986). These characteristics are indicative of high uncertainty avoidance cultures such as Finland is suggested to be (see Gudykunst & Ting-Toomey, 1988, p. 47; Hofstede, 1980).

Moreover, some of the communication characteristics typical of Finns indicate high personal distance between individuals. Finns have been described as task- and issue-oriented communicators, who concentrate on facts instead of personal relations, feelings or opinions (Salo-Lee & Winter-Tarvainen, 1995). This is exemplified by Finnish business negotiators, who are considered formal, distant, closed, serious, and nonverbally inexpressive by foreigners from several other Western cultures (Hiukka, 1992, p. 12). Politeness is emphasized in Finnish culture either negatively or indirectly by, for example, showing respect for the privacy of others, keeping distance between self and others, expressing self-irony, and avoidance of saying "no" (Salo-Lee, 1993, p. 84).

In their cross-cultural comparisons in instructional settings, McCroskey, Richmond, Sallinen, Fayer, and Barraclough (1995) found that Finnish students perceived their teachers to be less nonverbally immediate (mostly on a significant level) than did students from the United States, Puerto Rico and Australia. (See also McCroskey, Sallinen, Fayer, Richmond, & Barraclough, 1996.) However, self-reported data addressing nonverbal immediacy in general indicates a similar degree of immediacy for Finns and for Americans and a higher degree of immediacy for Finns than for Japanese (Ishii, Sallinen-Kuparinen, Klopf, & Thompson, 1991). In addition to the general notion that self-reported and observational data share only a certain amount of common variance, this finding may suggest that minimal nonverbal immediacy signals would be typical of Finns, especially in public and in formal encounters such as teaching or business negotiations, not however, in informal interpersonal settings.

Furthermore, in public encounters, Finns do not seem to expect high nonverbal expressiveness. The Finnish television audience, for example, has been reported to prefer a communicator style totally opposite to American ideals. A presidential candidate whose communicator style was characterized in an empirical study as shy, modest, embarrassed, passive, considering, inexpressive, and unenthusiastic, managed to provoke trust even to the extent that he was elected (see Sallinen-Kuparinen, 1987b).

To summarize, many of the findings reported above do not quite support classifying Finland as a low-context communication culture (see Hall, 1976). On the contrary, many of them refer to high-context communication culture. In addition, characteristics of high uncertainty avoidance culture (see Hofstede, 1980, 1983) as well as those of low-contact culture (Hall, 1976) could well be recognized in the studies reviewed above.

National culture serves as a broad context for communication, since characteristics of national culture are usually shared by a large group of people. Therefore, it is reasonable to assume that the communication characteristics of Finnish culture described above should, at least to some extent, be reflected in various communication contexts and subcontexts inside the Finnish culture. Hence, when interacting in public and in formal encounters, for example on television or in politics, Finns ought to be task- and issue-oriented, distant, silent, and unwilling to communicate. Appreciation of literal expression should be reflected in their speech. In addition, they ought to show moderately low levels of assertiveness and responsiveness and they should try to avoid conflicts. The relevance of these assumptions is explored in the next two sections, where characteristics of Finnish communication culture are examined in the context of television and especially on political television programs.

Culture in Television Context

In this article television is considered to be an environmental context of communication. The goal of television is to entice viewers. This aim affects the communication forms of television in many ways. The structure, schedule, narration and serialization of programs has been developed to maximize the number of viewers. Emphasis is placed on entertainment, drama, intimacy, and authenticity, on one hand, and to credibility as a news source on the other. These features reflect the functions of television in society in general. Therefore, some of the features in television communication, such as certain program types or forms of news, seem to reflect the global characteristics of the media world. However, television programs as well as television performance have been noticed to differ from one culture to another (see e.g., Cohen, 1987; Heinderyckx, 1993), indicating that cultural characteristics are reflected in communication displayed on television.

Most of the studies comparing television programs between various cultures have focused on television news broadcasts. The style of European and American news broadcasts, for example, is shown to be different. According to Steinbock (1990), European television news broadcasts are less entertaining, humoristic, concrete, and emotional, and they emphasize less personified drama than do American news broadcasts. When compared with American news anchors, the role and character of European news anchors is stressed to a much lesser degree: the news is not personified in the anchor as it is on American television.

On the other hand, there are also differences within Europe. Indeed, the role and style of newsreaders appeared as one of the most significant differences on television news broadcasts between eight Western European countries compared by Heinderyckx (1993). However, although the conformity to the format of the news broadcasts is dominant in a culture, there are also significant nuances in single television programs which cannot be explained only by cultural characteristics. These nuances have been suggested to be consequences of, amongst other things, broadcast time of the program, the position of the station on the market, and the target audience (Heinderyckx, 1993), in other words, elements which are representative of television as a part of the media world.

To summarize, both cultural characteristics and features which cross cultural borders and are typical of the format of television news broadcasts in general, seem to be reflected on national television news broadcasts. Many of the findings concerning the style of European news broadcasts are consistent with the characterizations of Finnish communication culture as a task- and issue-centered culture where emphasis is placed on facts rather than on feelings, personal opinions, and relationships between people. Hence, in spite of the global form of television news broadcasts, they seem to form a context, which also draws characteristics of the national communication culture to the foreground. Naturally, there is also variance in communication features between individual news broadcasts, but this variance is not discussed in this article.

Cultural Characteristics in Finnish Television Programs

Characteristics of the national communication culture seem to be reflected in many ways in the context of television in Finland. Instead of a certain kind of ease and fantasy characteristic of American television culture, realism, seriousness, and slowness are typical features of Finnish television. While American television expression seems very fast-paced for Finns, Finnish television programs seem to proceed too slowly for many foreigners. American scholars Slade and Barchak (1989) have described that seeing original Finnish productions is like watching paint dry.

Contrary to the style of television news broadcasts in the United States, Finnish broadcasts typically use a formal language code (Dellinger, 1995). Characteristics of femininity cultures, such as emphasis given to relationships at the expense of action, modesty (meaning simplicity), and caring for the weak, as well as a less significant and less personificated role of anchor are also evident (Levo-Henriksson, 1994). The role of anchor in Finnish television has been suggested to reflect collectivism in Finnish communication culture (see Levo-Henriksson, 1994). In a collectivistic culture with high task- and issue-orientation and high receiver centricity, emphasis is more likely given to the message than to the person of the anchor: an anchor is not expected to arouse attention by very individualistic behavior.

The American news style has been called a "commercial style" by Dellinger (1995). He noticed that Finnish viewers sometimes dislike or have difficulties in interpreting the style of CNN. For example, the welcoming smile of an anchor or his/her attempts to establish contact with audiences on a personal level were easily misinterpreted by Finnish viewers.

Based on analyses of 116 Finnish television programs (Isotalus, 1996), typical features of Finnish professional presenters' on-screen performances in nonfictional programs seem to be reliance on written communication, an aim at speaking fluently, the use of formal and elaborated language, message orientation, effacement of the personality of the presenter, a lack of affective utterances and avoidance of interruption. These are all characteristics typical of communication in public encounters in Finnish culture. Newsreaders and presenters of current affairs and sports programs in particular seem to adhere to the tradition of public speaking: their messages are formal and seem to be addressed to large audiences (Isotalus, 1996). These findings are in contradiction with the interpretation that television communication resembles ordinary and informal interpersonal communication rather than public speaking (see e.g., Hellweg, Pfau, & Brydon, 1992; Scannell, 1991, p. 3).

According to Sallinen-Kuparinen (1986), public speaking in the Finnish culture has primarily ritualistic and informative functions. Since television performance due to the large audience is one kind of public speaking, the norms of public speaking seem to be reflected in this context as well. Hence, as the programing policy of Finnish television has traditionally been informative, it may have encouraged the use of a communication style resembling that of public speaking. (Isotalus, 1996, p. 160.)

In the communication studies presented above, fairly static communication contexts of television have mainly been explored. This kind of context may emphasize the static communication features of Finnish culture instead of the more dynamic features typically associated with interpersonal interaction. However, these studies probably reflect the traditional trend in news broadcasts and in current affairs programs on Finnish television.

As is true in any culture, television culture is a dynamic system which changes over a period of time as a consequence of interaction between different cultures and subcultures. Recently, due to an essential organizational reform in Finnish network television which has led to increased competition between channels, the variance in the nature of communication on television programs has also increased. Certain programs have become more entertaining and the communicator style of presenters on these programs has turned to a more personable direction. These changes in television culture can most notably be seen on political programs.

Interactive Aspects of Culture and Subcultures

Political television programs reflect the practices of a specific communication context. This context constitutes a junction of national communication culture, political communication culture, and television communication culture. In addition, participants in political programs represent various subcultures according to factors such as political orientation, profession, gender, and age. As a consequence, interactants' goals and behavior on these programs may differ from the expectations each one has of the other, as well as from those of the television audiences.

Because of the competitive goals of participants, political programs seem to form a communication context which requires confrontation, assertiveness in presenting one's point of view and in sustaining an argument, challenging others' opinions and points of view, and sometimes even calling another person's character into question. However, this kind of communication is not characteristic of Finnish culture in public encounters.

In the following sections, an attempt is made to explore the extent to which national culture, political culture, and television culture are reflected in the communicative behavior of politicians and presenters in political television programs and in the expectations and evaluations concerning this behavior. The focus of empirical data is on programs broadcast in Finland during the 1994 presidential elections.

Culture as Co-created Context

Since the early 1960's, when television became a medium for politics and politicians, several attempts have been made to develop the slow, nonconfrontational conversation tradition of Finnish communication culture toward a more dynamic direction on Finnish television, most notably during the last decade. Indeed, it has been claimed that Finnish political television programs have been greatly influenced by the style characteristic of American presidential debates (Moring & Himmelstein, 1993).

During the most recent Finnish presidential elections in 1994, for example, political television programs were more dynamic, more argumentative, and more entertaining than was the norm. Furthermore, communication features which are untypical of communication in public encounters in Finnish culture were identifiable in presidential interviews. These appeared as confrontation-seeking strategies such as negative or critical remarks implying a lack of knowledge or the political incompetence of the candidate, and as a person-centered orientation, demonstrated by a great number of personal questions concerning issues such as religion, intimate relationships, character, and outward appearance of the candidate (Isotalus, 1995, p. 76). The keeping of a tight rein on the discussion by the host, a high percentage (56%) of the questions addressed to the candidates being competitive, a large number of questions being asked in a relatively short time period, and many questions which challenged the candidate, as well as a superficial and entertaining atmosphere were all characteristic features in many of the presidential interviews (Ruonala, 1995).

However, adopting new features into a communication culture may prove to be a long process. Findings of a case study (see Isotalus & Pörhölä, 1994; Pörhölä & Isotalus, 1995) examining the most popular television panel discussion of the eleven candidates ("The Great Presidential Panel Discussion") during Finland's presidential election of 1994 are used to illustrate more precisely the confrontation of the new and old kind of political conversation cultures. Reflecting an attempt to arouse more confrontation in the panel discussion, the host of this program, a well-known political journalist, gave a dominating impression by strictly controlling the time used by the candidates and the topics of discussion, by interrupting the participants repeatedly, and by carefully following a strict, predetermined plan for structuring the conversation.

Nevertheless, many of the characteristics typical of communication in public encounters in the Finnish culture were recognized on this program. The communication between the candidates, predominantly monologues, was mostly harmonious and nonconfrontational; arguing was rare. However, inconsistent with the features of traditional Finnish communication culture, the candidates occasionally had brief discussions during which they commented on each other and argued. Still, confrontation mainly occurred between the host and the candidates rather than between the candidates. (Isotalus & Pörhölä, 1994; Pörhölä & Isotalus, 1995.)

These findings suggest that in spite of shared environmental and cultural contexts, the understanding of the demands and constraints of the given context and of appropriate communicative behavior may be quite different for participants representing different subcultures and therefore playing different roles. In conclusion, the findings presented above suggest that the communication characteristics of various subcultures may occur simultaneously, and together with the communication characteristics of the national culture make the cultural communication context multifaceted and flexible. Thus, culture as context is not a static stage but rather a dynamic, open system, which is situationally co-created by interactants.

Culture as Expectancy-arousing Context

It has been presumed that there are cultural differences in expectations concerning contextual behavior. Burgoon (1995, p. 202) suggests that people from cultures that are more inexpressive and more reticent conversationally (such as Scandinavian cultures), may expect others to be less talkative and less dominant than would people from cultures that are more expressive and assertive. Further, in low-contact cultures (such as Finland), greater interaction distances may be expected than in high-contact cultures. In addition, cultures high in uncertainty avoidance (such as Finland) are likely to be intolerant of deviant behavior (Hofstede, 1980).

In Finnish communication culture, where receiver-centricity, preference of task- and issue-orientation, and conflict-avoidance are emphasized, and where dominating communicative behavior is rejected, the new style of the presenters displayed in the political programs discussed above seems to be problematic. Although this style may be typical of political and television cultures in many countries, it may go beyond the "tolerance range" of communicative acts of the Finnish national communication culture, and therefore may be considered to be an expectancy violation by the majority in the Finnish culture. A "tolerance range" refers to "the range for a given act beyond which the act is considered a violation and may invoke sanctions or disapprobation" (Burgoon, 1995, p. 197).

Indeed, many of the political programs broadcast during the 1994 elections were widely criticized in the press. Reflecting the task- and issue-oriented communication culture, a Finnish researcher of politics characterized the new style of Finnish political television interviews as carefully structured interrogations, where stress is placed on the politician's image and on his/her personal responses in certain situations instead of on the politics that he/she represents (Kanerva, 1994, p. 111). Further, in the research interviews of five presidential candidates who had participated in these programs (Mr. Martti Ahtisaari, Mr. Raimo Ilaskivi, Ms. Eeva Kuuskoski, Ms. Elisabeth Rehn, and Mr. Paavo Väyrynen), the candidates described the nature of these programs as schematized, formal, artificial, and fragmentary; they complained of questions which were irrelevant and of a far too personal nature, and of too short a time allowed for answering (Ruonala, 1995).

Presumably, the candidates and at least a part of the audience had based their contextual expectancies concerning communication in political television programs on the knowledge of the demands and constraints of public encounters in Finnish culture in general. Violating these expectancies, the presenters seemed to define the same context differently and followed the expectancies of the media world concerning political programs. As suggested in previous research, interactants evaluate each other negatively if they don't succeed in fulfilling each others' positive contextual expectancies (Burgoon, 1995; Spitzberg & Brunner, 1991).

However, contextual expectancies concerning television programs may vary according to the subculture of an audience. In studies focusing on the responses of young audiences, it was noted that instead of the harmonious communication and lengthy monologues characteristic of the Finnish presidential panel discussions, young people seemed to be more interested in the strong confrontations, arguments and opposite opinions of the candidates. They wanted to have their needs as young people directly addressed, and to see the candidates respond in an enthusiastic, excited, or irritated manner. (See Isotalus & Pörhölä, 1994; Pörhölä & Isotalus, 1995.)

The responses of young members of the audience may, first of all, reflect a certain subculture of youth. As such they may illustrate the different value structures of fragmented audiences. Concomitantly, they are also indicative of the multifaceted and dynamic nature of cultural context.

To summarize, the studies reviewed here suggest that some of the communication characteristics of Finnish culture are, indeed, reflected in the communication behavior of Finns in several communication contexts. When interacting on television, especially on political programs, Finns mainly seem to be task- and issue-oriented, conflict-avoiding, unassertive and unresponsive. They show respect for the speaker and they prefer polite listening. The extensive criticism that some of the television presenters encountered during the 1994 elections suggests that other kinds of communicative behavior are easily interpreted as expectancy-violation by the mainstream of Finnish audiences.

The communicative forms of political programs on Finnish television have traditionally been interviews and panel discussions with several participants. The choice of these communicative forms over dyadic debates illustrates the collectivistic nature of Finnish communication culture. Undoubtedly, interviews and panel discussions do not arouse strong confrontation between politicians in the same way as do dyadic debates. This fact may partly explain the differences in communication between Finnish and Anglo-American political programs.

Conclusions

In this article, the complicated interrelationships between culture and environmental context have been approached on the basis of empirical findings concerning Finnish communication culture. These findings raise the question whether different cultures, subcultures, and contexts directing one's behavior in a given communication situation, as well as one's expectations concerning this situation, are organized in a parallel or hierarchical fashion. On one hand, environmental contexts seem to set their own demands and constraints on communication. National culture as a communication context appears to be flexible, adapting to the demands of the environmental context and to the demands of subcultures as well. This suggests a parallel relationship between culture, subculture, and context. On the other hand, national communication culture seems to serve as a main context, which shapes environmental contexts. It has been shown that the nature of the same environmental context varies from one culture to another. The behavior and expectations of interactants seem to adapt flexibly to the given environmental context in the limits of the national culture. This suggests a hierarchical structure between national culture and environmental context. However, national culture includes several subcultures, which may set different kinds of demands and constraints on communication. This makes the interrelationships between culture, subculture, and context more complicated.

Contexts have been approached here as dynamic systems, which are co-created and negotiated by the interactants involved. It has been presumed that these negotiations are based on the understanding which the interactants have of the communication situation. This understanding, in turn, is closely related to expectations concerning other participants' behavior, relationships between participants, and the context itself. It has been suggested that cultural and subcultural differences between participants increase the amount of variance in these determinations. For example, a political journalist may understand a televised panel discussion of presidential candidates as a confrontation between opposite viewpoints in a television context, whereas politicians may understand the same situation as a public forum for image-building in the context of politics. The co-created context which is broadcast can be understood by television audiences as an interrogation containing attacking questions and hedging answers.

In previous literature concern has been expressed over whether the theory of speech communication adequately accounts for contextual and situational influences on human communication (e.g., Pettegrew, 1988, p. 337). Conceptualizing culture as context makes this question even more focused. The overwhelming majority of speech communication research has been conducted in the United States. When culture is seen as context, the inevitable conclusion is that major findings of this research may be applicable only in the mainstream of Anglo-American communication context. However, the theories of speech communication based on this research are widely applied among other nations and societies as well. Because of the ethnocentric biases of the studies these theories may lack external validity in other cultural contexts.

Although the focus of this article has been on culture and context, it should not be forgotten that communication cultures and contexts are realized through the communication behavior of unique individuals in unique communication situations. Naturally, a great amount of variance observed in human communication in various contexts can be explained by individual and situational factors. The recent approach in intercultural and cross-cultural research, where emphasis is placed on individual-level dimensions of culture (e.g., values and self-construals related with culture; see e.g., Gudykunst, Matsumoto, Ting-Toomey, Nishida, Kim, & Heyman, 1996; Kim, 1995) might help to get better understanding of the individual variability in communicative behavior in different cultural contexts. Research addressing the complicated interrelationships of culture, context, and situation, as well as individual variability in cultures, contexts and unique situations is, thus, warranted.

References

Argyle, M., Furnham, A., & Graham, J. A. (1981). *Social situations*. Cambridge: Cambridge University Press.

Berger, C. R. (1987). Communicating under uncertainty. In M. E. Roloff & G. R. Miller (Eds.), *Interpersonal processes: New directions in communication research* (pp. 39-62). Newbury Park, CA: Sage.

Burgoon, J. K. (1995). Cross-cultural and intercultural applications of expectancy violations theory. In R. L. Wiseman (Ed.), *Intercultural communication theory* (pp. 194-214). Thousand Oaks, CA: Sage.

Buttny, R. (1985). Accounts as a reconstruction of an event's context. *Communication Monographs, 52*, 57-77.

Carbaugh, D. (1995). "Are Americans really superficial?" Notes on Finnish and American cultures in linguistic action. In L. Salo-Lee (Ed.), *Kieli & kulttuuri oppimisessa ja opettamisessa* (pp. 53-60). Publications of the Department of Communication, 12. Jyväskylä, Finland: University of Jyväskylä.

Cohen, A. (1987). *The television news interview*. Newbury Park: Sage.

Dellinger, B. (1995). *Finnish views of CNN television news. A critical cross-cultural analysis of the American commercial discourse style*. Acta Wasaensia 43. Vaasa, Finland: University of Vaasa.

Goodwin, C., & Duranti, A. (1992). Rethinking context: An introduction. In A. Duranti & C. Goodwin (Eds.), *Rethinking context: Language as an interactive phenomenon* (pp. 1-42). Cambridge: Cambridge University Press.

Gudykunst, W. B., Matsumoto, Y., Ting-Toomey, S., Nishida, T., Kim, K., & Heyman, S. (1996). The influence of cultural individualism-collectivism, self construals, and individual values on communication styles across cultures. *Human Communication Research, 22,* 510-543.

Gudykunst, W. B., & Ting-Toomey, S., with Chua, E. (1988). *Culture and interpersonal communication.* Newbury Park, CA: Sage.

Hall, E. T. (1976). *Beyond culture.* New York: Doubleday.

Haslett, B. J. (1987). *Communication: Strategic action in context.* Hillsdale, NJ: Lawrence Erlbaum.

Heinderyckx, F. (1993). Television news programmes in Western Europe: A comparative study. *European Journal of Communication, 8,* 425-450.

Hellweg, S. A., Pfau, M., & Brydon, S. R. (1992). *Televised presidential debates.* New York: Praeger.

Hiukka, K. (1992, August). *Strengths, weaknesses, threats and opportunities of communication in intercultural business negotiations: How do Finns succeed as negotiators?* Paper presented at the World Communication Association Convention, Jyväskylä, Finland.

Hofstede, G. (1980). *Culture's consequences: International differences in work-related values.* Beverly Hills, CA: Sage.

Hofstede, G. (1983). Dimensions of national cultures in fifty countries and three regions. In J. Deregowski, S. Dzuirawiec, & R. Annis (Eds.), *Explications in cross-cultural psychology.* Lisse, The Netherlands: Swets & Zeitlinger.

Ishii, S., Sallinen-Kuparinen, A., Klopf, D., & Thompson, C. (1991). Differences in nonverbal immediacy between Japanese, Finns, and Americans. Otsume Women's University, Japan. *Annual Report, XXIII,* 47-55.

Isotalus, P. (1995). Suomalaisessa puhekulttuurissa monikulttuurinen televisio [Multicultural television in Finnish speech culture]. In L. Salo-Lee (Ed.), *Kieli & kulttuuri oppimisessa ja opettamisessa* (pp. 69-80). Publications of the Department of Communication, 12. Jyväskylä, Finland: University of Jyväskylä.

Isotalus, P. (1996). *Toimittaja kuvaruudussa. Televisioesiintyminen vuorovaikutuksen näkökulmasta* [Presenter on screen. Television performance as interaction]. Jyväskylä Studies in Communication, 5. Jyväskylä, Finland: University of Jyväskylä.

Isotalus, P. & Pörhölä, M. (1994). Mikä presidenttiehdokkaiden televisiokeskustelussa kiinnostaa nuoria? [What arouses young persons' interest in a television conversation of presidential candidates?] *Politiikka, 36,* 272-282.

Kanerva, J. (1994). *"Ryvettymisen hyvä puoli..." Suomalainen politiikka ja poliitikot televisiossa* ["The bright side of getting soiled..." Finnish politics and politicians on television]. Jyväskylä, Finland: University of Jyväskylä.

Katriel, T. (1995). From "context" to "contexts" in intercultural communication research. In R. L. Wiseman (Ed.), *Intercultural communication theory* (pp. 271-284). Thousand Oaks, CA: Sage.

Kim, M.-S. (1995). Toward a theory of conversational constraints: Focusing on individual-level dimensions of culture. In R. L. Wiseman (Ed.), *Intercultural communication theory* (pp. 148-169). Thousand Oaks, CA: Sage.

Lehtonen, J. (1986). Puhekasvatus ja sosiaaliset taidot [Communication education and social skills]. In L. Kirstinä (Ed.), *Puhumalla paras* (pp. 20-40). Äidinkielen opettajain liiton vuosikirja XXXIII. Helsinki, Finland: ÄOL.

Lehtonen, J., & Sajavaara, K. (1985). The silent Finn. In D. Tannen & M. Saville-Troike (Eds.), *Perspectives on silence* (pp. 193-201). Norwood, NJ: Ablex.

Levo-Henriksson, R. (1994). *Eyes upon wings. Culture in Finnish and US television news.* Helsinki, Finland: Finnish Broadcasting Company.

McCroskey, J. C., & Richmond, V. P. (1979). The impact of communication apprehension on individuals in organizations. *Communication Quarterly, 27,* 55-61.

McCroskey, J. C., & Richmond, V. P. (1987). Willingness to communicate. In J. C. McCroskey & J. S. Daly (Eds.), *Personality and interpersonal communication* (pp. 129-156). Newbury Park, CA: Sage.

McCroskey, J. C., Richmond, V. P., Sallinen, A., Fayer, J. M., & Barraclough, R. A. (1995). A cross-cultural and multi-behavioral analysis of the relationship between nonverbal immediacy and teacher evaluation. *Communication Education, 44,* 281-290.

McCroskey, J. C., Sallinen, A., Fayer, J. M., Richmond, V. P., & Barraclough, R. A. (1996). Nonverbal immediacy and cognitive learning: A cross-cultural investigation. *Communication Education, 45,* 200-211.

Moring, T., & Himmelstein, H. (1993). *Politiikkaa riisuttuna. Kampanjakulttuuri murroksessa televisioidun politiikan aikaan* [The culture of campaigning in tradition during the era of televised politics]. Helsinki, Finland: Finnish Broadcasting Company.

Okabe, R. (1983). Cultural assumptions of East and West. Japan and the United States. In W. B. Gudykunst (Ed.), *Intercultural communication theory. Current perspectives.* Beverly Hills, CA: Sage.

Pettegrew, L. S. (1988). The importance of context in applied communication research. *The Southern Speech Communication Journal, 53,* 331-338.

Pörhölä, M. (1995). *Yksin yleisön edessä. Esiintymisjännitykseen ja esiintymishalukkuuteen liittyvät kokemukset, käyttäytymispiirteet ja vireytyminen yleisöpuhetilanteessa* [Alone in front of an audience. Cognitive experiences, behavioral features and physiological arousal in speech anxiety and willingness to speak]. Jyväskylä Studies in Communication, 2. Jyväskylä, Finland: University of Jyväskylä.

Pörhölä, M., & Isotalus, P. (1995, August). *Talking heads talking politics. The relationship between audience interest and communication features in a presidential television debate.* Paper presented at the Nordic Conference of Mass Communication Research, Helsingør, Denmark.

Pörhölä, M., Isotalus, P., & Ovaskainen, T. (1993). Communication-elicited arousal in public speaking, small group, and dyadic contexts: Comparisons of change in heart rate. *Communication Research Reports, 10,* 29-37.

Ruonala, K.-M. (1995). *Presidenttiehdokkaat haastateltavina. Vuorovaikutuksen ja ehdokkaiden esiintymisen tarkastelua tv-haastattelutilanteissa vuoden 1994 presidentinvaaleissa* [Presidential candidates in television interviews. Interaction and performance of candidates in television interviews during the 1994 presidential election]. Unpublished master's thesis, University of Jyväskylä, Jyväskylä, Finland.

Sallinen-Kuparinen, A. (1986). *Finnish communication reticence. Perceptions and self-reported behavior.* Studia Philologica Jyväskyläensia 19. Jyväskylä, Finland: University of Jyväskylä.

Sallinen-Kuparinen, A. (1987a, February). *Culture and communicator image.* Paper presented at the Western Speech Communication Association Convention, Salt Lake City, UT.

Sallinen-Kuparinen, A. (1987b). Televisioesiintyminen, mediaretoriikka ja poliittinen vaikuttaminen [Television performance, media rhetoric, and political persuasion]. *Politiikka, 29,* 120-133.

Sallinen-Kuparinen, A., McCroskey, J. C., & Richmond, V. P. (1991). Willingness to communicate, communication apprehension, introversion, and self-reported communication competence: Finnish and American comparisons. *Communication Research Reports, 8,* 55-64.

Sallinen-Kuparinen, A., & Pörhölä, M. (1986). Assessment of arousal in speech communication research. In A. Sallinen-Kuparinen (Ed.), *Jyväskylä studies in speech communication* (pp. 57-83). Publications of the Department of Communication, 2. Jyväskylä, Finland: University of Jyväskylä.

Sallinen-Kuparinen, A., Thompson, C. A., Ishii, S., Park, M.-S., & Klopf, D. W. (1991, August). *An analysis of social style among disparate cultures.* Paper presented at the World Communication Association Convention, Jyväskylä, Finland.

Sallinen-Kuparinen, A., Thompson, C. A., & Klopf, D. W. (1991). Social styles of Finns and Americans. *Psychological Reports, 68,* 193-194.

Salo-Lee, L. (1993). 'Teillä on kaunis nappi' - small talk: Tyhjänpuhumista vai mielekästä viestintää? ['You have a nice button' - small talk: Empty talk or meaningful communication?] In J. Lehtonen (Ed.), *Kulttuurien kohtaaminen. Näkökulmia kulttuurienväliseen kanssakäymiseen* (pp. 77-90). Publications of the Department of Communication, 9. Jyväskylä, Finland: University of Jyväskylä.

Salo-Lee, L. & Winter-Tarvainen, A. (1995). Kriittiset tilanteet kulttuurien kohtaamisessa: Suomalaisten ja saksalaisten opiskelijoiden näkökulma [Critical incidents in intercultural encounters: Perspectives of Finnish and German students]. In L. Salo-Lee (Ed.), *Kieli & kulttuuri oppimisessa ja opettamisessa* (pp. 81-107). Publications of the Department of Communication, 12. Jyväskylä, Finland: University of Jyväskylä.

Scannell, P. (1991). Introduction: The relevance of talk. In P. Scannell (Ed.), *Broadcast talk* (pp. 1-13). London: Sage.

Slade, J., & Barchak, L. (1989). Public broadcasting in Finland: Inventing a national television programming policy. *Journal of Broadcasting & Electronic Media, 33,* 355-373.

Steinbock, D. 1990. *Amerikkalaiset TV-uutiset* [American television news broadcasts]. Helsinki, Finland: Finnish Broadcasting Company.

Spitzberg, B. H., & Brunner, C. C. (1991). Toward a theoretical integration of context and competence inference research. *Western Journal of Speech Communication, 55,* 28-46.

Stamp, G. H., Vangelisti, A. L., & Knapp, M. L. (1994). Criteria for developing and assessing theories of interpersonal communication. In F. L. Casmir (Ed.), *Building communication theories: A socio/cultural approach* (pp. 167-208). Hillsdale, NJ: Lawrence Erlbaum.

Chapter 22

Between Challenge and Burden: Changing Contexts in East Germany After Democratization

Romy Fröhlich
Institut für Journalistik und Kommunikationsforschung
Hochschule für Musik und Theater Hannover, Germany

In the beginning of the 21st century we must more than ever deal with the increasing complexity of our world. On the one hand, our world grows more and more complex. On the other hand, it seems to be smaller than ever. Wars far away affect our lives. Since environmental destruction or political movements do not stop at national borders, we will have to interact, communicate, and negotiate with our near and far neighbors in the world. Complexity has reached a new level and thus international exchange will reach a new dimension that has not been experienced in the past. In particular, the developments in Eastern Europe constitute a complete new context which will lead to new challenges for international communication, mass media, journalism, and professional communicators in general. And all of this of course will influence individual communication, too.

Eastern Europe is undergoing the transition from a totalitarian system to a democracy. In this process mass media play a very important role. Countries like Czechoslovakia and Poland have just begun to re-establish freedom of the press. For the republics of the former Soviet Union (CIS) this transition is even more difficult because freedom of the press has rarely existed in their history. Now at the end of our century, the Eastern print-media and electronic-media scene will change dramatically for the people and societies concerned. As state control ceases, former state-owned newspapers will be bought by commercial companies--perhaps Western ones--and a variety of new newspapers may be founded in the near future. Sooner or later, the Eastern media scene will resemble the Western one, no matter what new ideas or creative concepts are being discussed there at present.

But after centuries with party- or government-controlled mass media, the principle of freedom of the press or freedom of the media market cannot just be *established*. Horvat (1992) describes the difficulties as follows: "In Eastern Europe the entire system was changed, not only the ruling elites. Concepts which are familiar elsewhere, such as private property, enterprenurialism, banking system, etc., are a novelty in Eastern Europe. In this respect the democratization of the media differs the most from Asian or South American models, where the media, especially the print media, never left private or family hands.... In Eastern Europe, with scant tradition of private ownership and with the absence of financial resources and managerial skills, a smooth media transition is proving next to impossible" (p. 5).

As one result of changes, in Eastern Europe a new system of journalism education and training is required. The Eastern countries themselves feel strongly about this necessity. Thus, Eastern Europe now seeks Western help, professional consulting, and an exchange of concepts and ideas. The West is happy to help with this process. First contacts have begun, especially in Europe where the two systems and the people living in them have always been very close to each other geographically. Some professionals have already visited colleagues or professional journalism groups in Eastern Europe or welcomed them in their countries. During the meetings one often realizes that despite the translator, we have some problems understanding each other. The problem is not with language. The problem is understanding completely different concepts of journalism, journalism's role and function, and the skills required as well as completely different concepts of the public. It is also a problem of understanding totally different systems of education in general, and journalism education in particular. For example, in a communist society, *any* aspect of individualism is looked upon as negative. And we should not forget that the decades of cold war have just ended. In the near future, we will still have to deal with people in the East who have been raised with certain concepts about the "evil West." Honestly, haven't we in the West been raised in quite a similar manner, only with the picture reversed?

In this new situation, Eastern Europe needs Western help in a broader sense. Of course Eastern Europe needs financial aid and technical equipment, but perhaps more than anything else, it needs this know-how and consulting on the basis of *mutual understanding*. The differences between both systems even within one culture, like in Germany, cause a lot of misunderstandings. Very often it is the ignorance about the conditions of different socializations that leads to the frustrations on both sides. As a result of the lack of knowledge, both here and there, we deal with traditional and strong stereotypes. *Real mutual understanding* in the interaction between "East" and "West" requires one to know something more about the difficulties of long-term socialization in a totalitarian system suddenly meeting the unfamiliar values and rules of democracy.

Fundamentally, we still know nothing about how the new political context exactly influences Eastern journalists' and communicators' ideas of their present role in society. Finally the new context might force them to keep their old beliefs and to more than ever defend them against the new values. Thus, we first of all need to learn more about socialist journalism and the journalists themselves in order to keep from building new walls between us.

Research on Journalists: What We Know So Far

Research on journalists in general focuses on three questions: (1) Individual aspects of professional skills, behavior, and roles, (2) internal mechanisms of the media system (for example, the conditions in the process of selecting and producing news), and (3) the images and knowledge journalists have about their audiences as well as their relationships to society in general. Most of the research we are familiar with so far deals with one or more of these questions.

One of the first and most well-known research projects on the sociology and professional organization of the American journalists is Leo Rosten's study on Washington correspondents (Rosten, 1937). British journalists were surveyed by Jeremy Tunstall in 1970 (Tunstall, 1970, 1971). In Germany the first comprehensive journalist survey was conducted between 1973 and 1976 (Arbeitsgemeinschaft...., 1977). In the meantime we have quite a number of studies which compare journalism concepts of two nations, although the journalists studied were usually from two Western nations (Donsbach, 1982, 1983; Köcher, 1986). But there is little journalism research based on broader international or cultural comparisons (see for example McLeod & Hawley, 1964). Although results of these few surveys show great international conformity concerning professional standards or values, like freedom of the press, considerable national differences exist concerning role definitions and the individual perceptions of the function of journalism.[1]

While there are some national studies about expectations, views, and role definitions of journalism *students* (as a German example see Gruber, Koller, & Ruhl, 1974; American examples are Becker, Fruit, & Caudill, 1987) only one study has compared journalism *students* from different countries. In 1987, students from 22 countries were interviewed in an international survey (see Sparks & Splichal, 1989; also Donsbach, 1990). Ten Third World countries, three (at that time) socialist countries,[2] and nine Western industrialized countries[3] took part in the project. It concentrated on the attitudes of the students towards their future profession, their concepts of journalists' roles in society, and their motives for becoming a journalist.

This international study found significant differences between role definitions and individual motives of journalism students in different countries. According to the findings, the students' motives fell into three major categories. To one group of students, the belief in their own ability and talent was far more important than extrinsic motives such as job market or an "easy major." A second group valued most personal gratification, such as the chance to travel, to become well known or popular in the field or to earn good money. The third group of students named altruistic motives, such as changing society, influencing social or political processes, and exposing nuisances or scandals, as most important. Students' responses in Western industrialized countries and in India fell into the first or second group of motives more frequently than students' responses in socialist countries and Third World countries (Donsbach, 1990, p. 412). Against expectations, differences did not exist between the students from different countries concerning altruistic motives. We can then conclude altruistic motives are a general and intercultural component of journalism students' conception and interpretation of their job.

Answers to the question about qualifications and abilities needed to be a good journalist did also show differences between the two major groups of students.

Western and Indian students gave "ability to be critical" and "accuracy" as answers much more than students from Third World or socialist countries gave. "Objectivity" as a requirement for a good journalist appeared to be the same between the two groups, but in comparison with other qualifications, "objectivity" was of less importance. But these results cannot be so simply evaluated. One must consider the respective political and cultural contexts. Finally "objectivity" is defined differently among the 22 countries, and the realization of objectivity also differs within these different contexts. Thus, Donsbach, who directed the German part of this international project, describes some problems of the survey concerning the validity of answers given by Bulgarian, Polish, and Yugoslavian students. He points out that these students obviously had not been allowed to write their own opinion but rather had been forced to answer in a controlled manner. He argued, for example, the Bulgarian students said that they have complete freedom of the press in their country when obviously, because of the totalitarian regime, they couldn't. But this argument is only part of the story because a real consideration of political and cultural context(s) leads to a more detailed interpretation: Couldn't it be that the Bulgarian students really meant what they wrote? Isn't it possible that they really believe that their country has complete freedom of the press? We should consider that these young people did not decide to become bakers, sales(wo)men or physicists in a socialist country but instead journalists in a socialist country. The interesting questions behind these results is to what extent are the answers the result of coersion or of socialist socialization? Now, as democracy is on its way into the socialist countries of Eastern Europe, we have the opportunity to investigate and learn how strong socialist concepts of journalism still are despite (or because of) the changing cultural and political context.

When the Berlin wall fell, Germans had a good opportunity to examine more closely the differences between the communist and the capitalist concepts for "everything," including journalism and mass media. West Germans had to accept that for East Germans, it was and still is painful to learn that their ideas and concepts are no longer valid and respected. This is no exception for journalists, who also have "old" values, standards, and ideas in their heads.

The Former Context--Some Essentials about Socialist Journalism Education[4]

According to socialist ideology, "The Party" is the most advanced member of society. In the former GDR, as well as in other socialist countries, mass media played an important role in establishing and maintaining the omnipotence and all-embracing power of the communist party. Because journalism served as an important instrument for political guidance, journalists had to be functionaries of the communist party and the socialist state (see also Blaum, 1985, pp. 79, 98). Thus socialist journalists were taught that the press was a collective system of spokes(wo)men for mediating between the omniscient, controlling socialist leaders and, to some extent, the ignorant members of society. Their job was to support the "good" socialist ideology by emphasizing its benefits and positive achievements and by concealing, or at least downplaying, the problems (see also Blaum, 1985, pp. 79-80; 100-112). With this point of view it is legitimate to protect the public from anti-socialist tendencies, even if it means dealing with dishonest messages. Journalists, of course, were aware of that and accepted their function. People who chose to be journalists in these countries normally knew exactly what this would mean to them and it was necessary for them to be convinced of the concept.

Because of mass media's role in the socialist systems, specific requirements were necessary in journalism education. One of the most important qualifications for journalism students was their "active cooperation in shaping socialist society" and their "willingness to actively defend socialism" (Leszczensky & Filaretow, p. 16). This usually meant active membership in the communist party or the socialist youth organization "Freie Deutsche Jugend (FDJ)" (Free German Youth) (Blaum, 1985, p. 98). Thus journalism was not a "free access" profession, as it is in Western societies, nor was journalism instruction available to everyone.

While studying at the University, students often were already partial members of editorial staffs, working for newspapers, magazines or electronic media. This meant that the students already had permanent jobs as journalists when they finished their studies at the University and were never forced to find jobs by themselves. Everything was prepared for them. The recent political change has brought with it the freedom of jobseeking. As one can imagine, the new freedom in this respect is a burden which is causing severe problems.

The same is true for the economic situation of the students. As with every student in the GDR, journalism students did not have to worry about their financial situation. Education was free. Plus they received free housing and spending money. The amount of financial relief depended on the students' marital status and number of children. And again the new freedom is to the disadvantage of the students because it has, for the most part, brought an end to free housing and financial aid.

The Former Context--Implications for Self-assessment and Role-definition

The cultural and political context Eastern communicators had been socialized within is most different from the context of the Western World. As I pointed out above, the lack of belief in objective truth was programmed for socialist journalism and therefore for socialist journalism education. The students were taught that a journalist's job is the selection and distortion of facts which strongly support the welfare of the socialist society. Thus, journalists educated in former socialist countries bring with them different ideas and behaviors. One of my studies conducted October 2, 1990, at the university-level journalism program in Leipzig found that it made only little difference that people had had a certain period of time to become accustomed to the new system (Froehlich, 1995).[5] After nearly a year of experience with the new society and the system of freedom of the press, professional communicators and journalists still differed strongly from their Western colleagues concerning self-assessment and role-definition. It seems that now, perhaps more than ever, these former GDR journalists see their role as an altruistic one. Some of them may be overwhelmed by the new freedoms and the new system. They now think of supporting this system as an important part of their job. As in the old system, they again distinguish between facts which are in favor of the new system and those which are not.

Others may still--or now even more than ever--have respect for the "accomplishments" of socialism, such as "social security" and "full employment." Thus, they too distinguish between "good" and "bad" facts, this time to support the old system. The concept is always the same--to positively shape society. No wonder that East German journalism students are not very willing to work for *non-political* magazines (Froehlich, 1995, p. 9). This for example is completely different from what we know from North American and British journalism students (Donsbach, 1990, p. 416). Plus, for most of East German journalists an interest in writing and creative opportunity followed by the opportunity to work independently, highly influenced their decision to study journalism (Froehlich, 1995, p. 10). "Independence" as an extremely important motive is surprising. One should remember that most of the East German journalists had been educated before the political change. Then how could they have decided to become journalists for reasons concerning "independence?" We have to speculate. One possibility is that the journalists think of journalism as an *independent* profession because of their socialist socialization. They may still believe in socialism and may still have respect for its "accomplishments." Thus, they today define journalism like they always defined it--as an indepedent profession in the way the socialist system defined it as independent. Another possibility is that East German journalists are trying to prove their democratic sentiments. It seems perhaps they want to show that they had already "learned their lesson," giving the answer that "independence in journalism" is the most important thing for them. A third possibility could be that as a result of the political change the journalists are confused and unsure about their professional future. The most important question in such a situation is, "Will I have a chance in the new system despite the fact that I am considered to be a socialist journalist?" In this situation, a lot of them have asked themselves whether they should continue as journalists, or whether they should change professional paths completely. It may be that the journalists felt as if they made a second decision and now they wanted to be journalists because it presents a new opportunity to work independently and thus to work within a new context.

It is not surprising that, compared with international results, "political" motives seem to be much more important for journalists from the former GDR than for West German, British, and North American students (Froehlich, 1995, p. 11) which indicates East German journalists' orientation to the journalist's role as a *watchdog* or *controller* of the political elite. Comparatively few of them see the journalist as a *neutral and objective mediator* or regard a journalist's role as an *advocate*. This is contrary to the normal importance laid on the neutral and objective mediator role by Western journalists (Donsbach, 1990, p. 422). Given that obviously this is still valid for a lot of journalists educated and socialized in socialist countries, it is no wonder that they are extremely willing to transport values. This interpretation is supported through Horvat's (1992) description and estimation of the present situation of "Media Democracy and Media Freedom in Eastern Europe": "Now that a politically objective and unbiased journalism could be the order of the day, many East European journalists are uncertain. Their role perception is tied to the past.... They want to become a mouthpiece for the people. They are familiar and comfortable with a partisan press, with party alignments, and with propaganda. For many the lack of official guidelines spell chaos and abandonment" (p. 12). And this is exactly the reason why people in the East evaluate the new context of their social and political lives completely different from how we (would) do it. It makes it extremely important to always take into account the respective context people live in and are socialized in when communicating with each other.

This essay is only a glimpse into one aspect of the many professional changes communication in Eastern Europe is being faced with now. Despite the fact that communist East European countries all practiced Soviet-style journalism in education as well as in practice, and thus are comparable in many respects, the different cultures and press traditions of the numerous East European countries must be considered. This is especially important for future Western consulting concerning the diverse aspects of the press system such as the nature of ownership, communication or press laws, education, and professional ethics or standards. With the revolutionary process still going on in most East European countries, people are confronted with problems they never were confronted with before. They are threatened by unemployment and rising prices. Their living standard is lower than ever, and they have lost most of their social and political values. The new values democracy offers to them are not yet accepted overall as good ones. Instead, life seems to be disjointed. In this situation, East Europe is being required to establish a new society and to find new values by using the Western world, which not long ago was an enemy, as a pattern. The people there are required to achieve all of this without losing their identity as individuals. No wonder that a lot of East European journalists in this situation think of their role differently from the way Western ones do. Horvat (1992) finally gives a last reason for these differences: "Hardly any of the East European media players--including politicians, publishers, editors, journalists, and readers--thought until recently that they were participants in a *business* venture. In Eastern Europe the press had never been considered a commercial enterprise, papers had never been bought and sold on the open market. This new phenomenon, the new social and economic order, gives rise to many contradictions in Eastern Europe with regard to the social function and democratization of the media" (p. 13). We should keep these circumstances which result from the very specific East European context in mind and should understand the special background when meeting or working together with our new colleagues from the East. This will make it much easier to establish and maintain a fruitful exchange.

References

Arbeitsgemeinschaft für Kommunikationsforschung. (1977). *Schlußbericht. Synopse: Journalismus als Beruf* (Projektleitung Hans-Jürgen Weiß) [Final report. Synopsis: Journalism as a profession]. München: Arbeitsgemeinschaft für Kommunikationsforschung.

Becker, L. B., Jeffrey, W., & Caudill, S. L. (1987). *The training and hiring of journalists*. Noorwood, NJ: Ablex.

Blaum, V. (1985). *Ideologie und Fachkompetenz. Das journalistische Berufsbild in der DDR* [Ideology and competence. Job description of journalism in the GDR]. Köln: Nottbeck.

Donsbach, W. (1981). Legitimacy through competence rather than value judgement. The concept of professionalization reconsidered. *Gazette, 27,* 47-67.

Donsbach, W. (1982). *Legitimationsprobleme des Journalismus. Gesellschaftliche Rolle der Massenmedien und berufliche Einstellungen von Journalisten* [Journalism's problems with legitimacy. Social role of mass media and professional attitudes of journalists]. Freiburg, München: Alber.

Donsbach, W. (1983). Journalists' conceptions of their audience. Comparative indicators for the way British and German journalists define their relations to the public. *Gazette, 37,* 19-36.

Donsbach, W. (1990). Journalistik Studenten im internationalen Vergleich [An international comparison of journalism students]. *Publizistik, 35,* 409-427.

Fröhlich, R. (1995, July). *The challenge of democracy. Future journalists during times of change. The GDR Case.* Paper presented at the conference of the World Communication Association, Vancouver, B.C., Canada.

Gruber, T., Koller, B., & Rühl, M. (1974/75). Berufsziel: Journalist [Intended career: Journalism]. *Publizistik, 19+20,* 337-359.

Grubitzsch, J. (1990). Traditionen, Altlasten und Neuansätze der Leipziger Journalistenausbildung [Traditions, old burdens and reshaping of the Leipzig journalism program]. *Rundfunk und Fernsehen, 38,* 400-406.

Horvat, J. (1992, May). *Media democracy and the media freedom in Eastern Europe.* Paper presented at the 42nd annual conference of the International Communication Association, Miami, FL.

Karl-Marx-Universität Leipzig. (Ed.). (1976). *Universitätsführer.* Leipzig: Karl-Marx-Universität Leipzig.

Köcher, R. (1986). Bloodhounds and missionaries: Role definitions of German and British journalists. *European Journal of Communication, I,* 34-64.

Langenbucher, W. R., & Neufeldt, G. (1988). Journalistische Berufsvorstellungen im Wandel von drei Jahrzehnten [Professional expectations of journalist's in the course of three centuries]. In H. Wagner (Ed.), *Idee und Wirlichkeit des Journalismus. Beiträge aus Wissenschaft und Praxis* [Concept and reality of journalism. Contributions from research and profession] (pp. 257-272). München: Olzog.

Leszczensky, M., & Filaretow, B. (1990). *Hochschulstudium in der DDR. Statistischer Überblick* (University education in the GDR: A statistical overview). Hannover: HIS.

McLeod, J. M., & Hawley, S. E. (1964). Professionalization among newsmen. *Journalism Quarterly, 41*, 529-539.

Rosten, L. (1937). *The Washington correspondents*. New York: Harcourt, Brace.

Sparks, C., & Splichal, S. (1989). Journalistic education and professional socialisation. Summary of a survey study in 22 countries. *Gazette, 43*, 31-52.

Tunstall, J. (1970). *The Westminster Lobby correspondents: A sociology study of national journalism*. London: Routledge & Kegan Paul.

Tunstall, J. (1971). *Journalists at work: Specialist correspondents, the news organization, news sources and competitors-colleagues*. London: Constable.

Weaver, D., & Wilhoit, G. C. (1986). *The American journalist: A portrait of U. S. newspeople and their work*. Bloomington, IN: Indiana University Press.

Footnotes

[1] There is evidence that German journalists, for example, differ from British and American in terms of self-assessment and role definition. German journalists, more than British, think of journalism as a political task (Donsbach, 1983) and are said to be "missionaries" (Köcher, 1986) rather than neutral mediators. There is some evidence that this distinction is valid also for a German-American comparison or roles and self-assessment of journalists (Weaver & Wilhoit, 1986, p. 137). But according to Langenbucher and Neufeldt (1988), German journalists' picture of themselves as opinion leaders has changed in the course of the last thirty years. This "old" picture is more and more following the American and British journalism patterns, although differences still exist. For a more detailed overview of international comparison results, see Donsbach, 1981.

[2] Bulgaria, Poland and Yugoslavia.

[3] Including Germany, Great Britain and the United States.

[4] For detailed information about the only university-level journalism program in Leipzig, GDR, see Blaum, 1985, pp. 87-100 and Grubitzsch, 1990.

[5] This was about one year after the first so-called "Monday demonstrations," which took place in September of 1989 in the streets of Leipzig and which led to the collapse of the GDR. And October 2, 1990, was one day before the official unification of East and West Germany.

Section 6
Technological Context and the Applied Analysis of Communication Behavior

Chapter 23

Shifts in Identity: The Contextualizing Function of Communication Technologies

Denice Yanni
Fairfield University

But when it came to writing, Theuth declared: "Here is an accomplishment, my Lord the king, which will improve both the wisdom and the memory of the Egyptians. I have discovered a secure receipt for memory and wisdom." "Theuth, my paragon of inventors," replied the king, "the discoverer of an art is not the best judge of the good or harm which will accrue to those who practice it...Those who acquire it will cease to exercise their memory and become forgetful; they will rely on writing to bring things to their remembrance by external sign instead of on their own internal resources. What you have discovered is a receipt for recollection, not for memory. And as for wisdom, your pupils will have the reputation for it without the reality: they will receive a quantity of information without proper instruction, and in consequence be thought very knowledgeable when they are for the most part quite ignorant." Plato

Accompanying all communication shifts in history are forecasts of utopia and apocalypse. There are those who extol the virtues of the new medium, providing a litany of features that will only enlarge the human capacity for action. As well there are those who recount the demise of culture due to the pervasive influence of a reductionist technology affecting experiences of social relations, identity, knowledge, politics, memory, and the economy. Both accounts have in common an image of ideal human nature that will either be fully realized or thwarted by 'the machine in our midst.' It is an approach that can be identified today in popular discourse on computers where postulated "effects" are debated on everything from consumer behavior to education and from child's play to artistic expression.

The challenge of identifying and analyzing the influence of communication technologies extends beyond the terms of this dualism. The purpose of this essay is to present a constitutive perspective on the human-technology interface; one that argues for a reflexive relationship in which both humans and technologies define and extend each other. Special attention is directed toward expanding the concept of "context" since it has an instrumental role in determining the significance of communication shifts. Further, by examining how technologies affect perception, we will be better able to understand ourselves in context as we continually relate to new media.

Conceptualizing Context

The popularization of using "context" for the study of communication technologies belies the complexity of this concept. Use of the phrase, "in context," prompts studies with subjects such as the development of the computer in twentieth century France or television during the 1960s in the United States and assumes a conceptual framework without the requisite need to define the terms of analysis. Rather than consider context as a pre-existing condition into which an artifact is set, a constitutive perspective of communication technologies examines the reflexive nature of both categories--technology and context. In this way, we move from studying communication technologies in context to studying the contextualizing function of communication technologies. Significant scholarship has contributed to defining a more constitutive perspective (Innis, 1951; Eisenstein, 1979; Douglas, 1987; Marvin, 1988, 1989; Slack, 1987, 1989; Kramarae, 1988; Heyer, 1988; Poster, 1990; Woodward, 1993) thereby reframing the questions and provoking a more challenging analysis.

A Constitutive Perspective of Communication Technologies

Communication technologies are constitutive of both individual and collective identity. That is, they are factors in constructing subjective experience as well as social relations: "Technology...is an element in the culture and the personality systems as well" (Alexander, 1992, p. 314). While we cannot deny the material existence of these objects, neither can we deny their extension into consciousness. Referring to late twentieth century American society as "The Information Society" because of the growth of computers is an example of how we situate ourselves within the terms of a technical procedure. Technologies, then, function on both a concrete and abstract level; they are both empirical and discursive objects. This locates the experience of technology within various systems of meaning within a social structure.

Further consideration must be given to the fact that we are specifically discussing **communication** technologies which intensifies this reflexive function as it relates to the experience of self as well as cultural formation. Private and public identity is affected by changes in communicative practices:

> ...[S]ubjects are constituted in acts and structures of communication...[C]hanges in communication patterns involve changes in the subject. Changes in the configurations or wrappings of language alters the way the subject processes signs into meanings...The shift from oral and print wrapped language to electronically wrapped language thus reconfigures the subject's relation to the world. (Poster, 1990, p. 11)

Communication technologies play a role in mediating different experiences of subjectivity. Woodward (1993) echoes this interpretation by suggesting that the new information technologies "contribute to the conditions of **self-knowledge**..."

since they are factors in "the production of social/cultural environments" (164). Consequently, the contexts in which individuals self-define are continually being affected by practices of communication. As contexts change, so do ways of perceiving human identity.

By extension, cultural identity is also affected. The pioneering work of Harold Innis (1894-1952) specifically examined how the character of a technology affects the shaping of culture, demonstrating "...the significance of communication to the rise and decline of cultural traits" (1951, p. 33). His work inspired further scholarship that explored the cultural imprint of a specific communication technology (Havelock, 1982; Menache, 1990; Schudson, 1978; Douglas, 1987). Rather than merely identifying an artifact like the telephone or the television as 'invented' in a given historical period, this approach promotes a frame of reference which highlights the role of communication in cultivating different forms of human civilization. That is, communication technology is not merely a component in a cultural history, but "an agent of change" (Eisenstein, 1979) that has a definitive role in successive configurations of human society.

Reconceptualizing context in the study of communication technologies is important not only to an understanding of cultural formation but also social practice. In what ways are the on-going, everyday activities of society affected by these technologies? Carolyn Marvin (1989) refutes the "black-box or media-artifact" approach to analyzing communication history. Rather than studying each media form as a separate object with a distinct history, Marvin advocates a new context:

> If the focus of communication is defined as the expression of social relations, communication with new artifacts is the occasion for introducing new rules and procedures to express those relations....
>
> New communication technologies come to existing groups less as transformative agents than as opportunities or threats to be weighed and figured into the pursuit of on-going objectives...They come as elements to be absorbed into existing rules and expectations about the structure of social relations (p. 191).

While some studies select a media artifact as the unit of observation from which stems certain social effects, Marvin argues that this is a rather arbitrary starting point. Not only do technologies have various stages of development but also societies acknowledge, adopt, and adapt to new communication technologies in different ways. Where would one start with a study of how computers influence American society: Cybertext? Virtual reality? The Web? With what social group: The Elderly? African Americans? Girls in elementary school? As it relates to what activity: Politics? Consumerism? Education? We need to alter our perception of the interaction between technologies, not merely as objects, and society, not as historically homogenous, but both as mutually defining.

In addition, Marvin (1989) provides insight as to the character of effect on social groups. Her position concerning communication technologies is that they have a conservative rather than transformative function. In practice, this results in solidifying existing identities, objectives, and interactions. Hers is not a utopian embrace of new technologies. Rather, she charts how "habitual social intercourse is restructured in new media" (p. 191).

A final observation as to the mutual shaping of context and technology is evidenced in the work of Jennifer Daryl Slack (1989). She states that since technologies exist within a nexus of discourses, they can never be fully differentiated and studied as isolated objects:

> If context is truly constitutive, we can never completely separate object and context...'Technology' has no absolute identity; it is rather the ongoing production of identity empowered and empowering in articulated social relations (p. 338).

Technologies are always "objects in relationships" drawing their identity from interaction with different social forces.

Inherent to all theorists cited in the above discussion is an understanding of the material and symbolic identity of technology and its role in the production of meaning. They promote a constitutive perspective which refutes an absolutist understanding of context in favor of a more dynamic, reflexive approach which is codeterminous of human self-conception and social relations.

Communication Technology and Perception

As previously noted, the history of communication shifts in human society is characterized by claims of individual and social transformation. These transformations may be conceived of as apocalyptic or utopian and continue with the advent of each new shift. Such refrains are evident in popular discourse concerning computers:

> "Computers will make knowledge easily accessible to all people. It is a tool of equality."

> "Ownership determines access; consequently, economics determines who rides the 'information highway.'"

> "On-line exchanges fragment and isolate the human community."

> "On-line exchanges create communities-without-borders thereby realizing the development of a global society."

The purpose of this section is to explore how the material and symbolic existence of communication technologies affect the perception of change. Can a dynamic understanding of context promote a more accurate observation and interpretation of cultural change as it is mediated through technological processes? Are there similarities in the conceptual environment generated by each society in response to new media? What kinds of interpretations of cultural process are possible when technologies are contextualized according to a constitutive perspective? Responses to these questions require some knowledge of communication history. The following discussion will illustrate how a focus on historical shifts of communication from a constitutive perspective informs emerging understandings of new communication technologies.

The communication shift in the European community caused by the development of the printing press in the fifteenth century provides some interesting lessons to the current computer generation. This historical example is heuristic in that it identifies where to look and how to evaluate changes in the character of a culture in light of a new communication technology. In addition, it is a cautionary tale which advocates a critical analysis of current technological discourse concerning the computer. Rather than accept effects popularly ascribed to the computer, a constitutive perspective based on historical evidence encourages attention to the nature and level of influence.

Two contradictory effects attributed to computers are: 1. Computers result in an isolated experience of self, and 2. computers create communities-without-borders thereby realizing the global society. Examining these effects in light of studies concerning the printing press are illustrative.

1. Computers result in an isolated experience of self.

One of the concerns about computer use is the emphasis on the interface between the individual and the machine. It is considered a form of isolated activity which calls into question characteristics presumed inherent to human communication: Face-to-face exchanges, knowledge of personal demographics particular to participants, and at least partial control over who receives any given message. Consequently, children immersed in play with video games and adults who spend hours chatting 'on-line' raise an alarm in society. This seems to be a dangerous level of personal isolation, damaging to both the individual and the social collective. While computer mediated communication redefines context and promotes a more individualistic form of interaction, these changes were not initiated by the current technology.

The development of the printing press contributed to this evolution in communicative practices. In her classic study of the printing press, historian Elizabeth Eisenstein (1979) observes that a reading public was "more atomistic and individualistic" (p. 132). The expansion of cultural codes of communication to include not only oral literacy but also print literacy prompted changes now representative of computer literacy:

> Print was a major factor in the development of the sense of personal privacy that marks modern society. It provided books smaller and more portable than those common in a manuscript culture, setting the stage psychologically for solo reading in a quiet corner, and eventually for completely silent reading. The drift in human consciousness toward greater individualism had been served well by print. (Ong, 1982, p. 72)

The experience of books generated a new sense of self. It gradually eroded the need for traditional community gatherings in order to receive certain types of messages. Now, a solitary individual became engaged in the highly individualistic act of reading. This "drift in consciousness" is valued when associated with reading books but considered suspect in relation to computer use.

2. Computers create communities-without-borders.

Computers are extolled for their unique ability to extend beyond the physical parameters of communication in order to create community. This capability for borderless exchange is evidenced in the development of the World Wide Web which connects people by virtue of their interests rather than their citizenship. On both a national and an international level, on-line communities are being forged. The reconfiguration of human community is one of the effects of a shift in communication and strains of current changes were evident following the development of the printing press.

While an oral culture was dependent on close physical communities, books contributed to expanding these boundaries:

> ...even while local ties were loosened, links to larger collective units were being forged. Printed materials encouraged silent adherence to causes whose advocates could not be found in any one parish and who addressed an invisible public from afar. New forms of group identity began to compete with an older, more localized nexus of loyalties. (Eisenstein, 1979, p. 132)

The experience of communication-without-borders has its roots in the print culture and shares similar characteristics with the computer culture. An on-line community represents a new form of group identity. Individuals address "an invisible public from afar" but now receive an immediate response. A sense of collective identity may be experienced beyond "local ties" to family, neighborhood, and nation-state. Both are technologies that may be said "to disperse the self in the world" (Poster, 1990, p. 128) thereby creating 'virtual communities.'

The purpose of these examples is not to negate any substantive difference between the use of books and the use of computers. There are numerous differences. Nor should these examples provoke an attitude of 'nothing new under the sun.' The constitutive perspective suggests that there is always some variation by virtue of the mutually defining interaction between individual and social identity and technologies. Rather, the value of this approach lies in highlighting the necessity for critical, historical thought when evaluating the nature and scope of change associated with communication technologies.

Since technologies affect not only our material environment but also our conceptual environment, this is not an easy task. Innis (1951) refers to the "bias of communication" which means that the character of the dominant media technology in any given society influences perception. We experience ourselves and the world in the context of communication technologies:

> If a [cultural innovation] is basic, simply because it **is** so, a generation after it has been introduced, it becomes part of the world as given--part of the

shape of consciousness, you might say, rather than the content of consciousness" (Hardison, 1989, p. xii).

Forms of media affect ways of thinking. In her study of the printing press, Eisenstein (1979) not only provides an exhaustive account of change in early modern Europe but also conjectures that standardization of print affected the structure of laws, language, and thought (p. 8). This conveys some of the challenge to a student of cultural change. The popularly attributed effects of computers are superficial observations reflecting a clear bias of communication. As indicated, one approach to thinking beyond the technological "shape of consciousness" is knowledge of the historiography of communication. In addition to providing a comparative perspective, these studies are heuristic in that they identify points of entry to media and social systems for productive analysis.

Other theoretical implications of this "bias" are less benign. An uncritical acceptance of the popular terms for describing a particular shift in communication compromises rigorous analysis. A clear example of this is the discourse of globalism which heralds the "Information Society" in which all peoples are connected. But the concrete reality is less than persuasive when considering even basic telephone service: 80 percent of the world's telephones are located in 10 countries of North America and Europe serving a population of 750 million people; 30 percent of the phones are in the United States; 12 percent of the phones are in the developing world with a population of 2.8 billion people (Sussman, 1993). Issues concerning access, commercialization of information, social authority and privilege, and cultural identity continue to challenge assumptions conveyed in the seemingly innocent use of descriptions such as "the information superhighway," "the global society," and "the age of the Internet."

These generalizing terms abstract and universalize a communicative practice that is not relevant to the everyday, lived experience of vast numbers of people. While millions of people may have homepages on the Internet, billions do not. The desire to create a theoretical "grand narrative" which ignores these issues undermines the validity of diverse experiences and, ultimately, limits the value of the theory itself. In a material and symbolic manner, then, the world-view of a privileged few maintains dominance.

The privileging of experience may be more evident as a function of material existence but it also operates on an abstract level by reinforcing a particular perception of the world. Conceptual frameworks have normative as well as descriptive and prescriptive functions (Mowlana, 1984; Hamelink, 1993). Continually asserting the primacy of a concept without interrogating its meaning, normalizes its use. For example, the concept "information" is simply accepted as a given. We have no sense of the history of its use or even current meaning. What do we mean by information? Who creates information that is considered valuable? Trivial? Who has access to distributing information? Receiving it? Does information have social as well as commercial value? What is the relationship between communication and information? Between personal and cultural identity and information? What is the relationship between information and knowledge? How is information institutionalized? Eradicated? These are only some of the issues that need to be examined. Failure to do so promotes a normative understanding of communication technologies by perpetuating a singular perception:

> ...[it gives] a theoretical priority over just the radical differences of "ways" and "functioning," and over the highly differential character of being a "member" of the society (Williams, 1974, p. 114).

In order to chronicle cultural change, participants at all levels of the culture need to be taken into consideration be it only by not asserting universalizing characteristics of media effects.

Conclusion

> It appears that the very cognitive structure of the individual human being and the formal patterns of human social relations are intimately linked to the forms or systems of communication that are predominant in given eras. (Rowland, 1995, p. xi)

There is a metaphysical relationship between technology and humans. Each calls the other into being, shaping and re-shaping the terms of existence. This interface contributes to the production of contexts from which we develop systems of meaning. Rather than accept superficial accounts of change, this essay argues for greater specificity in analyzing the nature, level and relative power of change inherent to shifts in communication. It is a challenging endeavor because we must step out of the perceptual bias of our time in order to more accurately assess new projectories of identity and behavior. And it is a complex project for we must account for diverse human experiences in formulating theories with any explanatory power. Reneging on the intellectual commitment necessary for such a task may prove Plato correct: we may be thought very knowledgeable when we are for the most part quite ignorant.

References

Alexander, J. C. (1992). The promise of a cultural sociology: Technological discourse and the sacred and profane information machine. In R. Munch & N. J. Smelser (Eds.), *Theory of Culture*. Berkeley, CA: University of California Press.

Douglas, S. J. (1987). *Inventing American Broadcasting*. Baltimore, MD: John Hopkins University Press.

Eisenstein, E. (1979). *The printing press as an agent of change: Communications and cultural transformations in early-modern Europe* (Volumes I and II). New York: Cambridge University Press.

Hamelink, C. (1993). Globalism and national sovereignty. In K. Nordenstreng & H. Schiller (Eds.), *Beyond national sovereignty: International communication in the 1990s* (pp. 372-389). Norwood, NJ: Ablex Publishing Corporation.

Hardison, O. B. (1989). *Disappearing through the skylight: Culture and technology in the Twentieth Century.* New York: Viking Penguin, Inc.

Havelock, E. (1982). *The literate revolution in Greece and its cultural consequences.* Princeton, NJ: Princeton University Press.

Heyer, P. (1988). *Communications and history: Theories of media, knowledge, and civilization.* Westport, CT: Greenwood Press.

Innis, H. (1951). *The bias of communication.* Cheektowaga, NY: University of Toronto Press.

Kramarae, C. (Ed.). (1988). *Technology and women's voices: Keeping in touch.* New York: Routledge and Kegan Paul.

Marvin, C. (1988). *When old technologies were new.* New York: Oxford University Press.

Marvin, C. (1989). Experts, black boxes, and artifacts: New allegories for the history of electric media. In B. Dervin, L. Grossberg, B. O'Keefe, & E. Wartella (Eds.), *Rethinking communication: Paradigm exemplars* (pp. 189-198). Thousand Oaks, CA: Sage Publications.

Menache, S. (1990). *The vox dei: Communication in the middle ages.* New York: Oxford University Press.

Mowlana, H. (1984). The myths and realities of the "Information Age": A conceptual framework for theory and policy. *Telematics and Informatics, 1,* 427-438.

Ong, W. J. (1982). *Orality and literacy.* London: Methuen & Co.

Poster, M. (1990). *The mode of information: Poststructuralism and social context.* Cambridge, England: Polity Press.

Rowland, W. D. (1995). Forward. In D. Crowley & P. Heyer (Eds.), *Communication in history: Technology, culture, and society* (pp. xi-xiv). White Plains, NY: Longman Publishers.

Schudson, M. (1978). *Discovering the news: A social history of American newspapers.* New York: Basic Books.

Slack, J. D. (1989). Contextualizing technology. In B. Dervin, L. Grossberg, B. O'Keefe, & E. Wartella (Eds.), *Rethinking communication: Paradigm exemplars* (pp. 329-342). Thousand Oaks, CA: Sage Publications.

Slack, J. D., & Fejes, F. (Eds.). (1987). *The Ideology of the Information Age.* Norwood, NJ: Ablex Publishing Corp.

Sussman, L. (1993). Toward the universal interactive neighborhood. In K. Nordenstreng & H. Schiller (Eds.), *Beyond national sovereignty: International communication in the 1990s* (pp. 433-442). Norwood, NJ: Ablex Publishing Corp.

Williams, R. (1974). *Television: Technology and cultural form.* Hanover, NH: Wesleyan University Press.

Woodward, W. (1993). Toward a normative-contextualist theory of technology. *Critical Studies in Mass Communication, 10,* 158-178.